"...a comprehensive history of the tremendous influence the Italian culture has had upon our civilization. This book is a must-read..."
- Paul Rosetti, Editor, *The Italian Tribune*

" The Golden Milestone...really is a treasure trove...it covers an amazing sweep of Italic heritage and history."
- Bob Masullo, The Voice of Sacramento 88.7 FM

"Until you read the whole book, you'll never get a sense of the immense impact the Italian mind has had on...the world."
- Professor Fred Gardaphe, Ph.D.
 Director, Italian-American Studies Program,
 Stony Brook University, NY
 Former President, American Italian Historical Assoc.

About the Author – Russell R. Esposito

The author was born to an Italian-American family in New York City. Mr. Esposito graduated from the City College of New York and obtained an advanced degree from New York University. In addition to writing, he is also a Vice President and Chief Information Officer. Mr. Esposito has also been an instructor at the State University of New York, and Visiting Professor at Touro College. He frequently lectures on various business and information technology subjects, as well as on Italian culture and heritage.

*To my family and friends
who encouraged me to continue,
offered many ideas and demonstrated
extreme patience with me through
the years that I worked to
complete this book.*

The Golden Milestone

The Italian Heritage of Innovation and Contribution to Civilization

- 4th Edition -

St. Peter's in Rome inspired the dome on the U.S. Capitol Building.

Published by
THE NEW YORK LEARNING LIBRARY

www.nylearninglibrary.com

The Golden Milestone
The Italian Heritage of Innovation and Contribution to Civilization
(Fourth Edition)

Copyright © 2007 by Russell R. Esposito

Published in the United States of America by The New York Learning Library, New York (www.nylearninglibrary.com).

International Standard Book Number: 0-9671436-1-6
Library of Congress Control Number 00-191009

First Edition 2000
Second Edition 2002
Third Edition 2003
Fourth Edition 2007

Cover design by Mae Lincoln

Published and printed in the United States of America

Direct all inquiries to:
service@nylearninglibrary.com

CONTENTS

How to Use this Book:

The publisher highly recommends that you read this book, as you would any other, from start to finish. The book's text is highly cross-referenced to foster and reinforce learning and to provide logical associations. After you read it completely, the book's organization facilitates its use as a reference book for subsequent research. We hope you enjoy your reading, whether for academic study or personal knowledge and enrichment.

Note: Most chapters list subject entries **alphabetically**. However, at times exceptions are made and some chapters list subject entries **chronologically** in order to foster a better understanding of the subject's development.

က္သ

PREFACE
What was the Golden Milestone?

For over two millennia, the adage "all roads lead to Rome" has been well known to our civilization. Today, this expression has a *figurative* meaning that alludes to Rome as the cultural center that scholars, students, tourists and pilgrims flock to year round for intellectual and spiritual enlightenment. Majesty and mystique inexorably draw the souls of many along a road that leads to Rome. However, this adage was a *literal* maxim during the epochal era of the Roman Empire, since all major roads *actually did lead to Rome!*

The Romans created an advanced civilization and were undoubtedly master builders by any standard. They invented and perfected the use of concrete, which enabled them to construct the world's first complex system of roadways that spanned 60,000 miles (96,500 km) across a massive landscape, from Britain to Egypt and Spain to Asia. The Romans carefully engineered this lattice of roadways and accurately placed directional and distance milestones to aid travelers, commerce, communication and the movement of Roman armies. The Romans documented their vast road system with the world's first road maps. Their roadways radiated out from Rome to the most distant reaches of the Roman Empire and travel was protected under the aegis of Roman peacekeeping patrols. This vast Roman network of roadways was also literally the first "information highway." These roadways provided a very sound infrastructure that made communication frequent, efficient and dependable. The combination of massive scale, Roman security, and permanence from advanced engineering established the world's first large-scale information system.

In the Roman Forum, at the center of Rome, Emperor Augustus built a large column covered in gold with inscriptions indicating the major roads, directions and distances from Rome to every large city in the Empire. This golden column was called the "Miliarium Aureum," which is Latin for the "Golden Milestone." This "Milestone" was a monument that stood in the heart of the Roman Forum and dramatically symbolized the magnitude and influence of the Empire. It served as a clear reminder to all that Rome was at its center.

For almost 500 years the Roman Republic and Empire influenced and led all of Europe introducing literacy and an advanced civilization. Rome provided Europe with sophisticated legal and monetary systems, a complex formal government, advanced engineering, architecture, agriculture, medicine, and perhaps equally important, new standards for personal hygiene. Their society produced enduring influences that persist even to this day. For example, the powerful and long lasting influences of Roman law and medical arts are quite obvious when one considers that contemporary legal systems and medical professions still employ Latin, the language of the Romans.

Centuries after the Romans made their potent contributions, the Italian Renaissance brought civilization to still greater heights, advancing art, literature, science, mathematics, technology and demonstrating heroic new explorations across the Atlantic Ocean. Centuries later, once again in Rome, the nuclear age was ushered in when Enrico Fermi split the atom at the University of Rome in 1934.

This book takes its title from the previously described Roman monument, the "Golden Milestone," since that monument represented the achievements and influences of Rome and Italy that so greatly advanced mankind and world civilization.

OVERVIEW

We live in a world filled with astonishing invention and daunting discovery. Every day we awake to new ideas, technology and innovation, and experience the associated benefits of our rapidly advancing civilization. All nations, nationalities and peoples of this world have contributed to the miraculous age we now live in. Numerous volumes have been written on human progress. The purpose of this book is to focus on and examine the vast cultural and scientific contributions made by the Romans, Italians and Italian-Americans throughout the ages. It is a previously untold story of the countless heroic efforts over many centuries that culminated in contributions to civilization of epic proportions.

This book covers the broadest spectrum of human achievement from fine art to high technology. Italians invented the battery, barometer, radio, thermometer, nuclear reactor, telescope, piano, violin, ballet, opera, musical notation and accomplished a wealth of other important innovations. For example, few know that an Italian mathematician named Luca Pacioli invented double-entry accounting in the 15th century and that an Italian banker named Lorenzo Tonti invented life insurance in the 17th century. This book carefully documents how the telephone was first invented by Antonio Meucci, an Italian immigrant living in Staten Island, NY, who was unable to renew his patent due to financial problems and a sudden and serious injury. Years later, a similar patent was submitted by Alexander G. Bell.

At times recorded history has clouded and obscured the correct assignment of credit. The venerable explorer of North America, John Cabot, was Italian whose real name was Giovanni Cabotto. Similarly, the great mathematician Girolamo Cardano and the literary genius Francesco Petrarca both met the same historical fate when their names were changed to Jerome Cardan and Petrarch. No first name, simply Petrarch, like the celebrity pop-singers Madonna and Cher. Historians altered these names, which resulted in the obfuscation that this book now rectifies. For reasons uncertain, some editors of history seem to have demonstrated a peculiar penchant for eliminating vowels and anglicizing names.

Historical portrayals of America's beginnings typically fail to identify that important seminal events were the result of Italian immigrants and their efforts. The Italian mind significantly contributed to the birth of America. For example, traditional accounts of early American history neglect to illuminate the fact that main concepts in the American Declaration of Independence, written principally by Thomas Jefferson, were derived from his close friend and neighbor Filippo Mazzei. Mazzei was an Italian physician, businessman and American patriot who also wrote articles for Italian news publications, which frequently documented conditions in the American colonies. The concepts of *natural or unalienable rights* and the importance of *equality among men* are directly derived from Mazzei's writings in Italian. U.S. President John F. Kennedy in his book "A Nation of Immigrants" correctly ascribes the origins of the concept that *all men are created equal* to Mazzei. Mazzei may have developed these concepts from his knowledge of the Roman Republic where the concepts of *natural rights* and *equal votes among men* were socially and legally institutionalized.

Thomas Jefferson was enamored with Italian and Roman culture and was determined to build his new nation's capital using neoclassical architectural styles. He hired Italian sculptors to create the statues and monuments in the new American capital. The U.S. Capitol Building is an example of Palladian architecture, a style named after its inventor, the famous Renaissance architect Andrea Palladio. The building's massive central dome was inspired by the equivalent dome atop St. Peter's Basilica in Rome. Furthermore, Capitol Hill in Washington D.C. was named after the Capitoline Hill in Rome.

Jefferson clearly had an appreciation for world-class standards. Jefferson, always intent on acquiring the finest for his youthful America, also hired Italian musicians for the first professional U.S. Marine military band.

Further, America was not only discovered by an Italian, but was also named after an Italian merchant and explorer Amerigo Vespucci. The massive Hudson River in New York is named after Henry Hudson, however, it was actually discovered almost a century earlier by the Italian explorer Giovanni da Verrazano. Although the river is named after Henry Hudson, the imposing suspension bridge that looms above it is named after Verrazano. The Verrazano Narrows Bridge is the longest suspension bridge in the United States. Many formidable Italian innovators have contributed significantly to our modern world. The decades of world peace following World War II are attributed largely to an Italian physicist who left Italy after concluding that he would not offer scientific support to either the Nazi or Fascist governments of Europe. This Italian physicist and professor at the University of Rome, Dr. Enrico Fermi, was the first to transform and split the atom. Fortunately, Fermi decided to immigrate to the U.S. where he led a team that developed the first nuclear reactor and the first atomic bomb. Early possession of this technology allowed the U.S. to quickly end World War II, saving hundreds of thousands of lives on both sides that would have been tragically wasted in a prolonged invasion of Japan. This technology has also allowed the U.S. to maintain world police powers, thus fostering world peace. Had Fermi helped the Axis Powers during World War II, we would most likely be living in a totalitarian world under conditions we would all find unimaginable. It is a fact that Albert Einstein wrote a letter to U.S. President, Franklin D. Roosevelt, warning him that Adolf Hitler was trying to develop an atomic bomb and that the United States urgently needed to develop this technology *first*. Fermi, a Nobel Prize laureate, made it possible for the U.S. to win the ultimate race and stabilize the democratic world. The decades that have followed World War II have been thankfully unmarred by global conflict.

During the 20th century, nineteen Italian scholars and scientists were awarded the Nobel Prize in diverse disciplines such as: physics, chemistry, medicine, literature and one for peace. And another won the Fields Medal for mathematics. Italian physicist, Dr. Federico Faggin, while working for the Intel corporation developed the world's first computer microprocessor, and changed our lives forever. His initials (F.F.) are inscribed on the Intel 4004 chip. Italian-American scientists, such as Dr. Anthony Fauci and Dr. Robert Gallo, have gained international fame and recognition for their important medical discoveries. As we witness the dawn of the 21st century, Italian scientists and innovators continue to make very real contributions to civilization. At the start of the new millennium, Italians led both the European Space Agency and the European Union.

The chapters in this 4th edition have been very carefully researched over two decades of intensive study. This book illustrates how Italians and Italian-Americans in many ways "invented" civilization, and hopefully it will inspire others to continue the very human pursuits of exploration, discovery and invention.

Chapter I

AMERICAN GOVERNMENT

"E Pluribus Unum" ("Out of Many, One")
- Roman authors Horace and Virgil -

Declaration of Independence - Principles
Filippo Mazzei

The founding fathers of America had an acute appreciation and deep respect for the intellectual achievements of ancient Rome and the Italian Renaissance that followed. In England during the 18th century, interest in Roman and Italian art, architecture, literature and philosophy was at its zenith. The English aristocracy considered a tour of Italy, known then as the "Grand Tour," a necessary part of their education. In 1776, the literary giant Dr. Samuel Johnson said, "A man who has not been to Italy is always conscious of his inferiority." The famous German poet Johann Wolfgang von Goethe said in 1786, when he first arrived in Rome, "Now, at last, I have arrived in the First City of the World!" Even the great Shakespeare had written many of his plays with Italian characters, which were often set in Italy, for example, "The Merchant of Venice," "Romeo and Juliet," "Two Gentlemen from Verona" and "Julius Caesar." The English inhabitants of America shared this enduring interest and appreciation for Rome and Italy. They borrowed both Italian and Roman legal and philosophical concepts as they forged the foundations of their fledgling American government. They studied Roman laws regarding respect for property, personal freedoms along with the speeches of great Roman orators. It is well known that Thomas Jefferson was especially enamored with Italian culture and learned how to read and write in both Latin and Italian. Jefferson had great respect for the illustrious Roman orators and philosophers. He analyzed their writings, in particular Cicero's works. Jefferson's appreciation of Italian culture is also evident by the naming of his estate Monticello, which means a small mountain in Italian (*monte* means *mountain* and *cello* is a diminutive suffix). Also, Monticello was built using Italian and Roman architectural designs, which are described in detail in the "Art & Architecture - Contributions in America" chapter of this book.

Through business associates Jefferson corresponded with and later befriended an Italian immigrant named Filippo Mazzei (aka Philip Mazzei). Mazzei was an Italian physician, horticulturist, intellectual and businessman from Florence who was born in 1730. Led by an entrepreneurial spirit, Mazzei started an import and export business in London in 1757. After purchasing two "Franklin stoves" for export to the Grand Duke of Tuscany in Italy, Mazzei ultimately met Benjamin Franklin, John Adams and other influential people from America. Later, Mazzei decided to start a business in America and arrived in Virginia in 1773, where he met Thomas Jefferson who befriended Dr. Mazzei. Jefferson convinced Mazzei to build his own estate adjacent to Jefferson's Monticello home. Jefferson gave Mazzei 193 acres adjacent to Monticello and Mazzei purchased an additional 700 acres. On this land Mazzei built his estate, which he called Colle, meaning *hill* in Italian.

Over time, Mazzei became very involved in the American political environment and supported Thomas Jefferson and Patrick Henry during the American Revolution. Mazzei often wrote about the conditions in the American colonies for the Italian press. He understood that the lack of equality and freedom had caused the greatest of ancient republics to fail and wrote of the importance of these basic human needs. Mazzei wrote about the "natural rights of man" and that "All men are by nature equally free and independent." Mazzei continues: "This equality is necessary to establish a free government. Each one must be equal to the other in natural rights." Mazzei might have been influenced by the Roman legal system's precept of *natural law* that sought a fair and ideal justice for all citizens, subjects and foreigners. In the 3rd century, a prominent

Roman jurist and legal scholar, Domitius Ulpianus wrote, "according to the law of nature all men are equal." (See the chapter on "Law" for more information on the Roman legal system and how its *natural law* evolved into Rome's *common law*.)

Mazzei wrote many articles from 1774 to 1776 about the American colonies, his dissatisfaction with British rule and the importance of equality under the law for all men. He sometimes wrote these under the pseudonym of Furioso. With Mazzei's permission, Jefferson translated Mazzei's Italian articles and published the English text in the "Virginia Gazette." Further, the Jefferson Memorial Foundation, Inc. in Monticello, Virginia documented that Jefferson used an excerpt from Mazzei's work entitled "Instructions of the Freeholders of Albemarle County to their Delegates in Convention" in his own work to establish a new constitution for the state of Virginia.

Later, the Virginia Declaration of Independence, written by George Mason, was adopted by a Virginia Convention on June 12, 1776. The first paragraph reads: "That all Men are created equally free and independent, and have certain inherent natural Rights."

On July 4, 1776, the American Declaration of Independence was adopted in Philadelphia. The draft was written by Mazzei's neighbor, Thomas Jefferson and read: "That all Men are created equal, that they are endowed by their Creator with certain unalienable rights."

In his book "A Nation of Immigrants," U.S. President John F. Kennedy wrote, that the great doctrine "All men are created equal" in the Declaration of Independence originated with Filippo Mazzei, close friend of Thomas Jefferson. In a "New York Times Sunday Magazine" article (11/29/98), Eugene Foster, professor of pathology and historian stated, "The evidence suggests that he (Jefferson) was not an original thinker. His greatest skill was writing."

In 1788, Mazzei also published a very comprehensive and popular four-volume history of the American colonies and the American Revolution called "Recherches historiques et politiques sur les États-Unis del'Amérique septentrionale." It became the first history of the American Revolution published and was the first objective account that countered both British and French propaganda. His book was very successful in Europe, and as a result, Mazzei was offered, and accepted, an international diplomatic position from the King of Poland who admired Mazzei's efforts in America. Eventually, Filippo Mazzei, physician and surgeon, horticulturist, businessman, intellectual, American patriot, author and diplomat retired in Pisa in 1792 and died in 1816 at the ripe age of 86.

Jefferson was also very influenced by another Italian named Cesare Beccaria. Beccaria was born 1738 in Milan, Italy. He was an economist and philosopher. His most notable work was entitled "Crimes and Punishments" ("Dei delitti e delle pene"). This was a major work that was translated into 22 languages. The book covers the principles of a good government and legal system necessary for objective rules, order, peace and justice. Beccaria also described the importance of separating church from state and spoke out against capital punishment and torture. Jefferson often quotes Beccaria in his writings. Both John Adams and Thomas Jefferson owned copies of "Crimes and Punishments." John Adams read and carefully analyzed this book. His personal copy is kept in the rare book section of the Boston Public Library. Even his son, John Quincy Adams, 6th U.S. President (1825-1829) often complained that his Presidential duties kept him from his studies of both Cicero and Tacitus.

Thus, America was born and its fundamental character, which lives in the Declaration of Independence, is significantly shaped by the thinking and writings of influential Italians. The American founding fathers had the wisdom to learn from history and adopt the ideas and concepts of highly successful civilizations. Americans and Europeans owe much of their legal systems and stable civilizations to the Romans and these outspoken Italians. In fact, the word *civilization* has Latin roots. Latin was the spoken and written language of the Romans.

Declaration of Independence – Signers

William Paca

William Paca was born October 31, 1740 and died October 13, 1799. He was the second son of John and Elizabeth Smith Paca, and was part of his family's fourth generation that lived in Maryland. William's great-grandfather Robert immigrated to the American colonies in the 1657 from Italy. William was encouraged by his father to attend the College at Philadelphia and received his Bachelor of Arts in 1750. After graduation he was employed by Stephen Bradley, a well known lawyer in Annapolis, and pursued a legal profession.

William Paca led an esteemed public life. He served as an Annapolis councilman and mayor, a vestryman of St. Anne's Church, a delegate from Annapolis to the General Assembly and a delegate to the Continental Congress. Paca was one of the leading patriots of

Maryland. He opposed the Stamp Act in 1764, voted for the adoption of the Declaration of Independence in July 1776, and signed it August 2nd. Paca became a judge of the maritime Admiralty Court, and was later elected Governor of Maryland in November 1782, winning reelections in 1783 and 1784. George Washington appointed Paca as a Federal district judge in December 1789, a position he held until his death in 1799.

Caesar Rodney

Born October 7, 1728, Caesar Rodney was a patriot who held numerous public positions during his life, including delegate to the American Continental Congress, speaker of Delaware's Assembly, justice of the state's Supreme Court and President (Governor) of Delaware. He also signed the Declaration of Independence.

Caesar's heritage is both Italian and English. His Italian ancestry can be traced back to a family named Adelmare from Treviso. His father, Caesar Rodney, Sr. died in 1745 leaving Caesar Rodney, the oldest son, the duties of the family farm when he was only 17 years old. He soon demonstrated a keen interest in public affairs and at the age of 27 became High Sheriff of Kent County. Caesar Rodney continually held public appointments for the rest of his life.

He is also honored for his gallant 80 mile ride to Philadelphia in July 1776 when he was the de facto President (Governor) of Delaware. He rode horseback, sick with cancer and asthma, through a thunderstorm and still arrived in time to vote for Delaware's independence from England. Caesar Rodney died at his home on June 26, 1784, at the age of 56, after a highly distinguished life.

In January, 1999 the U.S. Mint selected the State of Delaware for the first coin to be minted in the new series of State Quarters. The coin's reverse side displays a portrait of Caesar's courageous horseback ride into history.

Legal System & Government of the U.S.
Roman Republic

Rome's ancient government was characterized by exemplary and unmatched efficiency. Rome unified the known world, spread concepts of advanced civilization, and established peace by their rule. This lasting peace, known as *Pax Romana* (Roman Peace) was a period of prosperity that lasted over 250 years (27 BC to 235 AD). The last chapter of this book "World Peace" describes *Pax Romana* in more detail.

The founding fathers of early America respected Rome's enduring accomplishments and sought to establish an equally successful republic. They based much of their newly formed American government on the social philosophies and legal system of the great Roman Republic. According to the British scholar and author, Michael Grant, the founding fathers designed the fundamentals of their new American constitution upon the balances and checks of Rome's legislative, executive and judicial branches. It is well known that Thomas Jefferson and John Adams studied the Roman system of laws and government and adapted these as models for their young republic. They were also strongly influenced by the great minds of their Italian intellectual contemporaries. In later years, U.S. President Abraham Lincoln understood the significance of the Roman Republic and Empire. He owned and read a four volume set of Edward Gibbon's "Decline and Fall of the Roman Empire" to better understand Rome's strengths and weaknesses. The passages below clearly illustrate how closely the U.S. form of government parallels the Roman Republic.

The early Roman Republic's government was headed by two magistrates elected for one year (called *consuls*). Similarly, the U.S. has two elected leaders, the President and Vice President. (In the U.S. they are actually elected by the *Electoral College,* which on occasion does not follow popular vote.) There was also a Roman Senate of 300 men (called *patricians*) selected by the two magistrates. The U.S. has a Senate of 100 leaders that are elected by popular vote. In Rome, the common people (called *plebeians*) were protected from very serious abuses by the *lex Valeria* (*Valerian law*) passed in 509 BC. *Valerian law* protected the life and rights of citizens, by providing an appeal process with an assembly of the people. Around 494 BC, the common people went on strike and consequently won the right to have government representation in *Tribunes*. This is similar to the U.S. House of Representatives. The *Tribunes* could veto magistrate actions that they considered unfair to the common people. This parallels the U.S. Congress when it over-rides the President with a two-thirds vote. Around 350 BC, the common people also gained access to the Roman Senate and the highest positions in government. Around 300 BC, the concept of *one man's vote being equal with any other man's vote* gained social and legal acceptance.

Much of America's Federal Government and principles of elections, equality of votes, veto powers, and the appeals process have been based upon the original Roman Republic's government. In their effort to be fair to all, Roman laws were carved on 12 wooden tablets and displayed for all to read. Even school children were required to learn these laws. The Roman legal system also allowed *freedom of thought* and stated that no one could be punished for what they thought. The Romans were so concerned with the rights of individuals that even slaves were protected by the law, and if mistreated they could bring a civil suit against a master.

As a result of the Social War from 90 BC to 88 BC, the Roman Republic granted citizenship throughout the Italian peninsula. Years later in 212 AD, the Roman Emperor Caracalla (aka Marcus Aurelius Antoninus) gave Roman citizenship to every freeborn subject in the entire Roman Empire, i.e. *Civis Romanus sum*. This is virtually the same as today's U.S. policy on U.S. protectorates, such as Puerto Rico. Although the Romans provided the first example of a large Republic with efficient and advanced government administration, credit must be given to the ancient Greeks who invented the first democracy. Yet, if the Romans had not accepted and preserved the Greek culture into their own society, many Greek concepts, works of art, literature and influences would have been lost.

America has another very important similarity to the Roman Empire, one that made Rome, as well as America highly successful. As the Roman Empire expanded throughout Europe, Asia and Egypt, the Romans came in contact with many different peoples, laws, customs and methods. The Romans were *extremely* practical people. When they learned of some new idea that they felt was useful, they would adopt it and assimilate the concept into their own methods or culture. The Roman Empire was a huge and successful "melting pot" of diverse people and ways. This term "melting pot" has often been used to describe how America assimilates immigrants from diverse cultural origins. In reality immigrants become Americans culturally in many ways, but still keep much of their own traditions. These are often modified and embraced by other Americans if they are perceived as having value in the American culture. Hence immigrants, and their unique ways, add to and improve the great eclectic American "melting pot." New York City is the quintessential American "melting pot" and, perhaps not by accident, is the financial capital of the world. In 1898, New York City had 43 newspapers- only 23 were in English.

As the Roman Empire entered into new territory and discovered its laws, the Romans would incorporate the local legal principles into a local legal framework, if the laws were practical for that territory. This practice is much the same in America where the state and local laws provide specific local legal autonomy. By allowing and at times embracing diversity, both Rome and America benefited and succeeded. The Roman poet and author Horace may have captured the importance of diversity and tolerance when he said this about immigrants, "They change their sky but not their soul, who cross the ocean." (Latin: Caelum non animum mutant qui trans mare current.")

The emblem of the Roman Republic.
The inscription SPQR (Senatus Populusque Romanus) represents "The Senate and People of Rome" and illustrates their unity.

Great Seal Inscriptions & Motto of the U.S.
Horace, Virgil and Roman Republic

The Great Seal of the United States has a bald eagle holding an olive branch in one claw and thirteen arrows in the other. In the eagle's beak is a scroll with the Latin inscription *E Pluribus Unum*, which means *Out of Many, One*. This was a well known Latin phrase in the 18th century and was a common theme in Europe at the time. The source of this phrase is the work "Epistle II" written by the famous Roman author and poet Horace. *E Pluribus Unum*, also appears in the poem "In Moretum" by another great author, the Roman poet Virgil. Since these two poets were contemporaries it is impossible to ascribe the origin to one of them.

The reverse side of the Great Seal has a triangle with an eye at its peak. Above the pyramid is the Latin phrase *Annuit Coeptis* meaning *He Favors Our Undertakings*. This phrase comes from Virgil's masterpiece "The Aeneid." In this work, the son of Venus, Aeneas, uses this phrase to ask the god Jupiter to favor his undertakings. This phrase also appears in Virgil's "Georgics," where the gods are again asked to favor undertakings. Also, below the seal's pyramid is the Latin phrase *Novus Ordo Seclorum* meaning the *New Order of the Ages*. Again this Latin phrase is taken from Virgil. In his "Eclogue IV," Virgil used that phrase in regard to the powerful Roman Empire and its rule and successes. In 1935, President Franklin D. Roosevelt ordered both sides of the Great Seal to be printed on the one dollar bill, since the *new order* concept was similar to his *new deal* administration that followed the great depression in the United Sates.

Also, *the U.S. Great Seal was inspired by the symbol of the Roman Republic* which had a similar eagle with out-stretched wings perched above four arrows and laurel leaves on both sides.

Business Motto of the U.S.
Rome
The U.S. business motto, "caveat emptor," is a Latin phrase that means "let the buyer beware." This was a famous Roman saying inscribed in Latin above a central marketplace in the City of Rome. There is good reason to subscribe to this Roman philosophy, especially since the American corollary sayings are: "A sucker is born every minute" and "Never give a sucker an even break."

"Capitol Hill" and "The Capitol" – U.S. capital
Rome
The early U.S. government selected a plateau that rests 88 feet (26.8 meters) above the Potomac river for its permanent capital, located in Washington, D.C. (District of Columbia). Although the terrain is not actually a hill, it is referred to as "Capitol Hill." The hill and the building "The Capitol" are spelled with a single letter "a" unlike the noun *capital*. This was inspired by the Roman Republic, which developed its capital on the seven hills of ancient Rome, the highest one being Capitoline hill (derived from the Roman Latin, *Capitolinus*, in turn derived from *capitalis*, Latin meaning *of the head*).

Marine Band - First U.S.
Sicilian Musicians

President Thomas Jefferson wanted a professional brass band to replace the simple and unprofessional fife-and-drum band used mostly for certain military events. He had the U.S. Navy recruit fourteen professional musicians from Sicily, Italy. On September 19, 1805, Gaetano Caruso, the organizer and the first musical director of the new band arrived at the Washington Navy Yard on the U.S. Frigate Chesapeake with thirteen other musicians who were also recruited from Sicily. Gaetano Caruso was also a known musical composer. They were hired with the rank and pay of sergeant-major and Caruso was later promoted to lieutenant and then to captain. Francis M. Scala from Naples joined the band in 1840 and became its musical director in 1861. Under his leadership the band grew to 25 pieces and performed for all government functions. This band officiated for President Lincoln's inauguration and also for his funeral. Scala made the band a highly trained and distinguished professional and military organization. He even trained the famous band composer John Philip Sousa when Sousa was a member of Scala's band. (Note: Sousa's parents were from Portugal and Bavaria.)

Italian musicians were often found in many government and military organizations as the country and its military branches grew. Emilio Cassi was the chief trumpeter for Theodore (Teddy) Roosevelt's "Rough Riders" during the Spanish-American war. Achille LaGuardia, bandmaster for the 11th Regiment U.S. Infantry during the 1880's, was the father of Fiorello H. LaGuardia, the beloved mayor of New York City.

"Pledge of Allegiance" to Honor Columbus
Columbus Day

Heard in every school throughout America, this pledge was originally written in 1892 to commemorate Columbus Day and the achievements of Christopher Columbus. It was written by Francis Bellamy of Rome, New York, however, he was not Italian. Although he intended it to be recited by all school children on Columbus Day, it has become part of everyday American culture. President Dwight D. Eisenhower added the words "under God" through legislation in 1954. These words were not in the original Bellamy text. The "Pledge of Allegiance" was not written by an Italian, however, it was inspired by the heroic achievements of a great Italian sailor, navigator and explorer.

New York City Mayors

Fiorello LaGuardia

LaGuardia was one of New York City's most beloved and admired mayors and served for three consecutive terms from 1933 to 1945. He was affectionately called "The Little Flower" (the meaning of Fiorello). He beautified the City, successfully fought organized crime, fought for child labor laws and women's rights, and greatly improved the City's vast operations. He even obtained a new charter for New York City in 1938. The venerated LaGuardia saw his popularity and fame increase further when he read the Sunday comics over the radio (at the time, a recent invention by Marconi) during a newspaper strike. A graduate of New York University Law School and a veteran (Lieutenant) of World War I, he was one of America's most admired and esteemed politicians. In New York City, LaGuardia Airport and LaGuardia Community College are named in his honor. After his dedicated service to the City, he became Director of the United Nations Relief and Rehabilitation Administration. Fiorello Henry LaGuardia was born in New York City on December 11, 1882 and died in the same city that loved him on September 20, 1947.

Rudolph W. Giuliani

Giuliani was born in Brooklyn in 1944, the grandson of Italian immigrants. He attended New York University Law School, graduating with *magna cum laude* honors in 1968. On November 3, 1993, Rudolph William Giuliani was elected New York City's 107th Mayor. New York is a city of over seven and a half million people. Giuliani has won national recognition by improving the overall quality-of-life, reducing street crime and successfully battling organized crime, notably in the carting industry, at the Jacob Javits Center and at the Fulton Fish Market. Under Mayor Giuliani's leadership, many new police tactics have been implemented and new regulations have ended parole for violent offenders. New York City is now the safest large city in America, according to the most recent FBI Crime Report. Giuliani also merged the NYPD with the Transit Police, implemented work-fare and reduced the welfare roles by 220,000. He also drastically reorganized many of the City's massive departments.

R. R. Esposito

After the tragic World Trade Center destruction by terrorists, Giuliani's strong leadership and tireless efforts to raise morale earned him the honor of "Time" magazine's *Person of the Year – 2001*. He was also knighted by Queen Elizabeth II at Buckingham Palace for his heroism and leadership in the face of the crisis.

Giuliani greatly admired former Mayor LaGuardia and had LaGuardia's desk resurrected from storage for his use and other NYC Mayors who follow.

Prior to his role as New York's Mayor, he was Associate U.S. Attorney General responsible for 30,000 Federal employees and a $1 billion budget. Giuliani's record as a prosecutor was incredibly successful: 4,152 convictions with only 25 reversals.

New York City Health Commissioner - First
Giovanni Ceccarini, MD

The Department of Health was created in 1870 and the governing committee consisted of four commissioners of the Sanitary Committee. Dr. Ceccarini was one of these first four commissioners and was also chosen to be the first Chairman of this governing Sanitary Committee. He was a well known and distinguished surgeon in the United States. He was active in the New York City community and with Cav. Egisto P. Fabbi (a partner of J. P. Morgan) had the Columbus monument erected in NYC's Central Park at Columbus Circle, located at the southwest entrance to the Park. At the same time another eminent Italian physician, Dr. Tullio Suzzara Verdi was the president of the Board of Health for the District of Columbia, the nation's Capitol, from 1871 to 1878.

New York State Governors

Mario M. Cuomo

Cuomo was born in Queens, New York City, June 15, 1932. He received his law degree, with *cum laude* honors, from St. John's University in 1956. He served as Lieutenant Governor of New York State from 1979 to 1982 and then as the 52nd Governor for 12 years from 1983 to 1995. New Yorkers received the largest tax cut in the State's history when Mario Cuomo served as Governor. He also gave them the first significant ethics law for public officials. His oratory powers are legendary and consequently he was selected as keynote speaker for the 1984 U.S. Presidential Democratic National Convention. Undoubtedly, the celebrated Roman philosopher and orator Cicero would have been impressed by Cuomo's public speaking prowess. Mario also set new records for public approval ratings in both his 1986 and 1990 bids for re-election, winning the highest percentage of votes and the largest victory margins of any candidate for second and third four-year gubernatorial terms in New York State history. During his three terms as Governor, he created more than a half-million jobs for New Yorkers. His economic development plan was the largest in the State's history with $32 billion in investments used to generate private sector growth. Governor Cuomo has authored numerous articles and essays, and has written and edited several books. His books include: "Forest Hills Diary," "Diaries of Mario M. Cuomo," "Lincoln on Democracy," "More Than Words," "The New York Idea: An Experiment in Democracy" and "Reason to Believe."

Alfred E. Smith (born Alfred Emanuele Ferrera)

Smith was the first Italian-American to be elected to the office of NYS governor (1919). He changed his name to avoid discrimination at a time when Italian immigrants were not accepted by much of established American society. His paternal grandfather was born in Genoa in 1808. Smith was also the first Italian-American to run for President of the United States.

Governor - First Women Elected
Ella Grasso

Ms. Ella Grasso was born Ella Tambussi in Windsor Locks, Connecticut, on May 10, 1919 to Italian immigrant parents. She attended St. Mary's elementary school, the prestigious Chaffee School and then Mount Holyoke College, earning both B.A. and M.A. degrees with *magna cum laude* honors and was also elected *Phi Beta Kappa*. In 1942, she married a school principal, Thomas Grasso and together they had two children.

In 1952, she won her first election to the General Assembly of Connecticut and never lost an election thereafter. She was Secretary of the State of Connecticut for twelve years, served two terms in the U.S. Congress, and was elected Connecticut's governor in 1974 and re-elected in 1978. She served as the State's governor until illness forced her to resign on December 31, 1980. In 1979, Ella was also elected chair of the Democratic Governors' Conference. Ella was dearly loved by her constituents for her honesty, dedication and success in helping the working class. She instituted a "people's lobby" where average citizens could speak out and be heard or seek help or advice. In a 1978 snowstorm, she demonstrated her true humanity and dedication by staying around the clock at a state armory where she directed emergency operations. When Connecticut had to economize, she returned a $7,000 raise she could not legally refuse, to the State's treasury. Ella was seen as a very caring almost maternal leader who loved her work and her constituents. Early in her career Ella Grasso wrote, "It is not enough to profess faith in the democratic process; we must do something about it." Thankfully, Ella actualized her own advice to the benefit of many. Ella Grasso lived in Windsor Locks, Connecticut, until she passed away in Hartford, Connecticut on February 5, 1981.

Vice President - First Woman Nominated
Geraldine Ferraro

In 1984, the daughter of an Italian immigrant family became the first woman to be nominated for Vice President by a major political party in the United States. She was born to Dominic and Antonetta Corrieri Ferraro on August 26, 1935 in Newburgh, N.Y. Her family saw more tragedy than the average immigrant family. She was named after a brother, Gerry, who died at the age of three in an automobile accident. Her father Dominic died of a heart attack when she was only seven years old.

Geraldine attended Marymount College on a scholarship, graduated in 1956 and subsequently earned her law degree in 1960 from Fordham University, while she was also teaching in the New York City public school system. Major milestones in her career include these accomplishments: Passed the NY bar exam 1961; Appointed Assistant U.S. District Attorney for Queens County in New York 1974; Elected U.S. House of Representatives 9th Congressional District in Queens, New York in 1978 and was re-elected two other times; Elected Secretary of the Democratic caucuses in 1980 and 1982; Chaired the Democratic Platform Committee charged with establishing the party's agenda for that year's presidential campaign 1984- as *Chairwoman she impressed party factions who requested she run as Vice President with Presidential nominee Walter F. Mondale.*

In 1960, she married Manhattan real estate developer John Zacarro and together they have three children. Although she and Walter Mondale lost the 1984 presidential election to the Republican incumbent Ronald Reagan, she broke a political "glass ceiling" for American women at a national level.

Supreme Court Justice

- **Antonin Scalia**

Scalia was born on March 11, 1936 in Trenton, N.J. His father was an Italian immigrant from Sicily who came to America as a teenager. His mother was the daughter of Italian immigrants. Antonin is essentially a first generation Italian-American born into a working class family who rose to the highest judicial office in the United States using his intellect and determination as his only vehicle to success. In 1986, under the Reagan administration, he became the first Italian-American appointed to the esteemed U.S. Supreme Court. Scalia's academic credentials are outstanding: Georgetown University and University of Fribourg (Switzerland), A.B., 1957; Harvard, LL.B., 1960; Sheldon Fellow, Harvard University, 1960-61; Editor of Harvard Law Review. He and Maureen McCarthy were married on September 10, 1960 and have nine children.

- **Samuel Anthony Alito, Jr.**

With early hopes as a youth of being a professional baseball player, a young New Jersey boy, and son of an immigrant father from Italy, had no idea exactly how different his final professional calling would be. No idea that he would someday hold the ultimate judicial position in the "free-world" – U.S. Supreme Court Justice (appointed January 31, 2006). His legal profession is marked by distinction. "The New York Times" (November 11, 2005) made these comments about Alito: "Alito...has made his mark with quiet distinction rather than showy display. He has cloaked his formidable intellect in modesty..." (More information will be available on Judge Alito and Judge Scalia in this book's next edition.)

Federal Bureau of Investigation (FBI) - Founder
Charles J. Bonaparte

Charles J. Bonaparte was an Italian-American born in Baltimore, Maryland on June 9, 1851 and died at Bella Vista near Baltimore on

June 28, 1921. He received a law degree from Harvard University and became the 46th Attorney General of the United States appointed by President Theodore (Teddy) Roosevelt in 1908. As the Attorney General at that time, Bonaparte had access only to temporary staff from the Treasury Department and found this to be ineffective for investigations. Thus, he petitioned the U.S. President for permanent staff. On July 28, 1908, in order to provide a permanent agency, President Roosevelt gave Bonaparte the executive order to create a unit of twenty-three men that were to be under Bonaparte's direction. Bonaparte implemented this early crime-fighting unit that eventually became the Federal Bureau of Investigation in 1935. Charles J. Bonaparte, a self-professed Italian-American, was named after his great-grandfather, Carlo Buonaparte, who was the father of the French Emperor Napoleon. The name *Bonaparte* is an Italian name. (Refer to the Military Leaders & Heroes section in the chapter on "Military Contributions" for more on Napoleon and his Italian heritage.)

Prior to his appointment as Attorney General, Bonaparte had been appointed by President Roosevelt as Secretary of the Navy and served for one year in 1905. Teddy kept him there for one year, until he could give Bonaparte the intended Attorney General position, where he would establish the foundation of what we know today as the FBI.

Secretary of Health, Education and Welfare
Joseph A. Califano Jr.

Califano is credited for reorganizing the massive U.S. Department of H.E.W., introducing major disease prevention programs, such as, alcoholism prevention, childhood immunizations and anti-smoking initiatives. During his tenure from 1977 to 1979, *he also issued the first Surgeon General's Report on Health Promotion and Disease Prevention.* His administrative improvements also included new computerized techniques used to monitor welfare, Medicare and Medicaid programs. The Department's name has since been changed to the Department of Health and Human Services. One of his well known quotes promoting preventive medicine is: "You, the individual, can do more for your health and well-being than any doctor, any hospital, any drug, and any exotic medical device."

Califano is currently the Chairman and President of the Center on Addiction and Substance Abuse at Columbia University in New York City. He is also on the faculty at Columbia University's Medical

School and School of Public Health. Further, Califano is a member of the Institute of Medicine of the National Academy of Sciences. He is a leading expert in understanding the dynamics of the American health care industry.

Califano has authored numerous books and articles. His books are: Governing America" (Simon and Schuster, 1981); "America's Health Care Revolution: Who Lives? Who Dies? Who Pays?" (Random House, 1986); "The Triumph and Tragedy of Lyndon Johnson: The White House Years" (Simon and Schuster, 1991); "Radical Surgery: What's Next for America's Health Care" (Random House, 1995). He has also written numerous articles for major publications, which include: "Journal of the American Medical Association," "The New England Journal of Medicine," "The New York Times," "The Washington Post," "Readers Digest" and "New Republic."

Lottery for Public Financing
Augustus

The lottery was invented in Rome during the 1st century BC, by either Emperor Augustus or Nero, and offered boats, houses and slaves as prizes. This ancient lottery was free to enter. The Emperor Augustus lived from 63 BC to 14 BC and was greatly admired for his wisdom, integrity and leadership. His real name was Octavian, but was given the name Augustus, which meant *the exalted one* in Latin. The word *august* in English similarly means *noble* or *eminent* and stems from these Latin origins. Centuries after Augustus, around the 12th century in Italy, citizens were charged for lottery participation. Still later lotteries spread to Germany (1498), France (1539), London (1569), and became a new and widely accepted means of public financing. Thanks to Augustus and today's money strapped state government comptrollers, it has now spread to every convenience store on the planet earth. In the United States almost every state has a lottery, sometimes called *lotto*. The words *lotto* and *lottery* are derived from the Italian word *lottoria,* which is further evidence of its origins.

Today millions of people play the lottery in the hope that somehow they will overcome the colossal pre-determined odds set against them. It is this author's personal belief that one is more likely to be stuck twice by lightning in the same spot than win the lottery. Nevertheless, it is far more important to inform others that this author does not play the lottery and is relying heavily on book sales for income.

ೞ

Chapter II

ART & ARCHITECTURE

"Art is long, life is short."
- Roman poet Seneca -
(Latin: Ars longa, vita brevis.
***Ars* also means proficiency or skill.)**

Art experts have estimated that 40% of the world's fine art is in Italy. Since Italian culture has produced a vast cornucopia of art, this chapter concentrates only on the most famous art and architecture and related developments in these two subjects. Although it is difficult to always separate art from architecture, the first half of this chapter focuses on art and the second half focuses on architecture. There are a few masters who appear in both sections of this chapter, notably Michelangelo and Leon Battista Alberti, since the two of them were venerated for both their artistic and architectural accomplishments.

ART: Early Development

First Realistic Art Styles to Appear in Paintings
Giotto

Giotto di Bondone, known simply as Giotto, was born 1267 in the small village of Vespignano, near Florence and died on January 8, 1337. *He is often called the single most influential artist in European history.* His works are most influential, since he was the first to abandon the Byzantine and Gothic art style and create very realistic paintings during the pre-Renaissance period. He was the first to include narrative drama in paintings, elevate the human form, and paint with realistic proportions and accurate pictorial space. Although he was an innovator, later artists benefited from more technical knowledge about anatomy and thus surpassed his anatomical painting abilities. Nevertheless, *Giotto was the first to introduce this very realistic art* style, which allowed others to follow through the 19th century. *He is clearly recognized as the first genius of art in the pre-Italian-Renaissance.*

Giotto painted many frescos for the church and nobility. He painted frescos of religious subjects in the Church at Assisi and in the Arena Chapel in Padua. The famous artist, architect and art historian Giorgio Vasari (1511-1574) describes Giotto's true artistic genius when he wrote a biography of Giotto. Vasari's famous account tells how Giotto drew, free-hand, a perfect red circle with one continuous stroke of his brush. Giotto drew this circle when a messenger sent by Pope Boniface VIII asked for a sample of his work. Giotto was a short man but was respected not only for his art, but also for his quick wit and practical jokes. The famous perfect red circle he drew for the Pope illustrates both his skill and sense of humor. Other artists would have been quite intimidated by a messenger *from the Pope* and would have quickly offered a very fine completed painting. Clearly, genius has its privileges, and Giotto recognized that his stature would allow him the liberty of some playfulness with the Pope's messenger. Incidentally, a simple red circle is the corporate logo used by the giant American Telecommunications company Lucent Technologies. One has to wonder if it was inspired by Giotto's famous red circle.

Giotto was an accomplished sculptor and architect, as well. Late in his life, he was appointed as the architect for the city of Florence and designed a famous bell tower (campanile) in red, white and green

R. R. Esposito

marble, which was almost 300 feet tall.

It is because Giotto observed and painted Halley's Comet, which appears in one of his paintings as a star, that the European Space Agency named one of its spacecraft after him. The *Giotto* spacecraft completed many successful missions, which included the recording of numerous photographs of the famous Halley's Comet.

Masaccio (aka Tommaso Guidi)

Masaccio was a painter and engraver born on December 21, 1401 in Castello San Giovanni di Valdarno and died in 1428. *He is considered the single most important and influential artist during the early Renaissance.* He pioneered an early system for perspective and three dimensions in his paintings. *He also is credited for introducing proper proportion and humanism into art.* Most of his work has been lost with the exception of about four pieces. Masaccio's most notable masterpieces include the beautiful frescos in the Brancacci Chapel in Florence. Art historians credit Masaccio for influencing the artistry of subsequent masters, including Michelangelo and Raphael.

Accurate Depth & Perspective in Sculpture
Donatello

Donato Niccolò di Betto Bardi was his full name. Donatello is a diminutive and endearing form of his name. Donatello was born in 1386 in Florence and died on December 13, 1466. He was the *first sculptor to explore depth and perspective, refining measurement* and distance to create very realistic three-dimensional forms, a distinct departure from the earlier medieval and Gothic statues. His human figures were realistic in that they were self-activating and functional, displaying anatomical correctness and position.

He was one of the towering masters of the Italian Renaissance. Donatello influenced both sculpture and painting throughout the Renaissance. He was also teacher and master for the young Michelangelo. When one sees Michelangelo's sculpture, the "Pieta" for example, it is difficult to understand how anyone could carve such life forms from a cold, lifeless stone. For these masterpieces to be possible there were several generations of dedicated geniuses who learned from each other. The master teaches the student, and the student surpasses his master, and then becomes the next master for the following generation. *Da Vinci once said that for the world to have progress, the student must surpass his master-* a noble concept. Donatello's master was the Gothic sculptor Lorenzo Ghiberti. It is said that Ghiberti's works broke new ground in offering correct perspective. He was transitional, moving from the Gothic style to the more naturalistic Renaissance style. Donatello further improved upon Ghiberti's innovation and advancements. Donatello's greatest works are the marble statues of "St. Mark" and "St. George." Donatello's famous statue "Zuccone" (aka "pumpkin" because of its bald head) also exemplifies his unique style.

He also developed a new, very shallow style of *relief*, called *schiacciato* (which means flattened out), which he used on the base of "St. George." Donatello also crafted his celebrated bronze statue "David," which was the first large-scale freestanding nude statue of the Renaissance. The nude statues were a way to illustrate the knowledge and ability of the sculptor to accurately re-create the human form in its entirety.

Rules for Linear Perspective (Drawing in 3D)
Renaissance Architecture
Rules for Surveying and Mapping a Land Area
Leon Battista Alberti

Although not as well known as da Vinci and Michelangelo, there was another great genius of the Renaissance. He was a quintessential Renaissance man or "universal man" who excelled in many intellectual areas. Leon Battista Alberti was born to a wealthy merchant-banker family in Genoa on February 14, 1401. He lived in Florence and died in Rome on April 25, 1472 after a very full and accomplished life. He was a writer, architect, humanist and principal originator of Renaissance art theory. He wrote several landmark treatises on different subjects all in the Italian language. Alberti was also an athlete and champion gymnast. History books assert that he could practically leap over a man's head with his feet held together- probably legendary hyperbole.

Alberti had friendships with artistic giants such as the sculptor Donatello and the architect Filippo Brunelleschi. He wrote two groundbreaking books. *In his book "De Pictura" ("On Painting"), published in 1435, Alberti was the first to establish a scientific system for linear perspective, which is used by most artists today.* This book had significant and lasting effects on painting and *relief* art, giving rise to the spatial characteristics of Renaissance style art. As a precursor to his monumental book "De Pictura," Alberti also wrote "Rules of Perspective" in 1412.

Some say he advanced the concepts of linear perspective in painting by building on the work of Filippo Brunelleschi, an early developer of the concept and technique. Brunelleschi was an architect, engineer, inventor and sculptor born in 1377 in Florence and died in 1446. Brunelleschi designed the church of Santa Maria degli Angeli in Rome and engineered the famous, massive dome atop the Santa Maria Del Fiore Cathedral in Florence. Brunelleschi also designed the esteemed Foundling Hospital in Florence in 1419. Refer to the 'Architecture' section of this chapter for more on Brunelleschi.

Alberti was also an architect, and in 1447 was appointed as the architectural adviser to Pope Nicholas V. He also designed several outstanding buildings, such as the facades of Santa Maria Novella and the Palazzo Rucellai in Florence, as well as the magnificent churches of Santa Andrea and San Sebastiano both in Mantua, Italy. After serious study of the venerable Roman architect Vitruvius, Alberti published in 1452 *"De re aedificatoria"* *("Ten Books on Architecture")* *that became a bible of architecture for at least the next 200 years.* He went beyond other authors who wrote how buildings *were* built- Alberti wrote how they *should* be built. His books are surpassed only by *Andrea Palladio's* "The Four Books of Architecture." Palladio *is considered the most influential architect in the history of architecture.* (Refer to the references on Palladio in the 'Architecture' section of this chapter).

Alberti also wrote a significant exposition on geography and *established a comprehensive rulebook for surveying and mapping topography.* Nothing had advanced this field of science since the works of antiquity. True to his "Renaissance man" nature, he learned this field from the famous Florentine cosmographer Paolo Toscanelli and then surpassed his master by producing groundbreaking works on the subject. There are additional significant Alberti contributions in three other chapters of this book: "Literature," "Mathematics," and "Technology and Science."

Color – New & Innovative Use
Titian
This master painter of the Italian Renaissance, known as Titian, was born in Pieve di Cadore, near Venice. Titian's actual name was

Tiziano Vecellio and was born around 1488 and died on August 27, 1576. *His innovative use of rich colors made his life-like paintings and portraits assume a special brilliance. He is considered one of the world's greatest master colorists.* As a young boy, Titian's special abilities drove him to paint with whatever material he could find. He would use the pulp and liquid pressed from flowers as paint. Titian painted prolifically until his death, mostly portraits and religious subjects. His most famous works include: "The Venus of Urbino," "The Rape of Europa," "Assumption," "Christ and the Pharisee," "The Entombment of Christ," "The Supper of Emmaus," "The Holy Family," "Christ Crowned with Thorns," "Presentation of the Virgin in the Temple," "Bacchus and Ariadne," "Venus Anadyomene," and "The Vendramin Family." The Smithsonian Museum's National Gallery of Art in Washington D.C. contains several of Titian's magnificent works including "Portrait of a Lady" (circa 1555). Giovanni Bellini who himself was an expert in color and lighting mentored the great Titain who became the ultimate master of color and natural qualities in paintings.

The illustrious Spanish artist El Greco, born in Crete, received his artistic training in Italy from Titian in Venice. El Greco later moved to Rome and at the age of thirty-six moved to Spain.

Chiaroscuro:
Dramatic Expression Using Light & Shade
Michelangelo Merisi Caravaggio

Caravaggio was born on September 28, 1573 in Caravaggio and died on July 18, 1610. He was one of the founders of Italian baroque style. *Caravaggio is famous for his use of light and shade (chiaroscuro) to create dramatic expression in his intensely realistic paintings. Art historians credit Caravaggio for discovering "chiaroscuro" in his paintings.* He painted many famous works of art, "Martyrdom of St. Maurice" (1581), "Bacchus" (1589), "Basket of Fruit" (1596), "Calling of St. Matthew" (1597), "Conversion of St. Paul" (1600) and "The Taking of Christ" (1602). For over 200 years "The Taking of Christ" was thought to be a lost work of art. In 1993, it was found in a Dublin dinning room of a Jesuit residence far from its creator's home in Caravaggio, Italy.

ART: The Masterpieces

"Birth of Venus"
Sandro Botticelli

Botticelli was born in Florence in 1445 and died on May 17, 1510. He is one of the great artists of the early Renaissance. His painting "Birth of Venus" depicts the goddess Venus standing on a scalloped shell as she is born from the sea. Many classic concepts and ideals are woven into the theme of this beautiful painting. The painting is often and humorously called "Venus on a Half Shell." Botticelli painted many portraits and religious works for the famous and powerful Medici family of Florence. His other well known painting "Primavera" is a large panel, as is the "Birth of Venus." Botticelli also painted frescos in the magnificent Sistine Chapel. The Smithsonian Museum's National Gallery of Art in Washington D.C. has several of his works including the "Madonna and Child" (1470).

His real name was Alessandro di Mariano Filipepi. It is understandable that Sandro may have been derived from Alessandro, but it is not as obvious why he chose Botticelli.

"David"
Michelangelo Buonaroti

This famous statue of white marble depicting the young biblical King David, standing unclothed and ready for battle with Goliath, was created by the Renaissance genius Michelangelo. It is considered a classic example of artistic perfection and wonderfully portrays the power and beauty of the human form. *This is one of the most recognizable statues in the world.* Michelangelo even designed the proportions of David's frame to be optimally viewed when looking somewhat up at this massive statue.

About Michelangelo Buonaroti

Michelangelo was one of the greatest artists of all times. He was a sculptor, painter and architect, born in Caprese on March 6, 1475 and died in Rome, February 18, 1564. Michelangelo was born to a noble family in Florence but of limited wealth. He began an apprenticeship in 1488 with Domenico Ghirlandaio. Michelangelo was enamored by his master's ability to create extremely life-like drawings. From 1489 to 1492 he studied sculpture in the palace of the Medici and later under the direction of Bertoldo, who had been a pupil of Donatello. Some say Donatello was also a mentor for Michelangelo. Michelangelo's most famous sculptures are the "Pieta" and "David." His most acclaimed paintings are the biblical scenes of the Book of Genesis on the ceiling of the Sistine Chapel and on the Chapel's wall where he painted the "The Last Judgement," behind the altar. As an accomplished architect, he also designed the Medici Chapel and made significant contributions to the plans for Saint Peter's Basilica and designed its massive dome. He also designed the Laurentian Library in Florence (1525), Piazza del Campidoglio in Rome (1538 to 1650) and the Sforza Chapel in Rome (1558). His ingenious and revolutionary architectural concepts were an inspiration to others who followed. Other works of Michelangelo are detailed later in this chapter, both in the Art and the Architecture sections.

"Last Supper"
Leonardo da Vinci

Da Vinci is credited for creating another one of the world's most famous paintings, "The Last Supper" (1498). It depicts Jesus with his disciples seated at a long table as they share their last supper together. This painting is a fresco style work of art and is housed at the Church of Santa Maria delle Grazie in Milan. The artist uses very clever symmetry and geometry to guide the viewer's eye to the central figure (Christ) in the painting. This painting portrays the story of Christ's last supper where he tells his apostles to "Take and eat, this is my body" (referring to bread) and "This is my blood" (referring to the wine), and finally instructs them "To do this in remembrance of me," establishing the Christian sacrament of Communion.

Since 1978 this painting was under careful scientific renovation and was returned to public display 21 years later on May 28, 1999. Since 1726 there have been six other restoration projects, but this recent project has been the most painstaking, and employed the most technologically advanced methods ever used to restore this priceless work of art to its original splendor. The famous art restorer Pinin Brambilla Barcilon was selected to restore the painting in 1978. On May 27, 1999, the "New York Times" reported that Mrs. Brambilla's dark brown hair has turned gray over the 21 year restoration period, a true labor of love for two decades. For more about da Vinci's life see the reference in this chapter to his painting "Mona Lisa."

Madonna Paintings,
"The School of Athens" and "Crucifixion"
Raphael (aka Raffaello Sanzio or Santi)

Raphael was born in Urbino, Italy on March 28, 1483 and died on April 6, 1520. He is well known for his numerous paintings of Madonnas, examples are his "Coronation of the Virgin" and "The Sistine Madonna." His works depict serene, graceful, poised and beautiful Madonnas. His father Giovanni Santi was an artist for the duke of Urbino and introduced Raphael to painting. Raphael's set of wall frescos in the Vatican entitled "The School of Athens" is a prized masterpiece, as well as his "Crucifixion" and others. He was also a noted architect and contributed to the design of St. Peter's Basilica along with Michelangelo and Donato Bramante. He succeeded Bramante as the chief architect of the Vatican in 1514. Raphael was influenced by Masaccio, Leonardo da Vinci, but mostly by Michelangelo.

"Mona Lisa"
Leonardo da Vinci

Da Vinci painted this world famous portrait of a woman with a mysterious smile and arms peacefully folded. It is a very intriguing painting that depicts a very soft landscape in the distant background that frames the kind face of this woman with a gentle and very curious smile. Experts now understand the artistic trick that da Vinci has played on us. The smile of "Mona Lisa" is so subtle that if you focus just on her mouth, the smile seems to disappear. Da Vinci combines the facial muscles that support a smile, and muscles that affect the eyes when smiling, with a very subtle smiling mouth. Taken together, and reinforced by facial shadows, her face smiles. However, focus on her mouth alone and her smile seems to fade. The twenty-four year old Lisa di Antonio Maria Gherardini Giocondo was Leonardo's subject for this portrait, which he completed in 1505 after three years of effort.

On February 7, 1963, the Metropolitan Museum of Art in New York City began an exhibit of the "Mona Lisa," on loan from the Louvre in Paris. On that opening day, 16,000 visitors waited on line for this exhibit. The "Mona Lisa" was protected by the U.S. Secret Service and was displayed behind bulletproof glass.

This painting has been extensively used commercially, more often than any other work of art, and sometimes altered.

About Leonardo da Vinci

Leonardo da Vinci is considered one of the world's greatest geniuses. Leonardo was born 1452 in Vinci, in the Tuscany region of Italy and died on May 2, 1519. He was the illegitimate son of a notary and a peasant woman. Leonardo was a brilliant painter, sculptor, draftsman, architect, engineer, anatomist, scientist and inventor. He was also an accomplished musician and a philosopher who wrote many insightful passages. Around 1467, at about the age of 15, da Vinci became a pupil of Verrocchio. It is at Verrocchio's studio that Leonardo met his other masters, the great Botticelli and Ghirlandaio. *Leonardo became a master colorist and also invented sfumato*, i.e. a smoky style of painting. He painted dozens of works of art, the most famous include: "Mona Lisa" (1503-1506), "The Last Supper" (1495-1497) and "St. John the Baptist (1504). His beautiful portrait of a woman, "Ginevra de' Benci" (1474), is on permanent display at the Smithsonian Museum's National Gallery of Art in Washington D.C. and is *the only Leonardo da Vinci work that can be seen in the Americas.* Leonardo's equestrian statue of Francesco Sforza is also a masterpiece and greatly impressed King Francis I of France. Consequently, the King then brought Leonardo to France in order to gain the benefits of this genius in art and architecture. The King had such great admiration for Leonardo that he allowed Leonardo to work on whatever projects he desired. The King also purchased Leonardo's famous "Mona Lisa" which now hangs in the Louvre in Paris. King Francis I also brought the celebrated Italian goldsmith Benvenuto Cellini to France, but tried and failed to convince the great Michelangelo to leave his beloved homeland in Italy.

Regarding the genius of Leonardo, it has been said, "... that it is as if he awoke in the midst of darkness while the others were all still asleep." His "Notebooks" are a treasury of art, anatomy, philosophy, science and inventions. They contain thousands of detail illustrations on every imaginable subject, including plant and animal biology, astronomy, geology, hydraulics, mechanics, optics, military weapons and fortifications, human and embryonic anatomy, philosophy, mathematics, studies on birds in flight, human flight, submarine inventions and linguistics. *Leonardo's study of human anatomy led him to draw a male figure with arms and legs outstretched standing inside of a square that is circumscribed by a circle. This drawing is one of the most recognizable and copied images in the world.* This famous drawing is also the centerpiece of this book's cover graphic. Many advertisements have used this drawing and the American

Museum of Natural History in New York City has a logo that is almost identical to Leonardo's image.

Many of Leonardo's more significant contributions included in his famous "Notebooks" are listed in the "Medicine, Biology & Health," "Technology and Science" and "Transportation" chapters of this book. When you read the variety of advances he conceived and how futuristic his inventions were, it becomes very clear why he is often considered the greatest genius who ever lived. Leonardo da Vinci was the consummate perfectionist and said on his deathbed in 1519: "I have offended God and mankind because my work did not reach the quality it should have."

Neoclassicism
Antonio Canova
Canova was born in Possagno in 1757 and died in Venice in 1822. *He was considered "the supreme minister of beauty" by his contemporaries and was the greatest sculptor of his time.* His early works were in the baroque style but after spending time in Rome he developed and advanced neoclassic art beyond all others. *Neoclassicism is a revival of ancient Roman and Greek styles.* Canova was venerated for his art internationally and his works are on display at the world's greatest museums. His first major artistic success was the statue "Apollo Crowning Himself." His later masterpieces were "Love and Psyche" (1793) exhibited at the Louvre in Paris, "Venus Victrix" (1807) exhibited at the Galleria Borghese in Rome and "Perseus with Medusa's Head" (1801) exhibited at the Metropolitan Museum of Art in New York City. (Incidentally, the first director of the Metropolitan Museum of Art in New York City was the famous Italian archeologist, Luigi Palma di Cesnola.). *Several of Canova's works were commissioned by the French Emperor Napoleon,* including "Venus Victrix," which was a voluptuous portrait of Pauline, the sister of Napoleon. His work "Love & Psyche" (also called "Cupid & Psyche" or "Eros & Psyche") is a very beautiful and touching sculpture of the god Psyche being revived by Cupid's kiss. Canova's art is considered among the greatest neoclassic art ever created. Later in this chapter you will read how Thomas Jefferson made the new American capital in Washington D.C. a neoclassical showpiece of the world. At Jefferson's request to hire Italian sculptors, a friend of Jefferson tried to convince Canova to work in America, but Canova would not leave Italy. Other talented Italian sculptors and artists were

hired and crafted most of the art and monuments in Washington D.C.

"Nude Sdraiato" - Mannerism in Modern Art
Amedeo Modigliani

Modigliani was a painter and sculptor born on July 12, 1884 in Leghorn, Italy and died on January 24, 1920. He developed an innovative style of elongated figures. His compelling works often display an unusual calm and gentle elegance. His highly sophisticated works are categorized within the *mannerism* school of art. He is well known for his feminine nudes (e.g. reclining "Nude") and wonderful portraits. He was influenced by Paul Cezanne, Pablo Picasso, Henri de Toulouse-Lautrec and Georges Rouault. His interest in sculpture was sparked by his friendship with Constantine Brancusi. His works have been displayed by leading museums such as the Guggenheim Museum and the Museum of Modern Art, both in New York City. Other collections are in Milan. His short life of only 35 years was the result of poverty, tuberculosis, alcohol and drug abuse.

"Pieta"
Michelangelo Buonaroti

This massive and dramatic sculpture of white marble was created by the genius of Michelangelo. It depicts Mary holding her deceased son Jesus after the crucifixion. It is housed in Saint Peter's Basilica. Michelangelo also contributed to this venerated basilica's architectural design and personally designed its lavish dome.

The "Pieta" (the "Pity") was on display at the 1964-1965 New York City World's Fair in Queens. As a youth, this author visited this World's Fair and had the opportunity to see the "Pieta." There were many remarkable things at that fair, but the "Pieta" left a very strong and vivid memory. The "Pieta" is synonymous with absolute perfection. Perfection in its composition and the emotion it evokes, as well as the human physiology it portrays. Michelangelo tried eight blocks of marble before he was satisfied enough to continue his efforts and complete the masterpiece. The figures of Jesus and Mary are incredibly natural and appear to be actual humans somehow frozen in time. For more about Michelangelo's life see the reference earlier in this chapter to his sculpture "David."

Sistine Chapel's Art
Vatican City, Rome

The Sistine Chapel was built as a private papal chapel for Pope Sixtus IV (1473-1484) by Giovannino de' Dolci. The chapel adjoins with St. Peter's Basilica, which is part of Vatican City. The walls of the Sistine Chapel were decorated by several Italian masters including Michelangelo, Botticelli, Ghirlandaio, Pinturicchio and Signorelli. (To learn more about the design and construction of Saint Peter's Basilica and Vatican City, refer to the ARCHITECTURE section of this chapter.)

From 1508 to 1512 Michelangelo painted the vaulted ceiling with biblical events from the "Book of Genesis," as commissioned by Pope Julius II. He painted the "Creation," the "Birth of Adam and Eve," the "Expulsion from Paradise," and many other scenes. Michelangelo painted while working on custom scaffolding 60 feet (18 meters) above the floor and painted over 10,000 square feet (930 square meters) of the ceiling. The "Creation" depicts the index finger of God pointing slightly downward toward Adam's finger bestowing life, mind and soul to our species.

This classic concept has been copied many times in many forms often commercially. For example, there is a famous scene in the blockbuster movie "E.T." when the cute alien named E.T. points his finger toward a boy's finger to heal his cut. This beautiful and classic concept of two fingers almost touching, conceived by Michelangelo in his "Creation," is reborn almost 500 years later in this emotional scene in the movie "E.T."

From 1534 to 1541, Michelangelo painted the "Last Judgment," an enormous fresco, on the entire wall behind the altar.

Other Famous Artists and Sculptors

The list of artists that follows is fairly representative of famous masters. However, there were dozens of others, particularly during the Italian Renaissance, that are not listed. Please refer to this book's bibliography for other books that offer additional information on the almost countless numbers of Italian masters. Also, it is easy to observe from the list of artists that follow, how often great masters came from families of talented artists. This is again a very prominent characteristic among the master violin builders that spanned generations, as you will read in the chapter on "Music."

Andrea Del Sarto (painter) born July 16, 1486 in Florence and died September 28, 1530. Del Sarto was a leading fresco artist in Florence during the High Renaissance period.

Fra Angelico (aka Beato Angelico & Guido di Pietro) (painter) born around 1387 in Vicchi and died on February 18, 1455. He painted mostly religious works and developed a notable unifying style for color and purity of line elements. *He was one of the master painters of the Renaissance.* Angelico was a monk who lived such an exemplary life that he was also called Beato, which means *blessed.*

Fra Bartolommeo (painter) born March 28, 1475 in Florence and died on October 31, 1517. He painted mostly religious subjects in the style of High Renaissance.

Bellini Family

- **Jacopo Bellini** (painter) born 1400 in Venice and died 1470. He was the father of Gentile Bellini and Giovanni Bellini. Most of his art has been lost but his greatest remaining contributions are his art notebooks that describe perspective, landscape and other topics relating to different painting techniques.

- **Gentile Bellini** (painter) born 1429 in Venice and died February 23, 1507. He painted Venetian life as it was at the time. Some of his later works included certain oriental characteristics, after he returned from a trip to Constantinople in 1479.

- **Giovanni Bellini** (painter) born 1430 in Venice and died November 1516. He was a master of color and lighting who later became the teacher of the great artist Titian. Titian (aka Tiziano Vecellio) became *one of the world's greatest master colorists.* Giovanni also taught the great painter Giorgione. He founded the Venetian school of painting that elevated Venice to the cultural level of Florence and Rome. Bellini became one of the greatest landscape painters of his time. His best known paintings are: "Christ's Blessing," "Giovanni Emo," "The Virgin and Child with Two Saints," "The Doge Barbarigo," "The Lamentation over the Body of Christ," "Virgin with Saints Mark, Benedict, Nicholas and Peter," "Madonna with Saints" and the "The Feast of the Gods."

Giovanni Lorenzo Bernini (sculptor, architect, painter and designer) born on December 7, 1598 in Naples and died on November 28, 1680. Bernini used action concepts and theatrical effects in his works and is *considered a founder of the Italian baroque style.* (Refer to the Architecture section of this chapter, Bernini also designed the grand Piazza of St. Peter's in Vatican City along with other famous structures).

Il Bronzino (painter and poet) born November 17, 1503 in Monticelli and died November 23, 1572. Noted for his portraits and elongated figures in the *early Mannerism* style.

Campi Brothers

- **Giulio Campi** (painter, architect and founder of the school of painters in Cremona) lived from 1500 to 1572. Among his students were his younger brothers who are listed below.
- **Antonio Campi** (painter) lived from 1536 to 1591.
- **Vincenzo Campi** (painter) lived from 1532 to 1591.
- **Bernardino Campi** (painter) lived from 1522 to 1590.

Canaletto (painter, etcher) born October 18, 1697 in Venice and died April 19, 1768. Best known for his accurate cityscapes and lively action scenes of London and Venice.

Vittore Carpaccio (painter) born 1450 in Venice and died 1522. He was noted for his use of color and detail in his St. George series of paintings.

Carracci Family

- **Ludovico Carracci** (painter) born April 21, 1555 in Bologna and died November 13, 1618. A pupil of Tintoretto, Ludovico Carracci and his artistic family members established a highly *prestigious painting academy* in Bologna called "Accademia degli Incamminati" in the 1580's. Translated into English it means the Academy of Progressives.
- **Annibale Carracci** (painter) born November 3, 1560 in Bologna and died July 15, 1609. He was Ludovico's brother and worked in his family's Academy and completed numerous masterpieces. *He is the most famous and accomplished Carracci and painted murals, ceilings and many large pieces.*
- **Agostino Carracci** (painter) born August 16, 1557 in Bologna and died February 23, 1602. Agostino was a cousin of the Carracci brothers who also worked in their Academy and was a notable painter in his own right.

Andrea del Castagno (painter) born 1421 in San Martino a Corella and died August 19, 1457. He was a Florentine artist in the early Renaissance who helped incorporate proper perspective and naturalism in religious paintings.

Giuseppe Castiglione (painter) lived from 1688 to 1766 was a Jesuit missionary who traveled to China in 1715 and *had a significant influence on Chinese painting.*

Benvenuto Cellini (goldsmith, sculptor and author) born November 3, 1500 in Florence and died there as well on February 13, 1571. *His works are considered among the finest of the Renaissance* and include these bronze works: "Nymph of Fontainebleau," on display at the Louvre, Paris; "Perseus and Medusa" on display at Loggia dei Lanzi, Florence and the beautiful gold statue "Saltcellar" portraying the goddess of earth with the god of the sea (Neptune), on display at Kunsthistorisches Museum, Vienna.

Cellini was commissioned by two Popes, Cosimo de' Medici and King Francis I who recognized his genius and convinced this celebrated Italian master to move to France for a five-year period. *Cellini's autobiography written between 1558 and 1562 is considered one of the most important documents of the period.*

For more about Cellini, refer to the chapters entitled "Literature" (Autobiography) and "Science & Technology" (Minted Coins & Metal Stamping).

Giovanni Cimabue (painter and mosaicist) born 1240 in Florence and died 1302. His works are a departure from the Byzantine painting to greater naturalism. He was the master of mosaics at the cathedral of Pisa.

Antonio Allegri da Correggio (painter) born 1489 or 1494 in Correggio and died March 5, 1534. *Correggio, one of the great Renaissance masters,* was influenced by da Vinci and subtly used soft colors in his works. Also, his decorated ceilings were completed through the use of his celebrated techniques.

Piero della Francesca (painter) born in Sansepolcro about 1412 and died there as well on October 12, 1492, the same day that Columbus discovered America. He was a leading artist and member of the Umbrian school who was known for his large magnificent frescos. Also, refer to the "Mathematics" chapter for more information on della Francesca.

Della Robbia Family
- **Luca Della Robbia** (sculptor) born 1399 or 1400 in Florence and died February 1482. Della Robbia perfected a technique for enameled terracotta using a special glaze of tin and other metals, often with gold highlights. He founded a family studio where his nephew Andrea and Andrea's three sons continued the tradition.
- **Andrea Della Robbia** (sculptor) born 1435 in Florence and died February 1525. Andrea della Robbia was the nephew of Luca. *Andrea crafted the famous medallions for the renowned Foundling*

Hospital in Florence. The Smithsonian Museum's National Gallery of Art in Washington D.C. has several of his pure white glazed terracotta works, notably "Madonna and Child with Cherubim" (1485). His three sons who are listed below followed in the family's artistic traditions.

- **Giovanni Della Robbia** (sculptor) born 1469 in Florence and died 1529.
- **Luca II Della Robbia** (sculptor) born 1480 in Florence and died 1550.
- **Girolamo Della Robbia** (sculptor) born 1488 in Florence and died 1566.

Domenichino (aka Domenico Zampieri) (painter) born October 1581 in Bologna and died April 6, 1641. Painted many frescos of landscapes, the best known is his "Hunt for Diana," 1618.

Duccio Di Buoninsegna (painter) born 1255 in Siena and died 1318. Founded the Sienese School of painting in Siena, Italy. He and Giotto were very influential in making the early transition from Gothic to Renaissance art.

Gaddi Family
- **Gaddo Gaddi** (painter and mosaicist) born 1260 in Florence and died 1333.
- **Taddeo Gaddi** (painter) born 1300 in Florence and died 1366. Son of Gaddo Gaddi and was a pupil and later assistant to Giotto. He became the chief Florentine painter after Giotto's death.
- **Agnolo Gaddi** (painter) born 1350 in Florence and died 1396. Son of Taddeo Gaddi and grandson of Gaddo Gaddi, Agnolo Gaddi painted in a style similar to Giotto.

Lorenzo Ghiberti (sculptor) born 1378 in Pelago and died December 1, 1455. *Donatello's master was the Gothic sculptor Lorenzo Ghiberti.* It is said that Ghiberti's works broke new ground in offering correct perspective. He was transitional, moving from the Gothic style to the more naturalistic Renaissance and human forms. Ghiberti *completed two very famous sets of bronze relief doors, "The Gates of Paradise," for the Baptistery in Florence.* The first set was made 1403-1424 and the second set from 1425-1452.

Domenico Ghirlandaio (aka Ghirlandajo) (painter) born 1449 in Florence and died January 11, 1494. He was born Domenico di Tommasio Bigardi and *the great Michelangelo studied in his studio.* Ghirlandaio was one of the principle figures in the early years of the Italian Renaissance. *He completed some of the frescos on the walls of the Sistine Chapel.* The Smithsonian Museum's National Gallery of

Art in Washington D.C. exhibits one of his religious works.

Giorgione (painter) born 1477 in Castelfranco and died 1511. Much of his work has been lost over time, but his innovation and use of color influenced many contemporaries. His masterpiece entitled the "Tempest," painted in 1505, is one of his greatest surviving paintings. Giovanni Bellini was his master. Bellini also taught Titian, who became the master of all master colorists.

Lorezetti Brothers

- **Pietro Lorezetti** (painter) born in Siena 1280 and died 1348. He was a major Sienese painter who was influenced by Giotto and Pisano.

- **Ambrogio Lorezetti** (painter) born in Siena date of birth uncertain and died about 1348. A major Sienese painter influenced by Giotto and Pisano. He was more creative than his brother Pietro Lorezetti and painted frescos of every day Italian life, such as allegories of government actions. He was a master of spatial depths as illustrated in his paintings.

Benedetto da Maiano (sculptor, architect) lived in Italy from 1442 to 1497. In their family studio in Florence, he worked with his younger brother Giuliano da Maiano on many architectural projects. He sculpted many religious works, including the marble pulpit at Santa Croce, Florence (1472-1476) and the marble altarpieces at Mastrogiudici Chapel, S. Anna dei Lombardi, Naples (1489) and at S. Fina Chapel, Cathedral, S. Gimignano.

Pinturicchio (aka Bernardino di Bette) (artist) born in Perugia in 1454 and died in Siena in 1513. Before working independently, he collaborated with Perugino (aka Pietro Vannucci) during his early career, most notably in the Sistine Chapel (1481-1483).

Antonio Pisano (aka Pisanello) (painter, medalmaker, miniaturist) born in Pisa around 1380 and probably died in Mantua around 1455. He is noted for his famous "Annunciazione" for the "Monumento Brenzoni" (1426).

Pollaiuolo Family

- **Jacopo Pollaiuolo** (goldsmith) born about 1410 in Florence, he was a well established goldsmith who trained his sons Antonio and Piero.

- **Antonio Pollaiuolo** (goldsmith, sculptor, engraver, painter) born about 1429 in Florence and died 1498. He was one of the first artists to perform anatomical dissections to improve the naturalism of his art. His figures in action positions are very realistic, e.g. "Dancing Nudes" (painting). His studio was one of the leading

studios in Florence.
- **Piero Pollaiuolo** (sculptor) born 1443 in Florence and died 1496. He was the brother of Antonio but less accomplished. {NOTE: There is another family member listed in the separate list of Architects at the end of this chapter. **Simone del Pollaiuolo** (architect) was the nephew of Antonio and Piero. *He is credited for designing sections of the famous Strozzi palace.*}

Jacopo Da Pontormo (painter) born May 24, 1494 in Pontormo and died January 2, 1557. He was one of the first Florentine Mannerists.

Luca Signorelli (painter) born in Cortona around 1455 and died there as well around 1523. He is noted for several masterpieces including the painting "Testamento e Morte di Mose" in the Sistine Chapel in Rome and the "Sacra Famiglia" in the illustrious Uffizi Palace in Florence. His "Educazione di Pan" was destroyed in Berlin in 1944 during World War II.

Guido Reni (painter and engraver) born 1575 in Bologna and died 1642. He was a student of Carracci and later opened a studio in Bologna. One of his most significant works "Aurora" was painted in 1613.

Giovanni Battista Tiepolo (painter) born March 5, 1696 in Venice and died March 27, 1770. He is noted for his large frescos. He painted in Italy, Wurzburg, Germany and Spain.

Tintoretto (aka Jacopo Robusti) (painter) born 1518 in Venice and died May 31, 1594. He was an expert colorist and Mannerist in the Venetian school. He was one of the last great Renaissance masters. His famous masterpieces include "The Crucifixion," "The Miracle of the Slave," "Marriage at Cana" and "Alvise Cornaro." His works are displayed in many world-renowned museums, such as the Scuola Grande di S. Rocco and the Accademia Museum, both of which are in Venice. Tintoretto's own self-portrait is in the famous Louvre museum in Paris.

Paolo Uccello (painter) born 1397 in Pratovecchio and died December 12, 1475. He was an early pioneer in developing a system of perspective.

Domenico Veneziano (painter) born probably 1400 in Venice and died 1461. He painted landscapes with rich colors, which displayed an innovative use of space.

Paolo Veronese (painter) born 1528 in Verona and died April 19, 1588. Veronese painted mostly religious themes and was an expert colorist.

Andrea del Verrocchio (sculptor and painter) born 1435 in Florence and died 1488. Much of his works have been lost, but the remaining works illustrate his ability to create great detail in his paintings and sculptures. *He was a leading figure in his time and taught the young Leonardo da Vinci* when Leonardo was about the age of 15 in 1467. Some say that in later years, Leonardo da Vinci provided some assistance when Verrocchio painted his "Baptism of Christ."

Giorgio Vasari (painter, architect and writer) born July 30, 1511 in Arezzo and died June 27, 1574. *As an architect he designed the famous Uffizi Palace in Florence.* He was also an accomplished artist who studied under Andrea del Sarto. *He was the leading biographer of the Renaissance artists and provided much information about their lives and times.* In 1550, he wrote his famous, "The Lives of the Most Eminent Italian Architects, Painters and Sculptors." The original Italian title of his famous book is "Le Vite de Più Eccelenti Pittori, Scultori, et Architettori."

Zuccaro Brothers (aka Zucchero or Zuccari)
- **Taddeo Zuccaro** (painter) born 1529 in Florence and died 1566. He painted frescos for the Vatican and in the Caprarola Palace.
- **Federigo Zuccaro** (painter) born 1543 in Florence and died 1609. With his brother Taddeo, Federigo also painted frescos for the Vatican and in the Caprarola Palace. He also was an early proponent of art theory analysis and *was one of the first to provide lectures and discussions on art.* Zucarro also painted portraits of Queen Elizabeth and Mary Stuart while in Great Britain and for Philip II while in Spain. *He is also credited for building the magnificent Zuccaro Palace.*

ARCHITECTURE:

Architectural Designs, Engineering & Construction

Roman Influences

Architecture throughout the world has been profoundly influenced by Etruscan, Roman and other Italian architects and engineers. The Romans were a civilization of skillful engineers and prolific builders. They understood the benefits of advanced engineering for civilian, commercial and military purposes. In fact, to advance in the ranks of the Roman army one had to be an engineer. Caesar himself was a skilled engineer. His army built roads, and also suspension and pontoon bridges. They also needed to understand swamp drainage and have access to fresh water supplies. Some Roman bridges and roads, such as the Appian Way, are still in use today. U.S. General Patton, a history buff, took great pride in marching his troops over Roman roads and bridges during World War II, since these historic structures were used by Caesar, Pompey, Maxentius and other great generals of Rome.

As the Roman Empire grew, new cities were built following a standard Roman plan for surrounding farmlands, roads, commercial areas, public parks, sewage systems, and aqueducts that provided fresh water supplies for the population. The early Romans greatly benefited from their neighbors, the Etruscans, who inhabited central Italy, which is now called Tuscany. The *Etruscans pioneered basic domes, vaulted ceilings and arches.* The Romans were the first to refine and perfect these technological achievements and employed them throughout their Empire in massive buildings. The significance of the dome and vaulted ceilings should not be underestimated. Prior to these inventions large buildings, such as older Greek temples were built with massive columns in the interior space to hold up the roof. The Roman domes and vaulted ceilings allowed for large, spacious interiors never seen before in human history. *Their architectural and engineering feats were unmatched by others until modern times.*

The Romans were the first to incorporate concrete, terra-cotta and fired bricks in their designs. This variety of new building materials allowed the Romans still greater freedom in design and construction. The *Romans invented concrete and this consequently accelerated their design complexity and building capabilities in every project, from dome to road construction. The Pantheon in Rome, built from 120 AD to124 AD, boasts a massive domed roof that is mostly poured concrete* (see the reference on the Pantheon later in this chapter). Also, the architectural terms such as *cupola* and *rotunda* are Italian words. In Italian *cupola* means *dome* and *rotunda* is something *round*. You will read about *rotunda* buildings later in this section. *The Romans also invented "pouzzolana cement" that would set and harden underwater, useful for the construction of bridges and sewers.*

The Romans also invented the *basilica*. In ancient Rome the *basilica* was a large building with many vaulted ceilings and domes, which was used to transact business and legal matters. These were usually rectangular in shape with a semicircular protruding apse that provided a regal entrance. The *basilica* also featured hallways with windows for light. *This is probably the earliest manifestation of the modern office building.* There are very early examples of *basilicas* in Pompeii and Rome. The Christians later built *basilicas* using the same fundamental layout and plans for their churches. The floor plan was so well conceived that its basic design has been used in church *basilicas* throughout the ages.

Byzantine architecture borrowed heavily from Roman designs and technical engineering knowledge. St. John's basilica built in the 5th century in Constantinople is an example of the strong Roman influence on Byzantine architecture. Constantinople was part of the Roman Empire and was the eastern capital of the Empire from 330 AD until about 497 AD when the Western Empire fell to barbarians. Also, the huge and famous Hagia Sophia (or Saint Sophia or Church of Holy Wisdom) in Constantinople, built by the Emperor Justinian I in 537 AD, relies on Roman designs and technology. Hagia Sophia is now a museum. It should be noted that the Byzantines developed new ways to place round domes on square buildings, thus improving on the earlier Roman dome design and construction methods. Byzantine architecture uses *pendentives* that bridge the corners of a square building in order to provide a circular base for the round dome.

The Romans greatly admired the Greeks for their math and science. However, the Romans were known for testing, improving and implementing ideas and theories, thus making new discoveries and turning them into practical applications. In particular, they turned theory into advanced architectural and engineering realities.

The Romans also discovered the ancient Lighthouse of Alexandria (400 feet or 122 meters high) on the island of Pharos, the first true lighthouse, which was built by the Greeks. The Romans understood its full potential and subsequently built improved lighthouses all around Italy's shore. After Rome captured Britain, *the Romans built the first lighthouses in northern Europe.* They built them at Dover and Boulogne to assist ships crossing the English Channel. The remains of the Dover lighthouse built by the Romans still stands today.

Many of the great Renaissance architects and artists visited Rome and benefited from the study of ancient ruins and classic designs. The venerable architects Brunelleschi, Alberti and Palladio, as well as the great sculptor Donatello, all visited Rome for this reason. A technological triumph was completed in 1446 when Filippo Brunelleschi completed the large dome of the Gothic cathedral St. Maria Del Fiore in Florence *without the use of any scaffolding.* Brunelleschi was inspired by Roman construction and architectural designs. (Refer to the later reference labeled, *About Filippo Brunelleschi,* for more on the genius behind the revolutionary construction of this dome.)

Brunelleschi's younger contemporary, Leon Battista Alberti, was strongly influenced by the great Roman architect Vitruvius who wrote the oldest known architectural work entitled "Ten Books of Architecture." Alberti completely rewrote Vitruvius's classic ten book architectural treatise and Albert's ten books became a "bible" of architecture and influenced others who followed him, such as Serlio, Palladio and Vignola, *who all wrote masterpieces on architecture that had enormous influences on world architecture.*

A final note needs to be said about Roman engineering. Roman cities were well planned with sewer systems, baths, aqueducts, homes with indoor plumbing and central heating. *Bathing and cleanliness were only known to the Romans,* while the rest of Europe did not generally bathe. After the fall of Rome, bathing was not a common activity in Europe and was thought to be physically unhealthy. It was also discouraged for religious reasons. The Western world did not experience any measure of cleanliness again until the 18th century.

Italian Renaissance Influences

Roman and Italian arches, vaulted ceilings, domes, columns, floor plans and other decorative forms were copied throughout Europe. For example, in the 1530's Leonardo da Vinci and other architects were brought to France by King Francis I for their architectural knowledge and talents. While many illustrious Italian architects influenced world architecture, Andrea Palladio stands as the giant of architecture. *Palladio for centuries has influenced architecture more than anyone in the history of architecture!* For example, even the U.S. Capitol Building is classified as Palladian style architecture.

During the Renaissance, the celebrated architect Andrea Palladio built churches, palaces, castles and villas in Italy. *Palladio was also a prolific writer, and his designs and architectural books have had a greater influence on European and early American architecture than any other architect or text.* His books became standard architectural texts for centuries. Palladio wrote the monumental architectural treatise entitled "The Four Books of Architecture" ("I Quattro Libri dell'Architettura"). *His palaces and villas are astonishing in that they boast magnificent exteriors, yet highly functional interiors.* He also introduced grand entrances with sets of columns that were matched above with balconies having corresponding column sets. (Also, see the section on Palaces and Villas later in this chapter.) His design style became known as *Palladian* or *Palladianism* and this architectural style is very common in Great Britian, the United States, Russia, Italy, France and Germany. In Northern Ireland, the well known Cooke Castle designed by James Wyatt is a classic example of Palladian architecture. There is also a section later in this chapter that addresses the enormous influence of Italian architects in Russia. Further, the next chapter in this book documents the great impact of Palladian style architecture on colonial and government buildings in the United States.

The famous English architect, Inigo Jones, visited Italy to study architecture and returned to England with Palladio's architectural books. He was greatly influenced by Italy's classic buildings and their beauty. Following Jones was the *Palladian* architect Sir Christopher Wren who planned Saint Paul's Cathedral in London, giving it many similarities to Italian monuments. Christopher Wren and John Wood, the designer of the streets of Bath, relied heavily on the books of Palladio and Serlio. Sabastiano Serlio (1475-1554), also a highly influential architect, wrote a set of five books on architecture, which had an enormous influence on western architecture and were widely read during his time. His books, as well as Palladio's books included geometry, mathematical perspective, theory and very detailed woodcuts of Roman and Italian architecture. These books were invaluable sources for architects of northern Europe, Russia and the United States, who had never been to Rome or experienced Italian architecture. Serlio also carefully documented the newer Tuscan and Composite style columns of Italy that supplemented the older Greek Doric, Ionic and Corinthian columns. These became the foundation for many architectural types for centuries to follow. Serlio also developed twelve temple designs of his own invention. Giocamo da Vignola born in Vignola in 1507 and died in Rome in 1573, was a contemporary of both Palladio and Serlio. Vignola, whose real name was Giacomo Barozzi, wrote another treatise widely read throughout Europe entitled "Orders of Architecture" which influenced many. Vignola is also known for his churches and for succeeding Michelangelo in 1564 as the architect overseeing the work at St. Peter's Cathedral. He also built many villas including one for Pope Julius III along with several religious buildings and gardens.

English landscape architecture has been similarly influenced by Italian gardens, paintings and architecture. In the 18th century, the formal English gardens were transformed to look more like picturesque Italian landscape and art, and frequently included miniature copies of Roman ruins. The English word *picturesque* is derived from the Italian word *pittoresco,* which means "in a manner of painters." Thus, the picturesque English garden evolved its layout and design to simulate the appearance of classic Italian painting. In this case, life imitates art.

About Andrea Palladio

Andrea Palladio developed a magnificent yet practical architectural style that has been emulated throughout the world and has earned him the respect awarded no other architect in the history of architecture. *He is considered to be the most influential architect in the history of architecture.* The German poet Johann Wolfgang von Goethe said this of Palladio, "There is something divine about his talent, something comparable to the power of a great poet." Palladio's revolutionary changes and style had an enormous influence on European and early American design. He developed new practical designs that renewed ancient classic architecture blended with Renaissance styles. Imposing examples of his work can be seen in Vicenza and other cities in the Veneto section near Venice where he built many villas for the aristocracy of his time. He was born November 30, 1508 in Padua and his real name was Andrea di Pietro della Gondola, but he became known as "Palladio." He was an apprentice to a stonecutter in Padua at the age of thirteen. At fifteen he worked for Giangiorgio Trissino, who ran a leading stonecutting and mason workshop in Vicenza. Trissino was his principle mentor, who helped to educate Andrea and also introduced him to the concepts of classical architecture. His association with Trissino introduced Andrea to the wealthy patrons of Vicenza, Padua and Venice. It was Trissino who gave the name Palladio to Andrea. The name has Greek roots meaning *wisdom* and was also a name used by Trissino in an epic poem that he composed.

Palladio also studied the works and books of the great Roman architect Vitruvius, as well as the eminent Donato Bramante, along with the Renaissance genius Leon Battista Alberti, who also wrote an influential text on architecture. In 1538, Palladio started his own workshop and began to build his famous series of villas and palaces for the nobles and aristocrats of Vicenza. He also completed three magnificent churches in Venice, San Giorgio Maggiore (1560 to 1580), Il Redentore (1576 to 1591) and Le Zitelle (S.M. della Presentazione). These churches have survived the centuries and are still visited by both scholars and tourists. Additionally, in Venice, Palladio designed the refectory (monastery dining room) for the Benedictine monastery of San Giorgio Maggiore, the cloister of the monastery of Santa Maria della Carita (now the Accademia Museum), and the facade of the church of San Francesco della Vigna. In Vicenza he also built: Palazzo Chiericati (1550 - 1580); Palazzo Thiene (1545); Teatro Olimpico (1584); Villa Trissino (1576); Villa Capra or Villa Rotunda (1566-1571), which was the model for Thomas Jefferson's Virginia residence Monticello. In Malcontenta he also built the Villa Foscari (1549-1563).

Palladio also originated a beautiful combination of windows, still called today, the *Palladian window*, after its creator. His design places two vertical rectangular windows on opposite sides of a larger (and more square) central window that is capped by a semicircular window. Look around and observe just how common this design remains, particularly in neo-Victorian style homes. Sometimes shutters replace the two side windows, but the effect is the same.

Palladio, an early adopter of movable type, was also an author and published several books including a guide to the classical ruins of Rome ("La Antichita di Roma," 1554) and a new translation of Caesar's "Commentaries" with his sons. Palladio also worked with Daniele Barbaro on a new edition of Vitruvius's "Ten Books of Architecture" (the oldest known books on architecture). In 1570, he published in Venice his enormously influential masterpiece "I Quattro Libri dell' Architettura" ("The Four Books of Architecture") which included 217 meticulous woodcut illustrations of houses, temples, villas, palaces and architectural orders. *This work has had an unparalleled influence on western architecture and is considered the most famous architectural book ever written. It has had over 40 editions and has been translated into every European language. It remains in print today* both in paperback and hardcover (e.g. Dover Publications, New York). In August of 1580 Palladio died near Venice in the town of Vicenza where he lived and completed many of his famous buildings.

About Filippo Brunelleschi

Filippo Brunelleschi, probably the greatest of all early Renaissance architects, was born in Florence in 1377 and died there as well in 1446. He began his career in Florence as a clockmaker and goldsmith and was not formally trained as an architect. However, his genius allowed him to pursue his interest in architecture. Brunelleschi became an advisor, early in his architectural career, offering new concepts for the cathedral Santa Maria Novella in Florence. The highlight of his career culminated in the construction of the tall and massive dome atop the famous Santa Maria Del Fiore cathedral in Florence. The majestic dome of Santa Maria Del Fiore can be seen from almost anywhere in Florence. The Roman Pantheon partially inspired the revolutionary solutions Brunelleschi used in his dome. Perhaps in deference to the master builders of Rome, Brunelleschi made the diameter inside of his dome 142 feet (43.2 meters), equal to the dome in the Roman Pantheon. Some say that Dante's nine rings of hell in his masterpiece, "The Divine Comedy," inspired the nine stone and wooden architectural rings inside the dome's supporting structure.

Brunelleschi accepted the challenge to build the massive dome that was originally designed for the Santa Maria Del Fiore cathedral in 1367 by the famous architect Neri di Fioravanti. However, the design and scale of the dome perplexed architects and engineers who were unable to propose a viable construction solution. Brunelleschi's solutions for constructing the dome introduced many revolutionary concepts. The dome he built uses precise interlocking sections that mathematically form a series of inverse cones. He devised a revolutionary set of stone and wooden interlocking structures in the hidden interior of the dome's shell, a kind of architectural chain, which supported the arching masonry during construction. This allowed Brunelleschi to build what is still the largest masonry dome in the world, 142 feet (43.2 meters) in diameter and 300 feet (90 meters) in height - and without an interior scaffold! In his day, architects used a complex and expensive wooden scaffold to support a masonry dome under construction as masons gradually laid the arching brickwork. When a dome was completed and the mortar fully cured, workers had to carefully let sand out of bags that the scaffold rested on. This gradually lowered the scaffold away from the dome's structure. If a scaffold was lowered asymmetrically, the resulting imbalance of the dome's structures often caused a total collapse of the dome. Brunelleschi's design eliminated the scaffold, and masons laid over four million bricks higher and higher, which were sustained by the architectural chains. Further, the marble lantern that rests atop the dome weighs over one million pounds. Brunelleschi's critics thought this weight would collapse the dome. However, Brunelleschi knew the lantern actually strengthened the dome by acting as a keystone that locked the eight sides of the dome together. He worked on the design challenges of the dome for 28 years and completed it in 1446, the same year he died. Brunelleschi also had to invent ingenious and specialized cranes and hoists for construction of the dome and the lantern as well.

Brunelleschi used mathematical perspectives to accomplish many architectural innovations and pioneered new concepts in building proportions and symmetry. He worked as an architect and engineer and developed new revolutionary changes for Renaissance architecture that incorporated great domed interior spaces. His other major projects include: Church of San Spirito, Florence (1434 - 1482); Ospedale Degli Innocenti (Foundling Hospital), Florence (1419 - 1445); Pazzi Chapel in the Franciscan church, Florence (1442 – 1461); St. Maria degli Angeli, an oratory in the Camaldolese Monastery, Florence (1434 – 1437); San Lorenzo, Florence (1421 - 1440); Sacrestia Vecchia ("Old Sacristy") a square building with hemispherical dome.

Arches - Keystone & Triumphal
Rome
The Romans invented the arch with the keystone as its architectural centerpiece of strength. The keystone is the inverted trapezoid shaped stone that rests at the top of the arch.

Romans used many styles of arches in many different types of construction. Roman Triumphal Arches were built throughout the Roman Empire as a symbol of unity and power. These were designed and built as majestic and imperial reminders that the territory was part of the Empire. These massive arches are decorated with columns, carvings of wreaths, torches, faces, animals and other designs. They feature inscriptions that explain the purpose and dedication of the arch. For example, in Rome the famous "Arch of Constantine" built in 313 AD was dedicated to the Emperor Constantine and stands at the location where he returned to Rome after his successful conquest over Maxentius. The battle with Maxentius, at the Milvian Bridge, is of great significance to Christians. It was just before the start of this battle that Constantine saw his legendary vision of a cross in the sky and as a result converted to Christianity. He then made Christianity the official religion of the entire Rome Empire. In turn, this event precipitated the

Triumphal Arch of Constantine in Rome

spread of Christianity throughout Europe for centuries. His success at this battle also gave him unequivocal control of the western Mediterranean region.

Other famous examples of Roman Triumphal arches include: the "Arch of Trajan" in Ancona, built in 115 AD to honor the Emperor Trajan who had the harbor built for the City of Ancona; the "Arch of Titus" in Rome, built in 81 AD to commemorate the capture of Jerusalem; and the "Arch of Septimius Severus" in Rome, built in 205 AD commemorating the Emperor's Parthian military campaigns. This arch has a tremendous triple arch, unique carvings and Roman

Composite style capitals on its columns. The entire monument is 69 feet (21 meters) high and 76 feet (23 meters) wide.

These types of arches have been copied by other countries and civilizations for the past 2000 years. The American Museum of Natural History in New York City uses a Roman Triumphal Arch as its front entrance. Another copy of a Roman arch, commissioned by Napoleon in 1806 and completed in 1836, is the famous "Arc de Triomphe" in Paris. It commemorates battle victories of the Revolutionary and Napoleonic periods and has a small museum, along with the tomb of the unknown soldier with an eternal flame under the arch. A smaller but famous Roman arch stands in New York City at Washington Square Park, facing north on prestigious Fifth Ave.

"Arc de Triomphe" in Paris, which is styled after the triumphal arches that were built by the Romans throughout Europe

R. R. Esposito

Aqueducts
Rome

As the Roman Republic expanded and prospered, its cities grew in size and the need to supply fresh water for its citizens required new solutions. The Romans were not the only builders of aqueducts but their quantity, engineering complexity and massive size cannot be compared to any others. The Romans built aqueducts throughout Europe for more than 500 years from 312 BC to 226 AD. Appius Claudius Caecus, who was the equivalent of a Roman congressman, constructed the first Roman aqueduct. The longest aqueduct built by the Romans was the Aqua Marcia built in 144 BC. A classic example of a Roman aqueduct is the Pont du Gard in Nimes, France. It was built in 14 AD and has three layers of arches that rest on top of each other and rises to a height of 173 feet (53 meters). It is one of the tallest aqueducts and has survived almost 2000 years and is well preserved. This aqueduct carried over 30 million gallons (114 million liters) of water every day over 31 miles (50 kilometers) with a very gradual downward pitch that was perfectly graded and expertly engineered. The total drop of the aqueduct from start to finish, over the 31 mile (50 kilometers) topography, was only 55 feet (17 meters)!

The water supply for the City of Rome, with a population of over a million citizens at its peak, included 11 major aqueducts. As a testament to their superb engineering, a Roman aqueduct called El Puente is still in use and carries water from the Rio Frio into the city of Segovia in Spain! This aqueduct is 128 feet (39 meters) in height and was built using perfectly fitted granite blocks. It has two tiers of 118 majestic rounded arches The word aqueduct is derived from the Latin word *aqua* (water) and *ducere* (to lead).

The Romans were also the *first plumbers* and used lead pipes with brass valves and fittings. Refer to the "Science & Technology" chapter for more information on this early Roman technology.

Basilica
Rome

For information on the invention of the basilica, please refer to the first entry of this ARCHITECTURE section, entitled Roman Influences.

Coliseum (Colosseum)
Rome

The Coliseum was originally known as the Flavian Amphitheater. It was built as an arena for plays, performances, and gladiators, but was also flooded for shows of mock sea battles. Gladiators were almost always prisoners of war or slaves and were considered somewhat uncivilized and subhuman. They fought until wounded or dead depending on the event that they entered. Sometimes if a gladiator fought unusually well he could be granted freedom. The Coliseum rises four stories high, each story illustrating a different architectural style: the first Doric, the second Ionic, the third Corinthian, and the fourth a Roman Composite style. It was built with imposing travertine stone. Today's estimates are that the structure held over 50,000 spectators. However, according to the "Chronographia," published in 354 AD, it held up to 87,000 spectators. Perhaps today's estimates contain some modern assumptions regarding the space needed for comfortable seating. It had eighty entrances and the audience could be vacated in ten minutes.

The Coliseum in Rome

R. R. Esposito

Over the centuries the Coliseum has been damaged by earthquakes and during the Middle Ages stones and marble were removed for new construction. The massive structure is a tribute to Italian advanced architecture, design and durability. The construction of the Coliseum was begun in Rome in 72 AD by Vespasian, the first of the Flavian emperors. It was completed in 80 AD and dedicated by Titus. Titus was a fair and just emperor who lived from 39 AD to 81 AD and is quoted as saying "Friends I have lost a day," when he had reflected after finishing a day without helping another.

Although the Coliseum was a fantastic architectural marvel, that attracted both citizens and tourists, the "Circuses," which were large chariot racetracks with stadium seating, were actually more commonly attended than events at the Coliseum. "Circus Maximus" was Rome's most famous racetrack. The English word *circus* is derived from these Roman buildings and events.

Columns - Roman and Italian

The Romans and Italians created new column designs from the original Greek designs (see the next page). The Greeks developed three styles of columns: Doric (fluted column with a simple capital on top), Ionic (fluted column with a scroll type capital on top) and Corinthian (fluted column with a very ornate leafy capital on top). *The Romans combined the Ionic with the Corinthian and developed a new Composite design.* This new design uses the scroll from the Ionic capital along with a Corinthian floral capital design at the bottom half of the capital. The famous "Arch of Titus" in Rome displays Composite capitals on its massive columns. *During the 16th century in Italy, another column and capital developed called Tuscan.* It is a simple but very elegant design that has been frequently used in later centuries in many other nations. *It is very commonly found in Britain and the United States.* This Tuscan type column rests on a pedestal or base. It has a simple un-fluted column that tapers slightly at the top with a square capital at the top.

During the Renaissance in Italy many column variations were used but the five types described above are the basis for most architectural column designs. In his highly influential set of five architectural books, the Renaissance architect Sebastiano Serlio documented the Composite and Tuscan style columns of Italy that supplemented the older Greek Doric, Ionic and Corinthian columns. (Also, in the chapter

"Art and Architecture: Contributions to America" read how Italian sculptors created unique column designs, using graceful corncobs and tobacco leaves in the capitals of columns, for buildings in Washington D.C.)

Types of columns:
Original Greek (top),
Roman Composite (bottom left),
Italian Tuscan (bottom right)

Concrete – Reinforced (new type)
Pier Luigi Nervi

Nervi was born June 21, 1891 in Sorvino in the Lombardy region and died in Rome, January 9, 1979. He received his degree in engineering from the University of Bologna. In the 1940's, he experimented with new building materials and invented a new type of reinforced concrete (ferrocemento), consisting of a steel mesh core covered with layers of mortar and concrete. This new construction material allowed Nervi to create revolutionary designs that were graceful yet strong. The Royal Institute of British Architects, the

R. R. Esposito

American Institute of Architects and the Academi d'Architecture awarded Nervi several Gold Medals for his imaginative and beautiful buildings. He was also a professor of engineering at the University of Rome from 1946 to 1961. Nervi designed over two dozen large projects including the Turin Exhibition Hall (1949), two circular Olympic stadiums in Rome (1957 to 1960), the Palazzo del Lavoro in Turin (1961), George Washington Bridge Bus Terminal in NYC (1962) and San Francisco cathedral (1970). He also co-designed the UNESCO building in Paris (1953) and the Pirelli skyscraper in Milan (1958).

The Romans invented *concrete* and a specialized concrete used in underwater construction. For more information refer to the first entry of this ARCHITECTURE section, called 'Architectural Designs, Engineering & Construction.'

Dome
Etruscan, Roman and Italian Renaissance

For information on the invention of the dome, please refer to the first entry of this ARCHITECTURE section, called Architectural Designs, Engineering & Construction.

Egyptian Sphinx Restoration and Preservation
Roman Republic

From 30 BC to the end of the 2nd century AD, the Romans freed the Sphinx from the sand that covered it and rebuilt sections that eroded and collapsed over the many centuries. Like the ancient Egyptians, the Romans romanticized the Sphinx and it was used as a gathering place and a backdrop for various performances and plays. The people of Busiris, a village located near the Sphinx, left a monument in honor of the Roman leaders, Emperor Nero and Claudius Babillus (a Governor), who were responsible for the restoration.

Most of the Roman restorations were applied to the two paws and sides of the Sphinx. The Romans revered history and did not remove any of the ancient Egyptian stones. Their restoration preserved the original ancient stonework under layers of new small brick sized stones, which they added to restore the shape and preserve the huge structure. Archaeologist Mark Lehner of the Oriental Institute of the University of Chicago documented the Roman work in 1979. Further, the Romans paved the sanctuary's floor of the Sphinx. Before the Romans, others made attempts to restore the Sphinx. However, the Roman restoration was the largest and most comprehensive effort in history. Roman technical engineering and construction expertise restored and saved this magnificent monument for our civilization to appreciate and study. Historians consistently credit the Romans as the master builders of all time. Their reconstruction project of the Sphinx restored features that were eroded and lost over a period of 2500 years. Commissioned by the Pharaoh Khafre, the Sphinx was built during the period 2613 BC - 2498 BC and lines up with the Pyramid of Khafre at the base of its causeway. The ancient Egyptians also demonstrated impressive building skills that were astonishing for their time, which have endured for over four thousand years. These massive, heavy structures are great accomplishments, but are much less sophisticated than the arches, vaulted ceilings, domes and basilicas engineered by the Romans.

Palaces and Villas

Italy is the home of many exquisite castles, palaces and villas, for example the Citadel in Ferrara, Ferrara Palaces, Palazzo Vecchio, Strozzi Palace, Uffizi Palace, Zucarro Palace, the Ducal Palace of Urbino and the very famous Palace of the Doges in Venice. There are also many magnificent Cornaro castles and villas around Venice on the mainland in the Vicenza section. Of the many castles and villas of this famous Venetian family, only 22 survived the test of time. For more than 1,000 years the vast wealth of the Cornaro family supported the arts by commissioning the artists and architects of Venice to create palaces, chapels, church art, villas, paintings and theaters.

The renowned 16th century architect Andrea Palladio designed many famous villas including the magnificent Villa Cornaro at Padua for Giorgio Cornaro. This famous villa boasts one of Palladio's new designs. This innovative design incorporated the use of a set of six columns at the entrance, with a balcony above supporting the roof with yet another set of matching columns directly above. This design of a double set of six columns is also used for the front entrance of the White House in Washington D.C. Earlier portions of this ARCHITECTURE section discuss Palladio in more detail. *He is renowned for being the world's most influential architect* and his style of architecture, called *Palladian*, is emulated worldwide. A noted example of *Palladian* architecture is the U.S. Capitol Building in

Washington, D.C. (Also, refer to the chapter "Art & Architecture - Contributions to America" for more information of the influence of Palladio on American architecture.)

The English words *palace* and *villa* are both derived from Rome's Latin language. The word *palace* is derived from the Palatine Hill in Rome, where the homes of Roman emperors stood. The name of the Palatine Hill in Latin was *Palatium*. The location of emperors' homes on this hill led to the use of *Palatium* to mean *the emperor's residence*. Over time, *Palatium* came to mean a royal residence. *Palatium* later evolved into *palais* in English after some changes in Old French. Finally, it became *palace* in modern English. The word *villa* is actually a Latin word which first described a large country home or dwelling, but later came to mean *town* or *village* (*Village* is another English word derived from the Latin word *villa*).

The English language also derived the word *villain* from the Latin word *villa*. This took some time to evolve. The Romans used the Latin word *villanus* for a peasant who lived in a village (*villa* in Latin). Over the centuries this evolved into *vilain* or *vilein* in medieval France and England. Because landowners and the wealthy looked down upon these poor peasants, the word *vilain* or *vilein* came to mean a crude or rough person, uneducated with poor manners. In time this negative and derogatory image was carried over to the modern English as the word *villain*, which now means *criminal* or *scoundrel*.

Pantheon
Roman Republic

The Pantheon in Rome was built by Emperor Hadrian (120 AD to 124 AD) as a temple and boasts a massive domed roof (142 feet or 43.2 meters) that is mostly poured concrete. The Pantheon contained *the world's largest interior space for 1500 years.* The dome boasted the largest span until Brunelleschi's dome at the Florence Cathedral was built from 1420 to 1436.

This building, including the domed roof and bronze doors, is well preserved for today's tourists. The Pantheon has been perfectly preserved, and for two thousand continuous years, it has been a place of worship. Originally, it was a place of worship for pre-Christian gods. When Christianity became the official religion of the Roman Empire it was re-dedicated to the Virgin Mary. The dome has an opening at its top (oculus) to emit light. The dome's engineering is an astonishing accomplishment with respect to its technology, as well as its durability. It was constructed using stepped concrete rings as its underlying structure. Not only is each ring smaller as you approach the top, but each is engineered with less density in the concrete. Pumice was used to lighten the mass of the concrete. Other Roman architecture included domes constructed of interlocking arches. Originally, the exterior masonry walls of the Pantheon's circular room, beneath the dome, were covered with exquisitely colored marble slabs. These were removed after the fall of Rome, during the "Dark Ages."

Pisa – The Leaning Tower
Bonanno Pisano

Bonanno Pisano began the construction of this famous tower on August 9, 1173 as the bell tower for the city's cathedral. This magnificent marble tower is 179 feet (55 meters) high and 50 feet (15 meters) wide. The tower is part of the famous Piazza del Duomo, or Dome Square, which includes the cathedral, the domed baptistery (baptismal fount) and the campanile (bell tower), better known as the "Leaning Tower."

This beautiful, elaborately decorated tower in Pisa has been leaning for over 800 years and is now 15 feet (4.6 meters) out of perpendicular. There is a popular belief that Galileo dropped weights from the leaning tower of Pisa as part of his famous experiments in gravity and speed. While this may be folklore, it is certain that while living in Pisa, Galileo built and used inclined planes for these experiments (see the "Science & Technology" chapter).

The tower was closed to visitors from 1990 to 2001, as engineers struggled to find a way to save the 800-year-old, 16,000 ton structure from eventual collapse. Over the centuries the tower persisted on advancing its lean toward the south. The project to stabilize the tower met with many engineering problems during the 11-year engineering project that cost over $30 million, until it was successfully completed. A cadre of architects, engineers and soil mechanics joined the team to save the tower. The complex project included temporarily placing 960 tons of lead ingots on the north side of the tower to help stabilize the tower. Then liquid nitrogen was pumped around the base to freeze ground water at minus 200 degrees Fahrenheit to prevent flooding, while 80 tons of soil was removed from underneath to gently persuade the tower to reduce its lean by 16 inches (400 mm), greatly increasing its stability. The top of the tower's south edge still leans out 15 feet (4.6 meters) past the base of the tower, so rest assured, it is still the

R. R. Esposito

leaning tower of Pisa. The change in the tower's lean is not perceptible to the 4 million annual visitors to the piazza, who can now once again climb to the top of the beautiful and amazing structure. Visitors must ascend 293 spiraling steps. And when you descend the tower, each time you turn on the north side the steps seem to go uphill even though they are actually taking you down. On June 17th 2001, the celebrated opera tenor Andrea Bocelli performed the official reopening, and engineers and architects believe the project will maintain the structure for at least 300 years. The opening was for a symbolic, single day to coincide with the feast of the patron saint of Pisa, San Ranieri. Only 200 school children gained access to the Romanesque tower. The tower was permanently reopened in June of 2002.

The tower has a very long and fascinating history since construction began over 800 years ago. Unfortunately, the original designers had not realized that beneath the construction site rested the soft silt remains of an old riverbed, causing the tower to sink, at first on the north side. These early engineering pioneers then made the columns and arches on the north side slightly taller to compensate for the lower north side, but stopped construction in 1178 after the fourth story was completed. Modern engineers using computer models now realize why they stopped. Had these early builders continued with another story the tower would have collapsed. Construction resumed in 1272, and as a result the tower pitched to the south, the direction it leans toward today. Because the tower pitched south, builders compensated by making the new stories with slightly taller columns and arches on the south side. However, these early engineers realized the instability of the tower and again stopped construction in 1278. Yet again around 1360, a new generation of engineers decided to tackle the tower's challenge and completed the belfry at the top, adding two extra steps on the south side. In 1838, architect Alessandro della Gherardesca excavated the walkway around the tower that has sunk below ground level. In the early 20th century, during Benito Mussolini's rule, engineers added 80 tons of concrete into the foundation, but the perplexing tower shifted still further south. Interestingly, the tower has a very dynamic nature that makes it move a bit north or south, depending on seasonal temperature, rain accumulation and wind.

The columns of the tower are unique to a regional style of architecture found in and around Pisa. Other examples of these columns can been seen on the nearby cathedral and baptistery (baptismal fount), which were both built from 1063 to 1160 before work on the tower began. The beautifully round baptistery structure has perfect acoustics that are frequently demonstrated to the amazement of visiting tourists. It is in this cathedral that Galileo first observed the principle of the motion of a pendulum and studied the physics of inertia (see the "Technology and Science" chapter).

Pisa is known as a center of fine art and has many beautiful architectural landmarks that exhibit very intricate designs.

The Leaning Tower of Pisa

Cathedral next to the Leaning Tower of Pisa

Baptistery (baptismal fount) of the Cathedral in Pisa

"The Golden Milestone" 63

Roadway System and the "Golden Milestone"
Rome

The Romans built a system of highways to connect Rome to the rest of the vast Empire that covered over 60,000 miles (96,500 km) from Egypt to Britain and across Europe! These roads were incredibly durable due to their advanced design. Roman roads were constructed using a four-layer design. The top layer was built using large flat stones, pebbles and sometimes concrete. *The Romans invented concrete long before the birth of Christ.* After the fall of the Roman Empire, building technology with concrete was lost until the advent of the 19th century. Roman road design also included specific orientation to aid travel, proper grading and even slightly arched centers of the road so rain would drain to the curb, where storm drains were sometimes installed as well. They served military, as well as commercial purposes and permitted reliable travel and communication to distant regions for centuries. The roadways were also literally the first "information highway," allowing travelers and messengers alike, safe and speedy transport, providing in reality an infrastructure for communication. (Refer to the "Preface" of this book that describes how the Roman system of roadways constituted the world's first "information highway.")

The Romans placed stone milestones on their major roads in intervals of a Roman mile. These milestones, round and octagon shaped columns, were placed 1000 "paces" apart, which equates to a distance of 4859 feet (1481 meters). Many have been found throughout Europe and the Middle East and range in height from 6 feet (1.8 meters) to 11 feet (3.3 meters). They bore inscriptions that indicated the distance and direction to Rome and the name of the builder or restorer of the road.

In the city of Rome, at the center of the Roman Forum, next to the Temple of Saturn stands the "Golden Milestone" where all major roads converged. Although today only the base remains, the "Golden Milestone" was a tall column covered in gold and had inscriptions marking highways and the distances to all major cities in the Empire. The "Golden Milestone" was the monument that became the focal point of all roads that led to, or originated from, Rome. The enormous number and massive extent of roads built, and the fact that they radiated out from Rome in every direction from the "Milestone," gives meaning to the expression "all roads lead to Rome." Emperor Augustus had the "Milestone" built and in Latin it was called,

"Miliarium Aureum." Among the many inscriptions on the "Milestone" was the famous Appian Way (Via Appia), the first of many great Roman highways to be constructed. This wide road was often used to quickly transport Roman soldiers and couriers to regions south of Rome. Sections of this flat stone roadway still exist today and have become a tourist attraction. Appius Claudius Caecus is credited with beginning its construction about 310 BC. The Flaminian Way was the most important road out of Rome that was used for travel to the north. As a testimony to their ingenious design, some Roman roads that were built or rebuilt still exist today.

In Great Britain, the Romans built Ermine Street, Fosse Way and Watling Street. They rebuilt Icknied Street and as a result it too can still be traveled today. In fact, the *Romans founded the city of London* and its original Roman name was Londinium. The Romans copied the design of the city of Rome and made Londinium the central point of all roads in southern England. As a result, all roads in southern England lead to London. In 43 AD, the Roman general Aulus Plautius and his troops crossed the Thames River by building the *first bridge in London* or Londinium as it was called at the time. The town and later city developed after the bridge was built that allowed easy access to both sides of the river. The *city of Bath in England was also founded by the Romans* who built stone and concrete baths over the natural hot springs and enjoyed these for almost 400 years. Some of these Roman baths still exist today. Later, the city of Bath was attacked and destroyed by the Angles and the Saxons from Germany.

Although the Romans did not found Paris, they completely rebuilt it during the first century. Archeologists have excavated many Roman baths and theaters in Paris. The wide straight roads that exist in Paris are the descendants of the broad roads that the Romans constructed in the city. These wide, durable roads joined with a vast roadway system for travel between Paris and distant Rome. Another good example is the Boulevard Saint Michel in Paris.

Rome –The City
Donato Bramante

Donato Bramante was born in 1444 near Urbino in Monte Asdruvaldo (now Fermignano) and died April 11, 1514 in Rome. Bramante was a town planner, architect and writer, whose real name was Donato d'Angelo. As a leading architect of his time, he developed the high renaissance style of architecture exhibited in his many buildings in Rome and Milan. *He also was revolutionary in that he used space to create illusions as in a painting or stage setting and inspired and influenced successive architects.* He achieved a grandiose style that eventually developed into Mannerism. *In 1503, Pope Julius II engaged Bramante to redesign and renew the Vatican complex. Ultimately, he developed the early 16th century plan to rebuild the City of Rome*, as well as the original design of St. Peter's Basilica. He also designed the round, domed and colonnaded cloister Tempietto of San Pietro in Montorio and the cloister San Maria Della Pace in Rome, which was inspired by the Coliseum and has similarities in appearance.

Appropriately known as the *Eternal City*, Rome was the center of the Roman Kingdom, Republic and Empire. It was also an important city during the Renaissance, and it is now the capital of Italy, as well as the seat of the Roman Catholic Church. All year long international visitors pour into the Eternal City. Visitors come for many reasons. They are tourists, pilgrims, artists, architects, sculptors, poets and other scholars who visit this city that has over 3,000 years of history, art and cultural achievements.

Two brothers, Romulus and Remus, founded the city of Rome. Legend has it that their father had been a ruler of a nearby land, probably in the Tuscany region, inhabited at the time by Etruscans, a highly civilized people. This ruler's opponent usurped his governing power and took the ruler's two boys and set them adrift in a basket down the Tiber River. A shepherd and his wife rescued them from the river and nursed them with the milk of a she-wolf. Much like the biblical story of Cain and Abel, Remus was slain by Romulus during the building of Rome and Romulus became its first ruler in 753 BC. Although no one knows the accuracy of this legend, it is true that Rome's first king was named Romulus.

Russian Palaces and Cathedrals Designed by Italian Architects

Roman and Italian architecture has had significant international influences even in Russia. Gaetano Chiaveri, Aristotle Fioravanti, Giovanni Mario Fontana, Giacomo Quarenghi and Bartolommeo Rastrelli were some of the many Italian architects that built many of the palaces and cathedrals in Russia for the Czars and their royal families. Bartolommeo Rastrelli's Italian Baroque contributions shaped much of St. Petersburg's elegance and beauty. Listed below in chronological order, are some of the many Italian contributions to great Russian architecture.

Cathedral of the Annunciation (built 1484-1489)
Architect - Aristotle Fioravanti

Ivan the Great, who lived from 1462 AD to 1505 AD, brought the Italian architect Aristotle Fioravanti from Bologna to Russia to construct a series of cathedrals in the Kremlin. The magnificent Cathedral of the Annunciation built from 1484 AD to 1489 AD is an excellent example of Italian style architecture and displays beautiful symmetry that includes many tall domes. It was *built as the seat of the Russian Orthodox Church and as a focal point for the Czar's official functions.* Ivan the Great was so impressed by the new Church and its beauty that when Fioravanti requested to return to Italy, Ivan imprisoned him to retain Fioravanti's talent and intellect in Russia. Unfortunately, Fioravanti died in captivity only a few years later. Marco Polo had a similar problem in China with Kublai Khan, which you will read about later in the "Exploration" chapter. Evidently it is possible to be admired to excess.

The Cathedral of the Annunciation is where Ivan the Great defiantly tore up the charter binding Moscow to Asian Mongol rule and changed the course of history for Russia. It is also where much Russian pageantry took place including the coronations of the Czars and funerals for royalty.

In Moscow, the ornate St. Basil's Cathedral was constructed from 1550 AD to 1560 AD, 65 years *after* Fioravanti's Cathedral of the Annunciation. St. Basil's exhibits larger domes with colorful and swirling line designs on them. These are sometimes called "onion domes" because of their shape. The Roman influence is not as obvious at this point. St. Basil's style is more ornate and has Byzantine characteristics, which are different from the Roman or Italian styles. However, Fioravanti's earlier churches influenced and reinforced the concept of multiple domes and other architectural concepts in Russia. Although "onion domes" are a Byzantine architectural feature, it was the Romans who invented and perfected the dome, and Fioravanti who first built a great Russian cathedral displaying multiple domes. (Refer to the first entry of this ARCHITECTURE section, entitled Architectural Designs, Engineering & Construction for more on the Roman influence on Byzantine buildings.)

Further, the magnificent Taj Mahal in India was built subsequent to Fioravanti's Cathedral of the Annunciation. The Taj Mahal with its massive domes was built over a 22 year period from 1631 to 1652 almost *50 years subsequent* to Fioravanti's Cathedral of the Annunciation. The Taj Mahal was built by the fifth Mughal emperor, Shah Jahan in memory of his second wife, Mumtaz Mahal, a Muslim Persian princess.

The Peter and Paul Fortress – Oldest Building in St. Petersburg (1703-1706)
Architect – DomenicoTrezzini

Commissioned in 1703 by Peter the Great, the original fortress had earth walls. In 1706, brick construction began under the direction of the Italian Domenico Trezzini who was both architect and engineer for the project. The fort, built on an island to protect the land from Swedish attack, is the oldest building in St. Petersburg. In later years it was also used as a high security political prison for such noted figures as Dostoyevsky, Gorky, Trotsky and Lenin's brother Alexander. At the center of the fortress stands the Peter and Paul Cathedral, also designed by Domenico Trezzini.

The Peter and Paul Cathedral – Burial Place for the Imperial House of Romanov (1712-1733)
Architect – DomenicoTrezzini

Built from 1712 to 1733 this majestic cathedral was designed by the architect Domenico Trezzini. It has been the official Russian burial place for all Russian rulers for over 200 years. All Romanovs were laid to rest here from Peter I to Alexander III with only two individual exceptions. One end of the cathedral is adorned by a dome capped with a cupola, and at the other end, a gilded bell tower rises above St. Petersburg.

The Catherine Palace (built 1752-1760)
Architect - Bartolommeo Rastrelli

The history of the Catherine Palace in the town of Tsarskoe Selo goes back at least to a wooden structure in 1702. Empress Catherine I ordered a stone palace in 1718. In later years, a more elaborate palace complex was constructed. The palace had been built and rebuilt many times at great expense to the royal families during the 18th century. Early architects were Zemtzov, Kvassov, Tchevakinski and the Italian Domenico Giuseppe Trezzini. However, in 1752 Bartolommeo Rastrelli designed and supervised the building of a very new style that also had to incorporate some of the earlier foundations and structures in the new plan. His finished palace with lavish designs and gilding dazzled Empress Elizabeth and her ministers. In later years, Czarina Catherine the Great of Russia used the palace. *Bartolommeo Rastrelli was also the architect for these other great Russian buildings*: The Winter Palace (built 1754-1762, Saint Petersburg), The Cathedral of the Smolny Convent (built 1748-1764, Saint Petersburg), Zimnii Palace, Stroganov Palaces (Saint Petersburg).

Alexander Palace (built 1794 to 1796)
Architect – Giacomo Quarenghi

In 1779, the Czarina of Russia, Catherine the Great invited Giacomo Quarenghi of Bergammo, Italy to build a palace for her grandson Alexander. The Czarina chose Quarenghi for his technical knowledge, great drawing skills and his artistic abilities. In 1796, he completed a magnificent palace for her grandson near the Catherine Palace in the town of Tsarskoe Selo. Since Alexander and his wife were childless, the throne eventually went to Nicholas I who used the palace to host many events including the historic event of Russia's first telegraph transmission. Of all the palaces he occupied, the Alexander Palace, then known as "The New Palace," became the favorite palace of Nicholas. About 1917, during the Russian revolution, the palace became a museum that documented the life style of the royal Romanov family.

Italians greatly contributed to Russian architecture, and it is interesting to note that even the royal family's name *Romanov* includes the word *Roman*. In fact, the famous name Romanov is derived from a Romanov ancestor with the given first name of Roman. The history of this name, according to The International Romanov Society follows. The family name Romanov is derived from Nikita Romanovick. His father was Roman Zacharin. Nikita evidently wanted his last name to include the distinguishing name *Roman* in it and changed his last name from Zacharin to Romanovich. It later was shortened to Romanov. Also, the Russian word *Czar* is derived from the name of the Roman Emperor *Caesar*. The Germans similarly derived *Kaiser* from the great Caesar as well.

Other Russian Palaces

The Menshikov Palace built in 1710 was designed by the architects Giovanni Mario Fontana and Gottfried Shadel. The Kunstkammer, built from 1718 to 1734, was designed by architects Mikhail Zemtsov, Gaetano Chiaveri, Georg Johann Mattarnovi and Nicolas Herbel.

St. Mark's Basilica in Venice

Saint Mark's Square and Basilica
Venice

At the center of Venice lies Saint Mark's Square (Piazza San Marco). The Square or Piazza is the focal point for the city's economic, political, religious and artistic life. On the eastern side of the piazza stands the Basilica of St. Mark, one of the world's most magnificent churches.

The Basilica of St. Mark reputedly contains the remains of its patron saint. Five gilded domes reflecting a Byzantine influence top its roof. This massive and beautiful basilica was built from the 9th to 11th centuries and contains rare gemstones, marble, decorated ceilings and panels, and many detailed, beautiful mosaics and enamels. On the grounds of the Basilica one can find replicas of four Hellenic style bronze horses (housed in basilica's museum) with origins that date from the time of the Roman Emperor Nero.

R. R. Esposito

The elegant Ponte Rialto Bridge in Venice

Other Major Landmarks of Venice
- The magnificent church of San Giorgio Maggiore was built on its own island directly across from St Mark's square. Its architect was Andrea Palladio. The church has had a monastery since 982, but the current buildings were built during the 16th century. Its tall bell tower (campanile) offers a fantastic view of Venice.
- The Church of Santa Maria di Salute, designed in 1630 by architect Baldasarre Longhena, is yet another majestic cathedral in Venice. It has vast multiple domes and was built at the edge of the water, adding to its beauty.
- One of the world's most famous bridges is the Ponte Rialto. It has beautiful multiple arches and spans the Grand Canal of Venice. The large covered bridge also has many famous shops.
- The beautiful Palazzo Ducale (14th – 15th centuries) was the palace of the *doges* (rulers) of Venice. Its architecture boasts pink marble and white stone. Inside hangs "Paradise," a massive painting by Tintoretto. The palace connects to an adjacent prison by the Bridge of Sighs, named so because of the sighs of prisoners who were walked across for trial.

Saint Peter's Basilica
Vatican City, Rome
St. Peter's Basilica is the largest Christian building in the world and its adjoining Sistine Chapel contains a wealth of priceless art, as

described in the ART section of this chapter. St. Peter's was built and modified from 1546 to 1590. Its massive size is surpassed only by its exquisite beauty. St. Peter's is a part of Vatican City, that is described in more detail later in this chapter. St. Peter's was designed by, Giacomo della Porta, Michelangelo, Raphael, Antonio da Sangallo and Donato Bramante, a towering figure in Renaissance architecture. Michelangelo conceived and designed the great and lavish dome atop the Basilica in 1546, which later inspired the central dome on the U.S. Capitol Building. The dome rises an incredible 390 feet (119 meters) above the floor, an interior distance greater than a football field (300 feet) stood on end. It is visible from all districts of Rome. The Basilica was finished in 1626 after more than a century of construction and contains many side chapels. Among the many famous works of art, St. Peter's contains Michelangelo's masterpiece sculpture, the "Pieta," which depicts the Blessed Mary holding Jesus after the Crucifixion. In the 4th century a basilica stood on the site of today's St Peter's Basilica. That first basilica built in 330 AD is believed to have contained the tomb of St. Peter, the founder of the Christian church.

St. Peter's Basilica in Rome

R. R. Esposito

Dimensions and Statistics of the Basilica:
364 feet (111 meters) wide, 730 feet (223 meters) long, 438 feet (134 meters) high (exterior), 800 chandeliers, 44 altars, 27 chapels, 11 domes, 778 columns, 395 statues, 290 windows, 135 mosaics. The basilica stands on approximately 5 acres (20,235 square meters). St. Peter's Square is also magnificent and was designed by Giovanni Lorenzo Bernini in the 17th century. It is described in the Vatican City reference later in this chapter.

Historic district of Santo Domingo in the Dominican Republic

Santo Domingo - Oldest Continuously Inhabited City in the Americas
Bartholomew Columbus

Bartholomew Columbus, the brother of Christopher Columbus, designed this city in a Roman grid fashion by constructing straight and broad streets. This city, the capital of the Dominican Republic in the Caribbean was settled in August of 1496 and is the oldest continuously inhabited city in the Americas. Santo Domingo has a perfect natural harbor and many beautiful historical buildings.

Monument to Christopher Columbus in front of
Santo Domingo's 500 year old church.

R. R. Esposito

Home built for Columbus in Santo Domingo,
but actually his son was the inhabitant.

Saxony's Largest Cathedral - Dresden, Germany
Architect - Gaetano Chiaveri
Built from 1738 to 1754, the Catholic Court Church (Katholische Hofkirche) designed by the Italian architect Gaetano Chiaveri is the largest church in Saxony. It has been designated as the Cathedral of the Dresden-Meissen Diocese since 1980. This magnificent cathedral is highly decorated both in and out. Guided tours and organ recitals offer visitors a sense of the church's rich beauty. The cathedral has an urn that contains the heart of Augustus the Strong, an artifact not for the weak-hearted.

Vatican City
Rome
The site of Vatican City was originally an ancient Roman city. The ancient city's wall can still be found around Vatican City on three of its four sides. Today's Vatican City was constructed during the Italian Renaissance and contains some of the most celebrated and beautiful buildings in the world. At the entrance to Vatican City, St. Peter's Square (Piazza San Pietro), inspires awe in all of its visitors. The Square itself was designed by Giovanni Lorenzo Bernini and is considered one of his greatest architectural accomplishments. Built in the 17th century, the lengthy colonnade in the Square that Bernini

designed is exceptionally graceful and geometrically exact. On the Square stands the internationally celebrated St. Peter's Basilica (see details earlier in this chapter) and the Vatican Palace, which has been the residence of Popes since the 14th century. The Sistine Chapel is the most famous section of the Vatican Palace (see details in the ART section of this chapter). The Palace today is actually a collection of several buildings.

Before the Palace was built, Pope Symmachus built a residence for himself, at the end of the 5th century, where today's St. Peter's Basilica stands. The buildings of Vatican City illustrate an extraordinary record of Italian history, art, architecture and engineering. The U.S. Library of Congress Vatican Exhibit documents these vast Italian achievements and offers additional insights regarding the art and architecture of Vatican City.

Vaulted Ceilings
Rome
For information on how vaulted ceilings were invented by the Romans, please refer to the first entry of this ARCHITECTURE section, entitled Architectural Designs, Engineering & Construction.

Other Famous Architects
The following is a representative list of other accomplished architects and designers. However, there are several from the 20th century who deserve special recognition for their achievements. Three eminent architects (Renzo Piano, Aldo Rossi, Robert Venturi) have all won the coveted international *Pritzker Architecture Prize*. Also, Carlo Scarpa has introduced many revolutionary concepts and has been compared to the great American architect Louis I. Kahn. Finally, Luigi Nervi invented a new type of reinforced concrete (ferrocemento), which revolutionized architectural designs in the 20th century. Nervi was awarded Gold Medals from the Royal Institute of British Architects, the American Institute of Architects and the Academi d'Architecture.

Leon Battista Alberti (author, artist, architect). For information about the great Alberti, see the reference to Rules for Linear Perspective - Drawing in Three Dimensions in the ART: Early Development section of this chapter.

Galeazzo Alessi (architect) born Perugia 1512 and died 1572. He was a leading architect in both Genoa and Milan. Alessi was highly influenced by Antonio da Sangall, Baldassare, Peruzzi and Michelangelo. His works include the cathedral St. Maria di Carignano in Genoa (1552 to 1603).

Banfi, Belgiojoso, Peressutti and Rogers (architectural partnership). This well known partnership of architects was established in Milan in 1932. All four were born in Italy and were all graduates of Milan Polytechnic. Gianluigi Banfi was born in Milan in 1910 and died in 1945. Lodovico Belgiojoso was born in Milan in 1909. Enrico Peressuiti was in born Milan in 1908 and died there as well in 1975. Ernesto Nathan Rogers was born in Trieste in 1909 and died in 1969. These four innovators helped to bring modern architecture to Italy, yet retained and blended traditional Italian classical elements in their work. Their work included every aspect of architecture, including interior design, industrial design and urban planning. They were also teachers and authors. Rogers made significant contributions to architectural journalism as the editor of the publication "Quadranted, Domus, Casabella Continuita." One of their significant works is the Torre Velasca in Milan, which was established in 1932 and built from 1957 to 1960.

Pietro Belluschi (architect, engineer) born in Ancona, Italy in 1899 and died 1994. Belluschi studied engineering at both the University of Rome and Cornell University. He was also Dean of Architecture and Planning at the renowned Massachusetts Institute of Technology from 1951 to 1965. In his fifty years of practice he designed over 1000 buildings.

Some of his larger projects include:
- Central Lutheran Church, Portland, Oregon (1951)
- Equitable Building, Portland, Oregon (1948)
- Peter Kerr House, Gearhart, Oregon (1941)

Giovanni Lorenzo Bernini (sculptor, architect, painter and designer) born in Naples on December 7, 1598 and died in Rome, November 28th, 1680. He was trained originally as a sculptor by his father who was a Florentine sculptor. He is renowned for designing the majestic Piazza of St. Peter's in the Vatican City, Rome (1667). His other significant projects include:
- Piazza Navona, Rome (17th century)
- Saint Andrea al Quirinale, Rome (1665)

Francesco Borromini (architect) born September 25, 1599 in Bissone and died August 3, 1667 in Rome. As a youth he learned how to be a

stonemason from his father Giovanni Domenico Castelli. Although Francesco's style was eclectic using unusual geometric shapes, he was a significant and revolutionary influence in his time.
His significant projects include:
* Saint Carlo Alle Quattro Fontane, Rome (1641)
* Saint Ivo della Sapienza, Rome (1650)

Arnolfo di Cambio (architect) born 1245, Colle di Valdelse and died 1310, Firenze.
His significant projects include:
* Florence Cathedral, Florence (1296 to 1462)
* Orvieto Cathedral, Orvieto (1290 to 1500)

Cola da Caprarola (architect) lived in Italy from 1508 to 1604.
His significant projects include: San Maria della Consolazione, Todi (1508).

Giancarlo de Carlo (architect) born in Genoa 1919.
His significant projects include: Free University, Urbino (1980).

Mario J. Ciampi (architect). His significant projects include:
University Art Museum, Berkeley, California (1971).

Domenico Fontana (architect and engineer) born in 1543 and died in Naples, 1607. Fontana was a leading contributor to the grand rebuilding of Rome during the Renaissance. In 1580, he built a (lesser known) Sistine Chapel in the Church of Santa Maria Maggiore in Rome. He also designed the Lateran Palace (1588), portions of the Vatican and its library (1588). With his brother, Giovanni Fontana, he built the great aqueduct and fountain Acqua Felice (1587) and the obelisk monument of St. Peter's Cathedral (1586). He built the majestic Royal Palace in Naples (1600) and designed grand improvements for the harbor that were completed after his death.

Guidetto Guidetti (architect) worked principally in Rome designing churches and is noted for his complex ornamentation and façades. He is also famous for executing projects for Michelangelo and for helping to mentor Giacomo Della Porta who became a leading architect of the late 16th century. Although his date of birth is unclear Guidetto Guidetti died in 1564.

Guarino Guarini (mathematician, architect) born in Modena 1624 and died in Milan 1683. He was ordained as a Theatine priest and did most of his architectural work for his religious order. Guarini was a leading mathematician in his time and used his mathematical expertise in his architecture, which often displayed sophisticated geometry. He was influenced by the revolutionary design concepts of Francesco Borromini. Most of his work was built in Milan, but he also designed buildings in Sicily, Paris, Portugal and Spain. His significant projects include:

- San Lorenzo,Turin (1666 to1679)
- Sindone Chapel,Turin (1667 to 1690).

Baldasarre Longhena (architect) born 1598 in Venice and died 1682. He worked in Venice and designed the Church of St. Maria della Salute. He also designed two of the most beautiful palaces on Venice's Grand Canal, the Ca' Pesaro and the Ca'Bon (now called Rezzonico). However, both were completed by other architects. He also designed the Church of St. Maria di Nazareth, except for the façade.

Benedetto da Maiano (architect, sculptor) lived in Italy from 1442 to 1497. He worked with his younger brother Giuliano da Maiano on many architectural projects in their family studio in Florence. Although Giuliano da Sangallo and Simone del Pollaiuolo probably designed the building, Benedetto da Maiano is credited with designing the first story of the famous Strozzi palace in Florence (1489 to 1539).

Giuseppe Mengoni (architect). His most notable project is the magnificent Galleria Vittorio Emanuele in Milan, which he designed in 1861 and was built from 1865 to 1877. This is a massive indoor shopping plaza enclosed with spacious glass domes above the walkways. On each end of this 640 foot (196 meter) complex one finds the Piazza della Scala and the Piazza della Duomo. A triumphal arch was added in 1877 as well.

Michelangelo (sculptor, painter and architect). For more information about Michelangelo's life and works see the reference to his sculpture "David" in the ART section of this chapter. As a master architect, Michelangelo also conceived and designed the great and lavish dome atop the St. Peter's Basilica in 1546, which later inspired the dome on the U.S. Capitol Building. He also designed the Laurentian Library in Florence (1525), the Sforza Chapel in Rome (1558) and the monumental Piazza del Campidoglio also in Rome along with its central sculpture (1538 to 1650).

Pier Luigi Nervi (architect) Refer to the section Concrete - Reinforced in the Architecture section of this chapter for more on Luigi Nervi.

Baldassare Peruzzi (architect, painter) born in Siena 1481 and died 1556. His career as a painter also allowed Peruzzi to assist Raphael and others. The architect and author Sebastiano Serlio used Peruzzi's notebooks to help write his famous and influential books on architecture. Peruzzi built Ossoli Palace, Rome (1525) and Palazzo Massimo, Rome (1527 to 1536).

Renzo Piano (architect) born in Genoa September 14, 1937. Piano graduated from Milan Polytechnic in 1964 and later taught there as well. Early in his career he worked with the great Louis I. Kahn in Philadelphia and soon after established a partnership with Richard Rogers, an Italian-English architect. Rogers was born in Florence in 1933, but graduated from both the Architectural Association School in London and Yale University in the United States. Piano and Rogers designed buildings in Italy, England and France. Their most well known building is the Pompidou Center in Paris (1972 to 1976). Piano's buildings were high-tech, but still incorporated comfort and practical design. Piano's many works include the Kansai Airport Terminal in Osaka Japan (1994). Piano now participates in the *Renzo Piano Workshop Foundation* and also collaborates with Peter Rice on public and civic projects under the auspices of the *Stadio Nuovo* organization. *In 1998 Renzo Piano won the coveted Pritzker Architecture Prize.*

Pollaiuolo Family

- **Simone del Pollaiuolo** (architect) born 1457 in Florence and died 1508. Simone del Pollaiuolo is credited with contributing to design of the grand Strozzi palace (Giuliano da Sangallo and Benedetto da Maiano were also contributing architects). There are three other family members listed in a separate list of artists in the ART section in this chapter. They are **Jacopo Pollaiuolo** (goldsmith), his sons **Antonio Pollaiuolo** (goldsmith, sculptor, engraver, painter) and **Piero Pollaiuolo** (sculptor). Simone del Pollaiuolo was the nephew of Antonio Pollaiuolo and Piero Pollaiuolo and the grandson of Jacopo Pollaiuolo.

Giacomo Della Porta (architect, sculptor) born at Porlizza on Lake Lugano in 1541 and died 1604. He was a leading architect of the late 16th century. Both his father and grandfather were sculptors. He was taught the science of architecture by Guidetto Guidetti, Giacomo Vignola and some say Michelangelo, as well. He worked on all the major building projects in Rome during his time including St. Peter's Basilica and was venerated for his technical abilities and creative attention to decorative detail. He succeeded Vignola as the official architect of St. Peter's. He also helped to move style from Renaissance to Baroque. Another of his major accomplishments was the Villa Aldobrandini in Frascati (1598 to1603).

Giulio Romano (aka Guilio Pippi) (architect, painter) born in 1492 and died in 1546. Romano was a principal assistant to the great Raphael. One of his major works is the Palazzo del Te in Mantua (1526 to 1534).

Aldo Rossi (architect, designer, artist and author) was born in Milan in 1931 and graduated from Milan Polytechnic in 1959. He spent most of his life in Venezia where he died in 1997. His family ran the famous Rossi bicycle company. Rossi taught at several distinguished universities: Milan Polytechnic, New York City's Cooper Union, Zurich's ETH and Venice's Instituto Universitario di Architettura. Also, in 1966 he published his major work on urban architecture entitled "L'Architettura della Citta" ("Architecture and the City") and delivered the Walter Gropius Lecture at Harvard University. *He won the coveted international Pritzker Architecture Prize in 1990.* He designed numerous famous projects throughout the world:

- Teatro del Mondo, a floating theatre, Venice (1979)
- Toronto Lighthouse Theatre on the banks of Lake Ontario (1987)
- Carlo Felice Theatre which is the National Opera House in Genoa
- The Pocono Pines Houses in Pocono, Pennsylvania
- Monumental arch for the city of Galveston, Texas
- Canary Wharf Offices, London
- University of Miami School of Architecture Building, Coral Gables, Florida
- Apartment buildings Sudliche Friedrichstadt, West Germany
- Rossi Cemetery, Modena
- Il Palazzo Hotel and Restaurant Complex in Fukuoka, Japan (1989)
- Palazzo Regionale (civic center), Perugia (1988)
- Molteni family funerary chapel, Giussano (1988)
- Town Hall, Borgoricco (1988)
- Centro Torri Shopping Center, Parma (1988)
- GFT office headquarters, the Casa Aurora building, Turin (GFT is the parent company for Giorgio Armani, Valentino and Emanuel Ungaro.) (1988)
- Deutsches Historisches Museum in West Berlin, Germany (1989)
- Rossi also designed: a sports arena, schools and shopping centers in Italy; an art gallery in Japan; a monastery restoration and expansion in Seville, Spain; several estates in Milan and Berlin; and a large residential complex in The Hague, Netherlands.

Da Sangallo Family
- **Antonio da Sangallo** (architect, engineer) born in Florence 1483 and died there as well in 1546. In 1520, Sangallo replaced Raphael as master of works on St. Peter's Basilica. In addition to his many projects and his devotion to the work at St. Peter's, he also completed the Farnese Palace in Rome (1534).

■ Antonio da Sangallo's uncles, **Giuliano da Sangallo** and **Antonio da Sangallo** (an uncle with his same name), were his architectural mentors. They were architects and had a design, engineering and sculpture business, which provided his technical and artistic training. His uncle Giuliano da Sangallo with Simone del Pollaiuolo designed most of the Strozzi Palace in Florence.
Carlo Scarpa (architect, artist, designer) born 1906 in Venice and died after an accident in 1978 while visiting Japan. Scarpa is buried in San Vito d'Altivole near Treviso in the "garden of the dead" at the Brion Tomb, which he designed (1970 to 1972) for the Brion family. The legendary Scarpa is known for his creative, colouristic and avant-garde modern styles. Scarpa also designed magnificent glass at the famous Venini glass studios on the Venetian Island of Murano. Dozens of his fantastic drawings are in museums in Verona, Venice and Palermo. Many architects today are still inspired by his unconventional and revolutionary works. He was also a master of renovating older traditional buildings into more functional forms and offered many novel styles and techniques for this purpose. He restored and reorganized the 14th century Castelvecchio in Verona (1956 to 1973) into a working municipal art museum, which is now the Museo di Castelvecchio. In Verona, he also designed the main premises and annexes of the Banca Popolare di Verona (1973 to 1981) that inspired international commentary due to its unique style and façade. He also renovated and transformed the 15th century Palazzo Abatellis in Palermo into the National Art Gallery of Sicily (1953 to 1954) and built a new gallery for the Antonio Canova Museum in Possagno (1955 to 1957). Influenced by Frank Lloyd Wright, Scarpa successfully built a freestanding house in a narrow urban space in Udine for the lawyer Luciano Veritti (1955 to 1961) that offers new spatial beauty and unique landscaping. In Venice, Scarpa designed: the Balboni house restoration (1964 to 1974); the showroom for the Olivetti company on the Piazza San Marco (1957 to 1958); he rebuilt the galleries and courtyard of the Fondazione Querini Stampalia, a research library and art collection housed in a 16th century palazzo (1961 to 1963) and he redesigned the medieval Ca' Foscari for the University of Venice. In Bologna, he designed the façade for the Gavina Showroom (1961 to 1963). In the 1950's, two great architects, Louis I. Kahn in the United States and Carlo Scarpa in Italy provided new directions and style for architects throughout the world.
Sabastiano Serlio (architect) born 1475 and died 1554. He was a highly influential architect who wrote a set of five books on

architecture, which had an enormous influence on western architecture and were widely read during his time. (For more on Sabastiano Serlio, see the reference, Italian Renaissance Influences earlier in this ARCHITECTURE section of this chapter).

Alessandro Specchi (architect) born in Rome, designed the famous Piazza di Spagna in Rome (1721 to 1725).

Giuseppi Terragni (architect) born in Meda in 1904 and died in Como 1943. Terragni attended both the Technical College in Como and the Milan Polytechnic. From 1927 until his death during World War II in 1943, he practiced with his brother Atiilia in Como. Giuseppi offered revolutionary designs and pioneered the modern architectural style in Italy, building many well known and architecturally significant buildings mostly in Como. Some of his last buildings combined Mediterranean style with modern. One of his significant works is the Casa del Fascio in Como (1936).

Clorindo Testa (architect, painter) born in Naples in 1923. Testa graduated from the Faculty of Architecture and Urbanism of the National University of Buenos Aires in 1948. He also studied painting in Italy. Testa is noted for bold forms and unique spatial manipulations, which are common to his paintings. He is also known for heavy concrete finishes on his buildings.

Giorgio Vasari (painter, architect and writer) born July 30, 1511 in Arezzo and died June 27, 1574. *As an architect he designed the famous Uffizi Palace in Florence.* He was also an accomplished artist who studied under Andrea del Sarto. *He was the leading biographer of the Renaissance artists and provided much information about their lives and times.* In 1550, he wrote his famous, "The Lives of the Most Eminent Italian Architects, Painters and Sculptors." The original Italian title of his famous book is "Le Vite de Più Eccelenti Pittori, Scultori, et Architettori."

Robert Venturi (architect, designer) was born in Philadelphia, Pennsylvania in 1925. Venturi is an Italian-American. He attended the Episcopal Academy in Philadelphia and graduated from Princeton University where he received a Bachelor of Arts and a Masters of Fine Arts. He was *awarded the Rome Prize Fellowship* to study at the American Academy in Rome and subsequently started his own practice in 1958 after working with Eero Saarinen and the great Louis I. Kahn. Venturi has said that Michelangelo, Palladio, Le Corbusier and Alvar Aalto also influenced him. He has written several books including "Complexity and Contradiction in Architecture" (1966) which has been translated into 16 languages, "Iconography and

Electronics Upon a Generic Architecture: A View from the Drafting Room" (1998) and also co-authored "Learning from Las Vegas" (1972). Venturi uses revolutionary ideas, forms and facades to bring new visions in architecture. He has also designed creative teapots, cuckoo clocks, dishes, plates and candlesticks. He has been awarded *honorary doctorates from 12 universities* including, Yale University (1979), Princeton University (1983) and the University of Rome (1993). Venturi has won numerous awards from organizations in the United States, Italy, England, Scotland and the USSR. *In 1991, Venturi won the coveted Pritzker Prize in architecture.*

Robert Venturi along with his two partners, Denise Scott Brown (wife) and John Rauch are among the leading architects in the world. Their firm has designed museums, housing complexes, residences, commercial buildings and other projects, such as:

- 1959 Gwynnedd Friends Meeting Elderly Housing, Gwynnedd, PA
- 1961 Vanna Venturi House, Chestnut Hill, PA
- 1961 Friends Neighborhood Guild House, Philadelphia, PA
- 1961 North Pennsylvania Visiting Nurses Association, Ambler, PA
- 1962 Vanna Venturi House at Chestnut Hill, Philadelphia, PA
- 1962 Hun School Dormitory, Princeton, NJ
- 1966 Fire Station No.4, Columbus, IN
- 1967 Lieb House, Loveladies, NJ
- 1967 Dixwell Fire Station, New Haven, NJ
- 1968 Humanities Building, State University of NY, Purchase, NY
- 1968 Wike House, Devon, PA
- 1970 Trubeck House, Nantucket Island, Massachusetts
- 1970 Wislocki House, Nantucket Island, Massachusetts
- 1970 Social Sciences Building State University of NY, Purchase, NY
- 1972 Franklin Court, Philadelphia, PA
- 1973 Brant House, Greenwich, CT
- 1973 Allen Memorial Art Museum, Oberlin, OH
- 1974 NAVFAC Community Center, Philadelphia, PA
- 1975 House in Tuckers Town, Bermuda
- 1975 Tucker House, Mount Kisco, New York
- 1976 BASCO Store, Concord, DE
- 1977 Best Products Showroom, Oxford Valley, PA
- 1978 Institute for Scientific Information Office, Philadelphia, PA
- 1979 BASCO Showroom, Oxford Valley, PA

- 1980 Tree House Children's Zoo, Philadelphia, PA
- 1980 Gordon Wu Hall Dormitory Butler College, Princeton, NJ
- 1982 Primate Center Philadelphia Zoo, Philadelphia, PA
- 1983 Lewis Thomas Laboratory, Princeton, NJ
- 1983 Molecular-Biology Lab Princeton University, NJ
- 1984 Izenour House, Stony Creek, CT
- 1985 High Styles Exhibition Whitney Museum of American Art, NY, NY
- 1985 Furness Library University of Pennsylvania, Philadelphia, PA
- 1991 Art Museum, Seattle, WA
- 1992 Whitehall Ferry Terminal, NY, NY

Giacomo Vignola (aka Giacomo Barozzio) (architect) born in Italy in 1507 and died in Rome in 1573. Vignola worked on many villas and churches along with other projects in many parts of Italy, but spent considerable time in Rome working with Michelangelo. He is also noted for the design of Villa Farnese in Caprarola, near Viterbo. He wrote a highly influential architectural treatise entitled "Orders of Architecture." (For more on Vignola, see the reference 'Italian Renaissance Influences' in the ARCHITECTURE section of this chapter.)

ᘓ

Chapter III

ART & ARCHITECTURE
Contributions to America

**"So long had he devoted his heart and strength
to this Capitol that his love and reverence
for it was not surpassed by even that of
Michelangelo for St. Peters."**
- U.S. Senator Justin S. Morrill -
**This comment coined the title "Michelangelo of the
US Capitol" for the artist Constantino Brumidi.**

ART:

Filippo Mazzei, American patriot, businessman, physician and author was Thomas Jefferson's neighbor and close friend in Virginia. When Jefferson became president he moved to Washington, D.C. and Dr. Mazzei retired in Italy. As President of the young America, Jefferson asked the Architect of the Capitol, Benjamin Latrobe, to write to Dr. Mazzei asking for assistance in hiring a skilled Italian sculptor to beautify and culturally enrich the country's Capitol. Mazzei had helped Jefferson write the Declaration of Independence (see chapter I) and Jefferson was asking for his assistance again. Mazzei traveled to Rome to try to convince the internationally renowned Antonio Canova to work in America. Canova would not leave Italy and Mazzei recruited two other talented sculptors, Giovanni Andrei and Giuseppe Franzoni, who arrived in America in March of 1806. Many Italian artists followed and much of America's great art, sculptures and monuments are the result of the labor of these talented immigrants. Jefferson's well known admiration of Italian and Roman art and culture led him to create a neoclassical capital for the new American government, as you will read more about in the ARCHITECTURE section of this chapter. Italian artists and sculptors completed many works as described in this section on ART. They also creatively changed the classic Greek and Roman columns to include graceful corncobs and tobacco leaves at the top of these columns in the capitals. When you visit the U.S. Capitol look carefully at the capitals at the top of the columns, often in the interiors of buildings, and you will find these inventive artistic changes. Giuseppe Franzoni was the first to make these changes in American columns.

Bald Eagle – First Statue
Giuseppe Franzoni
Franzoni was a sculptor and *artist who sculpted the first U.S. Eagle.* Interestingly, when Franzoni was asked to sculpt an eagle, he executed a statue of a European eagle. The American artist Charles W. Peale drew a North American bald eagle so that Franzoni could create the first sculpture of this American symbol. Franzoni completed many other works for the American government. Unfortunately, during the War of 1812 the English destroyed most of his works. Giuseppe Franzoni also carved the Claiborne tomb in the St. Louis Cemetery.

Capitol Building – Paintings, Murals and Ornamental Designs
- **Constantino Brumidi**
Brumidi was born in Rome on July 26, 1805 and graduated in 1824 from the Italian art school Accademia di San Luca. He had much experience as an artist for the Vatican and also collaborated in the

restoration of Renaissance masterpieces, such as Raphael's "Third Loggia." He migrated to the U.S. on September 18, 1852 and applied his artistic talents by adding culture and beauty to U.S. Capitol buildings. Most notably his paintings beautify the Senate and the House of Representatives Chambers and the ceiling of the Capitol Building's rotunda. He worked at the U.S. Capitol building for a quarter of a century from 1855 until his death on February 19, 1880 earning $10 a day. His death followed a fall from a scaffold while working on a fresco in late 1879. On February 19, 1952, Congress placed a tablet on Brumidi's tomb in Glenwood Cemetery, Washington D.C., with the artist's own words inscribed: "My only dream is to decorate the Capitol of the only nation in the world where there is freedom." Brumidi painted many portraits and frescos on walls and ceiling vaults and also created bronze ornaments and designed railings and balusters. His great artistic contributions add splendor, beauty and sophistication to the Capitol of the most powerful nation in the world.

Brumidi's greatest masterpiece is his painting on the inner dome above the U.S. Capitol Building's rotunda. His finished work is over 62 feet in diameter, covers 4664 square feet of the ceiling's surface, and is called the "Apotheosis of George Washington." Brumidi started painting this ceiling in 1863, and completed it eleven months later in 1864. He worked lying on his back, as Michelangelo had painted the ceiling of the Sistine Chapel. As a result of this masterpiece and his other works, *Brumidi is often called the "Michelangelo of the United States Capitol."*

Brumidi was a master cupola artist trained in Italy with experience working at the Vatican. He understood the difficulty of painting on a round surface with figures that require natural proportions and proper perspective from observers beneath the dome. Brumidi's painting combines classic mythological images with American principles. This masterpiece has Washington seated and flanked by two goddesses, one that represents Liberty and a second that represents Victory & Fame. Thirteen maidens represent the original American colonies. The painting also has imagery for War, Commerce, Art & Science, Marine, Mechanics and Agriculture. Visitors who enter the U.S. Capitol Building see this massive and magnificent work of art on the ceiling directly above. Incidentally, some may wonder about the meaning of *apotheosis*, this author did. The dictionary defines *apotheosis* to be synonymous with *epitome*, and *epitome* is defined as meaning *idealization and glorification.*

Brumidi also decorated, what is called in his honor, the Brumidi Corridors. This complex of corridors is on the first floor of the Senate wing in the United States Capitol building. These corridors have many interlocking, vaulted ceilings, archways and moldings. These features and entire walls display ornate decorations painted by Brumidi and his assistants. Themes often match the use of rooms. Brumidi used mythological figures, flora and fauna, small woodland animals hiding in the vines, monochrome profile portraits of famous early Americans and countless other artifacts and designs. These famous corridors also contain nine large paintings by Brumidi: "Authority Consults the Written Law" (1875), "Columbus and the Indian Maiden" (1875), "Bartholomé de Las Casas" (1876), "Bellona, Roman Goddess of War" (undated), "Cession of Louisiana" (1875), "The Signing of the First Treaty of Peace with Great Britain" (1874), "Benjamin Franklin" (undated), "John Fitch" (1876) and "Robert Fulton" (1873).

- **Filippo Costaggini**

After completing the ceiling of the U.S. Capitol's rotunda, Brumidi began a *frieze* border around the base of the dome using the American chronology starting with Columbus in the first panel of the *frieze* border. However, he died before he could complete the *frieze*. Filippo Costaggini, a graduate from the Italian art school Accademia di San Luca, as was Brumidi, completed almost 90% of the unfinished project. Unfortunately, budget disagreements with Congress prevented Costaggini from completing the last three panels. Congress instead hired the American artist Allyn Cox, who had won the Prix de Rome award and was trained in Italy, to complete the last 10%. Congress should have kept Costaggini as the artist, since the expenses paid to Mr. Cox for finishing the last three panels was more than what was paid for the first sixteen panels painted by Brumidi and Costaggini. The *frieze* border is 300 feet in circumference, 58 feet above the floor and each panel is over 8 feet high.

Capitol Building – Sculptures & Reliefs
- **Antonio Capellano**

Capellano carved two reliefs for the U.S. Capitol building. His carving "The Preservation of Captain Smith by Pocahontas, 1606" (1825) rests inside the main Rotunda of the U.S. Capitol above the west door. His carving "Fame and Peace Crowning George Washington" (1827) is on the outside wall (facing east) at the main entrance of the U.S. Capitol.

- **Antonio Capellano and Enrico Causici**

Antonio Capellano and Enrico Causici collaborated on four relief sculptures in the Capitol building's Rotunda. These are portraits of John Cabot (1828), Christopher Columbus (1824), Sir Walter Raleigh (1824) and René Robert Cavelier Sieur de La Salle (1829).

- **Pietro Cardelli**

Cardelli was from Rome and carved portrait busts of both Thomas Jefferson and James Madison for the Capitol. He also carved the shallow *bas reliefs* for the central triangular pediment of The Cabildo building in New Orleans in 1821 (see full reference on State art later in this chapter).

- **Enrico Causici**

Causici carved the relief "Conflict of Daniel Boone and the Indians, 1773" (1826-1827), which rests inside the main Rotunda of the U.S. Capitol above the south door and "Landing of the Pilgrims, 1620" (1825) above the east door. (As mentioned above, Antonio Capellano completed his work above the west door - and for the sake of complete record keeping, Nicolas Gevelot, probably not Italian, completed his work "William Penn Treaty with the Indians, 1682" (1827) over the north door.)

Causici carved other works for the Capitol including, "Liberty and the Eagle" (1817-1819) and the first statue of George Washington (described later in this chapter).

- **Carlo Franzoni**

Carlo Franzoni came to the U.S. around 1816 from Carrara, the marble center of Italy. Carrara is internationally famous for its marble and as the home of many distinguished sculptors. In 1817, Franzoni completed a classic sculpture entitled "Justice," which still rests in the old chamber of the Supreme Court. In 1819, he completed a beautiful statute "Clio - Muse of History" which can be seen at the north entrance of the famous Statuary Hall in the U.S. Capitol Building. Another famous work is his sculpture entitled the "Car of History" (1819). Here the artist created a work containing a clock within the marble sculpture. It is a beautifully detailed chariot driven by a classical style female figure. The clock still works and is also displayed in Statuary Hall. In the office of the Architect of the Capitol is a portrait of Carlo Franzoni, painted by Pietro Bonanni also from Carrara, Italy. Bonanni painted the original ceiling for the dome in Statuary Hall simulating the Roman Pantheon, but it has since been replaced by a fireproof ceiling. The Hall was previously used for the House of Representatives before it became Statuary Hall, which is a large Americana art museum, that houses historic statuary.

- **George Giannetti**

Giannetti worked for studios in Brooklyn and Washington D.C. before he and his two sons founded the Giannetti studio in Brentwood, Maryland. His firm worked for many years during the 20th century to restore much of the 19th century sandstone statues and reliefs in the U.S. Capitol that were caved by Luigi Persico, Attilio Piccirilli and other Italian sculptors. Although sandstone is not nearly as durable as marble, a parsimonious Congress had selected sandstone to save money only to spend even more several decades later for restoration. Giannetti also sculpted the large bronze eagle in the Federal Deposit Insurance Corporation. *It is the largest federal eagle ever sculpted.* His firm, now run by his sons, also restored the U.S. Capitol Building exterior in 1961 for the inauguration of President John F. Kennedy.

- **Luigi Persico**

Persico was originally from Naples. During the 1820's, he carved beautiful, deep reliefs over the main entrance (east) of the U.S. Capitol Building: "Columbus Discovering America," "Genius of America" and "War and Peace." During the 20th century, artisans from the Giannetti Firm had to restore these sandstone carvings. Sandstone was used at the time since Congress sought to reduce the costs of many building projects. Persico was also employed as a portrait sculptor for many public personalities.

- **Attilio Piccirilli**

Piccirilli and his brothers carved the Capitol building's south wing triangular pediment, facing east, with a work entitled "Apotheosis of Democracy." He worked from a plaster model (c.1915) by Paul Wayland Bartlett who was awarded the commission for this pediment, but could not actually create the stone artwork. The south wing houses the House of Representatives.

Also, Attilio Piccirilli was both the artist and sculptor of the large detailed bronze statue beautifully immortalizing the work, dedication and loyalty of the American postman. His celebrated statue "Present Day Postman" stands in the U.S. Post Office Building in Washington, D.C. (Refer to three other sections on, Federal Triangle, Lincoln Monument and State artwork for additional information on Piccirilli and his brothers.)

Notice the triangular pediment relief on the south wing
(House of Representatives) of the U.S. Capitol Building

- **Thomas Gagliardi (main sculptor), Guido Butti, Vincenzo Casoni, G. Caspero and Domenico Giampaoli**

Although Gagliardi was the main sculptor, Butti, Casoni, Caspero, Giampaoli and others contributed to the Capitol building's north wing triangular pediment, facing east, with a work entitled "The Progress of Civilization." They worked from a plaster model made in Rome (1854) by Thomas Crawford, who was awarded the commission for this pediment, but could not actually create the stone artwork. The stone artwork for the pediment was completed between 1855 and 1859. The north wing houses the Senate.

R. R. Esposito

Federal Triangle
Piccirilli Brothers and other Sculptors from Carrara

In 1926, Congress approved a massive complex of seven federal office buildings in Washington, D.C., known as the Federal Triangle. This complex rests on seventy acres circumscribed by Pennsylvania Avenue, Constitution Avenue and Fifteenth Street, NW. Federal Triangle includes the Departments of Commerce, the Interstate Commerce Commission, Departmental Auditorium, Department of Labor, the Post Office Department, the Bureau of Internal Revenue, the Department of Justice, the National Archives and the Federal Trade Commission. The statuary, reliefs and stone decorations for these buildings were crafted from Carrara marble by Carrara sculptors. The famous Piccirilli brothers from the Bronx were major contributors to the artwork in Federal Triangle. The John Donnelly Company, New York, who employed several Italian carvers, was also a major participant in this project.

Federal Triangle
Interstate Commerce Commission Building

Lincoln Memorial
Attilio Piccirilli

Sculptor Attilio Piccirilli and his five brothers from Italy founded a sculpting studio in New York City and carved the majestic statue "Seated Lincoln" in the Lincoln Memorial. They began their work in 1920 and completed the magnificent statue almost two years later in 1922. They shipped their completed work of art on four railroad cars from New York City to Washington D.C. The statue of Lincoln weighs 175 tons, is 19 feet high and is made of 7 blocks of marble, perfectly fitted together. Actually, over 20 sculptors at the Piccirilli studios were involved in shaping the giant blocks of marble, but the face, its expressive eyes, and other delicate features were carved by the master Attilio himself along with his brothers. The clay model of Lincoln they used for the statue was provided by Daniel Chester French, an American artist selected by the U.S. government to create the design. French was unable to execute the final marble masterpiece.

About the Piccirilli Studios in NYC

In 1866, Attilio Piccirilli was born in Massa Carrara, Italy. He came to New York City in April of 1888. His family and brothers joined him less than two years later. He and his five brothers soon established their first studio in a stable in Manhattan on 6th Ave. and 39th Street. At that time in the United States public art celebrating civil war heroes and other leaders was reaching a new pinnacle and the Piccirilli studio became an overnight success. They opened a new studio at 4467 East 142nd Street at the corner of Brook Ave. in the Bronx. They hired apprentice stone carvers and sculptors, and worked on many public works of art for decades. Concurrently, many American artists lived in Italy to learn their art and then returned to enjoy this new American atmosphere celebrating public statues and art. Leading American art firms such as McKim, Meade & White, and American sculptors Daniel Chester French and Augustus Saint-Gaudens were given commissions by the U.S. government. These artists would send their plaster and clay models to the Piccirilli studio in order to craft the final marble statues for public display. *For thirty-five years, the Piccirilli studio made most of Daniel Chester French's statues for him including the Lincoln Memorial.* This chapter includes other works of the great Attilio Piccirilli including those that were of his original designs. Piccirilli was also one of the founders of the Free Art School Leonardo da Vinci in New York City.

At the age of 79, Attilio Piccirilli died in New York City on

October 8, 1945. His younger brother Getulio, born in 1874, who helped found the studio died two days later. Attilio's older brother Ferruccio born 1864, also a sculptor, died seven days later. The tragic loss of three brothers within days of each other is indicative of their life-long bonds, as brothers and artists. They lost their will to live without each other. Ferruccio's son Bruno, born in New York carried on the family tradition. He was a sculptor and became a professor of Art at the prestigious Vassar College.

Seated Lincoln at the Lincoln Memorial

National Cathedral - Decorations
Italian Sculptors
The statues, ornaments and gargoyles on the façade of the National Cathedral in Washington D.C. are the handiwork of Italian marble and

stone sculptors. Some gargoyles are traditional looking creatures, but others are uniquely American, for example, Darth Vader and a political protestor. The building was started in 1907 and was not completed until 1990. Its sculptors include these Italians: Roger Morigi, Vincent Palumbo, Jack Fanfani and Constantine Safferies. Palumbo represents the 5th generation of marble sculptors in his family who were originally from Molfetta, Italy. Over the main entrance of the National Cathedral is a work entitled the "Creation." The American sculptor Frederick Hart was commissioned to complete the plaster model for the "Creation," but was unable to execute his design in stone for the Cathedral. Palumbo transformed the plaster model into the marble artwork that spans the top of three doorways for all visitors to enjoy. A young sculptor named Franco Minervini came to the U.S. from Molfetta, Italy in 1985 and trained under Palumbo. He continues to work with Palumbo on projects for the great Cathedral.

State of California – Decorations
Piccirilli Brothers

The detailed ornamental work for the California Building and its towers in San Diego's famous and picturesque Balboa Park were designed and crafted by Masaniello (Thomas) Piccirilli, Orazio (Horatio) Piccirilli, Attilio Piccirilli and Furio Piccirilli. The building is now the Museum of Man. Furio Piccirilli was also the sculptor of several statues on the facade of the San Diego Museum of Art.

State of Louisiana – Pediment Relief
Pietro Cardelli

In 1821, Cardelli carved the *bas reliefs* (shallow relief) for the central triangular pediment of The Cabildo building in New Orleans. This famous building was the main administration building for New Orleans, and is where Spain signed over the City and surrounding territory to France. It is also where France signed over the City and surrounding land (Louisiana Territory) to the United States. The original building was constructed between 1795 and 1799, before Cardelli carved the pediment's relief. It is now the Louisiana State Museum and was made a National Historic Landmark in 1963.

The California Building in San Diego's Balboa Park

The Cabildo, New Orleans, Louisiana

State of Michigan – Statues
Attilio Piccirilli

At the University of Michigan in Ann Arbor, Martha Cook Residence Hall (906 S. University Ave.) rests a sculpture by Attilio Piccirilli of the character Portia, from Shakespeare's "The Merchant of Venice."

State of New York - Statues
Attilio Piccirilli

Attilio Piccirilli was granted commissions for several famous sculptures in New York. He is the artist and sculptor for many NYC monuments, including, the "Fireman's Memorial Monument" at Riverside Drive, the "Maine Memorial Monument" at Columbus Circle in Central Park and three works for the famous Rockefeller Center across from St. Patrick's Cathedral. These works at Rockefeller Center are "Youth Leading Industry" in the International Building, the "Joy of Life" at the entrance of 15 West 48th Street and the *bas relief* (shallow relief) "Eternal Youth" above the entrance of Palazzo d'Italia, which was the first relief cast in glass in the United States.

Piccirilli also was the sculptor of the famous entrance pediments at the *New York Stock Exchange* and the Frick Reference Library, both in New York City. He also carved the stonework for the Washington Arch in New York City's Greenwich Village and the well known *lions in front of the New York Public Library*, Main Building on 5th Ave. These two lions, named "Patience" and "Fortitude," gained additional notoriety when they were featured in the block-buster movie "Ghost Busters" starring Bill Murray and Dan Aykroyd. Piccirilli also created the "Mothers' War Memorial" in the state capital at Albany, New York.

State of Virginia – Statues
Attilio Piccirilli

When a fire seriously damaged the University of Virginia, the trustees retained two architectural masters for the large restoration project. Attilio Piccirilli was selected to replace the damaged statuary of the buildings and Stanford White was the architect chosen to rebuild the structures. Piccirilli is also the artist and sculptor for other famous statuary including "The Spirit of Youth" for the Virginia Military Institute in Lexington and a portrait bust of Thomas Jefferson for the

R. R. Esposito

State Capital Building in Richmond. Piccirilli also sculpted a large statue of President James Monroe standing at Monroe's estate in Ash Lawn – Highland, near Charlottesville, and completed busts of Monroe and Thomas Jefferson for the Virginian Art Commission. Piccirilli's great talent to design and execute portrait busts and monuments has left a bountiful legacy of art for all Americans to enjoy.

Union Station in Washington D.C.

Union Station, Washington D.C. - Statues
Andrew E. Bernasconi

Built from 1905 to 1908 by Italian and other construction workers, the six large statues that decorate the U.S. Capitol's train station's façade were sculpted by Andrew E. Bernasconi between 1909 and 1911. This train station is one of the most magnificent stations in the United States.

U.S. Coin Designer/Engraver
Frank Gasparro

Gasparro joined the U.S. Mint as a junior engraver in 1942 and was its Chief Engraver from 1965 to 1981. He designed several congressional commemorative coins: the 1971 Eisenhower dollar, the 1979 Susan B. Anthony dollar, the reverse side of the 1964 Kennedy half-dollar, as well as the reverse side of the Lincoln penny in 1959 when it was changed to celebrate the 50th anniversary of the penny. His design of the Lincoln Memorial for the "tail" side of the penny competed against more than 20 other designs. However, his classic concept was selected for the coin. Gasparro never walked past a penny on the ground, without picking it up. He would say, "It's personal," friends who knew him recall. Gasparro died September 29, 2001 at the age of 92. He taught at the Samuel S. Fleisher Memorial Art School until his death. (Also, refer to reference on the Silver Dollar in the "Culture, Conventions and Traditions" chapter.)

Washington's First Statue & Portrait Bust
Enrico Causici

The first monument dedicated to George Washington in America is in Mount Vernon. The statue of Washington on top of the monument (a massive 160 foot tall column) is the first statue of George Washington ever made. It was designed and sculpted by Enrico Causici of Verona, Italy. He used three blocks of marble weighing seven tons each to complete his statue of Washington that stands 16 feet tall.

The artist Houdon may have painted the first portraits of George Washington. However, the Italian Ceracchi painted Washington's first *portrait bust* and influenced the future of *portrait bust* paintings in America. He also painted several other founding fathers of America.

Yale University, Connecticut, U.S.
Italian Sculptors and Stonemasons

The prestigious Yale University hired Italian sculptors and stonemasons to decorate the exteriors of new gothic buildings added to the campus. These masons carved very detailed stone statues and scenes. However, if you are ever at Yale, look closely at the statues, not all of them depict classic or elegant scenes and faces. You will see fat demons with tongues sticking out at you, ugly gargoyles, naked bottoms of old people, and other less than completely solemn works of art. The great Yale University did not feel it necessary to pay the sculptors and masons a wage that was commensurate with their arduous and artistic efforts. Consequently, the Italian artisans took this unfair treatment as an opportunity to have fun with the stubborn Yale administrators and exacted revenge by carving these undignified figures on the exterior of these new buildings.

Other Italian Artists & Sculptors in America

The references listed earlier in this chapter describe some of the more famous Italian masters who applied their talents to beautify America. The following is a list of other Italian artists and sculptors who helped create the American art heritage we now all enjoy. They often also taught in universities and art schools, training the next generation of Americans and Italian-Americans with specialized skills in painting or sculpting. They beautified churches, hotels, libraries, museums, airports, government and other public buildings. The list includes: Carlo Abate, Paolo Abbate, Vincent Aderente, Corrado Albrizio, Louis Bosa, Beniamino Bufano, Vincent Canade, Robert Cimbalo, Pompeo Coppini, Jon Corbina, Alfred D. Crimi, Stefano Cusumano, Nicola D'Ascenzo, Robert De Niro, Sr. (father of actor Robert De Niro), Henry DiSpirito, Alfeo Faggi, Ralph Fasanella, Achille Forgione, Jr., O. Louis Guglielmi, Batiste Madelena, Albino Manca, Ugo Mochi, August Mosca, Joseph Oddenino, Achille Peretti, Gottardo Piazzoni, Raimondo Puccinelli, John Recco, Tony Saleme, Antonio Salemme, Lucia and Attilio Salemme, Vincent Salerno, Concetta Scaravaglione, Salvatore Scarpitta, Frank Stella, Giuseppe (Joseph) Stella, Leonard Tantillo, Joseph F. Trovato.

ARCHITECTURE:

Capitol Buildings, Washington D.C.

Many buildings in the capitals of the world have copied classic Roman and Italian Renaissance architecture. The U.S. Supreme Court building is a very close copy of a well preserved Roman temple now called the "Maison Carree" in Nimes, France. Also, the Virginia State Capital building is closely modeled after the graceful "Maison Carree."

U.S. Supreme Court Building

The famous front of the *New York Stock Exchange (NYSE) also greatly resembles the "Maison Carree."* Incidentally, Piccirilli carved the pediment at the entrance of the NYSE as described in the ART portion of this chapter.

Thomas Jefferson was a great admirer of Italy and ancient Rome. Jefferson is largely responsible for the neo-classical buildings in Washington, D.C. that echo Roman and Italian architectural styles. He owned and read four translations of Palladio's famous "I Quattro Libri dell' Architettura" ("The Four Books of Architecture") and knew much about the ancient buildings in Rome. Jefferson used the Pantheon in Rome as a model for the University of Virginia Library. Furthermore, Jefferson gave the estate he built in Virginia the Italian name, Monticello, which means small mountain in Italian. When he built this estate he used the majestic La Rotunda in Vicenza designed by the great Andrea Palladio for its architectural inspiration. These two buildings with central domes have many obvious similarities and represent *Palladian* (or *Palladianism*) style architecture. This is an architectural style conceived by the celebrated Andrea Palladio. Palladio often used central domes in his works and was inspired by the ancient Roman Pantheon. Perhaps as a tribute to Jefferson's admiration of Italian architecture and culture, the Jefferson Memorial in Washington, D.C. has the appearance of a Roman temple and has a very close resemblance to the Pantheon in Rome.

The *U.S. Capitol Building is classified as Palladian* style architecture with a central rotunda flanked by the wings for the Senate (north) and the House of Representatives (south). The building's dome was inspired by and has many similarities with Saint Peter's Basilica in Rome. They both display massive domes with vertical exterior ribs that connect to very similar peaks. The dome on the U.S. Capitol Building also has an oculus (opening for light at its peak) similar to both Saint Peter's and the Roman Pantheon. Also, Saint Peter's has a giant plaza at its entrance to accommodate large public gatherings and the U.S. Capitol has the "The Mall" (or "great lawn") at its entrance for public groups to assemble.

The main entrance of the White House is designed with a specific style of second story balcony. The six supporting columns above and below the balcony are aligned. This is the design used by Andrea Palladio when he built the celebrated palace Villa Cornaro at Padua during the Renaissance. Palladio's double set of six columns was an exquisite innovation in architecture and was copied when the White House was built. The White House architects made a modification by making the balcony rounded, which adds to the building's charm. The rear entrance of the White House closely parallels the Villa Cornaro at S. Andrea di Casasagra in Treviso which was designed by architect Giorgio Massario. This villa's entrance and the White House rear entrance both have four columns and have four pairs of windows vertically arranged on each side of the entrance. In summary, two Cornaro family villas built during the Renaissance inspired the basic design of the U.S. White House.

In the center of the plaza *in front of Saint Peter's Basilica stands an obelisk monument in the same shape as the Washington Monument*, a tall, elongated pyramid that has a pencil appearance.

Many traditional American buildings with columns, domed roofs, Palladian windows and high exterior staircases that lead to the main entrances are incorrectly viewed as "early American" architecture. Unfortunately, in America there are no Roman ruins or Italian Renaissance buildings to remind us of the inspirational sources for much of America's traditional architectural style. In Europe there are many ancient Roman and Renaissance reminders of the origins of these architectural styles.

Statue of Liberty
Architect - Frederic Auguste Bertholdi

Almost every American knows that the Statue of Liberty in New York Harbor was a gift from France. The architect, Auguste Bertholdi, was a Frenchman with an Italian name. This is because his father was an Italian immigrant who moved to France where his son Auguste was born. Auguste Bertholdi said that he used his mother's face as the model for the statue. When visitors gaze at this majestic monument to American liberty, the face of an Italian mother is what comforts and welcomes them. Also, the Italian John Rapetti (1862-1936) worked in Paris with Bertholdi on the Statue of Liberty. Rapetti's name is engraved in the crown identifying him as one of the Statue's creators.

Statue of Liberty Renovation
Lee Iacocca

Lee Iacocca was appointed Chairman of the Statue of Liberty-Ellis Island Foundation by President Ronald Reagan to raise funds to restore these national landmarks. On the Statue of Liberty's centennial, July 4, 1986, the refurbished statue was dedicated with great fanfare including fabulous Grucci (Italian-American) fireworks blazing high over the evening sky of New York harbor. Iacocca's efforts made it possible for the Statue to be refurbished in time for its centennial.

Iacocca also held the national spotlight for his leadership roles at the Ford Motor Company and Chrysler Corporation. (Refer to the chapter on "Transportation" for more on the life of Lee Iacocca).

ༀ

Chapter IV

ASTRONOMY

"Eppur si muove" ("It does move all the same")
- In defiance Galileo murmured this phrase about the
earth's movement around the sun during his trial for heresy -

Inventor of the Telescope
Father of Modern Astronomy
Galileo Galilei

Galileo, known by his first name only, was an astronomer, inventor, physicist and mathematician. He was born February 15, 1564 in Pisa to a father, who was a famous lutanist and composer. His father, Vincenzo Galilei, wrote several books on music history and theory, one of which analyzed both old and modern music entitled, "Dialogo della musica antica e moderna," which was published in 1581. Vincenzo Galilei was also an experimenter by nature, and combined the practice and theory of music. He was the first to discover the correct ratios of string lengths to octaves. It had long been believed that the ratio was 2:1, but he proved that it was 4:1 by his experiments that hung weights from strings. Galileo was raised by a father who used mathematics and experimentation in his musical studies. Similarly, Galileo, in his own life, also used mathematics and experimentation to rock the foundations of the world's scientific, philosophical and religious establishments. (Refer to the entry on Opera in the "Music" chapter for more on Vincenzo Galileo.)

Galileo entered Pisa University as a medical student in 1581. He later decided to become a mathematician and from 1592 to 1610 was a professor of mathematics at Padua University. Galileo taught himself optics and ingeniously used the lenses available at the time to build a telescope with significant magnification. His passion to study the heavens drove him to experiment with optics, and ultimately, invent the modern telescope. In 1609, his first telescope had a magnification power of 30, which was a massive power for his day. Other very crude spyglasses existed at the time with double or triple magnification and were used by ship captains or by military leaders. There are two known examples of magnification spyglasses long before Galileo's powerful telescope. For example, Leonardo da Vinci studied optics and designed a telescope 100 years before Galileo, but the optics of his day prevented da Vinci from building one with much magnification. His designs and analysis included curved mirrors and glass hemispheres. DaVinci even developed a means of testing curved mirrored surfaces for quality anticipating the Hartmann optical method. The famous Arab scientist Alhazen documented an even earlier writing of a primitive magnifying lens around 1000 AD. The Roman emperor Nero (37 AD – 67 AD) used an emerald as a means of magnifying the view of events in large arenas. Also, Hans Lipperhey in Holland patented a primitive telescope in 1608, but it was based upon early Italian models. *Nevertheless, Galileo built the first modern telescope and was the first to build one powerful enough to study the heavens. Perhaps more importantly, Galileo used his new telescope to make new scientific discoveries that greatly enlightened the world.* (Refer to the "Science & Technology" chapter, for more information on Galileo, who is also considered the father of modern physics. He is also credited with introducing the scientific method to the world and Albert Einstein has called him the father of modern science.)

Using his new invention, Galileo systematically studied the sky. He made many fantastic astronomical discoveries and today he is considered the *Father of Modern Astronomy*. Galileo was the first to provide evidence that confirmed the theory of the great Polish astronomer Nicolaus Copernicus that the Sun, not the earth, was at the center of the solar system. Galileo's studies of the crescent phases of Venus provided the first evidence that the earth was not at the center of the solar system and that the earth moved around the sun.

After receiving approval from the Church's censures, Galileo published his discovery in a book he titled "Dialogue." He gave it this title because it was written in an interesting readable style that took the form of three men having a dialogue about our planetary system. In this way Galileo could say he was showing both opinions, earth centered and sun centered concepts and arguments, so that he would not offend the Church, which held tightly to the concept that the planetary system was earth centered. Galileo's book and discoveries were highly controversial, but there were some supporters in high political and religious offices. A good quote can be taken from the Vatican librarian, Cardinal Cesare Baronio who said that the Bible was a book about how one goes to heaven, not how Heaven goes. Cardinal Baronio believed science should explain, "how heaven goes."

Unfortunately for Galileo, most of his colleagues, political and religious contemporaries supported the ancient Greek theories about the planetary system based upon the thinking of Ptolemy. They denounced Galileo, discriminated against him professionally, and rejected his new discoveries. Still worse, Galileo's adversaries convinced Pope Urban VIII of the Roman Catholic Church that his new book and findings were heresy.

On June 22 in 1633, after several trial hearings, the Church ruled Galileo's discoveries and book to be in conflict with Church teachings. Galileo was told he must disclaim and retract his discovery that the earth moves around the sun in order to prevent spending the rest of his life in jail. A euphemistic term for this is called *ecclesiastical censure.* The Church had supported the 1500 year old ancient Greek theory of Ptolemy, which stated that the sun revolved around the earth. The Church taught that God made man on earth and because of this, the earth must be more important than the sun and so the earth had to stand still and the sun must revolve around the earth. Also, the Church was determined to support the centuries old constructs developed by the great St. Thomas Aquinas. St. Thomas logically integrated Aristotle's metaphysics and concepts of cosmology and perfection of the heavens with Christian doctrines in his masterpiece "Summa Theologica." St. Thomas' works reverberated throughout European universities since the 13th century and Galileo's book conflicted with the way "Summa Theologica" embraced Aristotle's cosmology. The Church also held that because Galileo's book was written in Italian and not Latin, he was trying to intentionally reach and appeal to a wider audience than academics.

The infirm 70 year old Galileo, stricken with arthritis and a heart condition was made to kneel and read a statement prepared by Church officials. He was forced to apologize, retract his beliefs and promise never to teach or publish his books again. Historical accounts show, however, that immediately after Galileo retracted his discovery during his trial, he rose from his knees and whispered, "Eppur si muove." Translated into English it means, "It does move all the same." Galileo was referring to the earth moving around the sun! Galileo was a disciplined scientist, but evidently also a spirited rebel. At the trial Galileo was sentenced to the prison dungeons. Fortunately, two of Galileo's supporters Cardinal Taddeo Barberini, and the Tuscan ambassador to Rome, Ambassador Francesco Niccolini convinced the Pope to soften Galileo's prison sentence. As a result, the Church placed the elderly Galileo under the Church's version of house arrest, first at the Tuscan embassy and later to his own villa in Arcetri (near Florence) for the rest of his life.

The aged Galileo was nevertheless a dedicated unstoppable scientist and during his confinement finished his last revolutionary book, which he titled "Two New Sciences" sometimes referred to as "Discourses." This book rejected Aristotle's theories on motion. Galileo developed pioneering studies on inertia, gravity and motion. Instead of thinking about *why* things moved, as in Aristotle's mental framework, Galileo studied *how* they moved – through empirical experiments, observations and mathematics. His new book was smuggled into Holland and published, where the reach of the Church was not quite so strong and somewhat mitigated by Protestant establishments. (Refer to the chapter on "Science and Technology" for more information on Galileo's studies on gravity and motion.)

Although technically forbidden to receive visitors while in confinement, Galileo had international visitors, including the eminent philosopher Thomas Hobbes and the poet John Milton. He also learned from many visitors that his banned book "Dialogue" was in high demand and that the market price had tripled since the Church's ban!

Galileo died almost a decade after his imprisonment on January 8, 1642. He is buried in a decorated and massive tomb at the church of Santa Croce where Michelangelo, a fellow Tuscan, is also buried. To the Church's credit, it did later take Galileo's books off the list of books Catholics are prohibited from reading. This occurred in 1832, 200 years after his trial. And in 1992, 350 years after his death, Pope John II somewhat reluctantly repudiated the Church's rejection of Galileo, and formally recognized his scientific discoveries.

It is interesting and significant to note that the Roman Catholic Church still exerts great influence over the secular world. In 1992, the pop music star Sinead O'Connor tore up a photograph of the Pope after her performance on the television show "Saturday Night Live." NBC was fined 1.5 million dollars by the U.S. Federal Communications Commission - and Sinead's music career was essentially over. Two weeks after her "Saturday Night Live" performance and photo-tearing stunt, she appeared at a Bob Dylan tribute concert at New York's Madison Square Garden, and was promptly booed off the stage by the outraged audience in attendance.

More on Leonardo da Vinci and the History of the Telescope

Galileo invented the first modern telescope and was the first to point it at the stars, and due to this is credited for being the founder of modern astronomy. However, as previously noted, da Vinci had designed a telescope 100 years earlier, but probably did not build or use one with the magnification he desired. In his time, optics and lens technologies were insufficient and da Vinci could design, but not build a powerful telescope. However, we should also note that Leonardo da Vinci might be the first person to have conceived of building a telescope specifically to study the heavens. In 1490, Leonardo wrote his "Codex Atlanticus," almost 75 years before Galileo's birth. In it he writes about the possibility of "... making glasses to see the Moon enlarged." One of Leonardo's "Notebooks" also contains a drawing that shows a long cylindrical telescope that looks very much like a modern one. Also, in his 1513 book "Codex Arundul," Leonardo says " ...in order to observe the nature of the planets, open the roof and bring the image of a single planet onto the base of a concave mirror. The image of the planet reflected by the base will show the surface of the planet much magnified." Leonardo may have first conceived the indoor modern observatory when he suggests, "open the roof." He also had a strong understanding of the sky and the moon and wrote that the moon's light is actually reflected light from the Sun. He also said "Il sole no si muove," which means, "The sun does not move." Leonardo was a giant in his time and described many correct astronomical concepts. He designed and anticipated the modern telescope. However, it was Galileo who actually built the first telescope capable of studying the sky. Galileo built and used his new invention to study the stars and was able to prove for the first time to the world the fallacy of many long held beliefs, and replaced them with the truths born of experimentation and discovery.

There are some who claim that the first inventor of the telescope was Dutch. There was a patent filed in Holland by Hans Lipperhey in

1608 for a primitive telescope. The optics in Galileo's telescope were 32 times stronger! Also, it has been documented that an earlier telescope with the inscription "Anno 1590" (Year 1590) was exported from Italy to Holland. Even the great Italian scientist and mathematician, Della Porta, designed a telescope as early as 1580. History shows that the earliest example of a telescope design was that of da Vinci around 1509 and that students of da Vinci built early telescopes, which explains how one was exported from Italy to Holland around the year 1590. Also, in the late 1500's, sophisticated glass-making and lens crafting was first developed in Venice. Eyeglass lenses were invented in Florence in the 13th century, as you will read later in this book in the "Medicine, Biology & Health" chapter. In summary, one thing is certain, that this magnificent instrument, the telescope, is purely an Italian invention. (For documentation on the history of the telescope see the Artbras Book, "Leonardo da Vinci," listed in this book's "Bibliography." The book shows telescope designs made by da Vinci in 1509 and discusses the 1590 telescope that was exported from Italy to Holland).

Galileo at age sixty

Also, Riccardo Giacconi and Bruno Rossi invented the X-Ray telescope. Giacconi won the 2002 Nobel Prize in physics. His contributions laid the *foundations of X-ray astronomy*, and consequently he is considered the father of X-ray astronomy. Refer to the "Science & Technology" chapter for more on Giacconi and Rossi.

Discovery: Moons of Jupiter, Moon Craters and Sunspots
Galileo Galilei

Galileo was the first to discover that Jupiter had a group of moons and noted that the ones closer to Jupiter moved faster than the ones further away. He also was the first to discover that the earth's moon has craters and in 1610 wrote "Starry Messenger," which described this discovery. It is also interesting to note that Galileo was also a student of art and a painter. In 1613, he was admitted to the well known Accademia del Disegno art school for young artists. This school taught its students how to use mathematics for proper scale and perspective in paintings and other forms of art. Galileo painted watercolors of the moon and illustrated craters he discovered. He also discovered that the sun was spotted with dark areas and he was the first to think these sunspots were related to the nature of the Sun itself. These irregular lunar features also challenged the Church's doctrine regarding the perfection of the heavens.

In 1989, the U.S. space agency NASA launched the Galileo spacecraft, named in Galileo's honor, to explore Jupiter and its moons. It reached Jupiter on December 7th 1995. The spacecraft's mission was highly successful and brought back vast amounts of information on Jupiter and its moons, Venus, and asteroid belts. The Galileo spacecraft collected much evidence to support the idea that vast quantities of water may exist on Europa, one of Jupiter's 16 known satellites. The Galileo spacecraft completed its primary goals and concluded its 14-year trip until September 2003 when it intentionally plunged into Jupiter as its planned finale.

Planetary moons are often called *satellites*. The word *satellite* is derived from the Latin word *satelles* meaning *attendant* or *guard*. In the mid-1600's English speaking people began to use the word *satellite* to describe someone who follows another person around, such as a constant travel companion or bodyguard. Eventually, the word was also applied to moons that follow planets around. Also, modern

R. R. Esposito

man-made satellites got their name because they, like the moon, orbit the earth.

First Solution for Measuring Longitude
Galileo Galilei

Although Galileo was a scientist and not a sailor, he was nevertheless aware of the navigation problems at sea and the lack of an accurate method for measuring longitude. He provided the first solution for the measurement of longitude using the movements of Jupiter and its satellites (moons). *He observed that the moons of Jupiter eclipsed 1000 times per year and that you could accurately set a clock based upon these movements, an important factor in measuring longitude.* He even invented headgear that included a telescope called a *celatone* to be used to measure longitude. Although he died in 1642, by 1650 his solution for measuring longitude became widely accepted. His new and accurate solution had such great impact that surveyors and mapmakers used his technique to redraw the maps of the entire world. *As a result of the new maps, King Louis XIV of France said that he lost more territory to accurate longitude measurements than to war with his enemies.* This may be history's greatest proof that "the pen is mightier than the sword." Incidentally, the state of Louisiana, USA is named after King Louis XIV.

Milky Way Galaxy
Galileo Galilei

On a clear and moonless night, the Milky Way galaxy can be observed as an almost hazy composition of stars clustered together. Our solar system, consisting of our sun and the nine planets that include earth, is just one of billions of solar systems in the Milky Way galaxy. Galileo was the first to conclude that the Milky Way galaxy consisted of massive clusters of stars. When you see our hazy galaxy in the night sky you are basically looking at our heavenly neighborhood. However, keep in mind that even though light travels over 186,000 miles per second, it takes several years for the light from nearby stars in our vast galaxy to reach earth. For example, the closest star to us is Alpha Centuri, which is 4.35 light years away. This means that light from this star has to travel 4.35 years before it reaches us on earth. Some stars are millions of light years away. Consequently, when you see stars in the evening sky you are looking at how these objects appeared hundreds, thousands, and even millions of years ago. If a nearby star vanished today you will not see the light go out in the night sky for many years. Although he lacked the necessary technology, Galileo actually tried to measure the speed of light using flashing lanterns on hilltops. However, he could not perceive any delay and was unable to measure light's speed on earth.

Rings of Saturn
Galileo Galilei

In 1610, Galileo was the first human to see the rings of Saturn. His telescope was not powerful enough to clearly observe these objects as rings. To Galileo they appeared as two small moons or planets. In 1655, the Dutch astronomer Christian Huygens was the first to identify the objects specifically as rings. In 1675, the Italian astronomer Giovanni Dominico Cassini was able to identify a gap in the rings of Saturn. This hole in the rings is now called the Cassini Division.

Discovery of Four of Saturn's Moons
Determined the Rotation of Mars,
Venus and Jupiter
Discovered the Gap in Saturn's Rings
Giovanni Domenico Cassini

Cassini was born June 8, 1625 in Perinaldo, near Genoa and died September 14, 1712 in Paris, France. He was educated at the Jesuit College in Genoa and then at the abbey of San Fructuoso both in Italy. Cassini did research from 1648 to 1669 at the Panzano Observatory, which is also in Italy. In 1650, he became professor of astronomy at the University of Bologna. Early in his career, he made several significant astronomical observations that were published. He also understood the importance of Galileo's new solution for measuring longitude that was based upon the movement of Jupiter and its moons. Consequently, while he was a professor at the University of Bologna, he performed careful studies and developed the most accurate measurements and timings of these celestial bodies for the purpose of measuring longitude. In the mid-1600's Cassini's success had allowed him to convince the Church to alter the building plans for the cathedral

Basilica San Petronio that was to be built in Bologna. He wanted a *cathedral observatory* built similar to the one the great astronomer Egnatio Danti was given at the Vatican itself, called the "Tower of the Winds" ("Torre dei Venti"). (Refer to the "Calendar" reference that follows this one for more on Danti and how these *cathedral observatories* worked.) Like Danti's earlier *cathedral observatory*, Cassini's observatory would let small rays of light shine on the floor, but Cassini wanted a larger and longer meridian line to be built into the marble floor. This would allow for more accurate astronomical calculations as the sunlight travels along the line on the cathedral floor. The new observatory at the Basilica San Petronio would also have a towering vaulted ceiling 90 feet above the floor. Cassini was granted his request and used this solar observatory to determine the spring equinox for identifying yearly dates for Easter, a religious holiday the Church was greatly interested in accurately dating. Additionally, he used the observatory in Bologna to determine the time for setting clocks, and also for other research and calculations that indirectly supported the findings of Galileo regarding the earth moving around the sun. Thanks to Cassini, the solar observatory at the Basilica San Petronio was used by many astronomers to make over 4,500 astronomical observations from 1655 to 1736. Solar observatories were built and used by numerous astronomers in other Italian churches and cathedrals, for example: Santa Maria degli Angeli in Rome, Santa Maria Del Fiore Cathedral in Florence and the Cathedral in Palermo.

Cassini was also an expert in hydraulics and engineering and was consulted regarding the flooding of the Po River. He also worked for the Pope as an expert on river management.

King Louis XIV of France was very impressed with Cassini's work, especially his charts and measurements of the movements of Jupiter and its moons. He invited Cassini to come to Paris. The senate of Bologna and the Pope agreed to let Cassini accept this invitation in 1669. Cassini went to France and became director of the Paris Observatory in 1671. He became a French citizen in 1671 at the age of forty-six.

While living in France, Cassini was the first to discover Saturn's four moons (1671-1684). He determined the rotation periods of Mars, Venus and Jupiter (1665-1666). In 1675, Cassini was able to identify a gap in the then known rings of Saturn. This gap or hole in the rings is now called the Cassini Division. Also, in 1672 he was the first to calculate the approximate distance of the sun from the earth. NASA named the Cassini spacecraft after this great astronomer. The spacecraft costing $3.4 billion reached Saturn in 2004 and studied its rings and moons. It also captured images of Saturn's northern hemisphere detailing its striking blue colors and other unique features.

Cassini was born and educated in Italy and made his first significant astronomical discoveries when he was professor of astronomy at the University of Bologna. However, since he made many of his discoveries while living in France, he is sometimes considered an Italian-French astronomer. As a result, his name is sometimes seen with a French spelling- Jacque Dominique Cassini.

Calendar (Julian & Gregorian) and Leap Year

Roman Senate and Julius Caesar

The ancient Egyptians were the first to develop a calendar with 365 days, which they correctly based upon their celestial studies. They celebrated the New Year on January 7th, the day of Sekhmet. The early Roman society and others celebrated the New Year in March, usually the 25th. This date had some agricultural significance, since it represents the start of spring. Later, Romans used January 1st for the start of their year, because it was the date the Roman consuls took over their duties. However, the start of the year for Romans often changed. Government officials sometimes changed the calendar to extend their terms in office! This created a very artificial calendar that was no longer synchronized with the moon and other astronomical events. Fortunately, modern politicians dare not suggest such an unsettling ploy in a democratic society, as they understand the importance and reverence placed upon professional sports schedules! In 153 BC, the Roman Senate decided to resynchronize the calendar with astronomy and set the year to start with January 1 once more. However, new tinkering by subsequent politicians put the calendar in disharmony again. In 46 BC, Julius Caesar decided to rid everyone of this calamitous calendar and again reset the calendar to start on January 1. The change has endured. *Caesar's new calendar even included the correct leap year calculation every four years.* Of course to accomplish this he had to make one year last 445 days! Remembering birthdays and anniversaries *then* was clearly very challenging, but did provide plausible excuses not available to the absent-minded in today's digital world. Caesar's actions won him the respect of others and the calendar is called the *Julian calendar* in his honor. Incidentally, the month of July is named after Julius Caesar and the month of August is named after Augustus Caesar, his adopted son. The names of four other months also have a Latin legacy. These are months seven (September), eight (October), nine (November) and ten (December). Remember the first month of the early Roman calendar was March, as discussed above, so their twelfth month was February, not December.

Dionysius Exiguus

The year 2000 in our present day calendar is the 2000th year since the birth of Christ. It is 2000 AD (Anno Domini) or the 2000th "Year of our Lord." Setting the first year of our calendar to the birth of Christ was done by Dionysius about 527 AD. Dionysius was a Roman monk, originally of Scythian birth, who lived in the early 500's and died about 545 AD. He was a scholar and monk living in Rome who studied and taught Greek philosophy and became a chronologist. Dionysius was trying to identify the true date of Easter and became more intrigued with the birth of Christ. Dionysius calculated that the birth of Christ coincided with the founding of Rome. He then made that year the beginning of his new era and set the year to 1 AD.

Actually, Dionysius setting the year to *one* (1 AD) and not *zero* (0 AD) is what caused purists to complain that all the gala celebrations on January 1st, 2000 were premature. They correctly contended that we had not finished the year 2000 right through December 31, 2000 and the start of the new millennium was actually January 1st, 2001. Dionysius should have had a *day one* in *year zero (0 AD)* to begin his new Christian era. But let us not be too harsh on Dionysius, the mathematical concept of *zero* did not exist in his day.

Some scholars suggest that Dionysius was a little off and that the birth of Christ was not 1 AD, but occurred in 3 BC or 4 BC. Nevertheless, his system was gradually adopted first in Italy and later in other parts of Christian regions. This so-called Christian Era, created by Dionysius, was soon adopted in England as a result of the Roman missionaries there. Charlemagne was the first ruler of Northern Europe to officially adopt it in the 8th century. This calendar is found in Saxony in the 7th century and in Gaul in the 8th century. It became generally accepted in Europe after 1000 AD.

Egnatio Pellegrino Rainaldi Danti and Pope Gregory XIII

Danti was born in Perugia in April, 1536 and died on October 19, 1586 in Alatri. Even in his day he was a well known mathematician and scientist who worked on correcting errors in the calendar. He invented astronomical instruments that he used to determine an accurate equinox. The resulting knowledge he acquired allowed him to discover in 1574 an eleven-day error in the calendar. In 1582, the Italian Pope Gregory XIII (born January 7, 1502 in Bologna) adopted Danti's correction, however, the Protestant governments in northern Europe and in North America refused to comply with the Catholic Pope's calendar. England finally adopted this correction to the Julian calendar, eliminating eleven days in September, 1752 and re-named their calendar the *Gregorian calendar* in deference to Pope Gregory XIII. It was not until the early 20th century that the Soviet Union (1916) and the Greek Orthodox Church (1924) conformed to this standard.

Danti is known for his correction to the calendar, but he also designed and built instruments for wind direction and surveying.

Early Cathedral Observatories

Danti was born almost 30 years before Galileo, and like Galileo, Danti was a pioneering astronomer. Because of Danti's success in correcting the calendar in 1582, the Roman Catholic Church rewarded him by building an observatory in the Vatican. The Vatican structure called the "Tower of the Winds" ("Torre dei Venti") allowed for a small one inch hole in the roof so that sunlight (sometimes moonlight) could shine a narrow beam onto the floor. Danti had a meridian line made in the marble floor that ran north-south. By tracking the sunlight's fine beam that moved across the line he was able to make astronomical calculations. When the sun was at its highest point in the sky during the summer solstice, the light would shine at one end of the line. Conversely, during the winter solstice the light would shine at the opposite end of the meridian line. This began the start of a concept that took root in European cathedrals, especially in Italy, as other *cathedral observatories* began to be built by the Church for the next two hundred years. These were sometimes called solar observatories since they were used mostly to track the movement of the sun. In stark contrast to the Church's censure of Galileo in 1633, the Church had also supported astronomers, since there was interest in accurately identifying religious events and holidays, especially Easter. For more on the development of *cathedral observatories* see the section on Giovanni Cassini that immediately precedes this reference on the calendar.

Calendar and Names for Days of the Week
Roman Empire
There are five planets in the sky that are visible to the human eye. Thousands of years ago the ancients were aware of these five planets, which look like bright stars to the naked eye. These five planets also move independently, unlike actual stars that have fixed relative positions to each other and form constellations. The independent movements of the planets are based upon their orbits, which gives them clear uniqueness and seemingly higher power than the stars.

Calendar - Names for Days of the Week

ITALIAN DAY OF WEEK	ENGLISH DAY OF WEEK
Lunedi (from the word luna meaning moon in both Latin and Italian)	Monday (from the English words for moon day)
Martedi (from the Roman god of war Mars, in Latin, Martius)	Tuesday (from Tiu's day. Tiu or Tyr was the Norse god of war, which follows the Roman use of Mars, also god of war)
Mercoledi (from the Roman god Mercury, god of speed and messenger of the gods)	Wednesday (from Odin's day or Wodin's day. Odin in Norse mythology was the ruler of the gods)
Giovedi (from the Roman god Jupiter, ruler of the Roman gods)	Thursday (from Thor's day. Norse god of thunder and eldest son Odin)
Venerdi (from the Roman god Venus, goddess of love and beauty)	Friday (from Freya's day. Freya is the Norse goddess of love, fertility and beauty, which follows the Roman use of Venus, also goddess of love and beauty)
Sabato (from the Roman god Saturn, in Latin, Saturni. The 6th planet from the sun is also the 6th day.)	Saturday (from the Roman god Saturn)
Domenica (from the Latin dominus or domino meaning god. This parallels God's day in the bible)	Sunday (from sun's day, the most powerful thing in the sky, thus closest to God, dominus in Latin)

The ancients venerated these five objects in the sky. If one includes the dazzling sun and the huge moon, there are seven visible celestial bodies that were known to the ancient world. The seven days of the week are based upon these seven bodies. *The Romans provided the original names for the days of the week used in Europe.* The preceding table shows the Italian version, which is basically a dialect of the Latin language of the Romans, and the corresponding English version. Although the English names are sometimes different than the Latin or Italian, they are based upon similar Norse or Saxon meanings or gods. All of the English names are derived in meaning from the Roman names except for Wednesday and Thursday.

Discovery of the Canals of Mars
Giovanni Virginio Schiaparelli

Schiaparelli, the astronomer, was born in Italy on March 14, 1835 and died on July 4, 1910. In 1881, he was the first to discover an interesting system of straight lines on the planet Mars. He called these lines *canali*, which is the Italian word for *channels*. However, the Italian word *canali* was incorrectly translated into the English word *canals* implying that these were crafted canals and not natural channels. This misinterpretation of the word, and the unusual straightness of the structures, generated much publicity and speculation that there was life on Mars. Modern astronomers cannot explain them, but doubt these geographic features ever contained water or were created by water erosion. Schiaparelli also discovered the asteroid Hesperia in 1861 *and proved that meteor swarms move through space in cometary orbits.* He was director of the Brera Observatory in Milan from 1862 to 1900.

First Map of the Moon
Giovanni Riccioli

This Italian astronomer lived from 1598 to 1671. Riccioli published a famous map of the moon in 1651 in his "Almagestum Novum" (or "New Almagest"). Many of the names used today for craters and other principle features of the moon come from his map and naming conventions. He also published astronomical tables in "Astronomia Reformata" in 1665. Riccioli and many other colleagues resented the controversial Galileo and rejected his new view of the solar system as threatening to their theories, teachings and status. This is evident in Riccioli's map of the moon, "New Almagest," which was published nine years after Galileo's death. Even though Galileo discovered the existence of craters on the moon, Riccioli's map names a very small crater only 9 miles across, after the great astronomer Galileo. By contrast Riccioli named a very large crater Ptolemaeus, 115 miles across, after the ancient Greek astronomer Ptolemy who believed that the earth was the center of the solar system and did not move. Many other notable individuals were assigned large craters by Riccioli, and his successors, who evidently felt obliged to continue the discrimination even after Galileo's death. Fortunately, the International Astronomical Union (IAU) of professional astronomers has named a very large crater on Mars after Galileo. They also named the moons of Jupiter, discovered by Galileo, the Galilean Satellites.

Discovery of First Multiple Star
Giovanni Riccioli

In 1650, Riccioli identified the first multiple star, Mizar (or Zeta Ursae Majoris). It is located in the North Pole constellation Ursa Major (or Great Bear) that includes about 20 major stars and the five famous stars that make up the Big Dipper. Ursa Major is the third largest constellation in the sky.

Discovery of the Tycho Brahe Supernova
Francisco Maurolico

Maurolico was born in Messina on September 16, 1494 and died there as well on July 22, 1575. Maurolico was a famous mathematician who lived most of his life in Sicily. He spent a few years in Rome and Naples, was ordained a priest in 1521, later became a Benedictine monk and also supervised the mint in Sicily. Maurolico studied several astronomical phenomena. Most notably he observed the supernova that appeared in the constellation Cassiopeia in 1572, known today as "Tycho's supernova." This supernova is named after the Danish astronomer Tycho Brahe (1546 - 1601) who, two years later, published the details of his own observations on this supernova in 1574. Maurolico's full details of his observations were never publicly published and evidence of their existence was only recently rediscovered.

Maurolico also developed and published methods for measuring the Earth in his "Cosmographia." These methods were later used by Jean Picard in measuring the earth's meridian in 1670. (Also, see the "Mathematics" chapter for more on Maurolico).

The astronomical terms *nova* and *supernova* are derived from the Latin word *novus*, which means *new*. A nova is a star that, over a period of just a few days, becomes 10-100 times brighter than it was, but returns to its previous magnitude after some varying months of time. Approximately 10-15 novas (or novae) occur in the Milky Way galaxy each year. A supernova is an explosive brightening of a star by a factor of about 1000. Unlike a nova, a supernova takes several years to gradually fade, and while it lasts, its effects dominate the entire galaxy in which it lies. About one supernova occurs in the Milky Way galaxy every 30 years. In actuality, new scientific knowledge has proven that these two events in the sky are not new stars as their name suggests. These were originally named *nova* because their brilliance made them appear to be new. Similarly, Tycho Brahe mistakenly thought he was observing a new star.

Interestingly enough, remnants of supernova explosions create one type of *nebula* in the sky. Nebula is actually a Latin word meaning *mist* or *cloud*. The most famous is the "Crab Nebula," the result of a supernova explosion witnessed by the Chinese in 1054. Nebulas (or nebulae) are also caused by other astronomical relatively diffuse condensations of gas and dust in space.

Stellar Spectral Classification
Angelo Secchi

Secchi was born on June 18, 1818 in Reggio, Italy. He joined the Jesuit order when he was only fifteen years of age and became an ordained priest in 1847. He lectured on physics at the Jesuit Collegio Romano and in 1852 founded a new observatory there. He was the first to use spectroscopy to classify stars. His four stellar classifications, based upon his spectroscopic studies, became the foundation for all future stellar classification systems. He also made contributions to solar physics and was the *first to assert that the sun's core is a gaseous state* and that the sun's core was hotter than its brilliant surface.

Secchi was elected to England's Royal Society and the Royal Astronomical Society, the French Academie des Sciences, Russia's Imperial Academy of St. Petersburg. He also presided over Italy's Accademia dei Nuovi Lincei and founded the Societa degli

Spettroscopisti Italiana. Secchi died in Rome on February 26, 1878.

Radio Astronomy
Gugliemo Marconi

Marconi's pioneering radio work and radio interference observations from solar origins provided the first information and stepping stone for others to develop radio astronomy.

Marconi's invention of the radio led to commercial radio-telephone service, which in turn led to a radio astronomy discovery. In the 1930's, the Bell Telephone company was seeking to improve their new transatlantic radio-telephone service and assigned Karl Jansky to investigate sources of radio static. Jansky's efforts led him to discover radio waves emanating from the Milky Way galaxy. (Refer to the chapter on "Science & Technology" for more on Marconi's invention of the radio, and Giacconi's invention of the X-Ray telescope.)

Discovery of the Ionosphere
Gugliemo Marconi

After inventing the radio (see "Science & Technology" chapter), Marconi was the first to provide cross-Atlantic radio transmissions and thereby inadvertently discovered the ionosphere. He performed this transmission in spite of many scientific objections stating that cross-Atlantic transmission was impossible since the earth's surface curves and radio waves transmit in a straight line. His opponents and critics claimed the radio transmissions would go straight off into space and never reach the other continent. Nevertheless, Marconi persisted and was successful, as a result of the previously unknown electrically charged layer of the atmosphere called the ionosphere. The ionosphere bounces waves back to earth increasing the usefulness of radio transmissions. His work was very controversial since the global transmission of radio communications threatened the business of the trans-Atlantic cable companies. Marconi's new invention threatened these companies in the same way that Galileo had threatened the Church's teachings and authority centuries before. However, both Marconi and Galileo had the integrity, persistence and courage to continue and succeed against all odds. Their stories provide powerful, inspirational lessons. (Note: In 1924, the English physicist, Appleton, provided a complete description of the ionosphere.)

First Explanation of Diffraction of Light
Francis Grimaldi

Grimaldi was born on April 2, 1618 in Bologna and died there as well on December 28, 1663. He was an astronomer who explained the principles of light diffraction in his publication "Physicomathesis de lumina," published in 1665, two years after his death. Diffraction is the spreading or bending of light waves as they pass through an aperture or round the edge of a barrier. This phenomenon of light gave considerable support to the wave theory of light.

Grimaldi also helped Riccioli, a close friend, in the completion of the first map of the moon.

Names of Our Planets

The Romans gave names to the seven planets that were known to them in honor of their most powerful gods. Their names for these planets are still in use in modern times. These seven planets were also used by ancient peoples to devise the seven-day week for the first calendar. (See the Calendar reference earlier in this chapter for more information on these planets and the names for the days of the week.)

Mercury

Mercury is the Roman name for the Greek and Roman god of speed. Hermes is the Greek name for Mercury. Since Mercury is closest to the sun and travels a brief orbit of only 88 days to circle the sun, understandably it is named after the fleet-footed messenger of the Greek and Roman god of speed.

Venus

Venus is the Roman name for the Greek and Roman goddess of love and beauty. The Greek name for Venus is Aphrodite. The planet may have this name since it is easily visible from earth and appears to the human eye as a very bright and beautiful star. When you can only see one large "star" in the sky, it is usually Venus that you are observing. Contrary to the romanticism associated with this planet's name, in reality Venus is made up of deadly gases.

Earth (not Roman or Italian)

Our planet is named earth in English and is derived from the old Anglo-Saxon word *eorthe*, which is derived from the Old High German *erdha*. The Romans did not name it after any god, since they had no means of knowing it was a planet. In Italian the word for *earth* is *terra*.

Mars

Mars is the Roman name for the Greek and Roman god of war. The planet Mars is appropriately named because of its red color that is symbolic of blood. The Greek name for Mars is Ares.

Jupiter

Because Jupiter is the largest planet in our solar system and visible from earth, it is appropriately named after Jupiter the ruler of the Roman gods. Jupiter is the Roman name for this Greek and Roman god who is the most powerful of the mythological gods. Zeus is the Greek name.

Saturn

Saturn is named after the Roman god of agriculture who settled in Italy and who assured equality among the people along with bountiful harvests. Saturn was also the god of time. Among the known planets to the Romans, Saturn takes the longest time to circle the earth. The Romans may have named it Saturn for its long orbital time factor. Also, it is the sixth planet from the sun and our sixth day of the week is Saturn's Day or Saturday as we know it.

Uranus (not Roman or Italian)

Uranus received its peculiar name when it was discovered in 1781. Uranus has no origin with Rome or Italy and is, fortunately or unfortunately, named after the Greek god of the sky, *Ouranos*. Uranus was discovered by William Herschel of England who had suggested that it be named George after King George III. Evidently, others in the scientific community felt Uranus was a better suited name, much to the delight of elementary school children in English speaking countries for generations.

Neptune

Neptune is the Roman name for the Greek and Roman god of sea. He is portrayed as a bearded giant holding his trident, a spear with three prongs. His lower torso is a fish's tail. Poseidon is his Greek name.

Pluto

Pluto is the Roman name for the Greek and Roman god of the underworld and ruler of the dead. The planet Pluto is furthest from the sun and may be suggestive of an underworld or distant forbidding place. The Greek name is Hades. Contrary to what we would like to believe, this planet is not named after that cute but dopey Disney dog character.

Chapter V

CULINARY CONTRIBUTIONS

**" A meal without wine is like
a day without sunshine."**
- Italian Proverb -

Big Mac
Jim Delligatti
James Delligatti, owner of a McDonald's franchise in Pittsburgh, Pennsylvania invented the McDonald's Big Mac classic sandwich that was officially introduced in 1967. Since then over 14 billion Big Macs have been sold, making it the most popular sandwich in the world.

Blimpie International Inc. - Sandwich Company
Anthony Conza, Peter DeCarlo and Angelo Baldassare
Three Italian-American high school friends, Anthony Conza, Peter DeCarlo and Angelo Baldassare founded Blimpie when they opened their first Blimpie restaurant in Hoboken, New Jersey on April 4, 1964. Blimpie International now operates a franchise of almost 2000 restaurants in 46 states in the U.S. and in 12 foreign countries.

R. R. Esposito

Broccoli
Broccoli Family of Calabria, Italy
The vegetable we know as broccoli was actually created in Italy from hybridized cauliflower and pea seeds. This successful bio-process was completed by the Broccoli family who then named their newly created plant after themselves. Seeds were brought to this country from Italy in the 1870's.

Albert Broccoli is a nephew to this Broccoli family. However, Albert is not famous for agriculture, but rather theater-culture. He *produced almost every James Bond movie*, as well as other very successful movies such as "Chitty Chitty Bang Bang."

He was born Alberto Romolo Broccoli (aka Chubby) in NYC, but spent most of his entire life in Beverly Hills. He was also life-long friend and confidant of the great suspense movie director Alfred Hitchcock. Although Albert has passed away, his daughter Barbara Broccoli's production company continues the tradition and still produces Bond movies.

Perhaps all this notoriety will change former U.S. President George H. W. Bush's negative opinion of broccoli. When he was the 41st president, his comment that he did not like broccoli caused broccoli producers to dump truckloads of this very healthy vegetable at the US Capitol in protest.

Chef Boy-ar-dee
Ettore Boiardi
The real Chef Boy-ar-dee is the Italian chef whose original name was Ettore (aka Hector) Boiardi. Ettore came to America from his hometown Emilia Romagna, Italy. He became a chef at the esteemed Plaza Hotel in Manhattan during the 1920's. He eventually opened a restaurant, named Il Giardino d'Italia in Cleveland, Ohio and began bottling his dinners and selling these to patrons to take home. By the 1930's he had a food canning business in Cleveland. A food distributor for the A & P supermarket chain learned of the chef's cooking, promoted his products, and the rest is history. Every American family knows the Chef Boy-ar-dee food brand for canned pasta dinners, pizza mix and sauce. During World War II, his company expanded by opening a Pennsylvania plant and Chef Boy-ar-dee became the largest supplier of food rations for the U.S. and Allied Forces.

Chicken Tetrazzini

This dish, with a white cream and cheese sauce, was named after the opera star, Luisa Tetrazzini. Born in Florence in 1871 she started singing at the age of three. Luisa made her debut at the age of 19 in 1890 as Inez in Meyerbeer's "L'Africana" at the Teatro Pagliano in Florence. She gained international fame when she made her debut at Covent Garden in 1907, and with the help of the famous musical composer Oscar Hammerstein, she signed with the Manhattan Opera House. On Christmas Eve 1910, she sang at the San Francisco Chronicle building, before a crowd of a quarter of a million people.

Chocolate Specialties

Ghiradelli Chocolate Company

Domingo Ghiradelli founded the Ghiradelli Chocolate Co. in San Francisco in 1852. The company's very popular gourmet chocolate outlet in San Francisco's Fisherman's Wharf area attracts scores of tourists daily. Their large brick building with the family name spelled out in brick letters faces the wharf and beckons chocolate aficionados. Ghiradelli was sold to the DeDomenico family who retained ownership until 1986, when it was sold again to the Quaker Oats Company. In 1996, the Stroh Brewing Company also bought an interest in the company. There are four Ghiradelli outlets in California, one of which is located in San Francisco's scenic Ghiradelli Square. If you crave gourmet chocolate while in the windy city of Chicago you can satisfy your desires by visiting their fifth outlet. In San Leandro, California, the Ghiradelli Chocolate Company operates a vast 230,000 square foot processing plant. The company also has an industrial foods division that sells chocolate chips, chocolate coatings, and cocoas to commercial bakers and the specialty coffee industry.

Perugina Company

Perugina manufactures a wide variety of upscale chocolate and other desert and bakery products. The most famous are their "Baci" chocolates. The word *baci* means *kiss* in Italian. These gourmet chocolates are the "chocolate kisses of Italy." Each one has a multilingual proverb printed on its inner wrapper. Of course these are always about love.

Chun King
Jeno Paulucci

After serving in World War II in the Pacific theater, Jeno Paulucci returned to the U.S. in 1946. He knew that American soldiers in the Pacific had learned about Chinese and oriental-style food and thought he could make some money by selling Chinese food from his car. He started by only selling canned bean sprouts. Jeno expanded gradually and found that he had hit upon a real demand. After several years of success, he ultimately opened a plant in Cambridge, Maryland in 1962. Chun King is now owned by ConAgra a multi-billion dollar food supplier.

"Ciao Italia" Television Program
Mary Ann Esposito

Mary Ann Esposito is the host and creator of the cooking program "Ciao Italia." This cooking show started its broadcast with the Public Broadcast Company in the U.S. in 1990 and demonstrates the art of Italian cooking. Mary Ann Esposito shows us all how to cook, as well as our Italian mothers and grandmothers. Mary Ann has written four best selling cook books: "Celebrations, Italian Style: Recipes and Menus for Special Occasions," "Ciao Italia: Traditional Italian Recipes from Family Kitchens," "What You Knead," "Nella Cucina: More Italian Cooking from the Host of Ciao Italia." Incidentally, the name *Esposito* is one of the most common names in Italy and no, Mary Ann is not related to this author. However, this author's sister is of course a relation and she is also an excellent cook. She always says: "Never trust a skinny cook." Also, this author's mother is a great cook as well and whenever we visit, she has a genetic need to ask that perennial Italian mother's question: "Do you want something to eat?"

Coffee Filter Paper and Mr. Coffee Machine
Vince Marotta

Morotta was an inventor who invented the "Mr. Coffee" machine, as well as the disposable filter paper that it uses. It is one of the most popular coffee makers in the world and many manufacturers have since copied the principle and design of his invention.

"Cucina Amore" Television Program
Nick Stellino
Nick Stellino began hosting the cooking program "Cucina Amore" for the Public Broadcast Company in the U.S. in 1995. He is originally from Sicily and his great recipes, humor and high-energy performances make this show a favorite.

Espresso Machine
Gaggia Company
In 1946, Achilles Gaggia, founder of the Italian company Gaggia, invented the modern espresso machine that passes steam through a filter to quickly make concentrated coffee. The original steam process called infusion was very slow. Hence this new invention was appropriately named *espresso*, which means *fast* in Italian. This author and his brother cannot visit their father without having at least two cups of espresso. Holidays require more.

Florentine
Catherine de' Medici
The youthful Catherine de' Medici, daughter of Lorenzo de' Medici II, Duke of Urbino, married Henry II of France in 1533. She left Florence, Italy for France knowing the inferior state of French cuisine at the time. Consequently, she brought her own chefs and frequently requested that spinach be added to most dishes. As a result, recipes that include spinach often include the descriptive term *Florentine*, such as Chicken Florentine, Eggs Florentine, etc.

Gallo - Largest Wine Producer in the World
Ernest and Julio Gallo
The California wine industry began to take shape around the 1850's and is largely the result of Italian immigrants who developed vineyards and wineries in the California valleys. The largest of these is the Ernest & Julio Gallo Winery in Modesto California, which was founded by Ernest and Julio Gallo, the sons of immigrants from Piedmont, Italy. Ernest and Julio learned wine making from their father Joseph Gallo, Sr. who founded the Gallo Wine Co. in 1909. The Ernest and Julio Gallo Winery was founded in 1933. The Gallo brothers were technical

innovators and pioneered the use of stainless steel winemaking vats and computerized blending applications. The Ernest and Julio Gallo Winery owns almost half of the vineyard acreage in California and has annual revenues of about $1 billion. Gallo has grown to be the largest wine producer in the world and sells over 100 million gallons of wine a year. Gallo supplies almost 30% of all the wine consumed in the United States. Gallo owns several subsidiaries including Bartles & Jaymes (wine coolers) and Hornsby's Pubdrafts (draft ciders). Gallo wines continue to win international acclaim at wine competitions throughout the world. Gallo has won 43 Gold Medals and many Double-Gold medals.

Ice Cream, Italian Ices and Gelato
Italy

The earliest mention of frozen dairy products dates back to the Roman Empire, China and India. However, in Italy in 1559 the first ice cream appears when ice and salt are added to the dessert to create the freezing combination necessary for ice cream. The popularity of Italian gelato and Italian ices, like the famous Marino brand, are further evidence that the Italians were the first to create and popularize flavored ices and ice cream. Gelato style Italian ice cream is actually made from milk and not heavy cream. It is a unique, delicious and heavenly treat. Gelato is a very creamy textured ice cream, available in every mouth-watering flavor imaginable, from traditional vanilla to cappuccino and cannoli flavors.

Ice Cream Cone
Italo Marchiony

Italo was an Italian immigrant to New Jersey who invented the ice cream cone in 1896 and received a U.S. patent for his new ice cream cone mold invention in 1903. One year later, a Syrian immigrant at the St. Louis Fair of 1904 named Ernest A. Hamwi claimed to be the first to put ice cream on a waffle type pastry. He was selling pastry when a nearby ice cream stand ran out of cups. Hamwi rolled warm pastries into cones and sold them to the ice cream vendor, except this event was a year subsequent to Italo's patent and Ernest did not invent the mold for making cones.

Pasta

Tuscany, Italy

Pasta and tools for making and cooking pasta existed in the Tuscany region of Italy around the time of Christ's birth, long before Marco Polo wrote about Chinese noodles in 1275. In the first century a chef named Apicius wrote a recipe in his cookbook for a meal that resembles lasagna. Around the year 1000 Martino Corno wrote a book, "De arte Coquinaria per vermicelli e maccaroni siciliani" ("The Art of Cooking Sicilian macaroni and Vermicelli"), that described how to cook pasta. Corno was a chef to the ruling Patriarch of Aquileia. Today, pasta is a deeply established part of American and other culinary cultures. If you ever travel to Italy you can learn everything you always wanted to know about the history of pasta by visiting the Historical Museum of Spaghetti in Pontedassio, Italy. The Barilla pasta company also operates a pasta museum in Parma, Italy. The Italian Ministry of Cultural Assets and Activities has declared the Barilla Historical Archives to offer considerable historical interest. Italians are also credited for *inventing tomato sauce*. There is nothing better on pasta than fresh homemade sauce, sometimes called *gravy* by Italian-Americans with Sicilian heritage.

Pastry

Italian pastries are well known for their variety, beautiful presentation and, of course, palatable pleasures. These gastronomical delights include: cannoli, pignoli cookies (with pine nuts), pasticciotti (cream puff), tiramisu dessert (originated in Venice), savoiardi (lady fingers), sfingi, sfogliatelle, Tuscan biscuits, biscotti and anisette cookies. If you ever visit Little Italy in Manhattan, make an effort to visit the famous Ferrara's on Grand Street for coffee and an incredible dessert experience. In Brooklyn, a visit to the notable Savarese Bakery on the corner of 60th Street and New Utrecht Avenue is highly recommended for their pastry and gelato.

Pizza

Raphael Esposito

Pizza is universally known and enjoyed by virtually everyone who has tried it. In ancient Greece and Rome, people baked flat breads with a variety of toppings. However, modern pizza, with tomato sauce and mozzarella cheese, is a regional dish of Naples, and it may simply be Italy's greatest culinary contribution to fast food. In 1889, Raphael Esposito, a well known pizzauola (pizza-maker) in Naples was asked to cook pizza for King Umberto and Queen Margarita. The King and Queen were curious and wanted to experience pizza, which was a common meal of the people in this region of Italy. Esposito cooked one typical round Neapolitan pie, but also prepared another, as a special gift for Queen Margarita of Naples. The special pie that he made had the usual red tomato sauce, but had mozzarella cheese left white on top and a few fresh green basil leaves placed at its center. Esposito combined these ingredients to achieve colors in his pie that would represent the national colors of Italy (red, white and green). He called it the Margarita pie in honor of his Queen. The King and Queen were very impressed with these pizza pies and a thank you letter was sent to Esposito on behalf of the King, who later ordered additional pies. Soon news spread that pizza had been accepted by *royal* taste buds and this helped to popularize the pizza styles made by Esposito throughout Italy.

If you ever travel to Naples, visit the Brandi Restaurant and Pizzeria where Esposito worked over a century ago. On display in this restaurant is the actual letter from the King's staff, thanking Raphael Esposito for his pizza. But you don't need to travel to Italy to feel connected with pizza history, just order a Neapolitan or Margarita pizza this Friday night and experience the same culinary delight that was first enjoyed by royalty over 100 years ago!

In the U.S., the best pizza pies are found in New York City, Boston, Chicago and San Francisco metropolitan areas, places where many Italian immigrants settled. A "New York Times" article (Nov. 6, 2002) credits Gennaro Lombardi for introducing pizza to NYC on Spring Street in 1905. Today there are over 2,700 pizzerias in the NYC metropolitan area. Some of the more famous pizzerias in NYC are: John's Pizza and Joe's Pizza both on Bleecker Street in Greenwich Village; Patsy's uptown on First Ave; and Louie & Ernie's on Crosby Ave, in the Bronx. Most other parts of the U.S. offer very poor facsimiles of pizza. Frozen commercial pizza should never be mistaken for *real* pizza.

Planters Peanut Company
Amedeo Obici and Mario Peruzzi
Obici and Peruzzi settled in Wilkes-Barre, Pennsylvania after

leaving their Italian homeland. They successfully owned and operated a small fruit and nut stand. Their success grew dramatically when Obici invented the electric automatic peanut roaster. This invention eliminated the time consuming and laborious task of shelling peanuts. The automatic peanut roaster included an electric motor that eliminated the manual work and gave them the ability to shell and roast peanuts on a vast scale. This allowed them to expand and finally establish the Planters Peanut Company in 1906. A public contest to design a trademark was advertised by the new company and a fourteen-year-old boy's entry, a drawing of a peanut person, took first prize. Professional artists later added some details and ultimately the peanut man, familiar on all Planters products, was born.

Pretzel
Italian Monk
Most people, if asked how the pretzel was invented, will reply that the pretzel is a creation of the Germans or the Pennsylvania Dutch in America. Actually, an Italian monk created the first pretzel. Centuries later the pretzel found its way to Germany and the United States. This monk, looking for a small reward or present to give children for memorizing prayers, designed the criss-cross shaped pretzel around 610 AD. The shape mimics the folded arms of the praying children. The word pretzel is actually derived from Latin and Italian words. A little present in Latin is *pretiole*. In Italian, *bracciatelli* means *small arms*. About 600 years after this Italian monk, a pretzel recipe reached Germany from Italy in the 13th century and the criss-crossed pretzel was called *bretzitella* in the Old High German language. *Bretzitella* is clearly a combination of the Latin (*pretiole*) and the Italian (*bracciatelli*) descriptive words for the food. Later, it became *brezel* in German and ultimately *pretzel* in English.

There is an interesting story about Austrian pretzel bakers. In the 16th century the Turkish Mongol emperor Babar attacked Vienna and was foiled by the city's surrounding stone wall. Babar decided to tunnel underneath the wall during the night, but was unaware that the pretzel bakers were up and working. The bakers alerted the military that then beat back the invasion. The Viennese pretzel bakers were given an official coat of arms by the city council for their help during the Turkish invasion. That Viennese coat of arms given to the bakers had a pretzel in the center. Consequently, today the baker's emblem is the pretzel.

Progresso Quality Foods Company
Vincent Taormina and Guiseppe Uddo

Around 1905, a Sicilian immigrant named Vincent Taormina arrived in New Orleans and began a small business importing foods from Italy to the U.S. Twenty years later in 1925 Vincent merged his growing business with his cousin, Guiseppe Uddo, another immigrant importer and together they formed the Uddo & Taormina Corporation of New Orleans. Vincent's son, Vincent Taormina, Jr. then started an importing business in New York City. By 1927 both the New Orleans and New York City companies were merged to form the Progresso Italian Food Corporation of New York City. Using an old family recipe, their first Progresso brand soups were introduced in 1949. Today the Progresso Quality Foods Company is a vast enterprise and offers excellent soups, sauces, beans, bread crumbs, tomato products, olive oils, vinegars and other products.

Ragu and Francesco Rinaldi Brands
Ralph Cantisano

Ralph Cantisano began selling spaghetti sauce door-to-door in 1937. His operation grew into one of the biggest brands in the category, namely the Ragu Packing Company. Cantisano sold Ragu to Chesebrough-Ponds in 1970, and then began another company. Cantisano and several former Ragu employees, including Mr. John LiDestri, founded Cantisano Foods. In 1982, Mr. Edward P. Salzano joined Cantisano Foods, bringing with him the Francesco Rinaldi brand name. Today, Cantisano Foods, and its proprietary label, Francesco Rinaldi, represent a multi-million-dollar manufacturing and packaging business.

Ronzoni Foods Company
Emanuele Ronzoni

Emanuele Ronzoni, a teenage immigrant from Italy, landed his first job in the United States in the early 1880's as a helper in a small macaroni factory. Gaining factory knowledge and saving his money, Emanuele finally opened his own small macaroni business. New immigrants from Italy during the 19th and 20th centuries created significant demand for macaroni products. By the early part of the 20th century, the Ronzoni Macaroni Company in Long Island City, Queens was well established and became incorporated. Through Emanuele's demand for quality the business flourished. When Emanuele Ronzoni died, he was succeeded by his son Emanuele, Jr., as president of the company. During the 1960's, a third generation of Ronzoni's, Angelo and Raymond (sons of Emanuele, Jr.,) began taking an active part in the business. The Ronzoni Macaroni Company later purchased a small spaghetti sauce business in 1965, which became the foundation of the ultramodern sauce facility, which Ronzoni opened in 1968 in Hicksville, Long Island. The Ronzoni Foods Company is now one of the leading pasta makers in the United States. In 1984, the Ronzoni Foods Company was acquired by General Foods who sold the company in 1990 to the Hershey Foods Corporation.

Sbarro
Gennaro Sbarro

In 1956, Gennaro Sbarro left Naples with his wife Carmela and their three sons, Joseph, Mario and Anthony, and immigrated to America to open a gourmet Italian delicatessen, called a salumeria, in Brooklyn. Today, the Company is under the leadership of the three sons. Carmela Sbarro still operates Sbarro's Salumeria delicatessen and is responsible for providing the homemade cheesecake to all stores. Since those small beginnings, smart business planning and a passion for high quality food has allowed Sbarro to grow into an international company with 1000 Sbarro restaurants in 27 countries throughout the world. Sbarro's new corporate headquarters is located in a beautifully designed building in Melville, New York.

Subway - Sandwich Company
Fred De Luca

Fred De Luca founded the Subway sandwich chain and now there are 14,067 stores in 71 countries. When Fred was only 17 years old, he was looking for a way to earn extra money to pay his college tuition. He borrowed $1000 from his friend, Dr. Peter Buck, a nuclear physicist, and opened Pete's Super Submarines on August 28, 1965 in Bridgeport, Connecticut. Fred did receive his Bachelor's Degree in 1971 and now is the President of one of the world's largest fast food chains. Dr. Buck is now a very wealthy partner whose $1000 loan was a fantastic investment.

Tropicana
Anthony Rossi

In 1947, Rossi founded a Florida fruit packaging company. Seven years later, in 1954, *he perfected a pasteurization process for fresh orange juice.* This allowed Rossi to produce fresh orange juice for the first time in a ready-to-serve package. In 1978, Rossi sold his Tropicana company to Beatrice Foods who later sold the company to PepsiCo in 1998. Tropicana is now the world's largest producer of fruit juices. Their fruit juice products are sold in 23 countries.

Other Noteworthy Italian Eating

Food Industry

There are virtually countless food-industry related products that are exported from Italy to the world's dinner table. Some of the well known brand names include: Auricchio cheese, Barilla pasta, Berio olive oil, Bertolli olive oil, Buitoni, Medaglia D'oro espresso coffee, Regina balsmic vinegar, Sclafani canned goods and mineral water from Acqua Panna, Fonte Santafiora and San Pellegrino. Here are some interesting facts about some of these companies.

- The Barilla pasta factory in Pedrignano is the largest pasta factory in the world. In 1998, Barilla supplied 9% of all of the pasta consumed in the United States.
- The natural spring in the mountain town of San Pellegrino gained fame when the great Leonardo da Vinci drank its water (the company was incorporated centuries later in 1899).
- Legend has it that the famous explorer Amerigo Vespucci drank from Acqua Panna's spring, and that a major Roman road was built to pass this spring to provide water for travelers.
- Gennaro Auricchio was born in 1877 in San Giuseppe Vesuviano near Naples. He founded the Auricchio company and invented *sharp rennet,* the ingredient that gives their cheese its distinctive, mouth watering flavor.

If your supermarket does not carry imported Italian products, look for an Italian food specialty store in your area. In New York, Connecticut and New Jersey, thirty A & S Specialty Food stores offer a variety of high quality, gourmet Italian products. For those who live or vacation on Long Island, a great place to shop for excellent food and the most friendly, helpful customer service is Primavera in Seaford. If you would rather not cook, there are many good restaurants in Little Italy in Manhattan, such as Umberto's, Angelo's and Paolucci's. Paolucci's walls are covered with signed photographs of celebrities, such as Billy Crystal, Ed Koch and Rudy Giuliani, praising the food. Of course the legendary Rao's in upper Manhattan on East 114th St. has heavenly food and the most elite patrons, but it is nearly impossible for the vast majority to get a table. Reservations are made six to twelve months in advance. Other great places in Manhattan are: Il Mulino in Greenwich Village - rated by Zagat as NYC's number one Italian restaurant for 18 straight years; Babbo in Greenwich Village; and Scalini Fedeli in TriBeCa.

However, just east of New York City, on Long Island, are several very fine Italian restaurants that include: Sempre Vivolo in Hauppauge; Piccolo in Huntington; Da Ugo in Rockville Center; La Piccola Liguria in Port Washington; Trattoria Diane in Roslyn and Butera's located in both Massapequa Park and Woodbury.

CR

Chapter VI

CULTURE, CONVENTIONS & TRADITIONS

"The die is cast."
- Julius Caesar -

American Medical Association's Journal ("JAMA") – First Woman Editor
Catherine De Angelis, MD, MPH

In 1998, Dr. Catherine DeAngelis became the first woman to edit the prestigious medical journal, "Journal of the American Medical Association" ("JAMA"), in its 116 years of history. She also holds the position of Editor-in-Chief of AMA's Division of Scientific Information and Multimedia. Dr. De Angelis is a highly distinguished physician, scientist, educator, chief editor, and has demonstrated her vision and creativity in her tenure as AMA's Editor-in-Chief of "Archives of Pediatrics & Adolescent Medicine." She has had a venerated 30-year career as a leading physician-scientist-educator, holding these highly respected positions:

- Founding Director of the Division of General Pediatrics at the University of Wisconsin and at the Johns Hopkins Medical Institutions.

- Deputy Chair and Residency Director of the Department of Pediatrics at the Johns Hopkins Medical Institutions.
- Vice Dean for Academic Affairs and Faculty at Johns Hopkins University School of Medicine.

"JAMA" publishes world renowned scientific papers on medicine that ultimately results in better health for people throughout the world. Dr. De Angelis will be guiding "JAMA" as it continues its most humane mission.

Dr. De Angelis was born in Pennsylvania in a working class family. Her father was a worker in a silk mill.

Amphitheater, Oldest Known
Pompeii

The world's oldest known amphitheater was built in Pompeii in 82 BC about the time when this city in central Italy became a colony of Rome. The amphitheater held 20,000 spectators, close to the entire population of the city. This arena has three levels supported by tall arches that surround the amphitheater. Roman amphitheaters were actually multi-storied buildings that were always constructed above ground, unlike Greek amphitheaters that were built into the sides of hills, below ground.

The city of Pompeii was destroyed in 79 AD by the sudden and violent eruption of Mount Vesuvius. The volcanic lava that poured down the mountain rushed the city of Pompeii so quickly that many residents were suddenly buried in ash or entombed in lava as they performed their daily tasks.

The citizens of Pompeii were frozen in time by the instantaneous precipitation of lava and ash. The city became a fantastic archeological site offering insights as to how people lived in the ancient Roman civilization. Many buildings, people and artifacts were preserved, sealed underground for almost 1800 years.

The many ruins of Pompeii were discovered under the volcanic ash by accident in 1748. The first systematic excavations began in 1860 under the direction of Giuseppe Fiorelli, a professor at the University of Naples, who invented the technique of pouring liquid plaster into empty cavities and between layers of solidified volcanic lava and ash.

The ruins of the ancient Roman city of Pompeii.

These empty spaces were created when victims' bodies and their artifacts decomposed over the centuries leaving gaps between the layers of lava and ash. Professor Fiorelli stopped workmen from digging whenever they came upon a hole in the ashes and then poured liquid plaster into the spaces. When the plaster hardened, he removed the exterior volcanic ash like a shell and produced casts of bodies in great detail, putting a human face on the last tragic moments of that day in 79 BC. Fiorelli's ground-breaking techniques are still used today, but with modern day liquid fillers.

Astrology, Spread through Europe
Tuscany and Rome

The ancient art of astrology was introduced to the early Romans by their Etruscan neighbors who lived in the central Italian region called Tuscany. The ancient Greeks and others practiced astrology before the Romans. However, the Romans spread the art of astrology to other parts of Europe as ideas and cultures traveled throughout the Empire during its 500-year existence. (The ancient Greeks referred to the Etruscans as Tyrrhenians)

Ancient Roman astrologers used the Latin word *cumsidus*, which meant *set alongside the stars* or being influenced by the stars. The positions of stars were "taken into consideration" for interpretation and predictions, and as a result, the English word *consider* was subsequently derived.

Broken Mirror Superstition
Rome

To the ancient peoples, things that caused reflections of your image contained something of you or of your future. To break a mirror meant some harm may come to yourself, or in some way this act may harm your future. The Romans felt that a person's health changed in seven-year cycles. Therefore to break a mirror would mean bad luck for the next seven year cycle. Since mirrors were also an expensive luxury it did not hurt matters to have servants or children fear these superstitions and be more careful not to break mirrors.

R. R. Esposito

Caesar, Kaiser, Czar, C-section, Salad, etc.

The prestigious and influential lives of Julius and Augustus Caesar gave the name "Caesar" a royal meaning throughout Europe for many centuries. From this name the German title of "Kaiser" and the Russian title of "Czar" developed. In Irish myths, "Cesar" was the name of the "Fir Bolg" tribe's chief wizard who used sorcery to save his tribe during battles, but ultimately the gods took his life and soul as payment. The Irish legend, "The Conquest of Ireland," states that the first people ever to "walk the virgin territory of Ireland" were from the tribe "Cessair," also an interesting similarity to the name of "Caesar."

Caesarean sections (*C-sections*) are so named because, according to legend, this is the method by which Julius Caesar was born.

Also, *Caesar Salad* is named after this very memorable emperor, presumably to make salad seem a bit more exciting.

Rome, its leaders and even its language, Latin, has had strong influences throughout all of Europe. The ancient Irish word for king *Ri* is actually derived from the Latin word for king, which is *Rex*.

Caesar and Expressions:
"The Die is Cast," "Crossing the Rubicon" and
"I Came, I Saw, I Conquered"
Julius Caesar

The expression "the die is cast" is actually a quote of Julius Caesar. He said this in 49 BC as he led his armies across the Rubicon River in northern Italy in defiance of the Roman government and its leaders. The Roman government ordered Caesar to disband his army after his highly successful campaign to capture Celtic Gaul (part of France). Roman leadership feared that Caesar's prestige and armies would allow him to return to Rome with enough power to attack and initiate a civil war and wrest control from them. When Caesar stated, "the die is cast," he was referring to the chances he was taking (as if he were rolling dice) by disobeying Rome's orders and hoping to use his army to usurp the Roman government's power. Incidentally, General Caesar was successful when he returned with his army to Rome and became Emperor Caesar. Caesar was not only a great military strategist and leader but was also an engineer, a talented writer and powerful orator.

Also, the expression "crossing the Rubicon," which means taking a dangerous and irreversible step, is derived from this moment in history when Caesar defiantly crossed the Rubicon River knowing a great battle was certain and imminent.

To describe the success of an earlier military campaign, Caesar said, "I came, I saw, I conquered." This famous quote originated with Julius Caesar when he addressed the Roman Senate after a conquest in Asia. In Latin, the quote is "veni, vidi, vici." The English word *video* is derived from the Latin word *vidi*.

Cherry Tree Introduced to Europe
Lucullus

The Roman General Lucullus (circa 110 BC - 56 BC) imported the first cherry trees from Asia Minor to Europe, bringing them to Rome in 79 BC. He learned of the plant during his massive Asian campaign.

Coin Toss
Julius Caesar

Caesar was the first to institute the coin toss as a decision-making method for civil and sometimes criminal disputes in the 1st century. Caesar's head was on the head side of the coin, so heads usually was for the affirmative decision. One must wonder if Caesar even tossed a coin and declared, "heads I win, tails you lose," as we have heard from our modern day hucksters. Incidentally, Caesar's full name was Gaius Julius Caesar.

"Cold Feet"
Lombardy, Italy

The expression to "have cold feet" originated around the year 1500 in the Lombardy region of Italy. During Medieval and Renaissance times, this region was the banking capital of Europe. The term originally meant that you were without money, but today it has a broader use, i.e. to back away from a situation. In Italian it is, *Avere piedi freddi*, and in Lombardy it still means to be without money.

Cologne (eau de Cologne)
Johann Maria Farina (aka Jean-Baptiste Farina)

In 1709, this Italian barber, who lived from 1685 to 1766, decided to market his fragrances in Cologne, Germany. His product became the first eau-de-Cologne (water of Cologne). It is interesting to note that Agrippina the wife of Claudius the Roman emperor founded the city of Cologne in 50 AD.

Convertible Sofa-Bed
Bernard Castro

Bernard Castro (1904-1991) emigrated from Italy and opened an upholstery shop in New York City. By 1931, he conceived his invention of a space-saving sofa that opens into a comfortable bed. He was committed to the best engineering and comfort, in conjunction with a featherweight lift that he promised even a child could open. By 1945, his vision was fulfilled and he started making the world's first convertible sofa-beds.

Today Castro offers over 60 styles, 800 fabrics and 60 leathers. Their sofas are sold in Castro Convertibles showrooms and their affiliate Krause's Custom Crafted Furniture stores nationwide.

Bernard's daughter, Bernadette Castro, is now the Commissioner of New York State Office of Parks, Recreation and Historic Preservation.

Cursive Handwriting
Aldus Manutius

Refer to the section on Latin and Its Influences in the "Language and Literature" chapter.

Diamond Engagement Ring
Venice

It is believed that in 860 AD Pope Nicholas I, born in Rome, made the engagement ring necessary for marriage and required that it had to be of a valued metal like gold or silver. Around the 13th century *medieval Italians started the custom of giving diamond* engagement rings to women. By the 15th century, *the Venetians* realized the intrinsic value of diamonds and learned how to precisely cut and polish them. They discovered that diamonds were the hardest known substance and *popularized the practice of giving diamond engagement rings throughout the world.* (Also, see the reference on Wedding Rings in this chapter.)

English Cities
Roman Empire

Many cities in England were founded by the Romans. The Romans founded London, which they had originally named Londinium. The city of Bath was also founded by the Romans who capitalized on the natural hot springs in the area and built elaborate baths. Several English cities developed from towns that were originally established as Roman camps and forts. Cities with names that include the words *chester* or *cester*, were established as a result of the presence of a Roman fort, for example, Chester, Gloucester and Manchester. The words *chester* and *cester* are derived from the Roman word *castrum*, which means *fort*.

Etiquette Book
Baldassare Castiglione

In 1478, a book by Baldassare Castiglione entitled "The Courtier" ("Il Cortegiano") covered customs and manners of polite society in the cultivated courts of Italy. This became a handbook on etiquette for all European gentlemen. The book also covered basic philosophies of life that encouraged family unity, fairness and honesty.

Forks & Spoons
Tuscany Region of Italy

Children in your family will be pleased to know that until fairly recently most people ate with their hands. Aristocrats ate with only three fingers not soiling the ring finger and pinkie. The three finger method originated with the Romans. Small forks for eating first appeared in the Tuscany region of Italy during the late 10th century and gained greater attention when first introduced in Venice in 1071. Forks were not generally accepted and the clergy condemned them claiming that only human hands were worthy of touching God's bounty. By the 14th century in England, highly decorative forks from Italy were a royal curiosity and not used for eating. Men who used forks were considered effeminate and women ridiculous. By the 17th century, Italy began to accept the fork, even though it was introduced in Venice in the early 11th century. The rest of Europe began accepting forks 100 years later in the 18th century.

Over two thousand years ago, the Romans introduced spoons to northern Europe as the Roman Empire spread throughout the continent. Slurping soup or stew from a bowl gradually gave way to the Roman custom of using a spoon.

Fountain Pen, First
Rome

The Romans created the first form of a fountain pen from the hollow tubular-stems of marsh grasses, especially from the jointed bamboo plant. The Romans cut one end to form a pen nib or ink point, and filled the tubular stem with ink that was squeezed out and down to the writing tip.

Glass Windows
Rome

Around 400 BC, the Romans were the first to make sheets of glass to be used for windows. By 50 BC they developed glass blowing for making cups and vessels. Around 200 AD it was common for the upper-class in Britain, then part of the Roman Empire, to have windows of Roman origin. Around 600 AD, in the colder climates of Germany, glass sheet creation became perfected. The Romans invented sheet glass but their warm Mediterranean climate made it less important than it was to the inhabitants of the northern, colder regions of Europe.

"God Bless You"
Pope Gregory I

In Italy during the 6th century, a plague was claiming many victims. A sneeze was often the precursor of the lethal illness. People's response to a sneeze was often, "Good luck to you," since the sneeze repelled an illness or bad spirit. Pope Gregory I replaced this response to a sneeze with the more urgent and potent phrase, "God bless you." This new expression subsequently spread throughout Europe and the Western world. Pope Gregory I was born in Rome about 540 AD and died on March 12, 604 AD.

Hand-Held Conair Hair Dryer
Leandro ("Lee") Rizzuto
In 1959, Rizzuto and his parents founded the Conair company when they invented hot rollers for drying and styling hair. Rizzuto is now chairman and president of Conair Corporation in Connecticut. In 1971, Conair introduced their professional hand-held hair dryer and today they sell hand-held hair dryers to millions of American households. The Rizzuto family is still the sole owner of this multi-million dollar corporation, which *also owns Cuisinart, the famous kitchen appliance and cookware manufacturing company.*

Handkerchief
Rome
The word *handkerchief* comes from the French word, *couvrechef*, which means covering the head. In the 16th century, these were originally linen head covers to protect women from the sun. Since women often held these in their hands they became *handkerchiefs* in English. Eventually, people realized that these handy little pieces of cloth were well suited for sudden sneezes. However, long before the French, the Romans invented the *sudarium* that had the dual purpose of wiping sweat from the brow and for wiping the nose. When the Roman Empire fell, the concept of a *sudarium* disappeared, and during the Dark and Middle Ages that followed, people just blew into the air or used sleeves, much like our children do today. The idea of a nose cloth did not return to the European culture until approximately 1503 in France.

Almost 500 years later, the use of a nose cloth was adopted by my sons in 1996 as a direct result of their mother's patience, persistence and sheer determination to overcome the natural tendency of boys to use any convenient article of clothing for this purpose.

Health Spa
Roman
In the 2nd century BC, the Romans were the first to build elaborate health spas. These spas contained gymnasiums, saunas, baths, gardens, shops, libraries and even art galleries. These were destroyed in 500 AD when barbarians from the north invaded Rome, which ultimately led to the fall of Rome and the "Dark Ages" that followed. The English word

vandal comes from an earlier unsuccessful group of invaders, the Vandals. The destruction of Roman high culture and cleanliness, combined with the rise of orthodox Christian beliefs set a new trend, that of being unwashed. Exposed flesh for bathing began to be considered sinful. Diseases grew to epidemic proportions in the "Dark Ages" and "Middle Ages" that followed the fall of Rome.

It is interesting to note that before Rome fell, the Romans would sell their soaps, made mostly of fats, as a laxative to the Gauls in France who did not have the same penchant for bathing. *This may be one of the earliest forms of creative marketing- "It's a soap - and – it's a laxative!"* (Refer also to the 'Soap' section later in this chapter.)

Horse Race, Oldest
Siena

Since the Middle Ages, Siena has been the home of the wild and tumultuous "Palio" horse race around the city's center. The seventeen well-defined neighborhoods or city wards of Siena, called *contrada*, originally practiced these races to stay trained and fit to aid the military for battle against the often domineering city of nearby Florence. Each *contrada* still provides a very strong social identity and influence in the lives of its people. The noisy crowds at this race wave the large colorful banners of their *contrada*. Jockeys similarly wear bright clothing with the representative colors of their *contrada*. Following a tradition from the 11th century, or earlier, when battle practice had no rules, the race also has no rules, except for one: jockeys can not touch the reins of an opposing horse. There really are no other rules and a *contrada's* horse may win the race by reaching the finish line, with or without the jockey! This is a tradition that dates back to ancient Rome, when chariot races had the same rule regarding getting the chariot to the finish line regardless of the presence of the driver. Chariot races in Roman *Circuses*, racetracks built with stadium seating, were far more popular events than those at the Coliseum.

"Ides of March"
Rome

The "Ides of March" was the day of March 15 on the ancient Roman calendar. It has become memorable in history because this is the day in 44 BC that Julius Caesar was assassinated by Senators and his friend Brutus. "Beware the ides of March" has become a modern day expression.

Italic Print & First Paperback Books
Aldine Press, Venice
Refer to the reference on this subject in the chapter on "Language and Literature."

Jacuzzi
Roy Jacuzzi
Centuries after the Romans built their famous baths, the Jacuzzi family invented the Jacuzzi hot tubs and spas. The Jacuzzi brothers, their wives and six daughters came to California from Italy in 1907. They supplied the U.S. military with propellers and in 1926 the Jacuzzi Brothers Incorporated developed the jet water pump that became the start of their Jacuzzi whirlpools and hot tubs. In 1968, Roy Jacuzzi actually invented the first whirlpool bath, and holds over 250 patents worldwide for pump and hydraulic systems, many for the agricultural pump industry.

Jeans
Genoa, Italy
A strong twilled cotton fabric was created in the town of Genoa. The French called this cloth "jeans," most probably derived from the first syllable of the Italian town's name. A softer fabric was later woven in the town of Nimes in France. This was known as "serge de Nimes" and Americans called this cloth "denim."

Library, First Public
Rome
There were certainly libraries before the time of ancient Rome, such as the great Mouseion Library of Alexandria in Egypt. It held papyrus and vellum scrolls, but was burned down in a civil war in the late 3rd century AD. However, it was the Romans who first built and operated public libraries for all of their citizens to use. The first three were established by Augustus in the city of Rome itself, and by the

time of Constantine, there were twenty-eight public libraries in operation. When the Roman Empire fell, after the onslaught of invading barbarians, libraries were destroyed and much of this knowledge base was lost. Around the end of the 5th century AD, the scholar Ammianus Marcellinus stated, "The libraries like tombs were closed forever." (Latin: "Bibliotecis sepulcrorum ritu in perpetuum clausis.")

Library & Museum Rules
Sir Anthony Panizzi

Panizzi was born in Italy in 1797 and died in 1879. During his ten-year tenure as chief librarian at the British Museum Library he developed his "91 rules," promulgated in 1839. This became the foundation for the Museum's book cataloging system. He also implemented the requirement of a book depository at the Museum for all books obtaining a copyright in Great Britain. The U.S. has also adopted a book depository requirement for American publishers. Publishers in the U.S. are required to send an actual book when applying for a U.S. Library of Congress catalogue number and a second copy to obtain a U.S. copyright.

Since 1984, The British Library offers The Panizzi Lectures for the study of the science of bibliography named so in honor of Panizzi. They have also instituted The Anthony Panizzi Foundation that supports lectures, research and other events. Panizzi was also a competent administrator and acquired a large purchase grant for the Museum. He supervised the building of the great circular Reading Room in the British Museum Library, constructed from 1853 to 1857.

Montessori Schools
Maria Montessori

These highly acclaimed schools are founded on the educational principles of the Italian educator and physician Maria Montessori who was born in Ancona, Italy in 1870 and died in 1952. Montessori type education is focused on preschool and early elementary school education. In 1907, she established a preschool center that began her development of educational programs that allowed children to be creative and develop their own ideas as part of a learning curriculum. A child's own natural interests and curiosity motivates learning in an environment that guides and focuses these creative energies. Dr. Montessori also published two books: "The Montessori Method" in 1912 and "The Secret of Childhood" in 1936.

Dr. Montessori was a pioneer in medicine as well. *She was the first woman to become a physician in modern Italy.* She graduated from the Medical School of the University of Rome and specialized in pediatrics and psychiatry. She also taught at the medical school of the University of Rome, and worked in its free clinics, becoming knowledgeable regarding early development problems in children. Dr. Montessori eventually applied some of the techniques that she developed for mentally challenged children to normal young children to advance their learning abilities. She was a highly talented researcher and educator who became famous throughout Europe and the United States, and later throughout the world, working in Africa, India, Sri Lanka and Pakistan. The first Montessori school in the U.S. was established in Tarrytown, NY in 1906.

Murano and Venetian Glass
Murano and Venice

Murano, and its larger neighboring city Venice, are world famous for their blown glass with characteristic color, delicacy and beauty. The glass masters, *battono,* from this part of Italy have created works of art in glass for almost a thousand years. Glass is heated, beaten, folded, swung, stretched, and blown to create these precious masterpieces. The Romans developed glass blowing technology and techniques that were passed through the ages to the Venetians. Early Venetians perfected this wonderful art form, but were also influenced by trade with other ancient glass blowing artisans in Syria, Egypt and the Orient. Murano is also famous for fabulous crystal, chandeliers, marble fireplace mantels and sculptures.

Nobel Prize – Medal Inscription
Virgil

This Latin inscription is used on the Nobel Prize medals: *Inventas vitam juvat excoluisse per artes.* It was taken from Virgil's epic work "Aeneid," 6th song, verse 663. Translated into English it means: *And they who bettered life on earth by newfound mastery.*

Opera Glasses
Nero

The Roman Emperor Nero (37 AD – 67 AD) used an emerald as a means of magnifying the view of events in large arenas. This is most probably the very first opera glass ever used. The Roman scholar, Pliny the Elder wrote "Emeralds are usually concave so that they may concentrate the visual rays. The Emperor Nero used an emerald to watch the gladiatorial combats."

Orphanage (Europe's First)
Florence

The famous Ospedale Degli Innocenti (Foundling Hospital) in Florence was the first orphanage established in Europe. The Hospital was designed by the eminent architect Filippo Brunelleschi who also designed the famous and massive dome atop the Maria Del Fiore Cathedral in Florence. Property for the orphanage was acquired from the Silk Merchants' Guild. The first great leader of the Medici family of Florence, Cosimo Medici born in 1389, had the Foundling Hospital built in 1444. Cosmo also built the first modern library for Florence. The artistic master Andrea della Robbia crafted the Hospital's celebrated medallions.

Pants
Venice

During the 16th century, a comic character in Italian folklore wore a goatee and loose trousers with a snug fit at the ankle. This character's name was Pantaleone, and the word pants is derived from his name. His name is mysteriously derived from St. Pantaleone, the patron saint of Venice. No one knows how this saint, who was beheaded in the 4th century by the Roman Emperor Diocletian, became associated in name with a comic goateed figure. At the time of Diocletian men did not wear trousers. Gradually, in the years to follow, pants came into use, probably influenced by Celtic peoples of western and central Europe that more often wore leg coverings, before the Romans.

Pockets were not invented until the late 16th century. First, these were merely a small sack, which was tucked into a garment or down into a man's codpiece. Later this evolved into a sack connected to the garment, i.e. pockets. Pockets certainly made pants considerably more comfortable. By the 18th century, knee breechers, a modified version of pantaloons began to be called pants in America.

Paparazzi (the word)
Federico Fellini
A character named Paparazzi in the Federico Fellini movie, "La Dolce Vita," photographed the rich and famous. This character's name has been applied to the maverick photographers who make a living taking and selling photographs of celebrities, preferably in embarrassing or compromising situations. Fortunately for the paparazzi, celebrities frequently put themselves in embarrassing situations and the supply is never greater than the public's voyeuristic demands.

Pet Names, Traditional
Rome
The common traditional names for dogs include *Rex* and *Fido*. *Rex* is the Latin word for *king*. *Fido* is derived from the Latin word *fidelis* meaning faithful or loyal. Both names are very appropriate given the well known dedication canines have for their masters.

U.S. President, Abraham Lincoln owned a yellow-brown dog named Fido that looked something like a beagle. The dog was given to a neighbor when Lincoln left Springfield, Illinois for Washington D.C. after he was elected President. Lincoln's son Tad had unsuccessfully pleaded to keep the dog, and had promised to care for him during the trip east to Washington. This is a familiar promise that all parents correctly evaluate as not particularly realistic.

Porcelain (China) Produced in Europe
Venice and Florence
The earliest porcelain was made in China about 620 AD. The first European manufacturing of Chinese style porcelain appeared in 1575 in Venice and Florence. It later spread to Germany and Austria. The famous Capo di Monte brand porcelain was first made in Naples and sponsored by Charles II, who was the King of Naples from 1743 to 1759. Capo di Monte uses an "N" with a crown for its trademark and is essentially synonymous with the Ginori porcelain made in the Doccia

factory, located on the old Doccia estate near Florence. The Marchese (Marquette) Carlo Ginori of Florence founded Ginori porcelain using his knowledge of chemistry and mineralogy to create porcelain works of art from the Tuscan clay hills. By 1735 his porcelain factory became highly influential in the small but growing porcelain industry of Europe that was inspired by porcelain from the orient. Carlo and his son Lorenzo developed and perfected their fine and delicate porcelain figurines to an art form. Even European royalty prized their work. During the late 18th and 19th centuries, Genori porcelain was commissioned by Marie Louise of Austria (wife of Napoleon), Franz II and later by the Khedive (Viceroy) of Egypt. Richard Genori has continued Carlo Ginori's two hundred year old tradition, and the Societe Richard Ceramica is the modern firm that produces Ginori and Capo di Monte porcelain.

Road Maps
Rome

The Romans were the first to build complex road systems using flat stones and concrete, which the Romans invented. They built over 60,000 miles of carefully engineered roadways from the Middle East to the northernmost reaches of the British Isles. Consequently, the Romans invented the first road maps, since these were required to document the extensive road system for travelers. They also carefully paced off distances between supply stations, towns and cities, and deployed a system of directional milestones to aid commerce and travel. Roman road engineering and construction were unsurpassed for many centuries to follow. (See the "Art & Architecture" chapter for information regarding the Roman Roadway System.)

Roman Numerals
Rome

Today, Roman numerals are often used to number and identify large divisions in any document or work, such as the chapters in this book. These numbers represent the numbering system used in ancient Rome, and have endured throughout history to our modern civilization. They are sometimes used for movie or other numbered series, for example, Rocky II, SuperBowl XXXIV. Here are Roman numerals with Arabic equivalents: I = 1, V = 5, X = 10, L = 50, C = 100, D =

500, M =1000. Roman numerals are derived from Latin, the language of the Romans, e.g., <u>centum</u> = C = 100 and <u>milliarius</u> = M = 1000. These Latin words are also used in the international metric system of weights and measures, e.g. *centi*meter and *milli*meter. Even the famous Irish welcome, *cead mille failte* has Latin (Roman) roots. These Celtic words mean *a hundred thousand welcomes*. The Latin words *cent mille factum* mean *a hundred thousand good deeds*.

Irish Celtic: *cead mille failte*

Roman Latin: *cent mille factum*

The French are credited for developing the metric system. In 1670, Gabriel Mouton, a French vicar, first conceived the system. In 1790, Louis XVI of France sponsored a study to reform the French system of weights and measures. This ultimately led to the development of the first metric system. Two hundred years later, the U.S. with the most advanced economy and technology on the planet, still has a citizenry that cannot comprehend the meaning of a metric meter. However, Americans are learning the meaning of a *liter of wine*. This is sobering evidence that American drinking prowess may be greater than its mathematical acumen.

Salt as Value
Rome

In his publication "Satyricon," the Roman author Petronius wrote that an underachieving soldier is "not worth his salt." Soldiers were given salt rations as salary called *salarium* or *salt money*. The English word *salary* itself comes from the Latin word *salarium*. In some cultures, including Celtic traditions, there is a superstition that if you run out of salt you will run out of money. Perhaps this is a legacy of the Roman salt salary for soldiers.

Also, because salt preserved meat and fish, and purified water somewhat, it was considered an essential item. Therefore, there are superstitions about accidentally spilling salt bringing bad luck, but throwing a small bit over your shoulder may bring or buy good luck.

Scissors
Rome

The first primitive scissors were invented around 1500 BC in ancient Egypt. These early scissors were made from a single piece of metal that was sharpened on two ends and then bent in half so that the two cutting edges passed each other when the scissor was squeezed. The scissors we use today, made from two connected cross blades was invented in Rome around 100 AD. Barbers and tailors used early scissors, however, scissors were not commonly used in Europe until the 1500's.

Shoes (Right and Left)
Rome
The professional shoemakers of Rome organized themselves into guilds and developed the first shoes that were crafted specifically for right and left feet around 200 BC. Roman soldiers also benefited from this innovation.

Shorthand
Marcus Tullius Tiro
In 63 BC, Marcus Tullius Tiro, a former slave of Cicero invented the oldest known system of shorthand writing.

Silver Dollar - "Miss Liberty Coins"
Antonio de Francisi
The U.S. "Miss Liberty" silver, one-dollar coins were minted in the 1920's and 1930's. In the last few decades these made neat little gifts that parents and grandparents would give their children and grandchildren. The average value is now about $100 dollars. Antonio de Francisi, an Italian immigrant from Palermo, did the master engraving for these "Miss Liberty" coins, and of course the model he used was the profile of his wife, Maria Teresa Cafarelli de Francisi. (Refer to the "Art & Architecture – Contributions to America" chapter for the reference on U.S. Mint Chief Engraver, F. Gasparro.)

Silver Spoon - "Born with a Silver Spoon"
Tuscany and Venice
During the 15th century, wealthy Tuscans (from Tuscany) and Venetians (from Venice) began the practice of giving silver *apostle*

spoons as christening gifts. These spoons were handcrafted with the image of the child's patron saint on the handle. Today's expression that describes a wealthy child, as being "born with a silver spoon in its mouth" originates from these wealthy Italians and their *apostle spoons*, which were usually made of silver.

Slapstick, Harlequin and Zany
Italy

Rough-housing comedic theater started with Greco-Roman performances, usually among clowns. However, the term *slapstick* is specifically derived from Italian performances where a flat double stick was invented and used to make a loud sound when struck. The two pieces of flat wood attached at the handle end would be used during comedic horseplay among performers who "slapped this stick," which amplified the sound making it audible for the audience.

The word *harlequin*, used to describe a specific kind of costumed clown, is derived from the famous Italian comedic performer Arlecchino of the Renaissance period. Similarly, the word *zany* is derived from Italian Renaissance performers termed *Zanni*. The *Zanni* (*Dei Zanni*) were usually servants, valets or clowns that often performed practical jokes. This Italian term is thought to be an abbreviated term derived from a certain Giovanni of Bergamo, who performed in the Lombardy region, where the *Zanni* character began.

Soap
Rome

Although it is difficult to identify the very first use of soap in antiquity, it was the ancient Romans who were the first to manufacture and widely use soap. The word *soap* is derived from Mount Sapo near the Tiber River in Rome. Soap was discovered by Roman women washing clothes in the Tiber River at the base of Mount Sapo. A temple at the top of Mount Sapo was used for animal sacrifices and fires. Rainwater washed the ashes (alkali) and animal fats (fatty acids) down the hill and into the clay of the Tiber River. Women noticed that the clay was an excellent cleaner. Later, Romans made higher quality soap from olive oil that was exported to other parts of Europe and the Mediterranean. (Refer also to the 'Health Spa' section of this chapter.)

Socks, Hose, Stockings
Rome

During the 1st century BC, Julius Caesar had his soldiers wear *hosa* of cloth or leather beneath their tunics to protect their legs from cold weather and thorn bushes during the invasion of Gaul (France). Similarly, the Roman women wore *soccus*, which covered the leg but not the foot. When the Romans traveled to the British Isles the local inhabitants called the *soccus* simply *soc*. The Anglo-Saxons learned to wear these under their rough leather boots to protect their feet. The Germans learned of the *soccus* and named them *socc*. Eventually the English word *sock* evolved. Stockings that covered the foot and leg to the knee were called *udo* by the Romans who first wore these around the 5th century under boots. Ironically, stockings were for soldiers, priests and young men, but not worn by women for many subsequent centuries. Women began wearing stockings around 600 AD.

Strawberry Fields Mosaic
Naples, Italy

On December 8, 1980, singer-songwriter and former Beatle, John Lennon, was murdered just outside the historic Dakota apartments where he lived. In 1985, his widow, Yoko Ono established a fund to maintain a small section of NYC's Central Park near the Dakota as a memorial park. The Strawberry Fields memorial park honors John Lennon and his pacifist ideals. The park's surrounding garden has species of plants from over 100 countries. At the center of Strawberry Fields is a black and white mosaic that is a gift from the city of Naples, Italy. At the mosaic's center is the word "Imagine," a reference to a Lennon song about world peace.

Teenage Mutant Ninja Turtles

These cute often comedic green turtle characters that appeared in cartoons and movies in the 1990's were named after four Italian Renaissance masters: Leonardo, Michelangelo, Raphael and Donatello. Refer to the "Art & Architecture" chapter for more information about these artists. There are references to Leonardo da Vinci in most chapters of this book.

Toast (Making a toast)
Rome
The Greeks were the first to drink to someone's health as far back as the 6th century BC. This became a practice since poisoning houseguests (obviously highly disliked houseguests) was a convenient method of eliminating one's foe. The host, taking the first drink, meant the jug was not poisoned and wishing good health was an added measure to express friendship. Later, the Romans also had the same concerns of being poisoned when taking a drink and therefore kept, for good reason, the Greek custom of drinking to good health and friendship. In the 1st century BC, the Romans added a variation to the custom and would dip a burnt piece of bread into the wine creating the present day "toast" to one's health.

Umbrella (waterproof)
Rome
As early as the 1st century AD, Roman women were the first to oil parasols to protect them from the rain. Previously, the parasol, although dating as far back as 1400 BC in Mesopotamia, was used as protection from the sun. Roman women often opened their umbrellas during rain at outdoor amphitheaters to the chagrin of many men with obstructed views. Their use of umbrellas at amphitheaters was contested by the unhappy males. However, the women prevailed when Emperor Domitian ruled in favor of women using their oiled parasols against the rain.

The English word *parasol* is derived from the Old Italian word *parasole*. *Parasole* was formed by combining two Italian words: *parare* meaning *to shield*, and *sole* meaning *sun*. The Italian word *sole* is a descendant of the Latin word *sol*. The Latin word *sol* is also the lexical parent of the English words *solar* and other related words such as *solarium* and *solstice*.

Unions (guilds)
Rome
From 200 BC to 400 BC, artisans in Rome formed professional guilds, creating the first organized unions. Shoemakers, perfumers, barbers and others organized into specialized guilds for each craft.

University – World's First
University of Bologna, Italy

The *world's first true university* with curriculum, standards, examinations and degrees was the University of Bologna. Bologna's instructors who could confer degrees upon graduates were called *collegia*. Women attended the University's schools and were also well represented among the university's faculty. Students from all over Europe attended Bologna and the student population was 10,000 by the 13th century. Bologna was founded in the 11th century and by the 12th century had a distinguished medical faculty as well. Bologna also founded the oldest university-based medical school in the world. (Refer to the 'Medical Schools – Oldest' section in the "Medicine, Biology and Health" chapter.)

The world's first public, state-funded university was the University of Naples founded in 1224 by Emperor Frederick II.

Valentine's Day
Roman Festival

In ancient Rome the fertility festival of Lupercalia was celebrated around February 15th. The Lupercalia festival celebrated the coming of spring according to the early Roman calendar. The activities were intended to ensure the fertility of crops, flocks and people.

In 496 AD, the Roman Catholic Church outlawed this "pagan" festival and replaced it with a Christian holiday. Pope Gelasius chose the martyred Bishop Valentine as a suitable replacement, because he had a legendary love story associated with his life. Bishop Valentine was condemned to death by a Roman Emperor. Legend has it that before his execution, Valentine wrote a letter to his jailer's daughter, with whom he had fallen in love. He allegedly signed the letter with a phrase that has endured over the centuries - "from your Valentine."

Vulcan
Rome

In the legendary television and movie series "Star Trek," the First Officer Mr. Spock, with the famous pointed ears and sometimes annoying logic, was a Vulcan from the planet Vulcan. Vulcan is the Roman name for the god of fire or blacksmith type metalworking. The Greek name for this god of fire is Hephaestus.

Vulcanization of Rubber (the word)
Rome

Vulcanization is an industrial process that requires a great amount of heat and strengthens natural rubber. It is appropriately named after the Roman god Vulcan, god of fire.

Wagon, Radio Flyer brand
Antonio Pasin

The most popular child's wagon in America is the red Radio Flyer wagon. It is the brainchild of Antonio Pasin, an Italian immigrant and carpenter. His family of skilled craftsmen sold a mule to purchase a ticket for Antonio to come to America in 1914 when he was only 16 years old. Three years after his arrival, in 1917, Antonio rented tools and a one-room carpentry shop and started making wagons. He made wagons at night and sold them during the day. By 1923, he founded the Liberty Coaster Company, which Antonio named after the Statue of Liberty. By 1930, the company operated under a new name, Radio Steel & Manufacturing, and was already the world's largest producer of "pull" or "coaster" wagons. The name *Radio* was a marketing idea Antonio had, since the world was amazed by Guglielmo Marconi's invention of the radio. *Flyer* was later added to the company's name, since it implied speed. The company was highly successful, even during the Great Depression they manufactured 1,500 wagons a day.

The Chicago based Radio Flyer Inc. employs 100 workers who manufacture about 8,000 wagons a day. Today, Antonio's three grandsons run the company and have introduced many models and styles for modern suburban living.

Wedding Cake - Eating Together
Rome

Instead of continuing an ancient practice of throwing wedding cake at the bride as a fertility gesture, the Romans adopted the more civilized practice of actually eating the wedding cake. (Had they continued to throw cake, the Romans might have invented slapstick. On a more serious note, the Renaissance Italians actually did invent slapstick; see the reference earlier in this chapter.) Furthermore, the Romans began the tradition of having the couple eat the cake *together*. Actually they ate the crumbs sprinkled over their heads as a compromise to those who so enjoyed the old days when the cake was flung at the bride to wish fertility.

After the fall of Rome, people began throwing wheat or rice grain, since Rome was destroyed by Germanic and other northern tribes, and the times of prosperity and good bakeries were over. Today, guests at weddings have stopped throwing rice, because the grain is unhealthy for birds that consume it. Instead birdseed is thrown by today's more enlightened wedding guests.

Wedding Ring & Friendship Ring
Rome, Greece

Placing a wedding ring on the finger next to the pinkie is a Roman tradition. The Romans believed there was some kind of nerve or vein that connected this finger directly to the heart. Placing a ring on this particular finger would bring bliss to the couple. The Greeks had an earlier tradition but probably used the middle finger for these rings. Unlike the Greeks, the Romans clearly used the finger next to the pinkie, which is our current tradition.

Also, a two thousand year old ring was discovered in the ancient Roman city of Pompeii, which is the oldest known "friendship" ring ever found. The ring had two hands joined together in a handshake pose. This motif was also used on some Roman coins to symbolize agreement and unity among the Roman Republic's leaders. (Also see the section on 'Diamond Engagement Rings' listed earlier in this chapter.)

"Who do you think you are, Mario Andretti ?"

This expression has been used by parent and police alike to get drivers to slow down. Mario Andretti was born in Montona, Italy, on February 28, 1940. When he was 14, Mario's interest in racing was sparked by a visit to Monza to see the great Alberto Ascari compete in the Italian Grand Prix. In 1955, his family immigrated to the United States, making their home in Nazareth, Pennsylvania. Mario is a master driver, but he is only one of many great Italian race car drivers. His son Michael, and Michael's son Marco are also professional drivers. An impressive list of Grand Prix drivers follows:

Michele Alboreto – born Italy 1956
Grand Prix Wins
- 1982 US GP
- 1983 US GP
- 1984 Belgian GP
- 1985 Canadian GP and German GP

Mario Andretti – born Italy 1940
World Driving Championship Win- 1978
Grand Prix Wins
- 1971 South African GP
- 1976 Japanese GP
- 1977 U.S. GP, Spanish GP, French GP and Italian GP
- 1978 Argentine GP, Belgian GP, Spanish GP, French GP, German GP and Dutch GP

Michael Andretti (Mario Andretti's son – born USA 1962)
World Driving Championship Wins - Best 11th 1993
Grand Prix
- 1993 3rd place Italian GP

Alberto Ascari - born Italy 1918
World Driving Championship Wins- 1952 and 1953
Grand Prix Wins
- 1951 German GP and Italian GP
- 1952 Belgian GP, French GP, British GP, German GP, Dutch GP and Italian GP
- 1953 Argentine GP, Dutch GP, Belgian GP, British GP and Swiss GP

Note: *Alberto Ascari has a record of wins unmatched by all but a few champion drivers. He is a racing legend, like Mario Andretti.*

Giancarlo Baghetti – born Italy 1934
World Driving Championship Wins - Best 9th 1961
Grand Prix Wins
- 1961 French GP

Mauro Baldi – born Italy 1954
World Driving Championship Wins- Best 16th 1983
Grand Prix

- 1983 5th place Dutch GP

Lorenzo Bandini – born Italy 1935
World Driving Championship Wins - Best 4th 1964
Grand Prix Wins
- 1964 Austrian GP

Fabrizio Barbazza – born Italy 1963
World Driving Championship Wins- Best 17th 1993
Grand Prix
- 1993 6th place European GP and San Marino GP

Lucien Bianchi - born Italy 1934
Grand Prix
- 1968 3rd place Monaco GP

Gino Bianco – born Italy 1916
Grand Prix
- 1952 18th place British GP

Felice Bonetto - born Italy 1903
World Driving Championship Wins- Best 8th 1951
Grand Prix
- 1951 3rd place Italian GP
- 1953 3rd place Dutch GP

Vittorio Brambilla – born Italy 1937
Grand Prix Wins
- 1975 Austrian GP

Giulio Cabianca – born Italy 1923
Grand Prix
- 1960 4th place 1960 Italian GP

Alex Caffi – born Italy 1963
Drivers Championship Wins- Best 16th 1989, 1990
Grand Prix
- 1989 4th place Monaco GP

Ivan Capelli – born Italy 1963
World Driving Championship Wins- Best 7th 1988
Grand Prix
- 1988 2nd place Portuguese GP
- 1990 2nd place French GP

Eugenio Castellotti - born Italy 1930
World Driving Championship Wins - Best 3rd 1955
Grand Prix
- 1955 2nd place Monaco GP
- 1956 2nd place French GP

Andrea Chiesa – born Italy 1964
Grand Prix
- 1992 20th place Spanish GP

Franco Comotti (aka Gianfranco Comotti) - born Italy 1906
Grand Prix
- 1952 12th place French GP

Andrea De Adamich – born Italy 1941
Grand Prix
- 1972 4th place Spanish GP
  1973 4th place Belgian GP

Elio De Angelis – born Italy 1958
Grand Prix Wins
- 1982 Austrian GP
- 1985 San Marino GP

Andrea De Cesaris – born Italy 1959
Grand Prix
- 1983 2nd place German GP and South African GP

Maria Teresa De Filippis - born Italy 1926
Grand Prix
- 1958 10th place Belgian GP

Piero Drogo – born Italy 1926
Grand Prix

- 1960 8th place Italian GP

Corrado Fabi - born Italy 1961
Grand Prix
- 1984 7th place US GP

Teo Fabi - born Italy 1955
World Driving Championship Wins- Best 9th 1987
Grand Prix
- 1984 3rd place U.S. East GP and Austrian GP

Luigi Fagioli - born Italy 1898
World Driving Championship Wins- Best 3rd 1950
Grand Prix Wins
- 1951 French GP (Shared with Fangio)

Guiseppe Farina - born Italy 1906
World Driving Championship Wins- 1950
Grand Prix Wins
- 1950 British GP, Swiss GP and Italian GP
- 1951 Belgian GP
- 1953 German GP

Giancarlo Fisichella – born Italy 1973
Grand Prix
- 1997 2nd place Belgian GP
- 1998 2nd place Monaco GP and Canadian GP
- 1999 2nd place Canadian GP
- 2000 2nd place Brazilian GP

Nanni Galli (aka Giovanni Giuseppe Gilberto Galli) - born Italy 1940
Grand Prix
- 1973 9th place Brazilian GP

Gerino Gerini – born Italy 1928
Grand Prix
- 1956 4th place Argentinean GP

Piercarlo Ghinzani – born Italy 1952
World Driving Championship Wins- Best 19th 1984
Grand Prix
- 1984 5th place U.S. GP

Bruno Giacomelli – born Italy 1952
World Driving Championship Wins- Best 15th 1981
Grand Prix
- 1981 3rd place U.S. Caesars Palace GP

Ignazio Giunti – born Italy 1941
Drivers Championship Wins- Best 17th 1970
Grand Prix
- 1970 4th place Belgian GP

Nicola Larini – born Italy 1964
World Driving Championship Wins- Best 14th 1994
Grand Prix
- 1994 2nd place San Marino GP

Giovanni Lavaggi – born Italy 1958
Grand Prix
- 1996 10th place Hungarian GP

Lella Lombardi – born Italy 1943
World Driving Championship Wins- Best 21st 1975
Grand Prix
- 1975 6th place Spanish GP

Umberto Maglioli – born Italy 1928
World Driving Championship Wins- Best 19th 1954
Grand Prix
- 1954 3rd place Italian GP.
- 1955 3rd place Argentinean GP

Sergio Mantovani – born Italy 1929
World Driving Championship Wins- Best 15th 1954
Grand Prix
- 1954 5th place German GP and Swiss GP

Pierluigi Martini – born Italy 1961
World Driving Championship Wins- Best 11th 1991
Grand Prix
- 1989 5th place British GP and Portuguese GP
- 1994 5th place Spanish GP and French GP

Arturo Merzario – born Italy 1943
World Drivers Championship Wins- Best 12th 1973
Grand Prix
- 1973 4th place Brazilian GP and South African GP
- 1974 4th place Italian GP

Stefano Modena – born Italy 1963
World Driving Championship Wins- Best 8th 1991
Grand Prix
- 1991 2nd place Canadian GP

Gianni Morbidelli – born Italy 1968
World Driving Championship Wins- Best 14th 1995
Grand Prix
- 1995 3rd place Australian GP

Andrea Montermini - born Italy 1964
Grand Prix
- 1995 8th place German GP

Luigi Musso – born Italy 1924
World Driving Championship Wins- Best 3rd 1957
Grand Prix Wins
- 1956 Argentinean GP (shared with Fangio)

Alessandro Nannini – born Italy 1958
Grand Prix Wins
- 1989 Japanese GP

Emanuele Naspetti – born Italy 1968
Grand Prix
- 1992 11th place Portuguese GP

Nello Pagani – born Italy 1911
Grand Prix
- 1950 7th place Swiss GP

Massimiliano Papis – born Italy 1969
Grand Prix
- 1995 7th place Italian GP

Riccardo Patrese – born Italy 1954
World Driving Championship Wins- Best 2nd 1992
Grand Prix Wins
- 1982 Monaco GP
- 1983 South African GP
- 1990 San Marino GP
- 1991 Mexican GP and Portuguese GP
- 1992 Japanese GP

Cesare Perdisa – born Italy 1932
World Driving Championship Wins- Best 15th 1956
Grand Prix
- 1955 3rd place Monaco GP
- 1956 3rd place Belgian GP

Luigi Piotti – born Italy 1913
Grand Prix
- 1956 6th place Italian GP

Renato Pirocchi - born Italy 1933
Grand Prix
- 1961 12th place Italian GP

Emanuele Pirro – born Italy 1962
World Driving Championship Wins- Best 18th 1991
Grand Prix
- 1991 6th place Monaco GP

Consalvo Sanesi – born Italy 1911
World Driving Championship Wins- Best 13th 1951
Grand Prix
- 1951 4th place Swiss GP

Ludovico Scarfiotti – born Italy 1933
World Driving Championship Wins- Best 10th 1966
Grand Prix Wins
- 1966 Italian GP

Giorgio Scarlatti – born Italy 1921
World Driving Championship Wins- Best 20th 1957
Grand Prix
- 1957 5th place Italian GP

Dorino Serafini – born Italy 1921
World Driving Championship Wins- Best 13th 1950
Grand Prix
- 1950 2nd place Italian GP

Gabriele Tarquini – born Italy 1962
World Driving Championship Wins- Best 26th 1989
Grand Prix
- 1989 6th place Mexican GP

Piero Taruffi – born Italy 1906
Grand Prix Wins
- 1952 Swiss GP

Nino Vaccarella – born Italy 1933
Grand Prix
- 1962 9th place Italian GP

Luigi Villeresi – born Italy 1909
World Driving Championship Wins- Best 5th 1951, 1953
Grand Prix
- 1953 2nd place Argentinean GP and Belgian GP

Alessandro Zanardi – born Italy 1966
World Driving Championship Wins- Best 20th 1993
Grand Prix
- 1993 6th place Brazilian GP

Renzo Zorzi – born Italy 1946
World Driving Championship Wins- Best 19th 1977
Grand Prix
- 1977 6th place Brazilian GP

Note: Since 1996, Michael Schumacher, born in Germany on January 3, 1969, has dominated Formula 1 racing and is considered to be the best Formula 1 driver of his generation. He has been racing with Ferrari since 1996.

Wishbone
Tuscany and Rome

The tradition of wishing on a hen's clavicle (wishbone) began about 400 BC in Etruria, a region of central Italy now called Tuscany. The belief comes from people's perception that hens have the power of premonition, since they cluck *before* laying an egg and *before* dawn. Therefore, the Etruscans wished upon an unbroken bone of this animal with perceived foresight. The Romans who followed many Etruscan life-styles (the Etruscans were highly urban and cultured) continued this practice, but started the practice of tugging for the larger half of the bone. *This is also where the expression "getting a lucky break" originates.*

R. R. Esposito

∽

Chapter VII

ECONOMICS, FINANCE and BUSINESS

"Modern capitalism...has its roots in Italy...
Italians laid the foundations for most of
the business institutions of today."
*- Raymond de Roover, author of "The Rise and Decline
of the Medici Bank" and professor at the
Harvard Graduate School of Business -*

Bank of America
Amadeo Peter Giannini

A. P. Giannini was born in San Jose, California in 1870, the son of immigrants from Genoa, Italy. He worked as a youth in a family run fruit market in San Francisco, California. By age thirty-four he opened his first bank, the Bank of Italy, to meet the needs of the Italian community in San Francisco. Little did Amadeo know that *his small bank would some day grow large enough to buy out the Bank of America and become one of the largest financial institutions in the world.* His early success with the Bank of Italy was the result of his dedicated focus on small businesses, individuals and their unique needs. His bank would often lend money to hard working Italian immigrants who were denied loans from other banks.

In 1906, a major earthquake in San Francisco ruptured gas mains and caused devastating fires in the city. Amadeo had the presence of mind to remove all bank records, money and gold from the bank and protect them from destruction by bringing them to his home in San Mateo. Other banks lost their records and money in the fire causing chaos for their customers. Working from his home, Amadeo commissioned shippers to buy new lumber in Oregon to rebuild the North Beach section of San Francisco where his customers lived and worked. Amadeo set up a temporary table at the Washington Street wharf where his customers could withdraw their money. He would lend money to others who were not his customers, some say if they had calluses on their hands. All of these hardworking and grateful people repaid their loans to Amadeo. The North Beach section started to rebuild and recover much more quickly than the rest of the City. Giannini's successes and fair business practices drew many new customers as the entire City began to rebuild, and his Bank of Italy grew into a large enterprise that ultimately bought out the Bank of America. The Bank of America, with assets of $572 billion is now the second largest bank behind CitiGroup's $751 billion.

Before Giannini's Bank of Italy, banks offered very limited services to consumers and primarily focused their services and products on larger businesses. *Giannini pioneered home mortgages, auto loans and other installment credit.* These banking services for the average consumer were not available until Giannini came along. His bank benefited from these unique new services that consumers needed.

Giannini was also somewhat of a "fiscal contrarian" and sometimes focused on risky and out-of-favor industries. Giannini's loans helped the fledgling California wine industry grow and establish itself. He financially supported Hollywood's film industry when it was young and unprofitable, creating a film industry loan division that helped Charlie Chaplin, Douglas Fairbanks and D.W. Griffith start United Artists. In later years, he lent money to Walt Disney when the "Snow White" production costs ran $2 million over budget.

Giannini has also been called the "architect" of nationwide banking that matured during the 1990's. His vision was that a statewide or nationwide bank would be less vulnerable to a single area's difficulties. He clearly saw the devastating effects of the San Francisco earthquake on local banks. A bank with large geographic coverage would be diversified and financially sound enough to easily assist troubled communities. Understandably, the first U.S. bank to have branches coast to coast was his Bank of America, which accomplished this goal through its $48 billion acquisition of NationsBank of Charlotte. His vision has also been realized on a national scale in the U.S. for the past twenty years and is reflected in international banking as well.

Giannini was an exceptionally wise man who realized the personal danger in excessive wealth. When he died at age 79, his estate was worth less than $500,000. Giannini could easily have been a billionaire, but he thought great wealth would change him, and also make him lose touch with the consumers he served. He accepted virtually no pay from the bank for many years, and upon being granted a $1.5 million bonus one year, he promptly gave it all to the University of California. Giannini once said, "Money itch is a bad thing. I never had that trouble."

Barnes & Noble - Largest Bookstore Chain
Leonard Riggio, Founder & Chairman

In 1958, Riggio was attending New York University at night and worked in the University's bookstore. Riggio believed he could operate a much better bookstore. In 1965, he took $5,000 in savings and loans and opened a competing bookstore. At the time Riggio was only 24 years old. His first store, SBX, was in Greenwich Village and mostly served local college students. After a few years of success he opened a few more small stores. In 1971, he convinced bankers into lending him $1.2 million to acquire the trade name Barnes & Noble and its single, ailing, century-old bookstore on Fifth Avenue, not far from New York University.

Leonard Riggio's great business sense, management style, and determination has built Barnes & Noble into a massive book retailer that subsequently purchased several other retailers. Riggio now owns and operates a virtual business empire. There are 500 Barnes & Noble superstores and 800 mall-based B. Daltons that sell almost $3 billion worth of merchandise annually. The cover story of the July 29, 1998 issue of "BusinessWeek," called Mr. Riggio "The Baron of Books." In that story, Leonard Berry, director of the Center for Retailing Studies at Texas A&M University said that Riggio "…was the first retailer to understand that the store is a stage and that retailing is great theater."

Currently, Riggio is chairman of Barnes & Noble, Inc., the parent company of Barnes & Noble Bookstores, B. Dalton Bookseller,

Doubleday Book Shops and Babbage's Etc. The Babbage's chain is one of the nation's largest video game retailers. Riggio is also the chairman of Barnes & Noble.com, which offers direct consumer Internet sales. He is also the chairman and major shareholder of several privately held companies, including Barnes & Noble College Bookstores, the largest operator of college bookstores in the U.S., serving more than 350 universities and colleges and MBS Textbook Exchange.

Among his other accomplishments and honors, Mr. Riggio has received the Ellis Island Medal of Honor and Yale's Frederick Douglass Medallion.

Borders - 2nd Largest Bookstore in the U.S.
Robert F. DiRomualdo, Former Chairman

DiRomualdo had been the Chairman of the Board (1996-2002) of Borders Group, Inc., and an officer since August 1994. He has been highly influential in the growth and success of Borders. DiRomualdo served as Chief Executive Officer from August 1994 until November 1998- and again, from April 1999 until November 1999, as interim President and Chief Executive Officer after the resignation of Philip M. Pfeffer.

Borders Group, Inc., is the parent company of Borders, Inc., which operates over 250 Borders Books and Music stores in the U.S. It is also the parent of Borders.com, its electronic commerce site that has access to over 650,000 titles and is teamed with Amazon.com. Borders Group, Inc. also owns Walden Book Company, Inc., which operates 900 Waldenbooks stores in malls in the U.S.

The Walden Books Company has an interesting history. It was originally founded by Lawrence Hoyt on March 4, 1933 during the Depression, the same day U.S. President Franklin D. Roosevelt closed the banks. The stores were not yet called Walden and were book rental stores. Hoyt opened his first store inside a Bridgeport, Connecticut department store charging only three cents a day to rent a popular novel. After decades of growth, the company had to transform its 250 rental stores to retail stores, since the paperback industry made very inexpensive books available for purchase to virtually everyone in the 1950's. In 1962, the company opened its first retail bookstore in Pennsylvania under the name The Walden Book Store, as a tribute to the literary classic "Walden" by Henry David Thoreau.

Double-Entry Accounting and World's Oldest Bank
Luca Pacioli (aka Luca di Borgo)

Pacioli was born in 1445 in Borgo San Sepolcro in Italy's Tuscany region and died about 1517. He was a mathematician who was also a Franciscan friar. Pacioli invented double-entry accounting. He worked in Venice as a tutor and also studied in Rome. He also taught mathematics in Perugia, Zara, Naples, Florence and Milan, and in 1494 wrote his epic work "Summa di arithmetica" often referred to simply as "Summa." This work is one of the first printed books on mathematics and represents a comprehensive text of all mathematical knowledge up to his time. *His book became a standard mathematics text and it also included his newly invented double-entry accounting system.* This became the foundation for all modern accounting systems that employ credits and debits to balance ledgers and statements.

During the Renaissance, Italy's businesses were highly successful and the Italian city-states became the bankers and financiers of Europe. Their use of double-entry accounting further advanced their banking and financial systems beyond anything that had ever existed. Italian wealth and advanced financial systems allowed them to establish banks throughout Europe. Lombard Street is the major financial street in London, equivalent in relevance to Wall Street in New York. Lombard Street was named after the Italian bankers who settled there from the Lombardy (or Lombardia) region of Italy.

Founded in 1472, twenty years before Columbus discovered America, the Banca Monte Dei Paschi di Siena is the *world's oldest bank.* The bank was established, by a charter of the city of Siena, as a public credit institution, and primarily offered very low cost loans for underdeveloped farm areas. Funds for the bank were raised from private sources, the city's hospital, local churches, and the sale of papal indulgences. Papal indulgences were truly the work of a medieval marketing mastermind. Today, the Monte Dei Paschi bank is a major international financial institution with 1800 branches and 28,000 employees. The bank also owns castles, palaces, a collection of ancient Etruscan coins, and an impressive Renaissance art collection.

Food Industry

Refer to the chapter "Culinary Contributions" for information on the many successful companies that were founded by enterprising Italian-Americans.

IBM - President, CEO and Chairman
Samuel J. Palmisano

Sam Palmisano became IBM's president and chief executive officer on March 1, 2002 and chairman of the board on January 1, 2003. The International Business Machines Corporation is one of the largest and most influential corporations in the world. Prior to his appointment as the head of IBM, Mr. Palmisano was IBM's president and chief operating officer. He has held numerous leadership positions, both domestic and international, since joining IBM in 1973. An interesting fact about Mr. Palmisano's youth is that he was a studio musician who played saxophone in a backup band for the famous Temptations singing group. If the reader of this book has a son who plays saxophone, as this author does, then let Sam Palmisano's life remind us all that, in life, anything is possible.

Life Insurance System, First
Lorenzo Tonti

In the 17th century, the Italian banker Lorenzo Tonti devised a financial plan or system for collecting premiums to provide life insurance for groups or associations of people. His system collected premiums that were invested for the group. His system was the first to incorporate life expectancies and laws of averages to set annuities and today it is called the *tontine* system in honor of its inventor. Tonti was a financial advisor to the French court at the time and consequently his system was first introduced in Paris. Shortly after the introduction of his system in France, the English Parliament passed the Tontine Act in 1693. This Act was based upon Tonti's financial principles but was applied to establish a system that marked the start of the English national debt. The Tontine Act raised money for long-term debt and paid the participants based upon the number of years of participation and the amount of each contribution. Lorenzo's financial system ultimately spread to all of Europe, America and the world. It served to *foster the actuary sciences*. Lorenzo Tonti had two famous sons, Alfonso and Enrico, who were both explorers in America and who founded a state and two cities. (Refer to the "Exploration" chapter in this book for more on Lorenzo's sons.)

Marine Insurance, First
Lombardia Region and Florence

The first premium-based insurance policies covering sea traffic appear to have been developed in Italy by the Lombards of the Lombardia region of northern Italy during medieval times. There are also extensive records of marine insurance to protect both merchants and the shipping industry dating back to Florence. The well known marine insurance, Ordinances of Florence, was passed in 1523.

Actual marine insurance companies were first established in Italy in the 17th century and further developed in the second half of the 18th century.

Mathematical Economics

Giovanni Ceva

Ceva was born in Milan December 7, 1647 and died in Mantua June 15, 1734. He studied hydraulics and applied mathematics. In 1711, he published "De re numeraria" and offered mathematical solutions for economic equilibrium in a pluri-metallic monetary system which represented a *pioneering work on mathematical economics.* Among other publications, he also wrote the "Geometrical Theorem on the Nature of Concurrency" in his larger work entitled "De lineis rectis" in 1678. (Also see the chapter on "Mathematics" for more on Ceva).

Francesco Paolo Cantelli

Cantelli was born December 20, 1875 in Palermo and died July 21, 1966 in Rome. He is known for founding the Istituto Italiano degli Attuari, which is dedicated to understanding the applications of mathematics and probability to economics. From 1930 to 1958, he was the editor of the Istituto's journal and during this time the journal became one of the leading journals in its field. He produced research in astronomy, celestial mechanics, probability, frequency distributions, actuarial science and applications of probability theory.

Pareto Optimum
Vilfredo F. D. Pareto

Pareto was born in Italy in 1848 and died in 1923. This illustrious economist spent the first 20 years of his professional life as an engineer, before turning his knowledge of mathematics to the study of economics. He is famous for his economic concept of providing the greatest amount of good for the largest number of people, often called *Pareto Optimum,* and now *taught in every economic academic curriculum.* This concept holds that an economic system has not reached optimum so long as it is possible to make one person better off without reducing benefits to another. Pareto wrote two groundbreaking books. His "Manuale di Economia Politico" (1906) is considered to be the foundation of modern economic welfare and "Cours d'economie Politique" (1896) uses mathematics to understand economic equilibrium. Pareto clearly subscribed to egalitarian beliefs. He is quoted as saying, "The man in whose power it might be to find out the means of alleviating the sufferings of the poor would have done a far greater deed than the one who contents himself solely with knowing the exact numbers of poor and wealthy people in society." Clearly, he believed that applying economics for human good was far more important than just reporting economic descriptions or statistics. A few decades later, the former President of Poland, Lech Walesa, expressed a similar sentiment when he said "...there is a declining world market for words....words are plentiful, but deeds are precious."

Pareto Analysis or "The 80/20 rule"
Vilfredo F. D. Pareto
In the 19th century, the economist Vilfredo Pareto (1848-1923) developed an income distribution principle. He postulated that 80% of a nation's income benefits only 20% of its population. This principle has been widely applied to other fields of study. For example, 80% of a company's profits are derived from 20% of its products, and 80% of all process failures are caused by 20% of all problem sources. Pareto analysis is often used by business and government decision makers when prioritizing strategies, projects and spending plans.

Savings Analysis and Financial Markets- *Nobel Prize*
Franco Modigliani
Born in Rome in 1918, Modigliani was the 1985 Nobel Laureate in Economics, which he received for his pioneering analyses of saving

and financial markets. He received a degree in law from the University of Rome in 1939 and a Doctorate of Social Science in NYC from the New School for Social Research in 1944. In 1948, he was awarded the prestigious Political Economy Fellowship at the University of Chicago. Dr. Modigliani has taught at the world's most prestigious institutions including Columbia University, The New School of Social Research, University of Illinois, Harvard University, Carnegie Institute of Technology (now Carnegie-Mellon) and Northwestern University. In 1962, he joined the Massachusetts Institute of Technology as professor of Economics and Finance. He has held the position of Institute Professor Emeritus since 1988.

In 1985, when Modigliani was awarded a Nobel Prize, he also received the prestigious James R. Killian Faculty Achievement Award from MIT and was made Knight of the Grand Cross of the Italian Republic. He is also a member of the United States National Academy of Sciences and of the American Academy of Arts and Sciences. Modigliani has also held the positions of President of the American Econometric Society, the American Economic Association and the American Finance Association and is honorary President of the International Economic Association. He has also served as a consultant to the United States Treasury, the U.S. Federal Reserve System and several European banks.

Dr. Modigliani has written ten books and numerous articles for academic and scholarly journals, including his recent "Manifesto Against Unemployment in Europe" (published by "BNL Quarterly Review, September 1998). His books include, "The Collected Papers of Franco Modigliani" (published in five volumes by MIT Press in 1980 and translated into many languages, including Chinese), "Capital Markets: Institutions and Instruments" by Frank J. Fabozzi and Franco Modigliani (1996), "Foundations of Financial Markets and Institutions" by Frank J. Fabozzi, Franco Modigliani and Michael G. Ferri (1997).

Stock Exchanges, Chairman and CEO

Richard Grasso

Grasso led the world's most powerful and influential financial exchange in the world, the NYSE, which was founded in 1792. Richard Grasso was born in Queens, New York City and now resides on nearby Long Island. He joined the New York Stock Exchange in 1968 and was Chairman and CEO 1995-2003. On March 29, 1999 the NYSE closed above 10,000 for the first time under the watch of Richard Grasso. Mayor of New York City, Rudolph W. Giuliani, helped Grasso swing the gavel to close that day's historic trading. The exchange broke a trading record on July 24, 2002, when over 2.81 billion shares were traded. (The NYSE traded over 1.8 billion shares valued over $68 billion on an average day in 2006.)

Under Grasso the Exchange had plans to build a new facility in New York City on the block bordered by Broad, William and Wall streets, and Exchange Place across from the current Exchange building. The new site was to include 650,000 square feet of space. New York City and New York State planned to construct an 800,000 square foot tower above the new NYSE facility. Construction was scheduled to be completed by 2004. The plans were put on hold after the attack on the nearby World Trade Center on September 11, 2001.

Frank Zarb

Frank Zarb grew up in an Italian-American home in Brooklyn. He was the Chairman and CEO of the National Association of Securities Dealers (NASD), the parent of both the NASDQ and American Stock Exchange (Amex), from 1997 to 2001 before retiring. In New York, Hofstra Unviersity's Frank Zarb School of Business is named so in his honor.

Salvatore F. Sodano

Salvatore F. Sodano was the Chairman and CEO (1999-2005) of the American Stock Exchange (Amex). Additionally, he is the Vice Chariman of the National Association of Securities Dealer (NASD), and has been an officer since 1997.

TV – First Woman to Head a Major Network
Patricia Fili-Krushel

From 1998-2000, Patricia Fili-Krushel was president of ABC Television and the first woman to ever head a major television network. Fili-Krushel had been president of ABC's daytime TV division (1993-1998) and previously held executive posts at Lifetime Television, and at the HBO cable entertainment network.

Wage and Labor Theories
Cesare Bonesana Beccaria

Beccaria was an economist, jurist and criminologist who lived from 1738 to 1794. He developed wage and labor analysis that anticipated similar thoughts of Adam Smith. Beccaria also influenced all of Europe and specifically Jeremy Bentham regarding the need for prison reform with his "Essay on Crimes and Punishments" published in 1764. In this work he made arguments against capital punishment and for humane and rehabilitative treatment of criminals, which precipitated prison reform in many parts of Europe. Beccaria's works were read by Thomas Jefferson and John Adams, founders of the new America. For more information of Beccaria's influence on America's founding fathers refer to the Principles of the Declaration of Independence section in the "American Government" chapter.

World Economics and Public Policy
Romano Prodi, Former President of the European Union

The industrial economist, university professor and Italian Prime Minister (1996 to 1998, and reelected 2006) Romano Prodi was unanimously elected as President of the European Commission Union (1999-2004). He is widely supported by European leaders and has the strong support of Great Britain's Prime Minister Tony Blair.

The Commission is the heart of the European Union that represents 19 nations on the continent. Under the guidance of Mr. Prodi, the Euro-Dollar had its debut in January of 2002 unifying the economic currency of Europe for the first time since the Roman Empire provided a common currency for Europe.

As former President, Mr Prodi oversaw the European Commission, which is the driving force in the European Union's institutional system. The Commission's role includes the following:

- It has the right to initiate draft legislation and therefore presents legislative proposals to Parliament and the Council;
- As the Union's executive body, it is responsible for implementing the European legislation (directives, regulations, decisions), budget and programs adopted by Parliament and the Council;
- It acts as guardian of the Treaties and, together with the Court of Justice, ensures that Community law is properly applied;
- It represents the Union on the international stage and negotiates international agreements, chiefly in the field of trade and cooperation.

Chapter VIII

EXPLORATION

"...a fountain which sends up oil."
- Marco Polo was the first European to document oil fields -

First European to Travel to China
Marco Polo

Marco Polo was born in Venice, Italy in 1254. In 1298, this Venetian explorer wrote a fascinating book about his astonishing adventures in the exotic and distant Far East, entitled "Description of the World." He wrote of new cities, temples, cultures and artifacts, such as silks, jewels, porcelain and more. Marco was the first European to document and describe an oil field when he wrote about "...a fountain which sends up oil." He visited the town of Saveh in Iran and wrote about their legend that the "Three Magi" of Christian fame were buried there. After leaving the city of Kerman in Iran they entered the "Desert of Emptiness" where they were attacked by nomad robbers who kidnapped some in their caravan including Marco. Luckily, he escaped to the safety of a nearby village. Later in Afghanistan he became seriously ill, probably with malaria, and the group could not travel for almost a year while he recovered. Marco and his group had to conquer high mountain passes crowned by glaciers and were often delayed by blizzards, rain and injury, which explains why it took almost four years to reach China. Their trip included mountain heights as high as 15,000 feet. At these altitudes, Marco wrote that "fire is not so bright," because of the thin air and lack of oxygen. His life and the accounts of his travels are so marvelous that they easily compare to a Hollywood production. In fact, at least three movies about Marco Polo came out of Hollywood. The first two movies featured Tyrone Power and Gary Cooper as Marco Polo.

Marco Polo's accounts of his daring explorations have been proven to be very accurate and there are many court and legal documents that support his life story and travels. His book that he titled "Description of the World," and is sometimes called "The Book of Sir Marco Polo," was translated and copied by hand into several languages. The book was read by many who were inspired to travel in search of new sea routes to China and the East Indies. *Two centuries later, his book was more widely published. Columbus read Marco's book and even used it as a reference to better understand eastern peoples and cultures.* The Biblioteca Colombina (library) in Seville, Spain houses the actual Marco Polo book that Columbus had read and contains notes written in the margins by Columbus himself.

Marco's father Nicolò and his uncle Maffeo traveled to Cathay (China) before him. After being away for many years, they returned to Italy in 1269. At the age of 17, Marco traveled with them for his first trip to China, leaving Venice in 1271. After reaching China early in 1275, Marco first met Kublai Khan, probably at his summer capital in Shangdu, about 200 miles northwest of Beijing. (In the poem "Kubla Khan" by Samuel Taylor Coleridge, the author created an Anglicized name for the city of Shangdu, when he wrote "In Xanadu did Kubla Khan, A stately pleasure dome decree...").

Kublai Khan was the grandson of the great warrior Genghis Khan who claimed most of Asia, from Iraq to China and Russia, as part of his Mongol Empire. Marco wrote that Kublai Khan was "..the most powerful man in people and in lands and in treasure that ever was in the world." This was probably close to the truth, at least for his time. Marco had reached 21 years of age when his father introduced him to Kublai Khan. Khan took an immediate liking to the youthful and charismatic Marco Polo. Khan wanted to learn about western culture and science and equally enjoyed sharing his culture's knowledge with the Italian explorers. Khan asked Marco to govern Yangchow, a large city of more than 250,000 people. Marco was also sent on missions to distant reaches of the Mongol Empire. Marco visited and documented fabulous accounts of Indochina, Tibet, Yunnan, Ceylon (now Sri Lanka) and Burma. These lands were very strange and exotic for the

Europeans of the time.

Marco also correctly documented that asbestos (a Latin word) was crafted from a mineral mined in China. Marco's European contemporaries had a poor understanding of asbestos. (Asbestos was used in ancient Rome and Greece but became a lost science in Europe after the fall of Rome when the "Dark Ages" ensued.) Medieval Europeans thought it was made from an animal, the salamander! Marco also wrote of a "black rock" that burned, coal. He was also fascinated with paper money, unknown in Europe at that time, and correctly wrote it was made from the ground up bark of mulberry trees. He also noted the custom of burning fake paper money to honor the dead, a ritual still practiced in China today.

Marco and his family prospered and became very wealthy while in China. However, they feared the Chinese nobility's jealousy and growing resentment toward Kublai Khan and his Mongol regime. The Polos realized it would be best to return to Italy, however, Khan did not want them to leave and would not allow it. Eventually, the Polo's found a way to leave when they persuaded Khan to let them escort a Chinese princess, Kokejin, on her journey to Persia for her wedding. She also was known by the wonderful name "Blue Princess," because her name meant she was like the sky. The princess was to be wedded to the Persian Khan, Arghun, the great-nephew of Kublai Khan. They convinced Kublai Khan that their experience as travelers would be needed to escape natural dangers and attacks from nomads. As expert navigators they could also maximize the use of sea routes. Khan gave the Polos two super-passports that were golden tablets, called *paitzu*. These would be honored by most rulers in the Mongol empire for safe passage and to obtain supplies. The Polos were outfitted with 14 ships that carried 600 passengers. Of the 600, only 18, including the Polo's and the Princes, survived the grueling ordeal. They met with the extremes of mountains and deserts, as well as disease, nomad attacks, and pirates on the open seas.

Marco and his family finally reached Venice after helping escort the princess to her destination. They had finally returned to Venice in 1295 after their 24 year odyssey. In Venice, Marco Polo joined the fight against the nearby warring state, Genoa, and was captured. While in prison Marco wrote his accounts of the Middle East, and Chinese Far East cultures, customs, peoples, precious stones, silks and temples, which ultimately amazed all of Europe. After his release in 1299 and safe return home, Marco married at age 45. He and his wife had three daughters. After a full life of discovery and adventure, Marco raised a family and died content about the age of 70 around the year 1323.

Europeans who read his book marveled, but some were incredulous. However, as Marco lay dying he said, "I did not write half of what I saw." And contrary to commom myth, pasta existed in Europe long before Marco visited China. See the "Culinary Contributions" chapter for more on pasta in Italy's history.

The prestigious "National Geographic," chronicled Marco's travels in great detail in a fabulous three part series in the May, June and July issues of 2001. Mike Edwards, an assistant editor, traveled with photographer, Michael Yamashita, and spent four years reliving Marco's journey from Venice to China. Edwards and Yamashita followed Marco's documented passage and experienced the same vistas, cities, monuments, peoples, and cultures that Marco had encountered. They found his book of 1298 to be amazingly accurate, finding ancient ruins, deserts and mountain passes that Marco encountered, but also found that some cities, cultures and peoples were very much unchanged in certain remote parts of Iran, Afghanistan and China. In Iran (formerly Persia) the "National Geographic" travelers were told that they needed a police escort through the "Desert of Emptiness." This is where the Polos were attacked by nomads early in their odyssey. They also discovered, as Marco did, in the Yunnan province of China, villagers who consider their gold teeth to be decorative displays, and others who celebrate certain feast days by eating *raw* pork. In the Gansu province the modern day travelers also saw the "Yellow Hat" sect of Tibetan Buddhist monks that marveled Marco. Both groups of travelers also witnessed the Bataks, people of Indonesia that were cannibals. Today only their museums tell this history. The flesh of the human palm was considered the most desired part to consume and was thought to have medicinal properties. If you can obtain copies of these three issues of "National Geographic" you will find fantastic photography and an enchanting account of Marco's life.

Marco was also the first European to learn about Japan, which he called *Cipangu*. He learned of this fantastic island from Chinese merchants and sailors who had traveled there. Marco learned that this island was far east of China and wrote it was "a great island....and the people have gold in very great abundance..." Columbus even wondered if one of the islands he first saw in the distance upon reaching the New World was the fabulous *Cipangu* that Marco Polo wrote about over 200 years before.

Professor John Larner of the University of Glasgow, a leading expert on Marco Polo stated, "Never before or since has any one man given such an immense body of new geographic knowledge to the West." Marco Polo was an expert explorer, navigator and geographer, but was also in many ways a pioneering anthropologist who brought a rich body of knowledge for both East and West worlds to share.

Discovery of the New World
Christopher Columbus (born Cristoforo Columbo)
Columbus was born about 1451 in Genoa, Italy. *Columbus was an exceptionally gifted navigator.* He was so confident and skilled in

Christopher Columbus Monument – UNESCO Building, Paris

R. R. Esposito

nautical navigation that he could brave the deadly Atlantic Ocean and not become lost at sea or literally sail in circles thousands of miles wide. *Navigation was extremely difficult in his day because there was still no way to measure longitude.* Over 100 years later, in the early 1600's, Galileo was the first to measure longitude using the moons of Jupiter as his clock. And even Galileo's method only worked at night and when the sky was clear. Columbus did not have the advantage of Galileo's science and knowledge. Nevertheless his own knowledge, skill and instincts allowed Columbus to successfully cross the formidable Atlantic Ocean with his three small wooden sailing vessels. This successful navigation was itself an amazing accomplishment. *On October 12, 1492 Columbus changed the course of history when he discovered the New World, landing on the island of San Salvador in the Bahamas.* He visited five islands in the Bahamas before he reached Cuba on October 18 and nearby Hispaniola (the island now shared by Haiti and Dominican Republic) on December 6.

On his second voyage in 1493 he discovered the Caribbean island of Dominica, the Leeward Islands, Virgin Islands and Puerto Rico before again arriving at Hispaniola where Columbus had left 40 men from the first voyage. He found all had perished and that "Indians" had destroyed the fort. Columbus established the first New World colony of Santo Domingo on the island of Hispaniola and became the governor of the island. Santo Domingo is now the oldest continuously inhabited city in the Americans. His brother Bartholomew Columbus designed the city in a standard Roman grid fashion.

His third voyage, in 1498, took Columbus to an island with three hills. Columbus named it Trinidad, after the Holy Trinity. Columbus was a very devout Christian and wished to spread Christianity to the new lands he explored. His fleet obtained fresh water and supplies on the south coast of Trinidad, which is less than 10 miles from the mainland of South America, where Venezuela now exists. He sailed close to the coast of Venezuela, discovered its Orinoco River and became *the first European to sight the continent of South America in 1498.* On his fourth voyage in 1502, he discovered the mainland of Central America, Honduras and Panama.

Columbus was not the first human to visit or inhabit the New World. However, he was the first one to bridge two hemispheres and realize the importance of the New World with all its possibilities and almost limitless opportunities. As such, historians also call Columbus the "inventor" of America. After Columbus's return and reports, all of Europe now understood there was a new vast continent. A New World was discovered, unlike the existing world of Europe, with centuries of fixed land ownership rights, religious prosecution and restrictions. He also brought back pineapples and other plants to Europe from the New World *heralding a new exchange of plants and animals between the continents.* Within a century after Columbus's historic trip, New World crops such as, potatoes, maize and tobacco had become common crops in Europe. Like many other great thinkers and pioneers, Columbus died poor and unrecognized for his fantastic achievements on May 20, 1506.

In 1998, a new monument honoring Columbus was erected in New York harbor by the Christopher Columbus Monument Committee (CCMC). CCMC unveiled a dramatic 6-story tall, sail shaped, bronze monument in Liberty State Park on the shore of Jersey City. The spectacular monument was erected permanently in the park, across from the Statue of Liberty and Ellis Islands. The monument called "La Vela di Columbo" ("The Sail of Columbus") is a gift to the United States from the Italian Gino Giannetti and the Italian city of Genoa (the birthplace of Columbus).

As of July 2006, there were 455 monuments to Columbus that were erected throughout the world, and the number increases almost monthly. Most are in North, South and Central America, but many are in Europe as well, including Italy, Spain, France, Germany, Ireland, Portugal and the United Kingdom. These monuments have inscriptions that refer to Columbus in different ways depending on the country's language. Here is a sample list:

Italian: Cristoforo Colombo
English: Christopher Columbus
Spanish (Castilian): Cristóbal Colón
Spanish (Catalan): Cristofor Colom
Portuguese: Cristóvão Colombo
French: Christophe Colomb
German: Christoph Kolumbus
Dutch: Christoffel Columbus

Discovery of the North American Shore
Giovanni Cabotto (John Cabot)

Cabotto was born in Genoa, Italy around 1450 and probably died in the early 1500's, but some say he lived until 1557. Cabotto, who was always accompanied by his son Sebastian on his voyages, reached the coast of Newfoundland in present day Canada on June 24, 1497. He

R. R. Esposito

first landed his ship The Matthew on Cape Breton Island, but thought he had reached the northeast coast of Asia. His discovery was five years after Columbus had reached several South American islands in 1492. *Cabotto sailed under the British flag and subsequently, Britain claimed all of North America* since Cabotto was the first to reach its mainland. During 1498 he sailed from Labrador all the way to Maryland.

Ironically, Christopher Columbus had first requested funding from King Henry VII of England, but was refused and then sought funding from Spain for his famous voyage in 1492. Five years later, in 1497, when Cabotto sought support for a voyage across the Atlantic, King Henry quickly agreed to his voyage.

It is interesting to note that both of these *early heroic explorers were sons of Italy and yet neither sailed for Italy.* There is a very simple explanation. Italy did not exist in the 1400's. Instead, there were several separate competing states that made up that boot shaped peninsula we now call Italy. The great Italian city-states of that time were Milan, Florence, Venice, the Papal States and Naples. The famed Renaissance author Niccolo Machiavelli, in his political analysis "The Discourses" places fault on the Church for Italy's inability to unify. He wrote:

> ...the church has kept and still keeps this country divided. Surely no country was ever happy or unified until it was all under the rule of a single republic or a single prince, as is the case with France and Spain. And the reason that Italy is not in the same situation and is not ruled by a single republic or a single prince is the church alone. Though located in Italy and holding temporal power in it, she has had neither the strength nor the ability to subjugate the Italian tyrants and become the ruler; on the other hand, when threatened with the loss of her temporal dominions, she has not been so weak as to be unable to bring in some foreign power to defend her from any Italian lord who had become too strong. We know this well from long experience, as when by means of Charlemagne she drove out the Longobards who had become the rulers of nearly all of Italy, or when in our own day she deprived the Venetians of power through the aid of France. Later she drove the French out through the aid of the Swiss. Thus, having lacked the strength to conquer Italy, and having refused to let others conquer her, the church has seen to it that the country cannot be dominated by a single ruler but has had many princes and lords instead.

Also, the Pope ruled the powerfully influential Papal States in central Italy (Rome and surrounding areas) and the Church probably did not embrace exploration to the "end of the world." New discoveries, peoples and cultures might have caused some contradictions with tradition and Church beliefs or created competitive spiritual organizations.

Furthermore, these city-states were basking in the light of the Italian Renaissance. Every aspect of intellectual thought, as well as commerce and trade were at a global zenith. These marvelous and progressive activities may have turned the Italians inward, as they focused on their own new revolutionary arts and sciences

It was not until 1870 that Giuseppe Garibaldi, the "George Washington of Italy," united these separate Italian city-states into the modern nation of Italy. The Vatican became a separate entity as a result of a treaty with Italy. Had Italy been a nation state in the 1400's, these explorers would most likely have sailed for their homeland and Americans would all be speaking Italian today. Perhaps the non-Italian immigrants arriving through Ellis Island would have had their names changed to include *more* vowels.

America's Name & Exploration of South America
Amerigo Vespucci (Americus Vespucius - Latin spelling)

Italians receive the distinction of discovering America and also for naming America, which is named after the Italian navigator and explorer Amerigo Vespucci. He was born in Florence, Italy, in 1454 and died in Spain on February 22, 1512. You may correctly ask why our continent and nation was not named after Christopher Columbus the discoverer. The name "America" is derived from Amerigo, who was incorrectly identified as the discoverer of the New World by a German cartographer, named Martin Waldseemüller. Vespucci made at least two voyages to the New World with Spanish (1499-1500) and Portuguese (1501-1502) expeditions. On his first voyage in 1499, Vespucci traveled with Alonso de Ojeda and discovered the mouth of the Amazon River and South America. This trip was actually after the earlier trips by Columbus in 1492, 1493 and 1498. However, Vespucci was the *first to set foot on the mainland of South America in 1499*. Columbus, on his 3rd voyage, was the *first to sight the mainland in 1498*, but did not explore Central America until his 4th voyage in 1502. To his credit, it was *Vespucci, not Columbus, who was the first to realize that he was exploring new continents*, not islands near China or India. He came to this realization after his second voyage in 1502. In all he had explored 6000 miles along the coast of South America. Waldseemüller suggested in his 1507 booklet "Cosmographiae Introductio" that the New World be named "Amerigo" after its discoverer. Waldseemüller also printed a map of South America calling it "America" for the first time. His writings explain how he derived the name "America" from "Amerigo the discoverer . . . as if it were the land of Americus or America." Later the name "America" was also applied to North America. Historians note that Waldseemüller probably never heard of Columbus or his travels. Had Waldseemüller known of Columbus, we probably would be living in the "United States of Columbia" and not "America" and the continents would then have been named "North Columbia" and "South Columbia." America's founders did, however, provide a correction, when they named the U.S. capital the District of Columbia.

Exploration of North American East Coast and Discovery of New York Harbor and Hudson River
Giovanni da Verrazzano

Giovanni da Verrazzano (or Verrazano) was born about 1485 near Florence and died about 1528. This Italian navigator and explorer lived in Italy and sailed for France. In 1524, Verrazzano landed at what is now present-day North Carolina. He then sailed north as far as Newfoundland. His journals described northeastern North America including the New York harbor area and Narragansett Bay. *Verrazzano was the first to prove that the land was a New World and not part of Asia.* The Verrazzano Bridge, which spans over the Hudson River in New York State, is named after this explorer. Opened in 1964, the total length of the Verrazzano Bridge in New York City makes it the longest suspension bridge in the United States.

Although the Hudson River in New York State is named after Henry Hudson, he reached New York in 1609 almost 85 years *after Verrazzano discovered New York harbor and the Hudson River.* Verrazzano also named the New York City area Rhode Island, which eventually became the name of the nearby state. (*Rhode* is a male Greek mythological figure that Verrazzano was obviously familiar with. In Greek mythology, the god and goddess of the sea, Poseidon and Amphitrite, married and their four children were Albion, Benthesicyme, Rhode and Triton. Rhode is sometimes spelled

Rhodos.)
   Verrazzano died after a second voyage in 1528. It is believed that he was killed and eaten by cannibals.

Largest Suspension Bridges in US

Name & Location	Total Length(ft.)	Main Span Length(ft.)	Height above Water(ft.)
Verrazzano Brooklyn-Staten Island in New York City	13,200	4,260	228
Golden Gate San Francisco, CA	9,266	4,200	220

Magellan's Companion and Historian
Antonio Pigafetta

   Like Marco Polo who documented his travels to China, Antonio Pigafetta documented Magellan's historic voyage that circumvented the globe. Ferdinand Magellan (c.1480-1521) was a Portuguese captain who launched a Spanish expedition to find a new route to the Spice Islands, north of Australia. During his voyage, Magellan discovered the passage between the Atlantic and Pacific Oceans at the tip of South America, which became known as the Straits of Magellan. He and his crew became the first Europeans to sail into the "new" ocean, which Magellan named "Pacific," meaning peaceful, because it appeared calm compared to the storms they weathered in the Atlantic Ocean. Actually, the Straits of Magellan and the Pacific Ocean can be just as fierce and challenging as the Atlantic Ocean, but Magellan's introduction to this body of water was relatively gentle. It took Magellan's crew three courageous years to circumnavigate the globe, which can now be accomplished in a few hours by NASA's Space Shuttle.

   Antonio Pigafetta was a navigator and historian, born in Vicenza, Italy around 1491. Due to his intelligence and bravery Pigafetta won the respect and trust of Magellan. Together they survived storms, attempted mutinies, fights between Portuguese and Spanish crew and near starvation. At times, they were forced to eat rats, ox hides and sawdust with worms. Magellan, however, did not survive the entire voyage and died in a conflict with natives on the Philippine Islands.

After Magellan's death, Pigafetta was recognized by the crew as their new leader for the return trip to Europe. Pigafetta was one of only several remaining survivors to be granted an audience with King Charles I. Pigafetta also met with King Frances I, and this historic meeting convinced Francis I to initiate France's entry into global exploration. Pigafetta was also inducted as a Knight of Rhodes.

Pigafetta's diary has enormous historic value, since it recounted the entire journey and included several illustrations depicting the islands and the coasts he encountered. The estimations and routes detailed in Pigafetta's manuscript proved the spherical shape of the Earth and also its rotation. His signed, 187-page manuscript, bound between wooded covers, was entitled "Account of the First Voyage Around the World -- Logbook" and was dated 1522. Sadly, Pigafetta, who survived the challenges of sailing around the globe, did not live a very long life after his return and died somewhere between 1526 and 1534.

In his diary Pigafetta detailed the hardships that were endured by the crew. Here is a passage that portraits their food shortages: "that thing we ate could no longer be called bread, for it was a sort of dust mixed with worms that had eaten up all the remaining substances and gave off a terrible stench due to its being soaked in mice urine. The water we were forced to drink was equally putrid and stinking; we even had to eat the hide of the rigging, but it had to be previously left to soak for four or five days. A rat would be sold for 30 ducats. Most men lay exhausted and many of them died. However, this huge sea that must have drawn deep sighs from Drake, remained merciful to us, so we named it Pacific." However, the rather disgusting remnants of food the crew consumed now pale in comparison to the list of bizarre things contestants regularly ingest on reality TV shows, such as "Fear Factor."

Explorer and Founder of the State of Illinois, U.S.
Enrico Tonti (aka Henry Di Tonti)

Tonti was born in Gaeta, south of Rome, in 1647 and moved to France as a youth when his family moved there. He explored the central U.S. for France and ultimately founded the state of Illinois in 1680. He also helped to establish the city of New Orleans in Louisiana and the first French settlement in Arkansas in 1683. Tontitown in Arkansas is named in his honor.

He did all this with one hand, since a metal hook replaced the hand blown off by a grenade in a war between France and Spain. His father, Lorenzo Tonti, was an Italian financier who invented the world's first life insurance system, still called the *tontine system* in honor of Tonti. (Refer to the "Economics, Finance and Business" chapter in this book for more on Lorenzo Tonti.)

Explorer and Founder of the City of Detroit, Michigan, U.S.
Alfonso Tonti (aka Alfonso Tonty)

Alfonso was the brother of Enrico Tonti who founded the state of Illinois. An explorer as his brother was, Alfonso founded the City of Detroit in 1704 and was the colonial governor for 12 years.

First Dirigible Flight over the North Pole
Umberto Nobile

Nobile was born in Lauro, Italy on January 24, 1885 and died July 29, 1978. He was an aeronautical engineer who flew over the North Pole with Roald Amundsen and Lincoln Ellsworth. Nobile was the pilot of their historic dirigible the "Norge." They flew 2,700 miles (4,300-kilometers) from Spitsbergen, Norway to Alaska. Nobile designed the "Norge," as well as another dirigible the "Italia." They flew over the pole on May 12, 1926.

Nobile was also Dean of Aeronautics at Lewis Holy Name School of Aeronautics, Lockport, Ill. from 1939 to 1942 and returned to Italy in 1943. He wrote a book about his explorations called "My Polar Flights."

The first plane that flew over the North Pole was piloted by Floyd Bennett who traveled with Richard E. Byrd on May 9, 1926, only two days before Nobile's flight in his dirigible.

Egyptian Archeology
Giovanni Battista Belzoni

Discovered the Tomb of King Seti I and Seven other Tombs

The Italian hydraulic engineer, explorer and archaeologist, Giovanni Battista Belzoni, was born on November 15, 1778 in Padua, Italy. He made significant contributions to archeology and Egyptology.

He was the first person to understand the Nile's flood patterns in the Valley of the Kings and realized that many tombs were under its flood debris, untouched since antiquity. In 1817, Belzoni discovered the tomb of Egyptian King Seti I. In the tomb, Belzoni found the richly ornate alabaster sarcophagus of this Pharaoh and fortunately documented all of his findings carefully, since much has now been destroyed. Born in 1291 BC, King Seti I lived a brief life and died at the age of 13 in 1278 BC.

Belzoni subsequently discovered seven more tombs in the Valley of the Kings. Subsequent to Belzoni's celebrated discoveries, other explorers entered many other tombs in the Valley of the Kings including the tombs of King Tut (Tutankhamen) in 1922 and the Rameses Pharaohs in later decades.

First to Enter the Temples of Abu Simbel

Belzoni was also the first man since antiquity to enter the Temples of Abu Simbel, after he and his workers freed them from the centuries of sand that covered them. Belzoni may have contributed to the actual labor since he was known for his incredible strength. As a youth he performed as a strongman in a circus where he also displayed his hydraulic inventions.

First to Enter the Great Pyramid of Khafre

In 1818, Belzoni became the first modern man to find the entrance and enter into the Khafre pyramid in Giza. As a result of this pyramid's geographic elevation it stands taller than any other. However, it is actually 10 meters shorter than the Great Pyramid built by Khufu, the father of Khafre. Apparently, Khafre was a good son and wanted his father's pyramid to remain the largest. The son should not be faulted because the terrain's height makes his pyramid *appear* taller than his father's pyramid. Some things never change. This story reminds this author of how his own two sons would stand as straight as possible to declare that they are finally taller than their father. Astute parents need to be mindful of the terrain to prevent from being unfairly dwarfed by their own prodigy. Pyramid building appears to be the same game, only on a much grander scale. Incidentally, the smallest pyramid is that of Menkaura, son of Khafre. And ironically all three pyramids were finished after the death of each king for whom they were built.

After Belzoni had made his many contributions to archeology in Egypt, he set off to explore Timbuktu in Africa. However, he unfortunately contracted severe dysentery and died on December 3, 1823 in the City of Gato.

European Space Agency – Director and Astronauts
Antonio Rodotà

Mr. Antonio Rodotà had over 30 years of leadership experience in the Italian electronics and aerospace industries before becoming the Director of the European Space Agency (1997-2003). In 1965, he was also the Italian delegate to NATO. Mr. Rodotà has also been a member of the High-performance Computer Group in the Italian Ministry of Research. Sadly he passed away in February 2006 at the age of 70.

Italian astronauts have also led space exploration in the 20th and 21st centuries. In 2001, Umberto Guidoni was the first European astronaut to visit the International Space Station. On April 24, 2001, Umberto Guidoni set foot on the International Space Station and was greeted via satellite communication by the European Union's Commission then President, Romano Prodi, as well as the then Director of the European Space Agency, Antonio Rodotà, both fellow Italians. Also, significant to note, the European Space Agency's first group of astronauts (1998) included three Italians out of the seven astronauts in the group. These astronauts are Umberto Guidoni, Paolo Nespoli and Roberto Vittori.

Mytilini (Mytilene), Greek City
Francesco Gattelusio

Well known for its scenic beaches and other natural beauties, Mytilini is the capital of the island of Lesvos (Lesbos), the third largest of the Greek islands. It was the homeland of several famous Greek philosophers and lyric poets, such as Sappho, Alcaeus and Pittakos. The city reached its height of prosperity in the early 6th century BC. During the Byzantine period, Mytilini suffered a series of raids, as was the fate of many Greek islands in the Aegean Sea at that time. The city and island was conquered and ruled after successive attacks by Persians, Athenians, Macedonians, Ptolemies and Romans. As a result of these conflicts and the city's overall instability, the population declined precipitously. Finally, in 1354, Francesco Gattelusio an adventurer from Genoa, Italy captured the city. The city and island experienced a second period of peace and prosperity under the rule of the Gattelusio family, yet retained its Byzantine traditions. For over

100 years until 1462, the benevolent Gattelusio family ruled peacefully and the city benefited in many ways. The fortress-castle built by Francesco Gattelusio in 1373 is one of the largest and best preserved in Greece. The city was plagued by more attacks from outsiders and succumbed to Turkish rule in 1462. The island of Lesvos was finally liberated and returned to Greece in 1913. Today, the fond memories of the Gattelusio family are still very much alive on this beautiful Greek island.

೫

Chapter IX

FASHION

"Stay small to remain great."
- the motto of Guccio Gucci -

Aurora Pens

Since 1919, Aurora is the oldest and most acclaimed Italian manufacturer of prestige writing instruments. They offer high fashion design with 14kt and 18kt solid gold writing nibs. Aurora has many beautiful pens and many models to choose from. Their handcrafted pens represent the highest quality writing instruments. The Optima model is their hallmark pen. Aurora also makes custom writing instruments for the very wealthy, with price tags as high as $10,000!

Canali

Two brothers, Giovanni and Giacomo Canali, who were dedicated to the manufacturing of high quality clothing, founded Canali in 1934. With the combined efforts of the next generation of Canali family tailors, sales grew significantly in the 1950's, and by the 1970's they were an international fashion company. Although their fashions can be purchased in over 1000 locations throughout the globe, their clothing is still all handmade in Italy and represents the highest quality. Canali headquarters is located in Sovico, near Milan, one of the most important fashion capitals of the world.

Dolce & Gabbana

Domenico Dolce was born September 13, 1958 in the village of Polizzi Generosa near Palermo, Sicily. His partner Stefano Gabbana was born November 14, 1962 in Venice. Dolce studied fashion design in Sicily and worked at his family's clothing factory, which is also located in Sicily. Gabbana studied graphic design and received no formal fashion education. The two men met in 1980 and started their own business in 1982, which by 1986 had won international acclaim. By 1989, they already opened their first boutique in Japan. Their company crafts men's and women's products, which include everything from neckties to lingerie. Their high standards in fashion earned them the coveted Woolmark Award in 1990.

Fendi

The luxury fashion firm of Fendi was established in 1925 by the husband and wife team of Edoardo and Adele Fendi. Initially, they opened a small workshop and sold leather and fur merchandise on Via del Plebiscito in the center of Rome. Later, as the business grew, they opened a shop on Via Piave in Rome in 1932. In the mid-1900's their five daughters Paola, Carla, Anna, Franca and Alda joined the family business and helped to make it an international success, using the double "F" logo (one is inverted) that is so well know today. Today, there are five Fendi shops that sell leather goods, fur, shoes and luggage on Via Borgognona in Rome alone. Around 1965, the president of Bloomingdale's, Marvin Traub, discovered Fendi's exquisite leather goods and introduced them in his stores in the United States. Fendi now has shops all over the world, and a large Fendi shop is located on New York's prestigious Fifth Avenue. Fendi also makes ready-to-wear clothing lines, such as "Fendissime," and sells perfumes as well.

Fila

With its corporate headquarters in Biella, Italy, Fila is a leading designer of active-wear, casual-wear, sportswear and athletic footwear. They offer well-styled, high quality clothing and professional running shoes. The winner of the 1999 Boston Marathon, Joseph Chebet, wore their running shoe, the "Fila Racer." This shoe, like Fila's other racer, "Adrenaline," represents the most highly engineered running equipment in the world. Fila offers clothing and accessories for many different sporting activities.

Gianfranco Ferre

Gianfranco Ferre was born in Legnano in 1944. Ferre has produced highly successful labels for men's wear, women fragrances and accessories. He became the artistic director of the House of Christian Dior in Paris in 1989.

Ferre's awards are numerous and easily identifiable in the available research material. These are listed below to illustrate his many accomplishments and some of the diverse awards that exist in the fashion industry.

- October 1982 "Occhio d'oro" award for the Spring/Summer 1983 women's collection
- March 1983 "Occhio d'oro" award for the Fall/Winter 1983-84 women's collection
- October 1984 "Occhio d'oro" award for the Spring/Summer 1985 women's collection
- March 1985 "Modepreis" award as best designer of the year for women's fashion, in Munich
- June 1985 "Cutty Sark Men's Fashion Award" as best designer of the year for men's fashion, in New York
- December 1985 Gold medal of civic merit from the Mayor of Milan
- January 1986 Honor of "Commendatore dell'Ordine al Merito della Republica Italiana" conferred by the President of the Italian Republic
- March 1986 "Occhio d'oro" award for the Fall/Winter 1986-87 women's collection
- March 1987 "Occhio d'oro" award for the Fall/Winter 1987-88 women's collection
- July 1989 "De d'or" for the first Christian Dior Haute Couture collection, in Paris
- October 1989 "Occhio d'oro" award as designer of the year in Italian fashion
- November 1989 Certificate of civic merit from his home town of Legnano, conferred by the Mayor
- December 1989 "Milanese dell'anno" (Milanese of the Year) award, in Milan
- March 1990 "I Grandi Protagonisti" award from the Italian Fur Association, in Milan

- October 1990 European "Lorenzo il Magnifico" award, in Florence
- June 1991 "Il Fiorino d'oro" awarded by the city of Florence
- December 1992 "Diva-Wollsiegel" trophy awarded for his great talent, in Vienna
- May 1993 "Senior Adviser" appointed for his artistic talent, in Beijing by the China Tiangong Clothing Science & Technological Development Group and the National Garments Research
- June 1993 "Pitti Immagine Uomo" presented by the mayor of Florence for his achievements in men's fashion
- November 1994 "Maschera d'oro" presented by the mayor of Campione d'Italia for his creative capability

Giorgio Armani

Giorgio Armani was born on July 11, 1934, in Piacenza, just south of Milan. He established his own men's label in 1974 and then expanded to women's wear. His sister Rosanna Armani headed the communication functions of the company. He is known for elegant but comfortable clothing. He has been bestowed many awards, most notably, the Neiman-Marcus Award (1979), and the CFDA International Award (1983). In the United States, Armani products are sold at over 2,000 locations, including the ultra posh Madison Avenue showroom in midtown Manhattan. When someone is seen "wearing an Armani suit," it is a clear expression of status.

Gucci

The Gucci family tradition of crafting beautiful luxury leather products began in 1930 when Guccio Gucci opened the first store in Florence. Guccio Gucci founded the company and his successors were all of his sons: Aldo, Ugo, Vasco and Rodolfo. They expanded the business to include new stores in Florence, Rome and Milan. Aldo and Rodolfo opened the first international Gucci shop in New York. Later, shops were opened in London, Palm Beach, Paris, Beverly Hills and Tokyo. In 1989, Rodolfo's son, Mauritzio Gucci, became President of the company. The family's great success is based upon their intense desire to produce only the highest quality leather goods. The company's founder Guccio Gucci conceived the Gucci motto, "Stay small to remain great."

Prada

Miuccia Prada founded Prada and designs fashions that are known for great style, yet remain comfortable to wear. In the 1980's, when Miuccia Prada was a political science and theatrical major, she decided to take over her grandfather's leather goods business. She transformed his business into a leading international fashion firm. Prada successfully launched a collection of women's clothing in 1988 and four years later, in 1992, introduced a second collection called Miu Miu. Not to rest on her laurels, Miuccia Prada launched her men's collection in 1994. Miuccia, who learned about fine fabrics from her mother, offers elegance and practicality to the world. Her great fashion vision and business skills have won her many international awards including: International Award from the CFDA (1994); VH1 Fashion Award for Designer of the Year (1994); VH1 Fashion Award for Best Second Collection for Miu Miu (1996).

Salvatore Ferragamo

Salvatore Ferragamo was an early fashion pioneer who was crafting luxury shoes in the 1920's. He provided footwear for the famous in Hollywood. Ferragamo was born in Bonito, near Naples. He was one of 14 children in a peasant family and knew that he wanted to design shoes when he was only nine years old.

Ferragamo made cowboy boots and Roman sandals for the Cecil B. de Mille epic movies. He was known as the "Shoemaker to the Stars." Ferragamo studied the anatomy of the foot and designed high fashion that was also comfortable. His wife continued his business after he died in 1960, and the business expanded to include clothing.

Italian shoes are luxury items known around the world. These include: Ferragamo, Calzature Santoni, Fendi, Prada, Gucci, Versace, Fratelli Rossett, Sergio Rossi and Bruno Magli. In the United States, Bruno Magli became a household word as a result of the murder trail of the famous football player O.J. Simpson. Bruno Magli shoeprints were left behind at the murder scene of Simpson's wife, Nicole Brown Simpson. It was proven that her husband, O.J., owned a pair of these unique luxury shoes the same size as the shoeprints found at the murder scene. In addition to this, there was a great deal of other evidence including much blood and DNA evidence. However, clever lawyers and a jury sympathetic to O.J., a football legend, let him freely walk out of the courtroom in his Bruno Magli shoes.

Valentino

The famous "V" logo of Valentino is internationally known. Valentino Garavani was born in Voghera, north of Milan on May 11, 1932. He opened his own shop in Rome in the 1960's in Via Condotti. His international debut took place in 1962 in Florence. He later partnered with Giammetti whose entrepreneurial genius allowed Valentino to expand his business. *He designed the lace mini-dress that Jacqueline Kennedy wore for her marriage to Aristotle Onassis.* Valentino went on to open boutiques in both Rome and Milan. In 1978, he started a perfume line in Paris. Later, he opened boutiques in the USA and Japan.

Versace

Gianni Versace was known as the *Prince of Fashion*, a title well deserved when one considers his accomplishments and the prestigious awards he received for revolutionizing the fashion industry. Gianni Versace was born in Reggio, Calabria on December 2, 1946. He started working in 1972 as a fashion designer in Milan, and in 1975 he presented his first leather collection for Complice. In 1982, Versace was awarded the coveted "L'Occhio d'Oro" for the best fashion designer of the Fall-Winter 1982-1983 season for women. In 1986, the President of the Italian Republic Francesco Cossiga awarded Versace with the "Commendatore della Repubblica Italiana." That same year he staged major shows in Chicago and Paris, and produced opera costumes for several international opera houses in Paris and Brussels. In 1987, Versace designed the costumes for "Leda and the Swan" at the famous La Scala opera house and also for several operas in Russia. That year he was awarded the "Maschera D'Argento" prize for his theater work. In 1993, the Council of Fashion Designers of America awarded Versace the "American Fashion Oscar" award. Versace also produced costumes for the Kennedy Center for the Performing Arts in Washington D.C. and the Metropolitan Opera House in New York. The master of art and fashion was tragically murdered in his South Beach home in Miami, Florida on July 23, 1997. Gianni's younger sister, Donatella Versace, continues his fashion empire, and she is currently designing new styles for the new millennium.

Zegna

Ermengildo Zegna men's clothing is internationally known for their harmonious blend of innovation and tradition. Zegna crafts formalwear, sportswear, outerwear, knitwear, leather goods, loungewear and other accessories. All of their formal garment lines are hand finished and represent the highest quality products. Ermengildo Zegna is known for his dedication to his hometown of Trivero, Italy. Ermengildo Zegna was an early environmentalist, and in the 1930's he supported the reforestation of the slopes of Mt. Rubello overlooking Trivero. He promoted the planting of hundreds of thousands of conifers and created a road, the Panoramica Zegna, to provide public access to the reclaimed slopes. He also developed Oasi Zegna, a unique wilderness preserve in the mountainous Italian northwestern pre-Alps. Ermengildo Zegna is also the exclusive sponsor of the Environmental Media Awards. To his credit, he made protecting the environment fashionable by focusing media attention on this important cause.

Chapter X

LANGUAGE & LITERATURE

"Love conquers all." ("Omnia vinci amore.")
- Roman poet Virgil from his *Eclogue* -

"Aeneid" (first national epic)
Virgil (aka Vergil)

Virgil was born near Muntua, Italy in 70 BC and died in 19 BC. His full name was Publius Vergilius Maro. He was a Roman poet, who lived during the time of Caesar Augustus, and dominated Latin literature in its golden age. Virgil wrote many e*clogues*, *bucolics* and g*eorgics*, but "Aeneid" (12 volumes), about the adventures of a Trojan warrior Aeneas, is his greatest work. Virgil's "Aeneid" was the *first successful national epic* written in the history of world literature. In "Aeneid," Virgil recounts the story of the Trojan horse, which concealed Greek warriors within the hollow of the large wooden beast that was presented as a gift to the city of Troy. The famous saying, "be wary of Greeks bearing gifts" comes from "Aeneid"- the warrior Aeneas states, "I am wary of Greeks, even bearing gifts." ("Timeo Danaos et dona ferentis.")

Virgil is credited for being the first to write, "Love conquers all, let us give in to love," which appears in one of his "Eclogues." Virgil was also the first to write that *time flys* when he penned, *"But meanwhile it is flying, irretrievable time is flying*," from one of his *georgics*. Some of the poetry used in Virgil's works became the Latin mottoes for the Great Seal of the United States, which appear on the US one dollar bill. (Refer to the chapter on "American Government" for more on Virgil.)

Autobiography
Girolamo Cardano,
Benvenuto Cellini,
St. Augustine

The modern autobiography was first created during the Italian Renaissance in the 16th century by two very famous and accomplished thinkers. The famous sculptor and goldsmith, Benvenuto Cellini, wrote his autobiography from 1558 to 1562, which was published in 1728. Girolamo Cardano (aka Jerome Cardan), physician and famous mathematician, wrote "Book of My Life" ("De propria vita") in 1575. These works were very unique. So much so, that the word *autobiography* did not become part of general English usage until the beginning of the 19th century.

The very first known autobiography was written by St. Augustine, bishop of the Christian church in the city of Hippo, located in the Roman Empire in Arab North Africa. Hippo is now known as the city of Annaba in Algeria. St. Augustine's autobiographical work entitled "Confessions" (399 AD) documents his childhood, education, philosophy and conversion to Christianity. He was the first to use the word *I* as we understand it today. In "Confessions," St. Augustine wrote "I carried inside me a cut and bleeding soul, and how to get rid of it I just didn't know. I sought every pleasure- the countryside, sports, fooling around, the peace of the garden, friends and good company, sex, reading. My soul floundered in the void- and came back upon me. For where could my heart flee from my heart? Where could I escape from myself?"

St. Augustine was born in Hippo near ancient Carthage on November 11th, 354 AD, but was completely romanized and lived much of his adult life in Italy, specifically in Milan and Rome. He was greatly influenced by the Roman poet Virgil, and in particular his literary masterpiece entitled "Aeneid." St. Augustine was baptized in Milan in 387 AD and taught there as well. He died in 430 AD. Amazingly, for over a thousand years, no other autobiographies were written until the works of Cellini and Cardano during the Italian Renaissance.

"The Betrothed"
Alessandro Manzoni

Manzoni was born in Milan, Italy in 1785 and died on May 22, 1873. He was a novelist and poet and his monumental religious composition "The Betrothed" (3 volumes) is considered a literary masterpiece. The operatic composer Giuseppe Verdi deeply admired Manzoni's works and wrote the opera "Requiem" for Manzoni. It was performed for the first time on the first anniversary of Manzoni's death, May 22, 1786.

"Divine Comedy"
Dante Alighieri

Dante was born in Florence somewhere between May 15 and June 15, 1265, to an aristocratic family. Dante is considered one of the greatest of Western literary geniuses, the others being Boccaccio, Petrarca, Shakespeare and Goethe. The author Henry James has called Dante the "greatest of literary artists." T.S. Eliot considered the last canto of the "Divine Comedy" to be "the highest point that poetry has reached or ever can reach." Dante was the first to write in Italian instead of Latin, which greatly influenced future European literature. Dante wrote in the Tuscan dialect of his time. His massive poem, "The Divine Comedy," chronicles Dante's trip through hell, purgatory and heaven. Dante creates almost 600 characters in this epic work. Virgil, the Roman poet, is Dante's guide through purgatory and hell, and Beatrice guides the poet through heaven. Beatrice is actually someone Dante met, when he was only 9 years old. He immediately fell in love with her. The poet had a love for her throughout his entire life, even though when they met only a few words were exchanged. She was most likely a woman named Beatrice Portinari. The poem is filled with hundreds of characters and many of the names are actual people that Dante knew. Dante originally entitled his poem, simply "Comedy" because it is a satirical work and contains many of his contemporaries who receive poetic justice in the novel. The word "divine" was added sometime in the 16th century, about 200 years after his death. *The work was a major departure for European literature and poetry because it was satirical in nature.* It is the first major piece of European literature that employed satire. Dante's "Divine Comedy" is also the source of this famous quote *"Abandon all hope, you who enter here,"* which quite often appears in pubs and bars with unsavory ambiance. Dante died on September 14, 1321 and his remains rest in a tomb in Ravenna, the town where he died.

Encyclopedia
Marcus Terentius Varro

The ancient Greeks wrote about many subjects but did not create encyclopedias in the modern sense. They wrote philosophical treatises, which were based upon conceiving knowledge within a philosophical mental model. The Romans, known for their very practical approach to the world, created the first multi-disciplinary knowledge-based encyclopedias. Varro who lived from 116 BC to about 21 BC is credited for its invention and is the author of over 620 works. His studies included medicine, music, grammar, astronomy, history, architecture and other subjects. Unfortunately, the only surviving works of his is a three volume set on farming entitled "De re rustica libri III" and parts of a 25-volume work, "On the Latin Language."

Another very early encyclopedia comes from Pliny the Elder, a Roman naturalist, who was born about 23 AD and died 79 AD. He wrote 37 volumes entitled "Historia Naturalis" covering many subjects including anthropology, botany, geography, mineralogy and zoology.

The famous Chinese encyclopedia of 1000 volumes did not appear until much later in 984 AD. Varro also predates Isidore of Seville (560 AD to 636 AD), the Spanish Saint who wrote an early encyclopedia call "Etymologies."

Again in 1522, the Italian Alessandro Alessandri (1461-1523) wrote "Dies Geniales" a non-sequential encyclopedia.

Fairy Tales

Italian authors have greatly influenced the evolution of European fairy tales, much more so than the Brothers Grimm (Germany), Charles Perrault (France), or Hans Christian Andersen (Denmark). In 1956, Italo Calvino's famous literary collection "Italian Folktales" (translated into English by George Martin) offered a comprehensive anthology of Italian fairy tales written in the 16ᵗʰ century. *Italian* authors like Basile, Boccaccio and Straparola wrote many of the original fairy tales that the world now tells its children, such as "Sleeping Beauty," "Cinderella," "Puss in Boots," "Pinocchio," "Rapunzel," "Red Riding Hood," and many others. In addition to authoring "Puss in Boots," Straparola is credited for publishing the first European collection of fairy tales ("Nights of Straparola") in 1550. In 1697, the Frenchman Charles Perrault published "Tales of Time Passed" and documented European fairy tales, almost 150 years *after* Straparola.

"Cinderella," "Rapunzel," "Sleeping Beauty," "Snow White"
Giovanni Battista Basile

Basile was born in Naples around 1575 and died on February 23, 1632. He had a checkered life as soldier, public official, poet and short-story writer. He wrote "Il Pentamerone" ("The Tale of Tales") which was a fantastic anthology of 50 folk tales written in the Neapolitan dialect. He creatively recorded and embellished upon centuries of Neapolitan and other Italian stories that were passed along in an oral tradition. This became an important source of inspiration for other European writers who followed.

"Cinderella"

"La Gatta Cenerentola" is one of the many stories in Basile's famous work "Il Pentamerone," which was published posthumously in 1634 or 1637. This is the earliest European version of the Cinderella story. The title "La Gatta Cenerentola" translated into English means "the cinder cat." The word *Cenerentola* is actually a combination of the Italian word for *cinder* followed by a feminine endearment suffix (*..tola*). The title implies a somewhat poor or unfortunate one by its association with cinders. The leading character in this Italian story is named Zezolla. Later European versions took the Italian title name, *Cenerentola,* and Anglicized it into *Cinderella*, which remains true to the original Italian meaning of cinders. In Basile's story, Zezolla (Cinderella) has an evil stepmother and stepsisters who make her work constantly and cook by the fireplace. She is metaphorically the *cinder cat*, as the title "La Gatta Cenerentola" implies.

Zezolla's father returns from traveling and gives fine gifts to his daughters except for Zezolla who receives a date tree, spade and a watering can. She lovingly tends the tree unaware that it has magical properties since it is from the "fairies of Sardinia." The tree grows rapidly and grants her wishes. As a result of her wishes she receives clothes, a white horse and many attendants. She goes to a social ball and loses a shoe that slipped from her foot as she fled at midnight. A prince, who admires Zezolla at the ball, finds the shoe and later discovers that only her foot fits into the shoe. The story ends with a happy ending when he marries her. The great operatic composer, Rossini wrote 39 operas, including one called "Cenerentola" ("Cinderella").

(Note: An older version of an unfortunate girl existed in China where a Chinese Cinderella gets her wish from magic fish bones. The story's scribe, Tuan Ch'eng Shih, implies that the story is older than his recording of it in 850 AD. Yeh-hsien is the Chinese Cinderella whose small foot, from being traditionally bound, is the only foot that fits the slipper).

"Petrosinella" or "Rapunzel"

The earliest version of this story was entitled "Petrosinella" and was written by Basile in 1632 and published again in his anthology, "Il Pentamerone" (1637). The heroine in his story was Petrosinella, a name derived from the Italian word "petrosine," a kind of parsley. In France, sixty years later (1697), Charlotte Rose de Caumont de la Force published her version of Basile's story and called it "Persinette." This French version was later translated into German by J. C. F. Schulz who changed the name of the heroine and story title to "Rapunzel." Schultz's story was later copied by the Grimm Brothers.

"Sleeping Beauty"

Basile's "Il Pentamerone" also contains the earliest version of the story of "Sleeping Beauty." In his story entitled "Sun, Moon and Talia"(Day 5, Tale 5), wise men forewarn a powerful king that his daughter is in danger of a poisonous flax splinter. He banishes all flax, but his daughter, Talia, still finds a spinning wheel and flax. She falls lifeless from the prick of a thorn beneath her fingernail. She is later awakened by a child she gave birth to while asleep. In the end, she lives happily with the nobleman who is also the father of her two children, named Sun and Moon. Interestingly, Basile named the children in his stories after objects in the sky long before modern Rock music stars and the Hollywood elite.

Charles Perrault (France) was influenced by Basile's original story and based his later story entitled "Sleeping Beauty" (1697) on "Sun, Moon and Talia" (1636). Later the Grimms (Germany) wrote "Briar Rose" which is simply another version of these earlier stories. Some say that Basile may have been inspired to write his original tale by an ancient story called "Perceforest" related to the mythical King Arthur during the Dark Ages.

"Snow White"
The oldest written version of this story is Basile's "The Young Slave," which is also published in his collection, "Il Pentamerone." There may have been an earlier Portuguese tale that existed in the oral tradition of storytelling. However, it was Basile's written story that inspired and propagated to other literature, for example, the Grimms' story of "Snow White."

"The Adventures of Pinocchio" ("Le Avventure Di Pinoccio")
Carlo Collodi
Collodi was born in Florence in 1826 and died there as well on October 26, 1890. The name "Collodi" is actually a pseudonym for the author's real name, Carlo Lorenzini. He took the name "Collodi" from the name of the town where his mother was born. He also had a colorful and checkered past. Collodi joined a seminary as a young man and later became involved with the movement for Italian national unification. He was a journalist in support of Italian independence and in 1848 founded the satirical journals "Il Lampione," and "La Scaramuccia." Collodi also wrote comedies and was a newspaper editor.

The first chapter of "The Adventures of Pinocchio" appeared in the "Giornale dei Bambini" in 1881 and was first translated into English in 1892 by M. A. Murray. Filmmakers, including Walt Disney, animated the story and now children throughout the world know "Pinocchio." It was in July 2001 that this classic story was reborn again in the high-tech movie version by Steven Spielberg, entitled "A.I. - Artificial Intelligence."

"Puss-In-Boots"
Gianfrancesco Straparola
(or Giovanni Francesco Straparola)
Straparola was born about 1480 in Caravaggio, Italy and died in 1557. In his story, "The Delightful Nights" ("Piacevole notti"), which

was published in Venice in 1553, a clever cat outwits the king to obtain riches for the cat's master (in Night 2, Fable 1). The story appears again almost a century later in Basile's work entitled "Il Pentamerone" (1637), in the story "Gagliuso"(in Day 2, Tale 4) and again five decades after Basile in the Frenchman Charles Perrault's "Tales of Time Passed" (1697).

Grammar, Italian

Leon Battista Alberti was born in Genoa on February 14, 1401 and died in Rome on April 25, 1472. He was a true multi-disciplined Renaissance man who also advanced the use of Italian instead of Latin for books and literature. He wrote two landmark books on Italian grammar using the Tuscan vernacular. His greatest literary contribution was written to advance public-spirited humanism, "De iciarchia" ("On the Man of Excellence and Ruler of His Family"). This literary work was also written in the Tuscan vernacular. Alberti further demonstrated his humanity and logic in his treatise "Della Famiglia" ("On the Family"). His superb writing skill in a comedy he wrote in Latin, when he was only 20, was so true to form that for over 100 years it was thought to be an original Latin Roman play. He also studied and advanced the writing of secret codes. Alberti was a genius who excelled in many diverse areas. (For additional information on Albert, the reader should refer to the "Art & Architecture," "Mathematics," and "Science and Technology" chapters in this book.)

"History of My Life"
Casanova

Casanova was a well educated man who traveled throughout Europe and wrote exaggerated accounts of his adventures, including his love life, which was entitled "History of My Life." His full name was Giovanni Giacomo Casanova De Seingalt. He was born in Venice in 1725 and died in 1798. He lived a somewhat mis-spent life making a living many ways including gambling, spying, and presumably some fraudulent activities. After his arrest in Italy, he subsequently escaped from a prison in Venice and went to Paris to become, of all things, the Director of Lottery. He obviously became the proverbial *fox watching the chicken coop*, since he accrued a fortune during this time and retired in a castle. His memoirs were not published until 1960.

Italian Literature - Influences on English Writers

The famous English poets Shakespeare, Chaucer, Dryden, Keats, Longfellow and Tennyson were all greatly influenced by Italian authors and poets, namely Petrarca (Petrarch), Boccaccio and Dante in particular. These three are considered to be among the most influential writers and scholars in the history of European literature and were a profound influence on later writers. Of special significance is Petrarca, whose influence on English Renaissance poetry is incalculable. Their most significant works are individually detailed in other sections of this chapter.

The great Boccaccio's masterpiece is his "Decameron" (see the reference on 'Short Stories' in this chapter for more on Boccaccio). However, his other works were also very influential. For example, his work "Filostrato" provided the plot for Chaucer's "Troilus and Criseyde," and Boccaccio's "Teseida" formed the basis of Chaucer's "Knight's Tale." Giovanni Boccaccio's celebrated "Decameron," is a collection of 100 tales. Over two hundred years after they were written, William Painter translated several of these tales into English in his book "Palace of Pleasure." One of Boccaccio's tales in Painter's translated work is "Giletta of Narbonne." Shakespeare used this story for his play "All's Well that Ends Well," about 250 years after the basic story was written by Boccaccio in 1353.

Boccaccio was a scholar and poet who also wrote a number of encyclopedic works in Latin ("De Genealogia deorum," "De claris mulieribus" and "De casibus virorum illustrium"), which were widely read in England. These became tragedy source books and references used by Chaucer, Lydgate ("The Fall of Princes"), Ferrers ("A Mirror for Magistrates") and others. *He is also credited for initiating Humanism during the Renaissance.* (Refer to the "Philosophy" chapter for more on Boccaccio.)

Shakespeare was highly influenced and enamored with Roman and Italian literature and culture. In fact, many of Shakespeare's plays borrow their plots from the Roman playwright Plautus (254 BC – 184 BC). Shakespeare even mentions Plautus in a line in "Hamlet," when Polonius states "Seneca cannot be too heavy, nor Plautus too light." Plautus wrote numerous plays of which only 21 survive. Many of his plots were Roman versions of original Greek comedies. These Roman comedies, with slapstick humor, were much less subtle than the older Greek versions.

Many of Shakespeare's plays have Italian characters and stories that take place in Italy. Because he so often wrote plays about Italy, many historians assume that Shakespeare most likely had traveled to Italian cities to gain the experience of their rich culture. *Shakespeare's lush and romantic poem "Venus and Adonis" was his most popular work during his own lifetime. The popularity of the poem was increased by the fact that it was written in an "Italianate" poetic style that was greatly admired* throughout Europe. This work was so popular that it went through nine editions in Shakespeare's lifetime alone. His contemporaries referred to this work more than any other. "The Rape of Lucrece" another famous poem of Shakespeare's took place in ancient Rome. Also, many of *Shakespeare's plays have Italian or Roman titles or characters, and these almost always have Acts that take place in Italy or ancient Rome, for example*:

- "Romeo & Juliet" (The original story was written by Luigi da Porto of Vicenza around 1520.)
- "Two Gentlemen of Verona"
- "The Merchant of Venice"
- "Julius Caesar"
- "Titus Andronicus"
- "Coriolanus"
- "Taming of the Shrew" (which takes place in Padua and the main characters are Lucentio, Petruchio, Baptista and Hortensio)
- "Othello, Moor of Venice" (part of the play takes place in Venice)
- "All's Well That Ends Well" (Act III & Act IV take place in Florence, and the plot was based on Boccaccio's "Giletta of Narbonne" as discussed above)
- "Cymbeline" (half of the play is in Rome or in Roman settlements in Britain)
- "Measure for Measure" (the main characters are Angelo, Duke Vincentio, Isabella and Lucio)
- "Much Ado About Nothing" (the main characters are Leonato, Antonio, Hero and Beatrice)
- "The Tempest" (the main characters are Prospero, Alonso, Antonio and Gonzalo)
- "Twelfth Night" or "What You Will" (the main characters are Olivia, Duke Orsino, Curio, Malvolio, Viola and Valentine)
- "Winter's Tale" (part of the play takes place in Sicily and the main characters are Paulina, Camillo, Leontes and Perdita)

Shakespeare may have been English, but Italian literature and culture powerfully influenced his genius and writing.

The famed English author, John Milton, used the imagery of Italian gardens that he gained from his tours of Italy in order to portray the Garden of Eden in his classic book "Paradise Lost." For more on Italian influences on English and European poets, also refer to the individual references that follow in this chapter on "Jerusalem Delivered" ("Gerusalemme liberata") by Torquato Tasso, "Orlando Furious" ("Orlando Furioso") by Ludovico Ariosto, and "Sonnets to Laura" by Francesco Petrarca.

In the 17th and 18th centuries the English aristocracy would not have considered their education complete without taking the "Grand Tour," as it was called then, of Italian cities. This tour was often called *giro*, the Italian word for *tour*. In 1776, the literary giant Dr. Samuel Johnson said, "A man who has not been to Italy is always conscious of his inferiority." The famous German poet Johann Wolfgang von Goethe said in 1786, when he first arrived in Rome, "Now, at last, I have arrived in the First City of the World!" The English Dilettanti Society was founded for gentlemen who completed the "Tour," and the Society encouraged others to take this cultural "Tour." The English novelist Jane Austen included in her works discussions about the strong Italian influence on England. In England, there was also a club called the Macaroni Club for the less enlightened populace who wanted to emulate the educated aristocracy, and took the "Tour" for status purposes or for the purpose of learning about fashion rather than for educational or scholarly reasons. The Macaroni Club had a significant flamboyant influence on English culture and fashion. This club also inspired the lyrics in the American patriotic song "Yankee Doodle" that states "...put a feather in his cap and called it Macaroni," which is a reference to the club's well known flamboyance.

During the 17th and 18th centuries, when the "Grand Tour" was part of English aristocracy's education, the various Italian city-states required health certificates before entering their borders. Travelers without proper health certificates or with signs of illness were required to be placed in quarantine for forty days. *Forty days* in Italian is *quaranta giorni*. The English word *quarantine* is derived from the Italian word *quaranta* as a result of travelers to Italy- but why *forty* days specifically? The Italians chose forty since this was the biblical period of time that Christ had sequestered himself in the wilderness.

Italy has not lost its power to draw visitors for tourism, culture, education, and scholarly pursuits to this day. According to the "Wall Street Journal" (June 17, 1999), the hotel industry in Italy generates more revenue than any other country in the world, except for the

United States. The "Journal" article also states that there are more hotel rooms in Italy than any other European country.

Italic Print & First Paperback Books
Aldine Press, Venice
The famous printing house, Aldine Press in Venice is credited with creating the first *italic* print. The words *italic* and *Italian* are derived from the same lexical roots. This printing house was also the first to produce small portable books that *were the first examples of modern paperback books.*

"Jerusalem Delivered" ("Gerusalemme liberata")
Torquato Tasso
Tasso was born in Sorrento and lived from 1544 to 1595. He was educated in Naples by Jesuits and studied law and philosophy at the University of Padua and at the University of Bologna. His father Bernardo Tasso was also a poet. He wrote several famous works but his greatest masterpiece was "Jerusalem Delivered." This epic poem about the exploits of Godfrey of Boulogne during the First Crusade is considered the greatest poem of the Counter-Reformation period. *This treasured work had a tremendous influence on English poets, most especially the great John Milton.* Tasso also wrote a beautiful play "Aminta" (1573) and another celebrated poem "Rinaldo" (1562). *Byron, Goethe, and other famous poets were influenced by Tasso and wrote of the legendary and failed love he had for Leonora d'Este.*

Latin and Its Influences
This section on Latin influences has three divisions:
- Source of European Literacy and Romance Languages, page 218
- Professional Terminology, page 221
- Other Modern Phrases, page 226

The Source of European Literacy and Romance Languages
Latin was the language of the Latium region of central Italy and its principle city, Rome. These ancient predecessors of modern Italians created and evolved the language of Latin, and its alphabet as well. It

is the alphabet that we still use today, and consequently the letters you recognize when reading this very book. Although the Roman alphabet is uniquely their own, they borrowed and modified both Phoenician and Greek alphabets to create the *A* to *Z* letters that we have inherited. The Etruscans, who also lived in central Italy in the Tuscany region, were advanced neighbors of the very early Romans. The Etruscans had their own spoken and written language before the Romans fully developed Latin. Their language was unique, but certain letters in their alphabet had similarities to Latin letters, which may have developed in part by the influence of Etruscan language and culture.

Latin continued as the spoken and written language of Rome when the Roman Kingdom was born in 753 BC. Later, the Roman Republic and the Roman Empire, consisting of the entire known western world, fostered and encouraged its use. The Romans subsequently *spread Latin and literacy throughout much of Europe for nine hundred years.* During the height of the Roman Republic and Empire from 100 BC to 500 AD, Romans traveled and migrated to distant provinces and territories of the Empire and thus introduced Latin to entire populations. The Romans also introduced literacy to tribal leaders in occupied territories of the Empire, teaching them how to read and write for the first time. At that time, northern and central Europe relied upon an oral tradition and had no written language. For example, the Celts were a large and fierce population, comprised of many individual tribes, in western and central Europe. Celtic tribes that were exposed to Latin brought some semblance of literacy to northern Europe as they increased their migration to the British Isles and Ireland. Their migration was exacerbated by Julius Caesar and his army who pushed the Celts from Gaul (now France), Spain and other parts of Europe. Celtic priests, the *druids,* were also teachers who used poetry to educate and maintain an oral tradition and culture. The *druids* also used a type of sign-language using five fingers to supplement oral communication. This sign-language is believed to have developed into early *ogham markings*, which were used among the Celts for short inscriptions such as grave markers and memorials from 500 AD to 700 AD. These markings did not employ letters, but consisted of a series of one to five short notches or longer slashes in conjunction with a few simple geometric shapes. *Ogham markings* later developed into cumbersome sets of straight lines based upon the Roman alphabet. These were cut into the edge of wood posts or long stone markers. From about 600 AD to 700 AD, *ogham markings* developed into *ogham script*, a rigid geometric form of the Roman Latin letters. There were over 300 posts or markers with *ogham markings* found in Ireland, predominantly in the south. The beautifully illustrated and celebrated Celtic "Book of Kells" (800 AD), a Latin religious text, retained some *ogham script* headings, but the text itself illustrates how *ogham script* evolved into Celtic *majuscule script,* a much closer form of the Latin alphabet. Other European tribes used a variety of runes or rudimentary markings that often had some mystical meaning and purpose as well, but all eventually embraced the Latin alphabet. Today, all European languages use Roman letters.

Ancient writing contained capital letters, but eventually scholars began using capitals and small letters, and writing with a slight slant and connecting some letters. However, the credit of inventing what's termed *Italian running hand* or *cursive handwriting* with its Roman capitals and small letters, is attributed to Aldus Manutius of Venice, who in 1495 first used this writing. Consequently, by the end of the 16th century, the old Roman capitals and Greek letterforms transformed into the twenty-six alphabet letters we know today, both for upper and lower-case letters.

Over the centuries of Roman rule, local language and grammatical structure in the Empire's territories also caused the development of Latin dialects. Since the populations in northern and central Europe were illiterate, Latin was transmitted orally, making it difficult to teach and maintain linguistic standards. Consequently, and much to their consternation, Romans were finding that a few different versions of Latin dialects were developing in different provinces. After the barbaric invasions of Rome, and the Empire's eventual collapse, communication became chaotic, commerce was limited and a single centralized government was no longer present to encourage Latin as a universal language. In fact, after the fall of Rome, commerce and communication was so negatively impacted that by 600 AD the monetary system collapsed and was replaced by barter throughout Europe. Latin dialects in these now isolated areas became increasingly divergent and were further changed by the influence of reciprocating barbaric invasions for centuries. Over these centuries of the Dark and Middle Ages, dialects of Latin slowly developed into Italian, French, Spanish, Portuguese and Rumanian, i.e. the Romance Languages. The English word *romance* is derived from the Latin colloquial word *romanice,* meaning "that which is descended from the Roman language (Latin)." Hence the definition of the term "Romance Language," which indicates that the language is derived from Latin. Serious literature continued to be written in Latin, but popular stories and fables of adventure, love and heroism were often written in a Latin dialect or *romanice* language. Consequently the word *romance* began to evolve with a new amorous or passionate meaning.

The first evidence of Latin dialects becoming new languages appeared around 800 AD when churches began offering sermons in the local dialects of Latin. Since Rome was the capital of the Roman Kingdom, Republic and Empire for over twelve centuries, Italy was central to Roman civilization. Understandably, Italian resembles Latin more than any other language. A linguistic examination of the number *four* provides a good example of how the Romance Languages are all dialects of Latin and that Italian has the most similarities to Latin. The English word *four* is *quattuor* in Latin, it is *quattro* in Italian, *quatre* in French, and *cuatro* in Spanish. In English (although not a Romance language) the prefix *quad*, meaning *four*, is also clearly derived from the Latin *quattuor*.

The spread of Latin by the Roman Empire throughout Europe promoted literacy and influenced all European languages. *About half of the words in the English language have some Latin origins.* In fact, the first dictionaries in England were Latin dictionaries that were used to help define the meaning of English words. The earliest one dates back to 1225 and had the Latin title of "Dictionarius." In the 1500's, a Latin dictionary published in London by Thomas Elyot was the first publication to use the actual English word *dictionary* in its title. During the 16th and 17th centuries, thousands of Latin words were directly added into the English language because many scholars read Latin and some still read Greek texts as well.

The common Latin heritage among European languages explains why English speaking people can understand many Italian, Spanish and French words. Many words in these languages are highly similar. (Also, refer to the earlier section in this chapter: 'Italian Literature - Influences on English Writers').

Professional Terminology

After the fall of Rome, church leadership, physicians, lawyers and other scholars continued to use Latin in their professions and thereby retained some standard communication on the continent. Latin became the universal language of the educated in general and continued its status as such throughout the Middle Ages, Renaissance and beyond.

Today physicians and other medical professionals throughout the world use Latin as a common technical language. Latin remains the official language of anatomy. The international Federative Committee on Anatomical Terminology states that only the Latin terms are to be used as a basis for creating new or revised medical nomenclatures in all languages. Here is a short list of common Latin words, anatomical terms and abbreviations that are used in the international world of medicine today. Very often Latin abbreviations, as shown in parentheses below, are more commonly used in prescriptions and in nursing notes.

ab ovo - from the egg; from the beginning
ad libitum (ad lib.) - at pleasure
ante cibum (a.c.) - before food
ante meridiem (a.m.) - morning
a posteriori - from effect to cause
a priori - from cause to effect
aqua (aq.) - water
aqua destillata (aq. dest.) - distilled water
aurio dextra (a.d.) - right ear
aurio laeva (a.l.) - left ear
aurio sinister (a.s.) - left ear
aures utrae (a.u.) - each ear
bis in die (b.i.d.) - twice daily
circa (cc.) - about
cum (c) – with (when abbreviated, the c has a horizontal line above it)
dentur tales doses, (d.t.d.) - give of such a dose
dies (d) - day
dilue (dil) - dilute
dispensa (disp.) - dispense
e.m.p. - as directed
errata - errors
ex aq. - in water
gramma (Gm or g) - gram
gutta (g.t.t.) - a drop
hora (h) - hour
hora somni (h.s.) - at bedtime
in articulo mortis - at the point of death
in extremis - at the point of death
in loco - in the place
in situ - in its original position
in vacuo - in a vacuum
liquor (liq.) - a liquor, solution

misce (M) - mix
mixtura (mixt.) - a mixture
more dictor (m. dict.) - as directed
nocturnal (noc.) - in the night
non repatur (non. rep.) - no refills
numerus (no.) - number
octarius (O or Oct.) - a pint
oculus dexter (o.d.) - right eye
oculus sinister (o.s.) - left eye
oculus uterque (o.u.) - each eye
post cibos (p.c.) - after meals
post meridiem (p.m.) - afternoon
per os (p.o.) - per mouth
pro re nata (p.r.n.) - as needed
pulvis (pulv) - a powder
quam volueris (q.v.) - as much as wanted
quater in die (q.i.d.) - four times a day
quiaque die (q.d.) - every day
quiaque hora (q.h.) - every hour
quoque alternis die (q.a.d.) - every other day
Rx - a recipe to take
repetatus (rep.) - let it be repeated
sataratus (sat.) - saturated
semis (ss.) - one-half
sine (s) - without
si opus sit (s.o.s.) - if there is need
solutio (sol.) - solution
statim (stat) - at once
stet - do not delete
sub rosa - confidentially
suppositorium (supp.) - suppository
syrupus (syr.) - syrup
tabella (tab.) - tablet
tal dos - such doses
ter in die (t.i.d.) - three times a day
tritura (trit.) - triturate
unguentum (ung.) - ointment
ut dictum (ut. dict.) - as directed
verbatim et literatim - word for word or letter for letter

Our legal systems still employ Latin. Many Roman legal concepts and Latin phrases are fundamental to our legal systems, such as, *subpoena, habeas corpus, pro bono, prima facie evidence, pro forma* and *ex post facto*. Below is a list of Latin terminology used by legal professionals. (Refer to the chapter on "Law" for information on how the Roman legal system influenced the world's legal systems.)

actio in personam - action against a person

ad hominem - to the man (used to declare that an aspect appeals to a person's interests or prejudices rather than to logic or reason.)

ad litem - for suit or action

amicus curiae - friend of the court

bona fide - in good faith

caveat emptor - let the buyer beware (from a famous sign posted by Roman marketplaces, now a common-law maxim)

corpus delicti - body of the crime (material evidence that crime has occurred.)

de jure - according to law or by right.

dura lex, sed lex. - the law is hard, but it is the law.

ex curia - out of court

ex lege - arising from the law; as a matter of law

ex post facto - from the deed afterwards (used to demonstrate increasing guilt and as in ex post facto laws.)

habeas corpus - you shall have the body. (used when a judge orders a person to appear before the court in order to determine if that person has been lawfully imprisoned.)

hoc indictumvolo - this is to be unsaid (withdraw a statement)

ignorantia legis neminem excusat - ignorance of the law excuses no one.

in camera - in chamber , in secret or closed session

in facie curiae - in the face or presence of the court

in loco parentis - in place of a parent

in personem - against the person

in rem - a lien on property or real estate

ipso facto - by the fact itself or by that very deed

jus gentium - law of nations, a concept of Roman law. It is the underpinning of the world's first international laws.

jus naturale - natural law (this was a concept of Roman law that inspired the *inalienable rights* in the U.S. Declaration of Independence.)

lex non scripta - unwritten law

lex scripta - written law

lis pendens - the pre-foreclosure state of a property when mortgage or taxes have not been paid for a period of time.

mala fide - in or with bad faith or treacherously

mala in se - bad or evil in itself

modus operandi (m.o.) - way of operating (of a person or thing)

modus vivendi - a way of living (usually a temporary arrangement whereby parties in dispute can carry on pending a final legal settlement.)

ne bis in idem - a person may not be punished twice for the same act or crime.

ne exeat - let him not go out from the jurisdiction of the court

noli-me-tangere - do not touch me (used as a warning against physical touching)

nolle prosequi - I do not wish to pursue (used when a prosecutor is dropping all or part of an indictment.)

nolo contendere - I do not wish to contend. (used as a temporary guilty plea, leaving open the option of denying alleged facts in later proceedings.)

non compos mentis - not having control of the mind (used to claim not legally responsible)

nunc pro tunc - now for then (indicates action in the present that should have been taken before.)

per se - in or by itself

prima facie - on first appearance or at first sight (as in prima facie evidence.)

pro forma - as a matter of form or formality

pro bono – for the good, meaning at no cost

pro tempore - for the time, temporarily

res gestae - things done, deeds or facts of a case that are admissible as evidence.

sine die - without a day (used to mean there is not a date for reconvening.)

sine qua non - without which not (used to claim an essential element or condition.)

sub judice - before the judge, court or under judicial consideration

subpoena - under penalty (used to summon a person to appear in court)

sui juris - of one's own right (used to mean capable of managing one's own affairs.)

For centuries Rome led the civilized world in all professions and as a result its language, Latin, has permeated all professions in our civilization. Roman philosophies, legal systems, medical science and its official religion, Christianity, have had enormous influences on all of Europe. This is quite evident since today's physicians, lawyers and Church leadership all continue to use the ancient language of Rome, Latin. And yes, even the motto of the U.S. Marine Corp is the Latin phrase *semper fidelis* which means *always faithful.*

Other Modern Phrases

Many Latin phrases are still used today even in non-Romance languages such as English: ad hoc, carpe diem, per se, per capita, per diem, caveat emptor, bona fide, de facto, ex cathedra, non sequitur, magna cum laude, magnum opus, mea culpa, modus operandi, pro forma, quid pro quo, P.M. (post meridian), A.M. (ante meridian), R.I.P (*requiescat in pace* meaning *rest in peace*), AD (*anno Domini*, meaning *in the year of our Lord*), i.e. (meaning *that is*), etc. Incidentally, *etc.* is an abbreviation of the Latin phrase *et cetera.*

The influence of the ancient Roman language, Latin, persists today in many other ways. Many of today's common proverbs were common Roman expressions that were often taken from the writing of Roman scholars and poets, such as Virgil, Seneca, Cicero and Horace. Some examples of Roman expressions include: "It is not quantity but quality that matters," "Better late than never," "To err is human," "There is no accounting for tastes," "Love conquers all," "Time is Flying," "Seize the day" and "Let the buyer beware." Throughout this chapter there are specific references to the Roman literary works that are the origins of these famous quotes.

In the "Proverbs and Quotations" chapter, there are many famous Latin and Italian quotes and references. In the chapter "Culture Conventions & Traditions" there is also a reference describing how the royal titles "Czar" and "Kaiser" evolved from the esteemed name of "Caesar." Further, in the "American Government" chapter, there are references to Latin expressions that were adopted as U.S. mottoes and are shown on the Great Seal of the United States.

"Meditations"
Marcus Aurelius

Marcus Aurelius, born 121 AD, was one of the greatest Roman

Emperors and is considered one of the great Stoic philosophers. His book, "Meditations," is a classic of the ancient world, and is *the most famous book ever written by a monarch.* Many of his contemporaries thought that he was the "Philosopher-king" envisioned by Plato in his work the "Republic." Aurelius, a fair and just ruler, died on March 17, 180 AD.

New Journalism - Founder
Gay Talese

Gay Talese is credited as one of the founders of the 1960's *new journalism-* a dramatic change to traditional journalistic style. This *new journalism* adds more interesting elements of story telling, such as intrigue, dialogue, scene description and variable viewpoints or perspectives. Talese is well known for his formal, elegant writing style and flawless research often on breaking news stories. He has been called a creative non-fiction writer.

Talese was born on February 7th, 1932 on the small resort island of Ocean City, New Jersey to Catherine and Joseph Talese, an Italian tailor who came to America in 1922. Gay Talese was a political and sports reporter for "The New York Times" from 1956 to 1965 where he often found his new writing style to be at odds with the stodgy management. Fortunately, the Sunday "New York Times Magazine" editor had an appreciation for Talese's unique talents and began to let his more unusual stories appear in the magazine section on Sunday. This new publicity propelled his career still further and he began writing for other magazines ranging from "Esquire" to "Reader's Digest."

A prolific writer, his books include "The Kingdom and the Power" (1969), "Fame and Obscurity" (1970), "The Best American Essays"- Editor with Robert Atwan (1987), "Honor Thy Father" (1992), "Unto the Sons" (1992), "Thy Neighbor's Wife" (1993), and "Writing Creative Nonfiction: The Literature of Reality" - with Barbara Lounsberry (1995).

Newspaper
Julius Caesar

The very first record of a regularly published newspaper is credited to Julius Caesar in 59 BC. These were hand copied and posted regularly on certain main buildings. These newspapers were also distributed at main buildings in Rome and also at buildings in principle towns in outlying provinces. Similar to modern newspapers, these carried major events, such as nominations for public office, legal judgements, military news, marriages and births, as well as obituaries.

Nobel Prize Winners in Literature

Giosuè Carducci was a poet and literary historian, born 1835 in Val di Castello, Italy and died in 1907. He was awarded the Nobel Prize in 1906 for his works "Hymn to Satan" and "Barbaric Odes." Some of his best poetry is in his work entitled "New Rhymes" ("Rime Nuove"). His style was different in the respect that he broke away from traditional romanticism. Carducci was the first Italian writer to win a Nobel Prize.

Grazia Deledda was born in Nuoro, Sardinia Island, Italy in 1875 and died in 1936. She wrote several novels about the life of Sardinian peasants and was awarded a Nobel Prize in 1926. Her novels included: "After the Divorce," "Cenere," "Ashes," "Elias Portulu," "The Flight into Egypt," "The Flower of Life," "The Mother," and "Reeds in the Wind."

Dario Fo was born in 1926 in Lago Maggiore, Italy. He received the Nobel Prize in 1997. His work shows the flaws and weakness of authority and the morality and intelligence of the common and underprivileged. Some of his well known plays include: "Accidental Death of an Anarchist," "Can't Pay," "Won't Pay," and "Female Parts."

Eugenio Montale was born in Genoa in 1896 and died in 1981. He was awarded a Nobel Prize in 1975 for his poetry. Montale published six books of poems from 1925 to 1976. He also translated other writers' works, e.g., T.S. Eliot and Shakespeare.

Luigi Pirandello is the inventor of *theater within a theater* and was awarded a Nobel Prize in 1934. (Refer to the section later in this chapter, Theater within a Theater, for more on Pirandello).

Salvatore Quasimodo was born in Syracuse, Sicily in 1901 and died in 1968. He was awarded a Nobel Prize in 1959 for his poetic works that deal with political and social reform entitled, "The Selected Writings of Salvatore Quasimodo."

"Odes"
Horace
This Roman poet and author was born in Venusia, Apulia (region) on December 8, 65 BC and is *considered one of the great lyric poets of all time.* He wrote under the patronage of Maecenas and even Augustus himself. Horace is best known for "Odes," but his other works include "Epistles," "Epodes," "Satires," and others. His real name was Quintus Horatius Flaccus. Horace died in 8 BC. The famous Latin saying used by the United States as a motto on its great seal, *"E Pluribus Unum" (Out of Many, One), comes from Horace's work entitled Epistles II.*

"Orlando Furious" ("Orlando Furioso")
Ludovico Ariosto
Ariosto was an epic and lyric poet who lived from 1474 to 1533. His greatest masterpiece, "Orlando Furious" (1532), *greatly influenced English writers such as, William Shakespeare, John Milton and George Gordon Byron.* Ariosto also wrote other great but less significant works: "The Pretenders" ("I Suppositi"), and "The Sorcerer" ("Il Negromante").

"The Prince"
Niccolo Machiavelli
Machiavelli was born to an aristocratic family in Florence in 1469 and died in 1527. *He is often referred to as the father of political science,* since his 16th century classic "The Prince" has value and relevance even in today's political and business world. Machiavelli held several high level diplomatic positions and learned how to manage people, politics and position. He also studied how leaders rule and how to be a successful leader. His 16th century epic, "The Prince," is a dissection of political power and management principles. This famous work is so insightful that many universities such as Cornell University's Graduate School of Business and Public Administration

used "The Prince" as required reading. Machiavelli is credited for also forming the Florentine militia, the first national army in Italy in 1506. Machiavelli also wrote "La Mandragola," a comedy in 1513.

Satire in Western Literature

The Italian poets and writers of the 13th century brought a profound change to European literature by introducing modern wit and satire as is clearly documented by the famous Renaissance historian Jacob Burckhardt. This is illustrated in the groundbreaking work by Dante, "The Divine Comedy" and by the many satirical novels produced by his contemporary Franco Sacchetti, also of Florence. By the 15th century, Florence, and the Papal Court became the centers of satire and wit, where social criticism became the social norm. According to Burckhardt, it was said that in Florence the people had "Sharp eyes and bad tongues." During the 15th century, the two most famous court jesters were Arlotto, a priest from Florence and Gonnella, a jester at the Court of Ferrara. The Italians introduced this revolutionary influence to Europe's literature, which had lost the beauty of Greek parody and Roman satire over the centuries. *The Roman poet Lucilius (about 180 BC -103 BC) wrote satires and many contend his works were the first to display a modern sense of witty social criticism.*

Short Story
Giovanni Boccaccio

Boccaccio was born (June or July, 1313) in Certaldo or in Florence and died in a small town outside of Florence on December 21, 1375. He is considered one of the greatest figures in European literature. Boccaccio is credited for initiating *Humanism* during the Renaissance. He was an Italian literary giant, the "father of Italian prose" and the inventor of the short story, as well. Boccaccio spent his youth in Naples and married a woman he called "La Fiammetta" ("The Flame"). He spent most of his adult life in Florence where he met and was greatly influenced by Petrarch (or Petrarca), another European literary giant. *Boccaccio was the first to write what are now called short stories.* His work "Decameron," is one of the most famous and readable books in world literature. He wrote "Decameron" from 1349 to 1351, during the bubonic plague in Florence that began in 1348. *His book contains 100 stories* both comedic and tragic and is the first documented collection of short stories in literature. The title "Decameron" means "Ten Days Work" in English. It is about a group of young people who tell stories in the countryside for 10 days. He also wrote "Diana's Hunt," "Filostrato," "Teseida," and other works. (Refer to the section in this chapter on 'Italian Literature – Influences on English Writers' for more about the celebrated works and influences of Boccaccio. Also, refer to the chapter in this book on "Philosophy.")

Sonnet and Sonnet Cycle
Giacomo da Lentini
Francesco Petrarca (aka Petrarch)

The 13th century Sicilian poet Giacomo da Lentini invented the sonnet, which is a 14-line poem with rhymes arranged in a fixed scheme. The literary giant, Francesco Petrarca, from Florence (1304-1374), invented the sonnet cycle, which was enthusiastically embraced, and rapidly spread throughout Europe. There have been several cycle variations since then, but the sonnet remains, as originally conceived by Lentini, a structured 14-line poem.

"Sonnets to Laura"
Francesco Petrarca (aka Petrarch)

Francesco Petrarca was a citizen of Florence, born in 1304 in Arezzo and died 1374. Petrarca was a scholar and writer who greatly influenced the literature of Western Europe. *The love lyrics in his "Sonnets to Laura" became stylistic models for poets in Italy, Spain, France and England for over 300 years.* These are called *Petrarchan sonnets* and are very common in English poetry. After Dante, Petrarca was one of the first great lyric poets to abandon Latin and use the Italian language instead. His other works include: "Triumphs," "On the Solitary Life," and "Rime." Petrarca is referred to as the "Laureate of the Civilized World." Refer to the section in this chapter on 'Italian Literature – Influences on English Writers' for more about the celebrated works and influences of Petrarca. Also, refer to the chapter in this book on "Philosophy." (For more information on the great Petrarca see, "Francesco Petrarca: The First Modern Scholar and Man of Letters" by James Harvey Robinson, Putnam, 1898).

Theater within a Theater – *Nobel Prize*
Luigi Pirandello

Pirandello was born in Agrigento, Sicily, Italy in 1867 and died in 1936. He wrote dozens of books and won the 1934 Nobel Prize in Literature for his dramatic and ingenious works. He is considered an important innovator in modern drama and is credited with inventing "theater within a theater" with his play "Six Characters in Search of An Author" (1921). This innovative play begins in the lobby outside a theater, with an actress playing an actress, rehearsing her lines for her play- a plot within the "Six Characters in Search of An Author" play. Pirandello mixes acting role of the actress with her real life personality, and the play concludes with the theatre management apologizing to the audience, but we are not sure which audience. Pirandello masterfully blurs the distinction between the play and reality.

R. R. Esposito

☙

Chapter XI

LAW

"Jus Commune" ("Common Law")
- Roman legal concept of "law common to all men and to nature," adopted by legal systems throughout the world -

First Legal System
Roman Empire

Roman law dates as far back as 753 BC, during the time of the early Roman Kingdom. Established during the early Roman Republic, about 450 BC, the "Law of the Twelve Tables" ("Lex duodecim tabularum") was engraved on bronze tablets and permanently displayed in public areas. The "Twelve Tables" is considered the first major codification of Roman Law. The "Twelve Tables" dealt with these legal areas: (1) preliminary trial proceedings, (2) trial proceedings, (3) enforcing judgments, (4) rights of fathers, (5) inheritance, (6) ownership of property, (7) real estate or land laws, (8) trusts, (9) public laws, (10) sacred or burial laws, and (11 and 12) supplementary legal subjects.

About 150 BC these laws were further developed and became known as "jus civile" ("civil law"). These laws applied exclusively to Roman citizens. As the Roman Republic became the Roman Empire in 27 BC with increasing territories, new commercial interests and treaties, legal system modifications were required. The Romans created "jus gentium" ("law of nations"). This was the world's first system of international law, and it evolved into the Roman concept of "natural law," that is, a "natural" and "common law" to all men and races. This legal construct was applied to all Roman citizens, subjects in provinces and foreigners. This Roman law states, "all men are equal." Over time these blended with "jus civile" (civil law) and became known as "Jus Commune" (Common Law) throughout Europe. The Roman legal system further developed during the time of the Roman Empire into what was called "Corpus Juris Civilis," ("The Body of Civil Law") and ultimately became the foundation for legal systems throughout much of the world. (These concepts of "natural law" and "equality among men" are what inspired Philip Mazzei, when he first wrote about the "natural rights of man" and that "all men are by nature equally free and independent." Mazzei introduced these concepts to Thomas Jefferson for use in the American "Declaration of Independence." Refer to the chapter on "American Government" for more on Mazzei.)

Roman Law covered many advanced civil issues, such as enactment of wills, family laws and rights of property. Disputes were settled in the courts. Around 200 AD, the Romans adopted "Sine Mano" marriages. These allowed a wife to retain the rights to her personal property and gave her the legal right to initiate a divorce from her husband. This is in sharp contrast to Greek civilization, where the wife had no legal rights or property. Further, Roman courts even used legal precedents, past rulings, and ultimately *case-law evolved* in their legal system, which was later adopted in Europe and the United States. Around 527 AD, the Emperor of the Eastern Roman Empire, Justinian, ordered all laws, statutes, rulings, significant cases and legal scholarly writings to be formally studied and systematically compiled into the first modern legal system. He commissioned ten Roman lawyers, including the famous Tribonianus and Theophilus, to reorganize the legal system. This commission of lawyers combined and organized three ancient Roman legal sources into one unified legal system for the entire Empire and was called "Corpus Juris Civilis," ("The Body of Civil Law"). "Corpus Juris Civilis" or sometimes referred to simply as the "Corpus" was based upon these Roman legal sources:

1) "Theodosian Code" (published in 438 AD) was transformed and updated into an orderly compendium. Consequently, the "Codex" was produced in 529 AD. The "Codex" represents the actual Roman laws and statutes.

2) A collection of legal scholarly writings, opinions and precedents that supported laws (the *responsa prudentum*) was transformed into the "Digest" (or "Pandects") which was published in 530 AD.

3) The commentaries of Gaius (published about 200 AD) were organized into a manual of law for legal students. This became the "Institutes of Ganius" published in 530 AD.

Thus the efforts of Justinian's legal commission produced a sophisticated legal system that included a new set of updated laws (the "Codex"), documentation of precedents for case law (the "Digest") and a set of texts for law students (the "Institutes of Ganius"). In 534 AD, all three bodies of work were revised, and a fourth document, the "Novellae" (or "Novels") was produced, containing later decisions made by Justinian's own courts.

The Roman Republic and Empire developed the *first true legal system* with complex criminal and civil laws including detailed administrative and judicial procedures. They were the first to provide academic study of the law as a science and invented the first true judicial system. Roman Law was spread to the distant reaches of the Empire throughout Europe for centuries, thereby *creating a common foundation for all European legal systems*. The later Roman legal system called the "Corpus Juris Civilis" ("The Body of Civil Law") is the basis of the Catholic Church's canon law (*ecclesia vivit lege romana*), and the foundation of legal systems throughout the civilized world, particularly those in Europe, Asia and the Americas (North, South and Central America). It would be difficult to exaggerate the significance and influence of the early Roman Law and the "Corpus Juris Civilis" on the world's legal systems.

Foundation of Modern Legal Systems
Roman Empire

The Roman legal system significantly influenced early legal texts that were written by other cultures throughout all of Europe. For example, Roman legal influences are found in the Celtic legal text "Brehon Laws" written between 800 AD and 900 AD in the Old Irish language. The Celts also wrote a "Marriage Law" text called "Cain Lanamna" around 900 AD to 1000 AD that has similarities to the Roman legal status of "Sine Mano" marriages, discussed earlier in this chapter.

When the Roman Empire was destroyed by the growing

populations of invading barbarians, the Dark Ages of ignorance ensued and the Roman legal system lost much of its influence until the Medieval Times. (Medieval Times represented the bridge between the Dark Ages and civilization's rebirth during the Italian Renaissance.) During Medieval times, Roman Law was studied and taught in universities. The University of Bologna (the world's first university) was the first to begin teaching Roman Law, and later other universities' teachings helped to re-establish the practice of Roman Law, especially in the area of civil law. British scholar, John Addington Symonds wrote that the Medieval Italians "became a race of statesmen and jurists." The re-adoption of Roman Law began to increase throughout Europe and was modified to meet the unique needs of various regions and cultures. Roman Law eventually became the foundation of law throughout Europe and provided common legal principles. These common legal principles became known as "Jus Commune" (Common Law). In Germany, actual Roman Law was used until around 1900 when a German national code was adopted, which was still fundamentally based upon Roman Law. Roman Law is also the foundation for the "Napoleonic Code" that governs the French legal system today and when first developed, in turn, influenced other national legal systems in Europe. In England, unlike the European mainland, rulers did not use actual Roman Law to govern. Instead their universities studied Roman Law and fashioned their own legal system using Roman legal principles and reasoning methods. The influence is clear when one considers that the English word *justice* is derived from the Roman Emperor's name, Justinian, who championed advances in the Roman legal system. (Also note these Latin to English translations: 1) jus = law; 2) justus = just or lawful; 3) justitia = justice). The Roman legal system was Europe's basic legal system until the 18th and 19th centuries when Europe's nations evolved and developed more independent and distinct legal systems. *Nevertheless, the Roman legal system provided the foundation for the development of all European legal systems, and later, the American legal system as well.* Latin, the language of the Romans, is still used today in American, British and other European legal systems. The "Language & Literature" chapter describes how modern legal systems still use the Latin language and Roman legal principles. Many legal principles today are still described in Latin terms demonstrating the powerful influence over the centuries of the Roman legal system. Also, refer to the "American Government" chapter, which describes how the Roman Republic's government and Italian philosophers influenced the American legal system.

Chapter XII

MATHEMATICS

"No human investigation can be called real science
if it cannot be demonstrated mathematically."
- Leonardo da Vinci -

Arabic Numerals
and Fibonacci Sequence Number Theory
Leonardo Fibonacci

Fibonacci was born about 1170 in Pisa, Italy and probably died there between 1240 and 1250. *He was a mathematician who was primarily responsible for the European adoption of Arabic numerals in place of Roman numerals.* He explained the advantages and the system in his book "Liber Abaci," written 1202. His father held a diplomatic post in Algeria representing the merchants of the Republic of Pisa. Fibonacci traveled with him to several Arab countries and recognized the enormous advantages of Arabic numerals and the Hindu-Arabic place-valued decimal system. His text "Liber Abaci" promoted this system and explained how it can be applied for commerce and surveying. "Liber Abaci" also included his study of simultaneous linear equations, which were probably of Arabic origin.

Fibonacci also made other significant mathematical contributions in other texts that he wrote such as, "Practica geometriae" (1220), "Flos"

(1225), and "Liber quadratorum" (1225), Fibonacci's most impressive piece of work. *Since the time of the ancient Greek mathematician Diophantus, Fibonacci was the only major contributor to number theory until the 17ᵗʰ century when others built upon his original concepts. Fibonacci's work in number theory was mostly unknown during the Middle ages. Three hundred years later, the world started to re-discover the same results.*

Unfortunately, other books he wrote have been lost over the centuries. His contributions include geometry and complex word problems, as well as mathematics for many practical purposes.

Fibonacci also conceived the numerical pattern of numbers, the *Fibonacci Sequence* that appears in a variety of connections in higher mathematics. This sequence (1, 1, 2, 3, 5, 8, 13, 21, 34, 55, etc.) is derived when each number is the sum of the two preceding numbers and *this sequence appears in many different areas of mathematics and science.*

The Fibonacci Quarterly is a modern journal devoted to studying mathematics related to this mathematical sequence.

Introduction of Western Mathematics to China
First Accurate Map of China's Location
Matteo Ricci

Ricci was born October 6, 1552 in Macerata, Italy and died May 11, 1610 in Peking, China. He was a Jesuit priest who learned mathematics from the Jesuit mathematician Christoph Klau Clavius. Ricci is credited for introducing Western mathematics to China by educating the Chinese on the logical construction in Euclid's Elements. Ricci introduced the Chinese to mathematical concepts that were radically different from Chinese mathematics. The reciprocal exchange of completely new and different mathematical concepts must have proved both intriguing and puzzling for all involved during these historic meetings.

In 1582, when Ricci was 30 years old, he moved from Italy to China. He took the name Li Matou and was well accepted by the Chinese. He lived in Macau, Chao-ch'ing, Shao-chou and Peking before he finally settled in Nanking during his later years. Throughout his life he studied mathematics, astronomy and geography. He was respected for his intellect, as well as his extraordinary memory and his art. He was also a landscape painter and one of his works has survived the centuries. Ricci eventually created the first world map showing an incredibly accurate geographical position of China on the globe. He called his map the "Great Map of Ten Thousand Countries." *European scholars at that time had no real understanding of China and did not even know if the country Marco Polo visited in 1271 called Cathay was the same as Ricci's China. Ricci correctly believed they were one and the same country.* However, Ricci's European contemporaries were not convinced these two lands were the same country, since Polo traveled to Cathay, 300 years earlier, *over a land route*, and Ricci arrived in China *by sea*. A few years later in 1602 a new overland journey to China was made by DeGoes, who was a Jesuit priest. He proved that Ricci was correct in his belief that Marco Polo's Cathay was the same country as the China that Ricci visited 300 years later. The discovery of America by Columbus in 1492 must have been truly a remarkable event at the time, when one considers that Europe did not even know where China was until Ricci's map was made about 100 years *after* Columbus.

Addition and Multiplication Rules with Complex Numbers
Rafael Bombelli
Bombelli was born January 1526 in Bologna and died about 1573, presumably in Rome. His giant contribution was that he was the *first to document the rules for addition and multiplication of complex numbers* and provided solutions for a cubic involving square roots of negative numbers. For more on Bombelli see the reference below on Algebra.

Algebra

Enrico Betti
Betti was born October 21, 1823 in Pistoia and died August 11, 1892 in Pisa. He is known for his work in algebra and topology. Betti made important contributions in the transition from classical to modern algebra.

Rafael Bombelli
Bombelli wrote a *very significant set of books on algebra and complex numbers* entitled "Algebra" in 1560 that was published in

1572. For more on Bombelli see the reference above on Rules for Addition and Multiplication of Complex Numbers.

Ettore Bortolotti

Bortolotti was born March 6, 1866 in Bologna and died there as well on February 17, 1947. He was mostly a *mathematical historian* who published in 1929, "Algebra" (Book 4) and "Algebra" (Book 5), which were *previously lost works of the famous mathematical giant Bombelli*. He also studied Torricelli's and Cataldi's works and edited Ruffini's complete works.

Pietro Antonio Cataldi

Cataldi was born April 15, 1548 in Bologna and died there as well on February 11, 1626. He wrote about 30 books on mathematics, and several more on other topics. From 1606 to 1617 he wrote "Practica aritmetica" in four parts covering new areas in algebra, square roots of numbers in an infinite series and continued fractions. In 1613, he further developed the concepts of continued fractions in "Trattato del modo brevissimo di trovar la radice quadra delli numeri." He also studied artillery trajectory and military applications of algebra.

Luca Pacioli

In 1494, Luca di Pacioli wrote "Algebra" which includes a study of the problems of cubic equations. The celebrated Pacioli also published a widely read comprehensive mathematics text "Summa di arithmetica" in 1494 and *invented double-entry accounting*. Refer to the Mathematics Education section in this chapter and the chapter on "Economics, Finance and Business" for more on Pacioli.

Algebra and the Father of Probability

Girolamo Cardano (aka Jerome Cardan)

Cardano, physician and mathematician, was born September 24, 1501 in Pavia and died September 21, 1576 in Rome. In 1545, he published the monumental mathematical work "Ars Magna" ("The Great Art") and provided algebraic solutions for both quartic and cubic equations. (The cubic solutions he published were actually developed by the famous Italian mathematician Tartaglia.) Around 1563 he wrote a groundbreaking book "Liber de Ludo Aleae" (published 1663) on games of chance and probability. Cardano was the first to study games of chance, such as dice rolling, and was the first to explain scientific probability governing the outcome of these games that were previously thought to be determined by "luck" or "fortune." *Consequently, he is considered the father of probability.* He wrote prolifically on many subjects including mathematics, medicine, philosophy and astronomy. Cardano was also a physician. He made important contributions to probability, hydrodynamics, mechanics and geology, and published two encyclopedias of natural science. Cardano also published and advocated methods of teaching the blind by sense of touch and the deaf by use of signs. Cardano also wrote one of the earliest known autobiographies when he published "Book of My Life" ("De propria vita") in 1575. (Refer to the "Language & Literature" chapter for more information on how Italians invented the autobiography). He was well known internationally and although he was Italian, he became known as Jerome Cardan in England. (Refer to the "Science & Technology" chapter for more on Cardano, the inventor of the gyroscope.)

Carlo Emilio Bonferroni
Bonferroni was born January 28, 1892 in Bergamo and died on August 18, 1960 in Florence. He is known for his research and contributions to probability theory.

Chair of Mathematics, First Woman
Maria Gaëtana Agnesi
Agnesi was born May 16, 1718 in Milan and died there as well on January 9, 1799. She is famous for her work in differential calculus. In 1750, at the University of Bologna, she became the first woman to occupy a chair of mathematics. Her research published as "Instituzioni analitiche ad uso della gioventù italiana" includes work on the cubic curve. *This has become known among mathematicians as the "Witch of Agnesi curve," since the Italian word "versiera" can mean both "curve" and "witch."*

Cubic and Cosa Equations
and Father of Ballistics

Tartaglia (aka Niccolo Fontana)

Tartaglia was born in Brescia around 1500 and died on December 13, 1557 in Venice. He was born Niccolo Fontana, the son of a modest mail rider and was nicknamed Tartaglia, which means *stammerer*. *There is an interesting story of how he overcame personal limitations to become a giant in mathematics.* When he was only 12 years old in 1512 his hometown was attacked and he was slashed across the face by a French soldier's sword cutting him through his jaw and palate. His mother cared for him, saving his life, but his injuries permanently affected his speech. As an adult he wore a beard to hide his ghastly scars. Tartaglia's personal strength allowed him to get beyond his poverty and personal problems. His dedication and love of mathematics allowed him to teach himself the subject and ultimately master it, going on to make significant contributions in the field. He is credited for being *the first to discover solutions to the cubic and cosa equations.* Another mathematical giant, Girolamo Cardano (aka Jerome Cardan), and his assistant Ferrari used Tartaglia's discovery to uncover more cubic proofs, and more importantly formulate the solution to the quartic equation.

Tartaglia also published the works of the Greek mathematicians Archimedes and Euclid in the Italian language and improved upon the formula for extracting roots, and *developed the process for rationalization of denominators.*

In 1537, Tartaglia also wrote a *groundbreaking book* entitled "Nova Scientia" ("The New Science") on artillery ballistic mathematics offering new methods and instruments. *He was the first to apply mathematics to artillery and is considered to be the father of ballistic science.* (Refer to the Science of Ballistics section in the "Military Contributions" chapter.)

Scipione dal Ferro

Dal Ferro was born on February 6, 1465 in Bologna and died there as well on November 5, 1526. In 1505, Dal Ferro was the first mathematician to solve some forms of the cubic equation by radicals. He taught at the University of Bologna and was a colleague of the great Pacioli.

Differential Calculus and Non-Euclidean Geometry Used by Albert Einstein

Gregorio Ricci (aka Gregorio Ricci-Curbastro)

Ricci was born on February 16, 1853 in Lugo, Italy and died August 7, 1925 in Bologna. He was a mathematician who from 1884 to 1894 was the primary *developer of absolute differential calculus.* This was the foundation of Tensor Calculus. In 1900, Ricci worked with his student, another Italian mathematician, Tullio Levi-Civita to complete Tensor Calculus. *Fifteen years later this was an indispensable tool necessary for Albert Einstein's formulation of the theory of relativity.*

Tullio Levi-Civita

Levi-Civita was born on March 29, 1873 in Padua and died December 29, 1941 in Rome. He studied the "Newtonian 3-Body Problem" in 1905, "regularization" in 1903, and developed the principles of "parallelism." *Tullio Levi-Civita is best known for his collaborative work with his mentor Ricci on absolute differential calculus and its applications,* which were used *by Albert Einstein to develop his revolutionary theory of relativity. Einstein corresponded with Levi-Civita who identified technical errors in Einstein's work with calculus.* Einstein had a good rapport with him and Levi-Civita was much more supportive of Einstein's ideas on relativity than Einstein's physics colleagues.

Levi-Civita was internationally recognized when he was bestowed an honorary membership to the London Mathematical Society, the Royal Society of Edinburgh and the Edinburgh Mathematical Society. He was awarded the Sylvester medal by the Royal Society of Edinburgh in 1922.

Levi-Civita, like Fermi, Fubini, Volterra and many other Italian scientists, was strongly and actively opposed to Fascism in Italy and the Nazis in Germany.

Luigi Bianchi

Bianchi was born on January 18, 1856 in Parma and died June 6, 1928 in Pisa. He made important contributions to differential geometry. His contributions to the development of non-Euclidean geometry were *used by Einstein to prove his general theory of relativity.* Bianchi was honored by many international mathematical organizations and elected an honorary member of the London Mathematical Society.

Tommaso Boggio

Boggio was born on December 22, 1877 in Valperga Canavese and died May 25, 1963 in Turin. He is known for his contributions in differential calculus for geometrical applications, mathematical physics and potential theory. Although Boggio made significant contributions to differential calculus, his work is not viewed as being specifically important to Einstein's work on relativity.

"Dini Condition"
Ulisse Dini

Dini was born on November 14, 1845 in Pisa and died there as well on October 28, 1918. Dini made important contributions to the theory of functions of a real variable and discovered a mathematical condition known today as the *"Dini condition." He also mentored the famous Luigi Bianchi who made significant contributions to non-euclidean geometries that were used by Albert Einstein to prove his general theory of relativity.*

Fields Medal Recipient and
U.S. National Academy of Sciences Membership
Enrico Bombieri

Bombieri was born on November 26, 1946 in Milan, Italy. In 1974 at the International Congress of Mathematicians held in Vancouver, Bombieri was awarded the coveted Fields Medal for his outstanding work. *Since there is no Nobel Prize in Mathematics offered, the Fields Medal is offered to recognize Mathematics on an international level.* Bombieri received the Fields Medal for his major contributions to the study of prime numbers, univalent functions, Bieberbach conjecture, theory of functions of several complex variables, theory of partial differential equations and minimal surfaces and theory on higher dimensions. In 1996, Bombieri was elected to membership of the U.S. National Academy of Sciences. The Academy stated: "Bombieri is one of the world's most versatile and distinguished mathematicians. He has significantly influenced number theory, algebraic geometry, partial differential equations, several complex variables and the theory of finite groups. His remarkable technical strength is complemented by an unerring instinct for the crucial problems in key areas of mathematics."

Fulkerson Prize Recipient
Michele Conforti
Michele Conforti is a professor at the University of Padua in Italy. In 1983, he received his Ph.D. in Operations Research from Carnegie Mellon University. His research interests are graph theory, combinatorial optimization and polyhedral combinatorics. In 2000, he and his co-authors G. Cornuejols and M. R. Rao, received the Fulkerson Prize (awarded by the American Mathematical Society) for their paper "Decomposition of Balanced Matrices."

Integral Calculus, Torricelli's Theorem and Analytical Geometry
During the 17th century, Italian mathematicians deserve recognition for their advances of the geometry of solids, taking this branch of mathematics well beyond where the ancient Greeks had left it.

Bonaventura Francesco Cavalieri
Integral Calculus
Cavalieri was born in 1598 in Milan and died on November 30, 1647 in Bologna. His method of treating indivisibles was a significant contribution to the development of integral calculus. He was celebrated in his time as one of the leading mathematicians. Cavalieri met and was inspired by Galileo who was a mathematics professor at the time of their meeting. In 1629, Cavalieri became the chairman of mathematics at the University of Bologna.
Analytical Geometry
In his book "Directorium Generale Uranometricum," Cavalieri introduced logarithms as a computational tool in Italy. He also published tables of logarithms of trigonometric functions for use by astronomers and texts on conic sections, trigonometry, optics, astronomy and astrology. Cavalieri also published a rule for calculating the focal length of lenses for the reflecting telescope.

Angelo Genocchi

Integral Calculus

Genocchi was born on March 5, 1817 in Piacenza and died March 7, 1889 in Turin. His contributions were in number theory, series and integral calculus. He was a prolific writer and published 176 articles mostly on differential and integral calculus.

Evangelista Torricelli

Integral Calculus and Torricelli's Theorem

Torricelli was born on October 15, 1608 in Faenza and died October 25, 1647 in Florence. He is most *famous for inventing the barometer in 1643 and being the first to sustain a man-made vacuum.* However, his work in analytical geometry *greatly contributed to the development of integral calculus* in 1644. Torricelli also worked as an assistant for Galileo from 1641 to 1642. Late in his life he also became a skilled lens grinder and developed a large business making telescopes and a type of microscope. Torricelli also developed a proof about the flow of liquid through an opening being proportional to the square root of the height of the liquid. Today this is known as *Torricelli's Theorem.* He also discovered how to calculate the length of the arc of the cycloid. Further, Torricelli applied infinitesimal mathematical methods, studied projectile motion, and published "Opera geometrica" in 1644.

Vincenzo Viviani

Analytical Geometry

Viviani was born on April 5, 1622 in Florence and died there as well on September 22, 1703. He worked on physics and geometry and was a student of the famous Torricelli, and a student and supporter of the giant Galileo. He was internationally recognized as a leading mathematician. Viviani stayed in Italy even though he had offers from the Kings of other European nations. In 1666, Louis XIV of France offered him a position at the Académie Royale and that same year John II Casimir of Poland offered him the position of Royal Astronomer. Also, in 1660 Vincenzo Viviani and Giovanni Alfonso Borelli were the first to accurately measure the velocity of sound by timing the difference between the flash and the sound of a cannon. (For more on Borelli see the "Medicine, Biology & Health," "Science & Technology," and "Transportation" chapters in this book.)

Geometry, General Advancements

Eugenio Beltrami

Beltrami was born on November 16, 1835 in Cremona and died June 4, 1899 in Rome. In 1868, he published "Essay on an interpretation of non-euclidean geometry," and made *the first mathematical transition between Euclidean and non-Euclidean geometry*, thus demonstrating their related properties. Beltrami also worked in many areas of scientific investigation, including optics, thermodynamics, elasticity, electricity and magnetism. His scientific investigations were published posthumously from 1902 to 1920 in his four volume work entitled, "Opere Matematiche."

Giuseppe Bruno

Bruno was born on June 21, 1828 in Mondovi and died February 4, 1893 in Turin. He was born into a poor family but won a scholarship to attend the Collegio Carlo Alberto. He taught at the Collegio Carlo Alberto, the Collegio Nazionale in Turin, the University of Turin, and also worked as a private tutor. Bruno wrote 21 papers, all on geometry, and dedicated much of his life to teaching. One of his students was the great Corrado Segre.

Enrico D'Ovidio

D'Ovidio was born on August 11, 1842 in Campobasso, and died on March 21, 1933 in Turin. He is noted for his work on Euclidean and non-Euclidean geometry, and published an important paper on the fundamental metric functions in geometry in 1877. D'Ovidio had two students who became famous mathematicians, Peano (1880-1883) and Corrado Segre (1883-1884). In Turin, D'Ovidio and Corrado Segre co-founded an important school of geometry. D'Ovidio was the recipient of many awards, was elected to the Academy of Sciences of Turin in 1878, and to the Accademia dei Lincei in 1883.

Giovanni Fagnano
(aka Giovanni Francesco Fagnano dei Toschi)

Giovanni Fagnano was born on January 31, 1715 in Sinigaglia and died there as well on May 14, 1797. His father, Giulio Fagnano, also a mathematician, worked on the mathematics of a triangle. Giovanni continued his father's work and also worked on the integration computing of integrals. Giovanni was also an ordained priest, as well.

Giulio Fagnano (aka Giulio Carlo Fagnano dei Toschi)

Giulio Fagnano was born on December 6, 1682 in Sinigaglia and died there as well on September 26, 1766. Fagnano worked on the mathematics of the triangle and advanced the great Bombelli's work on complex numbers. He devised ingenious analytic transformations that became the foundation for the theory of elliptic integrals. *His research also founded elliptic functions.* Giulio Fagnano was the father of Giovanni Fagnano, another great mathematician.

Luigi Guido Grandi

Grandi was born on October 1, 1671 in Cremona and died July 4, 1742 in Pisa. He wrote a number of works on geometric topics that included the circle, equilateral hyperbola, conical loxodrome, the *Witch of Agnesi curve*, curves of double curvature on the sphere, and the spherical surface. Grandi also worked on hydraulics and published works on mechanics and astronomy.

Giovanni Battista Guccia

Guccia was born on October 21, 1855 in Palermo and died there as well on October 29, 1914. His contributions include work on geometry, i.e. Cremona transformations, classification and properties of curves. He founded a mathematical publishing company and a mathematical society in Palermo, which is located on the Italian island of Sicily.

Lorenzo Mascheroni

Mascheroni was born on May 13, 1750 in Bergamo and died July 14, 1800 in Paris. In 1797, he proved that all Euclidean constructions can be made solely through the use of compasses, and that the use of a ruler was not necessary. In his 1790, "Adnotationes ad calculum integrale Euleri," he calculated Euler's constant to 32 decimal places, most of which are still correct today.

Michelangelo Ricci

Ricci was born on January 30, 1619 in Rome and died there as well on May 12, 1682. Ricci's most significant contribution was a 19 page paper "Exercitatio geometrica, De maximis et minimis" published in 1666. In this work on tangents, he also describes early examples of induction. Ricci also studied spirals, generalized cycloids and uses inverse operations for finding tangents and areas.

Giovanni Girolomo Saccheri

Saccheri was born on September 5, 1667 in Genoa and died October 25, 1733 in Milan. In 1773, a byproduct of Saccheri's analysis of a Euclidean mathematical problem entitled "Euclides ab Omni Naevo Vindicatus" *actually created an outline for non-Euclidean geometry.* His other work entitled "Logica Demonstrativa" (1697) advanced mathematical logic with definitions, postulates and demonstrations in the style of Euclid. His work entitled "Neo-statica" (1708) served to advance the mathematics of statics.

Beniamino Segre

Segre was born on February 16, 1903 in Turin and died October 22, 1977 in Frascati. Segre *published over 300 publications* on algebraic geometry, differential geometry, topology and differential equations. Segre made significant contributions to geometry and to geometries over fields other than the complex numbers. Segre lectured in London in 1950 and these lectures were published in his 1951 work entitled "Arithmetical Questions on Algebraic Varieties." In 1959, he published his major results and findings in "Le geometrie di Galois" and in 1965 published another work on ground-field mathematics. Beniamino Segre was a distant relative of another famous Italian mathematician, Corrado Segre.

Corrado Segre

Corrado Segre was born on August 20, 1863 in Saluzzo and died May 18, 1924 in Turin. *He made major contributions in mathematics.* He discovered an invariant of surfaces under bi-rational transformations for fourth order surfaces with sixteen double points in 1896. *This invariant today is now called the Zeuthen-Segre invariant.* Segre also introduced bicomplex points into geometry, identified a different type of complex geometry in 1912, and provided an extension of ideas of Darboux on surfaces using differential equations.

Luca Valerio

Valerio was born in 1552 in Naples and died on January 17, 1618 in Rome. His famous works are "De centro gravitatis" (1604), where Valerio uses early ideas of the quotient of limits with the geometry of Archimedes, and "Quadratura parabolae" (1606).

Giuseppe Veronese

Veronese was born on May 7, 1854 in Chioggia and died on July 17, 1917 in Padua. He provided *groundbreaking work that advanced and fostered the further study of geometry in higher dimensions.* In 1880, he described higher dimension mathematics using n-dimensional projective geometry.

Geometry, Algebraic

Eugenio Bertini

Bertini was born on November 8, 1846 in Forli and died February 24, 1933 in Pisa. He is known for his work in algebraic geometry. Bertini also fought in the war for Italian independence with Garibaldi, the "George Washington of Italy."

Guido Castelnuovo

Castelnuovo was born on August 14, 1865 in Venice and died April 27, 1952 in Rome. *In 1903, he published a significant work in algebraic geometry* entitled "Geometria analitica e proiettiva." He published numerous papers on algebra, and with the great Federigo Enriques, produced a classification of algebraic surfaces. In 1919, he wrote on probability in his work entitled "Calcolo della probabilitá" and in 1923 published works on the theory of relativity. *He received many international honors and was elected to the Académie des Sciences of Paris. In 1949, he became a senator of the Italian Republic.*

Gino Fano

Fano was born on January 5, 1871 in Mantua, Italy and died November 8, 1952 in Verona. He advanced finite, projective and algebraic geometry. Fano was one of the first people to set geometry in abstract terms even before D. Hilbert's work on abstract geometry.

Francesco Severi

Severi was born on April 13, 1879 in Arezzo and died December 8, 1961 in Rome. Severi *published over 400 works on mathematics.* His most important contributions are to algebraic geometry. He introduced the concept of algebraic equivalence, provided conditions for the linear equivalence of two curves on a surface F, discovered a base of algebraically independent curves on any surface, and advanced the theory of rational equivalence. Severi published his most significant work in his "Mathematische Annalen" in 1906. *In 1907, he and the illustrious Federigo Enriques worked on hyperelliptic surfaces in differential geometry and as a consequence won the Prix Bordin award from the French Academy.*

Geometry, Differential

Eugenio Beltrami

Beltrami was born on November 16, 1835 in Cremona and died June 4, 1899 in Rome. He is known for his work in differential geometry on curves and surfaces and in 1868 published a paper on an interpretation of non-Euclidean geometry. Beltrami also wrote a four volume work on optics, thermodynamics, elasticity, electricity and magnetism titled "Opere Matematiche," published posthumously about 1902.

Ernesto Cesàro

Cesàro was born on March 12, 1859 in Naples and died September 12, 1906 in Torre Annunziata. His most significant contribution was his development of intrinsic geometry, a specialization of differential geometry, which he discussed in his text "Lezione di geometria intrinseca," published in Naples in 1890. *His publication included curves that are now named after Cesàro.*

Federigo Enriques

Enriques was born on January 5, 1871 in Livorno and died June 14, 1946 in Rome. *Enriques is credited for making important contributions in geometry, and with Castelnuovo, produced a classification of algebraic surfaces.* In 1912, he gained international fame at the International Congress in Cambridge when his work was the centerpiece of H. F. Baker's presidential address. *Enriques is the recipient of many international honors.* In 1917, Enriques gained additional recognition when *he and Francesco Severi won the Prix Bordin award from the French Academy* for their work on hyperelliptic surfaces in differential geometry. From 1907 to 1913 Enriques was president of the Italian Philosophical Society and in 1911 organized the 4th International Congress of Philosophy in

Bologna. Enriques also received an honorary degree from the University of St. Andrews in Scotland.

Guido Fubini

Fubini was born on January 19, 1879 in Venice and died June 6, 1943 in New York City. He studied differential geometry, differential equations, analytic functions, functions of several complex variables, non-linear integral equations and calculus of variations. He also taught at the Politecnico and the University in Turin. Fubini also studied the accuracy of artillery projectory, acoustics and electricity. To escape the growing influence of Fascism, he immigrated to the U.S. and *accepted a position at the Institute of Advanced Study in Princeton in 1939. His most significant contributions were in the area of differential projective geometry using absolute differential calculus.*

Father of Mathematical Logic and
Devised Peano Axioms for Set Theory and Σ (sum)

Giuseppe Peano

Peano was the son of a farmer and was born on August 27, 1858 in a farmhouse in Cuneo and died April 20, 1932 in Turin. In 1889, Peano published "Arithmetices principia, nova methodo exposita" which included his *famous axioms* defining the natural numbers in terms of sets. In 1895, Peano *established the "Σ" membership sign* used in mathematical set theory.

Earlier in his career (1887) he discovered and published a solution for solving systems of linear differential equations using successive approximations. In 1888, Peano published the book "Geometrical Calculus" which includes a revolutionary chapter on mathematical logic. *Peano was one of the true giants in mathematics and is considered the <u>original founder</u> of mathematical logic* even though the German mathematical philosopher Gottlob Frege is sometimes considered similarly.

Leroy P. Steele Prize Recipients

Eugenio Calabi

Eugenio Calabi was awarded the coveted Leroy P. Steele Prize in

1991 by the American Mathematical Society for fundamental work on differential geometry. Eugenio Calabi is the only person to have held the position of Chairman of Mathematics at the prestigious University of Pennsylvania twice. He was the department's chairman from 1967 to 1968 and again from 1971 to 1973. Mathematicians Eugenio Calabi of the University of Pennsylvania and Shing-Tung Yau of Harvard University discovered so-called "Calabi-Yau manifolds." These manifolds are six-dimensional mathematical shapes that support string theory.

Gian-Carlo Rota

Rota was born in Vigevano and educated in Italy up to the age of thirteen. After coming to the United States in 1950, he graduated from Princeton University, received his doctorate from Yale University, and received a Postdoctoral Research Fellowship to undertake research at the Courant Institute at New York University. He taught at Harvard University, M.I.T. and Rockefeller University. He also worked as a consultant for the Rand Corporation (1966 to 1971) and Brookhaven National Laboratory (1969 to 1973). Rota received the Steele Prize from the American Mathematical Society in 1988. The Prize citation singles out his 1964 paper on "The Foundations of Combinatorial Theory" stating that it was "...the single paper most responsible for the revolution that incorporated combinatorics into the mainstream of modern mathematics."

In July 1998, Rota was named the Norbert Wiener Professor of Mathematics at M.I.T. He also won the James R. Killian Faculty Achievement Award at M.I.T. in 1996, which recognizes extraordinary professional accomplishments and service to M.I.T. Dr. Rota has been advisor to at least 44 graduate students and many undergraduates throughout his career. He was well liked and respected by both his students and colleagues.

Dr. Rota was author or coauthor of seven books on mathematics. His book, "Indiscrete Thoughts," on philosophy was nominated for the 1999 Edwin Goodwin Ballard Book Prize in phenomenology presented by the Society for Phenomenology and Existential Philosophy.

Mathematics Education

Piero Borgi

Borgi was born about 1424 in Venice and died around the year 1484. He wrote a very popular textbook on arithmetic that had over 17 editions and was the *most widely distributed arithmetic book* in Italy during the 15th century. Borgi wrote the following books: "Addiones in quibus etiam sunt replicae Mathei Boringii" in 1483, "Arithmetica" in 1484, "Libro de Abacho de arithmetica," and "De arte mathematiche."

Cesare Burali-Forti

Cesare Burali-Forti was born on August 13, 1861 in Arezzo and died January 21, 1931 in Turin. *He wrote over 200 publications* and was also a very dedicated teacher who joined and supported The Mathesis Italian Society of Mathematicians. The Society's mission is to improve mathematics instruction. Refer to the later section 'Set Theory Paradox' for more on Burali-Forti.

Count Guglielmo Libri

Guglielmo Libri was born on January 1, 1803 in Florence and died September 28, 1869 in Fiesole. Libri's family was one of the oldest in Florence, however, he fled to France in order avoid political problems. He became a French citizen in 1833 and was elected to the French Académie des Sciences. *Libri is famous for his documentation on the history of Italian mathematics* that he wrote from 1838 to 1841 in 4 volumes entitled: "Histoire des sciences mathématique en Italie." He documented mathematics from ancient Rome through the life of Galileo.

Luca Pacioli

Pacioli's famous 1494 book the "Summa di aritmetica" provides a comprehensive summary of the mathematics known at that time including arithmetic, algebra, geometry and trigonometry. *His book provided a foundation for significant advances in mathematics that followed in Europe.* DaVinci is said to have read his "Summa di aritmetica" when he studied geometry and mechanics. Pacioli also documented his *invention of double-entry accounting* in this great book. Refer to the chapter "Economics, Finance and Business" for more on Pacioli and his accounting innovation.

In 1509, Pacioli translated Euclid's Elements from ancient Greek to

Latin and it became the first printed edition of this body of work. He also wrote recreational problems, geometrical problems, and proverbs with Leonardo da Vinci.

Perspective (Laws of) and First Frequency Table

Leone Battista Alberti

Alberti was a Renaissance genius who lived from 1404 to 1472. In his famous book "De Pictura" ("On Painting"), published in 1435, Alberti was the first to establish a scientific system using mathematics for linear perspective that is currently used by most artists. This book on the "law of perspective" had significant and lasting effects on painting and relief art fostering the developing trend of accurate spatial characteristics in Renaissance style art. Alberti also wrote the first book on cryptography, which contains the *first example of a frequency table*. (Also, refer to the chapter on "Art & Architecture" for more information about Alberti.)

Piero della Francesca

Francesca was born in 1412 in Sansepolcro and died there as well on October 12, 1492. Although Francesca is *known for his significant contributions as an artist* during the Renaissance, he was also a mathematician who published several mathematical treatises, e.g. "Trattato d'abaco," "Libellus de quinque corporibus regularibus" and "De prospectiva pingendi." The last title is about perspectives in painting. (Also, refer to the chapter on "Art & Architecture" for more information on della Francesca).

Mechanics and Hydraulics

Giambattista Della Porta

Della Porta was born on November 15, 1535 near Naples and died there as well on February 4, 1615. Della Porta was a mathematician and scientist who also applied his skills in mechanics for practical inventions. *He was one of the first to have conceived a steam engine as described in his 1606 work entitled "De'spiritali."* Della Porta also wrote on cryptography, mechanics, and squaring the circle.

Another one of Della Porta's *significant contributions was to the development of the camera.* He wrote of the *camera obscura* in his famous 20 volume science encyclopedia, "Magia Naturalis," published in 1558 to 1589. He was the *first to suggest using a convex lens with the camera obscura* further advancing and perfecting this predecessor to the modern camera. *His major work, "Magia Naturalis,"* examines the natural world and explains how it can be altered through analysis and empirical experiment. This work covers a variety of topics from demonology to magnetism and the *camera obscura.* Della Porta even designed a telescope as early as 1580, but it was not nearly as powerful as Galileo's telescope built in 1609. Della Porta also wrote an agricultural encyclopedia entitled "Villae" (1583-1592), and a body of analysis on chemistry in a work entitled "De distillatione" (1609).

Della Porta formed a scientific society (Accademia dei Segreti) that was forced to cease operation by the Inquisition around 1578. In 1585, in an apparent attempt to become politically correct, he joined the Jesuit Order. However, this proclamation of faith was not enough to stop the Church from banning his publications from 1594 to 1598. (Refer to the "Astronomy" and "Science & Technology" chapters for more on the science and inventions of Della Porta.)

Paolo Frisi

Frisi was born on April 13, 1728 in Milan and died there as well on November 22, 1784. Studing kinematics and hydraulics, he supported and designed the canal built between Milan and Pavia. His writings popularized the works of Galileo, Cavalieri, Newton and d'Alembert. In 1762, he wrote a significant book on hydraulics entitled "Del modo di regolare I fiumi, e I torrenti."

Leonardo da Vinci

DaVinci was born on April 15, 1452 in Vinci (near Florence) and died May 2, 1519 in Cloux, Amboise, France. *He is considered one of the world's greatest geniuses* for his paintings, sculpture and scientific research in every academic subject imaginable. He was also a competent mathematician and had a passion for geometry that led him to study many geometric and mechanical concepts. Leonardo is said to have read Leon Battista Alberti's books on perspective and architecture, as well as Piero della Francesca's book on perspectives in painting. Leonardo studied Euclid and also read the celebrated Luca Pacioli's book "Summa di aritmetica" that provided a summary of the mathematics known at that time. *Leonardo subsequently developed his own research on geometry* and offered mechanical solutions, e.g. several methods of squaring the circle. Leonardo was a genius at combining mathematics and mechanics. He wrote in his "Notebooks," volume 1, chapter 20: "Mechanics is the paradise of the mathematical sciences, because by means of it one comes to the fruits of mathematics." DaVinci also wrote a book on the theory of mechanics circa 1498.

DaVinci is among the originators of the science of hydraulics and invented perhaps the earliest hydrometer for measuring atmospheric humidity. His designs for canalization of rivers have practical value even today.

This quote from Leonardo's text "Treatise on Painting," illustrates how profoundly important he considers mathematics: "No human investigation can be called real science if it cannot be demonstrated mathematically." ("Nessuna humana investigazione si pio dimandara vera scienzia s'essa non passa per le matematiche dimonstrazione.") Refer to the chapters on "Art & Architecture" and "Science & Technology" for more on da Vinci.

Francesco Siacci

Siacci published hundreds of academic papers and made major contributions to analytic mechanics and the physics of artillery ballistics. Refer to the Science of Ballistics section in the "Military Contributions" chapter for more on Siacci.

Evangelista Torricelli

Torricelli was a renowned mathematician and inventor. He is most *famous for inventing the barometer in 1643 and being the first to sustain a man-made vacuum.* He developed a proof about the flow of liquid through an opening being proportional to the square root of the height of the liquid. Today, this is known as *Torricelli's Theorem.* Refer to the section in this chapter on Integral Calculus and Torricelli's Theorem and also the Barometer section in the "Science & Technology" chapter for more on Torricelli.

(Also, refer to the last section, 'Other Contributions to Mathematics', in this chapter to read about other mathematicians who contributed to a variety of areas including Mechanics and Hydraulics.)

"Motion is Impossible Paradox"
Zeno of Elea

Zeno was born about 490 BC in the town of Elea in the Lucania region of Italy, as it was then called. The area that comprised Lucania is located in southern Italy. Zeno spent his entire life in southern Italy and in 430 BC died in Elea as well. Little is known for certain about Zeno's life, but he was certainly a philosopher, most probably of Greek extraction. Elea was essentially a Greek colony in ancient Italy. Some accounts state that Zeno wrote a book of forty paradoxes, some of which have perplexed mathematicians for centuries. However, Zeno developed four paradoxes, which have had a profound influence on the development of mathematics and the advanced mathematical concept of infinitesimals.

The summaries of his famous paradoxes logically prove that motion is impossible. If we are to travel a specific distance (or in mathematical terms "traverse a line segment") with specific start and end points, at some point in time, we must reach halfway to the midpoint. But before we can get to the midpoint we must at some point in time reach its midpoint, which is the 1/4 point. And before we can get to the 1/4 point we must in turn reach its midpoint, the 1/8 point. Since we are forever reaching, as a prerequisite, the midpoint of a smaller and smaller segment, and every segment has its own midpoint, we can never move and reach the end of the line segment. Consequently, his famous paradoxes logically prove that motion is impossible, since the paradoxes occur in all line segments even the minutest ones. This puzzle is great for occupying a group of young teenagers, Boy Scouts, Girl Scouts, etc. If you try this when they are older, they won't spend much time with you, they will just get in their cars and drive away proving motion is quite possible after all.

Statics
Guidobaldo Marchese del Monte

Del Monte was born on January 11, 1545 in Pesaro and died January 6, 1607 in Montebaroccio. His book on mathematical statics, "Liber mechanicorum," written in 1577 was *at the time considered the greatest work on the subject since the Greek mathematicians*. He was a long-term friend of Galileo for over 20 years, and Galileo had used some of del Monte's techniques in his own works as well. Del Monte also wrote two books on astronomy, "Planisphaeriorum" in 1579,

"Problematum astronomicorum" in 1609, and another book on perspective, "Perspectivae libri sex" in 1600. He was also interested in mechanics and invented mathematical instruments and compasses.

Solution for Quartic Equation
Lodovico Ferrari
Ferrari was born on February 2, 1522 in Bologna and died there as well on October 5, 1565. As a 14 year old youth, he was a simple servant for the mathematical giant Cardano. Because Ferrari could read and write, Cardano employed him as his secretary. When Cardano realized the youth was a very intellectually gifted boy, he taught Ferrari mathematics. Ferrari became a venerated mathematician and is famous for his work on the solution of the quartic equation in 1540. This solution was included in Cardano's 1545 groundbreaking publication "Ars Magna" ("The Great Art"). Refer to the section 'Algebra and the Father of Probability' in this chapter for more on the august mathematicians, Cardano and Tartaglia.

Set Theory Paradox, Discovery
Cesare Burali-Forti
Forti was born on August 13, 1861 in Arezzo and died January 21, 1931 in Turin. In 1897, Forti was the first to prove a set theory paradox. Two years later in 1899, the famed German mathematician Georg Cantor discovered a similar paradox. Forti worked on set theory, vector analysis, linear transformations and their applications to differential geometry. *He wrote over 200 publications* and was also a very dedicated teacher who joined and supported The Mathesis Italian Society of Mathematicians. The Society's mission is to improve mathematics instruction.

String Theory
To find information on the mathematics developed by Italians to support string theory, please refer to the reference on 'Physics- String Theory' in the chapter on "Science & Technology."

Other Significant Contributions to Mathematics

Stefano degli Angeli

Angeli was born on September 11, 1623 in Venice and died there as well on October 11, 1697. Angeli worked mostly on infinitesimals and studied spirals, parabolas and hyperbolas. In Venice he published "De infinitorum parabolis" in 1654, "De infinitorum spiralium spatiorum mensura" in 1660 and "De infinitorum cochlearum" in 1661. He published "Della gravita dell aria e fluidi" on fluid dynamics when he was the Chairman at the University of Padua.

Francesco Brioschi

Brioschi was born on December 22, 1824 in Milan and died there as well on December 14, 1897. In 1854, he published a major work entitled "Teoria dei determinanti" on the theory and application of determinants. He also discovered new results in the theory of transformation of elliptic and abelian functions.

Francesco Faà di Bruno

Faà di Bruno was born on March 29, 1825 in Piemonte and died March 27, 1888 in Turin. In 1876, he published a famous mathematical work on binary forms.

Felice Casorati

Casorati was born on December 17, 1835 in Pavia and died September 11, 1890 in Casteggio. Casorati is known for what later became known as the Casorati-Weierstrass theorem. Weierstrass proved this theorem in 1876, but Casorati offered his proof eight years earlier in his 1868 study on complex numbers.

Giovanni Ceva

Ceva was born on December 7, 1647 in Milan and died in Mantua June 15, 1734. In his "De lineis rectis," published in 1678, he documented his discovery of important geometric results for triangles. In 1728, he also published a significant work on hydraulics entitled "Opus hydrostaticum." He also published "Opuscula mathematica" in 1682 and "Geometria Motus" in 1692, which partially anticipated infinitesimal calculus. In 1711, Ceva wrote "De Re Nummeraria," *one of the first books on mathematical economic, which discusses the equilibrium of the monetary system.* (Refer to the chapter on

"Economics, Finance and Business" for more on Ceva).

Gian Francesco Malfatti

Malfatti was born in Ala, Trento in 1731 and died on October 9, 1807 in Ferrara. He is most noted for his contributions on equations of the fifth degree. Malfatti also made contributions regarding the mathematics of the triangle and circles.

Francisco Maurolico

Maurolico was born on September 16, 1494 in Messina and died there as well on July 22, 1575. Maurolico is noted for his original books on geometry, the theory of numbers optics, conics and mechanics. He also *provided a methodology for measuring the Earth* in his work "Cosmographia." In 1670, Jean Picard used his technique in measuring the earth's meridian. Maurolico *also used incomplete ancient manuscripts to reconstruct and restore significant books by famous Greek mathematicians, such as, Euclid, Archimedes, Theodosius, Menelaus, Autolycus and Apollonius.* His efforts saved these masterpieces for many subsequent generations to appreciate.

Pietro Mengoli

Mengoli was born 1626 in Bologna and died there as well in 1686. He is noted for his work on infinite series and harmonic series. *He wrote several books on a variety of subjects.* Mengoli wrote on infinite series in his "Novae quadraturae arithmeticae" (1650) and on limits in his "Geometriae speciosae elementa" (1659). He also wrote books on astronomy and on the theory of music in "Speculazioni di musica" (1670).

Alessandro Padoa

Padoa was born on October 14, 1868 in Venice and died November 25, 1937 in Genoa. He was the first to present a method to prove new concepts in primitive term theory and also made significant contributions in the areas of algebraic theory of whole numbers and deductive theory. Padoa presented these contributions in 1900 at the International Congress of Philosophy in Paris. He also discovered an important method in the mathematical theory of definition. *Padoa was internationally known and gave numerous lectures at the Universities of Brussels, Pavia, Berne, Padua, Cagliari and Genoa. He also presented lectures at Congresses in Paris, Cambridge, Livorno,*

Parma, Padua and Bologna. The Technical Institute in Genoa greatly benefited when he accepted a teaching position there.

Giovanni Poleni

Poleni was born on August 23, 1683 in Venice and died November 15, 1761 in Padua. Poleni made contributions to hydraulics, physics, astronomy, archaeology and meteorology. *He held many positions at the University of Padua including:* Chair of Astronomy in 1709, Professor of Physics in 1715, and Chair of Mathematics in 1719 replacing the famous Nicolaus Bernoulli II. In 1710, he was *also elected as Fellow of the Royal Society.* Poleni developed new methods for calculating the distance traveled by a ship at sea and offered new analysis of ship's anchors, cranes and windlasses. *These innovations won Poleni many awards and honors.*

Jacopo Francesco Riccati

Riccati was born on May 28, 1676 in Venice and died April 15, 1754 in Treviso. He gained international fame for his work and publications on new solutions for differential equations, lowering the order of equations, and separation of variables. Although he remained in Italy, *he had offers from Peter the Great* to become President of the St. Petersburg Academy of Science. Riccati also worked on cycloidal pendulums, the laws of resistance in a fluid, and differential geometry. *His work on hydraulics was valuable to the City of Venice during the construction of dikes along the canals.*

Vincenzo Riccati

Vincenzo Riccati was born on January 11, 1707 near Treviso in Castelfranco Veneto and died January 17, 1775 in Treviso. His contributions were in hyperbolic functions for solutions of cubics, their derivatives and exponential functions. *(Lambert is sometimes incorrectly credited as the first to introduce the hyperbolic functions, however, he did this subsequent to Riccati's contributions in 1770).* Riccati with Saladini also worked on the 'rose curves,' which was first postulated by Grandi. (Refer to the Geometry Advancements section for more on Grandi.) Vincenzo Riccati *also was an accomplished hydraulic engineer. His efforts and implementations of flood control projects saved the regions around Venice and Bologna.*

Paolo Ruffini

Ruffini was born on September 22, 1765 in Valentano, near Rome and died May 10, 1822 in Modena. He was a trained mathematician and physician studying at the University of Modena. In 1799, *he published a revolutionary and highly controversial theory of equations claiming that quintics could not be solved by radicals* as leading mathematicians had believed at the time. *Ruffini had to invent group theory* in his work to create his theorems and was the first to introduce the notion of the order of an element, conjugacy, the cycle decomposition of elements of permutation groups, and the notions of primitive and imprimitive. Like other great minds, ahead of their time, his mathematical contemporaries could not accept his revolutionary idea that a polynomial could not be solved in radicals. Niels Henrik Abel is sometimes incorrectly credited with Ruffini's ideas, since Ruffini was dismissed by peers who did not accept his theories into the mainstream mathematics of the time.

Ruffini, the physician, also published a scientific article on typhus based on his own experience with the disease in 1820. He also published several works on philosophy.

Giovanni Enrico Eugenio Vacca

Vacca was born on November 18, 1872 in Genoa and died January 6, 1953 in Rome. Vacca *published approximately 130 papers, 38 on mathematics theory, 45 on the history of mathematics, and 47 on Chinese culture.* Vacca's major paper on Fermat's method of descent represents one of his significant mathematical contributions. The great Giuseppe Peano presented this paper to the Academy of Sciences of Turin in 1928. Vacca was also deeply interested in Chinese culture. He spent from 1907 to 1908 in western China and in 1910 earned a Ph.D. in Florence on Chinese studies and later also taught Chinese language and literature at the University of Rome until he retired in 1947.

Giovanni Vailati

Vailati was born on April 24, 1863 in Cremona and died May 14, 1909 in Rome. He is known for his *contributions to mathematical logic and worked with the famous Giuseppe Peano. He gained international recognition for his essays on mechanics published from 1896 to 1898.* He also published works on the history and methodology of science and mechanics.

Vailati *was appointed as a permanent member at the First*

International Congress of Philosophy. He attended both the Second International Congress of Philosophy in Rome (1903) and the Third International Congress of Philosophy in Heidelberg (1908). The agenda of the third Congress was greatly influenced by Vailati's contributions to the committee.

Giuseppe Vitali

Vitali was born on August 26, 1875 in Ravenna and died February 29, 1932 in Bologna. He made significant contributions by his discoveries that include a theorem on set-covering, the notion of absolutely continuous functions, and a criteria for the closure of a system of orthogonal functions. Vitali also worked on a new absolute differential calculus and a new geometry of D. Hilbert spaces. *Vitali was appointed as Chairman of Mathematics at three major universities:* Modena (1923), Padua (1924) and Bologna (1930).

Vito Volterra

Volterra was born to a poor family on May 3,1860 in Anacona and died October 11, 1940 in Rome. His most famous contribution to mathematics was his work on *integral equations.* However, he also published works on partial differential equations, particularly the equation of cylindrical waves. *Today certain integral equations are called Volterra type in his honor.* In 1883, he conceived a relationship concept that a function can depend on a continuous set of values of another function.

Volterra fought against and opposed the Fascism that arose in the late 1920's and was made to resign from his position at the University of Rome in 1931 because he refused to take an oath of allegiance to the Fascist Government. Volterra earned his Ph.D. in Physics from the University of Pisa and in 1938 was also awarded an *honorary degree by the University of St. Andrews in Scotland* in recognition of his contribution to the field of mathematics.

꒐

Chapter XIII

MEDICINE, BIOLOGY & HEALTH

"If not for the intuition of Dr. Urbani…SARS would have spread farther and faster than it has, public health officials around the world say."
- New York Times, April 8, 2003 -

Anatomical and Pathological Terms
Italian Physicians and Researchers

About 100 anatomical and pathological terms have been named after, or named by, Italian physicians and biomedical researchers. The list below offers the names of many of these scientists (last name, first name) followed by the year of birth and death shown in parentheses. The most well known scientists are shown in bold type and they are detailed in specific entries throughout this chapter.

Albini, Giuseppe (1827 – 1911), Alè, G. (unknown), Alessandro, Giuseppe d' (unknown), Angelucci, Arnaldo (1854 – 1933), Aranzi, Giulio Cesare (1529 – 1589), Armanni, Luciano (1839 – 1903), Arslan, Michele (1904 – 1988), Ascoli, Alberto (1877 – 1957), Ascoli, Maurizio (1876 - unknown), Aselli, Gasparo (1581 – 1626), Aselli, Gasparo (1581 – 1626), Ayala, Giuseppe (1878 – 1943), Baccelli,

Guido (1832 – 1916), Bagolini, B. (unknown), Balduzzi, O. (unknown), Banti, Guido (1852 – 1925), Berlinghieri, Andrea Vaccà (1772 – 1826), Bertolotti, Mario (1876 - unknown), Bianco, Ida (1917 – unknown), Bignami, Amico (1862 – 1919), Biondi, Adolfo (1846 – 1917), Bozzolo, Camillo (1845 – 1920), Brusa, P. (unknown), Cacchi, Roberto (unknown), Campanacci, Mario (1932 – 1999), Cardarelli, Antonio (1831 – 1926), Cerletti, Ugo (1877 – 1963), Ciuffini (unknown), Comes, Rosario (unknown), Concato, Luigi Maria (1825 – 1882), Corno, Renzo (unknown), Cotugno, Domenico Felice Antonio (1736 – 1822), Dagnini, Giuseppe (1866 – 1928), Dagnini, Guido (1905 – unknown), De Crecchio, Luigi (1832 – 1894), De Toni, Giovanni (1895 – 1973), Dubini, Angelo (1813 – 1902), Ducrey, Agosto (1860 – 1940), **Eustachi, Bartolomeo (1510 – 1574), Falloppio, Gabriele (1523 – 1562)**, Fazio, E. (1849 – 1902), Fede, Francesco (unknown), Fermi, Claudio (1862 – unknown), Flajani, Giuseppe (1741 – 1808), Fontana, Felice (1730 – 1805), Giannuzzi, Giuseppe (1839 – 1867), **Golgi, Camillo (1844 – 1926)**, Gradenigo, Giuseppe Conte (1859 – 1926), Greppi, Enrico (1896 – unknown), Guglielmo, Giovanni Di (1886 – 1961), Maffucci, Angelo (1847 – 1903), Marchiafava, Ettore (1847 – 1935), Mazzoni, Vittorio (unknown), Mibelli, Vittorio (1860 – 1910), Micheli, Ferdinando (1872 – 1936), Miescher, Guido (1877 – 1961), Mistichelli, Domenico (unknown), Mondini, Carlo (1729 – 1803), Monteggia, Giovanni Battista (1762 – 1815), Mya, Giuseppe (1857 – 1911), Nazari, A. (unknown), Negri, Adelchi (1876 – 1912), Neri, Giovanni (unknown), Néri, Vincenzo (1882 – unknown), Oddi, Ruggero (1864 – 1913), Pacchioni, Antonio (1665 – 1726), Pellegrini, Augusto (1877 – unknown), Pellizzari, Celso (1851 – 1925), Perusini, Gaetano (1879 – 1915), Ramazzini, Bernardino (1633 – 1714), Ricci, Vincenzo (unknown), Rietti, Ferdinando (1890 – 1954), Riga, Antonio (1832 – 1919), Riva-Rocci, Scipione 91863 – 1937), Romano, C. (1923 – unknown), Scaglietti, Oscar (1906 – unknown), Scarpa, Antonio (1752 – 1832), Sertoli, Enrico (1842 – 1910), Signorelli, Angelo (1876 – 1953), Silengo, Margherita (unknown), Silvestroni, Ezio (1905 – 1990), **Spallanzani, Lazzaro (1729 – 1799)**, Splendore, Alfonso (1871 – 1953), Todaro, Francesco (1839 – 1918), Toffa (unknown), Torricelli, C. (unknown), Valsalva, Antonio Maria (1666 – 1723)

Aspirin – first isolated in pure form, salicylic acid
Raffaele Piria

The benefits of willow tree bark extract were known to the ancient Greeks. In 1828, salicin extract was first isolated by the French chemist Henri Leroux from willow bark. Raffaele Piria, an Italian chemist, first isolated *pure salicylic acid* in 1838 ushering in the modern age of aspirin. He derived this from methyl salicylate that was extracted from willow tree bark. A later form of aspirin (acetyl salicylic acid) was derived by Frederic Gerhardt in 1853 from the bark of a silver birch tree. In 1959, Hermann Kolbe at Marburg University succeeded in making it artificially. In 1899, Felix Hoffman made a stable form of aspirin at the Adolf von Bayer laboratories at Elberfeld. Today Bayer is a huge pharmaceutical corporation.

Autopsy and General Anatomy
Marcus Aurelius
Mondino of Bologna

Although Roman law prohibited autopsies, Emperor Marcus Aurelius, around 161 AD, allowed the Greek physician Galen (physician to the Emperor and elite gladiators) to perform autopsies secretly to advance his medical understanding. In later years, Mondino de Liucci (1275-1326) who taught at the University of Bologna advanced the concept of human autopsies, even though they were still generally outlawed. Mondino of Bologna dissected the human corpse for the first time in almost 1,500 years! *He wrote and published an autopsy manual in 1316, which enlightened many others for nearly two and a half centuries. His work became the official anatomy textbook of the universities and medical schools.* Following the advances made by Mondino, many other anatomists performed autopsies and performed research at universities, especially in Italy.

The study of human anatomy made further progress because of Italian artists. For example, the great Raphael (1488-1520) used the human skeleton to improve the accuracy of his sketches and assure proper posture. And of course, many famous anatomical descriptions and sketches were provided by Leonardo da Vinci (1442-1519). Also, Michelangelo (1475-1564) created many sketches of muscles and cadavers.

Biological Microscopy, Father of
Marcello Malpighi

The Italian anatomist, Marcello Malpighi is considered the Father of Biological Microscopy. He was born March 10, 1628 in Crevalcuore near Bologna and died November 30, 1694 in Rome. Malpighi received his M.D. and Ph.D. from University of Bologna in 1653. In the 17th century, Malpighi's work was far ahead of his time and his contemporaries. As a result, he and his work were widely criticized by his medical contemporaries. As a consequence, he suffered from bouts of depression. *Malpighi made a revolutionary breakthrough when he established the first procedures for preparing tissue for examination under a microscope.* He also completed revolutionary anatomical and embryological research on the circulatory system (refer to the Pulmonary Blood Circulation section later in this chapter). *His studies of glandular diseases were centuries ahead of his time; it took 200 years for these studies to be confirmed as correct by others in medical research.*

Malpighi is also famous for his ground-breaking research on the life cycle and activities of the silkworm in 1669. He was also interested in plant physiology and in 1675 and 1679, published "Anatome plantarum" which earned him international acclaim as the *founder of microscopic study of plant anatomy.*

Blind and Deaf – Education
Girolamo Cardano
(aka Jerome Cardan and Gironamo Cardano)

In the 16th century, the famous mathematician Cardano was the first to publish and advocate methods of teaching the blind by using the sense of touch and the deaf by using combinations of symbols or signs. He is credited for the original concept of communicating with and educating the deaf by using *sign language*. However, it was not until the 18th century, that the first school for the deaf was opened by Abbe Charles Michel de L'Eppe in Paris in 1755. (Also, refer to the chapter on "Mathematics" for more on Cardano and his mathematical genius.)

Body Temperature – First Measured
(Quantitative Measurements of Human Physiology)
Santorio Santorio

Santorio Santorio was born March 29, 1561 in Capodistria and died February 22, 1636 in Venice. Santorio studied at the University of Padua and received his M.D. in 1582. He was an Italian physician who, in 1626, was the *first to measure human body temperature using a thermometer*. Santorio was the *first to recognize the critical importance of physical measurement in medicine*. He introduced the use of precise instruments and measurements to add quantitative precision to the practice of medicine. In 1613, he wrote "De Medicina Statica" which analyzed the human metabolism and documented the need and significance of physiological measurement. In it he also reported his new studies on metabolism and perspiration using the new equipment that he invented for measurement. *His associates included the famous astronomer/physicist Galileo who is believed to have been one of Santorio's experimental subjects.* Galileo discovered new laws of physics regarding the pendulum and his influence probably led Santorio to use the pendulum's regular "beat" as a means of heart rate measurement. He also was the first to add a numerical scale to the thermoscope, which was the precursor to the thermometer. Also, refer to the entry 'Thermometer' in this chapter.

Brain Anatomy
Costanzo Varolio

Varolio published very early studies of the human brain anatomy in 1568.

Cancer and Virus Research - *Nobel Prize*
Renato Dulbecco

Dulbecco was born in 1914 in Catanzaro and graduated from the University of Turin, Italy receiving his M.D. in 1936 at the early age of twenty-two. In 1964, he received the coveted Albert Lasker Award for Medical Research, this is America's "Nobel Prize" in medicine. In 1975, Dulbecco won the *Nobel Prize* in medicine for his discoveries concerning the interaction between tumor viruses and the genetic material of the cell. Dr. Dulbecco opened new doors in genetic research with two of his groundbreaking discoveries. First, he discovered that the DNA of a virus permanently incorporates itself into another cell's genetic material, almost becoming a new gene of the infected cell. Second, he discovered that the new viral genes in the cell produce their own *messengers*, altering and interacting with the cellular DNA activity, thus affecting other cells in turn.

Dr. Dulbecco continues his association with The Salk Institute for Biological Studies after having served as its President from 1988 to 1992. He is the recipient of many international awards and honors and holds the following doctorates:

- Doctor of Science, Yale University (1968)
- Doctor of Laws, University of Glasgow (1970)
- Honoris Causa Doctorem Medicinae, Vrije Universiteit, Brussels (1978)
- Doctor of Science, Indiana University (1985)

Additionally, Dulbecco *invented new techniques* for studying animal viruses in the laboratory, and more importantly, he is also *credited with originating the Human Genome* Project. See the section, on Human Genome Project, for more information on Dr. Dulbecco.

Dr. Dulbecco has published extensively. His recent works include:

- Dulbecco, Renato, "The Biology of Mammary Cancer," article in "Current Topics in Biomedical Research," R. Kurth, W. K. Schwerdtfeger, editors, 1992
- Dulbecco, Renato, "The Genome Project," article in "The Diagnostic Challenge," E. P. Fisher and S. Kloje, editors, 1995

Clinical Examinations, Early
Giovanni Battista de Monte
At the University of Padua, Professor Giovanni Battista de Monte (1498-1552) became famous for his introduction of clinical instruction in Padua and included clinical patient bedside examinations in 1529.

Cloning, First Human Project Planned
Severino Antinori, MD
In January 2001, Dr. Severino Antinori, a famed Italian fertility specialist, announced that he will head a team to begin the first human cloning project. Dr. Antinori, director of Rome's International

Associated Research Institute, gained international recognition when he helped a 62-year-old woman conceive and give birth in 1994, *making her the oldest woman to give birth in history*. He describes human cloning as the "last frontier to overcome male sterility" troubling many infertile couples. Although cloning is not illegal in Italy, there are many skeptics and other opponents who have ethical and even religious concerns regarding human cloning. However, others support Dr. Antorini contending that cloning could mitigate the tragedy associated with some late term miscarriages and infant deaths during delivery by cloning the fetus. Supporters also argue that clones will differ greatly from their original donors. Clones will experience different parents, education, illnesses, and other life experiences, including different environmental exposures in the womb. Clones also have a slight difference in DNA due to the mitochondrial DNA of the de-nucleated egg used for the cloning process. Further, advocates say this science will yield to our understanding of stem-cells, and how to regenerate specific organ tissue for repair or transplantation.

Science may now be ahead of the law. Nations will need legislation to prohibit cloning for the almost science fiction sounding purposes of creating slaves, armies, or for the purpose of harvesting organs. All science has its bright and dark sides, but our civilization must be ready to evaluate scientific changes and legislate appropriately.

At a cloning conference held August 7th, 2001 by the National Academy of Sciences in Washington, D.C., Dr. Antinori's team announced their plans to clone a human in 2003. The team stated that they are working with 200 infertile couples from all over the world.

During an interview on August 10th, 2001, with the French daily newspaper, "Liberation," Dr. Antinori compared the condemnation of his work by the Vatican to the Church's heresy charges against Galileo during the 17th century. The Church has compared his cloning plans to Nazi type activities. The controversial doctor stated, "They can call me Hitler or Frankenstein. Personally, I prefer to compare myself to Galileo. I am a victim of intolerance."

The science of cloning a human is highly complex, and most experts doubt that Dr. Antinori has developed the necessary technology to succeed. The doctor will need great scientific prowess, as well as a healthy dose of good luck to reach his ambitious goal. This author's friend and associate, Thomas J. McAteer profoundly said, "It's good to be lucky, but it's better to be good." Undoubtedly, Dr. Antinori will need to be both.

Cold Cream
Rome

Credit must be given to Galen, the famous Greek physician, living in Rome who developed the first cold creams in Rome in the 2nd century. He recommended Romans make cold cream from white wax, rose essence, olive oil and lanolin (then called despyum).

Contact Lenses - Concept
Leonardo da Vinci

Da Vinci was the first to design a lens to fit on the eye to correct vision. He described this first contact lens in his "Code on the Eye." He explains that a short tube could be filled with water- the eye is then placed against the water, which refracts the light as a lens. The opposite end of the tube is sealed with flat glass. This is remarkably similar in concept to modern high-water-content soft contact lenses. How da Vinci conceived of this invention in the 15th century is beyond comprehension.

Cough Drop
Vincent R. Ciccone

Ciccone was the son of Italian immigrants and took his first job sweeping floors at the Charms Candy Company in Bloomfield, NJ at age 16. He eventually rose to chemist and candy-maker, and his inventions led him to file over twenty U.S. patents. Ciccone invented a method for combining medicines with hard candies without reducing the drug's effectiveness, a technique now commonly used in making cough drops and throat lozenges. *His inventions also contributed to the development of mass production of penicillin and revolutionized the manufacturing of hard candy and chocolate.* He also invented the "Blow Pop" lollipop with a bubble-gum center. Ciccone retired in 1990 as president and chief executive of the company, and passed away in 1997 at the age of 81.

Dentures
Etruria/Tuscany, Italy

Tuscany, the central region of Italy, was long ago called Etruria by the Romans. The Etruscan people who lived there (800 BC to 500 BC) *are considered the master dentists of the ancient world. History shows that their skills were lost after the fall of the Roman Empire and dentistry did not regain these dental skills until the 19th century.* The Etruscans crafted gold bridgework and would carve dentures from ivory and bone. Often Etruscan dentists performed an early form of organ donation. Good teeth of deceased individuals would be surgically removed and used with gold bridges for those who could afford this more natural looking denture. The Etruscans had a very advanced civilization with well developed technologies and were expert metallurgists at the time when their neighboring Romans were still organized into large tribes. The Etruscans developed very original artistry using bronze, gold and other metals. The first few kings of the early Roman Kingdom were probably Etruscans.

Electrical Nature of Nerves & Muscles Discovered
Luigi Galvani

Galvani was born September 9, 1737 in Bologna, Italy and died December 4, 1798. He received a medical degree from the University of Bologna and became a professor of anatomy there as well. Galvani added new revolutionary scientific knowledge based upon his experiments on the effects of electric impulses on muscle. Around 1771, Luigi Galvani demonstrated that a frog's legs would spasm from static electrical charges, and also, simply by connecting the nerve endings from one frog to a different frog's muscle. He termed this "animal electricity." Galvani was the first to discover the connection between life and electricity, paving the way for an entirely new area of biomedical research. The Galvanic electric process (i.e. *galvanization*) is named in honor of Galvani.

Eustachian Tube, Discovery of
Bartolommeo Eustachio

The Italian anatomist, Eustachio, who lived from 1524 to 1574, discovered the Eustachian tube and its function. The Eustachian tube is a narrow tube connecting the inside of the middle ear to the back of the throat. This tube allows periodic drainage of middle ear secretions and also functions to keep the air pressure in the middle ear equal to the atmospheric pressure surrounding us. This increases the performance of the eardrum and hearing. Eustachio wrote two books on anatomy, "Tabulae Anatomicae" (1552) and "Opuscula Anatomicae" (1564).

Eyeglasses
Salvino Armati
Alessandro della Spina

The invention of corrective spectacles around 1280 in Florence by Salvino Armati was exploited and marketed by his colleague Alessandro della Spina. Although Spina may have worked with Armati on the invention, it is possible that Armati invented eyeglasses and Spina heavily marketed them. They both were gaffers or glass blowers.

Centuries later, Venice became the center for eyeglass production in the 16th century and gradually over the decades eyeglasses became more commonplace throughout Europe and the world. Five hundred years after eyeglasses were first invented in Florence, the American inventor and writer, Benjamin Franklin, invented the bifocal eyeglasses in 1784.

The English word *lens* is derived from Italian. In Italian, the word for *lens* is *lente*. This is derived from another Italian word *lenticchie*, which means *lentil*. The first lenses were called *lenticchie* because the glass convex lens has the shape of the common lentil.

Fallopian Tube, Discovery and Condom Invention
Gabriele Fallopio

During the 16th century, a professor of anatomy at Padua University, Gabriele Fallopio (1523-1562) invented the condom to prevent the spread of venereal diseases and unwanted pregnancy. He made his condoms out of washed pig intestines and linen. This highly successful invention at the time was euphemistically called *overcoats*. Ironically, during the 16th century his invention was hailed, but centuries later, the more puritanical Americans supported by religious groups considered condoms immoral. *The U.S. Postal Service confiscated sixty-five thousand condoms in New York in the 1880s. Hundreds of manufacturers and mail order merchants were arrested for attempting to sell these "immoral" goods using the mail service.* A century later, in the 1990's, the U.S. Government funded programs to distribute free condoms for high school students, primarily to curb

HIV infection. The cultural pendulum can swing very broadly.

Fallopio also was the first to discover the movement of ova (egg) through a tube to the uterus. That tube, now named the *fallopian tube* is named in his honor.

Fertilization in the Lab and
Discovery that Semen is Necessary for Fertilization
Lazzaro Spallanzani

Spallanzani was the first to fertilize eggs in a laboratory using frogs' eggs in 1773. At that time spermatozoa had not yet been identified, but Spallanzani believed that semen was necessary to nourish or activate the already complete egg. *Spallanzani was certain that semen was needed for life.* During his experiments in 1779, he actually put tight pants on male frogs to keep them from fertilizing eggs. When the eggs did not fertilize, he proved that the sperm was needed and that other activities of the frog could not fertilize the egg. Perhaps, some tailor had a little fun crafting the frog pants for Spallanzani's experiment. This author's father was a tailor and he found this story humorous, picturing little Italian frogs looking quite continental in their tight pants. Believe it or not, fertilization of an egg was not *fully* understood *until 1875* when Oscar Hertwig (German embryologist) showed that the spermatozoon and egg were separate cells and their union was necessary for fertilization. (Also, refer to the section "Life..." later in this chapter for more on Spallanzani.)

Fluoride Treatments
Naples, Italy

Neapolitan dentists in 1802 realized that patients with certain tooth discoloration were cavity free. The spots turned out to be the result of high fluoride levels in the water and soil in certain sections surrounding Naples. Within a few decades both Italian and French dentists were recommending the use of fluoride lozenges sweetened with honey to reduce tooth decay.

Forensic Medicine
Fortunatus Fidelis

In 1598, the Italian scientist, Fortunatus Fidelis was the first person to practice modern forensic medicine. Forensic medicine is the application of medical knowledge to legal and criminal questions. Modern DNA analysis has added a powerful new weapon to the arsenal of forensic scientists.

Hospitals in the Western World, First
Roman Empire

Many historians credit the Romans for establishing the first civilian hospitals in the western world. The Romans were also the first to establish military medical services. Their medical and surgical sophistication was legendary. (Refer to the section on Military Services in the "Military Contributions" chapter.)

Human Genome Project
Renato Dulbecco and Charles DeLisi

On Columbus Day, 1985, Dr. Dulbecco of the Salk Institute publicized his idea of sequencing the entire human genome as a means of understanding the genetic origins of cancer and other diseases. He further advanced this concept in public lectures and in a commentary that he authored for "Science" magazine (March 1986). His efforts were the first to bring international attention to the idea of sequencing the entire genome, instead of piecemeal attempts to understand the genetic causes of specific diseases. Many opponents thought the idea was merely academic and not practical, due to the immense effort that would be needed. Today we know that Dr. Dulbecco (a 1975 Nobel Prize winner) was correct, since researchers are well on their way to completing this revolutionary genetic sequencing project. Also, see the section on Cancer and Virus Research for more on Dr. Dulbecco.

Also in the fall of 1985, Dr. Charles DeLisi read a report of the Department of Energy about the genetic consequences of the atom bombs dropped on Hiroshima and Nagasaki during World War II, and independently conceived and supported the idea of sequencing the entire human genome. DeLisi had worked for the National Cancer Institute of the National Institutes of Health. In 1985, Dr. DeLisi

R. R. Esposito

became head of the Department of Energy's Office of Health and Environmental Research, and used his personal convictions and position to initiate the now famous U.S. government human genome project.

Dr. DeLisi was, and still is, associated with the Department of Energy, Office of Health and Environmental Research. He is also Professor and Dean of the College of Engineering at Boston University. Dr. Delisi is an Italian-American, his father's family is from Palermo, Sicily and his mother's family is from the Abruzzi region.

Dr. DeLisi's publications include articles in numerous academic journals that include: "American Scientist," "Journal of Biophysics," "Computing in Science and Engineering," "Immunological Reviews," "Journal of Computational Chemistry," "Journal of Molecular Biology," "Biopolymers," "Science," "Protein Science," "Vaccines," and "Journal of the Franklin Institute."

Human Immunodeficiency Virus (HIV)
– Discovery & Diagnostic Screening
Robert C. Gallo

In 1984, Dr. Robert C. Gallo was Chief of the Tumor Cell Biology Laboratory (TCBL) of the National Cancer Institute when he co-discovered the HIV (or AIDS) virus. He also developed a diagnostic blood test to screen for the infectious disease. Dr. Gallo is credited for *safeguarding the world's blood supply and curtailing what would have been an international epidemic of this lethal disease.* Six years earlier, Dr. Gallo isolated and discovered the viral causes associated with certain types of childhood leukemia. For this research, the national government of Germany awarded the highest German prize for medicine, the *Paul Ehrlich Prize*, to Robert Gallo in 1999. Dr. Gallo founded and now heads The Institute of Human Virology at the University of Maryland as the first research institute in the United States to combine the disciplines of basic research, vaccine research, animal models, epidemiology, and clinical research to develop diagnostics and therapeutics in diseases due to chronic human viruses. Also, see the Rheumatism section in this chapter for Dr. Anthony Fauci's research on HIV.

Isometrics
George Siciliano (aka Charles Atlas)

Born in 1877 George Siciliano invented the technique or system of exercises that builds muscles by pushing and pulling arms or legs against another, called isometrics. In 1921 he originally called it "dynamic tension." Many organizations quickly adopted George Siciliano's techniques including the U.S. Navy and New York University, School of Medicine. These "no impact" exercises strengthen muscle and also have been applied to the science of physical therapy. George died in 1972 at the age of 85. Legend has it that he was inspired to build muscles when *a bully kicked sand in the face* of the young 97-pound George when on a date at the beach.

Life - Spontaneous Generation Disproved and Hermetic Sealing Discovery

Lazzaro Spallanzani

Spallanzani was born January 12, 1729 in Italy and died there as well on February 11, 1799. He was a biologist who in 1765 was the *first to perform experiments to disprove the ideas of spontaneous generation of life*. Spallanzani proved that life was not spontaneous by experimenting with sterilized "broths" sealed in flasks melted shut. The various "broths" remained sterile without life indefinitely. A second famous outcome of his experiments was that *Spallanzani was also the first to discover preserving by means of hermetic sealing*. For those of you who remember Johnny Carson's "The Tonight Show" (on NBC television), Carson played a comedic character called "Carnac the Magnificent," who referred to documents unviewed by anyone as "hermetically sealed in a mayonnaise jar." A use for hermetic sealing Spallanzani hadn't thought of in 1765.

In 1768, Spallanzani wrote that there is an inverse relationship between the regenerative power of living organisms and their age, i.e. the higher the organism's age, the lower its regenerative power. This principle regarding regenerative power is now called *Spallanzani's law*. This author safely assumes that middle-aged readers of this book are painfully aware of this *law*. Spallanzani studied the regenerative power of salamanders and snails, in particular the ability of snails to regenerate heads after decapitation. This explains why French snails have historically shown no fear of the guillotine. (Also, refer to the section "Fertilization..." in this chapter for more on Spallanzani.)

Francesco Redi

Before Spallanzani, another Italian named Francesco Redi was the *first to question the scientific belief in spontaneous generation of life.* Redi was a physician, naturalist, and poet who lived from 1626 to about 1698. Redi performed experiments to prove that plants and animals can only be created from others of their kind. His experiments with rotting meat proved that maggots were not spontaneously generated from the meat. Redi's experiments were not as extensive as Spallanzani's, and did not completely disprove the widely held belief of spontaneous generation of life. Spallanzani's experiments unequivocally proved that life cannot spontaneously occur without the presence of some kind of reproductive biology.

Liposuction
Giorgio Fischer

In 1974, Dr. Giorgio Fischer, an Italian gynecologist from Rome, invented liposuction. Dr. Fischer is the President of the International Academy of Cosmetic Surgery, Societa' Italiana di Chirurgia Estetica, and the Societa' Italiana di Liposcultura. In 1978, Dr. Illouz, a French plastic surgeon, made the first purely cosmetic use of the procedure.

Malaria Research - Proof that Mosquitoes Spread the Disease
Giovanni Lancisi

Lancisi was the first to claim that mosquitoes carried and transmitted the malaria disease to humans. He also had large swamps drained in Italy as a preventative measure. In 1898, three other Italian researchers, Amico Bignami, Giovanni Grassi and Giuseppe Bastianelli identified the malaria parasite's life cycle in infected human blood. They were also the first to prove that it is only the female mosquito that carries the parasite.

Medical Pathology, Father of
Giovanni Morgagni

Morgagni was born February 25, 1682 in Italy and died December 6, 1771. He completed early research on diseases of the ear in 1704 and later broadened his research to identify the causes of diseases through autopsy procedures. In 1706, he published "Adversaria Anatomica" a treatise on anatomy and diseases. In 1761, he published his pioneering study of pathology entitled "On the Causes of Diseases" and ushered in the scientific field of medical pathology.

Medical Schools - Oldest
Salerno School of Medicine
University of Bologna Medical School

Published in 1098 AD in Salerno, Italy by Nicholas of Salerno, "Antidotarum" represents a very early medical text of 2,650 medical prescriptions and the associated aliments that are relieved. The Salerno school of medicine also produced "Practica" in 1040 AD. Petrocellus authored this early important medical work. The school's most well known work is the "Regimen Sanitatis Salernitanum" ("Salerno Regimen of Health"). Twenty Salerno physicians also founded "Civitas Hippocratica" as a means to establish a formal medical school in Salerno in 1151 AD.

Salerno was also unique since it admitted women and Jews to the school even though many priests were engaged there as teachers of medicine. This offers an example of cooperation and tolerance that many religious factions should strive to emulate today.

Also, the *world's first true university* with curriculum, standards, examinations and degrees was the University of Bologna. Bologna was founded in the 11th century and by the 12th century founded the world's first university-based medical school. Bologna also admitted women and Jewish students. (Refer to the entry 'University – World's First' in the "Culture, Conventions and Traditions" chapter for more on Bologna.)

Salerno and Bologna are the oldest and most famous medieval medical schools in Western civilization and represented the most significant advances in medical knowledge since the ancient Greek physicians Hippocrates and Galen.

Nerve Cell Growth - *Nobel Prize*
Rita Levi-Montalcini

Rita Levi-Montalcini was born April 22, 1909 in Turin (Torino). Her father, Adamo Levi, was an electrical engineer and a gifted mathematician. Her mother, Adele Montalcini, was a talented painter. This Italian neurologist completed her medical degree and research at the University of Turin in 1947. She later held research positions at Washington University and University of St. Louis. Dr. Levi-Montalcini joined the Institute of Cell Biology in Rome in 1961 and received a *Nobel Prize* in 1986 for the discovery of a substance or growth factor that stimulates the growth of nerve cells. This substance is appropriately called *nerve growth factor* (NGF). In her experiments, she demonstrated that a few minutes after the addition of NGF, nerve fibers would grow out from the *ganglion* of the cell.

Nervous System Anatomy and Research Techniques- *Nobel Prize*
Camillo Golgi

Golgi was born near Brescia, Italy on July 7, 1843 and died in Pavia on January 26, 1926. He was an Italian physician and researcher. Golgi was a professor of medicine at the University of Pavia from 1880 to 1918. He received the 1906 *Nobel Prize* for new techniques in staining nerve tissue with silver nitrate for study under the microscope, now known as the *Golgi Method* in his honor. His new method of study allowed him to discover new structures in the nervous system, such as *Golgi cells* (1883), *Golgi apparatus or Golgi complex* (1909), and the *existence of synapses*. He also discovered that different protozoan organisms cause three different types of malaria.

The Historical Museum of the University of Pavia dedicated a hall in honor of Dr. Golgi, where more than eighty of his awards and honorary degrees are on display.

Operating Theater – First
University of Padua

In the late 1500's, the University of Padua's prestigious medical school was the first to construct a multi-tiered operating theater (six floors), the world's first such facility. It included a trap door in the floor that allowed the cadavers to be raised for anatomical studies and then lowered back down after the procedures to be burned in a furnace. The great Galileo began his college education studying medicine at the University of Pisa in 1581. He later decided to become a mathematician and from 1592 to 1610 was a professor of mathematics at the University of Padua. He, without a doubt, attended some of these anatomical studies in this operating theater.

Pulmonary Blood Circulation and Capillaries in Lungs - First Discoveries
Realdo Colombo
Marcello Malpighi

Colombo was born 1516 in Cremona and died 1559 in Rome. In 1546, at the famous University of Padua, *Realdo Colombo discovered the "lesser circulation of the blood" or "pulmonary blood circulation."* His research of blood circulation added to the understanding of his mentor, Versale. Columbo's work was later used by William Harvey (English) to prepare an outline of blood circulation (1628). However, Harvey still missed a very important aspect of the circulatory system; that is the connection between the arterial and venous systems via the capillaries. Another Italian, *Marcello Malpighi was the first to identify the capillaries in the lungs* and their connective purpose between the arterial and venous systems, which he wrote about in his "De pulmonibus," published in 1661.

Malpighi was the first to make extensive use of the microscope and was the first to discover many physiological elements of human, plant and insect life. (Refer to the Father of Biological Microscopy section earlier in this chapter.)

In addition to his pulmonary studies Colombo in 1559 was also the first to study and describe in the position and posture of the human embryo. He built upon basic studies performed by da Vinci who also investigated and documented the human embryo in the 15th century.

Rheumatism Researcher and the 5th Most Published Scientist in the World
Anthony Fauci

In 1984, Anthony Fauci, M.D. became the *Director of the National*

Institutes of Allergy and Infectious Diseases of the National Institutes of Health in the United States. He was born in 1940 in Brooklyn, NY and graduated Cornell University Medical College in 1966. He is an internationally celebrated scientist and is *a pioneer in the field of human immune response*. Dr. Fauci has developed therapies for several diseases and in 1985 Stanford University Arthritis Center Survey of the American Rheumatism Association *ranked Dr. Fauci's work as one of the most important advances in treating rheumatology in the last 20 years*. Dr. Fauci has also made basic contributions to the understanding and treatment of the HIV (or AIDS) virus. In 1995, the Institute for Scientific Information placed Dr. Fauci as the *fifth most published scientist in the world among more than 1 million scientists* for the period 1981-1994. *He has been awarded 20 honorary doctorate degrees* from universities in the United States and abroad. Dr. Fauci is a member of many professional organizations, serves on the editorial boards of many scientific journals, and is also editor of "Harrison's Principles of Internal Medicine." Dr. Fauci has edited, authored or co-authored, more than 960 scientific publications, including several textbooks. In 1977, he was also presented the American College of Physicians (ACP) *John Philips Memorial Award* for his distinguished contributions to clinical medicine.

SARS (Severe Acute Respiratory Syndrome)
Carlo Urbani

Dr. Urbani is credited with first diagnosing SARS in Johnny Chen, an American businessman, who was admitted to a hospital in Vietnam in February 2003. According to the "New York Times," April 8, 2003: "If not for the intuition of Dr. Urbani, Director of Infectious Diseases for the Western Pacific Region of the World Health Organization, the disease would have spread farther and faster than it has, public health officials around the world say." His early identification of SARS as a new disease quickly raised international attention, and allowed global surveillance to slow the spread of this serious and contagious disease.

Italian born, Dr. Urbani received his medical degree from the University of Ancona, Italy. Tragically, he died of SARS at the age of 46 in Bangkok, Thailand on March 29, 2003. Dr. Urbani was known as an expert clinical diagnostician, as well as a compassionate physician. Dr. Urbani, along with his colleagues, accepted the Nobel Peace Prize in 1999 on behalf of Doctors Without Borders. He was also president of the organization's chapter in Italy. Dr. Urbani is survived by a wife and three children.

Signal Molecule, Nitric Oxide Discovery – *Nobel Prize*
Louis Ignarro

Louis Ignarro was born May 31, 1941 in Brooklyn, NY. He is a first generation Italian-American. His father was a ship-builder from Naples and his mother came from Sicily as a young child. Ignarro received his B.A. from Columbia University (1962) and his Ph.D. from the University of Minnesota (1966). Both of his degrees are in pharmacology.

Ignarro was the recipient of the Nobel Prize in Medicine in 1998 for discovering that a gas (nitric oxide) can act as a signal molecule in the cardiovascular system. His discovery led to many new pharmacological innovations, and later, the proof that nitric oxide protects the heart, stimulates the brain and kills bacteria.

Ignarro is the recipient of many international honors and has been awarded honorary doctorates, including from major universities, such as Madrid, Lund, Gent and North Carolina. He is currently on the faculty of UCLA School of Medicine.

Spinal Biomechanics, Father of
Giovanni Alfonso Borelli

Because of his father's political difficulties, and perhaps some of his own, Borelli concealed his dates of birth and death; these are approximate: born January 28, 1608 in Naples and died December 31, 1679 in Rome. Leonardo da Vinci (1452-1519) was the first to seriously study and document the dynamics of spinal anatomy and spinal biomechanics. However, the distinction of "Father of Spinal Biomechanics" is with Borelli who in 1680 published "De Motu Animalium" representing the first extensive study on biomechanics. He provided the first detailed and comprehensive analysis of how the spine supports weight and motion.

There are several references to Borelli in this book under different areas of science. Borelli was a genius who studied many disciplines including mathematics, astronomy, medicine, physiology, geology and the mechanics of flight. He experimented with artificial wings and was the first to accurately measure the speed of sound with mathematician Vincenzo Viviani. He was educated as a physician receiving his M.D. in Naples, but worked in diverse areas of scientific investigation. In Pisa, he published works on anatomy and malignant fevers in 1649. Borelli even taught as Professor of mathematics at Pisa from 1656 to 1667. He also completed an important investigation of volcanoes. (For more on Borelli see the "Science & Technology" and "Transportation" chapters.)

Transgenics (Gene Transfer - Genetic Engineering)
Marialuisa Lavitrano

In October 2002, Dr. Marialuisa Lavitrano, a University of Milan immunologist and pathologist, and her associates created a new strain of swine that carries human genes in their hearts, livers and kidneys. This is a first step towards breeding animals capable of growing organs that could be transplanted into humans. Tests also indicate that the human genes present in the swine's central organs would be successfully passed along to later generations of pigs.

Dr. Lavitrano and her team successfully transferred the DNA of a human gene to swine sperm. The genetically altered sperm was then used to fertilize swine eggs. The fertilized embryos were implanted into sows to produce litters of pigs that carried the human gene. The DNA of a human gene called *decay accelerating factor* or *DAF* was used to alter the swine sperm. The *DAF* gene was chosen because it has been shown to help overcome rejection of pig organs by nonhuman primates. Dr. Lavitrano said that the new technique offers an efficient, low-cost way of genetically modifying pigs to express a human protein. Her team had previously demonstrated their transgenic technique, called *sperm-mediated gene transfer*, in mice. Dr. Randall S. Prather, a pig reproduction physiologist at the University of Missouri and a researcher said that Dr. Lavitrano's work is an advance because it demonstrates a simple way to add genes to the swine DNA. Dr. Prather helped develop an earlier, but costly and somewhat unreliable technique to eliminate a swine gene associated with transplantation rejection.

The ultimate goal is to find a way to accomplish the next step; that is, to eliminate the action of pig genes that would cause the human immune system to reject transplanted organs. Dr. Lavitrano said that five to seven pig genes will need to be silenced or replaced by human genes before useful organs could be harvested from pigs for the purpose of human transplantation. Dr. Lavitrano said, "With our efficiency we think we can add the other genes and breed the animals in about two years."

Pig tissue has been used to replace heart valves in humans, but replacing whole organs represents a significantly more complex challenge. It has been estimated that about 4,000 people die each year while awaiting human donor organs.

Valves in Veins
Giambattista Cannani

Giambattista Cannani performed many anatomical studies and discovered the valves in human veins about 1550. In 1603, Fabricio di Acquapendente also made significant studies of the valves in the veins.

Viral Mutations, Discovery of - *Nobel Prize*
Salvador Edward Luria

Salvador Edward Luria was born August 13, 1912 in Torino (Turin), Italy and died February 6, 1991 in Lexington, Massachusetts. After receiving his MD, *summa cum laude,* from the University of Turin in 1935, he migrated to the U.S. in 1940 and became a U.S. citizen in 1947. At the prestigious Massachusetts Institute of Technology (MIT) he was appointed a professor in 1959, Sedgwick Professor in 1964, and was the Director of the Center for Cancer Research. Luria's research work in the mutation of viruses and bacteria led to the 1969 *Nobel Prize* for research on the replication and genetic structure of viruses. He studied *bacteriophages* (a group of viruses that infect bacteria rather than ordinary cells) and was *the first to prove that viruses undergo permanent changes in their hereditary material and spontaneously create different mutant strains.* He wrote a textbook entitled "General Virology" in 1953 and a popular text for general audiences entitled "Life: The Unfinished Experiment" in 1973.

Among his many awards are these distinguished recognitions: Lepetit Prize (1935), Lenghi Prize of Accademia dei Lincei (1965), Louisa Gross Horwitz Prize of Columbia University (1969).

C8

Chapter XIV

MILITARY CONTRIBUTIONS

"Major Don Gentile is a one-man air force."
- U.S. General Dwight D. Eisenhower -

"Sergeant John Basilone is a one-man army."
- U.S. General Douglas MacArthur -

Atomic Bomb and Hydrogen Bomb
Enrico Fermi

Fermi ushered in the atomic age when he succeeded in transforming the nucleus of a uranium atom and simultaneously split the atom for the first time, in Rome in 1934. For his pioneering work he was awarded the Nobel Prize in 1938. Fermi led a team that built the first nuclear reactor (1939) and the first atomic bomb (1945). In 1941, Fermi was also the first to hypothesize that a hydrogen (or thermonuclear) bomb could be possible using fission to trigger a fusion chain reaction. After many years of research, the hydrogen bomb was developed and detonated in 1952. Fermi was against the building of the hydrogen bomb because of its massive destructive power, and although it was his brainchild, he did not participate in its creation.

Fermi was an Italian physicist who thankfully immigrated to the

United States just prior to World War II. One should shudder to think what the world would be like today, had Fermi been sympathetic to Benito Mussolini and Adolf Hitler and offered his talents to the Axis forces during World War II. In a very real way Fermi's support of the United States saved the world from oppression and set the stage for the next 50 years of peace without global conflict. If Fermi had helped the aggressors of World War II develop nuclear energy instead of the U.S., the world today would be a very different place, most assuredly less free and less peaceful. (NOTE: This entry is very brief, please refer to the "Science & Technology" chapter for more information on Dr. Fermi's fascinating life and how he ushered in the nuclear age and won a *Nobel Prize*).

Ballista and Mangonel
Rome

The Romans invented a giant missile launcher they called the *ballista*. It looked similar to a giant crossbow and could hurl large objects a distance of 1500 feet (457 meters). Large spears could be accurately shot into the ranks of the enemy. Heavy weights, usually stones up to 60 pounds (27 kilos), could smash through castle walls from a safe distance. *The word ballistics is derived from the name of this Roman weapon.*

The Romans also invented a catapult called the *mangonel*. It looked like a giant powerful mousetrap that used wound up rope at its center, instead of a spring, for powerful release action. Although it was less accurate than the *ballista*, the *mangonel* was lighter and could shoot stones or fire-bombs at the enemy. The very first catapult was invented in 399 BC by Dionysius the Elder of Syracuse. At the time, Syracuse was a Greek colony in Sicily.

Ballistics, Science of

Tartaglia (aka Noccolo Fontana)

Tartaglia, an eminent mathematician, lived from 1500 to 1575 and wrote a treatise in 1537 entitled "Nova Scientia" ("The New Science"). In this book he was the first to apply mathematics to artillery and initiated the science of ballistics. In "Nova Scientia" he also published the first firing tables. *As a result of his work, he is considered the father of ballistic science.* Tartaglia also designed a new compass used for surveying that was much more balanced than prior designs. He also invented a device called a *telemeter* that measures heights and distances, and also offered new methods for raising sunken ships. (Refer to the Cubic and Cosa Equations section in the "Mathematics" chapter for more on Tartaglia and his interesting life).

Galileo Galilei

Galileo lived from 1564 to 1642 and discovered the Law of Parabolic Path of Projectiles. Since Galileo was not only an astronomer, but was also a trained mathematician, he was able to conclude from experiments that projectiles follow the path of a parabola, as their fall curves down toward the earth.

Pietro Antonio Cataldi

Cataldi was a distinguished mathematician who published over 30 books covering various areas of mathematics and other subjects. He also studied artillery trajectory and military applications of algebra in his "Operetta di ordinanze quadre," published in 1618. (Refer to the Algebra section of the "Mathematics" chapter for more on Cataldi).

Guido Fubini

Fubini made major contributions in geometry and also studied the accuracy of artillery projectory, acoustics and electricity. (Refer to the Geometry, Differential section of the "Mathematics" chapter for more on Fubini).

Francesco Siacci

Siacci was born April 20, 1839 in Rome and died May 31, 1907 in Naples. Siacci was Professor of Mechanics at the University of Turin from 1871, Professor of Ballistics at the Military Academy from 1872 and Professor of Higher Mechanics at the University of Turin from 1875. *He published hundreds of papers* and made major contributions to analytic mechanics and mechanics of artillery ballistics. *His 1888 treatise on artillery ballistics was considered a masterpiece of analysis.* Siacci received many honors and was elected to many important scientific academies of Italy.

Biological Warfare
Leonardo da Vinci
Da Vinci first suggested bombs containing bacteria and also venoms in 1550. He stated that the bacteria could be obtained from rabid dogs or pigs, and venom from tarantulas or poisonous toads.

Civil War, American
During the Civil War, over 100 Italian-Americans served as Union officers in both the Army and Navy. This list includes four generals: Luigi Palma di Cesnola, Enrico Fardella, Eduardo Ferrero and Francis Spinola.

Italian Americans served in the nation's fight to save the Union throughout the Civil War. For example, the 39th New York Infantry, known as the Garibaldi Guard, included 150 Italian-Americans of its total complement of 850 men. Approximately 5,000 to 10,000 Italian-Americans fought during the Civil War and wore both "blue" and "gray" uniforms.

Camouflage
Rome
The earliest known use of camouflage used for military advantage is attributed to the Romans. Sailors in the Roman Navy wore blue uniforms to conceal their numbers aboard their vessels. The Roman Navy successfully fought enemy ships, as well as pirate ships that plagued commercial shipping. As the Roman naval ships approached pirate ships, their blue uniforms made it difficult for pirates to estimate the number of sailors that were about to board their ships – oops!

Firearms
Beretta
Beretta is the oldest industrial firm and the oldest gunmaker in the world. The company's full name is Fabbrica d'Armi Pietro Beretta S.p.A.. The company has roots that go back over 475 years. Random House publications, in New York, has just published a book on this company's rich history, entitled: "The World of Beretta - An International Legend."

Beretta has several contracts with the U.S. Navy, U.S. Army Reserve and U.S. National Guard, which purchase the Beretta Model 92F 9mm pistol as a standard issue sidearm. In two sales contracts (1995 and 1996), Beretta had sold 32,000 forty caliber (.40) pistols to the U.S. Immigration & Naturalization Service, making these combined purchases the largest purchase of pistols ever made by a federal law enforcement agency in the U.S.

The Beretta M9 has proven its renowned reliability in many military operations, such as, Desert Storm in Kuwait, Uphold Democracy in Haiti, Restore Hope in Somalia, Just Cause in Panama, Urgent Fury in Grenada, and Joint Endeavor in Bosnia.

Beretta is located in Gardone Val Trompia, near Milan, and is one of the world's leading manufacturers of sporting, military and personal-defense firearms.

Medical Services
Roman Empire

The Romans were the *first to establish military medical services* and paid for these with government taxes. Archeologists have found artifacts used by these military medical units in the battlefield that included analgesics, anesthetics, scalpels, sutures and clamps. In fact, the health care afforded to soldiers was so good that their life expectancy actually exceeded that of the average Roman citizen by approximately five years. Today, the United States military calls this a M.A.S.H. (Mobile Army Surgical Hospital) unit.

Many historians credit the Romans for establishing the first civilian hospitals in the western world. This is given further credence when one considers that the oldest medical school in the western world and the world's first university-based medical school were both established in Italy. (Refer to the chapter "Medicine, Biology & Health" for more information on this subject.)

Machine Guns
Leonardo da Vinci

Around 1480, da Vinci made several designs for machine guns. Each design allowed for rapid successive firing. One design contained 33 guns in a fan arrangement. Others contained a series of small cannons arranged in a turning cube or triangle. These designs allowed for rapid firing and reloading of each set of guns. The success of these inventions was limited, since they were somewhat cumbersome to implement, given the technology of the 15th century.

Military Leaders & Heroes

Many of the world's greatest military leaders and heroes were Italian or Roman. Here are a few of the more notable ones.

Napoleon Bonaparte

Napoleon Bonaparte was born August 15, 1769 on the island of Corsica and was considered a *Corsican-Italian. Corsica has a very long Italian history that exceeds over 650 years.* For almost 300 years, from the late 1000's until the 1312, it was subject to the Pope in Rome. From 1312 until 1768, a period that exceeds 450 years, it was ruled by the Italian city-state of Genoa, except when the French ruled for 100 years from 1458 to 1558. For many centuries the island of Corsica was part of Italian culture and politics in much the same way that the island of Sicily is today. In 1768, France took control of the island and it was in this anti-French environment that Napoleon was born.

Napoleon's original name was Napoleone Buonaparti in Corsica, but later living in France it was changed to Napoleon Bonaparte. His father's family was from Florence and his mother's family was originally from the Tuscany region of Italy and later spread to Naples and Florence. Napoleon hated the French who ostensibly oppressed the island of Corsica. His father was an anti-French lawyer.

Napoleon joined the French military and during the chaos of the French revolution rose in the ranks to Captain, then General and ultimately a self-proclaimed Emperor. He developed a military tactic that divided the enemy's army in half, and then deployed his entire army against one of the enemy halves. He was also known to be very intelligent, a fast thinker who knew how to mobilize and move an army quickly. *Napoleon conquered much of Europe* including Holland, Italy, Switzerland, Germany and Egypt. He also had major victories in Russia. By today's measurements Napoleon was only 5'2" tall, but this clearly did not stifle his ambitions.

Cesare Borgia

Cesare Borgia (c.1476 - 1507) was an illegitimate son of Pope Alexander VI. Early in his life Cesare was an Archbishop and later a

Cardinal. He was also a politician and by the age of 22 he became the Captain-General of the Roman Catholic Church. He ultimately became the military leader of the papal campaign to unite the warring states of Italy. In 1499, he successfully conquered the Romagna Region, Piombino, Camerino and Urbino in central Italy. His enemies joined forces to attempt to defeat him. However, Borgia skillfully plotted and lured the enemy leadership into the castle of Senigallia and had them executed.

Julius Caesar

Julius Caesar was born July 13, 100 BC. Caesar's full name was Gaius Julius Caesar. The month of July is named in honor of Julius Caesar. However, back in his day the month was called *Quintilis*. Caesar was a brilliant military strategist, but was also a talented writer and powerful orator. To describe the definitive success of his Asian military campaign, when he addressed the Roman Senate, Caesar uttered the famous, "I came, I saw, I conquered." (In Latin the quote is "veni, vidi, vici.") Later, Caesar's leadership led to another highly successful campaign to capture Gaul (now modern France). After this great success he returned to Rome to initiate a civil war and won control of the entire Empire. General Caesar then became Emperor Caesar. On March 15, the Ides of March, he was assassinated at the Senate house in the year 44 BC.

Fabius (aka Quintus Fabius Maximus)

The famous Roman General Fabius learned how to achieve victory without head-on confrontation. General Fabius achieved victories by delaying or avoiding large-scale confrontations and instead using evasion, delay, and small repeated attacks. Using these tactics, he defeated the great Hannibal in the Second Punic War. These tactics have become known as *Fabian tactics*.

Next time you make a telephone call and are put *on hold* by someone who does not wish to speak to you, remember they may be using a form of Fabian tactics. You will need strategy and tenacity to defeat a modern day version of General Fabius.

Giuseppe Garibaldi

Garibaldi was the son of a poor fisherman. He was born in Nice April 16, 1807 and died June 2, 1882, in Caprera where he is buried on the Italian island of Sardinia. He was known to be an honest, selfless man with great charismatic appeal. Garibaldi successfully fought the Austrians and several independent and papal states to unite Italy into one country under one government. Among his many famous victories, Garibaldi brought a small volunteer army of 1000 men to Sicily and defeated an army of 20,000 men. His movement for the reunification of Italy was called the *Risorgimento*. Garibaldi needed to be an effective military and political leader to unify the different regions under Victor Emmanuel II, who was proclaimed King of Italy in 1861. Garibaldi was elected to the Italian parliament in 1874. The reunification of Italy was clearly one of the most significant and influential political events in Europe during the 19th century.

U.S. President Abraham Lincoln tried, but without success, to recruit Garibaldi as a Major General during the American Civil War. Garibaldi was an admired and respected international freedom fighter. During the American and Soviet "Cold War" decades, Garibaldi was the only historical figure to appear on both American and Soviet postage stamps. Throughout his life, Garibaldi refused to accept all honors offered to him.

Dominic Salvatore Gentile (aka Don S. Gentile)

Dominic was born in Piqua, Ohio, on December 6, 1920. He was the son of Italian immigrants. His father was from the Abruzzi region of Italy and his mother was from Sicily. He was obsessed with flying from a very young age and ultimately joined the Royal Canadian Air Force after graduating from high school. Later, he transferred to the Royal Air Force. In 1942, he volunteered to fight with the British during World War II, and flew with the 133 Eagle Squadron. After proving himself and winning the British Distinguished Flying Cross, he transferred to the United States Army Air Corps in September of 1942. He became one of history's greatest flying aces, breaking the Allied "kill" record held from World War I, by the famous Captain Eddie Rickenbacker (26 kills). By April of 1944 he had destroyed 30 enemy planes! U.S. General Dwight D. Eisenhower called Major Gentile *a "one-man air force."* He has earned the title "Ace of Aces."

His astonishing awards include: Distinguished Service Cross, the Silver Star, the Distinguished Flying Cross, the Air Medal, the Presidential Unit Citation, the World War Two Victory Medal, the American Campaign Medal, the British Distinguished Flying Cross, the British Star, the British Eagle Squadron Crest, and other foreign medals and awards. In 1946, Major Gentile also received an honorary doctorate in aeronautics from Ohio Northern University. After the war

Major Gentile stayed with the U.S. Air Force as a test pilot and a Training Officer in the Fighter Gunnery Program. Tragically and ironically, he died in 1951 when his T-33 trainer crashed, killing Gentile and his student.

Pompey

Pompey (full name Cnaeus Pompeius Magnus) lived from 106 BC to 48 BC. He was one of Rome's greatest generals. Early in his military career, he saw success in battles within Sicily, Africa and Spain. Later, he put down the slave revolt by the great Spartacus. He became general in 67 BC and was commissioned to defeat and destroy the numerous pirates that plagued Mediterranean commerce and shipping. This difficult task was one of his greatest successes, which was followed by a successful campaign against Armenia. He next annexed Syria and Palestine and then began the Roman organization of the Eastern Empire when he defeated the Mithridates.

In 60 BC, Pompey became one of the three consuls or rulers of Rome. The rule of the First Triumvirate was formed and included Caesar, Crassus and Pompey. Pompey and Caesar always had a strained and jealous relationship, but Pompey's marriage to Caesar's daughter Julia kept their relationship healthy. However, when Julia died in 54 BC, the relationship between Pompey and Caesar deteriorated. In 49 BC, Caesar crossed the Rubicon with his troops, after his victory in Gaul, and initiated a civil war that concluded with Caesar as Rome's Emperor. Pompey wanted to restore the Republic government, but was defeated by Caesar's army at Pharsalus in 48 BC.

U.S. Four Star Generals

In 2005, Marine General Peter Pace became Chairman of the Joint Chiefs of Staff, the highest-ranking military officer in the U.S. He had been Vice Chairman under the previous Chairman, General Richard Myers. Brooklyn-born Peter Pace is a highly decorated officer having served his country in Vietnam, Somalia and Japan.

Marine General Anthony Zinni, the son of Italian immigrants, was in charge of Operation Desert Storm in December 2001. This four-day intensive military campaign was successfully waged by the United States and its allies against Iraq's invasion of Kuwait.

General Zinni was the Commander-in-Chief of U.S. Central Command with responsibility for U.S. troops in Saudi Arabia and the Gulf. This position in the Middle East is viewed as one of the most challenging in the U.S. military.

General Zinni is a highly decorated Vietnam War veteran and Four Star Marine General. General Zinni also served in the peacekeeping effort in Somalia in 1992, and as Chief of Staff and Deputy Commanding General for Operation Provide Comfort, which offered supplies and relief to the Kurds in Turkey and Iraq in 1991.

After the World Trade Center destruction by terrorists on September 11th 2001, retired General Zinni was sent to the Middle East to try and broker peace between the PLO and Israel. Unfortunately, tensions continue in the region as of this writing.

Revolution, American
Italian-American Patriots

Philip Mazzei wrote, "All men are by nature equally free and independent...equal to the other in natural rights." These words became the cornerstone of the American Declaration of Independence after some rewording by Thomas Jefferson. Signers of this noble document, who revolted against British rule, included other Italian-Americans, William Paca and Caesar Rodney. (Refer to the chapter on "American Government" for more information on these three Italian-American patriots.)

Mazzei worked alongside Thomas Jefferson and Patrick Henry, as three Italian regiments that totaled 1,500 men fought the war, in addition to other Italians who fought with other American revolutionary regiments.

Submarine
Leonardo da Vinci

In his famous "Notebooks," da Vinci designed a submarine that could be very effective for warfare. It consisted of a sealed chamber for divers and a tube to the surface for air that was attached to a round floatation device. The chamber had a propeller to allow travel below the surface.

Tank, Military
Leonardo da Vinci

His drawing of a circular, armored vehicle with a battery of cannons conceived the first military type tank. It had a conical roof, presumably to deflect projectiles and prevent easy boarding by the enemy. It took eight men to operate the tank's movement and armaments. Nevertheless, da Vinci once said, "War is madness."

U.S. Congressional Medal of Honor

Over 39 Italian-American servicemen have been awarded the U.S. Congressional Medal of Honor. These awards date as far back as the American Civil War, when Union General Luigi Palma di Cesnola received this honor. After the War, General Cesnola, who was also an archeologist, was appointed US Consul to Cyprus. There he completed excavations and discovered over 600 artifacts (circa 2500 BC to 300 AD). His collection was purchased by the Metropolitan Museum of Art in New York, and Cesnola became the museum's first director in 1879, a position he held until his death in 1904.

Sergeant John Basilone is the only Marine in U.S. history to receive the nation's two highest military honors. For his bravery in World War II, he was awarded both the U.S. Congressional Medal of Honor and the Navy Cross. Also, he was the first enlisted Marine to be awarded the Congressional Medal of Honor. Basilone saw battle at Guadalcanal (1942), but was killed during battle at Iwo Jima (1945). Basilone was called "a one-man army" by General Douglas MacArthur.

When he returned to the United States to receive the Congressional Medal of Honor from the President, he was heralded and toured the country to help finance the war through war bond sales. He refused a promotion to officer, and a post located in the U.S., and instead asked to return to the war, where he ultimately perished in heroic battle.

U.S. Distinguished Service Cross -'Bataan Rescue'

Colonel Henry Mucci trained his 6th Army Ranger Battalion in the mountains of New Guinea and turned them into an elite jungle fighting unit, one of the first American special operations forces. In December 1944, Mucci led his men thirty miles behind the line of Japanese troops, and rescued 513 American soldiers who survived three years of captivity in the notorious Japanese prison camp at Cabanatuan on the Bataan Peninsula. This became the *most daring rescue of World War II*. Colonel Mucci received the U.S. Distinguished Service Cross from General Douglas MacArthur. In February 2005, Miramax Films released "The Great Raid," a film about Mucci's audacious rescue.

∞

Chapter XV

MUSIC: Development, Instruments, Ballet & Opera

"Do, Re, Mi, Fa, So, La, Ti, Do"
- Guido d'Arezzo -

From the Middle Ages until the early 20th century, Italians were clearly the most influential musical innovators in the world. This chapter is divided into three main music sections: 1) Development - page 298; 2) Instruments - page 309; 3) Ballet & Opera - page 323

MUSIC: Development

Gregorian Chants
Pope Gregory of Rome

In the 6th century, a Roman monk who later became Pope Gregory the Great standardized and categorized the Church's music. His system identified particular songs for specific times of the year. His songs and their categorization were used by the Church unchanged until the 16th century. What became known as Gregorian Chants, named in his honor, are now one of the oldest bodies of music still in use. Since another Italian monk from Tuscany, who created musical notation, was not born until the 11th century, the music for these chants had to be memorized. The chants' words were written in Latin. However, only simple marks called *neumes* would indicate if the singer's voice needed to go up or down. To assure their standardization and longevity, Pope Gregory reorganized and enforced the use of standard hymns at the *schola cantorum*, the Church's singing school. It took ten years to groom a professional ecclesiastic singer, and as a result Gregory's standardized chants were flawlessly reproduced from generation to generation over the centuries without the use of written musical notation.

Inventor of Musical Staff, Notes and Octave System
Guido d'Arezzo

D'Arezzo lived from approximately 990 AD to 1080 AD and probably came from the town of Pomposa, but later moved to Arezzo. He was a Benedictine monk who *invented the musical notation we use today, around the year 1000 AD*. As a result of his invention, he was requested to move to Rome by Pope John XIX. *He designed the musical staff and located letters on each staff line*, which represented pitch. D'Arezzo also marked the sides of the staff to indicate the lines for the notes C and F. These evolved into the G clef and F clef signs that we use today to similarly indicate where the G and F notes are on the staff. He also *established the notes we use today from A to G and with this our octaves or eight note system* where the eighth note is the same letter as the first. In his manuscripts d'Arezzo states that he picked the seven notes (A through G), with the eighth note repeating with the first, to be in harmony with the weekly calendar. He is quoted as saying, "Just as after the course of seven days we start again from the same beginning, so that on the first and eighth days we always have the same name, so do we name the first and the eighth tones with the same letter...." His basic invention was so perfect that it is still used 1000 years later. However, his four-line staff evolved into today's five-line staff. He may have also invented the monochord, which was a single string on a wooden case with a movable bridge to teach music concepts and notation.

The significance of his invention of musical notation should not be underestimated. For the first time, singers could sight read music from scores and not have to learn from an oral tradition alone. Also, musical composers could now use his sophisticated system to document their music with limitless harmony and complexity using polyphonic melodies. Complex musical themes could now be conceived and documented and re-written adding layers of complexity for the first time in history. His musical notation for the first time gave musicians and composers a written language that could be universally understood.

Inventor of Solmization –
Do, Re, Mi, Fa , So, La, Ti, Do
Guido d'Arezzo

Guido d'Arezzo, the Benedictine monk who invented our musical notation system, also introduced solmization into musical theory, around 1026 AD. Solmization is the assignment of syllables to notes. He used the syllables *ut, re, mi, fa, sol, la, si, ut* to represent the eight notes in the scale. This developed into the solmization we use today: *do, re, mi, fa, so, la, ti, do.* But why did d'Arezzo use these original syllables or sounds? He took these from syllables in a Latin hymn called "ut queant laxis" from the Second Vespers of Saint John the Baptist. The leading syllables (bolded) in this hymn coincide with the musical scale. The hymn is "**Ut** queant laxis **Re**sonare fibris **Mi**ra gestorum **Fa**muli tuorum **Sol**ve pulluti **La**bii reatum Sante **I**oannes."

Inventor of Modern Major and Minor Scales
Gioseffe Zarlino

Zarlino was born in 1517 in Chioggia and died on February 4, 1590 in Venice. In 1558, he published the results of his research in "Institutioni Harmoniche" and defined the major and minor musical scales used today. He also defined the octave as having twelve halfsteps of equal temperament, as it remains today.

First Printed Music

Ottavio de' Petrucci

In 1501, Ottavio de' Petrucci of Venice was the first to print and publish music using movable type. He printed music with right-hand

and left-hand staves for keyboard. De' Petrucci printed music books for various kinds of masses, madrigals, songs and ballads. He was virtually the only music printer for decades and printed over sixty collections of music. His books were exported throughout Europe and to the New World as well. The popularity of his music books and sheet music reinforced the use of Italian words for musical terminology, which remains the standard in today's music.

Boethius
The very first record of written musical notation is credited to the Roman Boethius who used the first 15 letters of the alphabet as notes around 500 AD.

Liturgical Music
Giovanni Pierluigi da Palestrina
Known as the greatest composer of liturgical music of all time, Palestrina was born on a simple farm in Palestrina, 1514 or 1515 and died in Rome on February 2, 1594. He was the choirmaster at St. John Lateran and Santa Maria Maggiore. Palestrina was inspired by his acquaintance with Saint Philip Neri. Palestrina's major works include: "Canticle of C," "Lamentations," "Stabat Mater," the famous "Improperia," and the mass "Assumpta est Maria."

Musical Terminology
Italy
All musical terminology comes from the Italian language. (Examples: alto, bass, a cappella, adagio, allegretto, allegro, andante, cantata, crescendo, forte, fortissimo, impresario, maestro, mezzo, soprano, staccato, pianissimo, pianoforte, tempo, tenor, etc.).

Multiple Choir Technique
Andrea Gabrieli
Giovanni Gabrieli
Andrea Gabrieli lived from 1510 to 1586 and was a composer and organist. He wrote many forms of musical compositions, e.g. madrigals, motets, masses, ricercari and canzones. He was very influential in developing *multiple choir technique*. His nephew, the

Venetian, Giovanni Gabrieli who lived from 1555 to 1612, further developed this technique.

The madrigal, a song with two or more part harmony, was an Italian creation. The earliest forms were written for the words of great Italian poets, such as Petrarca, Ariosto and Tasso. Madrigals were very popular in Italy and this musical form later traveled to England, France, Spain and Germany. In England, Italian madrigals were altered by retaining the tunes, but replacing the poems of Petrarca with Shakespeare's works. The English soon began writing their own madrigals as they learned the multi-part harmony concepts.

Dynamic Indications and First Orchestration
Giovanni Gabrieli

The music Giovanni Gabrieli *published in 1597 was one of the earliest musical works to specify loudness, softness, tempo, other dynamic indications and instrumentation for an orchestra.* He had studied with the famous Flemish composer Orlando di Lasso who advanced polyphonic *a cappella* vocals. Giovanni Gabrieli is credited for *composing the first music written for orchestration.* In 1597, he wrote "Sacrae Symphoniae" and specified unique parts for each musical instrument. Prior to this, chamber music did not contain dynamic indications or assign differing harmonic musical scores for specific instruments. *Giovanni Gabrieli's innovations had enormous influences on all composers who followed.*

Note on Orlando di Lasso

Orlando di Lasso was one of the great composers of the Renaissance and is classified as a Flemish composer. However, his name suggests Italian heritage. Further, he was raised and received his musical education and training in Italy. As a boy singer he was in the service of the Vice King of Sicily. As a youth he moved to Italy, where he continued his musical training and by the age of 20 became a well known maestro in *a cappella* singing in Rome. In 1556, the Duke of Bavaria contracted with di Lasso, and subsequently he became the *a cappella* maestro for the Court of Munchen in 1564 where he lived until his death in 1594. His date of birth is unknown, but is believed to be around 1532.

"Fiori Musicali" Influenced J. S. Bach
Girolamo Frescobaldi

Frescobaldi was a famous organist and composer, born 1583 in Ferrara and died 1643 in Rome. He composed hundreds of works of music, one of his masterpieces is "Fiori Musicali" (1635), which later *influenced J.S. Bach* who was an admirer of Frescobaldi's music. In 1714, Bach had acquired a copy of "Fiori Musicali" but historians note that this famous copy was unfortunately lost during World War II. In his time Frescobaldi was so popular that a *crowd of thirty thousand gathered to hear him* play the organ at St. Peter's in Rome. Frescobaldi was the organist at Rome's Accademia di Santa Cecilia in 1604, and also the organist at St. Peter's in Rome until his death. His compositions for organ and harpsichord include: toccatas, capriccios, ricercars, fantasias and canzonas.

Sonata
Italy

The *sonata* originated in Italy during the 17th century. The early *sonata* was an instrumental work containing several sections usually for harpsichord, or for harpsichord and only one other instrument. The *sonata* is unlike the earlier *cantata*, which was a musical composition that was sung using multiple harmonies and accompanied by music.

By the early 18th century the *sonata* had evolved into a work of several separate movements. These *sonatas* were of two basic types: the somber, usually religious type was the *sonata da chiesa* (Italian for *church sonata*); and the *sonata* that used dance patterns was the *sonata da camera* (Italian for *chamber sonata*). These two types later merged and became the *sonata form* that represents the foundation for much classical music, including the *concerto* and *symphony* music.

The composer and harpsichord virtuoso Domenico Scarlatti composed over 500 *sonatas* for the harpsichord making important contributions to the development of the classical *sonata form*.

The classical *sonata form* movements usually express fast-slow-fast tempos. Typically, a quick *scherzo* is located before the last movement. During the 18th century, Hayden, Mozart and Beethoven all wrote and contributed to the development of the *sonata form*. After the invention and proliferation of the piano in the 18th century, *sonatas* were typically written for piano and infrequently harpsichords.

The First Concertos and Influences on J. S. Bach & Handel

The first *concerto grosso*, for a small group of soloists with a full supporting orchestra, was developed and written by three Italian masters: Archangelo Corelli (1653-1713), Giuseppe Torelli (1658-1709) and Antonio Vivaldi (1675-1741).

Archangelo Corelli

Born in 1653 in Fusignano near Milan, Corelli was a leading violinist and composer of his time. He died in January 1713 and was buried in the famous Pantheon in Rome, which was a show of immense respect. His beautiful and original *trio sonatas* and *concerti grossi* were an *immeasurable contribution to other composers, especially Handel,* who was a student of Corelli in Rome during 1707. Corelli's musical genius helped to evolve the baroque *concerto grosso* and *sonata forms.* He wrote many baroque pieces that were highly popular and was also a *highly accomplished violin virtuoso with innovative playing techniques.* Corelli was the director of violins at San Luigi dei Francesi in Rome for twenty-four years. J. S. Bach was born in 1685, thirty-two years after Corelli. Experts universally agree that *Bach's music was clearly influenced by Corelli's masterpieces.* Corelli was in the service of two Cardinals, the Catholic Queen Christina of Sweden and the Elector of Bavaria.

Giuseppe Torelli

Torelli was a composer and violinist born April 22, 1658 in Verona and died February 8, 1709 in Bologna. He began his career in Bologna where he performed in the San Petronio orchestra from 1686 to1696. Torelli later became the concertmaster for the Margrave of Brandenburg in Vienna from 1697 to 1699. He soon after returned to Bologna in 1701. Torelli made *significant contributions to the development of the concerto.* His concertos in *"Opus 8" (1709) are considered among the greatest achievements of baroque music.*

Antonio Vivaldi

J. S. Bach was greatly influenced by Vivaldi, and in fact, J. S. Bach arranged 10 concertos for Vivaldi. *Also,* Vivaldi helped develop the "concerti grossi" and the "three movement concerto."
About Antonio Vivaldi and his Masterpiece the "Four Seasons"

R. R. Esposito

Vivaldi was born March 4, 1678 in Venice and died July 28, 1741. As a composer and violin virtuoso, he was the *greatest master of Italian baroque music* during the 18th century. He composed over 450 concertos and sonatas and is known for beautiful melody, rhythm and clarity. The "Four Seasons," is probably his most famous work. Vivaldi's style *affected other composers of his time, most notably J.S. Bach, who used Vivaldi's musical models.*

Development of Classical Harmony and Influences on Handel and Others
Alessandro Scarlatti

Scarlatti was born May 2, 1660 in Palermo and died October 24, 1725. He was a prolific composer, writing in every musical category: 100 operas, 600 cantatas, 200 masses and other chamber and sacred music. The harmonies he used significantly advanced concepts of musical harmony for centuries to follow. He helped establish the "opera seria" and perfected the "aria da capo," as well as the three part overture. Queen Christina of Sweden loved opera with such great passion that she became Scarlatti's patron for four years. The German composer, George Friderc Handel traveled to Italy to meet Scarlatti and was greatly influenced by his work. Handel stayed in Italy for five years and wrote very popular operas in the Italian style. His Italian opera "Rinaldo" was a huge success in London in 1711, and he was later appointed as one of the three directors of the Royal Academy of Music. Alessandro Scarlatti's son, Domenico Scarlatti, later developed the foundation of modern keyboard technique. *Beethoven and Mozart followed the two Scarlatttis and took great musical inspiration from the sonatas of both father and son.*

Modern Keyboard Technique and Influences on Beethoven & Mozart
Domenico Scarlatti (aka Giuseppe Domenico Scarlatti)

Domenico Scarlatti, was the son of the famous Alessandro Scarlatti who had greatly influenced the work of Handel. Domenico was born October 26, 1685 in Naples and died July 23, 1757. He was a harpsichord virtuoso who wrote over 500 harpsichord sonatas. His music and keyboard technique became *the foundation of modern keyboard technique*, which also influenced the development of the harpsichord itself (also an Italian invention). Domenico performed in famous tours including London and Dublin in 1740. *Beethoven and Mozart* followed the two Scarlatttis and took great musical inspiration from the sonatas of both father and son. Incidentally, the Italian Lorenzo Da Ponte wrote many of Mozart's libretti and Beethoven was taught to play piano by an Italian musician and composer.

Violin Virtuoso & New Techniques Influencing Schumann and Liszt
Niccolo Paganini

Paganini was born on October 27, 1782 in Genoa and died on May 27, 1840. He was the leading violin virtuoso of his time, touring all of Europe. Paganini also composed music including 24 capricci (or caprices) for unaccompanied violin. *He was known for his brilliant technique*, especially *pizzicato*, fingering and improvisation. Paganini extended the way the violin is played by employing harmonics, and refining double and triple stops. He also revived various tunings (*scordatura*) for the violin for specialized effects. Paganini made his debut at age eleven in 1793. *Robert Schumann and Franz Liszt were greatly influenced by Paganini and adapted his music for the piano.*

Other Modern Composers & Notable Works

- **"The Pines of Rome"**
  Ottorino Respighi

  Respighi was born in 1879 and died in 1936. He was a composer of orchestral pieces, chamber music, operas and piano works. He is most notable for his symphonic romantic pieces: "Pines of Rome" (1924), "Fountains of Rome" (1917) and "Roman Festivals" (1929).

- **Pulitzer Prizes and NY Drama Critic Circle Award**
  Gian Carlo Menotti

  Menotti was born July 7, 1911 in Cadegliano, Italy and wrote chamber music, songs and operas. Menotti was also a music producer and librettist. He won the 1950 and 1954 Pulitzer Prize and the 1954 New York Drama Critic's Circle Award. His works include "The

Consul," "The Saint of Bleecker Street," and "Amahl and Night Visitors."

- ## Movie and Television Musical Scores
  ## Henry Mancini and Tony Esposito

The great musical genius Henry Mancini was born Enrico Nicola Mancini in Cleveland, Ohio on April 16, 1924. He was the *first composer to successfully merge popular songs with movie and television musical scores.* His career became meteoric in 1958 when he composed the score for the movie "Touch of Evil" produced by Orson Wells. Although he *composed scores for over 36 movies and television series,* he is most famous for the songs and scores of these major movie successes: "Breakfast at Tiffany's" (1961), "Days of Wine and Roses" (1962), "The Pink Panther" (1963), "A Shot in the Dark," (1964), "The Return of the Pink Panther" (1974), "The Pink Panther Strikes Again" (1976), "The Revenge of the Pink Panther" (1978), "10" (1979), "Victor/Victoria" (1982), "The Trail of the Pink Panther" (1982), "The Curse of the Pink Panther" (1983), "That's Life" (1986) and "Switch" (1991).

Mancini also wrote well known music for several television series including: "Peter Gunn" (1958), "Newhart" (1982) and "Remington Steele" (1982). The theme for "Peter Gunn" is a classic blues/jazz piece that is driving and hypnotic with a strong running base. This tune has been re-recorded by many artists including John Belushi and Dan Aykroyd on their "Blues Brothers" CDs. The very popular theme for "Newhart" is soft, melodic and tranquil. These two very different pieces are a good study in the diversity of Mancini's musical genius. Incredibly, Mancini was nominated for 72 Grammy awards and won 20 times.

Much of Mancini's music was co-written and jointly copyrighted with another Italian-American composer named Tony Esposito, not to be confused with the professional hockey player with the same name. Here is a list of compositions the two collaborated on:

"The Pink Panther" - by H. Mancini and T. Esposito © 1963.

"Moon River" - by H. Mancini and T. Esposito © 1961.

"Meggie's Theme" (aka "Anywhere The Heart Goes") - by H. Mancini and T. Esposito © 1983.

"Baby Elephant Walk" - H. Mancini and T. Esposito © 1961.

"The Sweetheart Tree" - H. Mancini and T. Esposito © 1965.

"Breakfast At Tiffany's"- H. Mancini and T. Esposito © 1961.

"Days Of Wine And Roses"- H. Mancini and T. Esposito © 1962.

"Softly" - H. Mancini and T. Esposito © 1960.
"Blackie's Tune" ("The Man Who Loved Women") - H. Mancini and T. Esposito © 1983.
"Slow Hot Wind" - H. Mancini and T. Esposito © 1963.
"Peter Gunn Theme" - H. Mancini and T. Esposito © 1958.
"Le Jazz Hot!"- H. Mancini and T. Esposito © 1981.
"Brass On Ivory" (dedicated to Doc Severinsen) - H. Mancini and T. Esposito © 1972.
"Charade" - H. Mancini and T. Esposito © 1963.
"A Cool Shade of Blue" - H. Mancini and T. Esposito © 1959.
"Mr. Lucky" - H. Mancini and T. Esposito © 1959.
"Fluter's Ball" - H. Mancini and T. Esposito © 1962.
"Dreamsville" - H. Mancini and T. Esposito © 1959.
"Dear Heart" - H. Mancini and T. Esposito © 1964.
"The Dancing Cat" - H. Mancini and T. Esposito © 1961.

- **"Charlie Brown / Peanuts" Television Musical Score**
  Vince Guaraldi

Vincent Anthony Guaraldi was born on July 17, 1928 in San Francisco. Vince, essentially a jazz composer and pianist, wrote the bouncy yet sophisticated theme music ("Linus & Lucy") for the "Charlie Brown" animated cartoons, as well as the entire score for each of the "Peanuts" television specials. His first big hit, "Cast Your Fate To the Wind" (1962), earned Guaraldi a Grammy Award and has since been recorded by dozens of other jazz musicians. Compared in success to Brubeck's "Take Five," Guaraldi's hit is one of the biggest selling jazz recordings. Sadly, Vince died suddenly at the age of 47 from a heart attack on February 6, 1976.

World's Most Famous Conductor and Musical Director
Arturo Toscanini

Toscanini was one of the world's greatest and most venerated music conductors. He was born March 25, 1867 in Parma, Italy and died January 16, 1957 in New York City. *He had the incredible ability to conduct from memory.* His performances included very energetic and dynamic interpretations of everything from Verdi to Wagner and Beethoven. His achievements are remarkable:

- Music Director of LaScala in Milan from 1898

- Music Director of Metropolitan Opera, New York City from 1908
- Conducted New York Philharmonic 1928 – 1936
- Director of NBC Symphony Orchestra 1937 – 1954. This symphony was organized specifically for Toscanini. Radio and television shows were produced to capitalize upon his fame and popularity. His television show was produced at NBC in New York City at studio 8H. NBC added four feet of sound proofing insulation around the entire studio to provide the best acoustics possible for the perfectionist Toscanini. Today, studio 8H is where the "Saturday Night Live" show is produced, and performing musical artists always welcome the opportunity to play in studio 8H because of the phenomenally good acoustics.

MUSIC: Instruments

Brass Instruments
Rome
Archeologists have uncovered Roman brass trumpet-like instruments. It is not certain whether the Romans were the first to invent brass instruments, but they were one of the earliest users, and certainly contributed to the development and perfection of these instruments. These were thought to be used by the Roman army and for official ceremonies.

Oboe
The earliest know form of the oboe dates to 50 BC in Rome.

Ocarina
Giuseppe Donati
The ocarina is a vessel-flute that first appeared about 10,000 years ago. The instrument has taken many forms in different parts of the world. In 1853, Giuseppe Donati of Budrio, Italy invented the modern 10-hole ocarina. Budrio has been the home of generations of ocarina builders since the 1850's, as well as the home of a succession of

Ocarina Orchestras. The current Ocarina Orchestra continues the long tradition of playing 7-part classical and opera music on tours across the globe.

Keyboard
Roman

Vitruvius, a very influential Roman architect and inventor in the 1st century BC, designed the keyboard. Some believe Hero of Alexandria (probably Greek) invented the key, but he lived *after* Vitruvius during the 1st century AD in Alexandria under Roman rule.

Vitruvius' greatest contribution to civilization was his 10 volume celebrated treatise entitled "De architectura" ("On Architecture"), that influenced architects for over 1500 years and was extensively used by Renaissance architects. His full name was Marcus Vitruvius Pollio, and he wrote extensively on many mechanical engineering subjects such as, hydraulics, clocks, and other civil and military designs.

Organ
Egypt and Rome

Some have credited the engineer Ktesibios (or Ctesibius), who lived in ancient Egypt in Alexandria, as the inventor of the organ in the year 265 BC. He either invented or improved the water or hydraulic organ. The famous Roman architect and engineer Vitruvius wrote about the organ invented by Ktesibios. However, the Romans invented or improved upon some of the earliest known organs. They were used in theatrical shows, ingeniously powered by an air-water mixture. The Roman organ, or "hydraulus," was powered by falling water that filled a funnel and developed a spinning whirlpool as the water fell into an enclosed chamber below (called an "Aeolian" chamber). The whirlpool caused the air-water mixture to fill the chamber and develop air pressure. Compressed air was forced out of the top of the chamber, and below the chamber the escaping water propelled a waterwheel. These two forces were used to operate the organ. There is a clay model from Carthage that has survived the centuries. Incredibly there is an actual organ that was rebuilt in 1931 and is in working order in the ancient Roman town of Aquincum, which is in present day Hungary. The organ was originally donated by Gaius Iulius Victorinus in 228

AD to the city's firemen's organization. There is also a hydraulic organ in the Quirinale area of Rome that was built in 1596 and restored several times from the 17th to the 19th centuries.

Organum, Harpsichord and Spinet
Giovanni Spinetti
The oldest ancestor of the harpsichord dates back to the 10th century in Italy and was called the organum. It was an oblong box about 30 centimeters (1 foot) long, and was used mostly for accompaniment with singing. Some have survived to this time. During the 15th century the harpsichord first appeared in Venice and early versions were trapezoidal in shape. In the 16th century, Giovanni Spinetti from Venice invented the spinet, which is a square shaped harpsichord. As a result of Spinetti and others, Venice became the first center of harpsichord manufacturing and its dominant shape eventually became wing-like, similar to a more modern grand piano. This wing shape actually follows the shape of the harp that rests horizontally within the wooden cabinetry of the instrument. The famous harpsichord composer, Domenico Scarlatti developed modern keyboard techniques and also advanced the development of the harpsichord.

The strings in harpsichords are plucked, and not struck by padded hammers as in the piano, a later Italian invention. Harpsichords produce notes with a constant volume and duration for each depression of a key. Therefore several harpsichords were played simultaneously to achieve *pianoforte* (*soft / loud*) effects.

Piano
Bartolomeo Cristofori
Cristofori was a harpsichord maker who also maintained dozens of musical instruments for the famous Grand Prince of Tuscany, Ferdinando de' Medici. In 1709, Cristofori created a brilliant musical innovation in Florence. He developed a revolutionary *percussion escapement* that caused hammers to strike the strings in a basic harpsichord cabinet and thus built the world's first piano. He built four pianos each with 49 keys, three of which still exist today. His new *percussion escapement* struck the strings with padded hammers instead

The world's first piano invented in Florence in 1709 by Cristofori

of plucking the strings with an unchangeable impact, as in the harpsichord. The sound was totally new and added expression to the musical piece based upon how hard each key was pressed, affecting the volume of each note played. Cristofori's new *percussion escapement* also allowed the musician to control the duration of each note by holding down the key. *For the first time the loudness and duration of each note would be affected by how the keys were struck by the musician.*

The English word *piano* is derived from the Italian word *pianoforte*, which was derived from the inventor's original term for the new instrument, *gravicembalo con piano e forte* (harpsichord that can play soft and loud). Cristofori gave his new instrument this name since it could be played *piano* (Italian for *soft*) or *forte* (Italian for *strong*) depending on how the musician pressed and held each key played. The great Cristofori was born in 1655 and died at the age of 77 in 1732.

In 1731 the Italian Lodovico Giustini wrote *the first compositions written specifically for the modern piano,* which he entitled "Sonate de Cimbalo di piano e forte."

Incredibly, the piano was outlawed in China during the rule of communist Chairman Mao Tse-tung (or Mao Zedong), because it was considered an instrument of the capitalist west. *Many pianos were destroyed by order of Mao* (1893 - 1976). Some survived on an island off the coast of China and the instrument eventually gained favor as some Chinese composers began to create piano arrangements for traditional Chinese music. Whenever the playful piano composition "chopsticks" is played, one can only image the consternation to Mao's eternal soul. Please do not confuse "chopsticks" with traditional Chinese music, Mao has suffered enough.

Violin
Northern Italy

The violin is an Italian invention that appeared for the first time in northern Italy around 1500. The first drawing of a violin dates back to a 1508 fresco painting in the town of Ferrara. The first written reference to the violin dates back to the 1523 accounting records of the town of Vercelli. Nearby lie the towns of Brescia and Cremona where the artisans produced these early violins. Cremona is the birthplace of the celebrated Amati family who made some of the finest violins ever crafted. Antonio Stradivari and other great violin makers were also born in Cremona. For over 450 years the city of Cremona has been and still is the leader of world-class stringed instruments. Cremona has produced the world's finest violins, cellos, violas and other stringed instruments. For generations, Cremona has been home to many families of artisans that have crafted magnificent musical instruments. The sound and quality of "Stradivarius" violins have never been reproduced. Violins that have been designed using the most modern sophisticated acoustic technology in the world still cannot equal the acoustic quality of Stradivari instruments. Cremona, Brescia, Naples and Venice are all home to many venerated violin and stringed instrument craftsman.

Ironically, here are three unusual stories of how world-renowned musicians have somehow managed to be incredibly forgetful:

- In the spring of 2001, the distinguished cellist, Lynn Harrell and former Principal of the Royal Academy of Music London, left a $4 million cello made by Stradivari when he exited a New York City taxicab. Harrell gave a $75 reward to the driver who returned the rare 17th century Stradivarius cello. After the cab driver bristled at the small reward for returning such a priceless instrument, Harrell increased the reward to $1000.

- In October of 1999, the world renowned cellist, Yo-Yo Ma was taking a taxicab to his performance in New York City and exited leaving his cello in the trunk. He telephoned the police who quickly radioed the cab using the fare receipt that Yo-Yo Ma had in his possession. The cello was recovered and the performance was saved from disaster. This instrument was made in Venice in 1733, and its estimated value is over $2 million.

- In 1967, David Margetts, who played second violin in the Roth String Quartette at the University of California at Los Angeles, left a Stradivarius violin, which belonged to the University, on the roof of his car and then drove off ! After 27 years, the violin turned up at a violin dealer's shop for repairs in 1994. The dealer recognized the rare violin and notified the University who was able to reclaim it after a lengthy court battle. This story appeared in the May/June 2001 issue of "Psychology Today" in an article about human memory.

So feel a little better the next time you leave your $20 umbrella in the back seat of a taxicab, at least it wasn't a rare and irreplaceable historic instrument.

Part 1 - Cremona, Italy

Amati Family

Amati violins are revered among the finest in the world. This famous Italian family of violin makers from Cremona was founded by Andrea Amati who lived from 1530 to 1578 (or 1611). He is the first recognized genius to craft superb violins. According to legend, Andrea would take a wooden mallet into the South Tyrol forest and strike trees that he liked and listened to the sound that they made. The trees he selected were then used to mill the wood Andrea used for his violins. Andrea and his sons Antonio (1550-1638) and Girolamo (1551-1635) crafted such venerated violins, violas and bass violins (violincelli) that the family gained international recognition.

Nicolo Amati (1596-1684), the grandson of Andrea and the son of Girolamo, was perhaps the most famous member of this distinguished family. *Nicolo's shop is where the great Antonio Stradivari and other masters learned the art of crafting fine violins and other stringed instruments.* Nicolo Amati was also the mentor for the patriarchs of three other famous families of violin makers: Andrea Guarneri, Francesco Ruggieri and Alessandro Gagliano. Continuing in this tradition, *the city of Cremora is still the source of the world's finest violins and other stringed instruments.* These fine instruments are hand crafted by highly specialized artisans, making Italy the leading supplier of the world's finest violins.

Two Amati-made violins are on display at the New York Metropolitan Museum of Art in the musical instruments department.

Guarneri Family

Andrea Guarneri (or Guarnieri) was the patriarch of another famous Italian family of violin makers. He was also born in Cremona about 1626 (died 1698) and studied under the famous Nicolo Amati. Andrea Guarneri had two sons, Pietro Giovanni (1655-1720) and Giuseppe (1666-1739/40?), who learned the art of designing and making superb violins from their father. Giuseppe's son, Giuseppe Antonio (1698-1744) carried on the tradition for a third generation and crafted some of the world's finest violins. Their instruments are also sometimes referred to by the Latin version of their name, i.e. Guarnerius.

Pietro and his nephew, Giuseppe Antonio, made the more esteemed violins in this family. Some musicians even prefer Giuseppe Antonio's violins to Stradivarius violins. A typical violin label of Guiseppe Antonio Guarneri would be: "Joseph Guarnerius fecit Cremonae anno 1737 IHS." The "IHS" is the Greek abbreviation for Jesus used to honor the Holy Name. The family is also sometimes referred to as Guarnerius del Gesu.

Antonio Stradivari

Stradivarius violins are the finest violins in existence, offering both visual and acoustic perfection. The master craftsman, Antonio Stradivari, born about 1644 in Cremona, designed and built these works of art. Starting at the age of 12, he learned his craft from the great Nicolo Amati. Modern scientific techniques have been used to analyze the Stradivarius violin characteristics, including design, wood and type of varnish. However, no other instruments have been made that equal the acoustic perfection of these priceless works of art. Stradivari's instruments, including violins, cellos, violas, lutes, guitars and mandolins, are in museums and private collections. Few are used by some very fortunate performing artists. Only about 650 in total have survived the centuries. It is not known how many he made, but some experts estimate that he made over a thousand violins in his lifetime. Stradivari spent his life where he was born in Cremona, Italy. It is here where he made his legendary violins and fittingly died there as well on December 18, 1737. His instruments are called "Stradivarius," since Stradivari inscribed this Latin version of his name on the instruments. The first violin labeled using his name was made in 1666.

Three Stradivari-made violins are on display at the New York Metropolitan Museum of Art, musical instruments department.

Violin scroll drawing by Antonio Stradivari (3D rendering added).

Carlo Bergonzi

Carlo was born in Cremona, Italy, in 1683 and died in 1747. Although other Bergonzi family members were also noted violin makers, Carlo was clearly the one outstanding artisan. Carlo Bergonzi's violins are often compared with the violins of the great Antonio Stradivari. In fact, Carlo Bergonzi apprenticed with Girolamo Amati (father of the great Nicolo Amati) and Giuseppe Guarneri, and eventually became the greatest pupil of the esteemed Antonio Stradivari. Bergonzi actually inherited Stadivaris violin workshop.

Ruggieri Family

Francesco Ruggieri was born about 1620 and died in 1695. Ruggieri studied under the great Nicolo Amati. Ruggieri's cellos, violins and violas represent instruments of the highest quality and are greatly admired for their rich, full tone and beautiful esthetics qualities. He is the most famous in his family of violin builders that he founded. His violins can be identified by several different signatures, e.g., Regeri, Ruger, Ruggeri, Ruggerius, or Rugier.

Francesco Ruggieri had two sons and a grandson who were also violin master artisans. However, their instruments are less esteemed than Francesco's works. His two sons are Vincenzo Ruggieri and Giacinto Giovanni Battista Ruggieri, who both built instruments from 1675 to 1730. Giacinto's son, Antonio Ruggieri, also continued the family tradition and built instruments from 1718 to 1726. This family's works should not be confused with those of the Rogeri family from Brescia. Both families worked during the same period of time.

Cremona's Great Legacy of Master Violin Builders
16th Century to the 18th Century

Andrea Amati
Andrea Amati's son / apprentice: Antonio Amati
Andrea Amati's son / apprentice: Girolamo Amati
Girolamo Amati's apprentice: Carlo Bergonzi
Girolamo Amati's son / apprentice: Nicolo Amati
Nicolo Amati's apprentice: Andrea Guarneri
Andrea Guarneri's son / apprentice: Pietro Giovanni Guarneri
Andrea Guarneri's son / apprentice: Giuseppe Guarneri
Guiseppe G.'s son / apprentice: Giuseppe Antonio Guarneri
Guiseppe G.'s apprentice: Carlo Bergonzi
Nicolo Amati's apprentice: Francesco Ruggieri
Francesco Ruggieri's son / apprentice: Vincenzo Ruggieri
Francesco Ruggieri's son / apprentice: Giacinto Giovanni Ruggieri
Giacinto Giovanni's son/apprentice: Antonio Ruggieri
Nicolo Amati's apprentice: Antonio Stradivari
Stradivari's apprentice: Carlo Bergonzi
Nicolo Amati's & Stradivari's apprentice: Alessandro Gagliano
Alessandro Gagliano's son / apprentice: Nicolo I Gagliano

Part 2 - Brescia, Italy

Gasparo Bertolotti (aka Gasparo da Salo)

Gasparo Bertolotti was a highly regarded violin designer and craftsman. He was born in 1542 in Brescia, Italy and died in 1609. Bertolotti is considered to be the founder of the Brescian school of violin makers. He was also known as Gasparo da Salo, because he was born at Salo on Lake Garda, Brescia, Italy. His violas and viola da gambas, often converted to violoncellos, are highly venerated. He trained and mentored Giovanni Paolo Maggini, who became yet another famous violin craftsman of the time.

Giovanni Paolo Maggini

Giovanni Paolo Maggini was born about 1580 in Botticino near Brescia and died in 1630. He studied with the famous master violin maker Gasparo Bertolotti (aka Gasparo da Salo) and continued the violin making legacy of the Brescian school. Maggini is known for his experimentation to improve tone quality and construction methods. *Many of his techniques and improvements are still in use today in violin building.* His instruments are known for their quality woods, mellow tones, and large beautifully shaped sound holes. Many have elaborate decorations on the back, such as the St. Andrew's Cross, a clover-leaf design, tableaux, medallions, crests, etc. Maggini built violins, violas, violoncellos, double basses and violas.

Part 3 - Naples, Italy

Gagliano Family

Alessandro Gagliano founded the Neapolitan school of violin building, and crafted instruments from about 1700 to 1735. He studied in Cremona with the two giants of his craft, Nicolo Amati and Antonio Stradivari. He later returned to Naples. His fine instruments are described as having a "mellow" quality. Although not many of his instruments have survived the ages, Alessandro Gagliano made violins, violas, cellos and double basses. His eldest son, Nicolo I, made instruments from about 1740 to 1780. They are of such fine quality that they have been mistaken for Stradivari violins. There were over a dozen violin makers with the name Gagliano, but Alessandro and Nicolo I were the most distinguished.

Modern Guitar Designers & Builders

John D'Angelico

The legendary John D'Angelico of New York City is the most celebrated archtop guitar and mandolin maker. His instruments are synonymous with the finest quality and some are valued at over $100,000. John was born in New York in 1905 and started his apprenticeship with his uncle at the age of nine. His uncle, Signor Ciani, was a noted guitar and mandolin maker in the traditional Italian style. Their shop was located at 40 Kenmore Street in New York City where they made all of their instruments by hand in limited quantities. *John D'Angelico also studied violin making, which influenced his archtop guitar concepts. His designs greatly influenced archtop guitars to follow.* His New Yorker Special (aka Teardrop style) guitars are especially beautiful, rare, and illustrate art deco design. He was an artist and master guitar craftsman. When John died in 1964, his apprentice James D'Aquisto continued the tradition of making only the finest custom guitars.

James D'Aquisto

James D'Aquisto of Greenport, Long Island, New York, studied under John D'Angelico. His Teardrop Solo and Centura models are among the finest guitars in existence. He made half a dozen, very rare seven string guitars, and one twelve-string guitar. D'Aquisto also built a unique blue archtop guitar, the D'Aquisto Centura Deluxe, which is considered to be a masterpiece of design and styling. James D'Aquisto, one of the world's finest guitar makers, passed away in 1995.

Robert Benedetto

Robert Benedetto was born in New York in October 1946. Robert comes from a family of gifted artisans. His father and grandfather were master cabinetmakers. Benedetto's grandfather was employed at the Steinway Piano Company. Robert's uncles were accomplished musicians and artists. He started playing guitar professionally at the age of 13. *Mr. Benedetto made his first archtop guitar in 1968 at the age of 21 and today his shop produces the most venerated of instruments.* He has crafted over 775 fine musical instruments, including over 460 archtops, and is internationally known for his superb violins, which are played by virtuosos in orchestras worldwide. Mr. Benedetto has crafted archtops, seven-string guitars, violins, violas, mandolins, semi-hollow electrics, solid body electric guitars and basses, and a single cello and classical guitar to date. Many celebrated jazz guitarists have endorsed his guitars by using and recording with them. These famous guitarists include: Bucky Pizzarelli, Ron Eschete, Jimmy Bruno, Howard Alden, Cal Collins, Jack Wilkins, John Pizzarelli, Jack Petersen, Johnny Smith, Chuck Wayne, Martin Taylor, Joe Diorio, Adrian Ingram, Frank Vignola, Royce Campbell, Kenny Burrell, Earl Klugh and Andy Summers. Mr. Benedetto is frequently profiled in books and magazines. His legendary instruments are included in countless recordings, books, videos, films and television soundtracks, as well as at concerts, museums and jazz festivals worldwide. His famous blue archtop guitar "La Cremona Azzurra" is an unusually loud and full sounding archtop. Only the D'Angelico Teardrop is known to have a loud sound with similar power, clarity and beauty.

The prestigious Guild Guitars company, subsidiary of Fender® Musical Instruments, has contracted with Mr. Benedetto to have him improve the design and construction of their archtop guitars. Further, a Guild-Benedetto archtop model will be developed and built at the Guild guitar shops. Mr. Benedetto has also written a landmark book in 1994 entitled "Making an Archtop Guitar," the first and only work of its kind. In 1996, he also produced a video on how to build archtop guitars called "Archtop Guitar Design & Construction." These two works offer priceless instruction and a foundation of knowledge that will benefit future generations of instrument designers and builders. Benedetto's first 30 years of archtop making are being documented by eminent jazz guitar historian Adrian Ingram in a soon to be published biography. Mr. Benedetto currently crafts a limited number (12-15) of archtop guitars annually. Buyers must wait almost three years for delivery. Prices range from $17,500 to $50,000.

How Robert Benedetto Fell In Love with Guitar Building

When Robert was about 12, his father took him to the old Gretsch guitar factory in Brooklyn, New York. He was invited there and given a tour by employee Carmine Coppolla, who was grateful to Bob's parents for selling a house in Hopatcong to his sister and her husband at the same low price Bob's parents had paid years earlier. Carmine Coppolla's sister had twelve children and little money. No one in the area would rent a house to this family with so many children, so Bob's parents sold the house to them, which was right next door to their own. Carmine heard that Bob's father had a son who was interested in the guitar, so he invited him and his son Bob on a tour of the factory. Bob recalls being absolutely overwhelmed by all those guitars under one roof. After that tour, he went home and began carving miniature guitars, which he still has in his possession today. Carmine told Bob to select a guitar and he picked the Chet Atkins "Nashville" model. Bob recalls, "I was so excited about getting that guitar. It was a real professional instrument. It was a kick to go on the job and take that guitar out of the case and strap it on. It made you want to play. I felt like a professional---I had a *real* guitar." He and his father visited that factory several times. It was where the great Bob Benedetto was first introduced to guitar building. In those early years, he cut up much of the family furniture to make his own guitars.

Robert Benedetto
13103 Waterford Run Drive, Riverview FL 33569-5732
Note: Robert Benedetto is a member of National Association of Music Merchants and the Guild of American Luthiers.

Mark Campellone

Mark Campellone was born August 29, 1954 in Providence, Rhode Island. His father's interest in music encouraged Mark to study music and later he repaired and built guitars. His archtop guitars and mandolins are all custom built and are highly esteemed for their quality of workmanship.

M. Campellone Guitars
5 Mapleville Road, Smithfield, RI 02828

Stephen Marchione

Stephen Marchione has used his experience repairing and restoring the most venerated D'Angelico and D'Aquisto guitars. He has built over 300 guitars and has built custom archtop guitars for jazz master Mark Whitfield and FarSide cartoonist Gary Larson.

Stephen Marchione, 20 W 20th Street #806, New York, NY 10011

John Monteleone

Monteleone's guitars and mandolins are all handmade and are highly esteemed since they offer the highest musical and aesthetic qualities. John took an early interest in making guitars at the age of 10 and began making his first guitar at 13. His father, Mario Monteleone, was a sculptor who attended the Beaux Arts Institute in Manhattan and in 1932 won the prestigious "Prix de Rome" design award from the American Academy in Rome. Mario, an accomplished sculptor, also built a New York City Harbor Scene that was displayed at the 1939-1940 New York City World's Fair. He also worked on exhibits for the 1964-1965 New York City World's Fair.

John's father Mario was influenced by his own uncle, John DeCesare, who was an architectural sculptor involved in designing lobbies and elevators for landmark buildings in Manhattan, such as the Empire State Building and the old New York Telephone building. John

DeCesare (John Monteleone's great uncle) also had a statue enlarging studio for stone and bronze statuary.

John is the third generation of gifted artisans in his family and recalls enjoying just watching his father work with his hands on statues. He is a self-taught guitar craftsman and got his professional start with the famous Mandolin Brothers music shop in Staten Island, New York City. This author interviewed John, and asked him what he thought had made him so successful in his profession. His reply offers profound advice for anyone with aspirations in any discipline. John said, "To be successful one needs both passion and vision." These are two powerful and necessary ingredients for any successful pursuit. John Monteleone, P.0 Box 52, Islip, N.Y. 11751

Note: Most of the guitar makers above have guitars they have built on display at the Smithsonian Museum in Washington D.C. Their guitars are exhibited in the Chinery Blue Guitar Collection in the American Museum Building. As the collection title indicates, all the guitars in this collection are actually blue in color.

MUSIC: Ballet & Opera

Ballet
Florence, Italy
The beginnings of ballet took place in the Italian courts in Florence during the late 1400's. The word *ballet* comes from the Italian word *ballare*, which means, *to dance*. The two earliest known ballets were written by Italians. The first was an Italian dance performance at the marriage of Gian Galeazzo, Duke of Milan, in 1489. The second ballet performance was given by the powerful Catherine de Medici of Italy for a wedding in Paris in 1581. It was called "Balet Comique de la Reine." The libretto and choreography were written by Balthazar de Beaujoyeulx. Beaujoyeulx was actually an Italian whose name was changed by history from Baltazarini di Belgiojoso. He left Italy for France around 1555. Baltazarini was a violin virtuoso and perhaps the best of his time. The violin at that time was a fairly recent Italian invention. French words are used for ballet terminology, because the

first ballet school was in France and the first books on ballet were published there as well.

Opera
Florence, Italy

Opera began in Florence by a group of scholars and musicians called the "Camerata Fiorentine." Vincenzo Galilei, the father of the great scientist Galileo Galilei, was a member of this founding group. The first opera is considered to be "Euridice" by Jacopo Peri, which was first performed at the Pitti Palace in Florence on October 6, 1600. Subsequently, in Rome and Venice the baroque style of opera appeared. The first open-air opera took place in Rome in 1606. The operatic term *aria* is Italian for *air*. Opera then spread throughout Italy, and Venice became the opera capital of the world. The famous composer and music director, Monteverdi, was highly instrumental in establishing opera in Venice. It was in Venice that opera received its name and was originally called *opera in musica*. Some music theorists believe the long and strong tradition of romantic Neapolitan songs provided much of the very early inspirations for opera.

Founder of Italian Opera and Developer of Modern Orchestration
Claudio Giovanni Antonio Monteverdi

Claudio Monteverdi was baptized on May 15, 1567 in Cremona, Italy and died on November 29, 1643. He was a composer and music director (*maestro di cappella*) at the famous St. Mark's Cathedral in Venice. Although he did not write the first opera, he is credited as the founder of Italian opera because he advanced many operatic concepts and music orchestration, including novel musical dissonance and other innovative uses of harmony. Many consider Monteverdi to be the *father of modern music*. His first opera, "Orfeo," was performed for a private audience in Mantua, Italy in 1607. He wrote many operas, including the opera "Adone" in 1639, which was performed at the world's first opera house, Teatro San Cassiano in Venice.

R. R. Esposito

First Opera House
Teatro San Cassiano
In 1637, Teatro San Cassiano became the first public opera house. It opened in Venice and was sponsored by the Tron family of Italy.

La Scala Opera House

"La Scala" Opera House
Milan, Italy
This opera house is considered one of the finest in the world. The great neoclassical architect Giuseppe Piermarini designed La Scala, which opened on August 3rd, 1778. The first opera was "L'Europa riconosciuta" by Antonio Salieri, which featured a libretto written by Mattia Verazi. During its early period the operas performed were closely linked to the tradition of Neapolitan opera buffa, whose leading composers included Giovanni Paisiello (1740-1816) and Domenico Cimarosa (1749-1801).

In 1997, La Scala was reorganized as a foundation, the Fondazione Teatro alla Scala, under the auspices of private ownership. The new organization has begun an integrated modernization plan.

La Scala is more than a theater for performances, it also includes professional schools for artistic training and students who aspire to work in opera theatres or in the entertainment industry. The training programs include specializations in ballet, singing, orchestral players, as well as theater management.

First Comic Opera
Marco Marazzoli
Vergilio Mazzochi

"Chi soffre, speri" was the first comic opera, which was written in 1639 by Marco Marazzoli and Vergilio Mazzochi. The term for comic opera is *opera buffa*. The Neapolitan, Giovanni Pergolesi, is known for his early *opera buffa* works, e.g. "La Serva Padrona" written in 1733. Domenica Cimarosa, who lived from 1749 to 1801, wrote almost 80 operas, some of which are excellent examples of early *opera buffa*.

"The Barber of Seville," "William Tell," "Cenerentola" (Operas)
Gioacchino Rossini

Rossini was born in Pesaro, Italy on February 29, 1792 and died November 13, 1868. The main character in "The Barber of Seville" is Figaro, the barber. He is a cunning servant who can outwit any aristocrat of his time. The outcome of his elaborate plans helps his former master win the heart of the beautiful woman he loves. Figaro is later used as a character in Mozart's opera "The Marriage of Figaro." Rossini wrote 39 operas including "William Tell" and "Cenerentola" ("Cinderella").

Rossini's main talent was in *opera buffa*, but he also wrote serious operas as well. He was a great influence on many, including the Italian composer Gaetano Donizetti (1797-1848) who wrote several notable operas. Later in life, Rossini moved to Paris where *he became a notable chef.* Still today in Paris, and elsewhere in French and Italian restaurants, there are dishes named after him by using the phrase *alla Rossini*, e.g. Cannelloni alla Rossini, Filet of Sole alla Rossini, Pheasant Suprême alla Rossini, Stuffed Turkey alla Rossini, and Macaroni Soup alla Rossini. Some are still made from his original recipes.

"Aida," "Otello," "Rigoletto," "Falstaff" and "La Traviata" (Operas)
Giuseppe Verdi

Verdi is considered one of the greatest composers of grand opera. He was born October 10, 1813 in Le Reneole, Italy and died January

27, 1901. Verdi composed many fabulous operas, twenty-seven in total. He is also known for his "Requiem Mass" and other sacred music. One of his most beautiful and moving arias, called *Questa o quella*, can be heard in "Rigoletto." In "Aida," the title character is a princess who falls in love with a warrior. By accident, he reveals military secrets to her and as a result she is condemned to death. She escapes but later dies with her lover. The play is well known for elaborate sets, costumes and props. "Aida" is singled out for these reasons, and because this author has an Aunt Aida, named after this opera by my grandfather who loved opera. Another aunt in this author's family is Aunt Norma, who is named after the opera, "Norma" written by Vincenzo Bellini. Aunt Aida is a wonderful baker and Aunt Norma a great cook. The family is never without great home cooked meals. A third aunt, Vitina, is not named after an opera, but ironically has great musical talent and taught herself to play piano.

This author's gastronomic good fortune (additionally blessed by his mother's cooking) is assured by his sister Mary and cousin Andrea who continue the family cooking and baking traditions with pride and excellence.

"Norma," " Il Pirata" and Other Operas that Influenced Chopin
Vincenzo Bellini

Bellini was born on November 3, 1801 in Catania, Sicily into a family of musicians. Bellini made significant contributions to opera and was known for his scores that combined both beautiful melody and deep expression. *Because of his strong melody treatments, he greatly influenced Chopin.* His aria *A te, o cara* in the opera "I Puritani" is an excellent example of his beautiful and expressive melodies. Bellini wrote wonderful operas and his "Oboe Concerto" is also a celebrated work. Bellini's most famous works are "Il Pirata," "I Capuletti i Montecchi," "La Sonnambula," "Norma" and "I Puritani." Bellini died in the midst of great success at the age of 34 on September 23, 1835 in Puteaux, France.

Incidentally, the name *Norma* and the English word *normal* are both derived from the Latin language used in ancient Rome. In ancient Rome, *norma* was the Latin word for a carpenter's square, the tool that guides a carpenter when building with right angles. In Latin, *norma* also meant a *standard* or *pattern*. Similarly, *normalis*, the Latin adjective formed from *norma*, had the literal meaning *forming a right angle*. Eventually, *normalis* in later Latin had the extended meaning *according to rule*. It is from this extended meaning that we derive the English word *normal*.

"Madame Butterfly," "La Boheme," "Tosca" and "La fanciulla del West" (Operas)
Giacomo Puccini

Puccini was born on December 28, 1858 in Lucca, Italy. *Puccini composed many of the world's most exquisite and beautiful operas* in the late 19th and early 20th centuries, e.g. "Madame Butterfly," "La Boheme," "Tosca," and "La fanciulla del West." The latter was written in New York City in 1910 and translates into "The Girl of the Golden West." A very sweet but powerful aria in this opera is called *Ch'ella mi creda*. Puccini started an opera called "Turandot," but it was left unfinished when he died on November 29, 1924.

"Pagliacci," "La Boheme" (Operas)
Ruggiero Leoncavallo

Leoncavallo was born on March 8, 1858 in Naples and died August 9, 1919. He is best known for the opera "Pagliacci" written in 1892. This is a classic example of Italian *verismo* opera based on a realistic story line. In Venice in 1897, Leoncavallo also wrote a lesser known "La Boheme." The famous "La Boheme" was of course written by Puccini in Torino in 1896.

Other Great Operas

"Adriana Lecouvreur" by Francesco Cilea (Milan, 1902)
"Andrea Chenier" by Umberto Giordano (Milan, 1896)
"Fedora" by Umberto Giordano (Milan, 1898)
"I Puritani" by Vincenzo Bellini (Parigi, 1835)
"La Gioconda" by Amilcare Ponchielli (Milan, 1876)
"La fille du regiment" by Gaetano Donizetti (Paris, 1840)
"Lucia di Lammermoor" by Gaetano Donizetti (Naples, 1835)

R. R. Esposito

Famous Opera Singers

Andrea Bocelli

Andrea Bocelli was born on September 22nd, 1958 on the family farm in Lajatico in the rural Tuscany region of Italy. He grew up among beautiful and pastoral vineyards and olive groves. His father still produces "Chianti Bocelli" wine from the family vineyard. Andrea studied piano, flute and saxophone, but had a passion to sing opera at an early age. He was born visually impaired, but while playing soccer with friends at the age of 12 he suffered a brain hemorrhage and completely lost his sight. Not easily deterred, Andrea attended the University of Pisa and received his Doctorate of Law. Later he approached the legendary tenor, Franco Corelli, who agreed to train Andrea for the opera. He paid for his own training by playing piano in bars and clubs where he also met Enrica his wife. They now have two boys, Amos and Mateo.

Andrea's early operatic performances with Zucchero and Pavarotti won him rave reviews. His very popular CDs, "Romanza," "Aria," and "Sogno" have made Bocelli an overnight recording success. On March 29, 1999, he performed at the Academy Awards ceremony where Italian actor-writer-director Roberto Benigni won two "Oscars" for Best Actor and Best Foreign Film for his movie box office hit "Life is Beautiful" ("La Vita è bella").

Italo Campanini

Campanini was one of the greatest tenors that ever lived. He was born in Parma in 1846 and died in Vigatto on November 22, 1896. He sang in Italy and Russia before his debut as Gennaro in the opera "Lucrezia Borgia" at the Academy of Music in New York on October 1, 1873. Campanini sang Italian and French operas and was also expert in Wagner's "Lohengrin." Campanini was known to have a brilliant voice with incredible range, power, and energy like no other singer of his time.

Enrico Caruso

Enrico Caruso was born on February 27, 1873 at home in a seven-story apartment building in Naples where his working-class family lived. Although his family was not financially rich, both his parents were rich in talent and had fine singing voices. His father, Marcellino Caruso, a mechanic in a local factory, had a deep bass voice. His mother, Anna Baldini, although known to suffer from poor health, had a lovely soprano voice. At a young age Caruso's talent was obvious and his mother encouraged his singing. He began formal voice training at the tender age of ten.

Caruso performed from the late 19th to the early 20th centuries throughout the world. His perfect voice with massive power, range and beauty makes experts describe him as the *greatest tenor in the history of opera.* He achieved fame when he played the part of Rodolfo in "La Boheme" in Milan. Caruso performed internationally and made his American debut in "Rigoletto" at the opening night of the Metropolitan Opera in New York City on Nov. 23, 1903. He was honored by opening each season at the Metropolitan Opera in New York City for the next 17 years. *His highly popular performances made the Metropolitan Opera Company in New York a financial success. Caruso's celebrated recordings sold so well that he also made the Victor Talking Machine financially successful as well.* He and his descendants made hundreds of thousands of dollars a year on royalties for these very popular records. His repertoire included over fifty famous operas. When Caruso died in Naples August 2, 1921, the entire world mourned his passing.

Giuseppe Mario, Count of Candia

Giuseppe Mario was born in Cagliari, Sardinia Island on October 17, 1810 and died in Rome on December 11, 1883. He was one of the greatest tenors in history. Mario toured in Boston, Philadelphia, New York and Washington. He married Giulia Grisi, another opera singer, and they often performed in operas together to the delight of their fans.

The Patti Family

▪ **Salvatore Patti** was born in Catania, Sicily and died about 1869 in Paris. He was a tenor, musical impresario and the father of the great Adelina Patti. His wife was Caterina Chiesa of Rome.

▪ **Adelina Patti** was the daughter of Salvatore and Caterina Patti. Adelina, by circumstance, was born in Madrid, Spain on February 10, 1843 and she died in Wales on September 27, 1919. *She was one of the world's greatest opera singers*, and was called "the last of the great divas." Adelina began her career at the age of nine and toured throughout the U.S. and Europe, but mostly in New York. Her career was a consistent string of successes, which came with phenomenal financial rewards. For example, she owned a $60,000 private railroad-car that she traveled in. On one tour of Mexico and the United States (1886-1887) she earned over $250,000.

- **Carlo Patti** was the older brother of the great Adelina Patti. He too was born in Madrid, Spain in 1842 and died in St. Louis, Missouri on March 17, 1873. Carlo was a violinist and conductor. He toured mostly in the United States and Mexico.

- **Carlotta Patti** was the older sister of the great Adelina Patti. Carlotta was born in Florence in 1836 and died in Paris on June 27, 1889. She was an eminent coloratura soprano and successfully toured the United States, England and Italy. Carlotta was an instant success at her debut and had an exceptionally brilliant career. Unfortunately Carlotta was physically lame. The First Commissioner of Health for NYC, the distinguished Dr. Giovanni Ceccarini, attempted to treat her but to no avail. This hindered her career in opera, since her limited ability to walk and stand hampered her stage abilities. (Refer to the chapter on "American Government" for more information on Dr. Ceccarini). Carlotta broke her hip as a child, which caused her condition. Some say that the Patti family members were all attractive, but that Carlotta was the most beautiful and her voice was superior to even that of Adelina.

Luciano Pavarotti
Pavarotti was born on October 12, 1935 in Modena, Italy. He is one of the world's greatest tenors and has been compared to Caruso by many. In his debut, Pavarotti played Rodolfo in "La Boheme" in 1961. He is an internationally acclaimed performer and has made many very successful CD's of opera and Neapolitan songs. In 1997 and 1998 he also performed with the popular rock singer Bryan Adams.

Renata Scotto
Scotto was born February 24, 1934 in Savona, Italy and is an operatic soprano. She has performed internationally, starting with the most famous opera houses: La Scala (1954), Covent Garden (1957) and Metropolitan Opera (1965). Her repertoire includes "La Boheme," "Madame Butterfly" and "Don Giovanni."

Renata Tebaldi

Tebaldi was born January 2, 1922 in Pesaro, Italy. She is a soprano who made her debut in 1944. Tebaldi has had many well known international performances: La Scala (1946), San Francisco (1950) and Metropolitan Opera (1955). Her repertoire includes "La Boheme," "Madame Butterfly," and "Tosca."

Luisa Tetrazzini

Tetrazzini was born in 1871 in Florence and died in 1940. She was a coloratura soprano and sang internationally, including at the Metropolitan Opera in New York City (1908). The dish "Chicken Tetrazzini" is named after her. (See the "Culinary Contributions" chapter for more on Luisa and her life).

ᘓ

Chapter XVI

PHILOSOPHY

"We honor Cicero, who taught us how to think."
- Voltaire -

Italy has a rich and diverse philosophical history. For this reason, the entries in this chapter are not alphabetized as most chapters are organized in this text, but instead are listed in chronological order to illustrate the evolutionary and developmental paths.

Inventor of Rhetoric
Empedocles

Of Greek descent, Empedocles lived in Agrigento, Sicily where he was born about 492 BC. At the time Agrigento was a Greek colony known as Acragas. Empedocles was primarily a natural philosopher, but was also a poet, physician and social reformer. Aristotle is said to have considered him the inventor of rhetoric, while Galen regarded him as the founder of the science of medicine in Italy. He anticipated the modern concept in physics that matter and energy cannot be created or destroyed, i.e. the principle of conservation of energy. Empedocles theorized that nothing really comes into being or is destroyed, but that changes in the ratio of four elements (fire, air, water and earth) merely transform the materials we experience.

The earliest theory of magnetism is often credited to Empedocles. He believed the invisible release and entry of a substance from iron produced magnetic affects. This was an early intuition of magnetic flow. Empedocles also offered a primitive theory of evolution, believing that at first all species were indistinguishable and had not even developed gender distinctions. He also theorized that all earthly life came from trees and vegetation and wrote of a simplified theory on survival of the fittest. Empedocles had a life-long interest in plants and embryology. His most well known work is entitled "On Nature," which was written as a didactic poem in three books on the subject of physical-cosmology.

Empedocles also formulated an optical theory that included light particles and stated that color is derived from the senses, produced by the appropriate rays entering the eye. Both theories were close to modern concepts in physics.

Stoic Philosophy
Cicero (aka Marcus Tullius Cicero, aka Tully)

Cicero was born in Arpino, Italy 106 BC and died on December 7, 43 BC. He was a Roman philosopher and one of the greatest thinkers and orators the world has known. His speeches to the Roman Senate are known for their powerful rhetorical style. Cicero's philosophical writings are of the Stoic school. His mastery and art form of Latin prose is unsurpassed. He was also a senatorial party leader who opposed Julius Caesar. Cicero was a defender of the rule of law and constitutional government and supported republican values during the civil wars of the Roman Republic. After Caesar's assassination, he delivered a famous series of speeches ("Philippics") against Mark Antony, who later had Cicero executed. He was also a lawyer and wrote on ethics and political theory. In the 19th century, the great French writer Voltaire stated "We honor Cicero, who taught us how to think."

Cicero also invented the memory technique that associates rooms in a home with concepts. By associating the main points of his speeches with different rooms in his home, he always remembered the main talking points in his legendary oratories. In his mind, he would move through the rooms and remember each part of his speech.

Political Science

Dante Alighieri

Dante was born in Florence in 1265 and died September 14, 1321. He is well known as the famous Italian poet and political philosopher whose greatest work was "The Divine Comedy." However, his literary works include strong philosophical treatises. His rigorously conceptualized treatise entitled "Monarchia," argues for a strong universal monarchy as the only solution to the detrimental political and economic factionalism of his day. In this treatise he *separates the Church from State* and argues why they should be separate and independent. He continues that the Church manages the spirit, but the State must also adhere to a moral philosophy. (Refer to the chapter on "Language & Literature" for more on Dante.)

Niccolo Machiavelli

Machiavelli is considered the *father of political science*. His masterpiece "The Prince" offered groundbreaking analysis on the requirements of political success. Refer to the chapter on "Language & Literature" for more on Machiavelli's work.

Humanism
Francesco Petrarca (or Petrarch) (1304 - 1374)
Giovanni Boccaccio (1313 - 1375)

Boccaccio and his older contemporary Petrarca (Petrarch) are credited as the forces that rekindled the study of classical works during the early Renaissance that initiated *humanism*. This concept embraces the spirit of intellectual freedom and refuted the church's doctrine that man was intrinsically bad and required salvation, which could only be obtained through the Church. *Humanism* also embraces man's free will, education, and the belief that man is intrinsically good-natured. *Humanism* conceptually opposed the medieval Church's total authority and fatalistic beliefs. Petrarca's philosophical concepts were influenced by the meaning and use of the Latin term *humanitas* by the Roman scholars Cicero and Varro. Pico della Mirandola also comprehensively expressed this idea in his "Oratio de dignitate hominis." Refer to the chapter "Language & Literature" for more information on Boccaccio and Petrarca. They are considered to be among the most influential figures in the history of western literature.

Father of Modern Philosophy of History
Giambattista Vico (aka Giovanni Battista Vico)

Vico was born in Naples on June 23, 1668 and died there as well on January 23, 1744. He spent his entire life in Naples. Vico is generally regarded as the founder of modern philosophy of history and is often considered the founder of the philosophy of culture and the philosophy of mythology. Many argue that *Vico was the most significant and influential of Italian philosophers.*

Vico has also written on epistemology, psychology and the philosophy of mathematics. His concepts on the dynamic study of history and culture were far in advance of his time, but they went unnoticed until the 19th century. He was the first to depart from the simple biographical and chronological accounts of history. *His concepts helped explain the birth, development and decay of civilizations, and included studies of their language, religion and myths.* He published his philosophy in his 1725 work "The New Science," which he rewrote completely and then published again in 1730 and again in 1744. "The New Science" is his most celebrated work, however, his work entitled "On the Most Ancient Wisdom" is also an important treatise.

Karl Marx discusses Vico's concepts in "Das Kapital." *Vico's dynamic and cyclical view of history was a strong influence on the Dialectical Materialism of Karl Marx.* Also, Leon Trotsky quotes Vico on the first page of his book "History of the Russian Revolution." Goethe read "The New Science" as well as Jacobi. Vico also greatly influenced other philosophers, such as Jules Michelet and Benedetto Croce. Coleridge was the first English writer to disseminate "Vichian" ideas.

When Irish author James Joyce wrote his classic "Finnegans Wake," he based the general structure and concepts on "The New Science" and referred to Vico several times, including in a Latin phrase (*a commodius vicus of recirculation*) that contained the Latin translation of the name Vico. Joyce greatly admired the Italian culture and moved to Trieste, Italy where he raised his family, naming his children Giorgio (born 1905) and Lucia Anna (born 1907).

The Philosophy Department of Emory University has an Institute for Vico Studies, which is dedicated to the study of his ideas and contributions. Vico was also an academic having been Professor of Rhetoric at the University of Naples beginning in 1699.

R. R. Esposito

Idealism and Positivism - Traditional

Most traditional Italian philosophy has been dominated by two schools of philosophical thinking that are diametrically opposed. One is the philosophy of idealism. Idealism is a metaphysical theory about the nature of reality. It presumes that there is a distinction between appearance and reality, in part based upon differences in individuals' perceptions and thoughts. For example, there is no certainty about what the true color red is. It may be different in each individual's mind. Further, the input tools (the eyes) to the mind may not perceive red the same. We know there are many males with common red/green deficiencies. These individuals view the world differently - one must ask which perception is in fact reality. Another metaphysical discussion would ask: what is the true nature of wax, solid or liquid. Its state depends on the temperature, but what is its true nature? Most Italian idealists founded their own new interpretations and critical elaborations on the writings of the German philosophers Immanuel Kant (1724 - 1804) and Georg Wilhelm Friedrich Hegel (1770 - 1831). These fundamental questions about reality date as far back as the Greek philosopher Aristotle.

Positivism, as a school of thought (similar to empiricism and naturalism) was introduced during the 19th century by the French sociologist Comte (1798 - 1857). Positivism attempts to describe the history of human thought in evolving stages. Comte called these stages: religious, metaphysical and scientific. The scientific stage is where most modern people feel most comfortable, and is clearly the most useful and practical. In later decades, Italian Marxism was an outgrowth of positivism, with some influences of idealism. Italian political scientists and philosophers have developed their own version of socialism, communism and Marxism. Positivism also is the basis for other modern and post-modernism philosophical theories.

In this chapter, several great Italian philosophers are profiled. Below are other notable figures who are categorized as *idealists* and *positivists*:

Idealism School of Thought – Notable Philosophers

Tommaso Campanella (1568-1639), Vincenzo Cuoco (1770-1823), Francesco De Sanctis (1817-1882), Marsilio Ficino (1433-1499), Vincenzo Gioberti (1801-1852), Antonio Labriola (1843-1904),

Giovanni Pico Della Mirandola (1463 1494), Antonio Rosmini-Serbati (1797-1855), Bertrando Spaventa (1817-1882), Augusto Vera (1813-1885).

Positivism School of Thought – Notable Philosophers

Niccola Abbagnano (1901-1990), Roberto Ardigo (1828-1920)*, Cesare Beccaria (1738-1794), Mario Calderoni (1879-1914), Carlo Cattaneo (1801-1869)*, Enrico Ferri (1846-1929), Gaetano Filangeri (1752-1788), Antonio Genovesi (1712-1769), Ludovico Geymonat (1908-1991), Melchiorre Gioja (1767-1829), Achille Loria (1857-1943), Cesare Lombroso (1835-1909), Gaetano Mosca (1858-1941), Vilfredo Pareto (1848-1923)**, Luigi Pareyson (born 1918) Pietro Pompanazzi (1462-1525), Gian Domenico Romagnosi (1765-1835), Bernardino Telesio (1509-1588), Giovanni Vailati (1863-1909), Galvano della Volpe (1895-1968), Pasquale Villari (1826-1917).

*Ardigo and Cattaneo were main figures and contributors to the positivist school during the 19th century.
**Pareto is famed as an economist, but his later sociological work was entitled "The Mind and Society" (1916), which critiqued political liberalism and supported a free market economy. Also, refer to the "Economics, Finance and Business" chapter for more on Pareto.

Idealism, Modern
Benedetto Croce

Croce was born February 25, 1866 in Pescasseroli, Italy, and lived most of his life in Naples, before passing away on November 20, 1952. *His works were landmarks of modern "idealism."* His most significant work, "Philosophy of the Spirit," was written from 1902 to 1917. He was also an historian and literary critic. Croce produced several other significant works including his "History as the Story of Liberty" in 1938. He was influenced by the great Vico.

Croce also founded "Critica" (1903 to 1944), a review of literature, history and philosophy. In 1944, this publication became "Quaderni della critica." In 1910, he became a senator and served for two years as minister of education. He staunchly and openly opposed Fascism. In 1943, he became a leader of the Liberal party in Italy.

Idealism, Education and Fascism
Giovanni Gentile

Gentile was born in 1875 and died in 1944. He and Croce led the revival of Italian idealist philosophy in the early 20th century. Gentile's concepts represented an extreme form of idealism, covering the subjects of: consciousness of experience, uniting thought and will, and objective knowledge. His philosophy, "actual idealism," is a form of neo-idealism and was developed in his book entitled "Teoria generale dello spirito come atto puro" ("The Theory of Mind as Pure Act") published in 1916.

He taught in several Italian universities and also wrote a number of influential books on education. Gentile also wrote a detailed history of modern Italian philosophy to illustrate how the concepts of German philosophers were similar to their Italian colleagues, leading to his belief in a single European tradition of philosophy.

Gentile became a senator in 1922 and for two years he served as minister of public instruction. It is in this position that he was able to reform the structure of public education.

He supported Fascism and has also been called the philosopher of Fascism.

Democratic Theory, Contributions
Norberto Bobbio

Bobbio was born in Turin in 1909 and was among Italy's most influential philosophers concerned with political science and law. He taught at the University of Turin, became a Life Senator in 1984, and gained international fame. Bobbio's main contribution has been to democratic theory and individual rights synthesized with socialist concerns aimed at equality and social justice.

Marxist Theorist
Lucio Colletti

Colletti was born in 1924 and became famous as the principal Italian Marxist theorist. He was a Professor of Philosophy at La Sapienza University in Rome. Colletti was a student of the great Galvano Della Volpe. He rejected much of traditional/classical Italian philosophy. Colletti critiqued Marxism and insisted on scientific methods for economic development, and later studied capitalism. It was in the late 1970's that he abandoned Marxism.

Communist Party Ideologist (Italian)
Antonio Gramsci

Gramsci was born on the island of Sardinia in 1891 and died in 1937. He was one of the founders and the principal ideologist of the Italian Communist Party. Gramsci was later imprisoned by Italian dictator Benito Mussolini for the rest of his life. As others have done in prison, Gramsci made the best use of his incarceration and wrote. He completed his "Prison Notebooks," which are regarded as one of the world's founding documents of Western Marxism. Gramsci was influenced by the works of Croce.

Post-Modernism Theorist
Gianni Vattimo

Vattimo was born in 1936 and is currently a professor at the University of Turin. He is the leading theorist of Italian post-modernism and is also a leading scholar of 19th and 20th century German philosophy. His works include studies of the organization of modern societies and the problems created by the effects of new technologies and the mass media. He believes that these developments can produce alienation and a fragmented society.

R. R. Esposito

∝

Chapter XVII

Proverbs & Quotations

"When you are at Rome live in the Roman style"
(Often quoted as "When in Rome, do as the Romans do")
- Saint Ambrose, patron Saint of Milan -

This chapter has four major sections:
- Latin Proverbs – Anonymous, page 341
- Quotations - Classical and Modern, page 343
- Latin Phrases, page 361
- Italian Proverbs, page 371

Well known proverbs and quotations are shown in bold print. (Also, refer to the "Language & Literature" chapter for information on medical and legal terms, and other influences of Latin.)

Latin Proverbs - Anonymous

The Book of Books (Liber librorum.) ~ Latin phrase for the Bible

Let the buyer beware. (caveat emptor)
~ a famous sign posted in Roman marketplaces, now a common-law maxim.

Beware of the dog! (Cave canem!)
~ A common inscription at the entrances and gates of Roman homes, a good example may be seen in the ancient city of Pompeii.

Let him be promoted to get him out of the way. (Promoveatur ut amoveatur.) ~ Roman emperors got rid of an unwanted person (persona non grata) by these means.

Not everything that is shining is gold. (Non omne quod nitet aurum est..) ~ ancient Latin proverb
Note: All that glitters is not gold.

One who sleeps doesn't sin. (Qui dormit, non peccat.)
~ ancient Roman saying

I count only the bright hours. (Horas non numero nisi serenas.)
~ A common Latin inscription on ancient sundials.

To the city and the globe. (Urbi et orbi.) ~ Vatican
Note: This phrase is often spoken by the Pope during his blessing, to indicate that the message is for the city (Rome) and the world.

Thus passes over the glory of the world. (Sic transit gloria mundi.)
~ Vatican
Note: Phrase spoke when a newly elected pope enters St. Peter's Basilica in Rome, since the glory has passed over to him.

The Senate and the Roman People (Senatus Populusque Romanus or S.P.Q.R.) ~ Used on buildings, signs and banners in ancient Rome to illustrate the unity between the Roman people and its rulers.

Silence gives consent. (Qui tacet, consentit) ~ ancient Roman saying

Words fly away, the written remains. (Verba volant, scripta manet.)
~ ancient Roman saying

Who, what, where, with what, why, how, when?
(Quis, quid, ubi, quibus auxiliis, cur, quomodo, quando?)
~ ancient Roman saying

Quotations - Classical and Modern
(Listed in Alphabetical Order by Author's Last Name.)

&

A man can do all things if he but wills them. ~ Leon Battista Alberti

&

A great flame follows a little spark. ~ Dante Alighieri, "The Divine Comedy"

Abandon all hope, ye who enter here! (Lasciate ogni speranza chi entrate. - Italian) ~ Dante Alighieri, "The Divine Comedy"

Consider your origin; you were not born to live like brutes, but to follow virtue and knowledge. ~ Dante Alighieri, "The Divine Comedy"

He listens well who takes notes. ~ Dante Alighieri, "The Divine Comedy"

&

Silence is a text easy to misread. ~ A. A. Attanasio, "The Eagle and the Sword"

&

If you are distressed by anything external, the pain is not due to the thing itself, but to your estimate of it; and this you have the power to revoke at any moment. ~ Marcus Aurelius

Look well into thyself; there is a source of strength, which will always spring up if thou wilt always look there. ~ Marcus Aurelius

In the morning, when you are sluggish about getting up, let this thought be present: 'I am rising to a man's work.' ~ Marcus Aurelius, "Meditations"

Never esteem anything as of advantage to you that will make you break your word or lose your self-respect. ~ Marcus Aurelius, "Meditations"

Nothing happens to anybody that he is not fitted by nature to bear. ~ Marcus Aurelius, "Meditations"

The universe is change; our life is what our thoughts make it. ~ Marcus Aurelius, "Meditations"

Think not disdainfully of death, but look on it with favor; for even death is one of the things that Nature wills. ~ Marcus Aurelius, "Meditations"

◊

Ninety percent of the game is half mental. ~ Yogi Berra

It ain't over, 'til it's over. ~ Yogi Berra

Nobody goes there anymore, it's too crowded. ~ Yogi Berra

Always go to other people's funerals, otherwise they won't go to yours. ~ Yogi Berra

The future ain't what is used to be. ~ Yogi Berra

It's déjà vu all over again. ~ Yogi Berra

When you come to a fork in the road, take it. ~ Yogi Berra

Nobody did nothin' to nobody. ~ Yogi Berra

Don't get me right, I'm just asking. ~ Yogi Berra

If you don't know where you are going, you might not get there. ~ Yogi Berra

Only in America. ~ Yogi Berra

❧

Nothing is unfortunate if you don't consider it unfortunate. (Nihil est miserum nisi cum putes.) ~ Boethius, "De consolatione philosohiae"
Note: U.S. President Abraham Lincoln stated this similarly, "People are about as happy as they fix their minds to be."

❧

If people only knew how hard I work to gain my mastery, it wouldn't seem so wonderful at all. ~ Michelangelo Buonarroti

❧

I found Rome a city of bricks and left it a city of marble. (Urbem latericiam invenit, marmoream reliquit) ~ Augustus Caesar, as quoted in "Augustus" by Suetonius

❧

The die is cast! (Alea iacta est!) ~ Julius Caesar
Note: Said by Caesar when he crossed the Rubicon river with his troops, and took his chances by starting a civil war in Rome. The word *die* refers to the chance taken when tossing dice.

I came, I saw, I conquered. (Veni, vidi, vici.) ~ Julius Caesar
Note: Spoken by Caesar to the Senate after a conquest in Asia.

Men willingly believe what they wish. ~ Julius Caesar, "De Bello Gallico" ("Gallic Wars")

And you, my Brutus. (Et tu, Brute.) ~ Julius Caesar
Note: Caesar said this when he realized his friend, Brutus, was among his assassins. The phrase is used in Shakespeare's play "Julius Caesar."

❧

You, the individual, can do more for your health and well being than any doctor, any hospital, any drug, and any exotic medical device. ~ Joseph A. Califano Jr., U.S. Secretary of Health, Education and Welfare (Now the U.S. Dept of Health and Human Services.)

After I'm dead I'd rather have people ask why I have no monument than why I have one. ~ Cato the Elder

Grasp the subject, the words will follow. ~ Cato the Elder

I think the first virtue is to restrain the tongue; he approaches nearest to gods who knows how to be silent, even though he is in the right.
~ Cato the Elder

We cannot control the evil tongues of others; but a good life enables us to disregard them. ~ Cato the Elder

☙

Everything has a small beginning. (Omnium rerum principia parva sunt.) ~ Marcus Tullius Cicero, "De finibus"

Habit is our second nature. (Consuetudo quasi altera natura.)
~ Marcus Tullius Cicero, "De finibus"

Our thoughts are free. (Liberae sunt nostrae cogitationes.)
~ Roman law book "Corpus Juris Civilis."
Note: A much older version written by Marcus Tullius Cicero, in his "Pro Milone" stated: Nobody should be punished for his thoughts. (Cogitationis poenam nemo patitur.)

A friend in need is a friend indeed. (Amicus certus in re incerta cernitur.) ~ The Roman author Ennius first stated this line, but it was made popular when he was quoted by Marcus Tullius Cicero

To everyone each his own. (suum cuique) ~ Marcus Tullius Cicero

Oh the times! Oh the customs! (O tempora! O mores!)
~ Marcus Tullius Cicero

May it be good, fortunate and prosperous! (Quod bonum, felix faustumque sit!) ~ Words spoken when the Roman senate opened its session. Quoted by Marcus Tullius Cicero, in "De divitatione"

Anybody can err, but only the fool persists in his fault. (Cuiusvis hominis est errare, nullius nisi insipientis in errore perseverare.) ~ Marcus Tullius Cicero, "Philippicae orationes."
Note: often quoted as, Errare humanum est, ignoscere divinum - to err is human, to forgive divine.

The force of habit is great. (Consuetudinis magna vis est.)
~ Marcus Tullius Cicero, "Tusculanae Disputationes"

To live is to think. (Vivere est cogitare.)
~ Marcus Tullius Cicero, "Tusculanae disputationes"

Nothing is more uncertain than the (mind of the) crowd. (Nihil est incertius volgo.) ~ Marcus Tullius Cicero, "Pro Murena"

Surmounted labors are pleasant. (Iucundi acti labores.)
~ Marcus Tullius Cicero, "De officiis"

A letter doesn't blush. ~ Marcus Tullius Cicero, "Epistulae, ad familiares"

What has been wrongly gained is wrongly lost.
~ Marcus Tullius Cicero, "Philippicae orationes"

Names are hateful. (Nomina sunt odiosa.)
~ Marcus Tullius Cicero, "Pro Roscio"

The extreme law is the greatest injustice. (Summum ius, summa iniuria.)
~ Marcus Tullius Cicero, "De officiis"

Laws are silent in times of war. (Silent enim leges inter arma.)
~ Marcus Tullius Cicero, "Pro Milone"

Live as brave men; and if fortune is adverse, front its blows with brave hearts. ~ Marcus Tullius Cicero

Natural ability without education has more often attained to glory and virtue than education without natural ability. ~ Marcus Tullius Cicero

Never go to excess, but let moderation be your guide.
~ Marcus Tullius Cicero

Reason should direct and appetite obeys. ~ Marcus Tullius Cicero

&

Liberty is a thing beyond all price. (Libertas inaestimabilis res est.)
~ "Corpus Juris Civilis"
Note: The "Digest" section of the great Roman legal system, "The
Body of Civil Law" ("Corpus Juris Civilis").

It is better that a crime is left unpunished than that an innocent man is
punished. (Satius est impunitum relinqui facinus nocentis, quam
innocentem damnari.) ~ "Corpus Juris Civilis"
Note: The "Digest" section of the great Roman legal system, "The
Body of Civil Law" ("Corpus Juris Civilis").

Not everything that is permitted is honest. (Non omne quod licet
honestum est.) ~ "Corpus Juris Civilis"
Note: The "Digest" section of the great Roman legal system, "The
Body of Civil Law" ("Corpus Juris Civilis").

The best interpreter of the law, is practice. (Optima enim est legum
interpres consuetudo.) ~ "Corpus Juris Civilis"
Note: The "Digest" section of the great Roman legal system, "The
Body of Civil Law" ("Corpus Juris Civilis").

&

All truths are easy to understand once they are discovered; the point is
to discover them. ~ Galileo Galilei

I do not feel obliged to believe that the same God who has endowed us
with sense, reason, and intellect has intended us to forgo their use.
~ Galileo Galilei

I have never met a man so ignorant that I couldn't learn something
from him. ~ Galileo Galilei

E Pluribus Unum (Out of Many, One.)
~ Horace, "Epistle Book II"

Seize the day! (Carpe diem!) ~ Horace, "Carmina"

Since nature cannot change, **true friendships are eternal.** (Quia natura mutari non potest idcirco verae amicitiae sempiternae sunt.) ~ Horace

Rare bird (rara avis) ~ Horace

Alas, the fleeting years (eheu fugaces anni) ~ Horace

Into the midst of things (in medias res) ~ Horace

Dire necessity (dira necessitas) ~ Horace

The concord of things through discord. (Rerum concordia discors.) ~ Horace, "Epistle"

Scattered remains (disiecta membra) ~ Horace

He who postpones the hour of living rightly is like the rustic who waits for the river to run out before he crosses. ~ Horace

He will always be a slave who does not know how to live upon a little. ~ Horace

Anger is a short madness. ~ Horace, "Epistle"

Remember when life's path is steep to keep your mind even. ~ Horace

Once a word has been allowed to escape, it cannot be recalled. ~ Horace, "Epistle"

They change their sky but not their soul, who cross the ocean. (Latin: Caelum non animum mutant qui trans mare current.") ~ Horace

✄

The trick is to make sure you don't die waiting for prosperity to come.
~Lee Iacocca

✄

The love of wealth grows as the wealth itself grew.
(Crescit amor nummi, quantum ipsa pecunia crevit.)
~ Iucenalis, "Saturae"

Who is to guard the guards themselves?
(Quis custodiet ipsos custodes?) ~ Iucenalis, "Saturae"

✄

You can't stay mad at somebody who makes you laugh. ~ Jay Leno

✄

It's better late than never. (Potius sero quam numquam.)
~ Livy, "Ab urbe condita"

Danger in delay. (Periculum in mora.)
~ Livy, "Ab urbe condita"

Woe to the conquered! (Vae victis!) ~Livy, "Praefatio"

✄

If winning isn't everything, why do they keep score?
~ Vince Lombardi

If you aren't fired with enthusiasm, you will be fired with enthusiasm.
~ Vince Lombardi

✄

Nothing can be created from nothing.(De nihilo nihil.)
~ Lucretius, "On the Nature of the Universe" or "De Rerum Natura"

What is food to one man is bitter poison to others.
~ Lucretius, "On the Nature of the Universe" or "De Rerum Natura"

ᘒ

When neither their property nor their honor is touched, the majority of men live content. ~ Niccolo Machiavelli, "The Prince"

ᘒ

Poor is the man whose pleasures depend on the permission of another.
~ Madonna

ᘒ

Conceal a flaw, and the world will imagine the worst.
~ Marcus Valerius Martialis, "Epigrams"

Why do strong arms fatigue themselves with frivolous dumbbells? To dig a vineyard is worthier exercise for men.
~ Marcus Valerius Martialis, "Epigrams"

A man who lives everywhere lives nowhere.
~ Marcus Valerius Martialis, "Epigrams"

Tomorrow's life is too late. Live today.
~ Marcus Valerius Martialis, "Epigrams"

Virtue extends our days: he lives two lives who relives his past with pleasure. ~ Marcus Valerius Martialis, "Epigrams"

ᘒ

If you drink, don't drive. Don't even putt. ~ Dean Martin

ᘒ

Reality is something you rise above. ~ Liza Minnelli

Never help a child with a task at which he feels he can succeed.
~ Maria Montessori

ॐ

Often the prickly thorn produces tender roses. (Saepe creat molles aspera spina rosas.) ~ Ovid

Dripping water hollows out a stone, a ring is worn away by use. (Gutta cavat lapidem, consumitur anulus usu.) ~ Ovid, "Ex Ponto"
Note:
The English Protestant martyr Hugh Latimer (c. 1485 - 1555) modified this as: The drop of rain maketh a hole in the stone, not by violence, but by oft falling. (Gutta cavat lapidem, non vi sed saepe cadendo.)

Although the power is lacking, the will is commendable. (Ut desint vires, tamen est laudanda voluntas.)
~ Ovid, "Ex Ponto"

ॐ

War is sweet for those who haven't experienced it. (Dulce bellum inexpertis.) ~ Pindaros

ॐ

He whom the gods love dies young. (or ..Only the good die young.)
~ Titus Maccius Plautus, "Bacchides"

You have hit the nail on the head. (Tetigisti acu.)
~ Titus Maccius Plautus, "Rudens"

Practice yourself what you preach.
~Titus Maccius Plautus, "Asinaria"

There are occasions when it is undoubtedly better to incur loss than to make gain. ~ Titus Maccius Plautus, "Captivi"

No guest is so welcome in a friend's house that he will not become a nuisance after three days.
~ Titus Maccius Plautus, "Miles Gloriosus" ("The Boastful Soldier")

No man is wise enough by himself.
~ Titus Maccius Plautus, "Miles Gloriosus" ("The Boastful Soldier")

Patience is the best remedy for every trouble.
~ Titus Maccius Plautus, "Rudens"

Not by age but by capacity is wisdom acquired.
~ Titus Maccius Plautus, "Trinummus"

What is yours is mine, and all mine is yours.
~ Titus Maccius Plautus, "Trinummus"

&

Not many, but much. (Non multa, sed multum.)
~ Plinius Iunior, "Epistulae" Note: Meaning, not quantity but quality.

&

With a grain of salt. (Cum grano salis.)
~ Pliny the Elder
Note: Pliny used this phrase in describing Pompey's discovery of an antidote for a poison (to be taken with a grain of salt). Once discovered, the phrase was quickly adopted by English writers.

In these matters the only certainty is that nothing is certain.
~ Pliny the Elder

Indeed, what is there that does not appear marvelous when it comes to our knowledge for the first time? How many things, too, are looked upon as quite impossible until they have been actually effected?
~ Pliny the Elder, "Natural History"
Note: Galileo, Columbus, Spallanzani, Marconi and Drs. Dulbecco and DeLisa are all good examples to remember.

The best plan is to profit by the folly of others.
~ Pliny the Elder, "Natural History"

An object in possession seldom retains the same charm that it had in pursuit. ~ Pliny the Younger, "Letters"

His only fault is that he has no fault. ~ Pliny the Younger, "Letters"

That indolent but agreeable condition of doing nothing.
~ Pliny the Younger, "Letters"

ଛ

Never get angry. Never make a threat. Reason with people.
~ Mario Puzo, "The Godfather"

ଛ

The clothes make the man. (Vestis virum reddit.)
~ Marcus Fabius Quintilianus

I do not live to eat, but eat to live. (Non ut edam vivo, sed vivam edo.)
~ Marcus Fabius Quintilianus, "Instituitio oratoria"

A liar needs a good memory. (Mendacem memorem esse oportet.)
~ Marcus Fabius Quintilianus, "DeInstitutione Oratoria"

When defeat is inevitable, it is wisest to yield.
~ Marcus Fabius Quintilianus

Those who wish to appear wise among fools, among the wise seem foolish. ~ Marcus Fabius Quintilianus, "De Institutione Oratoria"

ଛ

When you are at Rome live in the Roman style; when you are elsewhere live as they live elsewhere.
~ Saint Ambrose, patron Saint of Milan
Note: This well known advice was Saint Ambrose's answer to Saint Augustine when asked whether they should fast on Saturday as Romans did, or not fast, as in Milan.

❧

A timid dog barks more violently than it bites.(Canis timidus vehementius latrat quam mordet.) ~ Curtius Rufus

❧

Build castles in the air. (In aere aedificare.)
~ Saint Augustine, "Confessiones"
Note: A reminder of the temporal world within which we live.

O Lord, help me to be pure, but not yet. ~ Saint Augustine

I was in love with loving. ~ Saint Augustine, "Confessions"

❧

Where there is hatred, let me sow love. Where there is injury, pardon. Where there is doubt, faith. ~ Saint Francis of Assisi

❧

Do not look a gift horse in the mouth. (Noli equi dentes inspicere donati.) ~ Saint Jerome, "Commentarius in epistulam Pauli ad Ephesos"

Always do something, so that the devil always finds you occupied. (Facito aliquid operis, ut te semper diabolus inveniat occupatum.) ~ Saint Jerome, "Epistulae"
Note: Commonly paraphrased as: idleness is the devil's workshop.

The face is the mirror of the mind, and eyes without speaking confess the secrets of the heart. ~ Saint Jerome

A fat paunch never breeds fine thoughts. ~ Saint Jerome, "Letter"

An unstable pilot steers a leaking ship, and the blind is leading the blind straight to the pit. The ruler is like the ruled. ~ Saint Jerome, "Letter"

No athlete is crowned but in the sweat of his brow.
~ Saint Jerome, "Letter"

The friendship that can cease has never been real.
~ Saint Jerome, "Letter"

The scars of others should teach us caution.   ~ Saint Jerome, "Letter"

ॐ

Three things are necessary for the salvation of man: to know what he ought to believe; to know what he ought to desire; and to know what he ought to do.   ~ Saint Thomas Aquinas, "Two Precepts of Charity"

ॐ

Art is long, life is short. (Ars longa, vita brevis.)
~ Seneca, "De brevitate vitae," section 1
Note: Latin *ars* can also mean *proficiency* or *skill*.

We should learn as long as we may live. (Tamdiu discendum est, quamdiu vivas.) ~ Seneca, "Epistulae"
Note: Often summarized as "live and learn."

If you want to be loved, love. (Si vis amari, ama.) ~ Seneca, "Epistulae"

Poetic license. (Licentia poetica.) ~ Seneca, "Quaestiones naturales"

If one does not know to which port one is sailing, no wind is favorable. (Ignoranti, quem portum petat, nullus suus ventus est.)
~ Seneca, "Epistulae"

True joy is a serious thing. (Res severa est verum gaudium)
~ Seneca, "Epistulae"

Consult your friend on all things, especially on those, with respect to yourself. His counsel may then be useful where your own self-love might impair your judgment. ~ Seneca

Difficulties strengthen the mind, as labor does the body. ~ Seneca

Enjoy present pleasures in such a way as not to injure future ones.
~ Seneca

It is easier to exclude harmful passions than to rule them, and to deny them admittance than to control them after they have been admitted.
~ Seneca

Let tears flow of their own accord: their flowing is not inconsistent with inward peace and harmony. ~ Seneca

Most powerful is he who has himself in his own power. ~ Seneca

One should count each day a separate life. ~ Seneca

Toil to make yourself remarkable by some talent or other. ~ Seneca

While the fates permit, live happily; life speeds on with hurried step, and with winged days the wheel of the headlong year is turned.
~ Seneca

Rest without reading is like dying and being buried alive.
~ Seneca, "Epistulae"

We do not learn for school, but for life. ~ Seneca, "Epistulae"

As long as we are among humans, let us be humane.
~ Seneca, "De ira"

The important thing isn't how long you live, but how well you live.
~ Seneca, "Epistulae"

Nothing is so expensive as that which you have bought with pleas.
~ Seneca, "De beneficiis"

Nobody is laughed at, who laughs at himself.
~ Seneca, "De providentia"

Stern masters do not reign long. ~ Seneca, "Medea"

٧٤

Nothing in excess. (ne quid nimis.) ~ Terence, "Andria"

Said and done (dictum factum) ~ Terence, "Heautontimorumenos"

The wolf in the fable (lupus in fabula) ~ Terence

٧٤

The worst kind of enemies, those who can praise. (Pessimus inimicorum genus, laudantes.) ~ Cornelius Tacitus, "Agricola"

It is the rare fortune of these days that one may think what one likes and say what one thinks. ~ Cornelius Tacitus, "Histories"

Without anger or bias.(Sine ira et studio.)
~ Cornelius Tacitus, "Annales"

٧٤

Eternal city. (Urbs aeterna.) ~ Tibullus
Note: The universal description for Rome and sometimes stated as Roma aeterna, meaning Rome eternal.

٧٤

The longest part of the journey is said to be the passing of the gate.
~ Marcus Terentius Varro, "On Agriculture"
Note: Starting a project is often the hardest part of the project.

٧٤

Let him who wishes for peace prepare for war.
(Qui desiderat pacem, praeparet bellum.)
~ Vegetius, "Epitoma Rei Militaris," book 3, prologue
Note, often quoted as: Si vis pacem, para bellum. If you want peace, prepare for war.

Patience serves as a protection against wrongs as clothes do against cold. For if you put on more clothes as the cold increases, it will have no power to hurt you. So in like manner you must grow in patience when you meet with great wrongs, and they will then be powerless to vex your mind. ~ Leonardo da Vinci

You do ill if you praise, but worse if you censure what you do not understand. ~ Leonardo da Vinci

As a well-spent day brings happy sleep, so life well used brings happy death. ~ Leonardo da Vinci, "The Notebooks"

Intellectual passion dries out sensuality.
~ Leonardo da Vinci, "The Notebooks"

Iron rusts from disuse; stagnant water loses its purity and in cold weather becomes frozen; even so does inaction sap the vigor of the mind. ~ Leonardo da Vinci, "The Notebooks"

۸

Love conquers all and let us yield to love.
(Amor vincit omnia et nos cedamus amori.) ~ Virgil, "Eclogae"

But meanwhile, the irreplaceable time escapes. (Sed fugit interae, fugit irreparabile tempus..) ~ Virgil, "Georgica"
Note: Often quoted in the short form **"tempus fugit" and interpreted to mean "time flies."** Commonly found on grandfather clocks.

Mind moves matter (Mens agitat molem) ~ Virgil, "Aeneid"
Note: Often expressed as: mind over matter.

Annuit Coeptis (He Favors Our Undertakings.)
~ Virgil, "Aeneid"
Note: refer to the chapter on "American Government"

Novus Ordo Seclorum (New Order of the Ages.)
~ Virgil, "Eclogue IV"
Note: refer to the chapter on "American Government"

A snake lies in the grass. (Latet anguis in herba.) ~ Virgil, "Eclogae"

Whatever this may be, **I fear the Greeks even when they're bringing gifts.** (Quidquid id est timeo Danaos et dona ferentis.)
~ Virgil, "Aeneid" (from the famous story of the Trojan horse.)

And they who bettered life on earth by newfound mastery.
Inventas vitam juvat excoluisse per artes.
~ Virgil, "Aeneid," 6th song, verse 663
Note: This inscription, in Latin, is used on the Nobel Prize medals:

Hover between hope and fear. (Spemque metumque inter dubiis.)
~ Virgil, "Aeneid"

Fortune favors the brave. (Audentes fortuna iuvat.) ~ Virgil, "Aeneid"

They can conquer who believe they can. ~ Virgil

They can do all because they think they can. ~ Virgil

Death's brother, Sleep. ~ Virgil, "Aeneid"

Each of us bears his own Hell. ~ Virgil, "Aeneid"

I have known sorrow and learned to aid the wretched.
~ Virgil, "Aeneid"

It is easy to go down into hell; night and day, the gates of dark death stand wide; but to climb back again, to retrace one's steps to the upper air - there's the rub, the task. ~ Virgil, "Aeneid"

Yield not to evils, but attack all the more boldly. ~ Virgil, "Aeneid"

ॐ

Criticism comes easier than craftsmanship. ~ Zeuxis (Greek), as quoted in "Natural History" by Pliny the Elder (Roman)

Latin Phrases

Below is a list of the more common Latin phrases used in modern languages. Please also refer to the chapter "Language & Literature" for specific Latin uses for medical and legal terminology, as well.

a capite ad calcem - from head to toe (meaning very complete)
a fortiori - with stronger reason
a fronte praecipitium, a tergo lupi - a precipice (or cliff) in front, wolves behind
a maximis ad minima - from the greatest to the least
a posteriori - from what comes after (relating to reasoning based on deductions from observations or known facts)
a priori - from the previous (makes a presumption that is true as far as known, usually through reasoning of abstract ideas)
ab absurdo - from the absurd
ab aeterno - from eternity
ab asino lanam - wool from an ass (similar to 'silk from a sow's ear')
ab extra - from the outside
ab imo pectore - from the bottom of the chest
ab incunabulis - from infancy
ab initio - from the beginning
ab intra - from within
ab irato - from an angry man
ab initio - from the beginning
ab ovo usque ad mala - from egg to apples (meaning a full, several course meal)
ab origine - from the origin (or beginning)
absit invidia - let ill will be absent
ad absurdum - to the absurd
ad arbitrium - at pleasure
ad finem fidelis - faithful to the end
ad gloriam - for glory
ad gustum - to one's taste
ad hoc - with respect to this object or purpose (An ad hoc report is created for a specific or one time use. An ad hoc committee has a temporal existence for a specific project.)
ad infinitum - to infinity
ad litteram - to the letter
ad maiorem Dei gloriam - to the greater glory of God
ad nauseam - to the point of nausea or disgust from excess

ad populum - to the people
ad praesens ova cras pullis sunt meliora - eggs today are better than chickens tomorrow
ad rem - to the purpose or point
ad unguem - to the fingernail (meaning down to every detail)
ad utrumque paratus - prepared for either
ad valorem - in proportion to the value
ad verbum - verbatim or word for word
ad vitam aeternam - for eternal life
ad vitam aut culpam - for life or until a misdeed
advocatus diaboli - the devil's advocate (Also, used for the person designated to dispute before the papal court the claims of a candidate for canonization.)
aequo animo - with an equable (or calm) mind
aeternum vale - farewell forever
Agnus Dei - Lamb of God
alias (or dictus) - otherwise called
alieni generis - of a different kind
alieni juris - of another's law
aliquando bonus dormitat Homerus - sometimes even good Homer dozes
alter ego - another self
alma mater - nurturing mother
altissima quaeque flumina minimo sono labi - the deepest rivers flow with the least sound
alumnus - foster child
amantes sunt amentes - lovers are lunatics
amicus humani generis - friend of the human race
amicus usque ad aras - a friend all the way to the altars
amor nummi - love of money
amor patriae - love of country
animal disputans - an argumentative animal (human being)
animal rationale - a rational animal (human being)
annus mirabilis - a remarkable year
ante bellum - before the war
ante cibum - before food (instruction for taking medicine)
ante partum - before childbirth
apologia pro vita sua - a defense of his life
apparatus criticus - critical matter
aqua et igni interdictus - forbidden water and fire (banished)
aqua pura - pure water

aqua vitae - water of life (meaning alcohol)
arbiter bibendi - judge of drinking
arbiter elegantiae - master of taste
arcanum arcanorum - secret of secrets
arma non servant modum - armies do not preserve (show restraint)
arma tuentur pacem - arms maintain peace
arrectis auribus - with ears pricked up
ars amandi - the art of loving
ars artium - the art of arts (meaning logic)
ars moriendi - the art of dying
arte perire sua - to perish by one's own creation
artes perditae - lost arts
audaces fortuna iuvat - fortune helps the bold
audi et alteram partem - hear the other side too
aureo hamo piscari - to fish with a golden hook
aurora australis - the southern dawn
aurora borealis - the northern dawn
auspicium melioris aevi - omen of a better time
aurea mediocritas - the golden mean (moderation)
aut bibat aut abeat - let him either drink or depart
aut Caesar aut nihil - either Caesar or nothing
aut disce aut discede - either learn or leave
aut viam inveniam aut faciam - I will either find a way or make one
aut mors aut victoria - either death or victory
Ave Maria - hail Mary (Also, the name of a well known Roman
Catholic prayer based upon Gabriel's salutation when he greeted the
blessed mother Mary)
beatae memoriae - of blessed memory
bis vivit qui bene vivit - he lives twice who lives well
bona fide - in good faith
bonis avibus - under good birds (meaning under favorable signs)
bonum vinum laetificat cor hominis - good wine gladdens a person's
heart
Canis Major - Larger Dog (A constellation in the Southern
Hemisphere) Canis Minor - Smaller/Lesser Dog (A constellation in the
Southern Hemisphere)
caput mundi - head of the world (often used to mean Rome)
castigat ridendo mores - he corrects manners by laughing at them
casus belli - an occasion for war
casus foederis - an occasion for a treaty
causa sine qua non - a necessary cause

causa causans - an initiating cause

cave quid dicis, quando, et cui - beware what you say, when, and to whom

ceteris paribus - all other things being equal

circa - about

cito maturum, cito putridum - quickly ripe, quickly rotten

coitus interruptus - interrupted coitus (a method of birth control)

communi consensu - by common consent

compos mentis - of sound mind

compos sui - master of himself

con amore - with love

conditio sine qua non - a necessary condition

coniunctis viribus - with united powers

consensus - agreement

consensus gentium - agreement of the nations

contraria contrariis curantur - opposites are cured by opposites

coram populo - in public presence

cornucopia - horn of plenty

corrigenda - things to be corrected

credo quia absurdum est - I believe it because it is unreasonable

crocodilae lacrimae - crocodile tears (meaning false tears based on the false belief that crocodiles weep after eating their prey)

cum laude - with praise (a phrase added to college diplomas when students achieve specific grade point averages)

cum privilegio - with privilege

curriculum vitae - the course of one's life (also meaning resume)

custos morum - guardian of morals

dabit qui dedit - he who has given will give

damnat quod non intelligunt - they condemn what they do not understand

de asini umbra disceptare - arguing about the shadow of an ass (discusing something stupid)

de bono et malo - of good and bad

de die in diem - from day unto day

de facto - from the fact (or point of actual fact whether official or not)

de gustibus non est disputandum - it must not be disputed about taste

de minimis non curat praetor - a praetor does not care about petty matters

de novo - from a new

de profundis - out of the depths

de pilo pendet - it hangs by a hair

de fumo in flammam - out of the smoke into the fire (the situation worsened)

Dei gratia - by the grace of God

Deo favente - God being favorable or with God's favor

Deo gratias - thanks to God

Deo juvante - if God is helping or with God's help

Deo volente - God permitting

deus ex machina - a god from a machine (used in dramatic scenes when characters escape from impossible perilous situations.)

dictum factum - said, done

dies faustus - a day bringing good fortune

dies infaustus - a day bringing bad fortune

dies irae - day of wrath

divide et impera - divide and conquer

dixi - I have spoken

docendo discimus - we learn by teaching

doctus cum libro - learned with a book

dramatis personae - characters of the play

dum vita est spes est - while there's life, there's hope

dura lex sed lex - the law is hard, but it is the law

e contra - on the other hand

e contrario - on the contrary

ecce signum - behold the sign

editio princeps - first edition of a publication

editio vulgata - common edition

ego et rex meus - my king and I

eiusdem farinae - of the same flour

emeritus - having served his time (used to mean former or retired)

eo ipso - by that itself or by that fact

ergo - therefore

errare humanum estto - to err is human

erratum (plural errata) - error

et al. - and others

et hoc genus omne - and everything of this kind

et nunc et semper - now and forever

et sic de similibus - and so of similar things

et id genus omne - and everything of that kind

etiam atque etiam - again and again

ex animo - from the heart

ex cathedra - from the chair (meaning from the chair of the pope, also may mean from a high authority.)

ex libris - from the library of (sometimes stamped in books to indicate ownership)
ex mero motu - of simple impulse
ex more - according to custom
ex officio - out of one's duty or office or position
ex parte - from one part or side
ex post facto - from after the deed (used to mean in the light of subsequent events with retrospective action or force)
ex propriis - from one's own experiences
ex tempore - from the moment or extemporaneously
experientia docet - experience teaches
exitus acta probat - the end justifies the means
extra muros - outside the walls
facile princeps - easily the first or preeminent
facta non verba - deeds, not words
falsum in uno falsum in toto - false in one false in all (completely untrue)
Fata viam invenient - fate will find a way
fide, non armis - by faith, not arms
fides Punica - Punic (i.e. Carthaginian) faith, meaning treachery
fidus Achates - faithful Achates meaning a true friend (Achates was the faithful companion of Aeneas in Greek and Roman mythology)
folio verso - the reverse side of the page
fortis in Domino - strong in the Lord
fortuna caeca est - fortune is blind
functus officio - occupied with duty
genus homo - the human race
Gloria in Excelsis Deo - glory to God in the highest
gratia Dei - by the grace of God
helluo librorum - A glutton for books (bookworm)
hic et nunc - here and now
hic et ubique - here and everywhere (ubiquitously)
hic jacet - here lies (sometimes uses in epitaphs)
hoc tempore - at this time
hodie, non cras - today, not tomorrow
homo sapiens - wise man (meaning humans are the only creatures with intelligence)
honoris causa - because of honor
horribile dictu - horrible to speak
hostis humani generis - enemy of the human race
id est (abbreviated as i.e.) - that is

R. R. Esposito

ignis fatuus - foolish fire (meaning will-o'-the-wisp, which is a natural phenomenon sometimes observed on marshy ground or graveyards, appearing as a small bluish light. It is believed to be the flame of burning marsh gas, mostly methane, ignited by traces of hydrogen phosphide sometimes found near decaying organic matter.)
imperium et libertas - empire and freedom
in absentia - in (one's) absence
in aeternam - into eternity, meaning forever
in articulo mortis - at the point of death
in esse - in being or something that actually exists (opposite of the Latin term *in posse*)
in excelsis - in the highest
in extremis - in extreme situations or in an emergency. (in a religious context, to administer last rights *in extremis*, or near the point of death)
in forma pauperis - in the manner of a poor man
in loco parentis - in place of a parent
in medias res - into the middle of things
in memoriam - in memory of
in nuce - in a nutshell
in omnia paratus - prepared for all things
in perpetuum - forever
in pleno - in full
in posse - in possibility (meaning possible but not actual, the opposite of the Latin term *in esse*)
in propria persona - in one's own person
in re - in the matter of
in secula seculorum - unto the ages of the ages
in situ - in its original position
in terrorem - into terror (meaning a warning)
in toto - in the whole or complete
in transitu - in the course of transit
in utero - in the womb
in vitro - in glass (used as a way to describe fertilization in a test-tube or laboratory environment)
inter alia - among other things
inter nos - among us
intra muros - within the walls
ipsissima verba - the very words or the words themselves
ipso facto - by the fact itself
jus gentium - the law of nations
jure divino - by divine law

jure humano - by human law

jus gentium - law of nations, a concept of Roman law. It is the underpinning of the first international laws.

jus naturale - natural law jus naturale - natural law (this was a concept of Roman law that inspired the *unalienable rights* in the U.S. Declaration of Independence.)

lapsus calami - a slip of the pen

lapsus linguae - a slip of the tongue

laus Deo - praise to God

lex non scripta - unwritten law

lex scripta - written law

littera scripta manet - the written letter lasts

locum tenens - one holding the place of another or a substitute

lusus naturae - a freak of nature

magna cum laude - with great praise (a phrase added to college diplomas when students achieve specific grade point averages.)

lux ex oriente - light from the east

magnas inter opes inops - poor among great riches

Magna Charta - the great paper (or charter)

magnum bonum - great good (thing)

magnum opus - a great work

mala fide - in bad faith

mare clausum - a closed sea (A sea belonging to one nation)

materia medica - medical material

me duce tutus eris - under my leadership you will be safe

me iudice - I being judge (in my opinion)

mea culpa - my fault

memento mori - remember death (or any symbolic reminder of death; usually, skulls, hour-glasses, clocks and candles are the most common)

mens sibi conscia recti - a mind conscious of its own moral virtue

meo periculo - at my own peril

mihi cura futuri - my concern is the future

mirabile dictu - wonderful to say

modus operandi (m.o.) - way of operating (of a person or thing) or the way something works

modus vivendi - a way of living (usually a temporary arrangement whereby parties in dispute can carry on pending a final legal settlement)

nolens volens - unwilling, willing (modern willy-nilly, indecisive)

ne plus ultra - no more beyond (meaning nothing better)

non compos mentis - not in possession of one's senses

non sequitur - it does not follow (meaning a conclusion that does not logically follow from the premise or premises)

nosce te ipsum - know thyself

Nova Scotia - New Scotland

novus homo - a new man, usually in politics

nulli secundus - second to none

nunc aut numquam - now or never

panem et circenses - bread and circuses (From the Roman satirist, Juvenal who said, "Only two things does he and the modern citizen anxiously wish for, bread and the big match.")

Pater noster - Our Father (The Lord's prayer)

pater patriae - father of the country

pax in bello - peace in the midst of war

pax vobiscum - peace be with you

per annum - by the year or per year

per capita - by heads or individuals or per person

per diem - by the day or per day

per se - by itself

persona grata - an acceptable person (especially a diplomat acceptable to a foreign government)

persona non grata - an unwelcome person or unacceptable

poeta nascitur, non fit - the poet is born, not made

post cibum - after food (usually used as instruction for taking medicine)

post hoc ergo propter hoc - after it, therefore due to it (meaning a fallacy of confusing consequence with sequence or a coincidence without cause)

possunt quia posse videntur - they can because they think they can

post bellum, auxilium - aid after the war

post mortem - after death

prima facie - on first appearance or at first sight (as in prima facie evidence.)

primus inter pares - first among equals

pro forma - for form (a formality)

pro patria - for one's country

quid pro quo - what for what (meaning something for something or an equal exchange)

quidnunc - what now (a term for a meddler, busybody or gossip monger)

quo jure - by what legal right

quo modo - in what manner

quot homines tot sententiae - many people, so many opinions

requiescat in pace (R.I.P.) - rest in peace

rex regnant sed non gubernat - the king reigns but does not govern

sanctum sanctorum - holy of holies (meaning a private room or retreat)

semper idem - always the same thing

semper paratus - always prepared

sequens mirabitur aetas - the following age will be amazed

sic - thus

sine die - without a day, as not having a set date

sine qua non - without which not (a necessity)

status quo - the situation in which it was before (the existing condition or state of affairs)

suaviter in modo, fortiter in re - pleasantly in manner, resolute in action

sub rosa - under the rose (meaning hidden or secret)

sub sole nihil novi est - there is nothing new under the sun

sui generis - of one's own kind (unique, individual)

summa cum laude - with highest praise (used on diplomas when high grades are achieved)

summum bonum - the highest good

sursum corda - lift up your hearts

te judice - you being the judge (in your judgment)

tempus fugit - time flies

terrae filius - son of the soil (a man of lowly birth)

terra firma - solid earth (firmly on the ground)

terra incognita - an unknown land

ultima thule - farthest north (Thule was the ancient name for Norway)

una voce - with one voice, unanimously

urbs et orbis - city and world

vanitas vanitatum et omnia vanitas - vanity of vanities, and all is vanity

velle est posse - to be willing is to be able

verbum sapienti sat est - a word to the wise is sufficient

vestis virum facit - clothes make the man

via cruce - by way of the (Jesus's) cross

via media - a middle way or course

vice versa - in reverse or converse

victoria, non praeda - victory, not loot

virginibus puerisque - for girls and boys

virtute et fide - by virtue and faith

volens et potens, valens - willing and able

volente Deo - God willing

volo, non valeo - I am willing but unable
vox humana - human voice
vox populi - voice of the people

Italian Proverbs

Italian people say that proverbs are the wisdom of the people. The proverbs below may shed some light on the Italian personality and identity. Interpretations are provided below when needed.

Business & Money

L'occhio del padrone ingrassa il cavallo.
The eye of the owner makes the horse fat.
Interpretation: A business grows under the observant eye of its owner.

Il denaro è un buon servo e un cattivo padrone.
Money is a good servant, but a bad master.

I denari sono tondi e ruzzolano.
Money is round and meant to roll (i.e. spend it).

I debiti sono come i connigli.
Debts are like rabbits (i.e. they multiply).

Meglio un uovo oggi che una gallina domani.
Better an egg today than a chicken tomorrow.

Scopa nuova scopa bene.
A new broom sweeps well.
Interpretation: A new employee or associate behaves well.
Alternate interpretation and use: A new administration (or management) sweeps away the old establishment to bring in the new.

Family Life

Casa sporca, gente aspetta.
A messy house invites unexpected guests.

Chi incontra buona moglie ha gran fortuna.
Luck is the man who finds a good wife.

A padre avaro, figliolo prodigo.
A thrifty father, a prodigal son.

Friends & Enemies

Amico di tutti e di nessuno è tutt'uno.
A friend to all is a friend to none.

Dimmi con chi vai e ti dirò chi sei.
Tell me with whom you associate and I will tell you who you are.

Law & Lawyers

Fatta la legge, trovata la malizia.
Every law has a loophole.

Buoni avvocati sono cattivi vicini.
A good lawyer makes a bad neighbor.

Love

Amore e gelosia nacquero insieme.
Love and jealously are born together.
Interpretation: Without jealousy there is no love.

Planning

Non fare il passo piu lungo della gamba.
Don't make a step longer than your leg.
Interpretation: Don't bite off more than you can chew.

R. R. Esposito

Trouble

Il dire è una cosa, il fare è un'altra.
Troubles never come alone.

Chi semina spine, non vada scalzo.
If you scatter thorns, don't go barefoot.
Interpretation: If you spread trouble, expect trouble.

Ogni cuore ha il suo dolore.
Every heart has its own ache.

L'erba cattiva non muore mai.
Bad grass never dies.
Interpretation: The problem person always turns up.

La fame caccia il lupo dal bosco.
Hunger drives the wolf out of the woods.

Work

Con nulla non si fa nulla.
Of nothing comes nothing.

Quattordici mestieri, quindici infortuni.
Fourteen occupations, fifty accidents.
Interpretation: Too many different jobs prevent you from perfecting a
profession. Similar to: a jack-of-all-trades and a master-of-none.

Chi dorme non piglia pesci.
He who sleeps catches no fish.

Miscellaneous

L'abito non fa il monaco.
The habit doesn't make a monk.
Interpretation: Clothes don't make the man.

Ogni promessa è debito.
Every promise is a debt.

Il diavolo fa le pentole ma non i coperchi.
The devil makes the pots, but not the lids.
Interpretation: The devil teaches us his deeds, but not how to hide them.

Quando il gioco dei scacchi e finito, tutte le figure: fanti, dame, cavalieri, vescovo, re e la regina, tornano tutti nella stessa scatola.
When the chess game is over, the pawns, rooks, knights, bishops, kings, and queens all go back into the same box.
Interpretation: It means that regardless of your position in life, in the end (death), we all return to the same place, as mortals that we all are.

Tanti paesi, tanti costumi.
Many countries, many customs.

È meglio esser invidiato che compassionato.
It is better to be envied than pitied.

Ogni parola non vuol risposta.
Not every word deserves a response.
Interpretation: Not every statement or question deserves a response or answer.

L'unione fa la forza.
In union there is strength.

Bisogna navigare secondo il vento.
As the wind blows, you must set your sail.

Quando a Roma vai, fa come vedrai.
When in Rome, do as the Romans do.

La virtù è premio a se stessa.
Virtue is its own reward.

La fame muta le fave in mandorle.
Hunger makes hard beans sweet.

Roma non fu fatta in un giorno. Rome was not built in a day.

Il fatto non si può disfare.
What's done can't be undone.

Lupo non mangia lupo.
Wolves don't eat wolves.

Chi ama me, ama il mio cane.
Love me, love my dog.
Interpretation: Take the good with the bad in a relationship.

Tante volte al pozzo va la secchia ch'ella vi lascia il manico o l'orecchia.
A pitcher that goes to the well often is likely to get broken.

Che sarà, sarà.
What will be will be.

Nessuno è savio d'ogni tempo.
No one is wise at all times.

Il dire è una cosa, il fare è un'altra.
Saying is one thing, doing another.

Cuor forte rompe cattiva sorte.
Nothing is impossible to a willing heart.

Di buona volantà sta pieno l'inferno.
Hell is full of good intentions.

Chi s'aiuta, Dio l'aiuta.
Help yourself and God will help.

In bocca chiusa non entrano mosche.
A closed mouth catches no flies.

La storia si ripete.
History repeats itself.

Quando il gatto manca, i topi ballano.
When the cat is missing, the mice dance.
Interpretation: When the cat's away, the mice will play.

Il bugiardo deve avere buona memoria.
The liar needs a good memory.

Il tempo è un gran medico.
Time is a great healer.

R. R. Esposito

Chapter XVIII

RELIGION
Influences on Christianity

"His learning cannot be explained
without admitting a miracle."
- Pope John XXII about St. Thomas Aquinas -

Although most chapters in this text have entries listed in alphabetical order, entries in this chapter are basically organized in chronological order, so that the reader is able to understand the development of Christianity after the life of Christ.

Christmas Day
Roman Sun Festival

For centuries the date of Christ's birth was unknown. Few even cared to celebrate Christ's nativity, and those that did used a variety of different months for this purpose. The Church leadership in Rome decided, however, to celebrate Christ's birthday on December 25th to compete with the dominant and powerful religion in Rome, Mithraism. Roman followers of Mithraism recognized that life on earth could not exist without the sun, and annually celebrated during a sun worshiping festival on December 25th. The new Christian holiday on December 25th offered an alternative festivity to the sun-worshiping event. Later, Emperor Constantine officially declared Christmas to be on December 25th throughout the Roman Empire. Consequently, today *we celebrate Christmas on December 25th, in keeping with Roman tradition.*

Italians traditionally serve fish (13 dishes) on Christmas Eve since the symbol of a fish was the secret code Christians used to identify one another during the early days of the Church when Christians were persecuted. The number 13 represents the 12 apostles plus Christ.

Gift Giving on Christmas
Saturn - Roman god of Agriculture

In ancient Rome, the god Saturn was honored during the feast of Saturnalia from December 17th through December 23rd. During this merry feast, gifts were exchanged, banquets were served, schools and offices were closed and even slaves were served by their masters. This Roman tradition was adopted by the Christians who began to exchange gifts during their merry-making at Christmas time.

The Spread of Christianity in Europe

Roman Emperor Constantine

In 313 AD, Emperor Constantine issued a decree of toleration towards Christians throughout the empire. In 324 AD, Constantine made Christianity a state religion, although paganism was also tolerated. In 337 AD, Constantine converted to Christianity and was baptized. He unified the Church with the Roman Empire by making Christianity the official state religion and *permanently established December 25th as Christmas Day throughout the Roman Empire.* In fact, by the end of 4th century, all citizens of the Roman Empire were required to be Christians or at least they had to agree that they were Christians. This Roman decree making Christianity the official religion of the Empire helped to spread Christianity throughout all of Europe, because all of Europe was part of the Roman Empire. Christianity and Roman citizenship became somewhat inseparable concepts, and many became Christians as a first step to becoming culturally *romanized*. The Roman leadership also hoped that if Christianity was embraced throughout the Empire that this would have a unifying effect among the varied and dispersed peoples of the Empire. This proved to be a double-edged strategy. Its unifying effects were accompanied with resentment due to the coercive measures against pagans, which were encouraged by Christian leaders including St. Augustine. Also, Christian theology distracted Rome's intellectuals away from careers in politics, law and government, and also preached that earthly accomplishments and the needs of the Empire were secondary to spiritual life. This was in part the message in St. Augustine's influential book, "City of God," along with its anti-pagan messages. Thus Christianity contributed to the decline of the Roman Empire, although there were many other contributing factors, such as the growing barbarian populations supported by agricultural sciences taught to them, ironically by the Romans.

St. Patrick

St. Patrick was a Roman citizen of Briton, born in 387 AD. He lived a somewhat privileged romanized life in what we today call Scotland. At the time, the Roman Empire was in decline and its legions in Briton were returning to protect Rome. Thus security in Briton was reduced and Patrick's hometown was attacked. He was captured by the tribe of an Irish chieftain named Miliucc. St. Patrick first saw Ireland as Miliucc's slave. St. Patrick's story of survival and faith is nothing short of fascinating. After some time as a slave, he escaped from Ireland and ultimately became an ordained Roman bishop. He returned to Ireland to convert Ireland's many pagan tribes to Christianity, an incredible feat. St. Patrick's mission to spread Christianity to Ireland was the first of its kind to travel beyond the scope of the known Roman Empire. He was the first missionary bishop in history. St. Patrick's Roman Latin name was originally *Patricius*. St. Patrick died at Saul, Downpatrick, Ireland, March 17, 461 AD, which is the day his holiday is now celebrated.

Easter Sunday & The Cross
Roman Emperor Constantine

In ancient times, Easter was celebrated on Friday, Saturday and Sunday. It was the Roman Emperor Constantine who convened a council in 325 AD and decided that Easter would always be on the first Sunday after the first full moon (on or after the vernal equinox). *The same Roman council also made the cross the official symbol of Christianity.*

"Confessions" and "City of God"
Saint Augustine

It is impossible to speak of early Christianity and the foundation of Catholicism without mentioning St. Augustine, the Bishop of Hippo. St. Augustine was a provincial Roman born on November 11th, 354 AD near ancient Carthage in Thagaste, an inland city in the Roman province of North Africa, now in modern Algeria. In 395 AD, he became bishop of Hippo Regius (called Annaba in modern Algeria). He was completely romanized and lived from 383 AD to 389 AD in Rome and Milan. He was greatly influenced by the Roman thinkers, Cicero and Virgil, in particular Virgil's literary masterpiece "Aeneid." St. Augustine was baptized in Milan in 387 AD and taught there as well. St. Augustine only spoke and wrote in Latin and not in Greek, a language he disliked, although some scholars of his day still wrote works in Greek.

St. Augustine was a prolific thinker and writer, but his two masterpieces are "Confessions" (397 AD - 400 AD) and "City of God" (413 AD - 426 AD). His work entitled "Confessions" is also considered to be the first autobiography (refer to the "Language & Literature" chapter). He was a theological philosopher who conceived from the dialogues of Plato and Paul the doctrine of *original sin*, the sin all Christians inherit from the biblical Adam and Eve. St. Augustine also conceived the concept that all the un-baptized, including infants are condemned to hell, should they perish before receiving this sacrament. St. Augustine also founded the concept of *grace being a gift of God*, and developed an explanation for the Trinity. He also offered reconciliation for the perceived contradiction between the belief that God has a predestined plan for each of us, but nevertheless allows us to have free will or free decision. St. Augustine also believed, as other Christian and pagan thinkers of his time, that sexual activity and marriage were not totally congruent with philosophical thinking or religious life. By the end of his life in 430 AD, he had completed over a hundred works, many of which have survived.

Benedictine Order
St. Benedict

St. Benedict was born in the Umbrian town of Nursia, near Spoleto, Italy about 480 AD. He began to formulate his new Order while living at the abbey he founded in the city of Subiaco. He ultimately founded twelve other monasteries in and around Subiaco. Later, around 529 AD, he founded his 14th monastery, the famous Abbey of Monte Cassino that rests on a hilltop overlooking the city of Cassino, 80 miles (128 km) south of Rome, and 70 miles (112 km) north of Naples. In 530 AD, St. Benedict formally established his "Rule of St. Benedict" while at the Abbey of Monte Cassino, which eventually became the center of his Benedictine Order of monks. His "Rule" is actually comprised of many chapters concerning the obligations and life-style of the Benedictine monks. St. Benedict's "Rule" was revolutionary in many ways and required his monks to be active in both mind and body, and to be integrated with the community as a guiding help to all. One of St. Benedict's innovations was that manual labor was an essential activity for his monks. St. Benedict encouraged his monks to farm the land and raise livestock, which helped many poor regions experience agricultural success. The Benedictine monks were expected to become integrated with the community, in all respects, and to view the community as part of their extended family.

Prior to St. Benedict, individual monks were restricted to a specific task or singular activity. St. Benedict's new "Rule" required his Monks to be involved in many activities and this innovation helped to make his new Order highly successful. His monks also labored to help build many architectural successes throughout Western Europe. Many abbeys, churches, and cathedrals of Western Europe were in part possible because of the work offered by the Benedictine monks who were architects and builders. They are responsible for the construction of many English cathedrals, as well. St. Augustine (named in honor of the first St. Augustine born 354 AD) and his forty monks from the monastery of St. Andrew in Rome established the first Benedictine monastery in England at Canterbury in 597 AD. By the 9th century, Benedictine methods had become the only form of monastic life in Western Europe. And two hundred years later, even the Celtic monasteries in Scotland, Wales and Ireland had adopted the Benedictine "Rules."

Of course, St. Benedict's monks were also bound to partake in systematic reading and academic study. Many Benedictine monks became leading authors and scholars of their times. During meals, each monk took turns reading aloud for the group's educational benefit. These educated monks were also required to teach and thereby helped the community, young and old, gain access to educational facilities in monasteries and Christian universities. The Benedictine Order significantly helped raise the educational levels in parts of Europe during the Middle Ages, as people slowly lifted themselves out of the abyss of the Dark Ages that followed the fall of Rome.

St. Benedict's monks were taught not to be too somber but to be helpful and cheerful in their activities. They were taught to be efficient, parsimonious with conversation, prompt, humble and unquestioning to their superiors. St. Benedict died in 547 AD, and shortly after, so did his twin sister, St. Scholastica. They were both buried at the Abbey of Monte Cassino.

Over the centuries, the famous Abbey of Monte Cassino had been destroyed by battles, earthquakes and again in 1944 during World War II. It was rebuilt in 1964 by Pope Paul VI. The Latin motto of Monte Cassino is "Succisa Virescit" ("cut down, it grows green and strong again"). The famous Abbey of Monte Cassino is also where the great St. Thomas Aquinas received his education as a boy before attending the University of Naples in 1236. The University of Naples, founded in 1224, is the world's first secular, public university run by laypersons.

Franciscan Brotherhood
St. Francis of Assisi

In 1209, St. Francis of Assisi (Assisi is a city in Italy) published his rules for the Franciscan Brotherhood. St. Francis, like St. Benedict, came from the Umbrian region of Italy. In 1223, his rules were accepted by the Roman Catholic Church to establish a Catholic religious order. Franciscans are known for their devotion as educators and missionaries throughout the world. This author has heard many highly entertaining stories about Catholic high school education with Franciscan Brothers in the New York City area. Many New York area neighborhoods were challenging with many interesting, sometimes tough personalities. However, the Brothers were tougher and perhaps out of necessity.

"Summa Theologica" ("Sum of Theology")
St. Thomas Aquinas

St. Thomas Aquinas was born at Rocca Secca in the Kingdom of Naples in 1225 or 1227 and died in Fossa Nuova, Italy on March 7, 1274. He was a philosopher, theologian and one of the doctors (Angelicus Doctor) of the Roman Catholic Church. His genius, philosophy and writings in support of the Catholic doctrine has earned him the title *"Prince of Theologians."* Because of his philosophy, logic and writings supporting and explaining Catholicism, many consider St. Thomas to be "The Doctor of Catholic Truth," an honor bestowed upon St. Thomas and no other Doctor of the Church.

He was born to a privileged family. His father was Landulph, Count of Aquino, and his mother was Theodora, Countess of Teano. At the age of five St. Thomas began his education with Benedictine monks at the famous Abbey of Monte Cassino. Monte Cassino, located between Rome and Naples, is where the Benedictine Order was founded. His instructors recognized the genius in the boy and noted that *he could comprehend and remember whatever he read.* St. Thomas was a serious, dedicated student and was fervently religious. Incredibly, at the age of about eleven he began his academic education at the University of Naples.

St. Thomas is credited for writing over fifty works concerning and logically defending Roman Catholic doctrines. He had the ability to work on multiple projects and could simultaneously dictate to several scribes. *His masterpiece, "Summa Theologica," is a comprehensive, scientifically organized exposition of theology and is also a summary of Christian philosophy.* Although written in the 13th century, "Summa Theologica" still has great relevance 700 years later for modern readers. It is this massive work that has immortalized St. Thomas. Its brilliance and universality prompted Pope John XXII to say this about St. Thomas: "His learning cannot be explained without admitting a miracle." (in Latin, "Doctrina ejus non potroit esse sine Miraculo").

Theologians consider that the Roman Catholic Church has produced two monumental doctrines, one is the "Catechism" and the other is St. Thomas' "Summa Theologica." They beautifully complement each other in that the "Catechism" is for daily use and "Summa Theologica" provides the philosophical explanations and theological underpinnings that explain and support Catholicism. Because of his scholarly pursuits and accomplishments, St. Thomas is the patron of many Catholic universities, colleges and schools.

One unfortunate result of "Summa Theologica" was St. Thomas' integration of Aristotle's metaphysics and cosmology with Christianity. This conflicted with Galileo's celestial discoveries that proved a sun-centered solar system. Refer to the "Astronomy" chapter for more on Galileo, his discoveries, and conflicts with the Church.

Roman Catholic Church's Organization
Roman Empire and Italian Popes

After the Roman Emperor Constantine made Christianity the official religion of the entire Roman Empire, the Christian religion grew steadily. Later the organization that ran the new Roman Christian Church grew its organization by copying the structure of Roman government. The Pope and his Bishops function much like the Roman Emperor and his field Generals that were dispatched to various locations, reporting back to the Pope. The Church's Cardinals were similar to Roman Senators advising the Pope and the Emperor, respectively.

Interestingly, the word *cardinal* is derived from the Latin language of the Romans. The word *cardinal* is derived from the Latin word *cardo*, meaning *hinge*. Since a hinge is an active, central and significant piece of hardware, the Romans therefore gave the word *cardo* (*hinge*) an additional meaning of *something of importance*. Even today we use the word *hinge* when describing something important, as when we state an event *hinges upon* something else. The Romans also used the Latin word *cardinalis*, meaning *very important, primary* or *chief*. Subsequently, the Roman Catholic Church used *cardinalis* to refer to principal churches and priests. By the late Middle Ages, the word *cardinalis* was being used for a clergyman of the highest rank, next to the pope. Finally, the Latin word *cardinalis* became *cardinal* in English.

When the Church needed to select an official headquarters, it decided upon the Roman Empire's capital city, Rome, and located its Vatican there. The Bishop of Rome took on special significance and evolved into the Pontifex Maximus. Later this position evolved into that of the Pope. After the decline of the Roman Empire, the Church was the single most important reason that the Roman civilization, language, innovations, scholarship and laws survived. These survived even throughout the Dark and Middle Ages until they were given new life during Italy's great rebirth during the Renaissance.

The rebirth of the city of Rome and its civilization during the Renaissance was fostered and enabled by efficient local government and administration. In Italy during the Renaissance, the central administration of the Roman Catholic Church in Rome (*papal curia*) became one of the most efficient governments in Europe, as described by the U.S. Library of Congress Vatican Exhibit. The Roman Catholic Church copied the efficient Roman government model. The Popes and Cardinals built new streets and bridges across the Tiber River. They built hospitals, public squares, fountains and churches for their citizens. The geniuses of the time, Michelangelo, Raphael, Castiglione, Cellini, Giuliano da Sangallo, Domenico Fontana, and others lived and worked in Rome. Art, architecture, music and literature proliferated during this time. Because of its efficient government and the Roman Catholic Church's influential organization, Rome became a successful and prominent city. Many Popes worked to develop spiritual, as well as commercial and military capabilities, and strove to evolve the Church into a complete political state.

In addition to the Roman Empire's effect on the organization of the early Roman Catholic Church, Italian Popes had a consistent influence on the Church since the Renaissance. *For 456 consecutive years, from 1522 to 1978, every Pope was Italian.* These Italian Popes have had enormous influence on the Roman Catholic Church and the lives of millions of followers for *over 45 decades* or almost half of a millennium.

Spread of Christianity to China
Giulio Alenio

In 1635, the Italian Jesuit, Giulio Alenio, published the first story of the life of Christ in Chinese, bringing the ideas of Christianity to the Chinese people. Earlier, during the Ming dynasty, an Italian monk actually established a Catholic Church in the heart of China in its capital city with the permission of the Chinese Emperor.

First Naturalized U.S. Citizen to be Sainted,
Founder of the Order of the
Missionary Sisters of the Scared Heart,
Founder of Cabrini Medical Center
Saint Frances Xavier Cabrini

Maria Frances Cabrini was born to Agostino and Stella Cabrini on July 15, 1850 in the Lombardy region of Italy. She took formal religious vows in 1877 and only three years later founded the Missionary Sisters of the Sacred Heart of Jesus in 1880. *This was the first missionary order to admit women.* Mother Cabrini had the tenacity and organizational skills of a Roman general, and the administrative competence of a corporate executive. Under her leadership, this new order quickly grew, adding seven convents in seven years. Recognizing the value of Cabrini's strong leadership skills, Pope Leo XIIII requested that she relocate to the U.S. to help America's immigrants. With six other nuns, she moved to New York City in 1889. Her assignment in the U.S. was to establish charitable and religious organizations to assist impoverished immigrants, many of whom at the time were Italian.

Over a twenty-five year period, Mother Cabrini succeeded in establishing numerous schools, orphanages, hospitals and convents in the United States, England, Italy, France, Spain, Panama, Argentina and Brazil. Under her direction 67 organizations were established, staffed by 1500 nuns and other professionals. There are several colleges and universities throughout the world named Xavier in her honor.

Mother Cabrini founded four great hospitals, one in New York, another in Seattle, and two in Chicago. She founded Columbus Hospital in 1892 as a 10-bed facility with just 12 bottles of medicine, and staffed it with 7 sisters in a rented building in New York City. This small medical unit has grown into the famous 519-bed Cabrini Medical Center in the prestigious Gramercy Park section of Manhattan.

In 1909, Mother Cabrini became a naturalized U.S. citizen. Mother Cabrini died in Chicago on December 22, 1917. In 1946, she became the first American citizen to become a saint when Pope Pius XII canonized her. In 1950, the Pope named her "the patron saint to immigrants." The feast day of Saint Frances Xavier Cabrini is November 13.

✂

Chapter XIX

SCIENCE & TECHNOLOGY

"Galileo is the father of modern physics - indeed of modern science altogether."
- Albert Einstein -

Anemometer
Leonardo da Vinci

Da Vinci invented this device to measure wind speed, since he realized that wind had a flow similar to water. His anemometer has a vane hinged at the top and swings up a scale to show wind speed or force. His device looks very much like a modern one. A simpler version was invented in 1450 by Leon Battista Alberti.

First Atomic Transformation – *Nobel Prize*
First Atomic Reactor (or Nuclear Reactor)
Architect of the Atomic Bomb and
First Conceived the Hydrogen Bomb
Enrico Fermi

Enrico Fermi was born on September 29, 1901 in Rome to Ida Fermi and Alberto Fermi. His father Albert was a Chief Inspector of the

Ministry of Communications. Enrico showed a keen interest and ability in mathematics and physics as a young teenager and won a fellowship, Scuola Normale Superiore, at the University of Pisa in 1918. As a commentary to his genius, Fermi was soon teaching theoretical physics to his own physics instructor. Only four years later, in 1922, he earned his doctorate in physics at the early age of 21, and at the age of 26 Fermi became professor of theoretical physics at the University of Rome in 1927.

Fermi ushered in the atomic age when he succeeded in transforming the nucleus of a uranium atom and simultaneously split the atom for the first time, in Rome in 1934. For his pioneering work he was awarded the Nobel Prize in 1938. In his experiment, uranium was transformed into a new element that did not exist on the Periodic Table of Elements. Thus, Fermi was the first to demonstrate that elements may exist beyond the known Table of Elements. In his experiments, he systematically bombarded many elements, and finally uranium atoms, with "slow neutrons." He discovered that slowing the speed of neutrons, by passing them through a "light-element moderator," dramatically increased their effectiveness. This gave Fermi a technique that would allow him to release nuclear energy in a reactor, which he later invented in 1942.

Although Fermi was the first to develop the "slow neutron" technique that transformed the element uranium into a new and different element, he was unaware, at that time that the atom was also split, and that nuclear fission had taken place. His uranium sample had been wrapped in a sheet of metal foil that blocked the fission fragments that would have otherwise been detected by his equipment. Some historians assert that this was fortuitous and may have been divine intervention. Had the world understood in 1934 how to unleash nuclear energy, Adolf Hitler's Nazi Germany, aligned with the Italian dictator Benito Mussolini, would have gained the technology to build an atomic bomb in the mid-1930's. At that time Western Europe and the United States still slept, unprepared and unaware of the Axis power's military buildup. As fate would have it, in later years Fermi immigrated to the United States and led a scientific team that would develop the first nuclear reactor and ultimately the first atomic bomb.

In 1939, Fermi was the first to conceive of a nuclear chain-reaction that would unleash nuclear energy and designed the first nuclear reactor at Columbia University in the same year. He called the device a "pile" since the three-dimensional object had a number of components, and his fluency in English was still not optimal. This is why nuclear reactors are still sometimes referred to as "piles." His revolutionary work was then moved to the University of Chicago in 1942. The secret World War II project, called the Manhattan Project, was orchestrated under an unused squash court beneath the Stagg Field football stadium at the University of Chicago where Fermi led a team of scientists. *As a result of his leadership role, Fermi is credited with building the world's first atomic reactor. On December 2, 1942 his reactor reached critical point and the first man-made self-sustained atomic reaction occurred.* Fermi shut the reactor, called CP-1, down after 28 minutes of operation. A Hungarian scientist on his team, Eugene Wigner, opened a traditional straw-bottomed bottle (called a *fiasco* in Italian) of Chianti and offered a toast. After the toast a more serious communication transpired. In the throes of World War II, another one of Dr. Fermi's colleagues, Dr. Arthur Holly Compton, telephoned the head of U.S. National Defense Research Committee at Harvard, Dr. James B. Conant, with this secret message: "Jim, I think it will interest you to know that the first Italian navigator has landed in the United States." Fermi's groundbreaking success initiated the age of nuclear energy.

Fermi's Manhattan Project team continued their work and developed the first atomic bomb. *Fermi is considered the architect of the atomic bomb.* It was subsequently detonated at Alamogordo Air Base in New Mexico on July 16, 1945. Ten days later, on July 26, 1945, the Potsdam Declaration was issued by U.S. President Truman and other Allied leaders threatening "complete and utter destruction" of Japan if it did not unconditionally surrender. Unfortunately, Japan defiantly declared that it would not surrender and continued to wage war, escalating suicide missions against Allied ships and other forces. The first atomic bomb was then dropped, August 6, on Hiroshima. Unfortunately, Japan would still not surrender and did not believe another bomb of such power existed. Consequently, Japan suffered a second bomb, August 10, on Nagasaki, and finally surrendered ending World War II. Historians agree that had the U.S. not dropped these atomic bombs, at least 200,000 Allied lives would have been lost in a prolonged invasion of Japan, along with a similar loss of life for the Japanese. This loss of life was avoided by the two bombs and Japan's subsequent surrender.

One should shudder to think of what the world would be like today if Fermi was sympathetic to Mussolini and Hitler and had offered his talents to the Axis forces during World War II. Fermi and his team knew that Nazi scientists in Berlin were trying to develop nuclear weapons and had already succeeded in splitting a single uranium atom. In fact, there is a famous letter from Albert Einstein to President

Franklin D. Roosevelt warning that the U.S. must develop a nuclear bomb before Hitler's scientists. This letter prompted the U.S. to assemble the Manhattan Project team, which was led by Fermi. A very real and horrifying race existed between the Axis powers and the Fermi team of scientists organized by the United States. Fermi and his support of the U.S. saved the world from horrifying atomic strikes had Hitler developed the atomic bomb first. It was Fermi's work that led the effort to build the first atomic bomb in 1945.

In 1941, Fermi was also the first to hypothesize that a hydrogen (or thermonuclear) bomb could be possible using fission to trigger a fusion chain reaction. He theorized that a fission explosion could trigger a fusion reaction in deuterium, an isotope of hydrogen. However, *Fermi argued that a hydrogen bomb should not be built because of the great multiples of destructive power*. He stated the hydrogen bomb was "...a weapon which in the practical effect is almost one of genocide." In October of 1949, the General Advisory Committee to the U.S. Atomic Energy Commission held top secret meetings over several days to debate the ethics and feasibility of the hydrogen bomb. After these deliberations the U.S. Atomic Energy Commission (AEC) called for the research on the bomb to stop, partially because of technical problems and also because the U.S. AEC's Committee concluded that the weapon was unethical because of its incredible destructive power. President Truman, however, feared that even if the U.S. did not build the hydrogen bomb, the Soviet Union would do so. The U.S. Congress concurred and work on the bomb continued. Although Fermi did not work on the hydrogen bomb, a young scientist who had worked in Enrico Fermi's laboratory in Chicago, named Richard Garwin, came up with the basic technical design in 1951, according to Dr. Edward Teller, a senior colleague of Dr. Fermi. Three years after the U.S. AEC's recommendation, and after a total of seven years of research, the United States detonated the first hydrogen bomb on November 1, 1952, on Eniwetok Atoll in the South Pacific. The island of Elugelab in the Eniwetok Atoll was literally vaporized by the thermonuclear blast. The bomb left a crater in the ocean floor 200 feet deep and more than a mile across. The hydrogen bomb had an explosive yield of 10.4 megatons, 700 times the yield of the atomic bomb dropped on Hiroshima.

After the war, Fermi worked at the Los Alamos, New Mexico atomic bomb laboratory, again demonstrating his loyalty and patriotism to America, as he did in 1944 when he became a United States citizen. On November 16, 1954, U.S. President Dwight D. Eisenhower and the U.S. Atomic Energy Commission presented Enrico Fermi with a special

R. R. Esposito

award for his lifetime achievements in physics and particularly for leading the team that developed atomic energy. Fermi died of stomach cancer days later on November 28, 1954 at the early age of 53. The Enrico Fermi Presidential Award was subsequently established in 1956 as a memorial for his revolutionary breakthroughs that ushered in the nuclear age. Today, winners receive a citation signed by both the U.S. President and the U.S. Secretary of Energy, and a gold medal bearing the portrait of Enrico Fermi, along with a $100,000 honorarium. Further, in 1968, The Fermi National Accelerator Laboratory (FermiLab) was opened and named in honor of Fermi. It is operated by the Universities Research Association and funded mostly by the U.S. Department of Energy.

It is just an interesting historical note that in 1898 the Director of the U.S. Patent Office declared that the Office could be closed because everything that could be invented had already been invented. It was difficult for this administrator to image that only 36 years later the nuclear age would be born when Enrico Fermi working in Rome transformed and split an atom. One can only image what wonders will fill our world, 36 years from now, when we reach the year 2042! Let us hope and pray that we have the wisdom and strength to harness these new technologies for the global good and not to advance the dark side of any endeavor.

Sub-Atomic Particles Discovery – *Nobel Prize*
Carlo Rubbia
Rubbia was born in 1934 in Georizia, Italy. He won a Nobel Prize in 1984 for the discovery of W and Z field, sub-atomic particles, as proof of the weak-force theory in physics. He was a researcher at CERN (Conseil Européen pour la Recherche Nucléaire), the European nuclear research organization in Geneva, and was a professor at Harvard University.

Rubbia was appointed Director-General of Europe's CERN and served in this leadership capacity for five years from 1989 through 1993.

Automation, Early
Leonardo da Vinci
Da Vinci was revolutionary in that he designed several manufacturing devices that attempted to provide automation by using

weights that gradually descended, pulled by gravity, and turned gears. An example of this is his file-cutting machine that used weights for automation but also used a threaded shaft to automatically control the movement of the file blank through the machine as it is scored by the hammer. In the 16th century, Leonardo invented this machine to mass-produce and manufacture files. However, his advanced ideas were not applied to create this machinery until 1758, two hundred years later. (Note: The first handmade bronze files for grinding and shaping date back to Egypt circa 1500 BC.)

Also, although Gutenberg invented the movable type printing press almost fifty years earlier, da Vinci designed one that could be operated by one man instead of several. He was again far ahead of his time since printers did not adopt his concepts until the 17th century.

Ball Bearings
Leonardo da Vinci

In da Vinci's "Notebooks," he presents the first systematic study of friction and invented numerous designs for ball bearings. Again da Vinci's imagination was centuries ahead of his time. His world did not know of electric motors or combustion engines, and there was no need to greatly reduce friction. Nevertheless, he was thinking about frictionless machinery long before there were high-speed motors or engines that would require low friction devices, such as ball bearings.

Barometer
Evangelista Torricelli

Around 1640, two Italians, Gasparo Berti (physicist) and Galileo (mathematician/astronomer/inventor), first noticed that there was a physical limit that water could rise to when submerging a pipe with a closed top into water. However, Torricelli, a student of Galileo, understood that air pressure prevented the water from rising above 10 meters (32 feet) and by replacing water with mercury *invented the first barometer in 1643*. For more on Torricelli, refer to two sections in the "Mathematics" chapter: 1) Integral Calculus, Torricelli's Theorem and Analytical Geometry, 2) Mechanics and Hydraulics.

Barium Sulfide
Vincenzio Cascarido
Cascarido discovered barium sulfide in 1602. It is often used for plating and coating metals, for example, blue and brown coatings, or patinas.

Camera (Camera Obscura)
(Note: the English word *camera* is actually an Italian word, meaning *chamber*, since a camera is a hollow chamber.)

Leon Battista Alberti
The earliest mention of a camera device dates back to 15th century Italy. Alberti was the quintessential Renaissance man and is credited with inventing the camera obscura. He described its use in his 1435 book "De Pictura" and suggested this glass instrument be used as an aid in drawings. It was a dark box with a hole in it, which allowed the subject image to pass to the back of the box. There an inverted image would be seen. Artists would insert a piece of paper and sketch the image. (See the "Art & Architecture" chapter for more information on the famous Alberti.)

Giambattista Della Porta
Della Porta was born near Naples on November 15, 1535 and he died there on February 4, 1615. Giambattista Della Porta wrote of the camera obscura in his epic 20-volume science encyclopedia, "Magia Naturalis," published in 1589. *He was the first to suggest using a convex lens with the camera obscura* further advancing and perfecting this predecessor to the modern camera. He also designed a very early steam engine, described later in this chapter. (Refer also to the "Astronomy" and "Mathematics" chapters for more information on Della Porta.)

Amiello Barbaro
In the 16th century, Amiello Barbaro of Venice fitted the camera obscura box with a convergent lens to better focus and sharpen the image shown at the back of the box. *The modern camera differs only in that the photographic paper replaced the artist's pencil.* In the movie "Addicted to Love" the lead role played by Matthew Broderick uses a camera obscura to spy on a woman that he is in love with. In the

movie, his camera obscura projected the woman's image on the wall, large enough for this secret admirer to view her image clearly.

Candle
Rome

During the first century, Romans began making early candles of vegetable and animal fats. They considered these inferior to oil lamps, many of which were highly crafted works of art as well. There are many written accounts of starving soldiers eating their candles for nourishment. In later centuries English lighthouse keepers would sometimes eat candles, presumably when looking for an instant snack or perhaps from sheer boredom.

Capillary Action, Discovery
Leonardo da Vinci

Da Vinci is credited for discovering the capillary action of liquids in small tubes in 1490. This is the phenomenon where liquids seem to defy gravity and rise within a small tube without any source of energy or assistance from extraneous influences.

Carbon Paper for the Typewriter
Pellegrino Turri

In the early 1800's there were many forms of early typewriters that were being invented. However, a certain Pellegrino Turri was motivated to invention by his love for a woman who was stricken blind. She was the beautiful Countess Carolina Fantoni who had become blinded "in the flower of her youth and beauty." Turri invented (circa 1800 - 1808) a typing machine and carbon paper to allow the Countess to communicate with him, as well as others. The black carbon paper was essentially the ink of the machine that left its black ink marks on the white paper beneath it. His method of combining carbon paper with a typewriter was at least 65 years ahead of its time. As the Romans would have said, "Love conquers all."

Central Heating (Hypocaust System)
Rome

In the 1st century Roman engineers developed a central heating system they called the *hypocaust*. The system consisted of a basement wood or coal furnace, which evenly distributed heat throughout the home by means of terra cotta tubes in the walls and floors of homes. The *hypocaust* system also heated water for the indoor plumbing and baths. Large public buildings in Rome also benefited from this central heating system. After the fall of Rome, central heating in Europe disappeared during the Dark Ages for centuries.

Chemistry - Molecular
Stanislao Cannizzaro

Cannizzaro was an Italian chemist born in 1826 and died in 1910. He was a professor of chemistry at the universities of Palermo and Rome. He invented new ways to synthesize alcohol and his process is called *Cannizzaro's Reaction*. He also discovered cyanamid. Further, he also discovered a method of using Avogadro's Law to determine and distinguish atomic weights from molecular weights. (*Avagadro also discovered molecules and helped to define and popularize the word molecules.* Refer to the section on Molecules later in this chapter.)

Chemistry – Plastics and *Nobel Prize*
Giulio Natta

Natta was born in Imperia, Italy in 1903 and died in 1979. He graduated with a degree in Chemical Engineering from Polytechnic of Milan in 1924 and began teaching there in 1927, and later at Pavia University in 1933. He was Professor and Director of the Institute of Industrial Chemistry at Polytechnic of Milan from 1938 to 1974.

In 1938, Professor Natta began to study the production of synthetic rubber in Italy. In 1953, he also began working as a researcher for the large Italian chemical company, Montecatini. At the Montecatini laboratories, Natta created a thermoplastic material, isotactic polypropylene. Working with Natta, Montecatini was the first to produce isotactic polypropylene on an industrial scale in 1957.

Professor Natta won a Nobel Prize for Chemistry in 1963 for his research in the chemical structure and synthesis of polymers. *His polymer discoveries were significant, because they advanced the creation of various commercial plastic products.* His Nobel Prize was for research specifically in macromolecular chemistry and petrochemicals.

Professor Natta wrote and published over 700 research papers, of which about 500 relate to stereoregular polymers. He also holds a large number of patents in many different countries.

Natta has been distinguished by these honors:

- Life member of the New York Academy of Sciences (1961)
- National Member of the Accademia dei Lincei (1955)
- Belgian Chemical Society STAS medal (1962)
- Honorary Member of these Chemical Societies: Austrian (1960) Belgian (1962), Swiss (1963)
- Gold Medal from the town of Milan (1960)
- Gold Medal from the District of Milan (1962)
- Gold Medal from the President of the Italian Republic (1961)
- First International Gold Medal of the Synthetic Rubber Industry (1961)
- Gold Medal Society of Plastic Engineers - New York (1963)
- Perrin medal from the French Chemical Physical Society (1963)
- Lavoisier medal Chemical Society of France (1963)
- Perkin Gold Medal English Society of Dyers and Colourists (1963)
- John Scott award Board of Directors, City Trust of Philadelphia
- "Leonardus Vincius Florentinus Doctor Ingenieurs" Medal from FIDIIS, Paris (1971)
- Honorary member Industrial Chemical Society of Paris (1966)
- Honorary member Chemical Society of London (1970)
- Associated Foreign Member of the Académie des Sciences de l'Institut de France (1964)
- Member of the National Academy of XL, Rome (1964)
- Foreign member of the Academy of Sciences of Moscow, U.S.S.R. (1966)
- Honorary president of the Italian Section of the Society of Plastics Engineers (SPE)
- Gold medal of the Union of Italian Chemists (1964);
- Gold medal "Lomonosov" Moscow Academy of Sciences (1969)
- Gold Medal "Carl-Dietrich-Harries-Plakette" Deutsche Kautschuk Gesellschaft, Frankfurt/Main (1971)
- Honorary degree - University of Genoa (1964)
- Honorary degree - Polytechnic Institute of Brooklyn, New York (1964)
- Honorary degree - Catholic University of Louvain, Belgium (1965)

- Honorary degree - ESPI, University of Paris (1971)
- Honorary degree - Mainz University (1963)
- Honorary degree in pure chemistry - Turin University (1963)

Clock, First Modern
Milan, Italy

The first clock that had hours of equal increments was built in the 1330's for the church of St. Gothard in Milan. Prior to the clock at St. Gothard, medieval clocks had hours that varied from approximately 38 to 82 of today's minutes, and as such, were not particularly useful.

The word *clock* comes from a Latin word meaning *bell*, since very early clocks had no dial but chimed the hours. The Romans invented several types of water clocks (clepsydra), as early as the 2nd century BC. However, the first forms of water clocks date back to 5th century BC.

Clock Advancements
Giovanni de Dondi

The *first description of a clock's escapement mechanism*, which regulates the energy used to move the clock's mechanism, was provided by Giovanni de Dondi in 1364. He was an astronomer and physician who taught medicine at the University of Padua. He built a remarkable seven-dial clock that displayed time, the position of the planets, solar eclipses and other celestial movement. His original clock has been lost over the centuries but replicas have been built. It took over 200 years before anything was built to match the complexity of his magnificent clock.

Clock, First Pendulum
Galileo Galilei

In 1641, Galileo designed the first clock that kept time using a pendulum. This was the first reliable and accurate clock since the pendulum kept the clock's movements from random tempo changes. Although he did not build his clock, his son Vincenzio Galilei used his father's drawings to develop blueprints and build a model. The city fathers of Florence built a tower clock, based upon Galileo's invention of the pendulum clock. Most history books give credit to the Dutch scientist Christiaan Huygens who in 1656 built clocks with an escapement controlled by a pendulum; however, Galileo's design predates Huygens by a decade and a half.

Compass, Magnetic
Amalfi, Italy

The round, glass-covered, boxed magnetic compass that we use today as a directional aid was invented between 1295 and 1302 in Amalfi, most probably by a man named Flavio Gioia. This revolutionary invention allowed Amalfi to become a significant naval power in the early 14th century and dramatically enhanced the city's maritime trade. Early use of a ship's compass in Italy provided a dramatic competitive advantage and also contributed to the military and commercial success of Venice in the 13th and 14th centuries.

Although the Chinese had no real interest in maritime trade, they invented a type of compass made from a fish-shaped magnetized iron bar that was suspended in water in 1040 AD. They used this device to aid in the positioning of buildings, some say for *feng shui* aesthetic and spiritual benefits.

Compass, Proportional
Galileo Galilei

In 1597, Galileo invented the proportional compass. This invention is used to measure distances and heights using optics, the calibration markings on the device, and geometry. It had two calibrated arms that were joined at a pivot point and a third connecting arch between the two arms with calibrated markings. One arm had a needlepoint at the end, similar to modern mathematical compasses used for geometry. Galileo's device was used to measure the height of a tree or ship's mast without having to climb or scale the object to measure its height. It also was a pocket calculator, a type of slide-rule and the *first commercial scientific instrument to be crafted*. It was also used by the military to calculate the square root of troops for battlefield deployment, for the proper charge for specific cannon size, and by shipwrights who used it to test new hull designs using models built with the aid of the device.

Computer Research to Develop Artificial Intelligence (AI)
Floriana Esposito, Donato Malerba, Gianni Semeraro

Floriana Esposito has published over 100 articles in international journals on computer-based artificial intelligence, knowledge engineering, learning machines, mathematics for statistical pattern recognition, epidemiological modeling, and expert systems. Many of her articles were co-authored with Donato Malerba and Gianni Semeraro. *She is among the world's leading research scientists for computer based artificial intelligence.* Dr. Esposito received her degree in Electronic Physics from University of Bari (1970) and is Dean of Computer Science also at the University of Bari. At the University of Bari she is the head of the Laboratory for Knowledge Acquisition and Machine Learning in the Department of Informatics and is also Director of Interdepartmental Center for Logic and Applications. She is on the board of directors for the Italian Association for Artificial Intelligence. She is also a leader for the Italian national Machine Learning Group. Dr. Esposito is involved in research for many organizations including: European Science Foundation, University of California, University of Aberdeen, University of Paris, European Network on Computational Logic, and MilNet - US Defense Department. She is also part of the U.S. Navy's Artificial Intelligence Research Center at the Naval Research Laboratory (NRL). NRL is the Navy's corporate laboratory and conducts scientific research and advanced technological development in the areas of maritime applications, equipment, systems, oceanic, atmospheric, space sciences, and related technologies. She is among an elite group of scientists who perform research for the U.S. Navy.

Donato Malerba is Associate Professor for Computer Science at the University of Bari. He has published over 60 research publications on various aspects of artificial intelligence, mostly with Dr. Esposito. In 1987, he was awarded the IBM Italy Prize for the best thesis in Computer Science and has collaborated with the Italian national Machine Learning Group and the Institute of Computer Science, University of California. He has been involved with many world organizations and is a research scientist for the U.S. Navy's Artificial Intelligence Research Center at the NRL.

Giovanni Semeraro is Associate Professor at the University of Bari. His research focuses on many aspects of artificial intelligence, machine learning, applied mathematics, and distributed architectures for digital libraries on the Internet, and electronic commerce. He has published numerous articles on artificial intelligence and applied mathematics with Dr. Esposito. For his thesis on artificial intelligence he was awarded the TELECOM (Italian Telecommunication Company) Prize for the best thesis.

CPU – First Computer Microprocessor
Federico Faggin (Intel)

Federico Faggin was born on December 1, 1941 in Vicenza, Italy. He earned a doctorate in physics, with summa cum laude honors, from the University of Padua. Federico Faggin's contributions to the computer age and information technology are incalculable. Dr. Faggin developed the silicon gate integrated circuit, and built the world's first microprocessor, the Intel 4004 chip (1971). Federico Faggin's initials (F.F.) are inscribed on the Intel 4004 chip. Dr. Faggin led the team that built the Intel 4004, but his enormous personal contributions to the invention have earned him unique recognition. IEEE documents clearly show Dr. Faggin's dominating role in developing the Intel 4004 chip. He was awarded the IEEE W. Wallace McDowell award (1994) for developing the silicon gate integrated circuit and the first microprocessor, an award not shared with any others on the Intel 4004 development team. His other awards include the 1988 International Marconi Fellowship Award (Columbia University), the 1997 Kyoto Prize (Japan), and the Golden Medal for Science & Technology (Italy). He is also an inductee of the U.S. National Inventors Hall of Fame.

The invention of the microprocessor revolutionized computer technology allowing the fast, low energy, inexpensive computers that we now find ubiquitously.

Dr. Faggin also led the team that built the Intel 8088 processor, which became the foundation for all Intel Pentium processors. He also developed buried circuit and bootstrap load circuit technologies.

Dr. Faggin's inventive abilities and entrepreneurial spirit led him to leave Intel in 1974, and subsequently establish three highly successful technology companies. One of his companies, Synaptics, provides the unique touch-sensitive device used for navigation on the Apple iPOD, as well as touch pads for over 70% of the laptops in the world.

Diving Suit
Leonardo daVinci

DaVinci was the first to design an underwater diving suit. His design included a bell type helmet similar to those used centuries later.

Drinking Glasses
Rome

Romans invented glass blowing and used these techniques to make drinking cups of glass around 50 BC.

Electric Battery and Static Electricity Generator
Alessandro Volta

Volta was born February 18, 1745 in Como, Italy and died March 5, 1827. Volta was professor of physics at the University of Pavia for 25 years from 1779 to 1804. *In 1800, the first electric battery was invented by Volta* using zinc and copper plates. He demonstrated his invention at the Academy of Sciences in 1801 in Paris. Napoleon Bonaparte was so impressed, he bestowed Volta with the title of Count and also awarded him with a special commemorative gold medal. Volta built upon the knowledge base of two earlier Italian scientists who made electrical discoveries, Luigi Galvani and Giovanni Valentino Fabbroni. In 1771, anatomist Dr. Luigi Galvani, a friend of Volta, was the first to discover the electrical nature in nerves and muscles. In 1796, Giovanni Valentino Fabbroni discovered that if different metals were connected and immersed in water that one of them would oxidize, establishing an electro-chemical reaction.

Volta also made improvements upon Benjamin Franklin's glass pane electrometer, which measured differences in electrical potential. The English word "volt," used to measure units of electrical current, was named in honor of the great inventor, Volta.

In 1775, Volta invented the first static electric generator. It was an electrophorus device and produced charges of static electricity.

Volta invented many other electric devices involving static electricity and was awarded the Copley Medal of the Royal Society, and in 1791 was also elected to its membership. Also, his studies in chemistry and atmospheric electricity led him to *discover methane gas* in 1778.

Electric Generator and Electric Motor ("Pacinotti's Ring")

Antonio Pacinotti

In 1859, Antonio Pacinotti, a physics graduate from the University of Pisa, invented what became known as "Pacinotti's Ring." His invention was the world's first electric generator and the first electric motor as well. When cranked, it output electricity and functioned as a direct current electric generator. However, when battery current flowed into the "ring" it ran as an electric motor. His new invention included sixteen electromagnetic coils of silk insulated copper wire wound around a steel ring that spun on an axle. Small conductive brushes maintained connectivity as the sixteen sectors of the ring spun. Electric motors and generators (dynamos) that followed were all based upon his original invention.

Pacinotti was born in Pisa in 1841 and died in 1912. He was an instructor at the Bologna Institute of Technology and a professor of physics at the University of Pisa and the University of Cagliari as well. Pacinotti's invention in 1859 predates the 1869 commercialization of a generator by the Belgian, Zenobe Theophile Gramme, who is sometimes incorrectly credited for inventing the generator. Later the two men collaborated and made additional improvements to reduce the eddy currents in the generator's steel supports, further increasing the efficiency of the generator.

Today, Enel, with headquarters in Milan, is the largest electric utility by market value in the world, according to the "New York Times," May 2, 2003. Enel also owns CHI Energy, headquartered in Stamford, Connecticut. CHI Energy supplies energy for sixteen states in the U.S.

Electric Generator - Geothermal

Giovanni Conti

In 1903, the first geothermal power station was built by Giovanni Conti in Larderello, in the Tuscany region of Italy to generate electric energy from geothermal energy. The station successfully operated four incandescent lamps. Later, Conti greatly expanded this power station and supplied energy for the electric railway of central Italy. Conti's station was a huge success, however, it took over 50 years before another geothermal generating station was constructed. The second station was built in Wairakei, New Zealand in 1958.

An interesting historical note should be made regarding the use of geothermal energy. Niccolo Zeno an explorer from Florence traveled in the 15th century to Greenland and learned that in Greenland there were orange trees in greenhouses heated by natural geothermal heat. It is very likely that this natural source of clean energy is still vastly under-utilized. Beneath the earth's crust lies enormous energy stored in liquid magma.

Electric Motor
Antonio Pacinotti
(Refer to 'Electric Generator and Electric Motor' in this chapter.)

Electroplating
Luigi Brugnatelli

The Italian chemistry professor, Luigi Brugnatelli, invented electroplating in 1805. Using a diluted gold solution and a voltaic pile, he was able to produce inexpensive gilding and invented the electroplating process.

In the 2nd century BC the Romans invented a process for silver plating. They learned how to adhere silver foil to the surface of copper coins by discovering eutectic techniques that alloyed the silver and copper using specific solutions and temperatures.

Fax Machine
Giovanni Caselli

In the 1820's and 1840's the English made the first attempts at a crude needle telegraph to transmit graphic signs. Caselli's complex system was installed as the *first working* telegraph for graphics called the pantelegraph. It was put in operation in 1856 between Paris and Marseille. Caselli was also an ordained priest.

Fiberglass
Carlo Riva

Riva manufactured the first fiberglass in Venice in 1713. It was brought to the 1713 Academy of Science in Paris and exhibited by Rene de Reaumur.

Flight-Ejection System
Gino Santi

The rocket-propelled ejection seat used in fighter jets throughout the world was invented by Gino Santi in 1947 while working at a U.S. Army Air Force base in Dayton, Ohio. His later modifications included automatic parachute deployment, seat belts, and canopy break-away features. Santi was born in 1916 and died in 1997 at the age of 81.

Geological Sciences

Costanza Bonadonna, a physical volcanologist, was awarded the 2001 President's Award from the Geological Society of London. (The Society was founded in 1807.) Bonadonna, born in Italy, graduated in 1997 from the University of Pisa. She is currently a Research Assistant at Bristol University. Bonadonna has extensive experience in her field, having worked at the Volcano Observatory in Montserrat where she was responsible for monitoring suspended volcanic ash in relation to health risks.

Attilio C. Boriani, born in Italy, has been the Secretary General of the International Union of Geological Sciences since 1996. Since 1992, he had previously been a Vice President of the Union.

Domenico Giardini was born March 19, 1958 in Bologna. He studied physics at the University of Bologna, where he received his engineering degree in 1981 and his doctorate in 1987. Since 1997, Dr. Giardini has been Professor of Seismology and Geodynamics, and Director of the Swiss Seismological Service. Since 1992, he has been Director of the Global Seismic Hazard Assessment Program of the United Nations / International Decade for Natural Disaster Reduction (IDNDR). Since 1992, Dr. Giardini also coordinates research for INTAS, the European Union, UNESCO/IUGS and NATO. His prior positions include:
- Postdoctoral Fellow and Research Associate, Dept. of Geological Sciences, Harvard University (1982-1986)
- Researcher and Senior Researcher, Istituto Nazionale di Geofisica, Rome (1987-1992)
- Associate Professor of Seismology, University of Rome III (1992-1997)

Isabella Premoli-Silva, a palaeoceanography/micro-paleontology specialist from the University of Milan, and **Francesco Paolo Sassi**, a mineralogist from the University of Padua, are both Council Members of the European Union of Geosciences.

Also, refer to the entry in this chapter on 'Seismography for Earthquakes' for more information related to the geological sciences.

Glass Mirror
Rome and Venice

Although the Egyptians probably used polished metal as mirrors, it was the Romans in the 1st century who first used polished cheval glass, which also allowed for a full-sized reflection of the body. In the 14th century, the artisans in Venice (gaffers or glass blowers) perfected the process of making glass mirrors. Venice became a specialty center for mirrors in Europe. These early glass mirrors did not have high quality reflective characteristics and were also used to decorate swords and pendants on gold chains. In 1507, Orlando Galla of Venice made significant improvements in the manufacturing of glass mirrors. By 1648 most of Europe's mirrors and chandeliers were manufactured in the town of Murano near Venice.

Glass Windows
Rome

Around 400 BC, the Romans were the first to roll glass into sheets and use it for windows. However, the warm Mediterranean weather rendered glass windows less of a necessity and more of a curiosity. Most Roman glass was used in jewelry. They had no need for high quality clear sheet glass for windows, however, in colder regions a glass window offered more of a benefit. Consequently, the Germans perfected sheet glass for windows around 600 AD.

Grucci Fireworks – Pyrotechnics
Grucci Family

This Long Island, New York based Italian-American family owned business is the world's leading pyrotechnic company. They have won First Place - Medal Pyrotechnic World Fireworks Competition in Monte

Carlo. Grucci has also provided the firework displays for many prestigious events, e.g. the last seven consecutive U.S. Presidential Inaugurations in 1981, 1985, 1989, 1993, 1997, 2001 and 2005. The Grucci family also designed and executed displays for:

- The Brooklyn Bridge Centennial, New York, NY
- The Wedding of Sheik Hazza, Abu Dhabi, United Arab Emirates
- The Statue of Liberty Centennial, New York, NY
- The Smithsonian Institute 150th Anniversary, Washington, DC

Gyroscope Gimbal / Universal-Joint
Girolamo Cardano

The venerable mathematician Girolamo Cardano (aka Jerome Cardan) invented the *universal-joint* or *cardan-joint,* so named in his honor. He described it in his treatise "De Subtilitale" in 1550. This twin directional joint is also called a *gimbal.* Cardano used this to stabilize a ship's compass at sea. His *gimbal* design anticipated the gyroscope (invented by Jean Foucault in 1853) that uses the same *gimbal* or *universal-joint* to suspend the spinning wheel of a gyroscope.

There is a reference in Chinese literature to a perfume burner dating back to 100 BC that burned liquid fragrance inside a sphere that floated inside another sphere. This burner was so designed for safety and prevented spillage of the burning oil. This burner anticipated the *gimbal;* however, it was Cardano who invented the actual mechanical joint. (Refer to the "Mathematics" chapter for more on the eminent Cardano, the *Father of Probability.*)

Father of Modern Physics
Father of Modern Science
and the Scientific Method

Galileo Galilei

Galileo lived from 1564 to 1642 and did much to advance scientific thinking, which had not changed since the medieval era. He was the *first to pursue experimentation and quantitative methods.* Prior to his introduction of quantitative methods and experimentation, much of scientific thinking relied on philosophical theories and speculation without empirical studies. For example, Aristotle's theories and philosophies were held as beliefs without studies to support them.

R. R. Esposito

Aristotle was a great thinker and philosopher but he had not developed a way to measure and prove or disprove his theories. Galileo the scientist was the first to challenge and disprove Aristotle's theories on inertia and gravity. His careful experimentation not only made many scientific discoveries but also *introduced the scientific method to the world.* Instead of thinking about *why* things moved, as in Aristotle's mental framework, Galileo studied *how* they moved – through empirical experiments, observations and mathematics. His book entitled "Two New Sciences" (sometimes called "Discourses") gave mathematical explanations for gravity, inertia and other motions.

He is considered the Father of Modern Physics and also established mechanics as a science. Galileo discovered several laws of gravity (detailed in following sections of this chapter) and also demonstrated the laws of equilibrium, and certain principles of floatation.

Albert Einstein has been quoted to say: "Propositions arrived at purely by logical means are completely empty as regards reality. Because Galileo saw this, and particularly because he drummed it into the scientific world, he is the father of modern physics- indeed of modern science altogether." Also, refer to the "Astronomy" chapter for more on the amazing life of Galileo.

Bernardino Telesio

Telesio is also credited for advancing the empirical methods of science. He was born in Cosenza, Calabria in 1508 and died there as well in October 1588. He was an educated aristocrat and received his Ph.D. from Padua University. Telesio was the leading thinker of the Accademia Cosentina and strongly influenced their focus on using scientific observation and the study of nature. Later the Accademia Cosentina became the Accademia Telesiana as a result of his leadership and influence. He had a brother who was an Archbishop. Telesio was buried in the cathedral of Cosenza.

Gravity, First Studies of

Law of Inertia
Galileo Galilei

Before Galileo, Aristotle's writings about the characteristics of moving objects were accepted as fact. Aristotle wrote that when an object was moving, something had to continuously force the object to keep it moving. Instead of thinking about *why* things moved, as in Aristotle's mental framework, Galileo studied *how* they moved – through empirical experiments, observations and mathematics. Galileo's experiments led him to correctly theorize that as an object moved it would keep moving, and in the same direction, until something or some force stops it or makes it change direction. Galileo understood that moving objects keep moving by the nature of their own momentum or inertia. Something, like friction or an external force needs to intervene to make it change direction or stop. Long before there was space travel to provide a frictionless environment for experimentation, Galileo somehow conceived and developed controversial yet nevertheless correct concepts about inertia and gravity. Consider an object moving in space. It will move forever by the nature of its own momentum or inertia. There is no friction in space from contact or air resistance and it will travel in the same direction forever until some external force or object stops it or makes it change direction. His book entitled "Two New Science" (sometimes called "Discourses") gave mathematical explanations for gravity, inertia, projectiles, pendulums and other motions.

All of Galileo's ideas regarding gravity were contrary to the scientific thinking of his time. Until Galileo, many beliefs regarding gravity had not changed since the time of Aristotle. Consequently, Galileo became a very unpopular scientist of his time. He moved from Pisa to Padua and to Florence because of criticism and resistance against his work and writings.

Law of Parabolic Path of Projectiles
Galileo Galilei

Since Galileo was a trained mathematician, he was able to conclude from experiments that projectiles, such as cannon balls or arrows follow the path of a parabola, as their fall curves down toward the earth.

Law of Uniformly Accelerated Motion
(or Law of Falling Bodies)
Galileo Galilei

Galileo is credited for conducting the first scientific studies of gravity and again proved that traditional concepts were incorrect. Around 1604, Galileo timed the speed of falling objects by timing metal balls that he rolled down inclined planes (ramps). He discovered that all objects fall at the same speed when they have the same aerodynamics.

R. R. Esposito

The Earth's gravity causes objects to achieve acceleration of 32 feet (9.75 meters) per second squared. (Explanation: Gravity will accelerate any object at a rate of 32 feet per second, per second. After an object has been falling for one second, it will reach a speed of 32 feet per second. After two seconds its speed is 64 feet per second. After 3 seconds its speed is 96 feet per second, et cetera.) For centuries, traditional beliefs founded on the untested writings of the Greek philosopher Aristotle held that heavier objects fall faster than lighter ones. *It is incredible that it took centuries for someone (in this case Galileo) to actually test these beliefs and determine they were wrong.* It took another century for Newton to hypothesize that gravity is also the force that keeps the planets in their orbits.

Galileo did perform pendulum experiments at the cathedral of Pisa by swinging its chandelier as described in the section that follows. However, it is probably not true that he dropped weights from the Leaning Tower of Pisa to study gravity. This is most likely a popular folk legend. Galileo used inclined planes to study gravity.

Law of the Pendulum
Galileo Galilei

Using the chandelier in the cathedral of Pisa, Galileo discovered the Law of the Pendulum in 1583. This is also known as the isochronous property of the pendulum. Galileo studied the swinging of a chandelier and timed it with his own pulse, since there were no clocks with second hands in his day. He determined that regardless of the length of the pendulum's swing, the complete oscillation time was a constant. Consequently, his experiments became the basis for the use of a pendulum to provide the first reliable and accurate clocks for the world (refer to the section 'Clock, First Pendulum' in this chapter).

Herbarium
Luca Ghini

The term *herbarium* was originally used to describe a book made up of pages of dried plants that were usually medicinal in nature. The first herbarium, a collection of plants attached to pages of a book, was assembled in 1544 in Italy by Luca Ghini. This enabled scholars to study plants through the year and not just during the growing season. Today's herbarium is essentially a library of dried plant specimens. In the United States alone there are approximately 628 herbariums.

Hydraulic Motor
Agostino Ramelli

Ramelli was the first to introduce the hydraulic motor in 1588. He was also a military engineer under the service of Henry III, King of France and Poland. He lived from 1531 to about 1608. *He also published in Italian and French one of the most important books on machines in the Renaissance. Many of his inventions were successfully manufactured two and three centuries later.* Refer to the reference that follows in this chapter listed as "Reading Wheel" for more about Ramelli and his many inventions.

Hygrometer
Leonardo da Vinci

Around the year 1500, da Vinci built the first instrument for measuring atmospheric humidity. Sometimes the Italian Cardinal Nicola de Cusa is credited for this invention, but this is uncertain. In either case the invention was the process of measuring the weight of a ball of wool to which humidity would add weight.

Hydrostatic Balance
Galileo Galilei

In 1586, at the age of 22, Galileo invented the hydrostatic balance and wrote about it in his publication "La Bilancetta" ("The Little Balance"). His invention was a balance that weighed things in air and water and was so creative and inventive that the proportion of precious metals in an object could be read off directly from the scale's index. He understood that by measuring the *specific gravity* of an object, he could make a balance that would indicate the proportions in a composite metal.

Information Highway
Rome

Refer to the "Preface" of this book that delineates how the Roman system of roadways constituted the world's first "information highway."

R. R. Esposito

Internal Combustion Engine Contributions
Cristoforis, Barsanti, Mattecci, Murnigatti

Alphonse Beau De Rochas designed the modern internal combustion engine in 1862. However, many others developed earlier designs that he took and improved upon. These include four Italian inventors: Luigi Cristoforis (1823), Eugenio Barsanti (1854), Felice Mattecci (1854) and Murnigatti (c. 1850).

Ladder, Extension
Leonardo da Vinci

Da Vinci designed an extension ladder to scale the wall of an enemy fortress. The ladder uses a crank and toothed braces to lift the extension ladder up. His ladder looks exactly like the modern fire fighting extension ladder.

Luminous Objects
(Chemi-luminescent Solar Energy)
Vincenzo Cascariolo

In 1602, Cascariolo was a cobbler and alchemist who combined barium sulfate and powdered coal to invent luminous objects. He heated the mixture to coat an iron bar and discovered that after it cooled the object would glow in the dark for some period of time after exposure to the sun's rays. This method of storing solar energy quickly caught the interest of the clergy who recognized the immediate added value to religious objects that could glow in the dark. His mixture became known as *lapis solaris* or *sun stone*. Overnight, many new business opportunities arose for coated statues of saints, crucifixes and toys. Still today children of the 21st century, living in a "high-tech" age, continue to find this simple glowing characteristic of toys very intriguing.

Methane Gas Discovery
Alessandro Volta

Volta experimented with and studied atmospheric electricity. He performed experiments that included the ignition of gases by an electric spark in a closed vessel and discovered methane gas in 1778. He also invented the battery and the first static electric generator. See the reference on 'Electric Battery' earlier in this chapter for more information on Volta and his celebrated life.

Microwave Transmissions
Guglielmo Marconi

Marconi's experimentation with radio waves and short waves led him to produce the first man-made microwaves. In 1932, he installed the world's first microwave radio-telephone link between Vatican City and the Pope's summer residence at Castle Gandolfo.

His pioneering work with microwaves and the associated heat generated by them led to still further inventions by others. Others learned of his research and experimented with microwaves as a medical treatment for certain diseases. In deference to Marconi's early research with microwaves, these medical treatments were called *Marconi therapy*. (See the 'Radio' reference for more on Marconi, the inventor of the radio.)

Molecules, Discovery
and Avogadro's Law
Amadeo Avogadro

Avogadro was born on June 9, 1776 in Piedmont, Italy and died on July 9, 1856. He was a lawyer with a doctorate degree who later studied mathematics, physics and chemistry. In 1806, he began working as a demonstrator at the Academy of Turin. In 1820, he was appointed professor of mathematical physics and later became the chairman of physical chemistry at the University. Avogadro was the *first to identify molecules* as distinct from atoms in 1811. *His work also helped to define and popularize the word molecule.* Also, his experiments with gases concluded that equal volumes of gases under the same temperature and pressure have the same number of molecules. This has been named *Avogadro's Law*. However, his discovery was not generally accepted until two years after his death when in 1858, the Italian chemist, Stanislao Cannizzaro (1826–1910), constructed a concise, comprehensible system of atomic weights based upon it. Refer to the entry 'Chemistry – Molecular' in this chapter for more information on Stanislao Cannizzaro.

Molten Coins & Metal Stamping
Romans, Leonardo da Vinci and Benvenuto Cellini

In ancient Greece and China metals were heated and stamped for the creation of coins. However, the Romans invented molten molding around the 2nd century to make tools and coins.

Leonardo da Vinci invented an advanced stamping press with a screw mechanism, and the celebrated sculptor Cellini built upon da Vinci's ideas using a lever press.

Natural History Encyclopedia
Ulisse Aldrovandi

Aldrovandi, naturalist and physician, was born in Bologna, Italy on September 11, 1522. Although he created an extensive collection of flora, fauna and geological specimens, he never traveled and eventually died in his native city on May 4, 1605. In Bologna, he created one of the world's greatest collections of natural history. He became a *leading authority on natural history and wrote a 13-volume natural history encyclopedia.* Aldrovandi hired artists to illustrate thousands of specimens as well. He was also a professor of logic and natural history at the University of Bologna and founded a museum and a botanical garden in Bologna. In 1599, he also published his studies in ornithology.

In addition to being an inspector of pharmacies for Bologna, he also wrote "Le Antichita della Citta di Roma," which was basically a catalogue of the statues in Rome. Aldrovandi was once charged with heresy, but his brother Pompeo, a Cardinal, had him pardoned. There are certain advantages to a having a Cardinal in the family, especially so for scientists living in the 16th century.

Nitroglycerine
Ascanio Sobrero

Sobrero was an Italian chemist who lived from 1811 to 1870. He invented nitroglycerine in 1846 by combining glycerol with sulfuric and nitric acids creating trinitroglycerine or as it is commonly called, nitroglycerine. The Swede, Alfred Nobel, created dynamite by merely adapting nitroglycerine into porous silica or charcoal.

Odometer
Leonardo da Vinci & Vitruvius
Leonardo designed several devices that used wheels and gears to record the distance traveled. One used a pendulum type design. The famous Roman architect and engineer, Vitruvius, also designed an odometer that used gears to drop a pellet at specified distances to record distance.

Particle Physics – Discovery of Antiproton - *Nobel Prize*
Emilio Segrè
Emilio Segrè was born in Tivoli, Rome, on February 1, 1905, the son of Giuseppe Segrè, an Italian industrialist. Emilio won a Nobel Prize in 1959 for his experiments at the Radiation Laboratory at the University of California at Berkley that proved the existence of the antiproton.

Emilio taught at many prestigious universities including Columbia University, University of Illinois and the University of Rio de Janeiro. He is a member of the U.S. National Academy of Sciences, the Academy of Sciences at Heidelberg, the Accademia Nazionale dei Lincei and other professional societies. Segrè is the recipient of the Hofmann Medal of the German Chemical Society and the Cannizzaro Medal of the Italian Accademia dei Lincei. He is an Honorary Professor of San Marcos University in Peru and has an honorary doctorate degree from the University of Palermo.

Physics – String Theory
Gabrielle Veneziano
One of the most important directions of modern theoretical physics began in 1968 when Gabrielle Veneziano formulated *string theory* (now *superstring theory*). The famous physicist, Stephen Hawking, has helped us non-physicists better understand modern physics theory, including *string theory*, in his many popular books. However, it was Veneziano who originally devised this physics model as a method to explain the strong nuclear force and behavior of certain *hadrons* found in nuclear particle accelerators. Veneziano's model, which predates *quark theory*, explained the forces he observed in terms of strings.

Today his theoretical construct has become the newest theory to understand and unify the four fundamental forces of nature: gravity, electro-magnetism, strong nuclear (holds together the nuclei of atoms), and weak nuclear (radioactive decay and neutrino interactions). *Superstring* theory has also become the foundation of the *Theory of Everything* (TOE), which attempts to link together all the forces of nature, and to do so in a framework compatible with general relativity and quantum theory.

Gabrielle Veneziano is now a Senior Staff Member of the European Organization for Nuclear Research (CERN) and a member of the International Advisory Committee for the Pacific Institute for the Mathematical Sciences.

A leading *superstring* team works at the University of Torino. The Torino String Theory Group is part of the International School for Advanced Studies at the University of Torino. This School for Advanced Studies specializes in *superstring* theory and closely related areas in theoretical physics and mathematics. The school also offers a Ph.D. program in physics with a *superstring* theory specialization.

Mathematicians Eugenio Calabi of the University of Pennsylvania and Shing-Tung Yau of Harvard University discovered so-called "Calabi-Yau manifolds." Their manifolds are six-dimensional mathematical shapes that support string theory. Eugenio Calabi is the only person to have held the position of Chairman of Mathematics at the prestigious University of Pennsylvania twice. He was the department's chairman from 1967 to 1968 and again from 1971 to 1973. Eugenio Calabi has also been awarded the coveted Leroy P. Steele Prize in 1991 by the American Mathematical Society for fundamental work on differential geometry. (Refer to the "Mathematics" chapter for more recipients of the Steele Prize.)

Plumbing
Rome

The *periodic table of elements* used by the scientific community shows the chemical symbol of lead to be *Pb*. This is derived from the Latin word for *lead*, which was *plumbum*. Lead was used extensively by the Romans in their plumbing systems and hence the Latin word they used for *plumber* was *plumbarius,* clearly also the parent word of the English words *plumber* and *plumbing*. The Romans were the world's first true plumbers and manufactured lead and brass pipes that they connected with brass fittings and valves, well over two thousand years ago. Although in the last ten years modern plumbing systems have almost completely eliminated the use of lead, brass is still the best and most common metal used in modern valves and fittings.

The Romans manufactured pipes from flat plates of lead that were rolled closed. The seams were then welded tight. Brass valves were carefully crafted and the Romans even invented *mixing valves* to adjust the flow of water from two sources. These valves were also used for baths to control water temperature, just as we do today in our kitchens and bathrooms. Pipes and valves were manufactured in several large plants, and standards for diameter and thickness were developed so that Roman plumbers could order pipes and fittings from any manufacturing plant and find them to be compatible for installation. Pipes and fittings were stamped with the standards on their exterior surfaces just as modern plumbing supplies today. The Romans also designed and manufactured suction force pumps for buildings and ship use.

Roman plumbers used both atmospheric and hydrostatic pressure in their systems. Water was carried from mountain lakes and streams along aqueducts and water mains to building plumbing systems in homes and public buildings, as well as to ornamental fountains. Some aqueducts built over 2,000 years ago are still in use today, as discussed in the "Art & Architecture" chapter of this book.

Plumbing was also used extensively in Roman sanitary drainage systems and represented the best in the world until the 19th century. Roman public baths were engineering marvels with the finest craftsmanship. The Roman bath facilities built in Bath, England are still intact and the pools still hold water. The Romans founded the city of Bath and because of the natural springs there, they built several large resort type bath facilities, hence the city's name.

Roman plumbing traditions have endured for countless centuries and have been carried on by many generations of plumbers in Italy, America and elsewhere. A good example is the Scinto family in Southport, Connecticut that can boast at least three generations of Italian-American plumbers. The third generation of Scinto plumbers includes Chris Scinto, a professional engineer. His father, Jefferson Scinto, a highly skilled craftsman and designer is also a successful and knowledgeable businessman. His practical philosophy forged in the crucible of time and life experience is best expressed by his own straightforward proverb, "It's not how much money you make, it's how much you save." Prudent advice for anyone.

Radar
Guglielmo Marconi

Marconi accomplished pioneering work with radio beacons and with radar (an acronym for radio direction and ranging). He first foretold the use of radar and its applications during his lecture to the American Institute of Radio Engineers in New York in 1922. In 1934, at Sestri Levante, Italy, Marconi demonstrated his microwave radio beacon for ship navigation. In 1935, again in Italy, he gave a practical demonstration of the principles of radar.

Marconi later collaborated with two Americans (A.H. Taylor and L.C. Young) to further advance radar. They improved upon the concept with a more advanced method of localization.

The first radar system to be deployed was in 1936 under the direction of British physicist Sir Robert Watson-Watt at the Air Ministry, Bawdsey Research Station in Bawdsey Manor. By 1939, England established a system of radar stations along its south and east coasts to detect aggressors by air or sea. Also in 1939, two British scientists (Henry Boot and John T. Randall) were responsible for an important advance in radar technology during the start of World War II. They invented an electron tube called the resonant-cavity magnetron. This magnetron could generate ten kilowatts of power at ten centimeters, roughly a thousand times the output of the best U.S. electron tube using the same wavelength. (Refer to both the Radio and Microwave sections in this chapter for more on Marconi.)

Radio – *Nobel Prize*
Guglielmo Marconi

Marconi was born on April 25, 1874 in Bologna, Italy and died on July 20, 1937. He received a private education at Bologna, Florence and Leghorn, Italy. As a youth Marconi exhibited a strong interest and acumen in physical and electrical science. Marconi experimented at his father's country estate at Pontecchio where he succeeded in sending radio signals over a distance of one and a half miles. After years of study and experimentation Marconi succeeded in inventing the first practical radio system. In 1896, he demonstrated his invention to the chief engineer of the British post office and later that year Marconi was awarded the world's first patent for a system of wireless telegraphy. On March 27, 1899, Marconi demonstrated his new radio by sending a signal across the English Channel. He subsequently established the

Marconi Wireless Telegraph Company. Later in 1899, Marconi installed radio sets on two America's Cup yachts to broadcast this sporting event. This is the first time a sporting event was covered by radio announcements. More importantly, he introduced the power of radio communication to sea travel and shipping. Before this, ships at sea that ran into trouble were isolated from any help. Marine radios allowed radio transmissions to other ships or to land stations for help. These were fantastic successes, but Marconi's dream was to transmit signals across the vast Atlantic Ocean.

On December 12, 1901, Marconi realized the dream of his youth. He accomplished the first transatlantic radio communication, which took place between a transmitting station at Poldhu, on the English coast at Cornwall and Signal Hill in Newfoundland 2,000 miles away. His radio stations used approximately twenty 200-foot ship's masts in a circle for aerials. The aerials at Poldhu blew down in a storm and were replaced by aerials held up by a large canvas kite. This first transmission carried Morse code for the letter *S*. Marconi's transatlantic transmission was viewed as astonishing by most, but was a significant threat to the established cable-based telegraph companies. For example, the Anglo American Cable Company tried to order Marconi to cease radio operations in Newfoundland. However, their attempts to destroy or delay the advancement of his revolutionary invention failed. The Canadian government understood the future possibilities of Marconi's new radio and offered him a site to build a radio station at Glace Bay in Nova Scotia. Marconi accepted the invitation. One year later in 1902, the Glace Bay station was sending and receiving messages across the Atlantic.

After these successes, Marconi manufactured and sold radios to the Italian, German, British and French fleets. In 1912, when the luxury steamship the "Titanic" struck an iceberg and began to sink, the captain used this new invention, the radio, to send for help. The nearby ship "Carpathia" received the radio call for help and steamed towards the location of the "Titanic" and rescued its survivors and sixteen lifeboats. Prior to Marconi's invention, the survivors of the "Titanic" would have all perished in the frigid sea. After their rescue, the survivors participated in a special ceremony and presented a golden plaque as thanks to Marconi, because his invention saved their lives.

Marconi later improved radio technology by inventing ways to better control transmission frequencies and prevent interference among simultaneous broadcasts. *He also made major contributions to the development of short-wave radio.* He was awarded the *Nobel Prize in*

418   R. R. Esposito

physics in 1909. Marconi conceived and invented the very first radio set, transmitter and receiver. His invention not only radically changed the way the world communicates, but also precipitated discoveries in astronomy resulting from his radio transmissions (Also, see the sections on Radio Astronomy and the Ionosphere in the "Astronomy" chapter).

In 1920, Marconi established the first public broadcasting station in Britain at Writtle. This was the precursor to the BBC. His new broadcasting station stimulated the British demand for radios, and by 1925 there were 1,654,000 radio sets in Great Britain.

Radiometer
Macedonio Melloni
A radiometer measures the heating power of radiation. Melloni invented the first actual radiometer, which was called a thermopile in 1850. It used sets of electric thermocouples. (Thermometers measure heat but do not show the heating power of radiation, as does the radiometer).

Reading Wheel – First Information Workstation
Agostino Ramelli
Ramelli was an Italian engineer who lived from 1531 to 1608 and *published what is considered one of the most important books on machinery in the Renaissance.* At his own expense in Paris (1588), he published his masterpiece "The Various and Ingenious Machines of Agostino Ramelli" ("Le Diverse et Artificiose Machine del Capitano Agostino Ramelli"). His work is lavishly illustrated with 195 plates that carefully depict an incredible array of his own inventions including pumps, derricks, waterwheels, bridges, gear systems, looms, cranes, saws, foundry equipment, military machinery, fortifications and other devices. *The book was widely read and used by others.* Each item is fully described in his native Italian and in French as well. *Remarkably, many of the machines detailed by Ramelli were successfully manufactured and sold, two and three centuries later.*

Ramelli clearly understood the significance of these machines and inventions centuries before the world embraced these concepts. One of his interesting inventions is the "Reading Wheel." *This is the first attempt to create an information workstation* that quickly and easily brings information to the scholar. It is a specialized Ferris Wheel with many small lecterns that hold books in place and are made accessible to the reader without moving from the station. A series of gears keeps the lecterns upright. The lectern keeps each book in its position and always displays the open books as they were placed by the reader, who can refer to dozens, even hundreds of books, depending on the size of the wheel. Five hundred years later, the Internet, using databases and e-books, is an electronic version of Ramelli's first workstation. Ramelli would certainly be one to marvel at and appreciate the power of today's information age. He was also under the employ of Henry III, King of France and Poland as a military engineer.

Refrigeration (early form)
Zimara, the Italian
The first recorded use of food refrigeration was in Tivoli, Italy. The Emperor Hadrian's famous villa (120 AD) used snow tanks in the cellars to preserve food. In 1600, Zimara used a combination of saltpeter and snow to provide refrigeration.

Satellite Communication
Matra Marconi Space, UK, Ltd
This European company having origins with Marconi's radio communication companies is now Europe's leading satellite manufacturer. Matra Marconi Space has partnered with Teledesic Corporation to introduce the world's first satellite-based Internet services, providing continuous and ubiquitous worldwide communication using 30 low orbiting satellites. (Italian satellite manufacturer Alenia Spazio, a Finmeccanica company will also build some satellites for Teledesic.) Teledesic is privately owned by Microsoft's Bill Gates, Motorola, Boeing, Saudi Prince Alwaleed Bin Talal and Craig McCaw. Teledesic plans to begin service in 2005 and will provide wireless Internet communication from anywhere on the planet.

Scale with Dial (or Graduated Dial Balance)
Leonardo da Vinci
Scientific historians claim that *da Vinci was 350 years ahead of known techniques* for measuring weight when he invented the graduated

dial balance or the first automatic balance. Prior to da Vinci, scales for measuring weight were always based upon a suspended balance or balance beam. The Romans had invented a balance beam scale using a fixed pivot and measured weight equivalencies between the item being weighed and a standard weight on the opposite side of the balance. Before the Romans, earlier civilizations used suspended dishes to measure weight. Da Vinci was again revolutionary, since his scale directly measured weight and even included a graduated dial.

Seismography for Earthquakes
Italy

Seismographic instruments for measuring the intensity and characteristics of earthquakes were first invented and perfected in Italy. Below is a chronological review of the instrument:

- 1731 - Nicholas Cirillo was the first to use a mechanical device to study earthquakes. Cirillo used pendulums to investigate a series of earthquakes in Naples in 1731. He observed the amplitude of pendulum oscillations at locations around Naples where the shaking from Mt. Vesuvius was most and least severe. He found the amplitude to decrease with the inverse square of the distance from the mountain and published his research in 1747.
- 1751 - Andrea Bina suspended a pendulum, with a pointer attached to its hanging bob just above a container of very fine sand. The movement of the suspended pendulum bob recorded the earthquake's motions. The earthquake's nature, intensity, and the regularity of the swaying were recorded as the bob's pointer traced these characteristics in the sand.
- 1783 - F. Schiantarelli recorded the intensity of the 1783 earthquakes that occurred in the Calabria region. He was one of the first to record earthquake intensity. Schiantarelli did this by creating detail engravings. He and colleagues created 68 very detailed engravings of the landscape changes and building damage caused by the Calabrian earthquakes during February and March of 1783.
- 1856 - Luigi Palmieri was appointed Director of the Vesuvius Seismographic Observatory in 1855. One year later, he designed and installed the *first model of electromagnetic seismograph for continuous use* to track the occurrences and dynamics of the Mt. Vesuvius area. By the end of the 18th century, Ascanio Filomarino had built a mechanical seismograph, which was able to record the amplitude of the seismic

waves, the incoming direction of the earthquake, and its starting time.

- 1862 - Michele Baldacchini proposed studying changes in the seismic activity around Mt. Vesuvius to predict Vesuvian eruptions as a means to warn the surrounding population. Palmieri responded to Baldacchini's proposal and was the first to develop a plan of how to record and review seismic activity for this reason.
- 1875 - Filippo Cecchi invented a successful seismograph that was able to detect and record slight seismic activities. A. Cancani and G. Agamennone made particularly important improvements in the long-pendulum type seismometer instruments. Their instrument was so sophisticated that by the late 1800's they were recording Japanese earthquakes in Italy. These early Italian pendulum seismographic instruments recorded important planetary and seismic events. These early instruments marked seismic activity on smoked paper.
- 1895 - The long-pendulum seismometers pioneered by the Italians were improved upon by the Germans who designed light horizontal pendulums. In 1895, Vicentini (Italian) and Pacher (German) constructed the "Vicentini microsismografo," a mechanically-recording seismograph with sensitivity and magnification equal to the German instruments. In the late 1800's John Milne (English) also contributed to seismography with his work in Japan.
- 1874 - Michele de Rossi of Italy invented the first modern seismic intensity scale. Francois Forel of Switzerland independently published similar intensity scales, but seven years later in 1881. Rossi and Forel collaborated and produced the Rossi-Forel Scale in 1883. The Rossi-Forel Scale used ten degrees of intensity and became the first scale to be widely used internationally.
- 1902 - Giuseppe Mercalli improved upon the Rossi-Forel Scale. His improvements were further refined by A. Cancani, who created a twelve-degree scale of seismic intensity, because a ten-degree scale was insufficient. Cancani's scale had degree titles, e.g. "destructive."
- 1921 - Sieberg constructed a twelve-degree intensity scale with full descriptions of each degree. A version of this scale with slight modifications was published as the Mercalli-Cancani-Sieberg Scale, or MCS Scale, still in use in Southern Europe today. As of 1931, it has been called the Modified Mercalli Scale (MM Scale). In 1936, Charles Francis Richter of the California Institute of Technology offered a new scale with decimal fractions that is now commonly used to measure seismological *intensity or magnitude*. The Modified Mercalli Scale (MM Scale) assigns a degree to the *effects on the environment* of the earthquake. Both scales are used by seismologists.

Mercalli Seismographic Scale

I	instrumental	People do not feel any Earth movement.
II	lightest	A few people might notice movement if they are at rest and/or on the upper floors of tall buildings.
III	light	Many people indoors feel movement. Hanging objects swing back and forth. People outdoors might not realize that an earthquake is occurring.
IV	mediocre	Most people indoors feel movement. Hanging objects swing. Dishes, windows, and doors rattle. The earthquake feels like a heavy truck hitting the walls. A few people outdoors may feel movement. Parked cars rock.
V	strongly	Almost everyone feels movement. Sleeping people are awakened. Doors swing open or close. Dishes are broken. Pictures on the wall move. Small objects move or are turned over. Trees might shake. Liquids might spill out of open containers.
VI	strong	Everyone feels movement. People have trouble walking. Objects fall from shelves. Pictures fall off walls. Furniture moves. Plaster in walls might crack. Trees and bushes shake. Damage is slight in poorly built buildings. No structural damage.
VII	very strong	People have difficulty standing. Drivers feel their cars shaking. Some furniture breaks. Loose bricks fall from buildings. Damage is slight to moderate in well-built buildings; considerable in poorly built buildings.
VIII	violent	Drivers have trouble steering. Houses that are not bolted down might shift on their foundations. Tall structures such as towers and chimneys might twist and fall. Well-built buildings suffer slight damage. Poorly built structures suffer severe damage. Tree branches break. Hillsides might crack if the ground is wet. Water levels in wells might change.

IX	disastrous	Well-built buildings suffer considerable damage. Houses that are not bolted down move off their foundations. Some underground pipes are broken. The ground cracks. Reservoirs suffer serious damage.
X	most disastrous	Most buildings and their foundations are destroyed. Some bridges are destroyed. Dams are seriously damaged. Large landslides occur. Water is thrown on the banks of canals, rivers, lakes. The ground cracks in large areas. Railroad tracks are bent slightly.
XI	catastrophic	Most buildings collapse. Some bridges are destroyed. Large cracks appear in the ground. Underground pipelines are destroyed. Railroad tracks are badly bent.
XII	great catastrophe	Almost everything is destroyed. Objects are thrown into the air. The ground moves in waves or ripples. Large amounts of rock may move.

(Table continued from prior page)
The Mercalli Seismographic Scale, which provides descriptions

R. R. Esposito

Richter compared to Mercalli

Richter Magnitude	Energy in joule units	Mercalli Degree
< 3.5	< 1.6 E+7	I
3.5	1.6 E+7	II
4.2	7.5 E+8	III
4.5	4 E+9	IV
4.8	2.1 E+10	V
5.4	5.7 E+11	VI
6.1	2.8 E+13	VII
6.5	2.5 E+14	VIII
6.9	2.3 E+15	IX
7.3	2.1 E+16	X
8.1	> 1.7 E+18	XI
> 8.1		XII

Also, refer to the entry in this chapter on 'Geological Sciences' for related information.

Sewer Systems with Underground Mains
Tarquinius the Elder (Roman)

Although the Greeks dug isolated sewers, it was the Romans who first made this a standard for all public works. The Romans were the first to install complete sanitary systems with underground main sewers. The most famous was the Cloaca Maxima built in the 6th century. It was also designed to drain the marsh ground water on the land later used to build the Roman Forum. (Also refer to the 'Architecture' section in the "Art & Architecture" chapter for more on Roman engineering.)

The early Romans learned much from the Etruscans who lived in central Italy in the region called Tuscany. The Etruscans were experts in sewer designs, marsh drainage, land irrigation, canal construction, and complex city planning.

Silo (advanced and perfected)
Rome

The very first silos used for food storage were in the Middle East and China. However, the Romans built them with great technological expertise. These were accurately engineered to be airtight, as well.

Smokeless Candles
Antonio Meucci

This Italian inventor, while living in Staten Island, filed many patents including a patent for the first smokeless candles. Meucci also invented the telephone and filed a preliminary patent years before Alexander Graham Bell. Please read the incredible story about Meucci in the Telephone reference in this chapter.

Speed of Sound
Vincenzo Viviani
Giovanni Alfonso Borelli

Viviani was a mathematician who was born on April 5, 1622 in Florence and died there on September 22, 1703. At the age of sixteen, Viviani began his mentoring from Galileo. Viviani was a live-in companion for the aged Galileo, under house arrest by the Church for his books that contradicted Church teachings about the planetary system. Viviani demonstrated a strong mathematical intellect, and as a youth became Galileo's assistant during his final years. Later Viviani worked with the famous scientist/physician Giovanni Alfonso Borelli and in 1660 *accurately* measured the speed of sound to be 350 meters (1148 feet) per second. Borelli and Viviani did this by firing a canon and carefully timing the difference between the flash and the sound. This was not an easy task given the primitive state of clocks in the 1600's. Clearly, they devised their own method of timing the speed of sound. They succeeded and produced the first accurate measurement of the speed of sound. Before Viviani, this measurement was attempted by Pierre Gassendi who stated the speed of sound to be 478 meters or 1568 feet per second (off by 44% of the correct speed). Today the accepted speed of sound, measured at 0 degrees Celsius, is 331.29 meters (1087 feet) per second. (For more on Borelli see the "Medicine, Biology & Health" and "Transportation" chapters. For more on Viviani see the "Mathematics" chapter.)

Steam Engine
Giambattista Della Porta

Della Porta was one of those rare minds, a true Renaissance genius, and is listed in several other sections in this book. Della Porta was one of the first to design a steam engine. He documented how this would function in his 1606 work entitled "De'spiritali." *Almost two hundred years later, the first steam engines were built.* A revolutionary event in American history is the invention of the steamboat by Robert Fulton. His steamboat, the *Clermont*, made its first voyage from New York City, up the Hudson River, to Albany and back on August 17, 1807. The very first reference using steam to move or power things comes from Hero of Alexandria, Greece in the 1st century.

Della Porta was also the first to add a lens to the camera obscura (see the Camera section in this chapter and also the "Mathematics" chapter as well). He also designed a telescope as early as 1580 (see the "Astronomy" chapter).

Superconductor Electric Power Line, First
Italian-American Consortium

The world's first superconducting power line will be operational in Detroit, Michigan in a few years. An Italian-American consortium of companies will build this power line for the Detroit Edison utility company.

The American Superconductor company completed shipment of more than 18 miles of its superconducting wire to Pirelli Cables & Systems in August 2000. The wire was used by Pirelli to manufacture the first actual superconducting power line to be used in a utility power grid. Each superconducting wire is capable of carrying more than 100 times the power of a copper wire with the same dimensions. Pirelli's construction of the power line is quite complex, it consists of layers of superconductor wire woven around a hollow core. Liquid nitrogen is then pumped through the hollow core, providing cryogenic cooling for the wires. Several layers of thermal and electrical insulation are also necessary and specialized skid wires on the outside jacket of the cable are needed to help pull the cable through conduits and ductworks. When complete the cable has a capacity of 2400 amps.

American Superconductor company is located in Westborough, Massachusetts and Pirelli Cables and Systems company is located in Milan, Italy. *Pirelli is the world's largest supplier of power cable.*

Telephone
Antonio Meucci

The story of Antonio Meucci, inventor of the telephone, has only received attention and recognition in the last few years. On September 12, 2000, the Council of the City of New York unanimously passed Resolution 1566, which petitioned the U.S. Congress to acknowledge the primacy of Antonio Meucci in the invention of the telephone. The Council's Resolution quotes the former U.S. Secretary of State who said, near the close of the 19th century, "there exists sufficient proof to give priority to Meucci in the invention of the telephone." As a result, the U.S. House of Representatives issued Resolution 269 on September 25, 2001 that recognizes Antonio Meucci for "achievements and his work...in the invention of the telephone." On June 11, 2002, The U.S. House of Representatives unanimously passed Resolution 269. The passage of this congressional resolution has provided national recognition for Meucci and his work.

The story of Meucci, and how he invented the telephone years before Alexander G. Bell, is both fascinating and dramatic. The pages below detail the long journey of Meucci in his quest to complete and refine his telephone (or as he called it originally, the "teletrofono").

Meucci was an Italian-born inventor who worked on many different projects, inventions and patents. He was born in Florence on April 13, 1808 and attended the prestigious Academy of Fine Arts in Florence where he studied physics and science. He also studied Alessandro Volta's invention of the electric battery and static generator, and Luigi Galvani's discoveries about electricity in the nervous system of animals. In Florence, he was chief engineer at an opera house until 1835 when he and his wife moved to Havana, Cuba. At that time Havana was the cultural center of the New World. He accepted the position as chief engineer of the Teatro Tacon opera house, a new internationally acclaimed opera house in Cuba and his wife became the head of the costume department. Meucci was an inventor interested in many subjects. He developed an electroplating operation in Cuba for swords and armor, eliminating the need to ship these items to Europe. He also invented a water filtration system for the opera house where he worked. However, Meucci was most fascinated with electricity and began experimenting with new applications stemming from his knowledge of Volta's battery and Galvani's discovery of electric currents in the nerves. In 1849, he began experimenting with patients suffering from headaches by applying electricity. The patients held

428   R. R. Esposito

wires in each hand with cork insulators to prevent a strong shock. When treating a patient with his electric shock process, he noticed that the electrified wires amplified the patient's voice, as Meucci worked in the battery room a few rooms away from the patient. He was the first to transmit sounds over electrically charged wires in history and the first to discover this "electrophonic" effect. Twenty-five years later the inventor Elisha Gray in America rediscovered this phenomenon. Meucci's discovery gave him the idea of developing a "speaking telegraph," using electricity to communicate voices over distances. He then replaced the cork with a funnel and asked patients to speak into the funnel and later named his invention the "teletrofono." He was still far from inventing his long distance telephone system, but it was the beginning of his 20 years of research. *It is interesting to note that in 1849 when Meucci first performed these experiments and conceived the first telephone, Alexander G. Bell was only a 2 year old boy still living in Edinburgh, Scotland.*

In 1850, after a fire at the Teatro Tacon opera house, the Meuccis moved to the United States and became friends with "the George Washington" of Italy, Giuseppe Garibaldi. Meucci continued his work using different materials for diaphragms and ultimately incorporated electromagnets into his prototypes. He developed many types of diaphragms using animal skins, and parchment saturated with paraffin, bichromate of potassium and graphite, copper and other metals. He also tried diaphragms with and without holes in the center and some with wires touching the edges of the diaphragms as they passed through the holes. Meucci experimented with different shaped electromagnets, horseshoe shaped and cylindrical shaped. He sometimes bought components from a telegraph instrument manufacturer named Mr. Chester on Centre Street in Manhattan. Meucci made electromagnetic bobbins and magnetic vibrators and discovered what was later called the "Hall Effect," where charged conductors vibrate more strongly in their own magnetic fields. *His remarkable graphite-salt responder diaphragms preceded Thomas Edison's carbon button microphones by 24 years. The result of Meucci's research bore the fruit of early microphones and speakers.* He had his first working model by 1857, which he called his *teletrofono*. The prefix *tele* is the Greek word for *far*. This name, *teletrofono,* for his invention may be the earliest form of the word *telephone.*

In 1865, a description of Meucci's unpatented invention was printed in "L'eco d'Italia," an Italian language New York City newspaper. In 1867, Meucci had an artist create a technical drawing that illustrates two men siting "miles" apart using the hand-held ear and mouthpieces of his *teletrofono.* (This 1867 technical drawing appears on page 101 of the "3rd International Symposium on Telecommunication History, Record of Proceedings," editor Russell A. Pizer, assistant editor George W. Howard). Meucci had a working system that connected his workshop behind the house to his wife's upstairs bedroom, since she suffered from crippling arthritis. He also had another extension in Garibaldi's upstairs room. Living in a house with Garibaldi on Staten Island in New York City, he finished a refined working model. Unfortunately, in 1871 Meucci was on the Staten Island ferry "Westfield" when the boiler exploded, killing 100 people and seriously injuring Meucci who was in critical condition for two months and hospitalized for several months. During his time hospitalized, his wife, an arthritic invalid who needed income to live, had sold his telephone models for six dollars to a John Fleming of Clifton, New Jersey, a second hand dealer. When he finally recovered from his near death injuries, his finances were in disarray and he could not afford the expense of a complex patent. Consequently, Meucci filed a preliminary patent called a "caveat" which was classified as a "speaking telegraph." *In his 1871 "caveat," he made claim to his invention, which would be used for "communicating sound between distant places." In the "caveat" he stated that the users of the "speaking telegraph" would signal the distant party to pick up the phone by a telegraph signal.* In the "caveat" he stated that he would continue to perfect the invention using different metals and wire gages. The preliminary patent or "caveat" is supposed to be kept secret, but needs to be renewed each year. His first caveat patent was filed December 28, 1871 and was witnessed by Shirley McAndrew and Fred'k Harper in the U.S. Patent Office. He renewed his "caveat" in 1872 and 1873, but could not afford to renew the "caveat" in 1874. He and his associates were stunned when in 1876, Alexander Graham Bell, a speech teacher for the deaf, suddenly patented an "harmonic telegraph" which was essentially the same as Meucci's telephone. *Bell was a speech teacher who in 1874 (the same year Meucci's preliminary patent expired) took blueprints to the machine shop of Charles Williams at 109 Court Street and hired Thomas A. Watson, a highly skilled machinist, to build the invention shown on the blueprints. One history book states that Bell needed to hire a machinist to build the device since Bell was "not mechanically clever and needed help putting the thing together."* (The source of this quote is the book: "Once Upon a Telephone" by Ellen Stern and Emily Gwathmey, Harcourt Brace & Co, New York, San Diego and London, 1994.) Many believe that the blueprints were based upon Meucci's preliminary patent or "caveat" that expired in 1874. Bell and Watson then reverse-engineered the invention from the blueprints and filed a patent in 1876. In fact, according to the U.S. Library of Congress: "American Memory - Word and Deeds in American History" exhibit, Bell's *first* drawing of "his" invention was in 1876, *the same year of his patent.* This exhibit, showing Bell's drawing, can be viewed on the Internet. By any measure this drawing is crude and almost childlike and does not have any of the characteristics of a careful experimenter or inventor. The U.S. Library of Congress document states that it was drawn by Bell himself, and it is the earliest of his telephone drawings. Bell's 1876 drawing comes *nine years after Meucci's 1867 technical drawing,* which is on display at the Garibaldi-Meucci Museum in New York City and documented, as stated before, in the "3rd International Symposium on Telecommunication History, Record of Proceedings."

Meucci's first working telephone model in 1857 was 20 years earlier than Bell's first drawing in 1876, which was also the year of his patent. *It is virtually impossible to believe that Bell drew his first telephone, perfected it and filed a patent all in the same year.* There is much evidence to believe that Bell's patent was fraudulent because in 1874, Bell brought blue prints to Watson for him to build the invention for the "inventor"- highly peculiar, if not preposterous. In August of 1999, the History Channel television network broadcast a short historical vignette on Bell stating that a patent clerk admitted he had been paid $100 by Bell to look at another telephone patent filed within hours of Bell's. The broadcast showed a photograph of Bell's patent and how Bell hand wrote, in the margins of his own patent, new information that he had stolen from this other patent filed by Elisha Gray on the same day as Bell's filing. From all the evidence stated, Bell was probably not an inventor, had some connection in the U.S. Patent Office, was dishonest and did not invent the telephone. Although, others like Elisha Gray and Phillip Reis also made claims to the invention in 1876, only Meucci can be clearly credited as being *the first* to have a working system and filed the first preliminary patent in 1871.

To further complicate the old inventor's life, in 1874, Meucci sought to test his system on a large scale with the Western Union District Telegraph Company. He met with a Vice President of Western Union named W.B. Grant, who asked to keep and study the telephone models Meucci had showed him. However, after some time the Vice President and the models could no longer be found, much to the disappointment and concern of Meucci. Western Union representatives had told the aged immigrant who could hardly speak English that his models were somehow lost. Mr. Grant had given Meucci's models to a Henry W. Pope who shared them with his brother Franklin L. Pope a work associate of Thomas Edison, who was employed by Western Union. They studied the devices but could not understand or reverse engineer the components before Bell and Gray filed patents. A television broadcast by PBS (Public Broadcasting Service - US) stated that when Elisha Gray died in Newtonville, Massachusetts in 1901, a note was found with his belongings written by Gray himself. Gray's note said, "The history of the telephone will never be fully written... It is partly hidden away... and partly lying on the hearts and consciences of a few whose lips are sealed- some in death and others by a golden clasp whose grip is even tighter."

Because of the significant amount of convincing evidence supporting Meucci's claim, there was a well-publicized court battle between Meucci and Bell's many corporate financial backers. On October 12, 1885, a special dispatch of the "Baltimore Sun" stated, "The case of Antonio Meucci of Staten Island who claims to be the inventor of the telephone certainly deserves the attention of the government, the courts, and of all men who desire that justice shall be done." The newspaper continued its support of Meucci's case by saying that, "More than 50 affidavits have been made to prove the above claim. The case of Meucci, whatever may be adjudged as to his claim, is one that appears very strongly to the sympathies of everyone." (Source for this "Baltimore Sun" reference is also the "3rd International Symposium on Telecommunication History, Record of Proceedings, editor Russell A. Pizer, assistant editor George W. Howard.) In spite of all the evidence, Meucci lost the case against Bell's legal team that included M.I.T. engineers, because his patent had expired and the U.S. Patent Office clerk claimed that Meucci's preliminary patent was somehow "lost" by his office. The case was heard by Judge William Wallace. *Unfortunately, today's powerful Bell companies perpetuate the myth that their corporate founder, Alexander Bell, invented the telephone. The powerful propaganda disseminated by these companies will always be an obstacle to the historical facts.*

A small house on Staten Island in New York City where Meucci lived, and for a time shared with Guisseppe Garibaldi, is now a museum. The Garibaldi-Meucci Museum houses many artifacts of both famous men. (Garibaldi unified Italy fighting French, Austrian and Spanish interests. Refer to the "Military Innovations" chapter for more on Garibaldi.) The museum contains models of Meucci's telephones and copies of his preliminary patents, as well as drawings and documentation that date back to 1857, almost 20 years before Bell's patent in 1876. Unlike Bell, Meucci was a highly skilled inventor, engineer and craftsman. The museum displays a beautiful harpsichord Meucci built and a marvelous rocking chair he crafted. The museum also displays many other patents held by the great inventor Meucci for a wide variety of innovations, from new candle making machines to water filters. The museum contains a library with hundreds of books, several of which were used as references for this book. A trip to this museum is highly recommended for anyone interested in learning more about how the telephone was really invented.

Meucci also conceived of wireless communication by using salt water as a medium and experimented with earth batteries (by burying battery ground endplates) to use "aerial electricity." By the nature of these experiments he anticipated the radio that was later invented by Marconi in 1899. He also anticipated the modern LORAN marine navigation systems when he conceived a system of tone transmitters and onboard tone receivers that could be used to triangulate a position to reduce the navigation risks in fog and storm. LORAN was not invented for another 75 years. Meucci was a brilliant inventor who was cheated out of his rightful place in history by the greed of others and ill fate.

On a final note, the author's cousin Angelo points out that if Meucci had won the court case, what was called "Ma Bell" (a colloquial term for the Bell Telephone Company) might instead have been called "Mama Meucci."

Statue of Antonio Meucci, inventor of the first telephone
(Located on Staten Island, NY)

Telescope

Refer to 'Galileo' in the "Astronomy" chapter, as well as the entry 'X-Ray Telescope' in this chapter.

R. R. Esposito

Thermometer and Graduated Thermometer
Galileo, Santorio and Ferdinand II of Tuscany

Galileo is credited for inventing the thermometer in 1592. A colleague of Galileo, Santorio, invented the first *graduated* thermometer in 1611. Previous types of crude ungraduated thermometers were invented by the ancients as documented by Latin manuscripts, e.g. Philo of Byzantium. This knowledge was lost over the centuries and the thermometer had to be re-imagined and re-invented by Galileo.

In the 17th century, Grand Duke Ferdinand II of Tuscany (a region in central Italy) was the first to solve a problem related to atmospheric pressure by sealing off the upper end of the thermometer tube. This change in the instrument improved accuracy and led the way for others to experiment further with thermometers.

Over 100 years after Galileo's invention, Daniel Fahrenheit built upon this earlier knowledge and used mercury in a glass tube in 1714 to develop the modern thermometer we use today.

Three-Way Light Bulb
Alessandro Dandini

The Italian inventor Alessandro Dandini came to the U.S. in 1945 and patented more than 22 inventions, including the very practical three-way light bulb. He also patented the rigid retractable automobile top and a spherical reflective system to concentrate solar energy. Dandini held degrees in science, language arts, hydraulic engineering, classical literature, and also taught at the University of Nevada in Reno. Dandini died in 1991 at the grand age of 88.

Turbine - Hot Air & Steam
Leonardo da Vinci
Giovanni Branca

In 1480, da Vinci sketched a propeller fixed to a vertical axis in a chimney and designed the first hot air turbine. In his drawing, hot air would rise in the chimney and turn a propeller that activates a transmission gearing system that rotates a roasting spit.

In 1629, Giovanni Branca designed a rolling mill using a steam turbine and sets of gears. However, there was too much friction in the gear design to make it practical but his concept was correct and by the end of the century, mills in Spain and Germany operated on this design.

Turbine, Principle of the Water
Leonardo da Vinci

In 1510, Leonardo da Vinci was studying hydraulics and in his famous "Notebooks" he designed a horizontal water wheel that became the first water turbine to be invented.

Wind Tunnel Research
Founder of M.I.T. Engineering Department
Gaetano Lanza

Lanza was born in 1848 in the U.S. to a Sicilian immigrant family. He founded the engineering department at the eminent Massachusetts Institute of Technology in Cambridge. At M.I.T. he was a professor of mechanical engineering for 36 years. Lanza was also an inventor and in 1909 he developed an early wind tunnel. The first wind tunnel invented is attributed to the Wright brothers. Lanza died in 1928 at the age of 80, but his venerable legacies at M.I.T. continue.

X-Ray Telescope,
Father of X-Ray Astronomy and *Nobel Prize*
Riccardo Giacconi

Riccardo Giacconi was born in Genoa in 1931, and received his Ph.D. from the University of Milan. Giacconi was awarded the 2002 Nobel Prize in Physics for his pioneering contributions to astrophysics, which have led to the discovery of cosmic X-ray sources. In 1962, he was the first to detect a source of X-rays beyond our solar system and proved that the universe contains background radiation of X-ray light. Giacconi also constructed, with the assistance of the late Dr. Bruno B. Rossi, the first X-ray telescope. (Dr. Bruno B. Rossi was born in Venice and received his doctorate in physics at the University of Bologna in 1927. Rossi became an M.I.T. Institute Professor, a title reserved for scholars of special distinction. His accomplishments are forever recognized at M.I.T. by the Rossi Prize, awarded annually for original research in High Energy Astrophysics.) Their new invention, the X-ray telescope, provides astronomers with a revolutionary new tool that offers highly detailed images of the universe. Giacconi's contributions laid the foundations of X-ray astronomy, and consequently he is considered the father of X-ray astronomy.

In 1973, Giacconi joined the Harvard-Smithsonian Center for Astrophysics, and led the construction and operation of the powerful X-ray observatory, HEAO-2, also known as Einstein. In 1981, Giacconi became the first director of the Space Telescope Science Institute and held that position until 1993. He then became the director of the European Southern Observatory from 1994 to 2000. In 1999, he became president of Associated Universities, Inc., the operator of the National Radio Astronomy Observatory. He has simultaneously held positions as professor of physics and astronomy (1982-97) and research professor (since 1998) at Johns Hopkins University. Giacconi has been honored with many awards before winning the Nobel Prize. His most distinguished awards are:

- The Bruce Medal (1981)
- American Institute of Physics & American Astronomical Society, Dannie Heineman Prize for Astrophysics (1981)
- Franklin Institute, Elliot Cresson medal (1980)
- International Center for Relativistic Astrophysics, Marcel Grossmann Award (2000)
- Royal Astronomical Society, Gold medal (1982)
- Wolf Foundation, Wolf Prize (1987)
- American Association of Physics Teachers, Richtmeyer Memorial Lectureship (1975)
- American Astronomical Society, Henry Norris Russell Lectureship (1981)
- Robert Hofstadter Memorial Lecture, Stanford University (1998)

It's interesting to note that Dr. Riccardo Giacconi was born in Genoa, the birthplace of Columbus, and Dr. Bruno B. Rossi was born in Venice, the birthplace of Marco Polo. These two great Italian cities have produced four great explorers, both earthly and celestial.

Zamboni
Frank J. Zamboni
In 1949, Frank J. Zamboni (1901-1988), an Italian-American inventor and mechanic, invented the Zamboni Ice Resurfacing Machine. His invention, typically called "The Zamboni," is a highly efficient machine that is driven across ice rinks to repair the scratches and damage from ice skates. Anyone who has attended a hockey game has seen a Zamboni repair and resurface the ice between game periods.

In 1939, Frank Zamboni and his brother Lawrence built a large 20,000 square foot enclosed ice skating rink in Paramount, California. At the time, repairing and resurfacing rink ice was a labor-intensive task, and the Zamboni's large ice rink that accommodated 800 skaters required significant maintenance. In 1942, Zamboni modified an ordinary tractor to scrape and smooth his rink's ice in a single pass. His knowledge of refrigeration, along with his natural mechanical and innovative abilities, allowed him to perfect his invention over the years, using it on his own rink. In 1949, Zamboni started to build the "Model A Zamboni Ice Resurfacer" for sale to other rink owners. The Olympic skater, Sonja Henie, was one of his first customers and her purchase helped to market the new invention globally.

R. R. Esposito

❦

Chapter XX

SPORTS, THEATER
& ENTERTAINMENT

"Ninety percent of the game is half mental."
- Yogi Berra on baseball -

SPORTS HEROES AND LEADERS

Baseball

Yogi Berra

Born in the Italian district of St. Louis, Missouri on May 12, 1925, Yogi's real name was Lawrence Peter Berra. Early in his professional baseball career, Yogi became well known as a great Yankee catcher and home run hitter. He broke records in several areas: home runs by catchers (313), consecutive errorless games (148), and consecutive chances accepted (950). Yogi was unusual, he threw right-handed but batted lefty.

He started with the Yankees minor league as an outfielder in 1942 and started catching for them in 1949. He played as their catcher until 1963. As Phil Rizzuto might say, "Holy cow that's a lotta' years." The only interruption in his career occurred when he served in the U.S. Navy during World War II from 1943 to 1946. He was named the American League's Most Valuable Player, rare recognition for a catcher, in 1951, 1954 and 1955. Yogi played in 14 World Series from the 1940's to the 1960's. Also, he played in 75 World Series games, breaking another record for catchers. Yogi managed the Yankees in 1964 and coached the New York Mets from 1965 to 1972. He was their manager from 1972 to 1975. After that the Yankees hired him back as their coach. He again managed the Yankees from 1983 to 1985. In 1972, Yogi was elected to the Baseball Hall of Fame in Cooperstown, NY.

Yogi also gained enormous fame for his witty responses and advice. His recent autobiography, "When you come to a fork in the road - Take It" contains great baseball and personal stories, as well as many of his witty quotes. Also, refer to this book's chapter, "Proverbs and Quotations," for many of Yogi's great quotes.

In the last few years, Yogi also founded a new baseball museum. The Yogi Berra Museum & Learning Center is located on the campus of Montclair State University in Little Falls, New Jersey. The museum contains many fantastic baseball displays including a priceless collection of Yogi's personal artifacts. A trip is highly recommended.

Joe DiMaggio
(aka Joltin' Joe and The Yankee Clipper)

Joseph Paul DiMaggio was born November 25, 1914 in Martinez, California. Joe had an absolutely incredible life. He was one of the greatest outfielders in the history of baseball. Joe was also a prolific hitter, getting hits in 56 consecutive games in the 1941 season. Joe is *considered one of the best overall ball players that ever lived.* His famous 56 game hitting streak ended in a game against the Indians. However, Joe then got hits in the next 16 games. *DiMaggio got hits in 72 of these 73 games that season.*

DiMaggio was known for his boyish smile and charismatic nature. Joe's two brothers Vincent Paul and Dominic Paul were also major league outfielders. Off the field, the amazing Joe married the beautiful Marilyn Monroe on January 15, 1954, but their marriage lasted only nine months.

DiMaggio, who wore jersey number 5, was known as the "Yankee Clipper" since he played for the New York Yankees from 1936 to 1951 and helped them win nine World Series titles. Joe received the Most Valuable Player Award for the American League in 1939, 1941 and

1947. He was elected to the Baseball Hall of Fame in 1955. In his later years he worked as a public relations executive and television performer.

This author actually bumped into Joe DiMaggio on the streets of mid-town Manhattan in the 1970's. He kind of smiled and I of course looked and stared at the great Joltin' Joe, managing only some kind of unintelligible vocalization that even I did not understand.

On March 8, 1999 Joe died of lung cancer. The Westside Highway in New York City will be renamed DiMaggio Highway in honor of the great Yankee Clipper.

A. Bartlett Giamatti – Baseball Commissioner

Giamatti's distinguished and diverse professional life includes his position as President of Yale University, Commissioner of Baseball and President of the National Baseball League, succeeding Peter Ueberroth. Giamatti was Baseball Commissioner for five years from 1989 to 1994. He also graduated from Yale with *magna cum laude* honors and taught there until becoming its President from 1978 to 1986. As baseball commissioner, he stood by his ethics to enforce the 30-day suspension of Reds Manager Pete Rose against great opposition to this censure. Rose was suspended for gambling. Giamatti also supported the hiring of minority managers, coaches and executives. He made efforts to improve the family atmosphere at the parks with initiatives to reduce rowdy behavior.

Giamatti died of a heart attack on Martha's Vineyard, Massachusetts at the age of 51. A great quote of Giamatti's is about the legendary Yogi Berra: "Talking to Yogi Berra about baseball is like talking to Homer about the gods."

Tommy Lasorda

Just as Frank Sinatra is called the "Chairman of the Board," Tommy Lasorda has been bestowed the title of "Dean of Major League Baseball Managers." He is a legend in American Baseball. Tommy Lasorda spent 47 years of his 51 years in professional baseball with the Los Angeles Dodgers.

Tommy was manager of the LA Dodgers from 1976 to 1996. He managed his 3,000th game on May 10, 1996 at St. Louis, winning 3 to 2 in the 12th inning. Lasorda successfully managed the LA Dodgers in four World Series (1977, 1978, 1981, 1988) and six League Championship Series (1977, 1978, 1981, 1983, 1985, 1988) and two Division Series (1981,1995). He also managed the National League in

All-Star Games in 1978, 1979, 1982 and 1989. Also, he coached the All-Star Games in 1977, 1983, 1984, 1986 and 1993.

Tommy was also named *National League Manager of the Year by "The Sporting News." United Press International and Associated Press named him Manager of the Year in 1977, and he also won Associated Press Manager of the Year honors in 1981.* After retiring in 1996, he became team Vice President of the Los Angeles Dodgers and was *elected into the Baseball Hall of Fame.* Lasorda now has an active career as a lecturer on management and motivation for corporate executives and business leaders.

Billy Martin

Billy was born Alfred Manuel Pesano on May 16, 1928 in Berkeley California. Billy was known for his feisty personality and tremendous loyalty to the Yankee team that he managed. Martin was hired and fired five times during the time he managed the Yankees. He became the first Italian-American professional baseball manager to win a World Series when he led the New York Yankees to victory. Prior to being the Yankee manger he won the Most Valuable Player Award in the 1953 World Series when he batted .500, with 12 hits, 2 home runs, and 8 RBIs. The whole country mourned his death at the age of 61 on Christmas Day in 1989.

Mike Piazza

Mike was born on September 4, 1968 in Norristown, Pennsylvania. Mike's parents are Veronica and Vince. Vince is a first generation Sicilian. Mike has played for the LA Dodgers and NY Mets, and now plays for the San Diego Padres. He's a catcher with great hitting ability and has won many honors that include:

- N.L. Rookie Player of the Year, "The Sporting News"(1993)
- All-Star team, "The Sporting News" (1993-98)
- N.L. Silver Slugger team, "The Sporting News"(1993-98)
- N.L. Rookie of the Year, Baseball Writers' Association of America (1993)

Phil Rizzuto (aka The Scooter)

Rizzuto was born in New York City, the son of a trolley car conductor. He tried out for the NY Giants and Brooklyn Dodgers at the age of 16, but was not old enough to be taken seriously. Eventually, Phil Rizzuto became one of the best shortstops in major league history, playing for the Yankees in the 1940s and 1950s. During World War II he served in the U.S. Navy and played on the same team as another great shortstop, Pee Wee Reese. In 1950, Rizzuto won the American League MVP Award as he batted a career-high .324. He also won Best Major League Shortstop from "The Sporting News" from 1949 through 1952. Phil played errorless major league baseball for a record 21 consecutive World Series games. In 1956, he was hired for the Yankee broadcast booth. He worked as a Yankee broadcaster and his famous expression, "Holy Cow!" became a household expression. Phil wrote a book in 1993 about his life as a broadcaster that included his witticisms entitled, "O Holy Cow! The Selected Verse of Phil Rizzuto." On February 25, 1994 Phil *Rizzuto was elected to the Baseball Hall of Fame in Cooperstown, NY.*

This author attended a New York City public high school in the late 1960's in Queens and had the opportunity to meet another great Yankee announcer, Bob Sheppard. He was my speech teacher in 10th grade. Sheppard had legendary crystal clear speech, posture like a statue and longish silver hair. His is the distinctive and deep voice heard in Yankee Stadium since 1951- and he is still at it in 2003. I remember his charismatic appearance, but not much about his classroom work and some say I still have a "Queens" accent- my apologies to the celebrated Mr. Sheppard.

Joe Torre

Joe Torre was born in Brooklyn on July 18, 1940, in the Marine Park section, which is not far from the Verrazano Bridge. One of his sisters, Marguerite, is a nun who is now the Principal at Nativity of the Blessed Virgin Mary Elementary School in Ozone Park, Queens. She was one of my elementary school teachers in the early nineteen sixties. She also taught my brother whom she liked (apparently better than me)and gave him a bat signed by her brother Joe Torre who was then just a rookie. We were kids from south Queens without a lot of money and played baseball with that bat. Unfortunately, Joe's signature wore off long ago. I remember that bat being in my dad's garage for decades, but my father must have given it to a neighborhood kid some years ago.

Early in his career Joe Torre played with his brother Frank for the Milwaukee Braves. Joe demonstrated his superb catching and hitting skills. Joe returned to his native New York City and from 1974 to 1976 played for the Mets and was their manager from 1977 to 1981. He later became the Yankees manager and led them to four World Series wins, bringing their total to 26 World Series victories. In 2001 and 2003, Torre led the Yankees to their 39th World Series, but both times they were unable to capture the title. Torre's highlights are:

- Won the Gold Glove, 1965
- National League All-Star Team Member- 1963, 1964,1965,1966, 1967, 1970, 1973, 1974, 1975
- Managed Yankees to World Series wins in 1996, 1998, 1999, 2000
- Managed Yankees to an American League record 114 wins in 1998
- ESPY for Best Manager of the Year
- "The Sporting News" named Torre Sportsman of the Year

Bobby Valentine

Bobby was born in Stamford, Connecticut and while in high school played baseball, but excelled in football as well. He became the only three-time "All-State" football player in Connecticut history. Bobby eventually went on to play for Major League Baseball with the Angels, Padres, Mets and Mariners. After retiring as a player, Bobby continued in professional baseball wining accolades in many leadership positions:

- As Manager of the Texas Rangers, he was named UPI American League Manager of the Year (1986).
- First American to accept a management position in the Pacific League of Japan for the Chiba Lotte Marines (1994).
- Manager of the New York Mets (1996-2002), playing in the NYC Subway Series against the NY Yankees in 2000.

On Monday, October 8, 2001, Bobby Valentine was the Grand Marshall of the Columbus Day Parade in New York City. This was *the day after* the United States bombed the infamous terrorist organizations in Afghanistan that destroyed the World Trade Center on September 11, 2001. Many feared terrorist retaliation in New York City on Monday, Columbus Day, but the parade and Bobby courageously marched along fashionable Fifth Avenue on a beautifully clear and crisp day.

Bicycling

Champion Italian cyclists who have won the international *Tour de France* race are: Marco Pantani (1998), Felice Gimondi (1965), Gastone Nencini (1960), Fausto Coppi (1952), Fausto Coppi (1949), Gino Bartali (1948), Gino Bartali (1938), Ottavio Bottecchia (1925), Ottavio Bottecchia (1924). Also, in 1946, just after World War II, Giulio Breschi won the unofficial post-war tour in 1946 called "Ronde de France." The Tour de France winner from 1999 to 2003 is the

American cyclist, Lance Armstrong.

One of the world's most prestigious cycling race is the *Giro d'Italia*. It has been an annual event since 1909, and has been won by Italian cyclists from 1909 to 1949. Since 1949, the event has included many more international competitors, and as a result athletes from other nations have won about half the races since then.

Boxing

Rocky Graziano

Rocky was born Thomas Rocco Barbella on January 1, 1922 in New York City and died there as well on May 22, 1990. Rocky was the world middleweight boxing champion from 1947 to 1948. He was famous for his powerful right-hand punches and for his fighting tenacity. *In 1971 Graziano was inducted into the Boxing Hall of Fame.*

Rocky Marciano (aka The Brockton Blockbuster)

His real name was Rocco Francis Marchegiano. Rocky was born September 1, 1923 in Brockton, Massachusetts and died August 31, 1969 near Newton, Iowa in a plane crash. He held the world heavyweight boxing championship from September 23, 1952 to April 27, 1956. Marciano was undefeated in 49 professional fights and scored 43 knockouts.

Football

Vince Ferragamo

Vince was born on April 4, 1954 in Torrance, CA. During his career as quarterback he completed 730 of 1288 pass attempts, a remarkable 57 percent, for 9376 yards and 70 touchdowns. One of his most memorable greatest performances was in 1982 when he threw 509 yards against the Chicago Bears, the second highest yardage total registered in a single game in the NFL. Vince spent most of his career with the Los Angeles Rams, but finished his last few seasons with the Buffalo Bills and the Green Bay Packers. Vince founded The Vince Ferragamo Foundation, a non-profit public benefit corporation that helps fund qualified non-profit organizations. To date, the foundation has raised monies to benefit Special Olympics and other needy sports programs.

Daryl Lamonica

Daryl was born July 17, 1941 in Fresno, CA. He was known as the "Mad Bomber" because his very long passes dwarfed his opponents' defenses. Lamonica joined the AFL's Buffalo Bills out of the University of Notre Dame in 1963 and became one of the league's top quarterbacks after being traded to the Oakland Raiders in 1967. In his first season with the Raiders, he helped take them to the AFL Championship. He was named the league's player of the year in 1967 and 1969. Daryl remained with the Raiders until his retirement after completing the 1974 season. For his career, he threw 1,288 completions in 2,601 attempts for 19,154 yards and 164 touchdowns. He also scored 14 rushing touchdowns.

Vince Lombardi

Vincent Thomas Lombardi was born June 11, 1913 in Brooklyn, New York City and died September 3, 1970 in Washington, D.C. He got his start as an assistant coach at Fordham University in the Bronx, New York City (1947-1948). He later was coach at the United States Military Academy, West Point, N.Y. (1949-1953), and with the New York Giants of the NFL (1954-1958). In 1959, he became the head coach of the poor performing Green Bay Packers and led them to five championships in the National Football League. He worked as their head coach until 1967 and under his determined leadership they won two Super Bowl games against the American Football League in 1966 and 1967. *Vince is regarded as one of the greatest coaches in any sport and by most to be Football's Greatest Coach.* He believed in discipline, preparation, intensity and determination. And most of all, Lombardi knew how to motivate and build spirit in the team. *The winners of the Super-Bowl are given the coveted and famous "Lombardi Trophy," which is named in his honor.*

Lombardi's last year as general manager of the Packers was in 1968. He left to be head coach, general manager, and part owner of the Washington Redskins. In 1969, his leadership brought the resurrected team into a winning streak after losing 14 years. He died of cancer the following year in 1970. *In 1971, he was inducted into the Football Hall of Fame. One of his greatest quotes is: "If you aren't fired with enthusiasm, you'll be fired with enthusiasm." - Vince Lombardi*

R. R. Esposito

Dan Marino

In 1984, Marino was the highest rated NFL quarterback when he played for the Miami Dolphins. He passed for an incredible 47 touchdowns in his first 20 games. Just for comparison, it took the great Joe Namath three seasons to match this record. Dan played for 16 years and completed 4,763 out of 7,989 passes, 60% for a total of 58,913 yards with 408 touchdowns and 235 interceptions. Dan and his wife Claire have been instrumental in the founding of the Miami Children's Hospital Dan Marino Center, the Miami Children's Hospital Foundation and the Dan Marino Foundation.

Joe Montana

Joe was born May 11, 1956 in New Eagle and raised in Monongahela. Both towns are located in western Pennsylvania. One of football's greatest quarterbacks, Joe won four Superbowls with the San Francisco 49ers. He was also awarded Most Valuable Player in three Super-Bowls, more than any other player. Joe twice won NFL Most Valuable Player (1989,1990). He led the NFL in passing five times, and ranks 2nd all-time in passing efficiency (92.3). Joe was inducted into the Pro Football Hall of Fame in 2000.

Vinny Testaverde

Vinny Testaverde was born November 13, 1963 in Brooklyn and raised in Elmont, Long Island. When Vinny was quarterback of the University of Miami, he became the 52nd winner of college football's premier individual award, The Heisman Trophy (1986). He is Miami University's all-time leader in career touchdown passes, with 46. Vinny was the number one selection for the Tampa Bay Buccaneers, and later joined the New York Jets in 1998.

Gymnast

Mary Lou Retton

Mary Lou Retton was born Mary Lou Rettoni. At the 1984 Olympics in Los Angeles, at age 16, Mary Lou won five gold medals in women's gymnastics. In 1990, she broke two athletic records. She was the first American woman gymnast ever to win a gold medal in the Olympics, and she was the youngest athlete ever inducted into the Olympic Hall of Fame.

Hockey

Phil Esposito

Although he was born in Ontario, Canada on February 20, 1942, the legendary Phil Esposito was raised in a family of pure Italian heritage. After moving to the United States, Phil spent much of his hockey career with the Boston Bruins (1968-1978) playing center, wearing number 7. He played professional hockey for 18 years and has won two Stanley Cup Championships with the Bruins (1970 and 1972). Phil was the first NHL player to score 100 points in a season (126 in 1969). Phil also broke many Bruins team records:

- Most Career Hat Tricks: 26 (For those non-hockey fans, a hat trick is achieved when a player scores three or more goals in one game. This is not an easy task).
- For a Single Season:
  Most Goals: 76 (1970-71 season)
  Most Points: 152 (1970-71 season)
  Most Power Play Goals: 28 (1971-72 season)
- Most Points in a game: Phil Esposito (12/19/74) – tied with Bobby Orr (11/15/73).

In 1969 and 1974, Phil Esposito won the Hart Trophy, as the National Hockey League's Most Valuable Player for two seasons. He led the NHL in scoring for four seasons in a row (1971-1974) and was awarded the Art Ross Trophy each year for this accomplishment. Phil was also an NHL first team all-star player six times. He holds fourth place on the NHL all-time list for goals (717) and points (1,590). He was a star player in the 1972 Canada-Soviet series. Phil won the Lester Patrick Trophy, the Lester B. Pearson Award, and won the Art Ross Trophy five times.

In 1981, he retired from playing professional hockey while wearing a New York Ranger uniform. *In 1984, he was inducted into the Hockey Hall of Fame.* After retiring from playing, Phil became a sports analyst for the Madison Square Garden Network covering the New York Rangers telecasts for five years. He then left broadcasting to become the General Manager of the New York Rangers in 1986. Phil then went to Florida, and as President and General Manager, he brought the Lightning franchise to Tampa Bay, quickly succeeding in making the play-offs in only their fourth season of play. In 1998, Phil became a sports analyst for FOX Sports News. Phil's younger brother, Tony Esposito, was also a record breaking goal-tender in the NHL.

Tony Esposito

Tony was born Anthony James Esposito, on April 23, 1943, in Ontario, Canada. He is the younger brother of the great Phil Esposito. Growing up, the boys played hockey together, but since Tony was younger, he was often relegated to the goalie position by Phil. Phil became a great offense-man and consequently, Tony became a great NHL goalie. *In Tony's first full professional season with Montreal he earned a record of 15 shutouts and was honored with both the Calder Trophy (as the NHL's outstanding rookie) and the Vezina Trophy.*

Later moving to the United States, he played for 16 seasons with the Chicago BlackHawks and won 423 out of a total of 886 games in the NHL. (He lost only 307 and earned draws in 151). He also earned 76 shutouts (74 at Chicago), to place him among the best goalies in the NHL. Tony also was *awarded two more Vezina trophies in 1972 and 1974 and was named to the NHL All-star team in five seasons (1969, 1971, 1972, 1973 and 1979).*

Tony Esposito's greatest memory remains when Team Canada defeated the Soviet National Team in 1972 winning four games, losing three and tying one. Both Esposito brothers where an important part of what has been famed the "Series of the Century." *In a ceremony in Toronto on September 7, 1988, Tony was inducted into the Hockey Hall of Fame.* In Tony's honor, the Chicago BlackHawks retired his number 35.

Marathon Winners

Boston Marathon
- Gelindo Bordin from Italy won 1990.

European Marathon
- Stefano Baldini from Italy won 1998.

Madrid Millennium Marathon
- Stefano Baldini from Italy won 2001.

NYC Marathon
- Orlando Pizzolato from Italy won 1984 and 1985.
- Gianni Poli from Italy won 1986.
- Giacomo Leone from Italy won 1996.

- Franca Fiacconi from Italy won 1998.

Marathon Training Director
Gabriele Rosa, MD of Brescia, Italy is a well known athletic trainer who directs marathon running camps in the United States and Kenya. He has trained many marathon champions including Kenya's great Moses Tanui (World Champ 1990). About sixty elite athletes belong to the international group trained by Dr. Rosa.

Skiing

Alberto Tomba
Alberto Tomba, born December 19, 1966 in Bologna, is one of the greatest Olympic skiers of all time. He rose to the top of the skiing world as a daring, aggressive skier, and became the first skier to win in three different Olympic games (1988, 1992, 1994) winning 3 gold medals and 2 silver medals. In 1988, at the Calgary games, he won the Gold Medal in both the slalom and the giant slalom, becoming the first Alpine skier in eight years to win two gold medals during a single Olympics. In 1992, at the Albertville games, Tomba again won a Gold Medal in the giant slalom and took a Silver Medal in the slalom. In 1994, at Lillehammer, he won a Silver Medal in the slalom for his fifth and final Olympic medal. Tomba is the most decorated male Alpine skier in Olympic history. His successes were not restricted to Olympic Games. In 1995, Tomba won the World Cup for the overall men's title along with the slalom and giant slalom crowns. In 1996, Tomba won again in the slalom and giant slaloms at the World Cup.

Soccer
Soccer originated in Florence and evolved from the Renaissance game of *Calcio Fiorentino* (Florentine kickball), which is still played today. *Calcio* is based upon an ancient Greek and Roman game, modeled after military battle lines. The Romans introduced kicking into the Greek game of *harpaston* and called their game *harpastum*. The games *harpastum* and *calcio* are also the ancestors of modern football and rugby.

The Italian National Team won the Soccer World Cup 4 times. Italy won the World Cup in 1934, 1938, 1982 and 2006, a feat matched only by Brazil (4 wins), and Germany (3 wins) close behind.

Roberto Baggio

Roberto Baggio was born near Vicenza in the town of Caldogno on February 18, 1967. He has seven brothers and sisters, his brother Eddy also plays soccer professionally. He was born to Matilde and Fiorindo. His father, Fiorindo was an avid cyclist and recognized Roberto's soccer abilities at the tender age of nine.

In the 1993-1994 soccer season, Roberto Baggio was named Soccer European Player of the Year, and that season sports authorities and writers also voted him as Best Soccer Player of the World. As of October 2001, Baggio has played in 55 National Team Games making 29 goals. He has played professional sports for over 20 years and currently plays for Brescia. He is married to Andreina and has two children.

Giuseppe Meazza

Giuseppe Meazza (nicknam "Peppino) was born in Milan and played in the Soccer World Cup when Italy won in 1934 and in 1938. Meazza was Italy's most prolific goal scorer in the 1930's and his 33 goals in 53 appearances for the national team was a record until beaten by Luigi Riva. Meazza began playing the center-forward position with Inter-Milan in 1927, at the age of 17, and later played inside-forward. He scored 33 goals and in the 1929/1930 season was the Italian league's top scorer, a feat he repeated twice more. Meazza scored 355 goals at senior level during his career.

Gianni Rivera

Giovanni Rivera, or as everyone knows him, Gianni Rivera, was born in Alessandria on August 18, 1943. When playing for AC Milan he became the first Italian to win the European Soccer player of the Year in 1969. Rivera was Italy's golden boy of soccer during the 1960's. He is regarded as the greatest player that Milan ever had, Italian or foreign. After his soccer career, he entered politics and became a Member of Italian Parliament. He even formed part of the government as an Under-Secretary of State for the Defense Department.

Paolo Rossi

Paolo Rossi was born in Prato, September 23, 1956. Rossi was instrumental in 1982 when he scored 6 goals to help Italy win the World

Cup for a third time. His 6 goals were the most goals made in the 1982 World Cup.

Dino Zoff

Dino Zoff was one of the best soccer goalkeepers the world has ever seen. He has set many records for Italian and world soccer. He was also the goalkeeper to have kept a "clean sheet" (no goals conceded) for the longest time, from September 1972 to June 1974 (1142 minutes). In 1968, he was a member of Italy's European Championship winning team. Dino Zoff was team captain when Italy won the World Cup in 1982. At the time, he was 40 years old, making him the oldest player to win the World Cup. Zoff was also national team coach for Italy in 1999.

Swimming & Diving

Matt Biondi

Matt Biondi was born on October 8, 1965. He earned the most medals (eleven) of any Olympian in history, tying swimmer Mark Spitz and gun shooter Carl Osburn. Biondi and his teammate Tom Jager were the first U.S. swimmers to win gold medals in three Olympic Games (1984, 1988 and 1992). Each athlete swam in the games winning the 400 meter freestyle relay. Biondi won 7 medals in the 1988 Olympics, including 5 gold (2 individual, 3 relay). He has won a total of 11 Olympic medals (8 gold, 2 silver and a bronze) in 3 Olympics (1984, 1988, 1992). Biondi broke seven world records and 16 American records. He earned 15 international individual titles, 17 U.S. national titles and eight NCAA national titles. He is the current American record-holder in the 100 and 200 freestyle in yards and meters as well.

Klaus Dibiasi

Dibiasi was born October 6, 1947 and won distinction by winning three consecutive Olympic gold medals in the platform diving event (1968, 1972 and 1976).

Other international competitive swimmers:

*Men:*Luca Sacchi, Luis A. Laera, Emanuele Merisi, Emiliano Brembilla , Lorenzo Vismara , Andrea Righi, Massimiliano Eroli.
Women: Manuela Melchiorri, Roberta Felotti, Cristina Sossi, Ilaria Tocchini, Lorenza Vigarani.

Tennis

Jennifer Capriati

Jennifer was born March 29, 1976 in New York City. Her father, Stefano Capriati, was also an athlete who played soccer and grew up in Milan, Italy. Jennifer is a doubles and singles tennis champion who has earned millions of dollars during her professional career.

THEATER & ENTERTAINMENT

Alan Alda - Actor, Writer and Director.

Alan Alda was born Alphonso D'Abruzzo on January 28, 1936 in New York City. He is best known for his portrayal of Hawkeye Pierce on the award winning TV show "M*A*S*H" (1972–1983). He has also appeared in many other TV programs and in more than two dozen films, including "What Women Want" (2000), "Everyone Says I Love You" (1996), "Same Time Next Year" (1978), "The Four Seasons" (1981), The Object of My Affection (1998), "Crimes and Misdemeanors" (1989) and "Catch-22" (1970). For his performance in "M*A*S*H" he garnered an unprecedented number of awards. Alda was nominated for twenty-one Emmys, won five of these, and became the first person to win the award as an actor, writer and director. Also, for several years, Mr. Alda had been host of the "Scientific American Frontiers" program. Here is a partial list of his numerous awards:

- Emmy for Outstanding Lead Actor in a Comedy Series (1974)
- Emmy for Actor of the Year (1974)
- People's Choice for Favorite Male Television Performer (1975)
- Golden Globe for Best Actor in a Comedy or Musical (1975)
- Golden Globe for Best Actor in a Comedy or Musical (1976)
- Emmy for Outstanding Directing in a Comedy Series for Dear
- Sigmund (1977)
- Directors' Guild Award for Dear Sigmund (1977)
- Writers' Guild Award for the teleplay for Dear Sigmund (1977)
- Emmy for Outstanding Writing in a Comedy/Variety/Music Series for Inga (1979)
- People's Choice for Favorite Male Television Performer (1979)
- People's Choice for Favorite Male Television Performer (1980)
- People's Choice for Favorite All Around Male Entertainer (1980)

- Golden Globe Award for Best Actor in Comedy or Musical (1980)
- Emmy for Outstanding Lead Actor in a Comedy Series (1981-82)
- People's Choice for Favorite Male Television Performer (1981-82)
- Directors' Guild Award for The Life You Save (1981-82)
- Humanitas Writers Award (1980)

In 1976, Alan was appointed to serve on the National Commission for the Observance of International Women's Year, where he also co-chaired the Equal Rights Amendment Committee. In 1982, he was co-chair with Betty Ford of the National ERA Countdown Campaign. In 1985, he became a member of the Board of the Museum of Broadcasting.

Joseph Barbera - Cartoonist, Director and Producer

Barbera is the director, producer and co-founder of Hanna-Barbera Film Studios. This Hollywood studio is responsible for many classic and highly popular cartoons such as "Tom and Jerry," "Yogi Bear," "The Flintstones," "The Jetsons," "The Smurfs," and "Scooby-Doo." Barbera was a banker and amateur cartoonist. In 1957, he and Bill Hanna started their own animation studio that was so successful it ultimately won seven Oscars.

Roberto Benigni - Actor, Author, Director, Producer

Benigni was born October 27, 1952 in Misericordia, Arezzo, Italy. His recent movie box office hit "Life is Beautiful" ("La Vita è bella") *won countless international awards and two Oscar Awards in 1999 for Best Actor and also Best Foreign Film.* Benigni stole the Oscar evening when he walked across the backs of chairs to reach the stage to receive his first Oscar. The film has everything, great cinematography, acting, drama, plot and humor. Critics have compared Benigni to Woody Allen, since he has the ability to take a serious social subject and treat it with great intelligence and humor. Like Woody Allen, Roberto Benigni, writes, acts, directs, and on one occasion, even produced a movie. Mr. Benigni wrote and directed "Life is Beautiful" and also played the leading man. He has written, directed, and acted in these major productions: "La Vita è bella" aka "Life Is Beautiful" (1997), "Il Mostro" aka "The Monster" (1994), "Johnny Stecchino" aka "Johnny Toothpick" (1991), "Il Piccolo diavolo" aka "The Little Devil" (1988), "Non ci resta che piangere" aka "Nothing Left To Do But Cry" (1984) and "Tu mi turbi" aka "You Upset me" (1983). He has written over eight major films and acted in more than twenty. Benigni played the part of Ivo Salvini in Fellini's movie "La Voce della luna" aka "The Voice of the Moon" (1989).

Tony Bennett - Singer

Tony Bennett was born Anthony Dominick Benedetto in Astoria, Queens (New York City), in 1926. His father was an Italian immigrant who worked as a grocer in Queens. From an early age Tony showed talent for his drawings in addition to his singing. In fact, Tony still draws and paints today and has many successful art shows. In 1949, he auditioned for a revue at the old "Greenwich Village Inn." Bob Hope heard his performance and invited him to sing at the Paramount Theater. Bob Hope did not like his then stage name, Joe Bari, and asked Tony what his real name was. It was the great Bob Hope who told him to use Tony Bennett after hearing his real name was Anthony Benedetto.

Tony Bennett has the voice and personal charisma that can charm the world. His listeners span generations of music lovers from teenagers to seniors. Although his career started over 50 years ago, he recently performed on television in an "MTV Unplugged" session in 1994. Tony Bennett won the 1995 Grammy Award for Album of the Year and had already won four others in past years. He is most famous for his rendition of the song "I Left My Heart in San Francisco." In 1962, this song won him two Grammy awards: Record of the Year and Best Male Solo Vocal Performance. Some of his other very popular songs are: "Fly Me To The Moon," "Steppin' Out," "All of You," and "Body and Soul." In 1986, "Pulse!" magazine selected one of his albums as one of the 200 best albums of the decade and the number one vocal record.

Sonny Bono - Composer, Singer, Comedian

Sonny was born Salvatore Bono on February 16, 1935 in Detroit, Michigan. He started his show business career when he teamed up with his wife Cher and created the singing duo Sonny and Cher. He was a very astute businessman and a very talented songwriter. Sonny wrote many hit songs including, "The Beat Goes On" and "I Got You, Babe." Their top rated show, "Sonny & Cher Comedy Hour," lasted from 1971 to 1974. The show helped to give many new comics a start, such as Steve Martin and Teri Garr. After their divorce, they had a second show, the "Sonny & Cher Show," but it was not as successful. Sony appeared in over a dozen movies including, "Murder in Music City" (1979), "Airplane II: The Sequel" (1982) and "Hairspray" (1988). Sonny was also the Mayor of Palm Springs, California and in 1994 was elected to the office of U.S. Congressman. He died tragically in a skiing accident near Lake Tahoe on January 5, 1998.

Nicholas Cage - Actor

He was born Nicholas Coppola on January 7, 1964 in Long Beach, California, the nephew of movie director Francis Ford Coppola. Nicholas changed his last name to establish some independence from his uncle's fame and influence. Cage has been in over 30 major movies since he started his career over 20 years ago in 1982. In 1995, he won the Oscar for Best Actor for his role in "Leaving Las Vegas," as well as every other major acting award that year. Some of his other significant movies include: "Fast Times at Ridgemont High" (1982), "Peggy Sue Got Married" (1986), "Raising Arizona" (1987), "Moonstruck" (1988), "Red Rock West" (1994) and "Captain Corelli's Mandolin" (2001).

Frank Capra - Author, Director, Producer

Frank R. Capra was *one of Hollywood's most celebrated movie directors.* Capra was also a prolific screen writer and movie producer. Frank was born in Sicily on May 18, 1897, in the town of Bisaquino near Palermo and died September 3, 1991, in La Quinta, California. His working class family immigrated to California when he was six years old. He worked hard to help support the family and he *put himself through college, graduating with a degree in chemical engineering.* Capra also joined the U.S. Army and was promoted to the rank of Lieutenant. Frank wanted to be a movie director and started small by processing amateur films. Later his great talent allowed him to work on professional comedies including collaborations with the famous Hal Roach, Mack Sennett and Will Rogers. In addition to *making over 50 movies, many of them Oscar winners,* Capra used his talents while president (1935 – 1941) to save the Academy of Motion Picture Arts and Sciences from imminent demise and returned this important motion picture organization to its early glory. Frank was also a patriotic American and won awards for his series of defense films produced with the U.S. Signal Service Photographic Detachment entitled "Why We Fight" (1942-45). These films were used to communicate to the public the vital importance of supporting our troops during World War II.

Capra's greatest film, "It's a Wonderful Life" (1946) starring Jimmy Stewart, has become an American classic and is broadcast faithfully every Christmas. This movie is known and cherished by all Americans and has worldwide appeal and fame. Capra was a genius who could identify and understand very human conditions and then beautifully portray these in stories on the silver screen. In addition to his most famous classic "It's a Wonderful Life," some of his other well known productions include: "Arsenic and Old Lace" (1944), "Pocketful of Miracles" (1961), "A Hole in the Head" (1959), "Mr. Smith Goes to Washington" aka "Frank Capra's Mr. Smith Goes to Washington" (1939), "You Can't Take It with You" (1938), "Lost Horizon" (1937) and "It Happened One Night" (1934).

Capra also produced television shows that included "It Happened One Christmas" (1977) based upon the movie "It's a Wonderful Life," and "Hollywood" (1980) a television mini series. In 1982, Capra won the 10th American Film Institute Life Achievement Award. Unlike most of Hollywood's celebrities, Capra was married only once. He was a devoted family man and his marriage to Lucille lasted over 60 years until his passing.

Perry Como - Singer

Perry was born May 18, 1912 in Canonsburg, PA and died May 12, 2001 at the age of 87. He was a real-life singing barber, having owned his own barbershop in the small mining town where he was born. He unintentionally started his singing career when he helped organize a barbershop quartet. Como made dozens of albums and had a very successful television show, "The Perry Como Show." He sold more than 100 million records over his 60-year career, with 27 of his records going "gold." Perry was well known for his unique smooth voice and casual style, the sweaters that he always wore, and his marriage that lasted over 50 years, very unusual for Hollywood.

Francis Ford Coppola - Author, Director, Producer

Coppola was born April 7, 1939 in Detroit, Michigan. He grew up in suburban New York in a very Italian-American family. His father Carmine was a composer and musician and his mother Italia was an actress. He attended Hofstra University on Long Island, NY and UCLA Film School in California. He gained international acclaim for his Godfather series: "The Godfather" (1972), "The Godfather Part II" (1974) and "The Godfather Part III" (1990). In addition to the Godfather series, Coppola has been involved in the production, direction and sometimes writing of dozens of major films, some are listed here: "Finian's Rainbow" (1968), "Patton" (1970), "American Graffiti" (1973), "The Great Gatsby" (1974), "Apocalypse Now" (1979), "The Cotton Club" (1984), "Captain Eo" (1986), "Peggy Sue Got Married" (1986), "Dracula" aka "Bram Stoker's Dracula" (1992), "Shelley's Frankenstein" (1994) and "The Rainmaker" (1997). *Coppola* has been recognized by no less than *five Academy Awards, ten Oscar nominations and two Cannes Film Festival Palme d'Or Awards.* Incidentally, Coppola's nephew is Nicolas Cage, who changed his name from Coppola to Cage. Cage is an outstanding actor, in his own right, starring in numerous successful films.

Robert De Niro - Actor

Robert De Niro was born August 17, 1943 in New York City. A leading dramatic actor and Academy Award winner, De Niro's more significant films include: "The Godfather Part II" (1974; Academy Award), "Taxi Driver" (1976), "The Deer Hunter" (1979), "Raging Bull" (1980; Academy Award), "Goodfellas" (1990), "Cape Fear" (1991), "Casino" (1995), "Wag the Dog" (1997), "Analyze This" (1999), "Men of Honor (2000) and "Meet the Parents" (2000). He directed "A Bronx Tale" (1993) and runs his own movie production company, Tribeca Film Center. De Niro's first movie appearance was in "Greetings" in 1968. His career never faded, and he has been in movies almost every year since then.

Leonardo DiCaprio - Actor

Leonardo was born November 11, 1974 in Los Angeles, California. His parents are George and Irmelin DiCaprio. When his mother was pregnant with him, his parents were visiting the famous Uffizi museum in Italy. His mother felt a kick from the baby while admiring a Leonardo da Vinci painting. She then decided to name the baby Leonardo. Leonardo has been in thirteen movies, the most famous were "Titanic" (1997) and "William Shakespeare's Romeo and Juliet" (1996). He has also starred in five television shows including "Growing Pains" (1991-1992).

Jimmy Durante - Singer, Comedian, Actor

James Francis Durante was born February 10, 1893 and died January 29, 1980 in Santa Monica, California. Durante was loved by all for his comedy, singing and piano playing during a career that lasted over 60 years. He started his career when he was only 17 years old, playing the piano at Diamond Tony's Saloon in Brooklyn's Coney Island. In the 1920's he played in many clubs in New York City and founded with other vaudevillians the Club Durant in New York City in 1923. In the 1940's, he was the star of several radio programs, including "The Jimmy Durante Show" and "The Camel Comedy Caravan." He had Broadway roles in "Show Girl," "Jumbo," "The New Yorkers," and made movie appearances in "Roadhouse Nights," "Jumbo," and "Mad, Mad, Mad, Mad World." Durante appeared on many television shows in the 1950's, e.g. "The Four-Star Revue" and "The All-Star Revue." Durante had a rather large bulbous nose and the industry nicknamed him "Schnozzola." All of his own acts ended with a zestful closing: "Good night, Mrs. Calabash, wherever you are!"

Federico Fellini - Author, Director, Producer
Federico Fellini was born January 20, 1920 in Rimini, Italy and died October 31, 1993 in Rome. He produced/directed and in part wrote over two dozen films and received international acclaim for his intelligent productions and sophisticated subjects.

Fellini was honored with many awards: Grand Prize Venice Festival (1954), the New York Film Critics Circle Award (1956, 1961, 1974), Oscar for Best Foreign Film (1956, 1957, 1963, 1974). He received an *Honorary Doctor of Humane Letters from Columbia University* in 1970. Some of his more famous movies include "La Strada" (1954), "La Dolce Vita" (1960), "Satyricon" (1969) and "La Voce della Luna," aka "The Voice of the Moon" (1990).

Guy Lombardo - Band Leader
Guy was born in the City of London in Ontario Canada June 19th, 1902. His family comes from a small Italian island called Lipari. He was the bandleader for The Royal Canadians orchestra, which was formed in 1916. They were also known as the Lombardo Orchestra and their performances became a long-standing tradition on New Year's Eve in the United States. On New Year's Eve they played at the exquisite Waldorf-Astoria hotel in New York City from 1954 to 1979. For twenty-five years they helped the entire U.S. welcome in the New Year. Millions of viewers watched their New Year's Eve performance on television. They played a medley of hit songs but never failed to play their standard "Auld Lang Syne." Guy was not part of the last two broadcasts, he passed away in November 5, 1977. He also acted in two movies "Many Happy Returns" and "Meet the Band Leaders." He lived in Freeport, Long Island in New York, and in his honor Freeport dedicated a major road in the town- Guy Lombardo Boulevard.

Sophia Loren - Actress
Sophia Loren was born Sofia Scicolone in Rome on September 20, 1934. Already a striking young woman at the age of fourteen, she entered a beauty pageant wearing a pink evening gown made from

curtains and old black shoes covered in white paint - and was one of twelve girls to win among more than 200 contestants. Loren has starred in over thirty movies, which include: "Grumpier Old Men" (1995), "Ready to Wear" (1994), "Angela" (1990), "Running Away" (1989), "Courage" (1986), "Aurora" (1984), "Firepower" (1979), "Blood Feud" (1978), "A Special Day" (1977), "The Cassandra Crossing" (1976), "Man of La Mancha" (1972), "A Countess From Hong Kong" (1967), "Arabesque" (1966), "Lady L" (1965), "Operation Crossbow" (1965), "The Fall of the Roman Empire" (1964), "Marriage Italian Style" (1964), "Yesterday, Today and Tomorrow" (1964), "Five Miles to Midnight" (1963), "Madame" (1962), "El Cid" (1961), "Two Women" (1961), "A Breath of Scandal" (1960), "Heller in Pink Tights" (1960), "It Started in Naples" (1960), "The Millionairess" (1960), "The Black Orchid" (1959), "Desire Under the Elms" (1958), "Houseboat" (1958), "The Key" (1958), "The Gold of Naples" (1957), "Legend of the Lost"(1957), "The Pride and the Passion" (1957), and "What a Woman!" (1956). She has written several books including her autobiography, "Sophia Loren: Living and Loving" (1979). Her many awards include:

- 1958: Venice Film Festival: Best Actress, "The Black Orchid"
- 1958: Cannes Film Festival: Best Actress, "The Black Orchid"
- 1961: New York Film Critics Circle: Best Actress, "Two Women"
- 1961: Cannes Film Festival: Best Actress, "Two Women"
- 1961: British Film Academy: Best Foreign Actress, "Two Women"
- 1961: Oscar: Best Actress, "Two Women"
- 1963: Golden Globe: Female World Film Favorite
- 1964: Golden Globe: Female World Film Favorite
- 1968: Golden Globe: Female World Film Favorite
- 1976: Golden Globe: Female World Film Favorite
- 1977: NATO Star of the Year
- 1990: Honorary Cesar: Lifetime Achievement
- 1990: Honorary Oscar as "genuine treasure of world cinema"
- 1991: Honorary Cesar
- 1994: Berlin Film Festival: Silver Bear, Lifetime Achievement
- 1995: Cecil B. DeMille Award Hollywood Foreign Press Assoc.
- 1996: NATO Lifetime Achievement
- 1998: Venice Film Festival Golden Lion: Career Achievement
- 1999: David Di Donatello Prize: Career Achievement

"People" magazine said, "Loren's face is a gift from Mother Nature...Loren endures as the world's eighth natural wonder." Sophia

Loren's modesty and humor are evident. She is quoted as saying, "Everything you see I owe to spaghetti."

Madonna - Composer, Singer, Actor

She was born Madonna Ciccone on August 16, 1958 in Bay City, Michigan. She was married to Sean Penn for four years from August 16, 1985 to January 10, 1989. Madonna had a relationship with her fitness trainer, Carlos Leon, and as a result gave birth to a girl, Lourdes Maria Ciccone Leon on October 14, 1996. In 1991, "People" magazine included Madonna in their list of the 50 Most Beautiful People in the world.

Madonna has had many hit songs (e.g. "Like a Virgin," "Express Yourself," "Keep it Together," "Like a Prayer," "Vogue"). Madonna is also an accomplished actress and appeared in many films: "Chicago" (1998), "Happy Birthday Elizabeth: A Celebration of Life" (1997), "Evita" (1996), "Girl 6" (1996), "Blue in the Face" (1995), "Four Rooms" (1995), "Body of Evidence" (1993), "Dangerous Game" (1993), "A League of Their Own" (1992), "Shadows and Fog" (1992), "Madonna: Truth or Dare" (1991), "Dick Tracy" (1990), "Madonna: Blonde Ambition World Tour '90" (1990), "Bloodhounds of Broadway" (1989), "Who's That Girl" (1987), "Shanghai Surprise" (1986), "Certain Sacrifice" (1985), "Desperately Seeking Susan" (1985), "Vision Quest" (1985).

Henry Mancini & Tony Esposito - Composers

Please refer to the Development section of the "Music" chapter where you will find the countless classic pieces of this talented and versatile writing team.

Dean Martin - Singer, Actor, Comedian

Dean was born Dino Crocetti on June 7, 1917 in Steubenville, Ohio to Gaetano and Angela Crocetti. He dropped out from Steubenville High School in the 10th grade. Dean worked at many odd jobs and was even a fairly credible amateur welterweight boxer. He got his singing start like many others in small clubs and worked his way up. In 1944, Dean got a small 15 minute singing radio program called "Songs by Dean Martin." He and comedian Jerry Lewis hosted an NBC radio show called the "Martin and Lewis Show." Together they later made over 16 motion pictures. They are perhaps best remembered for their appearances on "The Colgate Comedy Hour" television show that began in 1950. The "Dean Martin Show" on NBC was one of the highest rated shows from 1965 to 1966. Dean Martin passed away on December 25, 1995.

Domenico Modugno - Composer, Singer

Domenico Modugno is considered the father of the Italian popular songwriters and was one of the greatest composers and performers in Europe. He was born January 9, 1928 in a small seaside village. His father taught him to play the guitar and he soon developed his love for music. Some of Modugno's early works included many Sicilian folk songs. His songs during that early period include: "Lu Pisce Spada," "Lu Minaturi," "La Sveglietta," "La Donna Riccia," "Lu Sciccareddu 'Mbriacu," and "Attimo D'Amuri." His later musical hits included "Lazzarella," "Sole Sole Sole," "Strada 'Nfosa," "Resta Cu'Mme," "Nisciuno Po' Sape'," and "Io Mammeta E Tu." Modugno's compositions modernized the older traditional style of the Neapolitan song. In 1958, his song "Volare" soon became an international bestseller and was translated into many languages. Millions of copies were sold in the U.S., and in 1958 Modugno won two Grammy Awards. "Billboard" awarded Modugno an Oscar for the best song of the year. During this period he wrote many hit singles, such as "Vecchio Frac," "Notte Di Luna Calante," and "Io." He won 1st prize at the Sanremo Festival in 1958, 1959, 1962, 1966, and took 2nd prize in 1960. Modugno wrote the music for these poems, "Le Morte Chitarre" and "Ora Che Sale Il Giorno," which were written by Salvatore Quasimodo, winner of a Nobel Prize in Literature. Modugno died in Lampedusa August 6, 1994 in his seaside home.

Al Pacino - Actor

Al Pacino was born April 25, 1940 in Manhattan, New York City. He studied at the Herbert Berghof Studio and the Actors Studio, both in New York City. Pacino is a leading dramatic actor who won a Tony Award early in his career for his Broadway debut in "Does a Tiger Wear a Necktie?" (1969). Pacino became a major star with his portrayal of Michael Corleone in "The Godfather" (1972) and its 1974 and 1990 sequels. He won his second Tony Award for his Broadway performance in "The Basic Training of Pavlo Hummel" (1977). His other more significant films include "The Panic in Needle Park" (1971), "Serpico" (1973), "Dog Day Afternoon" (1975), "And Justice for All" (1979), "Cruising" (1980), "Scarface" (1983), "Sea of Love" (1989), "Dick Tracy" (1990), "Carlito's Way" (1993), "Scent of a Woman" (1993), "Heat" (1995), "City Hall" (1996), "Devil's Advocate" (1997), "Donnie

R. R. Esposito

Brasco" (1997) and "The Insider" (1999). He won an Oscar and a Golden Globe for Best Actor in "Scent of a Woman" and received Oscar nominations for seven other performances. Pacino has been in movies almost every year since his debut in "Me, Natalie" (1969).

Joe Pesci - Actor

Joe Pesci was born February 9, 1943, in Newark, NJ. He started his career at the tender age of four on the radio. Pesci is well known for the energetic tough-guy characters he frequently plays in movies. His big break came when Martin Scorsese spotted him in "The Death Collector" (1975), and cast Pesci as Jake La Motta's brother in "Raging Bull" (1980). Pesci has been in over two dozen films. His performance with Marisa Tomei in "My Cousin Vinny" (1992) made it a classic comedy. Pesci also performed in several television programs including "Half-Nelson" (NBC, 1985), "Street Scenes: New York on Film" (AMC, 1992), "Tales from the Crypt" (HBO, 1992) and "The John Larroquette Show" (NBC, 1994). Pesci's movies include: "Lethal Weapon 4" (1998), "Gone Fishin'" (1997), "8 Heads in a Duffel Bag" (1997), "Casino" (1995), "Jimmy Hollywood" (1994), "With Honors" (1994), "A Bronx Tale" (1993), "Lethal Weapon 3" (1992), "My Cousin Vinny" (1992), "Home Alone 2: Lost in New York" (1992), "The Public Eye" (1992), "JFK" (1991), "The Super" (1991), "Home Alone" (1990), "Betsy's Wedding" (1990), "GoodFellas" (1990), "Lethal Weapon 2" (1989), "Man on Fire" (1987), "Once Upon a Time in America" (1984), "Tutti dentro" (1984), "Easy Money" (1983), "Dear Mr. Wonderful" (1982), "I'm Dancing as Fast as I Can" (1982), "Eureka" (1982), "Raging Bull" (1980) and "The Death Collector" (1975).

Mario Puzo - Author

Mario was born October 15, 1920, in "Hell's Kitchen" on Manhattan's upper West Side. He served in World War II and later attended New York's New School for Social Research and Columbia University. *His name became a household word when his novel "The Godfather" was a best seller, which became a blockbuster movie.* He has written many literary successes: "The Dark Arena," "The Fortunate Pilgrim," "Fools Die" (1978), "The Sicilian" (1984), "The Fourth K" (1991) and "The Last Don" (1996).

Mario has also written screenplays, including "Earthquake," "Superman," "The Sicilian," "The Cotton Club," and all three Godfather movies, for which he received two Academy Awards. Puzo collaborated with Coppola who directed and co-wrote "The Godfather Part II" (1974). Mario died on July 2, 1999 in his home in Bay Shore, Long Island, NY.

Martin Scorsese - Producer, Director

Scorsese was born November 17, 1942 in Queens, NYC into an Italian-American family. He began his adult life studying to be a priest. Scorsese left the seminary and was accepted into New York University's film school, where he received his degrees (B.A. English and M.A. in film). As a child he had asthma and spent many hours watching movies, which may have been the seed of his professional interests in filmmaking. He is one of the leading filmmakers in the United States. His movies include "Mean Streets," "Taxi Driver," "Alice Doesn't Live Here Anymore," "Raging Bull" (earned an Oscar for Robert De Niro), "After Hours," "The Color of Money" (earned Paul Newman his first Oscar), "The Last Temptation," "Cape Fear," "Age of Innocence," "Kundun," the Oscar-winning "GoodFellas" (based on the book "Wiseguys") and the television series "Alice." Released in 2003, Scorsese's "Gangs of New York," staring Leonardo DiCaprio, has won a Golden Globe award.

Frank Sinatra - Actor, Singer

His real name was Francis Albert Sinatra and he was born December 12, 1915 in Hoboken, NJ. He died May 14, 1998 of a heart attack. *Sinatra's fame and influence was so huge that he was affectionately called "Chairman of the Board."* He is famed for his recordings of many songs such as, "New York, New York" and "My Way." Sinatra is noted for his unique style of singing popular songs and love ballads using his own pauses and musical interpretations that branded his voice and performances. He stands above all in the pantheon of popular singers.

Sinatra appeared in many movies including: "Higher and Higher" (1943), "From Here to Eternity" (1953), "Guys and Dolls" (1955), "The Man with the Golden Arm" (1955), "Pal Joey" (1957), "Some Came Running" (1958), "The Manchurian Candidate" (1962), "Von Ryan's Express" (1965), "Tony Rome" (1967), "The Detective" (1968) and "The First Deadly Sin" (1981). He received an Academy Award for Best Supporting Actor in "From Here to Eternity."

Rudolph Valentino - Actor

Valentino was born Rodolfo Guglielmi in Castellaneta, Italy in 1895. In 1913 he immigrated to the United States and worked as a dancer. He was *one of Hollywood's first sex symbols* of the silver screen. In the early 1920's he became a box-office hit for his appearances in "The Sheik" and "Blood and Sand." He made eighteen movies from 1914 to 1926 before he died at he age of 31 of a ruptured appendix in New York City. *His funeral was at Saint Patrick's Cathedral in New York City where grieving fans caused a riot.*

His home in the Bayside section of Queens, New York City, near the Throgs Neck Bridge is now a notable Italian restaurant, "Café on the Green," that can provide an intimate dinner or a grand catered affair.

Other Noted Entertainers include:

Danny Aiello (actor), Don Ameche (actor), Frankie Avalon born Frank Avalone (singer), Ann Bancroft (actress), Jon Bon Jovi (singer), Ernest Borgnine (actor), Lorraine Bracco (actress), Jimmy Bruno (jazz guitarist), Russ Columbo (band leader, musician), Pat Cooper (comedian), Lou Costello (actor, comedian), Vic Damone (singer), Tony Danza (actor), Bobby Darin born Walden Cassotto (actor), Dom DeLuise (actor, comedian), Danny DeVito (actor, comedian), Jennifer Esposito (actress), Edie Falco (actress), Connie Francis born Concetta Franconero (singer), James Gandolfini (actor), Bob Grant (radio personality), Michael Imperioli (actor), Frankie Laine born Frank Lo Vecchio (singer), Mario Lanza (singer, actor), Julius LaRosa (singer), Jay Leno (comedian, talk show host), Richard Libertini (actor), Sophia Loren (actress), Susan Lucci (actress), Penny Marshall born Carole Penny Masciarelli (actress, comedian), Marcello Mastroianni (actor), Liza Minelli (actress, singer), Lou Monte (singer), Joe Pantoliano (actor), Bernadette Peters born Bernadette Lazarra (actress), Bucky Pizzarelli (jazz guitarist), John Pizzarelli (jazz guitarist), Paula Prentiss (actress), Louie Prima (composer, band leader, singer), Ray Romano (actor, comedian), Jimmy Roselli (singer), Bobby Rydell born Roberto Ridarelli (actor), Susan Sarandon (actress), Mira Sorvino (actress), Paul Sorvino (actor), Sylvester Stallone (actor, director), Connie Stevens (actress), Marisa Tomei, (actress) John Travolta (actor), Aida Turturro (actress), Jerry Vale (singer), Frankie Valli (singer) and Frank Vignola (jazz guitarist). Note: Refer to the "Music" chapter for information on famous opera singers.

౬౩

Chapter XXI

TRANSPORTATION

Toyota's 'Corolla' is actually a Latin word.
- The Latin word 'corolla' means small crown or garland -

Note: In ancient Rome, a garland or small leafy crown ('corolla') was awarded to actors as a special recognition. Sometimes actors were also given a monetary bonus or 'corollarium', which is a word derived from 'corolla.'

Airplane
Leonardo da Vinci

This genius of the Renaissance was an artist, astronomer, biologist, mathematician, scientist, inventor and more. *Da Vinci is credited for creating the earliest designs for flying machines in 1492.* His drawings include a helicopter with a screw type propeller above the cockpit. The basic concept of the modern airplane propeller was also conceived by this spinning invention. *Da Vinci somehow understood that a spinning device could lift a flying machine in the air.* He drafted many variations of winged machines including a 4-winged flying machine. He even *designed retractable landing gear* for his flying machines. The landing gear was designed to be in the down position before liftoff and retracted when in flight. The gear would again be lowered for landings to break the fall of landing and to prevent the movable wings from striking the ground. Modern landing gear keeps the propellers from hitting the ground and also clearly makes landing a lot less traumatic. It is amazing that da Vinci was not only trying to understand how man might fly, but even considered the details of *retractable* landing gear!

Some historians claim that Leonardo would have flown in the 1400's had he not been such a perfectionist and used a less sophisticated fixed wing to try to fly with. For an insight into da Vinci's driving personality one needs only to read this statement he made on his death bed in 1519: "I have offended God and mankind because my work did not reach the quality it should have."

Leonardo also anticipated the principle of "aerodynamic reciprocity" that Newton described nearly two hundred years later. In his famous "Notebooks" Leonardo says, "As much pressure is exerted by the object against the air as by the air against the body." Over 500 years ago da Vinci thought that man would some day fly. He wrote, "....you may know that man, with his great contrived wings, exerting effort against the resisting air, may conquer and subject it, and rise above it."

Centuries later, several Italian airplane manufactures built many models both for racing and for World War II fighters and bombers. These companies include: Caproni, Caproni-Campini, Fiat and Macchi/AerMacchi. Except for Fiat, they have all given way to the European Airbus consortium. Fiat still participates in large jet engine manufacturing with the U.S. (Refer to the 'Automobile Design & Manufacturing – Fiat' section later in this chapter.)

Airplane World Speed Records

Secondo Campini
Campini set a new air speed record in 1941 with his turboreactor airplane, flying at 500 kmh (310mph) from Turin in northern Italy to Rome. His plane the Caproni-Campini CC.2 used compressed air in three stages before reaching the combustion chamber. On November 30th his jet-propelled Caproni-Campini airplane was flown 475 kilometers (300 miles) in only 2 hours 11 minutes from Turin to Rome, by pilot Mario de Barnardini. The jet later became known as the N.1.

Fiat

Fiat's World War II fighter, the "CR.42 Falco," is considered one of the best biplane fighters ever built. It was used heavily by the Italian air force in 1940 and was exported to Belgium, Hungary and Sweden. The German Luftwaffe used 150 Falcos for night attack missions. Over 1,780 Falcos were built. A Fiat CR.42B prototype with an 1100hp DB601 engine has been called the fastest biplane fighter ever flown, with speeds of 520 km/h (323 mph). Today, FiatAvio collaborates with General Electric and Rolls Royce for jet engine development, and also operates a marine division.

Automobile Design & Manufacturing - Italian

Most of the world's finest luxury sports cars and fastest racecars are designed and manufactured in Italy. The names, Alfa Romeo, Bugatti, Fiat, Ferrari, Lamborghini, Lancia and Maserati are associated with high performance and classic beauty. Italian engineering, styling, and craftsmanship make these cars so desirable, that they are status symbols of the wealthiest lifestyles. Fiat is also a manufacturer of trucks and cars that are sold worldwide in the millions for the more common and practical purpose of basic transportation - without the hand-stitched leather, polished walnut dashboards and racing engines.

Interestingly, in the 15th century, Leonardo Da Vinci designed a three-wheel vehicle powered by springs and gears with a steering bar for the front wheel, anticipating the modern car. He also designed a vertical ratcheting jack for lifting heavy objects. The astonishing thing about his jack is that it looks almost exactly like the modern car jack that ratchets up to lift the car.

Alfa Romeo

Believe it or not, this prestige car company started out in 1906 making low cost cars and evolved into the luxury car manufacturer it is today. In the 1930's, Alfa won many international races, for example the coveted 1938 Vanderbilt Cup. In 1986, Alfa Romeo was bought by the Fiat Group and is now part of the Alfa Lancia division of Fiat.

Bugatti

Ettore Bugatti, born in 1882 and died 1947, founded the Bugatti Automobili company in Campogalliano (near Modena). Bugatti manufactured over 40 models, but the Type 35 racecar was the most famous Bugatti model. This model *won over 1000 races* from 1924 to 1940. The Type 35B was a high-performance model equipped with many advanced technologies for its time. It had a 24-valve engine, supercharger, brakes with cooling fins, aluminum wheels, all of which was wrapped in a new aerodynamic design. However, the Type 57 was their most commercially successful model. The Atlantic Type 57SC designed by Ettore's son Jean is *considered by most design experts to be the most beautiful car ever made.* The famous fashion designer Ralph Lauren owns a 1938 57SC, which was on display at NYC's Rockefeller Center (9/24/99 through 9/26/99) during the 4th Annual Louis Vuitton Car Classic Show. This author attended the show and even heard the powerful purr of this magnificent machine's engine.

The Bugatti Automobili company built several new, very beautiful, high performance sports cars in more recent years, such as the model EB110 GT (13 prototype cars with aluminum and composite chassis, 95 production cars) and the EB110 SS (31 production cars). Three EB112s were built, and the ItalDesign Company had built four cars independently of Bugatti. The market price to acquire one of these rare EB100s or EB112s is about $500,000. Bugatti Automobili no longer builds cars but there are discussions to possibly build EB112s with Lamborghini. Volkswagen bought the rights to use the Bugatti name from Bugatti International and built one EB118 so far. Volkswagen has plans to build 50 of these cars a year.

Ettore Bugatti had two other sons besides Jean who designed the famous Type 57SC. His son Carlo designed furniture and silver items, and lastly his son Rembrandt was a sculptor. In the summer of 1999, the Cleveland Museum of Art held an exhibition on the work of the entire Bugatti family, which had over eighty items on display. Today the Messier-Bugatti Company founded by Ettore Bugatti and George Messier of France manufactures wheels, brakes and hydraulic systems for aircraft.

Around 1938 the original Bugatti Automobili company built an *advanced high-speed prototype fighter plane* called the 100P, and the 110P with a slightly smaller wingspan. Photos of the 100P and 110P show a very *futuristic design* even by today's standards. It had forward swept wings, a twin tail in a "V" shape, and twin propellers mounted in-line that were powered by two supercharged engines (400HP each) that were mounted behind the pilot's cockpit.

Ferrari

In 1940, Ferrari was founded by the famous racecar driver Enzo Ferrari, who was born in 1898 in Modena, Italy. In 1905, his father took Enzo and his brother Alfredo Jr. to an automobile race in Bologna. Enzo quickly fell in love with racing. His first job in the business was with Alpha Romeo and he raced for them in the famous 1920 Targa Floria, finishing in second place. Ultimately, he established his own shop and the Ferrari automobile was born.

In addition to founding the famous Ferrari automobile company, Enzo Ferrari had a very distinguished life with much international recognition. He was awarded the *Dag Hammerskjold Peace Prize by the United Nations in 1962, the Columbus Prize in 1965, the Gold Medal from the Italian School of Art and Culture in 1970, the DeGasperi Award in 1987, Cavaliere award for sporting merit in 1924, the Commendatore award in 1927 and the Cavaliere del Lavoro in 1952.* He has also received honorary degrees: mechanical engineering from Bologna University (1960); and a degree in physics from Modena University (1988). Enzo Ferrari died in Modena on August 14, 1988 at the age of ninety.

Ferrari automobiles have won over 5,000 races and earned 25 world titles creating an impressive legend under Enzo's leadership from 1947 to 1988 alone. These include: nine Formula 1 Drivers' World titles, fourteen Manufacturers' World titles, eight Formula 1 Constructors' World Championships, nine wins at the Le Mans 24 Hours race, eight Mille Miglia wins, seven Targa Florio wins, and as of 2002, 148 wins in Formula 1 Grand Prix racing. Ferrari gained its logo, the Prancing Horse, when the father of a WWI Italian flying ace (Francesco Baracca- 36 kills) gave his son's squadron badge, which was the famous Prancing Horse on a yellow shield, to the young Enzo Ferrari.

Many of their models, like Ferrari's legendary "Testarossa," have been synonymous with high performance, luxury, wealth and prestige. In 1999, Ferrari unveiled their new "Ferrari 360 Modena," a stylishly sleek sports car that costs $180,000. The Fiat Group has purchased Ferrari.

Fiat

Fiat was founded in Turin in 1899, four years before the Ford Motor Company was created by Henry Ford in June 1903. The first car manufactured in the Turin factory was a 3.5 hp car. In 1902, Fiat's first racecar, the 24 HP Corsa, driven by Vincenzo Lancia (who later founded *the* Lancia car company) won the Sassi-Superga hill climb. *Fiat was racing cars in 1902 before Ford was making them in 1903.* (Incidentally, the Romans built and raced chariots in *circuses* two thousand years before Fiat raced cars.) By 1906 Fiat already had 2500 employees. In 1909, Fiat opened and operated its own automotive production plant in Poughkeepsie, New York. A few years later in 1911 Fiat developed the "Record" for the specific purpose of beating the world speed record. The "Record" had a massive 28,353cc displacement engine with almost 300 horsepower. It reached 290 km/h (180 mph) on Long Island, NY in April 1912. In 1919, Fiat made another automotive first. A convoy of twenty-three Fiat "15 Ter" lorries completed the *first motor vehicle crossing of the Sahara Desert.* And amazingly, no mechanical problems occurred during the 3000 kilometer (1863 mile) trip. In 1927, the Fiat "520" *introduced battery ignition and left hand drive.* Also that year, Fiat won the Monza Grand Prix with the "806 Corsa." In 1928, Fiat was the *first motor vehicle manufacturer in the world to adopt aluminum cylinder heads* on its engines as standard. In 1952, the "Campagnola" completed a coast-to-coast crossing of the African continent, setting a world record in a little over 11 days. Also in 1952, during the Geneva Show, Fiat introduced the "1900 Granluce" featuring the *first example of an automatic transmission that used a fluid coupling* device between the engine and clutch.

Fiat won "Car of the Year" for its "124" model in 1967, the "128" model in 1970 and the "127" model in 1972. In 1976, the "131 Abarth Rally" won the 1000 Lakes Rally.

Fiat is part of the Fiat Group, an industrial giant operating in 61 countries, which owns 1,063 companies and earns over $57 billion Euro-dollars annually as of 2002. The Fiat Group employs over 223,000 people throughout the world, of which 111,000 are outside Italy. The Fiat Group operates 242 production plants and 131 research and development facilities worldwide. The Fiat Group companies are organized into 10 operating sectors: Automobiles, Agricultural and Construction Machinery, Commercial Vehicles, Metallurgical Products, Components, Production Systems, Aviation, Publishing and Communications, Insurance and Services. The Fiat Group's aviation company, FiatAvio, designs and manufactures commercial aircraft engines with General Electric, Pratt & Whitney and Rolls Royce. FiatAvio is involved in almost all large aircraft engines that are manufactured for commercial aircraft with seating capacity of 100 or more, and manufactures many military aviation components as well. FiatAvio also builds turbo-generators for electricity producers. The Fiat Group has companies involved in everything from medical supplies (Sorin Biomedical) to nylon fabrics (Nylstar, Inc.).

Isotta-Fraschini

In 1910, the Isotta-Fraschini world class luxury car *introduced four-wheel brakes*. The car's single overhead cam with eight cylinders was wildly successful in numerous races. The young Enzo Ferrari and Alfieri Maserati were both Isotta-Fraschini's racecar drivers before developing their own car manufacturing companies.

Lamborghini

Ferruccio Lamborghini founded his company after World War II. His factory first made tractors but he later turned his interests to racecars. His first car was the "350GTV." Although one of the smaller car makers in the world, Lamborghini created many famous supercars like "Miura," "Countach," and the celebrated "Diablo." Later, Lamborghini entered boat racing with the Formula 1 boats. The company won more than 80 victories in 10 years and in 1994 a boat equipped with a Lamborghini engine won the Class 1 world championship. Their newest boat engine is the L804V4 for offshore racing. It is a V12 engine with 4 valves per cylinder, offers a massive 960 hp, and displacement of 8,200cc. Lamborghini was born in Renazzo di Cento, near Ferrara on April 28, 1916. He died at the age of 77 on February 20, 1993. Lamborghini has been purchased by Audi of the Volkswagen group.

Lancia

Founded in Turin, Italy in 1906 by Vincenzo Lancia, the Lancia company built luxury cars, won numerous races, and introduced many automotive innovations. In 1913, Lancia's "Theta" was the *first vehicle with a built-in electrical system*. In 1922, the Lambda was a revolutionary model. It had two technical breakthroughs, which the world automotive industry later copied: *a load bearing body and independent front suspension*. Also, Lancia engineers patented a flexible engine mounting system to reduce engine vibrations to the chassis and body. This feature was introduced in 1931 on the "Astura." In 1933, the "Augusta" was the first saloon style car in the world and was the *first vehicle with internal steering*.

The "Aurelia," viewed in 1950 at the Turin Motor Show, was *the first standard production V6 engine in the world.* The "Aurelia" won many races including the 1953 and 1954 Targa Florio, PanAmerican, and Mille Miglia races. Other Lancias ("Fulvia HF," "Lancia Stratos," "037," "Delta HF 4WD," and "Delta HF Integrale") dominated the rally racing scene for twenty years. Lancia was bought by Fiat in 1969.

Maserati

This famous status symbol has offered the world the highest standard in both automotive luxury and speed. The Maserati Quattroporte and 3200GT are world class luxury cars. Like many other Italian car manufacturers, Maserati was also founded by a famous racecar driver, Alfieri Maserati. Maserati has been acquired by the giant Fiat corporation and is part of the Fiat Group.

Other Manufacturers

Other Italian automobile manufacturers are Dallara, DeTomaso, Edonis, Minardi, Qvale, Pagani and Osca.

Italian automotive suppliers include Alessio, ANSA, Brembo, Ferodo, Fondmetal, Marangoni, Magneti, Marelli, MOMO, MSW, Nardi, O.Z.Racing, Pirelli, Sparco and Speedline.

Automobile Design & Manufacturing - American

Mini-Van and Chrysler Motor Corp.
Lee Iacocca

Iacocca, the American son of Italian immigrants, is credited for saving the Chrysler Motor Company from certain bankruptcy when he was their Chairman and CEO. He is also distinguished for *creating the first mini-vans for the auto industry* in 1983 while working at Chrysler. After rescuing Chrysler from certain financial disaster, he announced in 1984 that Chrysler's profits were 2.4 billion dollars. (Also see the chapter on "American Government" for more on Lee).

Mustang – Ford Motor Company
Lee Iacocca

Lee Iacocca conceived the very successful "Mustang" automobile for the Ford Motor Company, and later became the president of Ford.

His brilliant advertising campaign included the unveiling of the "Mustang" at the 1964 New York City World's Fair. Almost half a million cars were sold the first year. The "Mustang" has become a classic car and a part of Americana.

Automobile Tires and Cable Systems
Pirelli

In 1872, Pirelli was established in Milan by Giovanni Battista Pirelli, a twentyfour-year-old engineer, and a year later he set up the first general rubber goods factory. By 1879 Pirelli was manufacturing insulated telegraph wires, bicycle tires by 1890, and car tires by 1901. During the first few decades of the 1900's Pirelli expanded factories to Spain, Great Britain, Belgium and Argentina. In these years Pirelli tires were used in many auto-racing victories, and Pirelli boasts over 80 victories in international Grand Prix races, and 18 victories in partnership with Alfa Romeo and Ferrari in the renowned "Mille Miglia" races. In 1949, the "Cinturato" radial tire was born and the company was able to expand to Canada (1953), Mexico (1956), France (1957), Greece (1960) and Turkey (1960). In 1963, the German Veith tire company was acquired. The company continued to expand and set up cable manufacturing in Peru (1968), Australia (1975), the USA (1978), France (1980) and the Ivory Coast (1980). In 1982, at their Battipaglia plant in Italy, they began producing fiber optics. In the 1980's they acquired other tire manufacturers, such as Armstrong, and cable manufacturers, such as Standard Telephone. In recent years, Pirelli's Cable and Systems division purchased cable operations from Germany's Siemans Corporation and other cable companies, and also has a strategic alliance with Cisco Systems for telecommunications cable.

Today, Pirelli has plants in 24 countries on 5 continents. The Tire division has 22 factories, 20,000 employees with sales of $2.8 billion Euro-dollars in 2001. The Cable & Systems division has over 60 factories and 18,000 employees with sales of $4.7 billion Euro-dollars in 2001. Pirelli *manufactures more electrical power supply cable for utilities than any other manufacturer in the world.* They are also the power cable supplier for the new super-conducting power lines that are being installed in the United States (refer to the "Science & Technology" chapter).

Bicycle Manufacturers

Italian bicycle manufacturers include: Ablocco, Basso, Bellesi, Bianchi, Campagnolo, Cinelli, Ciocc, Colnago, De Rosa, Guerciotti, Masciaghi, Moser Cicli, Olmo Biciclette, Pinarello, Scapin, Somec and Viner. Most offer high performance components and racing models.

Bridge Designs

Leonardo da Vinci

Leonardo designed a two-level bridge that dedicated the upper level for pedestrians and the lower for vehicles. The bridge used trusses very similar to those used in the 19th century.

He also designed a rotating bridge to connect the mainland with an island fortress. The bridge could be swung across the water by means of windlasses. In New York City the "A" train travels across Jamaica Bay through the use of a similar rotating bridge that turns horizontally to allow sailboats passage through the bay.

Andrea Palladio

In 1570, the celebrated Italian architect Andrea Palladio designed a covered bridge with innovative construction that has become the most common style used in the United States. The basic principle uses the *king post truss*, where the longest timbers are used as diagonals. Over two hundred years later, in 1798, the American Theodore Burr of Connecticut used this design and patented it in 1817. Because of his patent, Burr is often incorrectly credited for developing this common bridge design. Refer to the "Art & Architecture" chapter of this book for more on Andrea Palladio and his unprecedented influences on Western architecture including the federal buildings of the U.S. Capitol.

Caterpillar/Tank Tracks (Improvements)
C. Bonnagente

Bonnagente improved upon the early design of this type of track in 1893. Two Americans, Holt and Best perfected this track by adding a driving wheel.

Bow of a Venetian Gondola

Gondola
Venice

The gondola is a grand symbol of Venice. It is as much a work of art, as it is a highly functional form of transportation. Building a gondola is a specialized science and requires many specialized skills and artisans. Its history goes back to 1094 when the gondola was first documented in writings. The specialized design of the gondola offers a very functional craft. An individual pilot (gondolier) can propel and steer this fairly large craft with passengers, even though the gondola weighs 600 kilos (1323 lbs.) and is 11 meters long (36 feet). It is unique in that its hull is asymmetrical, its port (left) side is longer than its starboard (right) side. Incidentally, the nautical term *starboard* is derived from the gondola's right side or *steer-board* side. The craft's unique oar (*forcale*) has a highly specialized and complex shape resembling a half screw that maximizes power and steering. The iron head at the gondola's bow is not there just for show, but is a counterweight to offset the weight of the gondolier. The six bars on the iron head represent the six sections of Venice and the one bar facing

R. R. Esposito

back represents the Giudecca Island. The head's curved shape is symbolic of the Grand Canal's curves. Gondolas are always black, since the city passed this color ordinance hundreds of years ago when some gondoliers were painting their gondolas with garish and unaesthetic colors. So, you can paint your gondola any color that you desire, as long as it is black. Henry Ford would certainly agree.

Front Wheel Drive (Early Prototype)
Bucciali Brothers
Although they did not invent this concept, they were among the first to build a prototype in 1931. Front wheel drive cars were conceived by Jean A. Gregoire and Pierre Fenaille in 1926. The Citroen's famous "7A" was the first mass produced front wheel drive car, which was introduced in 1934 in France.

Helicopter, First

Leonardo da Vinci
His very famous 15th century drawing of a flying machine with a screw type propeller above the cockpit looks very much like today's helicopter and inspired others to make models in the years that followed. These men include two Italian physicians, Carlo Forlanini (see reference below) and Giovanni Alfonso Borelli. In 1670, Borelli attempted to use artificial wings for flying. (See the Airplane reference for more on da Vinci and flight. For more on Borelli see the "Medicine, Biology & Health," and "Science & Technology" chapters.)

Enrico Forlanini & Pateras Pescara
Forlanini built and flew *the first helicopter* in 1877. The flight lasted a minute and the craft lifted 15 meters (50 feet). It was powered by a small steam engine. In the early 20th century, the Italian Pateras Pescara, as well as others in the United States perfected the craft to the point where it could endure flights of almost one hour at relatively low altitudes.

Highway Design- Modern
Leonardo da Vinci
DaVinci drew double tiers of roadways that anticipated today's modern elevated highways. He designed spiral loops to ascend and descend the upper and lower roadways, much like today's circular entrances and exit ramps to highways, which are often called jughandles. Again daVinci was designing the future 500 years before it actually came to pass.

Hydrofoil, First
Enrico Forlanini
Forlanini invented the *first true hydrofoil* in 1900 and his improved versions reached the incredible speed of 80 km/h (50 mph), as early as 1905. His invention was the first to lift and propel a "boat" with actual hydrofoils through the water. He also conceived the principle of the hydrofoil in 1898. In 1918, Alexander Graham Bell built, with Casey Baldwin, a hydrofoil that reached a speed of 100km/h (62 mph). (As with the telephone, again Alexander Graham Bell followed an earlier original Italian inventor.)

Motorcycle Design and Manufacturing - Italian
Italians have excelled in designing and manufacturing award-winning motorcycles for decades. Italian motorcycles have won awards for racing, engineering and styling. Here is a list of motorcycle companies in Italy:

Benelli made large 6 cylinder bikes in the 1970's and 1980's.

Bianchi claimed 95 victories in only 5 years, from 1925 to 1930.

Bimota not only makes motorcycles, but supplies frames for Harley-Davidson and Yamaha racing bikes.

Ducati has made many great motorcycles for decades. Their new "Monster" has a frame and gas tank design that makes the bike look a bit like a horse arching its back ready to kick. This author saw a beautiful 1999 model in red and black. The famous bike designer, Dr.

Fabio Taglioni joined Ducati in the 1950's and helped the company develop world class bikes. Ducati also pioneered the use of *desmonic valves*, which use geared rotating cams in lieu of lifters and springs. This innovation is a significant advantage when engines reach high revolutions per minute.

Gilera built the "Saturno" model that won the last Targa Florio (Sicilian Road Race) in the 1940's.

Morbidelli has manufactured a massive V8 engine for its bikes.

Moto Guzzi designed a flywheel in 1924 that was so sophisticated that it was used until the 1970's. They now offer a very wide range of big iron bikes over 900 cc's.

MV Augusta bikes reach speeds in excess of 280 km/h (175mph) and their new bikes still have an impressive appeal in terms of styling and performance.

Other Motorcycle Manufacturers
Other Italian motorcycle and scooter manufacturers include Aermacchi, Aprilia, Beta, Cagiva, Garelli, Ghezzi & Brian, Husqvarna, Italjet, Lambretta Laverda, Magni, Malaguti, Mondial, Moto Morini, Panilla, Piaggio, Vespa and VOR.

Other Motorcycle Suppliers
AGV helmets & gear, Alpinestars gear, Arrow exhausts, AXO helmets & gear, Bitubo shocks, Brembo brakes, Ceriani forks, Dainese helmets & gear, Dell'Orto carburetors, Devel helmets, Ferodo brake pads, Giannelli exhausts, GIVI luggage, Grimeca components, Jolly Moto exhausts, Leo Vince exhausts, Malossi tuning, MAPE engine parts, Marchesini wheels, Marzocchi forks, Nolan helmets, Nonfango luggage, Paioli forks, Pirelli tires, Polini tuning, Regina chains, SIDI gear, SPIDI gear, Termignoni exhausts and Verlicchi frames.

Note:
In the summer of 1998, the Guggenheim museum in New York City was literally filled with motorcycles for a very popular exhibit of engineering, history and design. All of the manufacturers listed above had bikes included in this unusual and exciting exhibit. This author

visited the Guggenheim and admits this was a very engaging piece of research. Two motorcycle museums, one in California and the other in Georgia were the source for most bikes in this fantastic exhibit.

Parachute
Leonardo da Vinci
Da Vinci is credited for inventing the parachute in 1480. In his "Notebooks," next to his illustration of a parachute in use, Leonardo writes: "If a man has a tent of linen without any apertures, twelve ells across and twelve in depth, he can throw himself down from any great height without injury." The first person to jump from an airplane with a modern parachute (and live to tell about it) was Captain Albert Berry, who jumped from a U.S. Army plane in 1912.

Ship Building
Leonardo da Vinci
Da Vinci studied the shapes of fish and water dynamics and designed new very sleek "spindle-shaped" hulls, similar to today's racing hulls. This was a great improvement over the round-bottomed vessels used in his time. He pioneered modern marine engineering and architecture.

He also designed a double-hulled ship anticipating modern double-hulls and modern bulkhead designs that compartmentalize the hull in order to isolate flooding.

Variable Speed Drive
Leonardo da Vinci
Da Vinci designed a three speed variable gear that anticipated many modern applications. He synchronized three different sized cogged wheels to one "lantern wheel" that allowed three different speeds. This is the basic principle used in the transmission of the modern automobiles, ships and other gear-driven devices.

෬

Chapter XXII

WORLD PEACE

"Pax Romana"
- This Latin phrase means "Peace of Rome,"
the world's longest period of peace -

U.N. Dag Hammerskjold Peace Prize
Enzo Ferrari

Racecar legend Enzo Ferrari was awarded the Dag Hammerskjold Peace Prize by the United Nations in 1962. For more information on his incredible international life refer to the "Transportation" chapter.

Nobel Prize for Peace
Ernesto T. Moneta

Ernesto Teodoro Moneta was born to aristocratic parents in Milan in 1833. During much of his early life he was involved (1848 to 1866) with the independence and unification of Italy, fighting alongside of the great Garibaldi in 1859 and later under General Sirtori in 1860. Ironically this patriotic, idealistic fighter, ultimately became a charismatic and dynamic pacifist. After his early years, Moneta became the editor of the daily newspaper "Il Secolo," a position he held from 1867 until 1895. The newspaper became a powerful and influential opinion shaper under his guidance.

By the turn of the century, Moneta retired as editor of "Il Secolo" and had finished over thirty years of research on war and peace. He then published his massive opus entitled "Le guerre, le insurrezioni e la pace nel secolo XIX" ("Wars, Insurrections and Peace in the Nineteenth Century") in 1903, 1904, 1906 and 1910. In the first volume, he describes the development of the international peace movement during the course of the 19th century. The major theme in this work details the lack of substantive results achieved by wars and militarism. Much of Moneta's life was then dedicated as a peace activist.

- In 1887, Moneta had helped to found, and then financially supported with his newspaper pension, the l'Unione lombarda per la pace e l'arbitrato internazionale (The Lombard Union for International Peace and Arbitration aka The Lombard Peace Union).
- In 1890, Moneta began publishing an annual almanac called "L'Amico della pace." He also continued to contribute editorial columns to "Il Secolo" and republished many of his earlier articles as pamphlets and periodicals. Moneta became convinced of the power of using propaganda for peace, and also printed simple one-page articles, which he distributed to rural schoolmasters.
- In 1895, Moneta became the Italian representative to the Commission of the International Peace Bureau.
- In 1898, he founded a review, "La Vita internazionale," which gained prestige throughout all of Italy.
- Moneta helped to found the Società per la pace e la giustizia internazionale (Society for International Peace and Justice), which lasted from 1887 until 1937.
- Moneta lectured at the newly founded Italian Popular University and attended peace congresses for many years.
- In 1906, he planned and had constructed a Pavilion for Peace at the Milan International Exposition, during which he presided over the 15th annual International Peace Congress.

In 1907, Moneta was awarded the Nobel Prize for Peace for his lifelong dedication to peace efforts. He died of pneumonia in 1918 at the age of eighty-five. A monument erected to him in 1925 displays the duality of this dynamic, charismatic and idealistic leader: "A partisan of Garibaldi's and as an apostle of peace."

World's Longest Period of Peace
Pax Romana (Peace of Rome)
The world's longest period of peace was the result of the unifying effect of the Roman Republic and the subsequent Empire. For over 250 years, from 27 BC to 235 AD, the whole Western world including the Byzantine world, was characterized by peace, technological advancement and great prosperity. This peace was the direct result of the effective and stable government of Rome. This period known as *Pax Romana*, included the very orderly succession of leaders that included the "Five Good Emperors" (Nerva, Trajan, Hadrian, Antoninus Pius and Marcus Aurelius). Their government provided predictability, law, commerce, prosperity, protection from wanton violence, and a reliable food supply for its citizens. As a result, the Britons, the Gauls, the Visigoths, the Vandals, the Slavs, and others relinquished their tribal loyalties to become Roman citizens. By participating in the Roman standards, society, and citizenship they gained the "Peace of Rome"- *Pax Romana*!

The efficient Roman government and vast communications capabilities, which spanned the known Western world, precipitated world peace, international trade, technology and commerce. The large Roman navy escorted and protected commercial shipping and other travelers at sea. The Roman army similarly protected land travelers over 60,000 miles of Roman roads. The many cities of the Roman Republic and Empire prospered as a result of peace and efficient commerce. The capital city, Rome, became truly an international showcase and city. With a population of approximately one million, it drew people from all over the world seeking access to education, commerce and entertainment. The height of *Pax Romana* was characterized by the lack of any major wars and great technological development that lasted for two hundred years spanning the reign of Emperor Constantine in 27 BC to the death of Emperor Marcus Aurelius in 180 AD. The famous historian Edward Gibbon who authored "The Decline and Fall of the Roman Empire" states in his book that *Pax Romana* was "...the period in the history of the world during which the human race was the most happy and prosperous." Even during our "civilized" 20th century, our world has known two world wars, horrific systematized torture, and mass murder of millions, such as the holocaust in Germany, as well as, wars in: Korea, Vietnam, Arab-Israeli, Iraq, Bosnia, Kosovo and Africa. Our 21st century has experienced global terrorism that our civilization now works to eradicate.

The "American Government" chapter of this book describes the Roman Republic's government in detail and how its design guided the formation of America's democratic government. America's founding fathers applied principles of government that were first developed and perfected over the centuries by the Roman Republic. The New World in America was founded upon the lessons learned from an older order. Let us hope the new "Pax Americana" with global alliances will prevail, endure and bring our world and civilization to new heights for the benefit of all mankind.

Italy Travel Guide

Introduction

This unique 'Italy Travel Guide' organizes points of interest that appear in the chapters of this book by Italian city- unlike the entries in this book's chapters, which are organized by subject. This guide also includes many other attractions and points of interest for travelers touring Italy's principle destinations. This guide combines the background and context of a city's history with its best attractions, to produce a uniquely comprehensive guide. If you are planning a trip to Italy, use this guide to enhance your appreciation as you visit the many regions and attractions of Italy. Conversely, if you are not planning a trip, this guide will offer a virtual tour that will enlighten your understanding of Italy. This guide offers a thorough review of the attractions in and around the major Italian cities. However, it is important to realize that there are other attractions and points of interest in Italy, as well as the beautifully scenic Italian countryside that is only fully appreciated when the human eye captures its panoramic beauty.

Map of Italy

R. R. Esposito

Bologna

What to See in Bologna

- The world's first true university with curriculum, standards, examinations and degrees was the University of Bologna, which was founded in the 11th century. Bologna's instructors, who could confer degrees upon graduates, were called *collegia*. In the 13th century, Bologna also founded the oldest university-based medical school in the world. The Archiginnasio is the University's oldest official building.

- Archaeological Museum (Museo Civico Archeologico) houses one of Italy's major Egyptian collections, and includes mummies and sarcophagi, as well as Greco-Roman works of art.

- Basilica di San Domenico dates back to the 13th century. The basilica houses the beautiful tomb of St. Domenico, in front of the chapel Cappella della Madonna. This sculptured tomb is a Renaissance masterpiece, which is a joint effort by several sculptors including Pisano and the young Michelangelo. Also, the choir stalls are a significant work of art that were carved by Damiano da Bergamo in the 16th century.

- The Basilica di San Petronio contains 22 chapels. The most interesting one is the Bolognini Chapel (Cappella Bolognini), which is located 4th on the left as one enters. It is decorated with some of the best Italian Gothic frescos.

- The National Picture Gallery (Pinacoteca Nazionale di Bologna) houses the most significant works of art produced in Bologna from the 14th to 17th centuries. The gallery also houses works by other major Italian artists, such as Raphael and Giotto.

Who is from Bologna

- The Italian anatomist, Marcello Malpighi is considered the Father of Biological Microscopy. He was born March 10, 1628 in Crevalcuore near Bologna. He received his M.D. and Ph.D. from the University of Bologna in 1653.

- Luigi Galvani was born September 9, 1737 in Bologna and died December 4, 1798. He received a medical degree from the University of Bologna and became a professor of anatomy there as well. Galvani contributed revolutionary, scientific knowledge based upon his experiments on the effects of electric impulses on muscle. He was the first to discover the connection between life and electricity, paving the way for an entirely new area of biomedical research.

- Guglielmo Marconi was born April 25, 1874 in Bologna. After years of study and experimentation Marconi succeeded in inventing the first practical radio system. On December 12, 1901, Marconi realized the dream of his youth. He accomplished the first transatlantic radio communication, which took place between a transmitting station at Poldhu, on the English coast at Cornwall, and Signal Hill in Newfoundland 2000 miles away. He was awarded the Nobel Prize in physics in 1909.

- Rafael Bombelli was born January 1526 in Bologna and died about 1573, presumably in Rome. His giant contribution was that he was the first to document the rules for addition and multiplication of complex numbers.

- Ulisse Aldrovandi, naturalist and physician, was born in Bologna on September 11, 1522. Although he created an extensive collection of flora, fauna and geological specimens, he never traveled and eventually died in his native city, Bologna on May 4, 1605. In Bologna, he created one of the world's greatest collections of natural history. He became a leading authority in natural history and wrote a 13-volume natural history encyclopedia.

- Ivan the Great, who lived from 1462 AD to 1505 AD, brought the Italian architect Aristotle Fioravanti from Bologna to Russia to construct a series of cathedrals in the Kremlin. The magnificent Cathedral of the Annunciation built from 1484 AD to 1489 AD is an excellent example of Italian style architecture and displays beautiful symmetry and many domes.

Carrara

What to See in Carrara
- Carrara is internationally famous for its flawless white marble and also as the home of many distinguished sculptors. Carrara's marble quarries are the world's oldest industrial site in continuous use. The Romans operated quarries there over two thousand years ago. A Carrara marble quarry is the source for Michelangelo's "David." The sculptor also had a home there, which still stands in the city's cathedral square. Quarries are open to the public in nearby Colonnata and Fantiscritta.

- Carrara's Marble Museum has over 300 samples of marble from all over the world. The museum also has information about the area's geology and other architectural, industrial and technical exhibits.

Who is from Carrara
- In 1866, Attilio Piccirilli was born in Carrara. Sculptor Attilio Piccirilli and his five brothers from Carrara founded a sculpting studio in New York City and carved the majestic statue "Seated Lincoln" at the Lincoln Memorial, as well as many other works in the United States.

Cremona

What to See in Cremona
- The Museo Stradivariano is a museum dedicated to Antonio Stradivari. It houses drawings, models and violins crafted by the master. Stradivari is buried in Piazza Roma in Cremona.
- The Palazzo del Comune is a major building on the city's square and contains violins by Stradivari, Nicolo Amati and Guarnieri.
- Continuing in this tradition, the city of Cremona is still the source of the world's finest violins and other stringed instruments. You can make a reservation to visit a violin workshop on Via Sicardo near the Piazza del Comune in the city's historical center.

Who is from Cremona
- The famous Amati family of violin makers was founded in Cremona by Andrea Amati who lived from 1530 to 1578 (or 1611). He is the first recognized genius to craft superb violins. Amati violins are revered among the finest in the world.
- Nicolo Amati (1596-1684), the grandson of Andrea Amati and the son of Girolamo, was perhaps the most famous member of this distinguished family of violin makers. Nicolo's shop is where the great Antonio Stradivari and other masters learned the art of crafting fine violins and other stringed instruments.
- Stradivarius violins are the finest violins in existence, offering both visual and acoustic perfection. The master craftsman, Antonio Stradivari, born about 1644 in Cremona, designed and built these works of art. No other violins have been made that equal the acoustic perfection of these priceless instruments.

- Claudio Monteverdi was born in Cremona. (See the section on Venice in this chapter for details of Monteverdi's life and accomplishments.)

Florence / Firenze

What to See in Florence

- The Piazza della Signoria is at the heart of Florence's social and political life. On this famous plaza stands the palace, Palazzo Vecchio, which contains works by Michelangelo, Vasari, Bronzino, Ghirlandaio and others. Prominently displayed in front of the palace is a replica of the grand statue "David" by Michelangelo. The original is in Florence, but is housed inside the Galleria dell' Accademia (Academy of Fine Arts). Tourists wander through the magnificent courtyards in the area to experience Florence.

- There are many museums in Florence, but the most famous is the Uffizi. The Uffizi is one of the greatest art museums in the world. It contains countless masterpieces from masters such as, Botticelli, Caravaggio, Giotto, Michelangelo, Raphael, Titian, Vasari, Goya, Rembrandt and many others. Among the many masterpieces, it houses Botticelli's famous "The Birth of Venus" (1485).

- Almost as great as the Uffizi, Florence's Bargello is also an important art gallery. Among the many masterpieces, it houses Donatello's "David" (1430) and his "St. George" (1416). The museum also has a room dedicated to Michelangelo.

- The church of San Lorenzo was rebuilt by Brunelleschi and contains a highly innovative staircase and other works by Michelangelo, including the tomb he carved for the Duke of Nemours (1520-1534).

- The church of Santa Maria del Carmine contains the Brancacci chapel, which displays the early works of Masaccio that revolutionized perspective and narrative drama in paintings. Both da Vinci and Michelangelo visited the chapel to study these works.

- The church of Santa Maria Novella designed by Leon Battista Alberti (1456-1470) contains Masaccio's famous "Trinity" and other works by Ghirlandaio.

- The palace, Palazzo Pitti contains two art galleries, one of which is the Galleria Palatina. This magnificent gallery contains works by Botticelli, Titian, Tintoretto, Raphael, Caravaggio and others, as well as Antonio Canova's "Venus Italica" (1810), which was commissioned by Napoleon.

- The Galleria dell' Accademia (Academy of Fine Arts) was founded in 1563 and houses one of the finest art collections in the world. Probably the most famous piece in the museum is the grand statue "David" by Michelangelo. This famous statue of white marble depicts the young biblical King David standing unclothed and ready for battle with Goliath. A classic example of the weak overcoming the strong. It is considered a classic example of artistic perfection and wonderfully portrays the power and beauty of the human form. This is one of the most recognizable statues in the world. Michelangelo was one of the greatest artists of all times. He was a sculptor, painter and architect, who was born just outside of Florence in the village of Caprese on March 6, 1475.
- The church of Santa Croce, founded in 1294, contains the tombs of Galileo, Machiavelli and Michelangelo. Amazingly, the church also contains frescos by Giotto and the church's adjacent chapel was designed by Brunelleschi.
- The world's first orphanage, Spedale degli Innocenti, was founded in Florence in 1444. Part of the building is still an orphanage and another section houses several paintings by Renaissance masters, such as della Robbia and Donatello.
- The Santa Maria Del Fiore cathedral is probably the most photographed image in Florence. In particular, its massive dome towers above the city. See the reference below about its architect and engineer, Filippo Brunelleschi, for more information.

Who is from Florence

- Filippo Brunelleschi, probably the greatest of all early Renaissance architects, was born in Florence in 1377. Brunelleschi accepted the challenge to build the massive dome that was originally designed for the Santa Maria Del Fiore cathedral in 1367 by the famous architect Neri di Fioravanti. Brunelleschi built what is still the largest masonry dome in the world, measuring 142 feet (43.2 meters) in diameter and 300 feet (90 meters) in height. He built the dome for Santa Maria Del Fiore without the use of a scaffold! Brunelleschi's design eliminated the supporting scaffold, and masons laid over 4 million bricks higher and higher, sustained by the architectural "chains." Further, the marble lantern that rests atop the dome weighs over one million pounds.

Tourists can climb an interior staircase to the top of the massive structure for a panoramic view of Florence.

- Giotto di Bondone, known simply as Giotto, was born in 1267 in the small village of Vespignano, near Florence and died on January 8, 1337. He is often called the single most influential artist in European history.

- Donatello was born in 1386 in Florence and died on December 13, 1466. He was the first sculptor to explore depth and perspective, refining measurement and distance to create very realistic three-dimensional forms, unlike the earlier medieval and gothic statues.

- Leon Battista Alberti was a quintessential Renaissance man or "universal man" who excelled in many intellectual areas. He was born to a wealthy merchant-banker family in Genoa on February 14, 1401. He lived in Florence and died in Rome on April 25, 1472 after a very full and accomplished life. He was a writer, architect, humanist, and principal originator of Renaissance art theory. In his book "De Pictura" ("On Painting"), published in 1435, Alberti was the first to establish a scientific system for linear perspective that is currently used by most artists.

- America is named after the Italian navigator and explorer Amerigo Vespucci. He was born in Florence in 1454. He was the first to realize that he was exploring new continents, not islands near China or India.

- Giovanni da Verrazzano (or Verrazano) was born about 1485 near Florence and died about 1528. Verrazzano was the first to prove that the land was a New World and not part of Asia. The Verrazzano Bridge, which spans over the Hudson River in New York City, is named after this explorer.

- Dante was born in Florence somewhere between May 15 and June 15, 1265, to an aristocratic family. Dante is considered one of the greatest of Western literary geniuses, the others being Boccaccio, Petrarca, Shakespeare and Goethe. Dante's massive poem, "The Divine Comedy" is considered a literary masterpiece.

- Giovanni Boccaccio was born (June or July, 1313) in Certaldo or in Florence and died in a small town outside of Florence on December 21, 1375. He is considered one of the greatest figures in European literature. Boccaccio was an Italian literary giant, the "father of Italian prose" and the inventor of the short story, as well. He spent most of his adult life in Florence where he met and was greatly influenced by Petrarch (or Petrarca), another European literary giant.

- Francesco Petrarca was a citizen of Florence. Petrarca was a scholar and writer who greatly influenced the literature of Western Europe. The love lyrics in his "Sonnets to Laura" became stylistic models for poets in Italy, Spain, France, and England for over 300 years. These are called Petrarchan sonnets and are very common in English poetry.
- Carlo Collodi was born in Florence in 1826 and died there as well on October 26, 1890. He wrote the fairy tale "The Adventures of Pinocchio" in 1881, which was first translated into English in 1892.
- Bartolomeo Cristofori was a harpsichord maker who also maintained dozens of musical instruments for the famous Grand Prince of Tuscany, Ferdinando de' Medici. In 1709, Cristofori created a brilliant musical innovation in Florence. He invented and built the world's first piano.
- The modern autobiography was first created during the Italian Renaissance in the 16th century. The famous sculptor and goldsmith, Benvenuto Cellini, wrote his autobiography from 1558 to 1562, which was published in 1728. Cellini was born in Florence in 1500 and died in 1571.
- Through business associates Jefferson corresponded with and later befriended an Italian immigrant named Filippo Mazzei (aka Philip Mazzei). Mazzei was an Italian physician, horticulturist, intellectual, and businessman from Florence who was born in 1730. The great doctrine "All men are created equal" in the American Declaration of Independence originated with Filippo Mazzei, close friend of Thomas Jefferson.
- The invention of corrective spectacles (eyeglasses) around 1280 in Florence by Salvino Armati was exploited and marketed by his colleague Alessandro della Spina. Centuries later, Venice became the center for eyeglass production in the 16th century and gradually over the decades eyeglasses became more commonplace throughout Europe and the world.
- Antonio Meucci worked on many different projects, inventions and patents. He has been credited as the original inventor of the telephone. Meucci was born in Florence on April 13, 1808 and attended the prestigious Academy of Fine Arts in Florence where he studied physics and science. In NYC, he invented the first telephone and the U.S. House of Representatives passed Resolution 269 recognizing Meucci as the true inventor of the telephone.

- L. Tetrazzini was born 1871 in Florence and died in 1940. She was a coloratura soprano and sang internationally, including at the Metropolitan Opera in New York City (1908). The dish "Chicken Tetrazzini" is named after Luisa Tetrazzini.
- The Gucci family tradition of crafting beautiful luxury leather products began in 1930 when Guccio Gucci opened his first store in Florence.

Other Interesting Information

- The first premium-based insurance policies covering sea traffic appear to have been developed in Italy by the Lombards of the Lombardia region of northern Italy during medieval times. The well known marine insurance, Ordinances of Florence, was passed in 1523.
- The beginnings of ballet took place in the Italian courts in Florence during the late 1400's. The word ballet comes from the Italian word *ballare*, which means, *to dance*. Italian composers wrote the two earliest known ballets.
- Opera began in Florence by a group of scholars and musicians called the "Camerata Fiorentine." Vicenzo Galilei, the father of the great scientist Galileo Galilei, was a member of this founding group.

Genoa / Genova

What to See in Genoa

- After extensive renovations, the Acquario di Genova (Genoa Aquarium) reopened in 1992 on the 500th anniversary of Columbus's discovery of the New World. This is the largest aquarium in Europe, containing over 40 tanks, and boasts exhibits of species from all over the globe. You can reach the aquarium within a 15-minute walk from Stazione Principe (Prince Station).
- Genoa is well known for its medieval churches. The Cattedrale di San Lorenzo and Campanile (Cathedral of San Lorenzo and Bell-tower) is by far the largest in the city. This beautiful cathedral's facade boasts black and white marble bands in a style common to Pisa. The cathedral dates back to the 13th century, and the campanile (bell tower) dates back to the 16th century. The Cappella di San Giovanni (Chapel of John the Baptist) is also of interest, it is said to contain the remains of the saint for whom it is named, as well as other relics.

- On Via Garibaldi one can find the Palazzo Tursi (Number 9), now home to municipal offices. It houses many historical documents of Genoa including letters written by Christopher Columbus and a violin that was owned by Niccolo Paganini.
- The Galleria Nazionale (National Gallery), originally a 16th century palace, now houses many notable works of art including Antonello da Messina's "Ecce Homo" and Giovanni Pisano's "Guistizia." The gallery is also known for its collection of silver works, furniture, ceramics and other art.

Who is from Genoa

- Christopher Columbus was born about 1451 in Genoa. Columbus was an exceptionally gifted navigator. On October 12, 1492 Columbus changed the course of history when he discovered the New World, landing on the island of San Salvador in the Bahamas. There is a small stone house in Genoa, next to the Porta Soprana, which is purported to be the childhood home of Columbus.
- Giovanni Cabotto (John Cabot) was born in Genoa around 1450. Cabotto discovered the North American shore when he reached the coast of Newfoundland in present day Canada on June 24, 1497.
- Niccolo Paganini was born on October 27, 1782 in Genoa and died on May 27, 1840. He was the leading violin virtuoso of his time, touring all of Europe. He also composed music including 24 capricci (or caprices) for unaccompanied violin. Paganini was known for his brilliant technique, especially pizzicato, fingering and improvisation. He extended the way the violin is played.
- Eugenio Montale was born in Genoa in 1896. He was awarded a Nobel Prize in 1975 for his poetry. Montale published six books of poems from 1925 to 1976.

Other Interesting Information

A strong twilled cotton fabric was created in the town of Genoa. The French called this cloth "jeans," most probably derived from the first syllable of the Italian town's name. A softer fabric was later woven in the town of Nimes in France. This was known as "serge de Nimes" and Americans called this cloth "denim."

Milan / Milano

What to See in Milan

- One of Leonardo da Vinci's most famous paintings is the "Last Supper" ("Cenacolo"), which is in the cathedral Santa Maria delle Grazie in Milan. Incidentally, Leonardo's other masterpiece, the "Mona Lisa," hangs in the Louvre in Paris.

- The Leonardo da Vinci National Museum of Science & Technology (Museo Nazionale della Scienza e della Tecnica Leonardo da Vinci) contains many models of da Vinci's inventions. There are also many other interesting exhibits on science, astronomy and physics.

- La Scala opera house is considered one of the finest in the world. The great neoclassical architect Giuseppe Piermarini designed La Scala, which opened on August 3, 1778.

- The magnificent Galleria Vittorio Emanuele was designed in 1861 by architect Giuseppe Mengoni. Construction began in 1865 and was completed in 1877. However, Mengoni fell from a scaffold and died tragically a year before its completion. This massive and ornate indoor shopping plaza is enclosed with spacious glass domes and vaulted ceilings above the walkways. A triumphal arch was added to the Galleria in 1877 as well. The Galleria has many stylish shops, boutiques, cafes and restaurants. Numerous beautiful mosaics cover the floor. These include graceful patterns, as well as works of art that depict the four continents of earth, the twelve heavenly signs of the zodiac, as well as the human endeavors in art, agriculture, science and industry. Tourists can be seen stepping on the genitals of the Taurus the Bull mosaic for good luck. (Perhaps not such good luck for the bull.) The Galleria is also known as Il Salotto Milano, meaning Milan's drawing room. On each end of this 640 foot (196 meter) complex one finds the Piazza della Scala and the Piazza della Duomo.

- The Piazza della Duomo is connected to Milan's massive Gothic cathedral, Duomo, which is crowned with graceful tall spires, and lies at the city's center. Housed in the Palazzo Reale, is a museum that documents the six centuries of the Duomo's history and includes many historical artifacts

- The Pirelli headquarters building was designed by Ponti and Nervi. It is an elegant and innovative skyscraper built in 1959.

496 R. R. Esposito

- The Pinacoteca Ambrosiana is home to a priceless collection of over 30,000 historic documents and manuscripts, such as an early edition (1353) of Dante's "Divine Comedy," da Vinci's "Atlantic Codex" (15th century), and a 5th century edition of "Iliad." The museum also includes an art gallery that features paintings by masters, such as da Vinci, Caravaggio, Titian and Botticelli.
- The finest art museum in Milan is the Palazzo di Brera. It includes works by Mantegna, Bellini, Raphael, Tintoretto and Caravaggio. The museum offers one of the best art galleries in Italy.
- The 4th century Basilica di Sant'Eustorgio has a bell tower that was built in the 13th century. In 1305, the tower received a clock, which was the first tower clock in the world. The first clock that had hours of equal increments was built in the 1330's for the church of St. Gothard in Milan. Prior to the clock at St. Gothard, medieval clocks had hours that varied from approximately 38 to 82 of today's minutes, and as such, were not particularly useful. A legend maintains that during the 3rd century the Basilica di Sant'Eustorgio contained the tomb of the Three Wise Men of Christian fame. (The word *clock* comes from a Latin word meaning *bell*, since very early clocks had no dial but chimed the hours.)

Who is from Milan
- Enrico Bombieri was born on November 26, 1946 in Milan. In 1974 at the International Congress of Mathematicians held in Vancouver, Bombieri was awarded the coveted Fields Medal for his outstanding work. Since there is no Nobel Prize in Mathematics offered, the Fields Medal is offered to recognize Mathematics on an international level.
- In 1872, Pirelli was established in Milan by Giovanni Battista Pirelli, a twentyfour-year-old engineer, and a year later he set up the first general rubber goods factory. Today Pirelli is known for automobile tires, racing tires, and it is the world's largest supplier of electrical power supply cable used by utility companies. Their sleek headquarters building in Milan is a well known icon of modern industrialization.
- Ernesto Teodoro Moneta was born in Milan in 1833. During much of his early life he was involved (1848 to 1866) with the independence and unification of Italy, fighting alongside of the great Garibaldi in 1859 and later under General Sirtori in 1860. Later in life he became

an active pacifist. In 1907, Moneta was awarded the Nobel Prize for Peace for his lifelong dedication to peace efforts.

Other Interesting Information
- In 313 AD, in Milan, the Roman Emperor Constantine declared his Edict of Milan that made Christianity a lawful religion. This edict, in part, was the result of the Emperor's religious vision during a successful battle and his subsequent conversion to Christianity. The other driving factor behind the edict was that the Emperor was using Christianity as a means to unify the growing disparity throughout the Roman Empire. The Romans colonized Milan in 222 BC. Its original Roman name was *Mediolanum*, meaning *city in the middle of the plain*.

Naples / Napoli

What to See in Naples
- The Museo Archeologico Nazionale is one of Italy's most important museums. It houses many Roman artifacts and art including artifacts from nearby Pompeii.
- The Museo de Capodimonte houses a magnificent collection of paintings by Botticelli, Titian, Raphael and others. The museum was originally the Capodimonte palace and is located in a park-like setting.
- In the Brandi Restaurant in Naples, Raphael Esposito invented a new pizza pie as a special gift for Queen Margarita of Naples and called it the Margarita pie in her honor. He also helped to popularize the Neapolitan pizza style in Italy during the late 19th century.
- The city's Aquarium (Acquario) is located in Villa Comunale, a municipal park. The Aquarium was established in the 1800's and is the oldest aquarium in Europe. It offers exhibits on approximately 200 marine species of plants and fish that are indigenous to the Bay of Naples.
- San Lorenzo Maggiore is the greatest of Naples's "layered" historical churches. It was built in 1265 over a 6th century basilica, which was built over other ancient Roman structural remains and artifacts. The church foundations are actually built upon walls of the basilica law courts of ancient Naples (Neapolis), which date back to 600 BC. The church contains nine chapels with inlaid marble and the highlight is the Tino da Camaino's canopy tomb of Catherine of

Austria (circa 1320's). In 1341, Boccaccio first met King Robert of Anjou's daughter Maria in this church. She became immortalized as "Fiammetta" in his famous writings.

▪ The famous Abbey of Monte Cassino, located on a hill 70 miles (112 km) north of Naples, is where the great St. Thomas Aquinas received his education as a boy. He later attended the University of Naples in 1236. The University of Naples was founded in 1224 and is now one of Europe's oldest.

Who is from Naples

▪ Giambattista Basile was born in Naples around 1575. He wrote "Il Pentamerone" ("The Tale of Tales") which was a fantastic anthology of 50 folk tales written in the Neapolitan dialect. His tales include the original stories of "Cinderella," "Rapunzel," "Sleeping Beauty," and "Snow White."

▪ Torquato Tasso was born in Sorrento and lived from 1544 to 1595. Sorrento is on the Gulf of Naples, about 35 miles (56 km) south of Naples. He wrote several famous works, but his greatest masterpiece was "Jerusalem Delivered." This treasured work had a tremendous influence on English poets, most especially the great John Milton.

▪ Giambattista Della Porta was born on November 15, 1535 near Naples. He was one of the first to have conceived a steam engine as described in his 1606 work entitled "De'spiritali." Another one of Della Porta's significant contributions was to the development of the camera. He was the first to suggest using a convex lens with the *camera obscura.*

▪ Alessandro Gagliano founded the Neapolitan school of violin building, and crafted instruments from about 1700 to 1735. He studied in Cremona with the two giants of his craft, Nicolo Amati and Antonio Stradivari. He later returned to Naples. His fine instruments are described as having a "mellow" quality.

▪ Enrico Caruso was born to a poor family on February 27, 1873 in Naples. His perfect voice with massive power, range and beauty makes experts describe him as the greatest tenor in the history of opera.

▪ Giambattista Vico was born in Naples on June 23, 1668 and died there as well on January 23, 1744. Vico spent his entire life in Naples. Vico is generally regarded as the founder of modern philosophy of history and is often considered the founder of the philosophy of culture and the philosophy of mythology. His concepts helped explain the birth, development and decay of civilizations, and included studies of their language, religion and myths.

Other Interesting Information

- Neapolitan dentists in 1802 realized that patients with certain tooth discoloration were cavity free. The spots turned out to be the result of high fluoride levels in the water and soil in certain sections surrounding Naples. They were the first to promote fluoride treatments.
- The world's first secular university founded and run by laypersons, was the University of Naples founded in 1224 by emperor Frederick II.

Padua / Padova

What to See in Padua

- Padua is a small city, which is located just outside of Venice. Padua's chapel Cappella degli Scrovegni was built in 1303 by Enrico Scrovegni for his deceased father. The chapel's interior is covered entirely with frescos that were painted by the great Giotto.
- The Basilica di Sant'Antonio, also known as Il Santo, was built in 1232. It is one of Italy's most important churches. The structure's architecture exhibits Byzantine influences, and inside the altar features magnificent reliefs carved by Donatello.
- A tour of the Padua University offers a glimpse into the beginnings of one of the world's first universities and medical schools. Padua is Italy's second oldest university, founded in 1222. Only the University of Bologna is older, which is the world's first university. The University of Bologna also started the world's first university-based medical school. In the late 1500's, the University of Padua's prestigious medical school was the first to construct a multi-tiered operating theater (six floors), the world's first such facility. During the 16th century, the famous Gabriele Fallopio was a student and instructor there. Although Galileo entered Pisa University as a medical student in 1581, he later decided to become a mathematician, and from 1592 to 1610 was a professor of mathematics at Padua University. In Padua, Galileo's passion for physics and astronomy was nurtured. The lectern he used from 1592 to 1610 as professor is on display at the University. The great Petrarca (Petrarch) also lectured at Padua.

Who is from Padua

- Andrea Palladio was born on November 30, 1508 in Padua, and his original birth name was Andrea di Pietro della Gondola. He is considered the most influential architect in history. Palladio designed many famous villas including the magnificent Villa Cornaro at Padua for Giorgio Cornaro. This famous villa boasts one of Palladio's new designs. This innovation used a set of six columns at the entrance with a balcony above supporting the roof with another set of matching columns directly above. This design of a double set of six columns is also used for the front entrance of the White House in Washington D.C. The U.S. Capitol Building is classified as Palladian style architecture with a central rotunda flanked by the wings for the Senate (north) and the House of Representatives (south). Much of Palladio's work was completed in Venice and Vicenza.

- During the 16th century, a professor of anatomy at Padua University, Gabriele Fallopio (1523-1562) invented the condom to prevent the spread of venereal diseases and unwanted pregnancy. Fallopio also was the first to discover the movement of ova (egg) through a tube to the uterus. That tube is named the *fallopian tube* in his honor.

- In 1546, at the famous Padua University, Realdo Colombo discovered the "lesser circulation of the blood" or "pulmonary blood circulation."

Other Interesting Information

- The first description of a clock's escapement mechanism, which regulates the energy used to move the clock's internal mechanism, was provided by Giovanni de Dondi in 1364. He was an astronomer and physician who taught medicine at the Padua University. He built a remarkable seven-dial clock that displayed time, the position of the planets, solar eclipses and other celestial movement. It took over 200 years before anything was built to match the complexity of his clock.

Pisa

What to See in Pisa

▪ Construction began on the Leaning Tower of Pisa on August 9, 1173 as the bell tower for the city's cathedral. The complete tower was finished in the 14th century. It was closed to visitors from 1990 to 2001, during which time its foundation was rebuilt and the tower was slightly straightened. The top of the tower's south edge still leans out 15 feet (4.6 meters) past the base of the tower. The tower and its cathedral are part of the Piazza del Duomo. This piazza (plaza) surrounds the visitor with beautiful historic buildings that are arranged on the plaza with specific and intentional symmetries and geometries that add to the plaza's overall ambiance.

Who is from Pisa

▪ Galileo, known by his first name only, was an astronomer, inventor, physicist and mathematician. He was born on February 15, 1564 in Pisa. Galileo entered Pisa University as a medical student in 1581. He later decided to become a mathematician, and from 1592 to 1610 was a professor of mathematics at Padua University. Galileo invented the telescope, made many astronomical discoveries, and was the first to study gravity scientifically. He is considered the father of modern physics and science. In 1641, Galileo also designed the first clock that kept time using a pendulum.

▪ Leonardo Fibonacci was born about 1170 in Pisa and probably died there between 1240 and 1250. He was a mathematician who was primarily responsible for the European adoption of Arabic numerals in place of Roman numerals. Fibonacci explained the advantages and the system in his book "Liber Abaci," which was written in 1202.

▪ In 1859, Antonio Pacinotti, a physics graduate from the University of Pisa, invented what became known as "Pacinotti's Ring." His invention was the world's first electric generator and the first electric motor as well.

R. R. Esposito

Pompeii

What to See in Pompeii

- The world's oldest known amphitheater was built in Pompeii in 82 BC about the time when this city in central Italy became a colony of Rome. The amphitheater held 20,000 spectators, close to the entire population of the city. The city of Pompeii was destroyed in 79 AD by the sudden and violent eruption of Mount Vesuvius. The volcanic lava that poured down the mountain rushed the city of Pompeii so quickly that many residents were suddenly buried in ash or entombed in lava as they performed their daily tasks. The many ruins of Pompeii were discovered under the volcanic ash by accident in 1748. Tourists can walk through the city streets and buildings, and examine what life was like in this Roman colony over 2000 years ago.

Rome / Roma

Rome, known as "the eternal city," is the birthplace of modern western civilization in so many different ways, as the chapters of this book clearly delineate. Rome developed into a great republic and eventually an empire that influenced all of Europe, providing a common culture and institutions that in many ways have endured to the 21st century. During its centuries of existence it became the home of many great poets, artists, architects, engineers, jurists, leaders and scientists. Rome offers tourists from all over the world elegant art and architecture of great historic importance.

What to See in Rome

The Ancient District – Rome's Center

- The Capitol of ancient Rome was built on the southern summit of Capitoline Hill (Capitolinus in Latin). From this hill's name, the English word *capital* is derived, as well as the term *Capitol Hill* as a designation for the US Capitol Building in Washington DC. The Capitol was the civic and political heart of ancient Rome. The Capitol had government and civic buildings, religious temples and public plazas. The Capitol has been rebuilt over the many past centuries. For example, the Temple of Jupiter's remaining foundations and podium now lie beneath the palace, Palazzo Caffarelli, which was built in the 16th century. During the 12th century, the senatorial palace, Palazzo Senatorio, was built over the ancient Roman Tabularium (Public Hall of Records). The palace was rebuilt in the 16th century during the Renaissance when Michelangelo designed the Palazzo Senatorio's new façade with its monumental twin staircases. This palace is now Rome's municipal center and town hall.

Today, the centerpiece of the Capitol is the Capitol Plaza, (Piazza del Campidoglio) and its surrounding structures. The plaza is framed on three sides by palaces (Palazzo Senatorio, Palazzo Nuovo and Palazzo dei Conservatori) and the fourth side provides access to the plaza by the imposing Cordonata staircase. Michelangelo designed the entire area, which includes the Cordonata staircase, the trapezoidal plaza and its elegant elliptical paving, and the three palaces that surround the plaza. The trapezoidal shape of the Capitol Plaza accentuates the panoramic view of the three palaces, since the Cordonata staircase is the plaza's entrance, which is situated at the wide base of the trapezoid. At the center of the Capitol Plaza is a copy of the ancient equestrian statue of the great Roman Emperor Marcus Aurelius. The original 2nd century statue, by an unknown sculptor, is housed in the Capitoline Museum. The Palazzo Nuovo and the Palazzo dei Conservatori that flank the Capitol Plaza comprise the famous Capitoline Museum, which contains some of the greatest Roman and Renaissance art in the world, including works by Tintoretto, Caravaggio, Bernini, Titian, Van Dyck, Rubens and others.

The church of Santa Maria d'Aracoeli was also built on Capitoline Hill in the 13th century for the Franciscans. The church is built on the site where the Roman Temple of Juno stood. Its exterior is quite simple, but the church's Bufalini Chapel contains masterpiece frescoes of scenes illustrating St. Bernardino of Siena and St. Francis by the Renaissance master Pinturicchio.

Also, located on Capitoline Hill stands the massive and imposing Victor Emmanuel Monument, which was inaugurated in 1911 in honor of Victor Emmanuel II, the first king of a unified Italy.

▪ The ancient Roman Forum was built at the eastern base of Capitoline Hill. As Rome grew, the Forum became Rome's political, commercial, and legal center, while Capitoline Hill became a religious center. The Forum's basilicas were the office buildings of Rome and the first in the world. The Basilica of Constantine still displays three vast barrel-vaulted ceilings and was the Forum's largest building. The

R. R. Esposito

Curia is reconstructed and was originally Rome's Senate House. Rome's leaders gave public speeches at the Rostra where public discussions were also held. The nearby House of Vestal Virgins contains the remains of a courtyard lined with ancient statues, and nearby is the Temple of Vesta. The Temple of Saturn is located at the western end of the Forum, behind the Rostra. At the center of the Roman Forum, next to the Temple of Saturn, stood the Golden Milestone where all major roads converged. Today only a small base remains with the inscription: Miliarium Aureum. However, the Golden Milestone was a tall column covered in gold and had inscriptions marking highways and the distances to all major cities in the Empire. Among the many inscriptions on the Milestone was the famous Appian Way (Via Appia Antica), first of many great Roman highways that were constructed. This wide road was often used to quickly transport Roman soldiers and couriers to regions south of Rome. Sections of this flat stone roadway still exist today and have become a tourist attraction. Also, in the Forum are the Arch of Septimus Severus and the Arch of Titus. The Arch of Constantine is at the eastern end of the Forum next to the Coliseum. This arch is of special interest. The Arch of Constantine, built in 313 AD, was dedicated to the Emperor Constantine and stands at the location where he returned to Rome after his successful conquest over Maxentius. This battle with Maxentius, at the Milvian Bridge, is of great significant to Christians. Just prior to the start of this battle Constantine saw his legendary vision of a cross in the sky and as a result converted to Christianity. He then made Christianity the official religion of the entire Roman Empire spreading the Christian belief throughout Europe.

▪ Just outside the eastern end of the Roman Forum is the Coliseum, originally known as the Flavian Amphitheater. It was built as an arena for plays, performances and gladiator combat, but was also flooded for shows of mock sea battles. Today's estimates are that the structure held over 50,000 spectators. However, according to the "Chronographia," published in 354 AD, it held up to 87,000 spectators. It had eighty entrances and the audience could be vacated in ten minutes. Immediately east of the Coliseum is the Golden House of Nero (Domus Aurea). Built by Nero in 68 AD, the original palace, one of the most opulent ever built in the world, contained 250 rooms and covered over 200 acres. Today only 30 rooms are open to the public, as well as some sculptures that have survived the centuries.

▪ Just a few blocks north of the Coliseum (several blocks northeast of the Forum) is the church San Pietro in Vincoli (St. Peter in Chains), which was founded in the 5th century to house the chains that bound St. Peter in Palestine. They are preserved under glass. The church also contains Michelangelo's "Moses," which is one of the world's most famous sculptures. The famous Renaissance painter and art historian, Vasari, wrote "No modern work will ever equal it in beauty, no, nor ancient either."

- Directly south of the Forum is the Palatine Hill (Palatinus in Latin) where Roman aristocrats and emperors lived for 400 years. The lavish homes of the Roman Emperors stood on Palatine Hill. The English word *palace* is derived from the name of Palatine Hill. Wandering through the palace built by Domitian on Palatine Hill, one encounters the Domus Augusta (private wing) and the Domus Flavia (public wing) with its beautiful colored marble pavement pattern.

- At the southern base of the Palatine Hill is the Circus Maximus. The Circus Maximus is a large elongated field with the remnants of tiered benches that once accommodated 250,000 spectators who watched chariot races and other sporting events. Its stone and marble were pilfered during the Renaissance for new building material. Today, one of Rome's most exclusive residential areas surrounds the Circus Maximus.

- Directly north and adjacent to the Roman Forum are the Imperial Forums (Fori Imperiali). The Imperial Forums were built by Julius Caesar to relieve overcrowding of the original Roman Forum. These were built with more flamboyance and were to represent the power and wealth of the Empire. The vast Trajan's Market is within the Imperial Forums. In its day, the market offered shoppers goods and merchandise from the far corners of the Empire. Much of the huge, tall shopping complex still stands.

Northwest of the Ancient District (Centro Storico city section)
- Roughly a mile (about 2 kilometers) northwest of the Capitol is the Pantheon. It was built by Emperor Hadrian (120 AD to 124 AD) as a temple and boasts a massive domed roof (142 feet or 43.2 meters) that is mostly poured concrete. In the 4th century it became a Christian church and it contains the tombs of Italian monarchs, as well as the tomb of Raphael. The Pantheon contained *the world's largest interior space for 1500 years.* The dome boasted the largest span until Brunelleschi's dome at the Florence Cathedral, which was constructed from 1420 to 1436. The Pantheon inspired many later buildings including the University of Virginia Library, which is a close copy.

The Romans also invented concrete, the architectural dome, as well as the vaulted ceiling by perfecting the arch, which allowed new architectural designs and spacious interiors, like the Pantheon.

▪ Near the Pantheon are government offices, the Italian Parliament (housed in the Palazzo Montecitorio), and the stock exchange that has the ancient Temple of Hadrian for its building's façade.

▪ A few blocks behind the Pantheon is the Piazza della Minerva that has a tall obelisk set upon an elephant sculpture by Bernini. On this piazza stands the church, Santa Maria sopra Minerva, which contains works by Michelangelo and Bernini.

▪ A few blocks east of the Pantheon is the palace, Palazzo Doria Pamphilj that contains an art gallery with several masterpieces.

▪ A few blocks west of the Pantheon is the famous Piazza Navona. This grand, elongated piazza is two blocks long and provides a romantic setting. The piazza is lined with palaces, cafes and three elaborate fountains. Two splendid fountains are the Fontana dei Quattro Fiumi and the Fontana del Moro, both have statues designed by Bernini.

North of the Ancient District

▪ About 2 miles (3 kilometers) north of the Ancient District is the Palazzo di Spagna. Built in the 17th century to house the Spanish Embassy to the Vatican, the Palazzo di Spagna stands on the bow-tie shaped plaza, Piazza di Spagna, which boast the famous Spanish Steps. The colossal steps have been a favorite site for tourists since the 18th century. Several blocks south of the Palazzo di Spagna is another grand plaza, the Piazza Trevi that contains Rome's largest and most famous fountain, the Trevi fountain with Neptune as its most central figure. About a half mile (1 kilometer) east of the Palazzo di Spagna is the church Santa Maria della Vittoria that contains one of Bernini's greatest sculptures, "Ecstasy of St. Teresa" (1646).

▪ Just north of the Palazzo di Spagna is the Museo e Galleria Borghese, which contains works by Caravaggio, Rubens, Titian, and also Bernini's finest works including "Apollo and Daphne" (1624), "The Rape of Proserpina" (1622) and "David" (1623). The gallery also houses Canova's neo-classical sculpture, "Venus Victrix" (1805), which is a semi-nude statue of Napoleon's sister Pauline reclining on a chaise lounge. Her husband Prince Camillo Borghese kept it locked away from view.

Northeast of the Ancient District

▪ Several blocks northeast of the ancient district is the Basilica Santa Maria Maggiore, which is one of Rome's four major basilicas. It was originally built in the 4th century with changes made during the 14th and 18th centuries. The campanile (bell tower) is Rome's tallest. The basilica is especially noted for the 5th century Roman mosaics and its coffered ceiling, said to have been gilded with gold brought from the New World. The church also contains the tomb of Bernini, one of Italy's greatest sculptor/architects. Ironically, the man whose art helped beautify the City of Rome is buried in a very simple tomb not easily found (near the altar's right). The Basilica Santa Maria Maggiore is located in Rome, but is actually part of Vatican City and not Italy.

▪ The Diocletian Bath (Terme di Diocleziano) and its Octagonal Hall (Aula Ottagona) are located near Piazza dei Cinquecento, which fronts Rome's main railroad station. This museum occupies part of the 3rd century AD Baths of Diocletian and part of a Renaissance convent. The Diocletian Baths were the largest thermal baths in the world. Today the structure houses a vast collection of funereal art works, such as sarcophagi, and other related artifacts dating back to the 3rd century. The Octagonal Hall contains Roman art notably from the 2nd century.

South of the Ancient District

▪ South of the ancient district stand several beautiful churches. The Basilica San Clemente is one of the more splendid buildings. Just two blocks southeast of the Coliseum stands San Clemente, an historical "layered-church." In the 1st century AD, a house became the foundation for a 4th century church upon which San Clemente stands today. Within it one discovers well-preserved frescoes from the 9th to the 11th centuries, and a magnificent bronze-orange mosaic from the 12th century.

▪ The Basilica San Giovanni Laterano, several blocks southeast of the Coliseum, was built in 314 AD by Emperor Constantine and is the official church (not St. Peter's) of the diocese of Rome, where the Pope celebrates mass on holidays. The Basilica San Giovanni Laterano is located in Rome, but is actually part of Vatican City and not Italy.

▪ Across the street from San Giovanni Laterano is the Palace of the Holy Steps (Santuario della Scala Santa). These 28 marble steps are alleged to be the original steps that Christ climbed at Pontius Pilate's villa in Jerusalem. According to a medieval tradition, the steps were allegedly brought from Jerusalem to Rome by Constantine's mother, Helen, in 326 AD. Since 1589 the steps have been in this location where Pilgrims from all over the world come to climb on their knees. Although the steps are one of the holiest sites in Christendom, some historians maintain that they probably date only to the 4th century AD. Nevertheless, these steps are a kind of "stairway to heaven" for many of the faithful.

- The church Santa Sabina is just a few blocks south of the *Ancient District* and is one of Rome's most beautiful churches. Dating from 422 AD, Santa Sabina is the best example of Paleochristian art, that is, the art of the first Christians. Its original wooden doors from that time, miraculously still intact, display fine carved Biblical scenes, including one of the Crucifixion. This historical carving of the Crucifixion is one of the earliest references of this event in the world. This carving is located on a door at the end of a 15th century porch. Santa Sabina is built on the site of the temple of Juno Regina and the twenty-four Corinthian columns may have come from the Temple of Juno. The highly delicate windows were pieced together from 9th century fragments.

- Less than a mile (one kilometer) directly south of the Coliseum stand the remains of the Roman Baths of Caracalla that were built in the 3rd century. This complex had once covered an area of 26 acres and had a capacity for about 1600 occupants. It contained art galleries, gymnasiums, gardens, libraries, conference rooms, shops and food courts. The baths had cold (*frigidarium*), warm (*tepidarium*), and hot (*caldarium*) water rooms to choose from, as well as an open-air swimming pool (*natatio*). The ultimate day spa!

- A few miles south of the *Ancient District* is the Museum of Roman Civilization, which houses two fascinating scale models of the city of Rome from two different eras. One model reconstructs the early Republican Rome, the other is a display of imperial Rome in the 4th century AD. These fascinating displays include many detailed reconstructions, such as Circus Maximus, the Coliseum and the Baths of Diocletian. The museum is a kind of virtual tour of ancient Rome.

- A few miles (several kilometers) south of the *Ancient District* are the Catacombs of San Callisto, which contain the remains of early Christians, popes and saints. These vast catacombs are essentially ancient underground cemeteries and are open to the public. The catacombs were the first cemeteries of the Christian community of Rome. They are the burial place of 16 popes in the 3rd century. The complex is a network of galleries and rooms that stretch for nearly 12 miles (19 km).

▪ The Basilica of St. Paul Outside the Walls (Basilica di San Paolo Fuori le Mura) is located in the Portuense section of Rome a few miles (several kilometers) south of the *Ancient District*, and beyond the original walls of the ancient city, hence named 'outside the walls.' The structure's origins go back to the time of Constantine (324 AD). St. Paul Outside the Walls is one of Rome's great churches and it is believed that the tomb of St. Paul rests beneath the church's altar. It is the second largest church in Rome after St. Peter's, and is one of the most elegant churches in Rome. Its unusual windows appear to be stained glass, but these are actually made from translucent alabaster. The triumphal arch leading to the altar is decorated with 5th century mosaics, including mosaic portraits of every Pope beginning with St. Peter. There are even blank areas ready for future popes. It also contains a magnificent 12th century candelabra by Vassalletto, who is also responsible for the remarkable cloisters, containing twisted pairs of columns enclosing a rose garden. St. Paul is located in Rome, but is actually part of Vatican City and not Italy.

West of the Ancient District - Across the Tiber River

▪ Ponte St. Angelo is one of Rome's most ancient bridges and certainly its most beautiful. Emperor Hadrian commissioned the bridge and its three graceful arches. The bridge spans the Tiber River and connects to Castel St. Angelo on the river's west bank. The ten statues of angels on the bridge were created by the Bernini Studio and School from 1598 to 1660.

▪ Castel St. Angelo, on the west bank of the Tiber River, is located just a short walk east of Vatican City. Castel St. Angelo has a long and fascinating history. It was originally built in the 2nd century as the tomb for Emperor Hadrian and his descendants, and also has been a repository for the ashes of cremated Roman emperors. During the Middle Ages it became a fortress to protect the Popes should the Vatican be threatened by attack. A tunnel connects Castel St. Angelo with the Vatican palace. During the Renaissance, the Church added a chapel by Michelangelo to its peak and various loggias by Bramante. Over the centuries St. Angelo has been used for many different and interesting purposes and a visit is recommended.

▪ Vatican City lies a few miles (several kilometers) west of Rome's ancient district and just west of the Tiber River. Vatican City is the seat of the Roman Catholic Church and exists as an independent political entity with a population of about 700 residents. The Vatican occupies 106 acres and is surrounded by high walls patrolled by Vatican guards. The Vatican has its own post office, currency, banks, judicial system, radio station and shops. The site of Vatican City was originally an ancient Roman city. Pope Julius II engaged Donato Bramante to redesign and renew the Vatican palace complex. The Vatican Palace today is actually a complex of several buildings, most notably, St. Peter's Basilica and the Sistine Chapel. Ultimately, he developed the early 16th century plan to rebuild the City of Rome, as well as the original design of St. Peter's Basilica.

St. Peter's Square (Piazza San Pietro) at the entrance to Vatican City inspires awe in all its visitors. The Square itself was designed by Giovanni Lorenzo Bernini and is considered to be one of his greatest architectural accomplishments.

Saint Peter's Basilica was designed by several famous architects including Michelangelo who personally designed its lavish dome. Inside, the extravagant posts and canopy (baldacchino) over the tomb of St. Peter was designed and carved by Bernini. The "Pieta" is a massive and dramatic sculpture of white marble that was created by the genius of Michelangelo. It depicts Mary holding her deceased son Jesus after the Crucifixion. It is housed in Saint Peter's Basilica.

The venerated Sistine Chapel was painted by Michelangelo from 1508 to 1512. He covered the Chapel's vaulted ceiling with paintings of biblical events from the "Book of Genesis," as commissioned by Pope Julius II. From 1534 to 1541, Michelangelo painted the "Last Judgment," an enormous fresco, on the entire wall behind the altar.

Vatican Museums are housed in palaces built by Renaissance Popes and include the Raphael Rooms and other wings that house Egyptian, Greek, Roman, and Renaissance art including masterpieces by Giotto, Bellini, Michelangelo, da Vinci and others.

Who is from Rome

- Among the many great leaders of ancient Rome are Julius Caesar, Constantine, Hadrian, Marcus Aurelius, Cicero (the legendary philosopher, statesman, jurist and orator), the great architect Vitruvius, as well as legendary writers such as Seneca, Homer and Virgil.

Cicero invented the memory technique that associates rooms in a home with concepts. By associating the main points of his speeches with different rooms in his home, he always remembered the main talking points in his legendary oratories. In his mind, he would move through the rooms and remember each part of his speech.

- Constantine Brumidi was born in Rome on July 26, 1805 and graduated in 1824 from the Italian art school Accademia di San Luca. He had much experience as an artist for the Vatican and also collaborated in the restoration of Renaissance masterpieces, such as Raphael's "Third Loggia." He migrated to the U.S. on September 18, 1852 and applied his artistic talents by adding culture and beauty to U.S. Capitol buildings. He became known as "the Michelangelo of the U.S. Capitol."
- Enrico Fermi was born on September 29, 1901 in Rome. He ushered in the atomic age when he succeeded in transforming the nucleus of a uranium atom and simultaneously split the atom for the first time, at the University of Rome in 1934. For his pioneering work he was awarded the Nobel Prize in 1938. Fermi led a team that built the first nuclear reactor (1939) and the first atomic bomb (1945).

Other Interesting Information

- The prestigious and influential lives of Julius and Augustus Caesar gave the name "Caesar" a royal meaning throughout Europe for many centuries. From this name the German title of "Kaiser" and the Russian title of "Czar" developed. The expression "the die is cast" is actually a quote of Julius Caesar. To describe the success of an earlier military campaign, Caesar said, "I came, I saw, I conquered." This famous quote originated with Julius Caesar when he addressed the Roman Senate after a conquest in Asia. In Latin, the quote is "veni, vidi, vici."
- Roman law dates as far back as 753 BC, during the time of the early Roman Kingdom. Established during the early Roman Republic, about 450 BC, the "Law of the Twelve Tables." This evolved into the world's first legal system, which became the foundation of all the legal systems in the western world.
- The Church leadership in ancient Rome decided to celebrate Christ's birthday on December 25th to compete with the dominant and powerful religion in Rome, Mithraism. The new Christian holiday on December 25th offered an alternative festivity to the sun worshiping event. In ancient Rome, the god Saturn was honored during the feast of Saturnalia from December 17th through December 23rd. During this merry feast, gifts were exchanged and banquets were served. This Roman tradition was adopted by the Christians who began to exchange gifts during their merry-making at Christmas time.

- The world's longest period of peace was the result of the unifying effect of the Roman Republic and the subsequent Empire. For over 250 years, from 27 BC to 235 AD, the whole Western world including the Byzantine world, was characterized by peace, technological advancement and great prosperity. This peace was the direct result of the effective and stable government of Rome. This period is known as *Pax Romana*. The famous historian Edward Gibbon who authored "The Decline and Fall of the Roman Empire" states in his book that *Pax Romana* was "...the period in the history of the world during which the human race was the most happy and prosperous."

Sardinia

What to See in Sardinia

- The beautiful island of Sardinia has been described by D. H. Lawrence as an island "left outside of time and history." This island of natural and timeless beauty has been home to ancient Phoenicians, Carthaginians, Greeks, Romans, Arabs, Byzantines, Spaniards and others. It has a long, rich history and retains much of its ancient ruins, buildings and cultures. Among its natural wonders, its famous Blue Grotto draws thousands of tourists from the mainland of Italy. It is only accessible by boat, and visitors must lie flat on boats to clear the low rock formations at the grotto's entrance, however, the grotto is well worth the trip. Sardinia is also the home of Grazia Deledda, who won the Nobel Prize for Literature in 1926.
- Genna Maria Archaeological Museum and Park in Villanovaforru houses artifacts that span a millennium of history, from 400 BC to 600 AD.
- The museum Antiquarium Turritano outside of Sassari displays archaeological findings from the excavations of the ancient Roman city Turris Libisonis, as well as other collections.

Sicily / Sicilia

What to See in Sicily

▪ Sicily's Valley of the Temples (Valle dei Templi) can be found just south of the city of Agrigento. In this area stand the remains of nine ancient Greek temples. The Temple of Hercules dates back to 600 BC.

▪ In the city of Palermo is the church Santa Maria dell'Ammiraglio (La Martorana), founded in 1143, is known for its glorious Byzantine mosaics. Palermo is also the home to the International Puppet Museum (Museo Internazionale delle Marionette). Sicilian puppets (*pupi*) have been considered among the finest of marionette art for centuries. The museum's collection includes Sicilian marionettes and many from a variety of other countries, including English *Punch and Judy* marionettes. Palermo's Palazzo Abatellis houses the Regional Gallery (Galleria Regionale della Sicilia), which displays the evolution of art in Sicily from the 13th to 18th centuries.

▪ The small Ortygia Island has been inhabited for many thousands of years and is rich with history and legend. It offers some of the most charming vistas in Sicily. In Greek mythology, Ortygia is said to have been ruled by Calypso (daughter of Atlas) the sea nymph who detained Ulysses (Odysseus) for 7 years. Ortygia's Duomo was built over the ruins of the Temple of Minerva, which was built in the 5th century BC. It was converted into a Christian basilica in the 7th century AD.

▪ Syracuse's archaeological park, the Archaeological Zone (Zona Archeologica) contains the city's most important attractions. The park contains the 5th century BC Greek Theater (Teatro Greco), which was one of the great theaters of the classical period where plays by the great Euripides were performed. In this theater, the Italian Institute of Ancient Drama presents classical plays by Euripides, Aeschylus and Sophocles. Near the entrance to the Greek Theater is the most famous of the ancient stone quarries, the Paradise Quarry (Latomia del Paradiso). A large quarry cave, nearly 200 feet (61 meters) long, has acoustics that make a whispered voice sound like a shout. The park's Roman Amphitheater (Anfiteatro Romano) was created at the time of Augustus. It ranks among the top five amphitheaters left by the Romans in Italy. To the east of the Archaeological Zone lie the Catacombs of St. John (Catacombe di San Giovanni). The entrance is below the Chiesa di San Giovanni, which was established in the 3rd

century AD. These catacombs include the crypt of St. Marcianus, which is beneath the alleged first cathedral built in Sicily.

The Paolo Orsi Regional Archaeological Museum (Museo Archeologico Regionale Paolo Orsi) of Syracuse is one of the most important archaeological museums in southern Italy. It spans Greek, Roman, and early Christian periods and displays sculpture, coins and other archaeological remains. The museum is known for its statues that include: Venus Anadyomene rising from the sea (200 BC), an earthware mother suckling two babes (600 BC) and fine pre-Greek vases.

▪ Taormina is well known for its beautiful beaches and resorts. The best and most popular beach is Lido Mazzaro. The Greek Amphitheater (Teatro Greco) is a popular tourist attraction and offers a view of Mt. Etna and the seacoast. Taormina also has a very scenic, flower-filled Public Garden (Giardino Pubblico) that overlooks the coast.

▪ Lipari is the largest of the Aeolian Islands and its only real town is also named Lipari. It has two beaches, one of which also functions as a harbor. Lapari has a 16th century Spanish castle and an archaeological park with evidence of the island's continuous civilizations dating back to 1700 BC. The Museo Archeologico Eoliano is one of Sicily's major archaeological museums and houses artifacts from the Stone and Bronze ages, relics from Greek and Roman acropolises, and one of the world's finest Neolithic collections. The oldest artifacts date back to 4200 BC.

Who is from Sicily

▪ Of Greek descent, Empedocles lived in Agrigento, Sicily where he was born about 492 BC. At the time Agrigento was a Greek colony known as Acragas. Empedocles was primarily a natural philosopher, but was also a poet, physician and social reformer. Aristotle is said to have considered him the inventor of rhetoric, while Galen regarded him as the founder of the science of medicine in Italy. He anticipated the modern concept in physics that matter and energy cannot be created or destroyed, i.e. the principle of conservation of energy.

▪ The 13th century Sicilian poet Giacomo da Lentini invented the sonnet, a 14-line poem with rhymes arranged in a fixed scheme. The literary giant, Francesco Petrarca, from Florence (1304-1374), invented the sonnet cycle, which was enthusiastically embraced, and rapidly spread throughout Europe. There have been several cycle variations since then, but the sonnet remains, as originally conceived by Lentini, a structured 14-line poem.

- Alessandro Scarlatti was born on May 2, 1660 in Palermo and died on October 24, 1725. He was a prolific composer, writing in every musical category: 100 operas, 600 cantatas, 200 masses and other chamber and sacred music. The harmonies he used significantly advanced concepts of musical harmony for centuries to follow. He helped establish the "opera seria" and perfected the "aria da capo," as well as the three part overture. The German composer, George Friderc Handel traveled to Italy to meet Scarlatti and was greatly influenced by his work. Handel stayed in Italy for five years and wrote very popular operas in the Italian style. His son Domenico Scarlatti was a harpsichord virtuoso who wrote over 500 harpsichord sonatas. His music and keyboard technique became *the foundation of modern keyboard technique* and also influenced the development of the harpsichord itself. He performed in famous tours including London and Dublin in 1740. *Beethoven and Mozart* followed the two Scarlatttis and took great musical inspiration from the sonatas of both father and son.

- Vincenzo Bellini was born on November 3, 1801 in Catania into a family of musicians. Bellini made significant contributions to opera and was known for his scores that combined both beautiful melody and deep expression. *Because of his strong melody treatments, he greatly influenced Chopin.*

- Salvatore Patti was born in Catania and died about 1869 in Paris. He was a tenor, musical impresario, and the father of the great opera singer Adelina Patti. She was one of the world's greatest opera singers, and was called "the last of the great divas."

- Luigi Pirandello was born in Agrigento, Sicily, Italy in 1867 and died in 1936. He wrote dozens of books and won the 1934 Nobel Prize in Literature for his dramatic and ingenious works. Pirandello is the inventor of *theater within a theater* and was awarded a Nobel Prize in 1934.

- Salvatore Quasimodo was born in Syracuse, Sicily in 1901 and died in 1968. He was awarded a Nobel Prize in 1959 for his poetic works dealing with political and social reform entitled, "The Selected Writings of Salvatore Quasimodo."

- Frank R. Capra was *one of Hollywood's most celebrated movie directors.* Capra was also a prolific screen writer and movie producer. Frank was born in Sicily on May 18, 1897, in the town of Bisaquino near Palermo and died September 3, 1991, in La Quinta, California. He

R. R. Esposito

made *over 50 movies, many of them Oscar winners*. Capra's greatest film, "It's a Wonderful Life" (1946) starring Jimmy Stewart, has become an American classic and is broadcast faithfully every Christmas.

▪ Around 1905, a Sicilian immigrant named Vincent Taormina arrived in New Orleans and began a small business importing foods from Italy to the U.S. Vincent merged his growing business with his cousin, Guiseppe Uddo. By 1927 both the New Orleans and New York City companies were merged to form the Progresso Italian Food Corporation of New York City. Today the Progresso Quality Foods Company is a vast enterprise and offers high-quality soups, sauces, beans, breadcrumbs, tomato products, olive oils, vinegars and other products.

▪ President Thomas Jefferson wanted a professional brass band to replace the simple and unprofessional fife-and-drum band used mostly for certain military events. On September 19, 1805, Gaetano Caruso, the organizer and the first musical director of the new band arrived at the Washington Navy Yard on the U.S. Frigate Chesapeake with thirteen other musicians recruited from Sicily. They formed the first U.S. Marine Band.

▪ Domenico Dolce was born on September 13, 1958 in the village of Polizzi Generosa near Palermo, Sicily. His partner Stefano Gabbana was born on November 14, 1962 in Venice. In Sicily, Dolce studied fashion design and worked at his family's clothing factory. Together they founded the international fashion firm Dolce & Gabbana.

Siena

What to See in Siena
▪ Since the Middle Ages, Siena has been the home of the wild and tumultuous "Palio" horse race around the city's center. In Siena riders originally practiced these races to stay trained and fit to aid the military for battle. Following a tradition from the 11th century, or earlier, when battle practice had no rules, the race also has no rules, except for one: jockeys cannot touch the reins of an opposing horse. A *contrada's* horse may win the race by reaching the finish line, with or without the jockey! This is a tradition that dates back to ancient Rome, when chariot races had the same rule regarding getting the

chariot to the finish line regardless of the presence of the driver. The race takes place every year on July 2 and August 16 at 7:00 PM.

- One of Italy's greatest cathedrals is Siena'a Duomo. The cathedral contains sculptures by masters such as Michelangelo, Donatello and Pisano. It contains an inlaid marble floor masterpiece and fantastic black and marble pillars that support a vaulted ceiling.

Sorrento

What to See in Sorrento

- The natural beauty of the Sorrento peninsula offers one of the most picturesque areas in the Mediterranean. Sorrento, on the Bay of Naples, offers a dramatic view of Mount Vesuvius in the background. Mount Vesuvius, still an active volcano, buried the Roman city of Pompeii in 79 AD. A trip to Pompeii or a ferry ride to Capri will enhance a visit to Sorrento. Sorrento also offers magnificent beaches, marinas, restaurants and shops. Sorrento's best beach is Punta del Capo.

Who is from Sorrento

- Torquato Tasso was born in Sorrento and lived from 1544 to 1595. He was educated in Naples by Jesuits and studied law and philosophy at the University of Padua and at the University of Bologna. Tasso wrote several famous works but his greatest masterpiece was "Jerusalem Delivered." This treasured work had a tremendous influence on English poets, most especially the great John Milton.
- Enrico Caruso was born to a poor family on February 27, 1873 in Naples, Italy and died there as well on August 2, 1921. He performed from the late 19th to the early 20th centuries throughout the world. His perfect voice with massive power, range and beauty makes experts describe him as the *greatest tenor in the history of opera.*

Tivoli

What to See in Tivoli
- Just west of Tivoli lies Hadrian's Villa, one of the largest and most elaborate villas ever built by the Roman Empire. The villa contains the remains of two baths, libraries, gardens and a theater. A great place to relax for a nearby get-away from bustling Rome. Tivoli also offers a place to relax as one roams through Renaissance villas and ancient temples.

Turin / Torino

What to See in Turin
- In the city's cathedral, Cattedrale di San Giovanni, rests the famous Christian medieval relic, *The Shroud of Turin*. It is kept in a silver case that sits inside an iron box within a marble coffer. Although many Christians believe it is the image of Christ's face created when the cloth was used to cover his face at death, carbon dating indicates the shroud is no older than the 12th century. Nevertheless, the Shroud remains an important and world-renowned Christian artifact.
- The Armeria Reale museum contains one of the most extensive collections of arms and armory in the world.
- A few miles outside of the city is the Museo dell'Automobile, which contains classic cars made by Bugatti, Maserati, Lancia, Fiat and other cars from around the world.
- The Egyptian Museum (Museo Egizio) & Galleria Sabauda are housed in the 17th century Science Academy Building. The collection within the Egyptian Museum is one of the best in the world. The statues of Ramses II and Amenhotep II are highlights. Another prized exhibit is the *Royal Papyrus* that chronicles the Egyptian monarchs from the 1st to the 17th dynasty.
- The Galleria Sabauda presents one of Italy's finest art collections. The largest exhibit is Italian, but there are many fine examples of Flemish art as well. Some of the museum's pieces include: Van Dyck's "Three Children of Charles I," Botticelli's "Venus," Memling's "Passion of Christ," Rembrandt's "Sleeping Old Man," Duccio's "Virgin and Child," Mantegna's "Holy Conversation," Jan van

Eyck's "The Stigmata of Francis of Assisi," Veronese's "Dinner in the House of the Pharisee," and Bellotto's "Views of Turin."

- The Mole Antonelliana is Milan's answer to the Eiffel Tower in Paris. It was built in the 19th century by Alessandro Antonelli. The tower rises to a height of 548 feet (167 meters) and for a time it was the tallest building in the world. At its base is a Cinema Museum.

Other Interesting Information

- In the Piazza San Carlo's northwest corner is the Galleria San Federico shopping arcade. In a café in the arcade Antonio Benedetto Carpano invented vermouth in 1786, still a popular drink in Turin.

Venice / Venezia

What to See in Venice

- At the center of Venice lies Saint Mark's Square (Piazza San Marco). The Square or Piazza is the focal point for the city's economic, political, religious and artistic life. Napoleon called the Square, " the most elegant drawing room in Europe." In the center of the plaza stands the city's famous clock tower, Torre dell'Orologio, and at the plaza's edge stands the bell tower, Campanile di San Marco, that offers an elevator ride to the top for a panoramic view of the city. On the eastern side of the piazza stands the Basilica of St. Mark, one of the world's most magnificent churches. The Basilica of St. Mark reputedly contains the remains of its patron saint. Five gilded domes reflecting a Byzantine influence top its roof. This massive and beautiful basilica was built from the 9th to 11th centuries and contains rare gemstones, marble, decorated ceilings and panels, along with many detailed and beautiful mosaics and enamels. Visitors should note the famous mosaics about the Basilica's entrance, as well as the four horses above them.

- The magnificent church of San Giorgio Maggiore was built on its own island directly across from St Mark's square. Its architect was Andrea Palladio. The church has had a monastery since 982, but the current buildings were built during the 16th century. Its tall bell tower (campanile) offers a fantastic view of Venice.

- The Church of Santa Maria di Salute, designed in 1630 by architect Baldasarre Longhena, is yet another majestic cathedral in central Venice. It has vast multiple domes and was built at the edge of the water, which enhances its beauty. The church contains paintings by Titian ("St. Mark Enthroned with Saints"- 1512; "Cane and Abel" ceiling painting- 1540-1549), as well as a major work by Tintoretto ("The Wedding of Cana- 1551).

- Santa Maria Gloriosa dei Frari is a vast gothic church that contains the "Assumption of the Virgin" (1518) by Titian, the "Modonna and Child" (1488) by Bellini and what is called the 'Monk's Choir' a three-tiered set of choir benches carved in 1468 with bas-reliefs of Venetian city scenes and saints. The church also contains a pyramid-shaped tomb where Canova rests. The great neo-classical sculptor Canova died in 1822.

- One of the world's most famous bridges is the Ponte Rialto. It has beautiful multiple arches and spans the Grand Canal of Venice. The large covered bridge also has many famous shops. Venetian gondolas are also a unique and beautiful way to travel on the canal.

- The beautiful Palazzo Ducale ($14^{th} - 15^{th}$ centuries) was the palace of the *doges* (rulers) of Venice. Its fantastic architecture boasts pink marble and white stone. Inside hangs Tintoretto's paintings "Paradise," "Three Graces," and "Bacchus and Ariadne," as well as Veronese's "Rape of Europa" and "Triumph of Venice." Tintoretto's "Paradise" is said to be the world's largest oil painting. The palace connects to a prison by the Bridge of Sighs (1660), named so because of the sighs of prisoners who were walked across for trial. Casanova was once imprisoned there and made a spectacular escape from the palace through a hole in the roof.

- In 1807, Napoleon relocated a well-know art collection to the Accademia museum and enriched the collection with many new additions. A visit to the Accademia offers a tour of art that spans over 500 years, from medieval Byzantine to Renaissance and Baroque periods. The Accademia's courtyard was designed by Palladio in 1561.

- The island of Torcello boasts the oldest building in the Venetian lagoon. The cathedral of Santa Maria dell'Assunta was founded in 639 AD. It houses a Roman sarcophagus and Medieval mosaics.

Who is from Venice

- Marco Polo was born in Venice, Italy in 1254. In 1298, this Venetian explorer wrote a fascinating book about his astonishing adventures in the exotic and distant Far East, entitled "Description of the World." He wrote of new cities, temples, cultures and artifacts, such as silks, jewels, porcelain and more. He had finally returned to Venice in 1295 after his 24 year odyssey.

- Casanova was a well-educated man who traveled Europe and wrote exaggerated accounts of his adventures including his love life, entitled "History of My Life." His full name was Giovanni Giacomo Casanova De Seingalt. He was born in Venice in 1725 and died in 1798.

- Claudio Monteverdi was born in Cremona and was baptized there on May 15, 1567. He was a composer and music director (*maestro di cappella*) at the famous St. Mark's Cathedral in Venice. Although he did not write the first opera, he is credited as the founder of Italian opera because he advanced many concepts in opera and music orchestration, including novel musical dissonance and other innovative uses of harmony. Many consider Monteverdi to be the *father of modern music*.

- Murano, and its larger neighboring city Venice, are world famous for their blown glass with characteristic color, delicacy and beauty. The glass masters, *battono*, from this part of Italy have created works of art in glass for almost a thousand years.

- Titian was a master painter of the Italian Renaissance. He was born in Pieve di Cadore, near Venice. Titian's actual name was Tiziano Vecellio. He was born circa 1488 and died on August 27, 1576. His innovative use of rich colors made his lifelike paintings and portraits assume a special brilliance. He is considered to be one of the world's greatest master colorists.

- Andrea Palladio is considered the most influential architect in the history of architecture. Palladio's revolutionary changes and style had an enormous influence on European and early American design. He developed new practical designs that recreated ancient classic architecture blended with Renaissance styles. Imposing examples of his work can be seen in Venice and nearby Vicenza, as well as in other cities in the Veneto section surrounding Venice where Palladio built many villas for the aristocracy of his time. He completed three magnificent churches in Venice: San Giorgio Maggiore (1560 to1580), Il Redentore (1576 to 1591) and Le Zitelle (S.M. della Presentazione).

- Carlo Scarpa (architect, artist, designer) was born 1906 in Venice. Scarpa is buried in San Vito d'Altivole near Treviso in the "garden of the dead" at the Brion Tomb, which he designed (1970 to 1972) for the Brion family. The legendary Scarpa is known for his creative, coloristic and avant-garde modern styles. Scarpa also designed magnificent glass at the famous Venini glass studios on the Venetian

Island of Murano. Dozens of his fantastic drawings are at museums in Verona, Venice and Palermo. Many architects today are still inspired by his unconventional and revolutionary works. Carlo Scarpa has introduced many revolutionary concepts and has been compared to the great American architect Louis I. Kahn.

Other Interesting Information
- Around the 13th century medieval Italians started the custom of giving diamond engagement rings to women. By the 15th century, the Venetians realized the intrinsic value of diamonds and learned how to precisely cut and polish them. They discovered that diamonds were the hardest known substance and popularized the practice of giving diamond engagement rings throughout the world.
- Small forks for eating first appeared in the Tuscany region of Italy during the late 10th century and gained greater attention when first introduced in Venice in 1071. Forks were not generally accepted and the clergy condemned them claiming that only human hands were worthy of touching God's bounty. By the 17th century, Italy began to accept the fork, even though it was introduced in Venice in the early 11th century.
- In 1637, Teatro San Cassiano became the first public opera house in the world. It opened in Venice and was sponsored by the Tron family of Italy. Opera quickly became very popular and several other opera houses and opera performing companies developed in Venice.

Verona

What to See in Verona
- The Arena in Verona (Arena di Verona) was completed in 30 AD. This enormous Roman amphitheater still hosts many major musical events. Only two Roman amphitheaters are larger, the Coliseum in Rome and the Santa Maria Capua Vetere, outside of Naples.
- San Zeno Maggiore is an ornate cathedral built from 1123 to 1135. Highlights are the forty-eight 11th and 12th century bronze panels on the west doors, the altarpiece, the nave ceiling and the cloister.
- Castelvecchio, built 1355-1375, houses one of the finest art museums. The museum contains Bellini's "St. Jerome," Giovanni Francesco Caroto's smiling red-haired boy, Tintoretto's "Madonna

Nursing the Child and Nativity," and Veronese's "Deposition from the Cross," and "Pala Bevilacqua Lazise."

- Teatro Romano (Roman Theater) is a 1st century Roman theater that offers entrancing views of the city and a Roman bridge that has survived the ages. Above the theater is the 10th century Santi Siro e Libera church, and in its cloister of St. Jerome is the Archaeological Museum, with fine mosaics and Etruscan bronzes.

- Designed in the 14th century by Agostino Giusti., the Giardino Giusti is one of Italy's oldest and most famous gardens. These beautiful Italian gardens with grottoes, statues, fountains, and Roman remains also offer an incomparable view of the city. Goethe commented on the great cypress trees. The garden includes a complex maze of myrtle hedges that is one of the most unusual in Europe. The garden is located near the Roman Theater.

Who is from Verona

- Shakespeare's play, "Romeo and Juliet," was originally written by Luigi da Porto of Vicenza around 1520. Tourists can visit Casa di Giulietta (House of Juliet) located at 23 Via Cappello, where Romeo allegedly climbed to Juliet's balcony, which is accessible to tourists. The building is a restored 13th century inn. A few blocks away is the alleged Casa di Romeo (House of Romeo) at 2 Via Arche Scaligeri, which has been converted into a fine, atmospheric restaurant called the Osteria dal Duca. At 5 Via del Pontiere lies a tomb that is called Tomba de Giulietta (Tomb of Juliet).

Vicenza

What to See in Vicenza

The Piazza dei Signori is lined by Andrea Palladio's beautiful buildings. Palladio is the world's most influential architect. Although he was born in Padua, Vicenza is Palladio's adopted city and boasts many works by this great architect. In Vicenza Palladio built: Palazzo Chiericati (1550 to1580); Palazzo Thiene (1545); Teatro Olimpico (1584); Villa Trissino (1576); Villa Capra or Villa Rotunda (1566 to 1571), which was the model for Thomas Jefferson's Virginia residence that he named Monticello.

Vinci

What to See in Vinci

▪ The Museo Leonardiano (Museum of Leonardo), housed in a 13th century castle, contains many artifacts of Vinci's most famous son, Leonardo da Vinci. The museum contains da Vinci's notebooks and many of his models including his bicycle, car, armored tank and machine gun. Most models are re-creations based upon his drawings.

Who is from Vinci

▪ Leonardo da Vinci is considered one of the world's greatest geniuses. Leonardo was born in 1452 in Vinci about 20 miles from Florence in the Tuscany region of Italy. At the time, Florence was the richest city in Europe. Da Vinci was the illegitimate son of a notary and a peasant woman. Leonardo was a brilliant painter, sculptor, draftsman, architect, engineer, anatomist, scientist, inventor and futurist. Leonardo is famous for painting the "Mona Lisa" (in the Louvre in Paris) and the "Last Supper" (in Milan).

APPENDIX 1

Nobel Prize Recipients

Camillo Golgi, Medicine, 1906
Giosuè Carducci, Literature, 1906
Ernesto T. Moneta, Peace, 1907
Guglielmo Marconi, Physics, 1909
Grazia Deledda, Literature, 1926
Luigi Pirandello, Literature, 1934
Enrico Fermi, Physics, 1938
Emilio Segrè, Physics, 1959
Salvatore Quasimodo, Literature, 1959
Giulio Natta, Chemistry, 1963
Salvador Edward Luria, Medicine, 1969
Renato Dulbecco, Medicine, 1975
Eugenio Montale, Literature, 1975
Carlo Rubbia, Physics, 1984
Franco Modigliani, Economics, 1985
Rita Levi-Montalcini, Medicine, 1986
Dario Fo, Literature, 1997
Louis Ignarro, Medicine, 1998
Riccardo Giacconi, Physics, 2002

Fields Medal for Mathematics Recipient
(There is no Nobel Prize category for mathematics. However, the Fields Medal is the equivalent international honor.)
Erico Bombieri was awarded the Fields Medal at the International Congress of Mathematicians that was held in Vancouver in 1974.

APPENDIX 2 - Illustrations

Scenic grape arbor from the beautiful island of Capri.

ACKNOWLEDGEMENTS and CREDITS

Many individuals have made contributions that have greatly improved this book. The author is very grateful for their efforts and expresses his sincere thanks below.

First, thanks to my brother and sister, my sons and wife who all offered their critical reviews of this book during its evolution and helped to significantly improve this book in many ways. Phil Gandolfo, Richard Spinello and Paul Vegoda offered important and careful reviews of the 1st edition, as Michael Grieco did for the 2nd and 3rd editions. Vincent Scicchitano's review of the chapter on sports also helped to clarify passages and biographical facts for the 3rd edition.

Several contributions that improved and clarified some portions of the text were provided by Lewis M. Elia, Secretary and Treasurer of the Italian Cultural Institute of the NY Capital District; Dr. Barbara Wolanin, Curator of the U.S. Office of the Architect of the Capitol and staff; Frank Lancetti of the Italian Cultural Society, Washington DC; and Thomas Adamo and James E. Celeberti both of the Museum of Italian Culture, Garden City, New York.

A special thanks is extended to Thomas Adamo for his help editing the 3rd edition. Contributions to the 4th edition made by Barbara Richardson are difficult to overstate. Her astonishing attention to detail and breadth of knowledge have greatly improved this edition. Thank you Barbara for lightning fast responses and very helpful insights.

Many thanks to several individuals who helped with other important graphic and artistic components:

- Nina Araujo authored photographs of Italy including: Pompeii photos and the grape arbor in Capri.
- Bridgeman Library, British Museum of London, Galileo portrait.
- Caroline Esposito provided much guidance, technical support for advanced page layout techniques, and assistance with the formidable index.
- Chris Cadieux authored many of the photographs of Italy including: Roman Triumphal Arch, Coliseum, Leaning Tower of Pisa, Pisa Cathedral, Pisa Baptistery, St. Mark's Cathedral, St. Peter's Cathedral (close-up) and the Rialto Bridge. Chris also provided original artwork for the Stradivari scroll, Roman Emblem and the Cristofori piano, as well as digital enhancements for all page artwork.
- Joseph Esposito authored the photographs of the "Arc de Triomphe" and the Columbus Monument, both in Paris.

- Lori Margaret Haughie created the gondola illustration.
- Mae Lincoln designed the book cover.
- Jack Schmitt authored the photograph of the La Scala opera house.
- Mary Spinello created the illustrations of the five classic columns.

Finally, thanks to my family and parents who encouraged me throughout this long journey from start to finish and demonstrated extreme patience with me over the years.

READERS' FEEDBACK

Almost two decades of research culminated in the "The Golden Milestone." Each edition contains new items with more complete and detailed information. Our readers are welcome to offer suggestions or provide new items for future editions. Please feel free to send email to the following address: **service@nylearninglibrary.com**

BIBLIOGRAPHY

Numerous encyclopedias and news services were used to verify and enrich the contents of this book. Additionally, many specialized books and other references were valuable sources of information: these are listed below.

Artabras Book, "Leonardo da Vinci," New York, Reynal & Company

Avery, Catherine B., "The New Century Classical Handbook," New York, Appleton-Century-Crofts, Inc., 1962

Bandon, Alexandra, "Seven Inventors Who Remade the Future," New York Times Magazine," January 4, 1998

Browne, Malcolm W., "Power Line Makes Use of a Miracle of Physics," "New York Times," November 3, 1998

Bruckner, D.J.R., "The Day the Nuclear Age Was Born," "New York Times," November 30, 1982

Bunyon, Patrick, "All Around the Town-- Amazing Facts & Curiosities," New York, Fordham University Press, 1999

Burckhardt, Jacob, "The Civilization of the Renaissance in Italy," New York, Harper Torchbooks of Harper & Row, 1958

Cahill, Thomas, "How the Irish Saved Civilization," Doubleday, New York, 1995

Claiborne, Craig, "Gastronomic Lore in Italy's Pasta Museum," "New York Times," July 1977

Consentino, Andrew J. and Glassie, Henry H., "The Capitol Image Painters in Washington, 1800-1915," Washington, DC, Smithsonian Institution Press, 1983

Covington, Richard, "The Leaning Tower Straightens Up," "Smithsonian," Washington, DC, June 2001

Doherty, Jim, "In Praise of Pianos..." in "Smithsonian," Washington, DC, March 2000

Dudar, Helen, "The Grandeur that Was Rome," "Smithsonian," Washington, DC, April 2000

Durant, Will, "The Renaissance: A History of Civilization in Italy from Petrarch to the Death of Titian (1304 to 1576), New York, Simon & Schuster, 1953

Edwards, Mike and Yamashita, Michael, "Marco Polo I," "National Geographic," May 2001

Edwards, Mike and Yamashita, Michael, "Marco Polo II," "National Geographic," June 2001

Edwards, Mike and Yamashita, Michael, "Marco Polo III," "National Geographic," July 2001

Faggin, Federico; Hoff Jr., Marcian E.; Mazor, Stanley, and Shima, Masatoshi, "The History of the 4004", IEEE Micro journal published by IEEE Computer Society, December 1996

Foster, Eugene, "Tabloid History," "New York Times Magazine ," November 29, 1998

French, Howard W., "Walking the Streets Columbus Built," "New York Times," November 3, 1991

Grant, Michael, "History of Rome," New York, Charles Scribner's Sons, 1978

Grun, Bernard, "The Timetables of History," New York, Touchstone of Simon and Schuster, 1982

Heilbron, Dr. John L., "The Sun in the Church," Cambridge, Harvard, 1999

Hirsch, Kett and Trefil, "The Dictionary of Cultural Literacy," Boston, Houghton Mifflin Company, 1988

Jackson, Devon, "The Cubby File," "New York Times Magazine," December 29, 1996

Jefferson Memorial Foundation, Inc., Monticello, Virginia

Jensen, Cheryl, "Bugatti: Generations of Artistry," "New York Times," July 30, 1999

Kennedy, John F., "A Nation of Immigrants," New York, Harper & Row, 1964

King, Ross, "Brunelleschi's Dome," New York, Penguin Books, 2000

Lane, Hana Umlauf (editor), "The World Almanac Book of Who," New York, World Almanac Publications, 1980

Levey and Greenhall, "The Concise Columbia Encyclopedia," New York, Avon Books (for Columbia University Press), 1983

Litton, Helen, "The Celts an Illustrated History," Dublin, Wolfhound Press, 1997

Lombardo, Vincent, "Attilio Piccirilli, Life of an American Sculptor," New York, Pitman, 1944

Machiavelli, Niccolo, "The Prince," "The Discourses" addendum, New York, Penguin Classics, 1973

Maine, Henry Sir, "Ancient Law," London, J. M. Dent, Everyman's Library, 1963

Messadie, Gerald, "Great Scientific Discoveries," New York, Chambers, 1991

Messadie, Gerald, "Great Inventions Through History," New York, Chambers, 1991

Messadie, Gerald, "Great Modern Inventions," New York, Chambers, 1991

Mlodinow, Leonard, "Euclid's Window," New York, Touchstone, 2001

Morris, William, "Your Heritage of Words," New York, Dell Publishing, 1975
Murphy, Francis X., "A Non-Italian Pope?" in "New York Times," August 8, 1978
"Oxford Dictionary of Quotations," Oxford, Oxford University Press, 1980

Paganelli, Sergio, "Musical Instruments from the Renaissance to the19th Century," London, Hamlyn, 1970

Panati, Charles, "Panati's Extraordinary Origins of Everyday Things," New York, Perennial Library of Harper & Row, 1989

Pescosolido, Carl A., Gleason, Pamela, "The Proud Italians: Our Great Civilizers," Latium Publishing Company, 1991 (Distributed by the National Italian-American Foundation)

Pizer, Russell A., editor and Howard, George W., assistant editor, "3rd International Symposium on Telecommunication History, Record of Proceedings" (For further information, contact Herbert J. Hackenberg, Executive Director, Telecommunications History Group, Inc., P.O. Box 8719, Denver, CO 80201-8719; telephone 1-303-296-1221)

Sagan, Carl, "Broca's Brain," New York, Ballantine, 1993

Sagan, Carl, "Pale Blue Dot," New York, Random House, 1994

Scarre, Chris (editor), "Smithsonian Timelines of the Ancient World," London, Dorling Kindersley, 1993

Schiavo, Giovanni Ermenegildo, "The Italian-American History" Volume I, New York, Arno Press (A New York Times Company), 1975

Shepherd, Steven, "The Mysterious Technology of the Violin," "American Heritage of Invention & Technology," NY, NY, Spring 2000

Siano, Joseph, "The Elite Rub Fenders With A Fast Crowd," "New York Times," Automobiles Section, September 25, 1999

Sobel, Dava, "Galileo's Daughter," New York, Penguin Books, 2000

Sobel, Dava, "Longitude: the true story of a lone genius who solved the greatest scientific problem of his time," New York, Penguin Books, 1996

Soria, Regina, "American Artists of Italian Heritage, 1776-1945," Cranbury, NJ, Associated University Presses, 1993

Soria, Regina, "The Role of the Artist of Italian Heritage in the Shaping of America," paper, College of Notre Dame, Maryland.

Stern, Ellen and Gwathmey, Emily, "Once Upon a Telephone," New York, San Diego and London, Harcourt Brace & Co, 1994

Thompson, David and Nagel, Alan F., "The Three Crowns of Florence," New York, Harper & Row, 1972

Taylor, Ken & Joules, "The Little Book of Celtic Myths & Legends," London, Siena, 1999

Van Gelder, Lawrence, feature "Footlights- Art History," "New York Times," November 3, 1998

Waterhouse, Ellis, "Italian Baroque Painting," London, Phaidon Press, 1969

West, Paul, "The Secret Lives of Words," New York, Harcourt, 2000

Winchester, Simon, "The Professor and the Madman," New York, HarperPerennial, 1999

Wundram, Manfred, "Art of the Renaissance," New York, Universe Books, 1972

Zens, Marty and Schansberg, David, "Country Scene Digest," Milwaukee, WI, Ideals Publishing Corp., 1979

Bank, oldest, 177
"Barber of Seville," 326
Barbera, Joseph, 454
Barilla, 137
Barnes & Noble, 175
Barometer, 392
Baseball, 439-444
Basile, Giovanni, 211
Basilica, 53
Basilone, John, 297
Battery, Electric, 401
Beccaria, Cesare, 8,183
Beethoven, 305
Bellini, Vincenzo, 327
Beltrami, Eugenio, 247,251
Belzoni, Giovanni, 196,197
Benedetto, Robert, 320
Benedictine Order, 380
Benigni, Roberto, 454
Bennett, Tony, 455
Beretta, 290
Berra, Yogi, 344,439
Bertholdi, Auguste, 104
"Betrothed, The," 209
Bianchi, Luigi, 243
Bicycle, 444,475
Big Mac, 126
Biological Microscopy, 268
Biological Warfare, 289
"Birth of Venus," 29
Blimpie, 126
Blind and Deaf – Education, 268
Bobbio, Norberto, 339
Boccaccio, Giovanni,
 215,230,335
Bocelli, Andrea, 329
Body Temperature, 269
Bologna, University, 280
Bombelli, Rafael, 239
Bombieri, Enrico, 244
Bonaparte, Charles, 20

Bonaparte, Napoleon, 292
Bono, Sonny, 455
Book of Kells, 220
Borders Books, 176
Borelli, Giovanni, 284,426
Borgia, Cesare, 292
Botticelli, Sandro, 29
Boxing, 445
Brain Anatomy, 269
Bramante, Donato, 65
Brass Instruments, 309
Bridge Designs, 475
Broccoli, 127
Broken Mirror Superstition, 142
Brumidi, Constantino, 87
Brunelleschi, Filippo, 45,49,50
Bugatti, 468

C

Cabotto, Giovanni, 190-192
Cabrini, 385
Caesar, Julius, 43,116,143,144,149,
 227,293,345
Cage, Nicholas, 456
Calculus, 243,245,246
Calendar (Julian & Gregorian), 116
Calendar, Days the Week, 119
Califano, Joseph, 21
California, carvings, 96,97
Camera (Camera Obscura), 393
Camouflage, 290
Campellone, M., 322
Campini, 467
Canali, 200
Cancer Research - Nobel Prize, 269
Candle, 394
Candles, Smokeless, 426
Canova, Antonio, 33
Capillaries in Lungs, 282
Capillary Action Discovery, 394
Capitol Hill (US), 14

Capra, Frank, 456
Capriati, Jennifer, 453
Caravaggio, 28
Carbon Paper, 394
Cardano, Girolamo, 208, 240, 268,406
Carducci, Giosue, 228
Caruso, Enrico, 329
Casanova, 214
Cassini, Gap in Saturn's Rings, 114
Castro,
  Bernard and Bernadette, 145
Cathedral Observatories, 118
Cathedral of the Annunciation (Russia), 66
Catherine Palace (Russia), 67
Causici, Enrico, 90,100
Cavalieri, B.F., 245
Cellini, Benvenuto, 208
Celtic language, 143,156,219,220
Cement, 43,55
"Cenerentola," 211,326
Central Heating, 395
CERN, 391,415
"Charlie Brown" music, 308
Chaucer, 215
Chef Boy-ar-dee, 127
Chemistry, Nobel Prize, 395
Cherry Tree, 144
Chiaroscuro, 28
Chicken Tetrazzini, 128
China,
  Christianity, 385
  Exploration, 184-188
  Map, 238
  Mathematics, 228
Chocolate Specialties, 128
Choir Technique, 301
Chun King, 129
Chopin, 311

Christmas Day, 377-378
Chrysler, 473
Cicero, 7,334,346-348
"Cinderella," 211,326
Civil War, American, 290
Clock Advancements, 397
Clock, First Pendulum, 397
Coffee Filter Paper, 129
Clinical examinations, 270
Cloning, 270
Coin Toss, 144
Coins, Molten, 413
Cold Cream, 272
"Cold Feet," 144
Coliseum (Colosseum), 54-55
Colletti, Lucio, 339
Collodi, Carlo, 213
Cologne (eau de Cologne), 144
Color, Art, 27
Columbus, Christopher, 188-190
Columns, Roman and Italian, 55-56
Comic Opera, First, 325
Common Law, 233
Communist Theory, 339,340
Como, Perry, 457
Compass,
  Magnetic, 398; Proportional, 398
Computer Research, 399-400
Conair Hair Dryer, 148
Concerto, 304
Concrete
  Invented, 43
  Reinforced, 56
Condom, 274
Conductor, Musical, 308
"Confessions," 380
Constantine, Emperor, 378,379
Contact Lenses – Concept, 272
Convertible sofa bed, 145
Coppola, Francis Ford, 457
Corelli, Archangelo, 304

Cosa Equation, 242
Cough Drop, 272
CPU, First Microprocessor, 400
Cristofori, B., 311
Croce, Benedetto, 338
"Crucifixion, The," 31
Cubic equation, 242
Cuomo, Mario, 17
Cursive Handwriting, 220
Czar, 142

D
D'Angelico, John, 319
D'Aquisto, James, 320
D'Arezzo, Guido, 299-300
Da Vinci, see *Vinci*
Dag Hammerskjold Prize, 481
Dante Alighieri, 209,215,335,343
Danti,
  Egnatio Pellegrino Rainaldi,
  117
"David," 29
De Niro, Robert, 458
Declaration of Independence, US,
  6-10
Deledda, Grazia, 228
DeLisi, Charles, MD, 276
Della Porta, Giambattista, 111,
  255,393,427
Democratic theory, 339
Dentures, 272
Detroit, 196
Diamond Engagement Ring, 145
DiCaprio, Leonardo, 458
DiMaggio, Joe, 440
Dini condition (math), 244
Dionysius Exiguus, 117
Dirigible, 196
DiRomualdo, Robert F. 176
"Divine Comedy, The," 209
Diving Suit, 400

Dolce & Gabbana, 201
Dome, 57
Donatello, 25
Double-Entry Accounting, 177
Drinking Glasses, 401
Ducati, 478
Dulbecco, Renato, 269,276
Durante, Jimmy, 458

E
"E Pluribus Unum," 13
Earthquakes, 421
Easter Sunday, 379
Economics, Mathematical,
  179,260
Egyptian Archeology, 196-197
Egyptian Sphinx, 57
Einstein, Albert, 243,387
Electric,
  Battery, 401
  Generator, 402
  Motor, 402
Electrical Biology, 273
Electroplating, 403
Emblem, Roman Republic, 13
Empedocles, 333
Encyclopedia,
  Natural History, 413
  Inventor, 210
English Cities, 146
English Writers, 215
Enriques, F., 251
Esposito,
  Floriana, 399
  Mary Ann, 129
  Phil, 448
  Raphael, 132
  Tony (Hockey), 449
  Tony (Music), 307
Espresso Machine, 130
Etiquette, 146

Generator, Electric, Geothermal, 402
Genocchi, Angelo, 246
Gentile, Don, 294
Gentile, Giovanni, 339
Geological Sciences, 404
Geometry, 243,245-252
Ghiradelli, 128
Giacconi, Riccardo, 436
Giamatti, A. Bartlett, 341
Gianfranco Ferre, 202
Giannini, A.P., 173
Gimbal(s), 405
Giorgio Armani, see Armani
Giotto, 24
Giuliani, Rudolf, 16
Glass Mirror, 405
Glass Windows, 147,405
"God Bless You," 147
Goethe, 6,217
Golden Milestone, 1,64
Golgi, Camillo, 281
Gondola, 476
Governor – First Women, 18
Governor, NYS, 17-18
Gramsci, Antonio, 340
Grasso, Ella, 18
Grasso, Richard, 181
Gravity, First Studies, 407
Graziano, Rocky, 445
Gregorian Chants, 298
Grucci, 405
Guaraldi, Vince, 308
Gucci, 203
Guidoni, Umberto, 190
Guitar, 319-323
Gyroscope Gimbal(s), 406

H
Halley's Comet, 25
Handel, 304,305
Handkerchief, 148

Harmony, Development, 305
Harpsichord, 311
Health Commissioner, NYC, 17
Health Spa, 148
Helicopter, First, 477
Herbarium, 409
Hermetic Sealing, 278
Highway Design, Modern, 478
Highway System, First, 56
History, Philosophy, 336
"History of My Life," 214
HIV Virus
  Discovery & Screening, 277
Hobbs, Thomas, 109
Hockey, 448,449
Horace, 13,229,349
Horse Race, 149
Hospitals, 276
Hudson River, 193
Human Clinical Examinations,
  270
Humanism, 335
Human Genome Project, 276
Hydraulic Motor, 410
Hydraulics, 255-257
Hydrofoil, First, 478
Hydrogen Bomb, 287,387
Hydrostatic Balance, 410
Hygrometer, 410
Hypocaust, see central heat

I
Iacocca, Lee, 104,473
IBM, 178
Ice Cream, 131
Ice Cream Cone, 131
Ices, Italian, 131
Idealism, 337-339
"Ides of March," 149
Ignarro, Louis, 284
"Il Pirata," 327

Illinois, 195
Inertia, 407
Information Highway, see Preface
Insurance,
  Life, 178
  Marine, 179
Ionosphere, 123
Isometrics, 278
Isotta-Fraschini, 472
Italian Grammar, 214
Italian Proverbs, 371
Italic Print, 218

J
Jacuzzi, 150
JAMA, 139
Jeans, 150
Jefferson, Thomas, 4,7,8,11,15,
  33,86,103
"Jerusalem Delivered," 218
Johnson, Samuel, 6, 217
Journalism, New, 227
Joyce, James, 336
Jupiter, 112-115,119,124
Jupiter, Moons of, 112
Justinian, Emperor, 234-236

K
"Kaiser," 142
Kennedy, J.F., 8
Keyboard, 305,310
Khan, Kublai, 185-187

L
"La Boheme," 328
"La fanciulla del West," 328
"La Scala," 309,325
"La Traviata," 326
Ladder, Extension, 411
LaGuardia, Fiorello, 16
Lamborghini, 472

Lamonica, Daryl, 446
Lancia, 472
Lasorda, Tommy, 441
"Last Supper, The," 30
Latin
  Influences, 218-226
  Phrases, 226,361-370
  Proverbs & Quotes, 341,342
  Professional Terminology,
    221-225
Leap Year, 116
Legal System,
  First, 233-236,348
  U.S., 10-13
Lennon, John, 159
Leroy P. Steele Prize, 252
Levi-Cevita, Tullio, 243
Levi-Montalcini, Rita, 281
Library, First Public, 150
Library & Museum Rules, 151
Life, Spontaneous Generation, 278
Light Bulb, Three-Way, 435
Light, Diffraction of, 124
Lincoln Memorial, 94,95
Liposuction, 279
Liszt, Franz, 306
Literature, Nobel Prize Winners,
  228
Liturgical Music, 301
Logic, Mathematics, 252
Lombardi, Vince, 350,446
Lombardo, Guy, 459
London, 65
Longitude, 112
Loren, Sophia, 459
Lottery, 22
Louisiana (relief carving), 96,97
Luminous Objects, 411
Luria, Salvador Edward, 286

R. R. Esposito

M

M.I.T., 253,436
Machiavelli, Niccolo, 229,335
Machine Gun, 291
"Madame Butterfly," 328
Madonna, 461
Madonna Paintings, 31
Magellan's historian, 194
Malaria Research, 279
Malpighi, Marello, 268,282
Mancini, Henry, 307
Mangonel, 288
Mannerism in Modern Art, 34
Manzoni, Alessandro, 209
Marathon wins, 449
Marchione, S., 322
Marciano, Rocky, 445
Marconi, Guglielmo, 123,412,417
Marino, Dan, 447
Mars, 114,119,120,124
Martin, Billy, 442
Martin, Dean, 461
Marx, Carl, 336
Marxism, Theory, 339
Masaccio, 25
Maserati, 473
Mathematics Education, 254
Mathematics Logic, 242
Mayors, NYC, 16
Mazzei, Filippo, 4,6-8,86,87
Mechanics, Science, 255
Medical Schools, Oldest, 280
"Meditations," 226
Metal, Molten, 413
Methane Gas Discovery, 411
Metric system, 156
Metropolitan Museum of Art, 297
Meucci, Antonio, 3,426,428-434
Michelangelo, 29,34,35,72,79
Michigan, 98,196
Microwave Transmissions, 412

Military Leaders, 292
Military Medical Services, 291
Milky Way Galaxy, 113
Milton, John, 109,216,218,229
Mini-vans, 473
Modigliani,
  Amedeo, 34
  Franco, 180
Modino of Bologna, 267
Modugno, Domenico, 462
Molecules – Discovery, 412
"Mona Lisa," 31
Moneta, Ernesto, 481
Montale, Eugenio, 228
Montana, Joe, 447
Monteleone, John, 322
Monteverdi, 324
Moon Craters, 112
Moon, Map, 120
Morgagni, Giovanni, 280
Motion Paradox, 258
Motorcycle – Italian, 478
Mozart, 305,326
Mr. Coffee Machine, 129
Mucci, Henry, 297
Multiple Star, 121
Multiplication Rules, 239
Murano Glass, 152
Musical
  Conductor, 308
  Notation & Octaves, 299
  Scales, 300
  Terminology, 301
Mustang, 473
Mytilini, 198

N

Napoleon, 21,292
NASD/NASDQ, 182
Natta, Giulio, 395

R. R. Esposito